THE ESSAYISTIC SPIRIT

THE ESSAYISTIC SPIRIT
Literature, Modern Criticism, and the Essay

CLAIRE DE OBALDIA

CLARENDON PRESS · OXFORD
1995

Oxford University Press, Walton Street, Oxford OX2 6DP

Oxford   New York
Athens   Auckland   Bangkok   Bombay
Calcutta   Cape Town   Dar es Salaam   Delhi
Florence   Hong Kong   Istanbul   Karachi
Kuala Lumpur   Madras   Madrid   Melbourne
Mexico City   Nairobi   Paris   Singapore
Taipei   Tokyo   Toronto
and associated companies in
Berlin   Ibadan

Oxford is a trade mark of Oxford University Press

Published in the United States
by Oxford University Press Inc., New York

British Library Cataloguing in Publication Data
Data available

Library of Congress Cataloging in Publication Data
De Obalida, Claire.
The essayistic spirit : literature, modern criticism, and the
essay / Claire de Obalida.
Includes bibliographical references.
1. Essay.   2. Criticism.   3. Literature, Modern—History and
criticism.   I. Title.
PN4500.D35   1995
809.4—dc20   *94-39236*
ISBN 0-19-815194-2

1 3 5 7 9 10 8 6 4 2

Typeset by Graphicraft Typesetters Ltd., Hong Kong
Printed in Great Britain
on acid-free paper by
Bookcraft Ltd
Midsomer Norton, Bath

Acknowledgements

MY WARMEST thanks go to Ann Jefferson, Terence Cave, Dunstan Ward, and my family for their unfailing support and encouragement throughout the lengthy writing and rewriting of the thesis from which this book originated.

C.d.O.

Contents

1. LITERATURE *IN POTENTIA*   I

   1. The Essay as a Marginal Genre   I
   2. Synchronic Approach to the Potentially Literary:
       Style, Imagination, Fiction, and the Novel   8
   3. Diachronic Approach to the Potentially Literary   16
   4. Montaigne's *Essais* and the Essay   28
       1. The *Essais* and the Essayistic   28
       2. The Montaignian Essay   38
   5. Essaying the Essay   57

2. MONTAIGNE'S *ESSAIS*: A POETICS OF THE MARGIN   65

   1. A 'Para-doxical' genre   65
   2. Second Nature   80

3. PHILOSOPHICAL ESSAYISM   99

   1. The Essay as a Parergon   99
       1. Lukács   102
          1. Introducing the Essay   102
          2. The Essay as an Art-Form   104
          3. The Essay Not (Yet) as Art-Form, or as Parergon   107
       2. Adorno   113
          1. Essaying the Pre-Text   113
          2. Essaying as 'Unmethodical Method'   115
          3. The Critique of Ideology   118
   2. The Logic of the Parergon   125
   3. Postscript: Paratextual Criticism   137

4. THE GLOSSES OF ROLAND BARTHES:
   THE ENCYCLOPEDIC AND THE NOVELISTIC   146

   1. Playing with Systems   146
   2. The Order of Disorder   156
   3. 'This is not your Place'   175
   4. 'Almost a Novel'   181

5. NOVELS 'WITHOUT QUALITIES'   193

   1. From Essay to (Essayistic) Novel   193
   2. 'Monstrous Essays'   206

1. Sleepwalkers and Men Without Qualities   206
2. Essay, *Bildungsroman*, and Polyphonic Novel   223
3. Essay(istic) or Novel(istic)?   236

6. POSTSCRIPT: BORGES, OR THE ESSAYISTIC SPIRIT   247

1. The Essayist as Master of Modern Fiction   247
2. The World as Tlön   260
   1. A Game of Shifting Mirrors   260
   2. Tlön and 'Tlön'   262
3. Deliberate Techniques of Anachronism   270

BIBLIOGRAPHY   283

INDEXES   307

I
Literature in potentia

I.I. THE ESSAY AS A MARGINAL GENRE

The intensive concern with generic studies in recent times has clearly shown that despite—or perhaps because of—striking progress in this field, the question of 'genre' remains one of the most difficult in literary theory. Whether approached synchronically or diachronically or both, 'genre' remains a notion with frustratingly blurred edges. Nevertheless, while a broad agreement does seem to exist as to what is meant by 'poem', 'play' and, to some extent, 'novel', the essay always appears as a particularly problematic form of writing, even—or especially—where the seemingly more specific category of the so-called 'literary essay' is concerned. Divergences in the descriptions of the genre, whether they are based on a historical perspective or on the study of the form at any one time, are extreme. Some argue that the fluctuations in the meaning of the word 'essay' are due to the fact that the genre varies greatly from one country to the next. Others—and this is the case for most histories of the essay—do not even present it as a genre: they concentrate rather on individual essayists, with a marked emphasis on the biographical and socio-cultural context; indeed, they seem to assume that each essay-structure is unique to the individual essayist, that there is no essay but only essays, as many essays as there are essayists. This could well be justified by the fact that most definitions of the essay refer back to the official founder of the genre, to Montaigne, whose *Essais* he himself described as 'the only book of its kind in the world', not just in the sense of being referable to one unmistakable author but in the sense of being the expression of the author's *essence* ('a book of one substance with its author, proper to me and a limb of my life'), an indissociable extension of himself.[1] Some theorists have gone so far as to appropriate Montaigne's famous claim to the uniqueness of the species not only to assert that there are as many essays as there are essayists, but even more literally that no one has ever written essays after Montaigne, that his are the only essays that exist in the proper sense of the word.[2] And yet some criterion must have determined the possibility of grouping together in one family the impressive list that makes up what the average reader of literature

---

[1] Montaigne, 'On the Affection of Fathers for their Children', *Essays*, II. 8, p. 433 ['C'est le seul livre au monde de son espece', 'De l'affection des peres aux enfans', *Essais*, II. viii, p. 364*c*]; and 'On Giving the Lie', *Essays*, II. 18, p. 755 ['Livre consubstantiel à son autheur', 'Du dementir', *Essais*, II. xviii, p. 648*c*].

[2] This interpretation is represented above all by Peter Schon, the German author of a classic work on the formal sources of the *Essais* in antiquity and humanism entitled *Vorformen des Essays in Antike und Humanismus: Ein Beitrag zur Entstehungsgeschichte der 'Essais' von Montaigne* (1954).

has come to recognize as the 'great tradition' of essayists—Montaigne, Bacon, Sainte-Beuve, Renan, Alain, Barthes, Addison, Steele, Johnson, Lamb, Hazlitt, Orwell, Woolf, Eliot, Emerson, Benn, Mann, Unamuno, Ortega, Borges, etc. The very act of selecting given texts as typical essays, however varied, suggests that over and above the different potentialities of the form there must remain something called 'the essay' which can be identified by a set of distinctive features. For only the constancy of these features can allow the definition of the word 'essay' to be roughly the same, whether one looks it up in an English, German, French, Spanish, or Spanish-American dictionary.

However, a closer look at this superficial dictionary definition of the essay shows the existing consensus to lie in an agreement on the uncircumventable indeterminacy of the genre. In fact, the one commonly accepted fact about the essay is that indeterminacy is germane to its essence. The overt etymological evidence, always triumphantly brandished at some point or other in studies on the essay, is a constant reminder of what we are all supposed to know and should under no circumstances be allowed to forget: that the word 'essay' comes from the French *essai* and *essayer*, to attempt, to experiment, to try out, and further back from the Latin *exagium*, 'weighing' an object or an idea, examining it from various angles, but never exhaustively or systematically:

The essay is a very flexible form and has been so ever since it originated with the 16th-century French writer Montaigne. He used it as a means of exploring himself and his ideas about human experience, and his essays were, in a sense, a means of thinking on paper, of trying things out in writing. And he deliberately emphasized their tentative and informal quality by calling them *essais*.[3]

The essay is an essentially ambulatory and fragmentary prose form. Its direction and pace, the tracks it chooses to follow, can be changed at will; hence its fragmentary or 'paratactic' structure. Rather than progressing in a linear and planned fashion, the essay develops around a number of topics which offer themselves along the way. And this sauntering from one topic to the next together with the way in which each topic is informally 'tried out' suggests a tentativeness, a looseness, in short a randomness which seems to elude the unifying conception—syntactic, semantic, and pragmatic—of a recognizable generic identity. Indeed the apparent randomness of the syntax which is usually encapsulated by the notion of 'play' seems to go hand in hand with an apparently equal randomness in the (semantic) choice of subject-matter: the range of 'topics' available to the essay is potentially infinite—from the most serious to the most trivial—and this subverts the principle according to which a genre designates certain kinds of material as acceptable while excluding others. This indeterminacy also inevitably affects the pragmatic dimension of the 'contract' between writer and reader. The very word 'essay' disorientates the reader's horizon of expectations, for if it is associated with

[3] Carl Klaus, 'Essay', in Robert Scholes and Carl Klaus (eds.), *Elements of Literature* (1991), 4.

the authority and authenticity of someone who speaks in his or her own name, it also disclaims all responsibility with regard to what is after all only 'tried out' and which is therefore closer, in a sense, to the 'as if' of fiction. As with the idea that each essay is the only one of its kind, favouring the etymological definition quickly raises the question of whether the essay can be regarded as a genre at all, or whether it might not represent the very denial of genre.

For all that, the hypothesis of the essay's a- or anti-genericness is most often tackled from the point of view of literature, and thus of genre. The essay's resistance to resolving itself into identifiable generic contours tends to be justified above all by the fact that it combines a seemingly arbitrary mixture of literary characteristics. Its ability to incorporate the qualities of any one of the three Aristotelian categories of the lyric, the dramatic, and the epic—or, even more typically, of all three together—makes it a literary hybrid. Its connection with the category of the lyric or the 'poetic' is usually seen to underlie both its fragmentary or 'paratactic' structure—one which, unlike that of logically ordered discourse, indulges in the use of associations, images, metaphors—and foregrounds the self (the essayist himself) in the process of essaying. An essay is 'poetic' to the extent that its author appears to be talking to himself rather than to others. Thus the poetic essay will characteristically take the form of a meditation 'overheard' by the reader.[4] The dramatic dimension, on the other hand, can be identified with the essay's use of dialogue—not so much in the form of the recorded speech of a play as in that of indirect imitation. In this, the essay comes closest to a genre which, since Plato's dialogues, has been used time and again as a means of presenting ideas from the point of view of an author who 'is present, if at all, only to perform the duties of a director'.[5] It is through the act of 'weighing' mentioned above, of approaching the matter from different angles, of choosing arguments for and against in the manner of the heuristic and dialectical method of question and answer, that the topic under investigation becomes the object of a dialogue. From the epic, finally, the essay is understood to borrow the feature of story-telling in the locatable form, first of all, of examples or *exempla*—the short narratives supposed to illustrate or deliver moral injunctions at the time of Montaigne's *Essais*—but also for the gratification of the essayist's more general inclination to narrate or relate rather than to teach [*Je n'enseigne point, je raconte*[6]]. This turns the author into a narrator who 'reports directly to us on persons and events': either on his own experience, when the highly personal, autobiographical dimension prevails, or on others' when a more impersonal, journalistic 'story' is involved.[7] The essay, then, may be narrative, dramatic, or poetic—depending on which alliance prevails—or it may be all

---

[4] Ibid. 5; and 'When we are meditating, we are in a sense engaged in a conversation with ourselves' (p. 24).

[5] Ibid. 5.

[6] 'I am not teaching, I am relating', Montaigne, 'On Repenting', *Essays*, III. 2, p. 909 ['Du repentir', *Essais*, III. ii, p. 784*b*].

[7] Klaus, 'Essay', 5, 15–16.

three. Its ability to overlap with these categories is such that when examining 'The Essay *and* Other Forms of Literature', some theorists refer spontaneously to 'The Essay *as* Poem', 'The Essay *as* Play', and 'The Essay *as* Story' (emphasis added).[8] All the above contributes to turning the essay into a 'baggy monster' which can be stretched in any direction.[9] And this could well explain the neglect of the genre in literary studies. On the other hand, another much more obvious prose form—the novel—can from the outset claim to be an open-ended, heterogeneous, anti- or a-generic form that subverts and redistributes existing categories in this way. As Maupassant's famous comment goes, 'the critic who dares to write "this is a novel, this is not" seems to be blessed with a perspicacity that very much resembles incompetence.'[10] Still, the 'bagginess' of the novel has not prevented its role from being diametrically opposed to the minor, marginal role of the essay in literary studies.

The problem, in the end, seems to be that the very notions of literature and genre remain a question for the essay, even though the latter is seen to partake of the literary, and notwithstanding its overt categorization as 'literary essay'. One cannot but be aware that unlike the novel, which in the course of its history has so quickly progressed from its status as a marginal (un- or sub-literary) genre to become a respectable genre, and ultimately to embody the notion of literature itself in most readers' and writers' minds, the essay has made little progress from its very similar starting-point and continues to be excluded from the realm of literature. Or rather, to complicate matters, the divide between the literary and the extraliterary operates within the province of the essay itself. This boundary corresponds first of all to an evaluative divergence between individual essays and the essay as a genre. The works of the essayists listed above have in fact been admitted to the canon of literary works, yet this has done nothing for the promotion of the genre itself. As Claudio Guillén deplores, 'even within the bounds of Western literature, the tripartite division into narrative, drama, and lyric has been insufficient for several centuries now. The rise of the essay as a genuine—certainly, since Montaigne, not spurious or marginal—literary genre has made the point quite clear.'[11] Similarly, Alastair Fowler, who in his book never questions the literary status of the *Essais*, has to yield to the evidence that the essay is one of the few genres to which 'ambiguity of literary status is confined'.[12] It is obvious that, as with any other genre, the essay's potential contribution to literature is dependent upon the arbitrary criteria of value that determine canons. The boundaries which regiment inclusions and exclusions into and from the realm of literature shift in

---

[8] Klaus in 'Essay', but also German theorists referred to further on in this chapter.

[9] Cf. Geoffrey Hartman, 'Literary Commentary as Literature', in *Criticism in the Wilderness: The Study of Literature Today* (1980), 195: 'So much of contemporary intellectual life consists in reading these all-purpose forms, these baggy miniature monsters which like certain demons are only too serviceable.'

[10] In his 1887 preface to *Pierre et Jean*.

[11] Claudio Guillén, *Literature as System: Essays toward the Theory of Literary History* (1971), 114.

[12] Alastair Fowler, *Kinds of Literature: An Introduction to the Theory of Genres and Modes* (1982), 11.

history, so that like other forms of its kind, the essay is likely to appear on one or the other side of the literary margin according to the period. Montaigne's *Essais*, for example, emerge at a time when the conception of literature is a much broader one, art being then an all-encompassing notion which can be used interchangeably with science simply to designate a particular body of knowledge or skill.[13] Also, as Fowler himself points out, a work can become literature 'by default', that is, when it is no longer useful or valuable in a practical or scientific way, when it has 'ceased to function as a treatise' and can therefore be enjoyed for 'its intellectual qualities' or its 'poetic vision'.[14] This no doubt has a role to play in the unequivocally literary status of the *Essais* to this day, despite a leading tendency to exclude such forms from the mainstream. In the end, however, the real nature of the divergence seems to have more to do with the fact that the tension between what we identify today as the literary and the extraliterary is inherent in the very logic of the genre. On the one hand, the form of the essay makes it a member of literature and does, for some theorists, grant it the right to establish itself as a fourth literary genre alongside the other three.[15] On the other hand, the content of the essay, the fact that it is concerned with ideas ultimately addressed directly by an author to a reader, assigns the genre primarily to the category of didactic, expository, or critical writing. In so far as 'the essay's essential quality is persuasion', in so far as 'in its purest form, it is an argument',[16] the aesthetic organization of the material remains subordinated to the treatment of an event or situation that exists in time and space, of an idea or text which the essayist is ultimately committed to telling the 'truth' about, a truth which he himself is answerable for. The result of this conflict between form and content is that the essay 'goes unrecognized either as knowledge or as art'.[17] From the point of view of science or philosophy, the essay is too 'artistic', too concerned with the strategies of writing itself; yet this does not suffice boldly to admit the genre into the realm of so-called creative or imaginative literature.

The essay, then, is not so much excluded from the realm of literature as relegated to the latter's margins. Its borderline position between the purely literary and the purely scientific or philosophical gives it a recognizable affinity to those other genres which Alastair Fowler most appropriately groups under the concept of 'literature *in potentia*':

[13] See Rosalie L. Colie, *The Resources of Kind: Genre-Theory in the Renaissance* (1973), 8; and Ann E. Imbrie, 'Defining Nonfiction Genres', in Barbara Kiefer Lewalski (ed.), *Renaissance Genres: Essays on Theory, History, and Interpretation* (1986).

[14] Fowler, *Kinds of Literature*, 11–12.

[15] e.g. Carl Klaus in his introduction: 'We have prepared critical introductions to the four forms of literature—essay, fiction, poetry and drama—that have dominated our culture for hundreds of years' ('Essay', p. xxvii). This is also the approach chosen by Klaus Weissenberger in 'Essay', *Prosakunst ohne Erzählen: Die Gattungen der nicht-fiktionalen Kunstprosa* (1985).

[16] Klaus, 'Essay', 5. See also p. 6 and p. xxx ('The essay in its purest form uses words to establish ideas addressed directly to the reader. The essay is associated with persuasion'), and the section entitled 'The Essay as Argument: Persuasion'.

[17] Graham Good, *The Observing Self: Rediscovering the Essay* (1988), 15.

According to the central conception, 'literature' refers to a certain group of genres, whose exemplars are therefore by definition literary, at least in aspiration. These central genres comprise the poetic kinds, the dramatic, and some of the prose kinds. . . . Round this nucleus spreads a looser plasma of neighboring forms: essay, biography, dialogue, history, and others. They are, so to say, literature *in potentia*.[18]

Among these 'neighboring forms'—to which one could add the autobiography, the letter, the sermon, the maxim, the aphorism, etc.—the essay is a particularly good specimen, for as well as being one member of the group it seems mostly to function as a generic term for the group as a whole. Indeed, concrete examples of the genre easily justify the use of the word essay as 'a catch-all for non-fictional prose works of a limited length'.[19] They show how freely it cuts across the boundaries of kindred forms, thus encroaching on and therefore sharing and combining a number of their respective features. In the same way that a theoretical inventory of existing essays will include the narrative, dramatic, or meditative essay, it will also include the historical, the biographical, the autobiographical, the aphoristic, the epistolary, or the dialogic essay. In fact, since the essay tends to exploit some of these potentially literary forms as vehicles for the literary organization of its material, this second category can be regarded as a sub-category, one which can in turn be broken down into yet another sub-category when the adjective in front of the word 'essay' is made to denote the range of the essayist's more subtle rhetorical attitude towards his object (as in the case of the associative, the polemical, the meditative, the sententious, the personal, or the reflective essay—to name but a few[20]). For example, the dialogue is the natural vehicle of the essay's dramatic dimension; but the 'dialogic' can also be associated with the letter and with the 'polemical'. As for the narrative aspect of our genre, it is bound to encompass at least the autobiographical (which can in turn be associated with the personal or with the reflective), the biographical, and history. Above all—and as with literary genres where 'narrative essay' and 'essay as story' were used more or less interchangeably—the fundamental indeterminacy of the essay enables it to overlap with *and* to be cast directly as one of its neighbouring forms. As well as the variety of texts associated with the great tradition of essayists referred to above, a typical list of examples thus also incorporates Plato's *Dialogues*, Seneca's *Epistles to Lucilius*, St Augustine's *Confessions*, Donne's *Sermons*, Descartes's *Méditations philosophiques*, Pascal's *Pensées*, La Rochefoucauld's *Maximes*, Diderot's *Encyclopédie* and *Lettres philosophiques*, Schlegel's *Fragments* and Novalis's drafts, Nietzsche's *Aphorisms*, Schopenhauer's *Parerga and Paralipomena*, the texts of the mystics, Kierkegaard's imaginary diaries and short stories, Surrealist Manifestos, Barthes and Leiris's self-portraits—and

[18] Fowler, *Kinds of Literature*, 5. This term is also used by Michel Beaujour in 'Genus Universum', *Glyph*, 7 (1980), 27.

[19] Klaus, 'Essay', 4.

[20] This taxonomic frenzy prevails above all in German studies: see e.g. the section entitled '*Einteilungsvorschläge*' (pp. 639–48) of Ludwig Rohner's *Der deutsche Essay: Materialien zur Geschichte und Ästhetik einer literarischen Gattung* (1966).

so forth. What this inventory serves to illustrate is the essay's ability to take on multiple aspects and/or the diversity of forms that have been identified as essays. For corpuses and traditions tend to be constituted retrospectively: apart from Montaigne and Bacon, very few of these 'essayists' would have defined their texts as 'essays' at the time of writing. Of course, the link between the essay and these other forms is not as arbitrary and accidental as the idea of shapelessness or 'bagginess' may lead one to believe. A look at existing investigations into the sources or precursor forms of the essay which often constitute a major part of a theorist's initial attempt to define or at least to situate the genre,[21] suggests that in most cases these examples are simply the forms or genres in which the essay is supposed to have existed in its 'latent state'. The works of Plato, Cicero, and Horace are all considered to have contributed to the spirit and form of the essay, as are those of Seneca and Plutarch.[22] The literature of compilation alone from which the essay originally arises comprises fables, anecdotes, similes, sententiae, and *florilegia* as well as the *exempla* of antiquity. From there, the development of the essay as described in histories of literature or of the essay is reliant on a growing variety of forms that include the dialogue, the diatribe, the letter, the paradox, the encomium, the aphorism, the treatise, the sermon, travel literature, the character-sketch, etc. Also, it is to be expected that the variety of these genetically-related forms is further determined and modulated by the evolution of respective traditions. The exact nature of the connection between our genre and these so-called 'essay-relatives', however, remains confused, as suggested by the terms and phrases usually employed to describe this connection, such as 'out-growth', what 'enters into the texture of the essay', 'combination', 'elder sisters' and 'twins', 'overlap', 'absorption', 'merges', etc. These essay-relatives are in other words presented both as antecedents and as kindred forms: they antedate the essay and thus make possible the latter's rise as a genre; yet they continue to exist alongside it in a way that promotes the idea that the essay is 'like' these forms from which it also borrows elements, and vice versa.[23] Given this confusion, the survey of the essay as the paradigm of 'literature *in potentia*', to which I want to devote the rest of this chapter, will also necessarily apply to some extent to these other forms. Moreover, we will see that the 'marginality' of the essay with regard to literature revolves around the same ambivalent relationship as that, observed above in the context of non-fiction, between kindred, overlapping forms or essay-relatives and precursor forms or antecedents. The notion of 'literature *in potentia*' which the

---

[21] Either in specific sections of studies or histories on the essay—all of which will be listed in the last section of this chapter—or in specialized works on the subject, such as Peter Schon's study referred to previously.

[22] Seneca's *Epistles to Lucilius*, as Bacon observed, 'are but Essaies,—That is dispersed Meditacons, thoughe conveyed in the forme of Epistles' (quoted in Douglas Bush, 'Essays and Characters', *OHEL* v. *English Literature in the Earlier Seventeenth Century (1600–1660)* (Oxford, 1962), 193).

[23] See e.g. chs. 3 and 4—*Spielraum der Gattung* ('The Scope of the Genre') and *Abgrenzungen* ('Delimitations')—in Rohner's *Der deutsche Essay*.

essay exemplifies must therefore be tackled from both a synchronic and a dia-chronic perspective.

I.2. SYNCHRONIC APPROACH TO THE POTENTIALLY LITERARY: STYLE, IMAGINATION, FICTION, AND THE NOVEL

The literary attribute that most immediately comes to mind when thinking about the essay and/or of essay-relatives is a certain concern with style. The essay, no matter what form it chooses to appear in, is considered to be literary first and foremost by virtue of being well or elegantly written. In this respect, the decisive influence of figures such as Plato, Cicero, Plutarch, or Seneca for the emergence of the genre has to do primarily with acquiring the ability to express thoughts artis-tically, with the gradual refinement of an 'art of imaginative prose'.[24] What is aimed at is a fusion of thought and style; and a judicious use of the dramatic, narrative, and poetic elements referred to above is one way, precisely, of achieving this fusion. The mastering of rhetorical and poetic devices (antithesis, hyperbole, oxymoron, the use of tropes, the attention to prosody and rhythm, etc.), all of which are already used with great sophistication in Montaigne's *Essais*, contribute to expressing 'finest thought' in 'finest prose'.[25] Nevertheless, one knows that if style is the most immediate index of the essay's contribution to literature, it is also what most easily discredits the genre when seen, as it often is, as promoting literariness at its most artificial, vacuous, or frivolous. 'Pleasure', according to Virginia Woolf in her essay on 'The Modern Essay', is the principle to which everything in the essay should be subordinated.[26] 'Yet'—she warns in her own most literary essayistic style—

if the essay admits . . . of sudden boldness and metaphor, and can be polished till every atom of its surface shines, there are dangers in that too. We are soon in sight of ornament. Soon the current, which is the life-blood of literature, runs slow; and instead of sparkling and flashing and moving with a quieter impulse which has a deeper excitement, words coagulate together in frozen sprays which, like the grapes on a Christmas-tree, glitter for a single night, but are dusty and garish the day after. The temptation to decorate is great where the theme may be of the slightest.[27]

The most obvious pitfall for the essay, then, is an over-eager inclination towards style which self-indulgently prompts it to be 'a trifle "literary"', 'giving the sense

---

[24] See Elbert N. S. Thompson, *The Seventeenth-Century English Essay* (1926), 18; and the whole of Laurence Stapleton's *The Elected Circle: Studies in the Art of Prose* (1973).

[25] Thompson, *The Seventeenth-Century English Essay*, 140.

[26] Virginia Woolf, 'The Modern Essay', in *The Common Reader*, i (1984), 211.

[27] Ibid. 214. Cf. also p. 215: 'we cannot help feeling anxious . . . lest the material may give out under the craftsman's fingers. The ingot is so small, the manipulation so incessant.'

of being fabricated ... rather than a direct reaction to life'.[28] It is understood, however, that style described in this way is only the most superficial aspect of what the essay and literature have in common. To emphasize the genre's belletristic aspirations is 'not yet to have said anything at all about its essential nature', as Georg Lukács points out in his essay on the essay. For one would otherwise be implying that 'whatever is well written is a work of art', and this would have to include such things as 'a well-written advertisement or news item'.[29] Virginia Woolf herself cannot but agree to this despite the significance which she ascribes to 'pleasure' in essay-writing and essay-reading. Her continuing interest in the genre is determined more seriously by the conviction, shared by most essayists, that the essay bears within it a potential for artistic purity that can rival that of a poem or a novel.[30] At its best, it is 'the imaginative recreation of a culture, a period or an individual', the essayist being 'guided by an instinct to create for himself'.[31] The most eloquent account of this active, creative role which likens the essayist to the artist is to be found in Georg Lukács's essay on the essay via the analogy of portrait-painting, the main points of which have since been transcribed in clearer terms by Graham Good in his own work on the essay. Lukács draws a parallel between essay-writing and portrait-painting in a way that turns the former into a half-mimetic, half-creative experience, one that 'aims at a kind of truth, as well as imaginative response'.[32] The essayist strives for and manages to create a 'likeness' of his object in just the same way that a portraitist creates the 'likeness' of his sitter.[33] This paradoxical operation is done by 'observing and recording the "traits" of the object until some kind of vital configuration of aspects makes the separate objective features come to life as a likeness'.[34] Most significantly, portrait-painting—and by extension essay-writing—includes the artist as well as the model: in 'representing the likeness of his sitter', the portraitist and by extension the essayist 'also represents his own likeness in his painting' so that 'the created image is both "like" the sitter and "like" the artist; it is a convergence of individual identities'.[35] What Lukács calls the 'struggle (of the essay) for truth' will thus take the form of an 'incarnation'—whether of 'a man, an epoch, or a form', and the success of this

[28] Bonamy Dobrée (in relation to the *Tatler*), 'Essayists and Controversialists', *OHEL* vii. *English Literature in the Early Eighteenth Century (1700–1740)* (Oxford, 1959), 80.

[29] Georg Lukács, 'On the Nature and Form of the Essay', in *Soul and Form* (1974), 2 ['Über Wesen und Form des Essays', *Die Seele und die Formen*, 4–5].

[30] Addison's essays, for example, 'fully entitle him to the rank of a great poet', according to Macaulay as quoted and endorsed by Virginia Woolf in her 'Addison', *The Common Reader*, i. 96.

[31] Good on Virginia Woolf ('Virginia Woolf: Angles of Vision'), *The Observing Self*, 116; and Virginia Woolf's introduction to *The Common Reader*, i. 1. (*NB*: it is the 'common reader', in fact, who is 'guided by an instinct to create for himself'.)

[32] Good, *The Observing Self*, 17.   [33] Ibid. 21.

[34] Ibid. 185. In relation to this conception of portrait-painting and/as essay-writing, see also Good's discussion (pp. 17–18) of the notions of 'configuration' and 'constellation' used respectively by Max Bense and Walter Benjamin, another two very important German theorists (and practitioners) of the essay whom I will not be dealing with directly.

[35] Ibid. 21 and 185.

struggle, the capacity of 'the written text (to) convey to us this suggestion of that particular life' will depend 'on the intensity of the work and its vision'.[36] So if the essayist's imagination 'must carry [him] out of [himself] into the feelings of others', as one of Lukács's English predecessors—William Hazlitt—writes,[37] it must also carry him or her into the atmosphere of other places, events, or books. Only by projecting his imagination can the essayist breathe (new) life into and release the essence of his object in a way that yields a more intense sense of truth than would a simple description. Graham Good's discussion of some of Henry James's travel essays turns James's 'poetics of description', his use of memory and sense of place, into a perfect illustration of the way in which the core of identity of a particular event or location can be released. More familiar perhaps is Virginia Woolf's phenomenological view of reading and criticism (which Good also discusses) as an immersion into the world of the author in an attempt to become him or her and hence to do justice to his or her unique individuality.[38] In fact, criticism for Lukács, as for most German theorists, is not just one aspect of the essay but the essence itself of the genre, and the work of art is its most natural object.[39] In Lukács's piece, the question of the essay's belonging to the realm of literature on the basis of a shared attitude towards life is therefore raised in terms of the essential nature of criticism as a work of art, that is, of the essay's acquisition of the creative independence or autonomy endemic to the work of art which it discusses. Now, if the idea that criticism is at the core of all essays goes more or less without saying, the identification of criticism with the essay, on the other hand, could be said to involve a *type* of criticism—of 'modern' criticism—freed (or in the process of freeing itself) from its traditional, subordinating role. Lukács's location of the essay between the mimetic and the creative is a reminder that the rules which bind the essay to its object (typically expressed by the 'on' or 'of' of its title) are by no means inflexible. Since Montaigne's *Essais*, no one will deny the essayist the right to quote from the original without being required to provide the corresponding references or footnotes, for example, or indeed to quote at all accurately: the essayist's chosen object serves mostly as a pretext for the discussion of subjects

[36] Lukács, 'On the Nature and Form of the Essay', 11 (preceded by 'the really significant portraits give us, besides all other artistic sensations, also this: the life of a human being who once was really alive, forcing us to feel that his life was exactly as shown by the lines and colours of the painting') ['Über Wesen und Form des Essays', 24–5].

[37] William Hazlitt, in 'Essay upon the Principles of Human Action', quoted in Stapleton, *The Elected Circle*, 94.

[38] Cf. also Henry James, for whom the critic's life is 'heroic, for it is immensely vicarious. He has to understand for others, to answer for them; he is always under arms. . . . (The critic) deals with life at second hand as well as at first; that is, he deals with the experience of others, which he resolves into his own', 'The Science of Criticism', in Roger Gard (ed.), *The Critical Muse: Selected Literary Criticism* (1987), 294.

[39] The 'critical' thus transcends the four main (but not mutually exclusive) essayistic activities distinguished by Graham Good—travelling (ambulatory form), pondering, reading, and remembering—and which for him correspond to four principal types of essay—the travel essay, the moral essay, the critical essay, and the autobiographical essay, and to four (interconnected) objects: books and places, mores, and memories (*The Observing Self*, pp. xi–xii).

that are close to his heart. From the outset, then, the essay is characterized by the very combination of so-called 'critical' and 'poetic' intertextuality practised by modern criticism: where critical intertextuality is 'declared' and implies a hierarchy between primary and secondary discourse, the poetic type is tacit and places primary and secondary discourse on one level.[40] In this respect, the influence of English Impressionist criticism (above all that of Walter Pater and Oscar Wilde) on Lukács's approach is unmistakable, as is the influence, further back, of early German Romantic theories. The essay becomes the most appropriate vehicle for the fusion of criticism and 'poetry' heralded by Friedrich Schlegel and Novalis and for the kind of criticism advocated by Oscar Wilde in his 'The Critic as Artist', one in which 'the critic occupies the same relation to the work of art that he criticizes as the artist does to the visible world of form and colour, or the unseen world of passion and of thought', and which 'treats the work of art simply as a starting-point for a new creation'.[41]

I will come back to the implications of this fundamental question of the essay's critical function. Meanwhile the essay's licence—or the injunction it receives—to 'create anew' suggests that there is but one step from the aesthetic or literary treatment of the subject-matter to the properly fictional dimension of the essay's emancipation from its mimetic constraints. The standard definition of the essay as a short, non-fictional prose form does suggest that fiction has probably for some time been the most determining criterion for the inclusion and exclusion of genres into and from the sphere of literature. With regard to the canonization of great essays, this would substantiate the view that 'some things are literature simply by virtue of being fiction . . . while other things, non-fiction, only become literature by being particularly good'.[42] Still, the distinction between 'being fiction' and 'being particularly good' is arguably more apparent than real. Approaches to great essayists as (creative) writers presuppose a continuity rather than an alternative between what is 'fictional' and what is 'good', since both appeal to the notions of imagination, invention, creativity, and originality adumbrated above. Moreover, if great essays are not fictional as such, examples where in one way or the other 'imaginative re-creation' implies 'fiction' are rife. The essayist's very act of letting his imagination carry him out into the life of other individuals, of places or scenes, is often the motor for the conception of hypothetical characters in correspondingly hypothetical contexts. In Montaigne's *Essais*, true stories are interspersed with passages in which the essayist invites the reader to imagine a man in this or that situation (often introduced by expressions such as 'let us consider') and by extension to speculate with him on the physical and spiritual characteristics of man in general. In a sense, such quasi-fictional compositions are those of a quasi-narrator, sometimes even of a completely fictional narrator. The English periodical essay, in

---

[40] For the concepts of 'critical' and 'poetic' intertextuality, see Leyla Perrone-Moisés, 'L'intertextualité critique' (especially pp. 372–3); and Laurent Jenny, 'La Stratégie de la forme' in *Poétique*, 27 (1976).

[41] Oscar Wilde, 'The Critic as Artist' in *Plays, Prose Writings and Poems* (1930), 24–5 and 27–8.

[42] Quoted in Fowler, *Kinds of Literature*, 17.

fact, is probably the best-known kind of essay to mark the transition from the elaboration of the 'type'—in the tradition of the literary genre of the 'character'—to that of the fictional figure. The most famous examples are of course *The Tatler*, in which Steele and Addison introduce characters supposed to represent the main sectors of English society from the point of view of a fictional author-editor borrowed from Swift's pamphlets. This game with the fiction/reality divide is extended by the 'letters to the editor'—some of which are entirely fictitious—and reflected upon in the essay 542 of *The Spectator*. In *The Rambler*, occasionally in *The Adventurer* and *The Idler*, Samuel Johnson will in turn adopt all of Addison and Steele's main innovations: the fictional author-editor and other characters, but also the allegories, dream-visions, letters, and tales that support the fiction-making. Later on, Charles Lamb's 'The Essays of Elia', the first series in *The London Magazine*, are also cast as if written by Elia, a semi-autobiographical, semi-fictional—and therefore unreliable—narrator, while William Hazlitt's essays, which, according to Graham Good, can all be seen as 'characterizations' of one kind or another (whether of an idea, a scene, an event, or a work of art) also 'recurrently weave threads of fiction in a web of truth'.[43] In every case, the exploitation of fictional resources and strategies which manifests the essayist's apparent emancipation from mimeticism can actually be said to be motivated by an acute perception of reality's potential, and therefore ultimately to make possible a 'more intense perception of truth'.[44]

In this, one immediately recognizes the spirit of another prose form, that of the novel itself, from *Don Quixote* onwards. Indeed, it seems from the above that a good essay is one which skilfully handles the main constituents of the novel—the portrayal of characters and scene. For Henry James, the best critic is one who makes things 'as vivid and as free as the novelist makes his puppets'; equally for Virginia Woolf, Walter Pater is an exemplary essayist not so much for the wealth of his knowledge as for his 'vision' which 'remains with us', 'a vision, such as we get in a good novel where everything contributes to bring the writer's conception as a whole before us'.[45] The idea that good essay-writing should require the talents of good fiction, and especially in the form of the novel, is not arbitrary. In the

---

[43] Graham Good, 'Hazlitt: Ventures of the Self', in *The Observing Self*, 85; and Hugh Walker on Charles Lamb, *The English Essay and Essayists* (1915), 236. See also Graham Good's chapter on Johnson ('Johnson: The Correction of Error'), as well as Douglas Bush, 'Essays and Characters', *OHEL* v. *English Literature in the Earlier Seventeenth Century (1600–1660)* (Oxford, 1962); James Sutherland, 'Essays, Letters, and Journals', *OHEL* vi. *English Literature of the Late Seventeenth Century* (Oxford, 1969); Bonamy Dobrée, 'Essayists and Controversialists', in *OHEL* vii. *English Literature in the Early Eighteenth Century' (1700–1740)*; and, esp. on Hazlitt and Lamb, Ian Jack, in *OHEL* x. *English Literature 1815–1832* (Oxford, 1963).

[44] William Hazlitt, quoted from his *Round Table* in Good, *The Observing Self*, 87: 'imitation interests, then, by exciting a more intense perception of truth'.

[45] James, 'The Science of Criticism', 294; and Woolf, 'The Modern Essay', 213. See also Woolf, *The Common Reader*, i. 1. Wayne C. Booth is also tempted to assimilate the essay with the novel because of Montaigne as a 'created fictional character': the only obstacle to this assimilation has nothing to do with the status of fiction, but with the fact that 'there is no sustained narrative in the *Essais*', *The Rhetoric of Fiction*, 2nd edn. (1983), 228.

previous section I established a first parallel between essay and novel on the basis of their common ability to combine literary modes. But the real convergence lies in the historical and philosophical conjuncture which determines the emergence of the two genres at roughly the same period. In the same way that the essay is usually seen to have two founders, the Frenchman (or Continental) Montaigne and the Englishman Bacon, one can say that the rise of the novel occurs in two great moments or stages. One moment corresponds to the Continental appearance of the genre in the Renaissance (Cervantes is usually thought to be the first proper novelist), the other to the emergence of the English novel in the early eighteenth century. Ian Watt's still-celebrated book *The Rise of the Novel: Studies of Defoe, Richardson and Fielding* has made the circumstances surrounding the rise of the English novel more familiar to us. But his examination clearly applies to the rise of the novel in general, for he argues from the point of view of the parallel manifestation of the philosophical and literary innovations that have resulted from 'the vast transformation of Western civilization since the Renaissance'.[46] What his study indirectly corroborates, is that the essay is a form of art 'historically, philosophically, and to some extent formally akin to realistic fiction',[47] both of which go hand in hand with the rise of bourgeois individualism. According to Watt, the transformation of Western civilization at the time of the Renaissance lies mainly in a philosophical shift from universals to particulars. The unified world picture of the Middle Ages is replaced by a 'modern' world which presents us essentially with an aggregate of particular individuals. Correspondingly, modern philosophical realism which originates mainly in Descartes and Locke (but also includes Hume and Berkeley) is elaborated from the position that reality is apprehended above all by the senses; that the pursuit of truth is a wholly individual matter, a question of individual experience, which is always unique and therefore always new.[48] The novel, which deals with particular experiences at particular times and in particular places, is supposed to be the form of literature which most fully reflects the 'general temper' of this philosophical realism which is 'critical, anti-traditional, and innovating' with regard to 'the body of past assumptions and traditional beliefs'; it is 'the logical literary vehicle' of a culture which, in the last few centuries, has valorized novelty and originality to an unprecedented degree, rejecting all the pre-formed, ready-made models.[49]

This, however, could be said just as well of the essay, despite Watt's remark that 'it is significant that the trend in favour of originality found its first powerful expression in England, and in the eighteenth century'[50] (which also curiously disregards the role of the Continental novel). Montaigne's *Essais* are an equally

[46] Ian Watt, *The Rise of the Novel: Studies in Defoe, Richardson and Fielding* (1979), 34.

[47] Good, *The Observing Self*, 14.

[48] See 'Realism and the Novel Form', in Watt, *The Rise of the Novel*.

[49] Ibid. 13–14. These ready-made models would have been drawn mainly from mythology, history, and legend.

[50] Ibid. 15.

typical product, in the Renaissance, of the transition from a collective tradition to the focus on individuality and originality. This collective tradition is embodied by the various works of compilation—collections of commonplaces, of 'sentences' and 'adages' amongst other prose miscellanies—the 'ready-made models' that constitute the general cultural and ethical models at the time of the genre's development. Unlike literary works, these compilations, catalogues, lists, etc., offer themselves 'vertically' rather than 'horizontally'. They are 'not intended for . . . consecutive reading, since their function is 'transitive and instrumental';[51] they are consulted rather than read. The collective memory or encyclopedia which they form makes them essentially neutral, anonymous, or 'transindividual' texts: texts without authors or with more than one author, or texts which by dint of being passed on from generation to generation as sources of reference have lost, so to speak, their author. Now, the *Essais* are generated precisely as a reaction against the assimilated accumulation of classical learning (a 'memory-oriented' culture) which they confront in a reflexive or critical manner, and which goes hand in hand with the promotion of a textual subject.[52] They seem to embody more directly than any other genre of the period the modern assumption associated mainly with Descartes that truth is a matter of individual experience and consciousness. Like the novel, they favour particular experiences at particular times and at particular places and stress the fact that 'the senses are the beginning and the end of human knowledge'.[53] In fact, in both the French and the English tradition, the essay and its 'relatives' (the letter, the dialogue, the meditation, the inquiry, etc.) could be described as the *most immediate* literary vehicles of the new philosophy described by Ian Watt, that is, of a new, more popular manner of philosophizing which, like the science of the time, purports to be predominantly empirical (a knowledge based on experience), and which gives prominence to man's 'natural faculties' of judgement and places ordinary life and common man as everybody knows them at the centre of its investigations. In the same way that 'everything is the stuff of fiction',[54] everything can be said to be the stuff of the essay. One recognizes the popularizing or vulgarizing of philosophical, scientific, and generally cultural themes as a constant in the life of the essay from Montaigne (who is the first to write in the vernacular) to Virginia Woolf, who entitles her best-known volume of essays after Johnson's notion of 'the common reader'.[55] Through the use of such literary structures (which turns

[51] Michel Beaujour, *Poetics of the Literary Self-Portrait* (1991), 112.

[52] The textual subject 'comes into being as the side-product of the humanist's gathering, deciphering and classifying of ancient textual fragments in order to make them operative in the new culture of print', Beaujour, 'Genus Universum', 26. See also Colie, *The Resources of Kind*, 35–6; and François Rigolot, *Le Texte de la Renaissance: Des rhétoriqueurs à Montaigne* (1982), 174 and 258.

[53] Montaigne, 'An Apology of Raymond Sebond', *Essays*, II. 12, p. 663 ['Les sens sont le commencement et la fin de l'humaine cognoissance', *Essais*, II. xii, p. 572a].

[54] Virginia Woolf, quoted in Georgia Johnston, 'The Whole Achievement in Virginia Woolf's *Common Reader*', in Alexander J. Butrym (ed.), *Essays on the Essay: Redefining the Genre* (1989), 152.

[55] 'I rejoice to concur with the common reader; for by the common sense of readers, uncorrupted by literary prejudices, after all the refinements of subtlety and the dogmatism of learning, must be finally decided all claim to poetical honours', quoted from Samuel Johnson by Virginia Woolf in her preface to *The Common Reader*, i. 1.

philosophers into men of letters if not into literary artists[56]), the aim is to attract the attention of a fast-growing audience which finds philosophical treatises and dissertations too difficult to read, to 'compromise between the wits and the less educated, between the belles-lettres and religious instruction' thus catering, like the novel, for the 'public's taste for informative, improving, entertaining, and easy reading'.[57]

So a first conclusion can be drawn with regard to the status of the essay as 'literature *in potentia*'. It appears that the various techniques of literature, of fiction, and of the novel in particular (notably the central elements of character, setting, and consciousness) are the means by which some of the individual essays referred to above are supposed to have proven their excellence. At the same time, however, those are the very means by which the genre is also seen to take 'fictive *license*' with its material,[58] an idea which suggests a deviation from the normal rule and which reinterprets the complicity between essay and literature/art as the permissive and barely tolerated borrowing of a minor genre from an older, more established brother. On the one hand, then, it is the 'potentiality' of the essay's potentially literary status which awards it its real value. On the other, this potentiality stretches the essay to its limits, beyond the province of its true nature. Of course, the similarities between essay and fiction/novel can only be measured against differences: the lack of an overall plot and of a continuity in the existence of characters are an obvious criterion of differentiation. Above all, the essayist's stance towards his (or her) material, what he means by it, is not the same. For plot and character tend to be used as local illustrations for some point or other in the essay, and in the last instance, the essayist will use any such material as an indirect means or pretext to talk about himself (or herself) as a (real) person: everything will be subordinated to the self-definition of the essayist. 'Rarely if ever do the fictions seriously interfere with the genuineness of [the essayist's] confidences', for the 'disguises' of the essayist are 'usually transparent'.[59] Or are they? To essay, according to standard definitions, is to try out things and oneself in writing, or— from Lukács's perspective—to define and create oneself in the very process of defining and creating the object at hand. Thus the genre foregrounds, perhaps as no other genre does, the relationship between imagination and writing, between the person of the essayist made of flesh and blood and the essayist as defined or

---

[56] As has been said e.g. of Berkeley on the basis of his dialogues: 'whatever the philosophical merit of these dialogues may be, in all of them Berkeley shows himself a triumphant literary artist', Dobrée, 'The Philosophers', *OHEL* vii. *English Literature in the Early Eighteenth Century (1700–1740)* (Oxford, 1959), 283.

[57] Watt, *The Rise of the Novel*, 57, and the whole of that chapter entitled 'The Reading Public and the Rise of the Novel'. In her preface to *The Common Reader*, i. 1, Virginia Woolf defines Dr Johnson's 'common reader' (and by extension the essayist as she would like him or her to be) as one who 'differs from the critic and the scholar. He is worse educated, and nature has not gifted him so generously. He reads for his own pleasure rather than impart knowledge or correct the opinions of others'. See also Q. D. Leavis, *Fiction and the Reading Public* (1965); and Terry Eagleton, *The Function of Criticism: From 'The Spectator' to Post-Structuralism* (1984).

[58] George Core, 'Stretching the Limits of the Essay', in Butrym (ed.), *Essays on the Essay*, 215.

[59] Walker (on Charles Lamb), *The English Essay and Essayists*, 236.

created out of words alone. In this sense, 'the particular personality conveyed in an essay is always in some sense a *fiction*.'[60] The contract between essayist and reader may be transparent, yet 'as we read we must continually adjust ourselves to the emerging aspects of the essayist's *fictional self*.'[61] What this necessary adjustment to the 'emerging aspects of the essayist's fictional self' perhaps also underlines is that the prevailing view of the essay's potentially literary status tends to be a diachronic rather than a synchronic one: the essay is, and it is not literature; or rather the essay *is not yet* literature. In this second, most pervasive conception of the essay as literature *in potentia*, the (static) difference between the literary and the extraliterary expressed by the opposition is/is not, is grasped as the temporal and therefore dynamic difference of the 'is not yet'. It is to this most familiar and at the same time most complicated approach that I want to devote the next two sections.

1.3. DIACHRONIC APPROACH TO THE POTENTIALLY LITERARY

The priority granted to the essay's etymological sense of 'rehearsal' in most definitions of the genre has without a doubt a great deal to do with the tendency to conceive the essay as a precursor. The perception of the affinities between the essay and the three literary genres in those terms (and especially the novel, since as well as being a narrative and a fiction it is first and foremost a prose form) is betrayed by phrases gleaned from interpretations of individual essays such as 'moving the essay towards fiction'; a 'possibility in prose that approaches fiction'; 'a sort of "prose poetry" which can be seen as partial efforts in the direction of the novel'; or 'experiments which stop short of the borderline of the novel', etc.[62] The idea that the novel exists 'latently' in the essay operates equally at the level of literary history. With regard both to the Continental and to the English novel, and whether this is viewed from the perspective of the novel (Ian Watt or Mikhail Bakhtin), from that of the essay (Hugh Walker or Bonamy Dobrée), or both (in histories of literature), the novel which develops alongside the essay also seems to rise *from* the essay. This seems to be in keeping with the widely accepted view that literature's generic innovations usually involve an elevation or canonization of inferior, sub-literary forms, which turns the essay into a 'simple form' (waiting to be) absorbed into a more complex one.[63] In the Oxford history of early eighteenth-century English literature, for example, the whole series of *The Tatler* is described as being full of 'scattered adumbrations' of the short story or of the novel: even

---

[60] Klaus, 'Essay', 6.   [61] Ibid. 8.

[62] Core, 'Stretching the Limits of the Essay', 208; and Stapleton, *The Elected Circle*, 117, 146, and 157.

[63] This is a view attributed above all to Russian Formalists, here Victor Shklovsky as quoted in René Wellek and Austin Warren, *Theory of Literature*, 3rd edn. (1982), 235. For 'simple forms', see André Jolles, *Einfache Formen* (*Formes simples* (1972) in the French trans.) which focuses on nine pre-literary forms (not including the essay).

though 'they are not yet a short story', they are 'the plot for one, or for a short novel'.[64] For Ian Watt and Bonamy Dobrée also, *The Tatler* and *The Spectator* prepare the way for the novel: 'Steele and Addison used all the devices the earlier essayists had taught them—the philosophical thought, the description, the character, and so on, and they developed and welded them together till their volumes seemed half-way to the novel.'[65] What the argument of the essay as a precursor recognizably does is to turn the relationship between essay and novel into a *progression*, and therefore the essay into a supplement or residue which can be discarded once the intended goal has been reached. The idea that the English novel 'drew to itself the more imaginative talent which had used the periodical essay as a medium for dreams, allegories, short-stories and character sketches', and therefore has to answer for the 'decline of the type (of essay) inherited by Steele', is concomitant with the conviction that in the end, 'the (periodical) essay was itself responsible for its own weakening'; that 'it had been one of the means to its own undoing'.[66] So it is the novel which could in a sense be said to mark the culmination of the tradition of 'imaginative prose' referred to in the previous section. The novel makes the (literary) essay redundant precisely because it develops the latter's imaginative or fictional techniques to their full potential. Ultimately, it appears to be a successful 'reworking' of the essay not least by virtue of representing a further (more sophisticated because more indirect) stage in the embodiment of the philosophy that underlies both genres.

When thinking about the essay, the prevalence of the etymological sense of 'rehearsal' results in the displacement of the noun 'the essay'—which denotes a genre in its own right—by the verb 'to essay', which denotes a relationship of transitivity and dependence. Thus, the idea of the essay 'preparing for the novel' or conversely of the novel trying itself out in the essay, implies a shift of perspective from an autonomous literary genre to an act (the act of essaying) that is only justified by its leading up to something else: the genre is presented in terms of what it is not, or not yet. This shift from 'the essay' to 'essaying' recognizably operates simultaneously at the level of literary history and of the individual writer's work when the latter comprises essays written before the literature 'proper'. In both cases, the autonomy of the 'literary essay' is undermined or at least considerably shaken by a retrospective evaluation which post-dates the advent of the literary genre and casts the essays of essayists (Addison and Steele) but also of essayists and 'creative writers' (Virginia Woolf or Jorge Luis Borges) as 'finger

---

[64] Dobrée, 'Steele', *OHEL* vii. *English Literature in the Early Eighteenth Century' (1700–1740)* (Oxford, 1959), 79–80. See also John Hollowell, *Fact and Fiction: The New Journalism and the Nonfiction Novel* (1971).

[65] Bonamy Dobrée, *English Essayists* (1946), 21; cf. also Ian Watt: 'The periodical essay did much in forming a taste that the novel, too, could cater for', and 'the public's taste for informative, improving, entertaining, and easy reading had not as yet found an appropriate fictional form' (*The Rise of the Novel*, 56 and 57).

[66] Hugh Walker, in 'The Early Reviewers of the Nineteenth Century: Some of their Victims, and Others', *The English Essay and Essayists*, 193.

exercises, drills . . . for the novelist's [or creative writer's] sensibility'.[67] In other words, the approach to the (literary) essay seems sooner or later to be contaminated by the hazier connotations of 'essaying' or essayism in general, connotations which emphasize the pre- or sub-literary function of the genre. The literary potential of the essay as a 'short, non-fictional prose form' acquires its meaning in so far as the essay strives towards a form which, especially in the case of the novel, is no longer 'short' and no longer non-fictional. In the first instance, the scope and size of the essay and of essay-relatives enhances its quality as supplement or by-product.[68] For the marginality and indeterminacy of the essay is perceived as combining both the form's inner fragmentariness and its quality as a fragment. Its condition is to herald a state or moment which has not yet been accomplished but which also foreshadows the completion and totalization generally associated with art and more particularly, in literature itself, with narrative continuity. So my earlier consideration of the essay's paratactic structure as one borrowed from poetry is here ignored or taken over by a tendency to merge the essay—however 'complete'—with the body of drafts and 'notes towards' that surround an author's 'work'. The resonance of the draft is, in a sense, extratextual: it operates where and as long as the writing has not yet begun. Accordingly, the pre-literary and pre-generic position of the essay is justified by the unstructured—the not-yet-rhetorically-structured—quality of the draft. In the case of the essay specifically, the 'not-yet-written' is endemic to a form which is seen to go no further than the exploration or essaying of the conditions of its meaning, this side of the writing itself. Moreover, in the case of the essay this is encouraged by the supposedly spontaneous and 'natural' style of a genre which is often thought (at least in the original form of the 'familiar essay') to try out its ideas according to the order in which they come to mind, thus remaining closest to the informality of speech. Hence the use of the dialogue (including in the letter-form) as a central component of the essay, a dialogue which, conformably with the role ascribed to parataxis, is not looked upon here as the expression of a literary (dramatic) procedure, but on the contrary as the negation of literariness. This 'artless' quality of the essay, which adds to the label of formlessness that of the unwritten, becomes a definite reason for banning the form from the realm of literature, since prior to involving the question of aesthetic autonomy and wholeness which applies equally to other forms of art, it is understood that literature is first and foremost a class of texts. Ultimately, the kind of progress involved in the passage from the unwritten to the written recognizably overlaps with the 'positivistic' consideration of the draft in traditional genetic studies, that is, with the point of view of a linear progression which leads from incoherence and incompleteness to the totalizing mastery of meaning, to a final(ized) text that materializes through the filling in of gaps or the reduction of the play of differences. The passage from the non-fictional to the

---

[67] Mark Shorer on *The Death of the Moth*, quoted in Vijay L. Sharma, *Virginia Woolf as Literary Critic: A Revaluation* (1977), 12.

[68] See Jean Lafond, *Les Formes brèves de la prose et le discours continu* (*XVIe–XVIIe siècles*) (1984).

fictional, however, is equally important. For the allocation of the essay to the pre-literary strongly appeals to the idea of 'skeleton' or 'outline', with material that remains abstract and external to the work as long as it has not been creatively embodied. In a sense, the essay is the type of draft which is most naturally associated with reflection, with theory. It stands for the body of the author's ideas that have yet to be 'fleshed out'. And this fleshing out is exactly what the novel prospectively provides, by presenting the idea(s) in the form of a continuous plot and substantial characters ready to act them out, and by replacing the total or partial fusion of essayist and author with the proper aesthetic distance of a fully-fledged narrator.

The essayist is strongly urged, then, to 'move on' to literature 'proper'. For there is no escaping the fact that 'to essay' has a strong amateurish connotation: anyone can try their luck at essays even—or perhaps especially—if they are not blessed with creative genius, the essay being 'a sort of testing ground where aspirants for literary fame might prove their skill'.[69] If he or she fails to make the leap, 'the essayist, unlike the novelist, the poet, and the playwright, must be content in his self-imposed role of second-class citizen'.[70] The only strategy left in his power, apparently, is the exploitation of the falsely modest claims of a *captatio benevolentia* which enables him or her to write, like Barthes, 'I must admit . . . that I have produced *only* essays'.[71] We have seen that the criteria of value that underlie this 'only' are numerous and contradictory. The essayist, in a word, is either too frivolous or too serious; either way, he oversteps the mark. 'Frivolous', superficial, and trivial because he only touches upon his subject here and there, 'impressionistically'; because he writes mere 'anecdotes of the intellect'.[72] He refuses to 'develop', to go deeper into the matter at hand. This goes together with the essay's enormous range of potential topics, with its concern with the common man and the common reader which gives it licence to stoop to the most trivial, with its propensity to popularize or vulgarize.[73] At its worst, the essay resembles gossip: 'the bad essay', writes Theodor W. Adorno, 'chats about people instead of opening up the matter at hand; in this the essay form is somewhat complicitous.'[74] Finally, the essayist's tendency (mentioned in the previous section) to indulge in too 'arty' a style can again be taken as the sign of a lack of skill or mastery. At the other end of the scale, however, the reluctance to consider the essay as literature can equally well be justified by its artlessness—by an informality also verging (or so it seems) on a lack of literary skill. In this case, in fact, the essay is above all accused of

---

[69] Thompson, *The Seventeenth-Century English Essay*, 139.

[70] E. B. White, quoted in Core, 'Stretching the Limits of the Essay', 215–16.

[71] Quoted in O. B. Hardison, Jr., 'Binding Proteus: An Essay on the Essay', in Alexander J. Butrym (ed.), *Essays on the Essay: Redefining the Genre* (1989), 14.

[72] Quoted from Ralph Waldo Emerson in Stapleton, *The Elected Circle*, 182.

[73] Cf. A 'highly miscellaneous fare that ranges from cooking recipes to conumdrums', in Alexander J. Butrym (ed.), *Essays on the Essay* (1989).

[74] Theodor W. Adorno, 'The Essay as Form', *New German Critique*, 32 (1984), 154 ['Der Essay als Form', in *Noten zur Literatur*, i (1958), 15].

excessive seriousness when synonymous with criticism, with ideas, with theory—with reflection. The various ways in which the essay signals its transitory position in the margins of a work to come is clinched by the concretely paratextual status of a genre which functions like a paratext when it has not been published literally as a paratext. For Gérard Genette—an expert on paratextuality—the paratext encompasses two (related) categories: that of the 'epitext' which includes drafts, autobiographies, diaries, letters, interviews, and other self-commentaries (of the 'How I wrote this book'-type[75]) and which is to be found immediately outside the periphery of the literary work, and, a bit further 'in', the 'peritext': the titles, prefaces, footnotes, conclusions that can be found immediately within the periphery of the literary work. As a rehearsal, the essay operates like a preliminary paratext (draft or foreword/preface) but also like a post-liminary paratext when its metalinguistic, critical role is at stake.[76] In Montaigne's *Essais*, this critical role begins 'peritextually', so to speak, as a development of notes or glosses in the margins of the existing intertext. Instances where the essay is cast as another form (the epitextual genres of the autobiography, the diary, or the letter which recognizably overlap with the 'neighbouring' forms examined in the previous section) show the essay's ability to function 'as' a paratext. This ability is reinforced by the genre's tendency to be published (often retrospectively) in the peritextual form of the preface (Barthes's, for example) in the same way that prefaces are sometimes retrospectively published as essays (Henry James's, for example). The essay's appropriation of the concretely paratextual, which provides the essayist with the various roles of annotator, editor, or prefacier, reinforces the features of literary 'secondariness' flaunted from the outset by the paratext's position. Indeed, the paratext is a fragment in relation to the text which it (re)presents; it conveys the non-exhaustive, the unwritten, the extratextual, the non-fictional. In rehearsing the work, the foreword or preface, for example, only skims over a subject which then remains to be developed. It is not-yet-written or extratextual in the sense that it favours the abstract, the theoretical, or the critical: to give an 'idea' of the literary work in a preface or in a conclusion is to 'tell' rather than to 'show'. Whatever the emphasis, the paratext draws attention to its secondary role with regard to the literary work which it both introduces and repeats, and therefore to its dispensability.[77]

So far, then, the progression from essay to literature has led to the marginalization of the essay in a way that turns the latter into a raw material always about to be absorbed and transformed. The smoothing over of the essay's disorderly fragmentariness and the working of the non-fictional into the fictional and of the

---

[75] This also encompasses all other oral and public performances by the author such as interviews, lectures, etc. (Gérard Genette, *Seuils* (1987), 10).

[76] For the 'metatextual' function of the paratext, see Gérard Genette, *Palimpsestes: La Littérature au second degré* (1982), 15.

[77] This, of course, also applies to the case where the prefatory material (however brilliant) is provided by another author.

abstract into the concrete already initiated within the essay are the mark of a transformation that is especially effective when the end-product is the novel itself, that is, a fictional prose form which develops predominantly in the narrative mode. And yet the novel has another, much more conspicuous way of taking the essay over and making it redundant as a genre: this is by incorporating it as such into its own texture. The novel, in fact, displays to an unprecedented degree the capacity of all literary genres to integrate short non-fictional prose forms like the essay (letters, diaries) and/or 'peritexts' (prefaces, conclusions, footnotes)—as early Continental and English novels testify. Since the beginning of this century, literary genres which exhibit essayistic material in this fashion have often been referred to as 'essayistic' novels, plays, or poems. The novel remains the genre to which the adjective 'essayistic' is most recurrently applied, and mainly in German literary criticism with reference above all to German Romantic novelists (Jean Paul and Schlegel), to Goethe, and to novelists of (roughly) the first half of the century such as Thomas Mann, Alfred Döblin, Robert Musil, Hermann Broch, Hermann Hesse, etc., who have also been described as 'post-Romantic' novelists. This choice of novelists, to which one has also added French and English exponents such as André Gide, Marcel Proust, James Joyce, or Aldous Huxley, indicates that the essayistic novel cuts across the established categories of the *Bildungsroman* (the novel of 'formation', 'education', or 'initiation' theorized by the German Romantics, Hegel, Georg Lukács, and Mikhail Bakhtin) and, more broadly, of the polyphonic novel (a novel which, for Mikhail Bakhtin, is instituted by Dostoyevsky and 'contrapuntually' confronts a multiplicity of 'voices'); and indeed, the theoretical characterization of the essayistic novel in German literary criticism brings together features which have been ascribed to both categories. What the essayistic novel is seen to foreground above all, is generic mixture or hybridism: since the integration of the essay-fragment into its fictional frame is not done by way of a dissolution, the demarcation of the essayistic material results in a confrontation between the cognitive and the aesthetic, theory and practice, potentiality and actualization, fragment and whole, poem and prose (the paratactic structure of the essay is also perceived as the structure of poetry), which brings about the disruption of narrative sequence. For theorists of the polyphonic novel, this confrontation occurs as the novel puts into dialogue and thus relativizes all those discourses—including its own—which assume they are the only voice of truth. From the point of view of the *Bildungsroman*, these tensions reflect the examination of the problematic relationship between the subject's (hero's) potential (which encompasses the particular as well as the virtuality of theory) and his self-realization in the world (the universal, 'practice', or narrative actualization). Either way, the essayistic novel is one which seems to hover between an idea and its concretization, between the 'not-yet-written' quality of the fragment and the 'writing out' of narrative. So the presence of locatable essayistic material in the novel goes hand in hand with a generalized 'self-essaying' or essayistic attitude, that is, with a blatant reflection or 'philosophizing' on the conditions of its realization or on the conditions 'in potentia' of its (the novel's) own meaning. The essayistic novel appears in other words to magnify the main qualities—or 'lack of qualities', to follow the logic of Robert Musil's famous novel—of the essay which it incorporates. And this no doubt explains why, along with all the other examples enumerated in the course of this chapter, prototypes of the essayistic novel such as Goethe's *Wilhelm Meister* novels, Jean Paul's *Titan*, Broch's *The Sleepwalkers* [*Die Schlafwandler*], Musil's *The Man Without Qualities* [*Der Mann ohne Eigenschaften*], Proust's *Remembrance of Things Past* [*À la Recherche du Temps Perdu*], Gide's *Les Faux-monnayeurs*, Joyce's *Ulysses*, Huxley's *Point Counter Point*, etc., are also included as typical manifestations of the essay, and therefore also identified with the genre.[78]

There is little doubt, then, that the act of essaying which, because of its etymological credentials, passes off as the essence of the essay, as its irreducible core, is least definitional of genre itself. By definition, one might say, the act of essaying can be applied to any (other) genre. The implications of this identification of the essay with the 'essayistic' or 'essayism' seems to me to be most usefully discussed from the point of view of Alastair Fowler's distinction between genre (or what Fowler calls 'kind'[79]) and mode. Any kind may be extended as a mode, according to Fowler, and the idea of 'modal extension' is used to draw attention to 'the structurally dependent status of mode vis-à-vis kind'. The main difference between the two, he writes, is that 'the terms for kinds, perhaps in keeping with their obvious external embodiment, can always be put in noun form, whereas modal terms tend to be adjectival'.[80] Modes involve a more elusive generic idea than kind. They are said to select 'only the corresponding kind's features'—which may amount to nothing more than 'tinges of generic colour'—a selection 'from which the overall external structure is absent'.[81] Most significantly, the independent consideration of these modal features from the unifying, regulating concept of an 'overall external structure' obeys a diachronic logic. Fowler contends that the mode is likely to supplant the genre only when the latter has become obsolete or 'outmoded', modes being the 'distillations, from these relatively evanescent forms, of the permanently valuable features': 'Thus they have achieved independence of contingent embodiments and may continue to all ages, incorporated in almost any external form, long after the antecedent kind has passed away.'[82] In some of the German studies most concerned with the essayistic novel, this proposition is in fact radicalized by the conviction that rather than giving way to the essayistic historically, the essay is from the start nothing other than the embodiment or

---

[78] For a bibliography on the essayistic novel, see Ch. 5.

[79] 'Kinds may be characterized by any of the elements of the generic repertoire' (Fowler, *Kinds of Literature*, 88).

[80] Ibid.   [81] Ibid. 107–8.   [82] Ibid. 111.

[83] Gerhard Haas, in *Studien zur Form des Essays und zu seinen Vorformen im Roman* (1966), 39–40, describes the form of the essay as a 'sum of its discreet features', indeed as an 'extrapolation' of the essayistic style or 'attitude'. Bruno Berger, *Der Essay: Form und Geschichte* (1964), 189, also talks about the essay as the 'external form' of the essayistic (however, he also dogmatically asserts on p. 115 that 'pseudo-essays'—as opposed to 'ideal' essays—'can be unmasked', though it is not at all clear how he

extrapolation of the essayistic.[83] In this perspective, the 'absence' of the 'overall external structure'—Fowler's 'kind'—is not one which follows from a process of selection whereby the mode remains 'structurally dependent vis-a-vis kind', but on the contrary one which is to be filled—extrapolated—a posteriori.

The question of the essay's relation to its mode thus reinforces what my diachronic approach to the notion of literature *in potentia* has yielded so far: everything about the overlap between essay and literature/novel points to the superfluousness or 'outmodedness' of the essay. No genre can be said to exist in its 'pure' state. But in the case of the essay, the question of delimitation, of where the genre begins and where it stops, what it includes and what it excludes, seems particularly acute. The fact that 'there is no genre that takes so many shapes and that refuses so systematically to resolve itself, finally, into its own shape'[84] is betrayed from the outset by theorists' striking resistance to referring to '*the* essay'. The pervasive use of adjectives in front of the word 'essay' is the first sign of this resistance (as in the dialogic, epistolary, autobiographical essay, or the narrative, dramatic, poetic essay). Pushed to its most absurd limit, the 'essayistic essay' is the closest one comes to referring to 'the' essay![85] As noted above, the ultimate expression of this resistance occurs when the adjective has displaced the word 'essay' altogether and replaced it with its own derived noun: the essay is then a dialogue, a letter, an autobiography, etc.; or a poem, a play, a story, a novel; it becomes a catch-all for genres on both sides of the literary margin. Everything about the essay contributes to looking at it—or for it—in other genres, which turns evanescence and obsolescence into its very substance. Ultimately, this must be because the essayistic supplements something which is already present in the genres in relation to which it is defined. The novel is a case in point. Using the term 'essayistic novel' in critical or theoretical discourse to draw attention to the distinct presence of the essay only stresses the fact that the essayistic novel, the *Bildungsroman* or the polyphonic novel are not so much a type of novel (one which like other genres deserves to be called 'essayistic' because it does not readily fall into a clear-cut category), or a novel 'in crisis' (the crisis of the narrative syntagm), but *the* novel in all its typicality. From the outset, the novel is the most 'naturally' essayistic genre. It is the baggiest, the most indeterminate, the most 'imperialistic' literary genre in that without scruple it colonizes and annexes surrounding territories. It is the most reflexive and critical in that it constantly questions its own form. The 'essayistic' thus appears simply to foreground the essence of the novel. In the works of Roland Barthes and Mikhail Bakhtin, in fact, what I have described

---

proposes to do so). Michael Hamburger claims that 'the essay is a style rather than a form' ('Essay über den Essay', *Akzente*, 12 (1965), 291), and this is further elaborated in Dieter Bachmann's *Essay und Essayismus* (1969) which revolves around the distortion which 'essayism' (the essence of the essay) goes through when transposed into the concrete form of an essay.

[84] Hardison, 'Binding Proteus: An Essay on the Essay', 12.

[85] See '"The Essay as Essay" or as "Essayistic Essay"' in Robert Scholes and Carl Klaus (eds.), *Elements of the Essay* (1969).

as the 'essayistic' or 'essayism' is presented as the 'novelistic' or 'novelness', and is associated with the indeterminacy, open-endedness, and generic criticism typical of the progressive, boundless, and non-canonic genre of the novel. In this sense, the 'novelistic' and the conception of German 'Romanticism'—also derived from the novel [*Roman*]—converge; for like the essayistic, the novelistic, novelness, or the 'Romantic', are notions which are not confined to the genre of the novel but can be made to apply to any other genre. The absorption of the essay (and of genres like the essay) by literary genres then becomes the unmistakable sign of the novel's supremacy and of the resulting 'novelization' or Romanticization of all genres, characteristic of our modern times. But in the end, does not the displacement of the essay by the essayistic and/or by the novelistic mode, which reflects a problematization and expansion of the text 'because the usual idea of the text as a closed, hermetic structure that is always adequate to itself is brought into question',[86] point to the supremacy of 'literariness' itself? As Gérard Genette points out, the paratext—which the essay exemplifies—is a 'class of texts' but also an 'aspect of textuality', and '*a fortiori* an aspect of literariness'.[87] The ease with which theorists like Carl Klaus (and Robert Scholes) interchangeably use the essay as play, poem, or story for what they otherwise refer to as the dramatic, the poetic, and the narrative essay, comes at first from recognizing the essayistic features of these literary genres at their most 'artful', i.e. self-conscious. But this rapidly gives way to the recognition of the inherently essayistic features of 'every form of literature', and although it is only hinted at in the last, concluding section ('Approaching an Essay') of the two versions of their book, this acknowledgement appears as the real (albeit retrospective) justification for their (and any) interest in the essay:

We hope to encourage the study of the essay as a literary form 1) because the form has great vitality and is represented by many good works 2) the more obviously artful kinds of literature share some of the essential qualities of the essay and cannot be fully understood without reference to their essayistic dimensions. With that in mind, we have tried to relate the elements of the essay to the other literary forms.

And:

When you read poetry, drama and fiction, be alert for the essayistic dimension of these literary forms. The ability to analyze the essay with sense and sensitivity will stand in good stead in dealing with every form of literature.[88]

The inherently essayistic dimension of literary genres seems indeed to be the key to the initial desire (shared long before by Alfred Kerr and the German Romantics) to acknowledge the essay and other critical or didactic prose works as a fourth

[86] Katherina Clark and Michael Holquist, *Mikhail Bakhtin* (1984), 297.

[87] Genette, *Palimpsestes*, 15.

[88] In the introductory (and unpaginated) 'On the Nature and Purpose of this Text', and p. 86 of *Elements of the Essay* (1969 edn.). This second quotation is repeated word for word in the 1991 edn., p. 39, except that 'be alert to the essayistic dimension of these literary forms' becomes 'be alert to the essay-like dimensions of these literary forms'.

literary category, or as what Fowler also calls 'extended literature'.[89] 'Extension' presupposes that art—the literary—is germane to the critical genre of the essay and that conversely criticism is germane to art. Scholes and Klaus's apparent promotion of the form to a genre its own right, that is, with rights equal to the other three categories, is founded on a vision of the essay, the story, the play, and the poem as 'four points on a *continuum* of literary possibilities' which overlap and cross-fertilize one another, the idea being that literature involves both formal beauty and truth and that the essay is only 'the form *most directly* concerned with truth' (emphasis added).[90] The interpretation of this difference as only a difference in degree or emphasis is also that established by Northrop Frye between the 'thematic' ('literature with an ideal or conceptual interest') and the 'fictional' modes ('dianoia' and 'mythos'):

It is easy to say that some literary works are fictional and others thematic in their main emphasis. But clearly there is no such thing as *a* fictional or *a* thematic work of literature. . . . Every work of literature has both a fictional and a thematic aspect, and the question of which is more important is often simply a matter of opinion or emphasis in interpretation.[91]

Approaching the essay as a fourth literary genre in order to do justice to it as a genre in its own right thus paradoxically amounts to confirming the suspicion that this fourth genre has been created from a desire to supplement something, the 'thematic', which is already there in the first place, since 'mythos' and 'dianoia' emerge as complementary aspects of all literature. But what this logic of supplementation seems to suggest above all, is that from not (yet) being 'up' to literature, the notion of literature *in potentia* which the essay epitomizes may on the contrary be synonymous with the magnification or blowing up of literary properties, with the supra-literary or the essence itself of all literature.[92] And this accordingly raises the question of whether the a-genericness of the essay might not be synonymous with its status as the 'matrix of all generic possibilities', as one Barthes critic persuasively argues:

One can say that the essay is not *a* genre like any other, and perhaps not a *genre* at all. . . . Nor is the essay a mixture of genres. It does not mix genres, it complicates them: the genres are, in a way, its (the essay's) 'fallout', the historically determined actualizations of what is potentially woven into the essay. The latter appears, then, as the moment of writing *before* the genre, before genericness—or as the matrix of all generic possibilities. What if, finally, the Essay belongs in the last instance to the genre of the *Other* by which the *genres* communicate with each other? . . . The essay would be neither non-being as Nothing nor being as Everything, but the figure of Alterity, the Other that generates all other (genres).[93]

---

[89] Fowler, *Kinds of Literature*, 9.   [90] Scholes and Klaus (eds.), *Elements of the Essay*, 2.

[91] Northrop Frye, *Anatomy of Criticism: Four Essays* (1957), 52–3. See also Paul Hernadi, *Beyond Genre: New Directions in Literary Classifications* (1972), 99; and Northrop Frye's *The Secular Scripture: A Study of the Structure of Romance* (1976).

[92] This is also Dominique Noguez's conclusion to 'Qu'est-ce que la paralittérature?' ('What is Paraliterature?'), in *Scolies*, 2 (1972), 37.

[93] Réda Bensmaïa, *The Barthes Effect: The Essay as Reflective Text* (1987), 91–2.

The logical conclusion of this diachronic approach to the essay is the recognition of its complete dispersal or dissemination, one which is inscribed in its very logic. But this is the theoretical conclusion. We know that in practice, the coexistence of the essay and literary genres has not led to the disappearance of the former. The essay has 'survived' the emergence of the novel at the level of literary history (some of the essayists who post-date the advent of the novel are considered to be the finest of all) just as it survives at the level of writers' individual works (many novelists continue to write essays alongside and/or after their production of fiction). As with the relationship between the essay and the other paraliterary forms in which it was supposed to exist latently, the 'latent' existence of the novel in the essay does not preclude the continued existence of the former alongside the latter. From the transitive point of view implied in the verb 'to essay', the English periodical essay is 'weakened' by the rise of the novel and must prepare to 'perish'. But in point of fact, this weakening forces the essay to 'find fresh strength elsewhere', to be 'transformed'—in this case into the modern review and the modern magazine.[94] Thus, 'it may with some justice be said that Steele unwittingly prepared the way for the novel; but to claim that he was feeling towards it, even when he invented the Coverley group . . . is almost certainly untrue. He aimed at some finality in a certain genre, and he achieved it.'[95] Virginia Woolf's discussion on Addison in one of her essays already makes the point quite categorically, all the more so, perhaps, as the autonomous value of her own essays with regard to her fiction is indirectly at stake. She begins by putting forward the accepted view that 'if we wish to find anything more vivid than Addison's best portraits, we must go either to Shakespeare or to Cervantes', and that 'we have not the least doubt that if Addison had written a novel on an extensive plan it would have been superior to any that we possess'.[96] Yet she does so only in order to counter that:

To call Addison on the strength of his essays a great poet, or to prophesy that if he had written a novel on an extensive plan it would have been 'superior to any that we possess', is to confuse him with the drums and trumpets. . . . The Sir Roger de Coverley papers are those which have the most resemblance, on the surface, to a novel. But their merit consists in the fact that they do not adumbrate, or initiate, or anticipate anything; they exist, perfect, complete, entire in themselves. To read them as if they were a first hesitating experiment containing the seed of greatness to come is to miss the peculiar point of them.

And she concludes:

The novel is not a development from that model, for the good reason that no development along these lines is possible. . . . The form of the essay admits of its own particular perfection; and if anything is perfect the exact dimensions of its perfection become immaterial.[97]

[94] Walker, *The English Essay and Essayists*, 193.

[95] Dobrée, 'Steele', *OHEL* vii. *English Literature in the Early Eighteenth Century (1700–1740)* (Oxford, 1959), 80.

[96] Woolf, 'Addison', 95–6.

[97] Ibid. 102–4. Cf. also Laurence Stapleton on De Quincey: 'But if De Quincey's writing is suggestive to a novelist, the novel form was not a possible one for De Quincey' (*The Elected Circle*, 59).

The identification of the essay with the preliminary paratexts of the draft and the preface discussed above must also be reconsidered along these lines. For the logic of the paratext is from the outset an inherently paradoxical one. In so far as the paratext (and paraliterature) is an 'uncertain zone between inside and outside', a zone of exclusion and inclusion without a rigorous limit either towards the inside (the text) or towards the outside (the world's discourse on the text)',[98] the issue of whether we are dealing with a by-product, a supplement, or with an autonomous form is germane to its very essence. The prefix 'para' of 'paraliterary' immediately conveys the dual meaning of 'against' as 'alongside', 'parallel to', and as 'counter', as opposition; it immediately raises the question of whether the relationship between the centre and the periphery is one of continuity, of homogeneity, or on the contrary one of heterogeneity. The answer, of course, is: 'both'. Not only is the paratext an 'aspect of all textuality' and a class of text; it is a genre in its own right.[99] In this one recognizes the paradoxical logic of the fragment as a genre, as theorized and practised by the early German Romantics. The fragment is at once a detached piece and an autonomous whole, a 'microcosm' and an 'analogon': 'A fragment, like a miniature work of art, has to be entirely isolated from the surrounding world and be complete in itself like a porcupine.'[100] The fragment can be part of a whole which exists; or part of a whole which it does not yet—or no longer—belong to; alternatively, there can be an absolute hiatus between fragment and whole.[101] The relationship between draft and 'completed' text is not to be regarded (only) as a linear progression leading to a finalized text through the filling in of gaps or the reduction of the play of differences. The drafts are not so much residues as different versions of the text outside the chronological rationale of a 'before' and 'after', of cause and effect.[102] And this, of course, applies all the more obviously to the preface which rehearses a work that it also already embodies to some extent. In fact, it is precisely because the paratext stands for or 're-presents' the text, that it makes the text accessible to the reader without his or her having

---

[98] Genette, *Seuils*, 8.   [99] Genette, *Palimpsestes*, 15.

[100] Friedrich Schlegel, *Athenäum Fragments*, 206, in Wheeler (ed.), 48 ['Ein Fragment muss gleich einem kleinen Kunstwerke von der umgebenden Welt ganz abgesondert und in sich selbst vollendet sein wie ein Igel', *Athenäums-Fragmente*, in Wolfdietrich Rasch (ed.), *Friedrich Schlegel: Kritische Schriften* (1970), 47]. For the Romantic fragment as 'microcosm' and 'analogon', see Philippe Lacoue-Labarthe and Jean-Luc Nancy, *L'Absolu littéraire: Théorie de la littérature du Romantisme allemand* (1978), ('Le Fragment'), 67–9.

[101] See Lawrence Kritzman (ed.), *Fragments: Incompletion and Discontinuity* (1981); Maurice Blanchot, *Le Livre à venir* (1959), and *L'Entretien infini* (1969); Steven Ungar, 'Parts and Holes: Heraclitus/Nietzsche/Blanchot', *Sub-stance*, 14 (1976), 126–41; Jefferson Humphries, 'The Otherness in Common/Places', *L'Esprit Créateur*, 24 (1984), 48–56; Philip Beitchman, 'The Fragmentary Word', *Sub-stance*, 39 (1983), 58–74; one volume of *Études Françaises* dedicated to the fragment: 'Le Fragment/La Somme'; and Lucien Dällenbach's *The Mirror in the Text* (1989). The connection between fragment and 'writing' is also at the centre of the whole of Jacques Derrida's work.

[102] On the draft as the text's 'other', see Jean Levaillant, *Écriture et génétique textuelle: Valéry à l'œuvre* (1982), esp. pp. 13–15; Jean Bellemin-Noël, *Le Texte et l'avant-texte: Les Brouillons d'un poème de Milosz* (1972), 15, and *Vers l'inconscient du texte* (1979); and Julia Kristeva's 'génotexte' and 'phénotexte' in *Révolution du langage poétique* (1974).

to read it.[103] The paradoxical logic of the fragment and by extension of the paratext which determines the essay, ultimately makes possible the dual appraisal of its paratactical structure as an affiliation to the literary genre of poetry *and* as the expression of the not-yet-written, the pre-literary and even pre-generic. Actually, we will see that art itself is at the root of the artless quality of Montaigne's *Essais* and of the natural, speech-like spontaneity one ascribes to the genre. The continuous revisions which Montaigne made to his text are a constant reminder of this dependence of artlessness on art, of the fact that the unstudied spontaneity of the style is the result of much skill (especially in a genre which starts off as being 'a trifle literary'[104]). The fragmentariness of the essay is the manifestation of a 'methodically unmethodical' organization,[105] the vehicle, as Aldous Huxley writes in the preface to his own *Collected Essays*, of 'free association artistically controlled'; in appearance 'one damned thing after another' but in reality the attempt 'to say everything at once in as near an approach to contrapuntual simultaneity as the nature of literary art will allow of'.[106]

1.4. MONTAIGNE'S *ESSAIS* AND THE ESSAY

1.4.1. The Essais *and the Essayistic*

It would be difficult to pursue this introduction without examining more closely the links which I have provided between the above conception of the essay and the original model of the *Essais* themselves. Choosing Montaigne as the original model of the genre does not altogether go without saying. For as I pointed out above, the genre is usually seen to have not one but two founders, Montaigne and Bacon, corresponding to two slightly different traditions of essays. Nevertheless, and for reasons which have not only to do with chronological precedence, the *Essais* remain the work that has determined implicitly if not explicitly all subsequent definitions (including the dictionary definition) of and approaches to the genre. The most striking fact about the *Essais* is that despite the unshakeable literary status which they have enjoyed ever since their appearance, they are founded on the tension described above between mode and genre, whereby the genre is in fact defined predominantly in terms of the mode. Whether the mode is given diachronic precedence over the genre (when the latter is seen as an extrapolation of the former) or whether it is regarded as the only surviving feature of the genre,

---

[103] As stated by Antoine Compagnon, who chooses the word 'perigraphy' rather than 'paratextuality', in *La Seconde Main, ou Le Travail de la citation* (1979), 328.

[104] Dobrée, *OHEL* vii. *English Literature in the Early Eighteenth Century*, 80—quoted and discussed in my previous section.

[105] Adorno, 'The Essay as Form', 161 ['Methodisch unmethodisch', 'Der Essay als Form', 29].

[106] Aldous Huxley, preface to the *Collected Essays* (1960), pp. vii and ix. Cf. also Graham Good: 'the essay's open-minded approach to experience is balanced by aesthetic pattern and closure' (*The Observing Self*, 14).

the 'dialectic of centre and margin' is already present at the heart of the founding text's very logic.[107] This can be put down to Montaigne's ambiguous use of the term 'Essai'. Montaigne does not use the word as a generic concept but as a structural or methodological principle in keeping with the etymological meaning—in keeping, that is, with the modal sense. Here is one of the passages in which the term most clearly covers that meaning: 'Our power of judgement is a tool to be used on all subjects; it can be applied anywhere. That is why I seize on any sort of occasion for employing it in the assays I am making of it here. If it concerns a subject which I do not understand at all, that is the very reason why I assay my judgement on it.'[108] It is significant that the term 'essai' should appear in the plural rather than in the singular when employed as the title of these miscellaneous and seemingly loosely connected writings, as is the fact that Montaigne is inclined to use the word as a verb. This does not stop him from insisting on the unity of his writings and from appealing time and again to the centralizing (recentring) power of the book which his essays make up. Only this (generic) unity is a unity 'in excess': 'My book is ever one: except that, to avoid the purchaser's going away empty-handed when a new edition is brought out, I allow myself, since it is merely a piece of badly joined marquetry, to tack on some additional ornaments [*quelque embleme supernuméraire*].'[109] From its genesis as notes in the margins of other texts, the genre becomes what it is through addition, supplementation, in other words by expanding on its own margins, so that the 'full' status which it acquires depends on an increasing marginality and (typographically visible) decentring.[110] So, one might say, the *Essais* are one by being permanently decentred and marginal to themselves. We are left, then, with a term which is neither completely covered by the verbal (modal), etymological sense of 'to essay', nor completely by the unifying generic utilization towards which it nevertheless gestures. Graham Good puts it in a nutshell:

With Montaigne the 'essai' is still a sketchy concept, a kind of linking medium between the established forms of the 'sentence' or quotation on one side, and the 'book' on the other . . . the term 'essai' . . . hovers between the then established usage as 'attempt' or 'trial' and an anticipation of the generic usage.[111]

The genre's difference from itself—the relationship between genre (the unity of the 'book') and mode—is perceived here as a 'temporal' difference or deferment. In fact, the *Essais*, the very concept of which mediates between method and genre, process and product, record the fundamental anachronism, paradoxicality, and, in

---

[107] François Rigolot, 'Montaigne et la poétique de la marge', *Actes du Colloque International Montaigne* (1980), 162.
[108] Montaigne, 'On Democritus and Heraclitus', *Essays*, I. 50, p. 337 ['De Democritus et Heraclitus', *Essais*, I. l, p. 289a].
[109] Montaigne, 'On Vanity', *Essays*, III. 9, p. 1091 ['De la vanité', *Essais*, III. ix, p. 941c].
[110] See Michel Beaujour, '"Considérations sur Ciceron". L'Alongeail comme marque générique: la lettre et l'essai', in *Actes du Colloque International Montaigne* (1980), 35.
[111] Good, *The Observing Self*, 28.

a sense, 'impossibility' of Renaissance literature at large, a paradoxicality manifest in the tension, at every level, between openness and closure, gloss and book. Indeed, Renaissance books are seen to 'feed on their own impossibility as they mediate the passage from medieval dogmatic and logical certainties' (the reign of the collective and universal subject discussed above) to 'the self-assured epistemological hubris of the classical age' (the birth of the individual subject later identified with the formulation of the Cartesian ego).[112] Renaissance texts are the product, concretely, of a dismemberment and a reconfiguration of the discursive system largely prompted by the typographical revolution of the time. This transmutation of the discursive system leads to a reshuffling and displacement of generic boundaries which brings about a proliferation of 'functionally primitive extrasystemic texts' that are no longer mere source books to be consulted but *'premature* products', 'works in progress' that strive to be (re-)integrated into a new totalizing epistemological system or 'encyclopedia' encapsulated by the idea of a Book-to-come. Thanks to the extended and ongoing process of addition and revision made possible by the advent of printing, these open-ended texts are thus said to function as the 'shapeless raw material for a future literature', as the 'disconnected entries' of this new system, as fragments which will be discarded with the advent of the Book.[113] On the other hand, the fragmentariness of the work-in-progress, its embryonic, 'neotenous' state,[114] is also the permanent feature of a book which cannot be brought to completion, however extended the process of addition and revision. The 'suspension' of both the writer and his text 'between an original wholeness (illusory, no doubt, but imaginatively potent) and a future reintegration' is itself permanent and thus subverts the very notion of anachronism, 'exile' being—as Terence Cave writes—'the condition of the dislocated *topos* eternally seeking reintegration'. Renaissance texts are doomed to everlasting wandering and digression towards a Book or encyclopedia which no longer represents a totalizing system of knowledge but 'centrifugally' 'reverts to the fragments of which it is composed'.[115] In short, the Renaissance text's difference from itself which the essay epitomizes turns out to involve not so much a temporary difference due to be resolved (like the draft by the finalized work) as a potentially endless deferment or *différance*, in the Derridean sense, of a Book which is at once embodied and endlessly gestured towards.

The 'modal' overrun of the particular genre or 'book' of the *Essais* which precludes generic self-identity must therefore be approached from this broader perspective, and take into account a conjuncture where the notion of Genre in the

---

[112] Beaujour, 'Genus Universum', 30. For the significance of 'paradox' in the Renaissance, see esp. Rosalie L. Colie, *Paradoxica Epidemica: The Renaissance Tradition of Paradox* (1966); Alfred Glauser, *Montaigne paradoxal* (1972); and Margaret McGowan's *Montaigne's Deceits: The Art of Persuasion in the 'Essais'* (1974).

[113] All quoted from Beaujour, 'Genus Universum', 26–9.

[114] 'The functional primitiveness of the new book might be called "neoteny"' (ibid. 27).

[115] Terence Cave, *The Cornucopian Text: Problems of Writing in the French Renaissance* (1979), 325, 326, and 332.

absolute sense of the essence of literature (implied by the notion of the Book) supersedes that of individual genres. Within this broader perspective, in fact, the *Essais* tend to be seen as the most typically transitory and 'a-generic' model of writing of the period.[116] For in this climate of generalized epistemological anxiety which the reorganization of the discursive system reflects, the *Essais* are above all the paradigm of a fundamentally sceptical motivation which determines their open-endedness, their rejection of closure or anti-systematic bias. By 'system', one usually understands a collective entity or a hierarchically organized construct subsumed under an overarching idea or concept that determines both the interrelation between the parts and the function of each part within the whole. In 'trying themselves out' without resolving themselves, the *Essais* emphatically reject the deductive and therefore highly systematic method of scholastic philosophy. Their openness is the formal externalization of Montaigne's famous motto 'What do I know?' [*Que scay-je?*[117]] which prompts acute critical reflection at the heart of all fields of knowledge and suspends the possibility of a universal epistemological synthesis associated with the encyclopedia—both past and future. Montaigne himself is considered to be the most significant figure in the Renaissance revival of ancient Greek scepticism, and in particular of the Pyrrhonian movement which begins in theology, is then extended to philosophy, science, and all areas of human knowledge, and which holds that human reason cannot achieve certainty in any area whatsoever.[118] All this casts a new, more resolutely sceptical light upon my previous outline of the already self-evidently critical transition from 'Scholastic' to 'modern' (philosophical) realism drawn from Ian Watt's book, *The Rise of the Novel*. On the one hand, the individual, personal experience which Montaigne opposes to the universal and anonymous knowledge of tradition only implies that 'the generality which is lost at one level is regained at another', for it is the essayist's 'universal being' [*mon estre universel*[119]] which is at stake. Through his personal experience, the essayist is still aiming at giving the reader access to the 'human condition' (to 'man') in so far as 'every man bears the whole Form of the human condition'.[120] Only this knowledge must be defined in terms of an oxymoron, that of the 'universal particular' where neither term is meant to have precedence over the other.[121] In this respect, the comparison between essay and portrait considered earlier is illuminating, since the portrait is 'the permanent record of a temporary impression': at its best, the individual face of the sitter epitomizes

---

[116] 'The *Essais* are unique in the history of literature: they do not partake of any genre, but of a transitory form between genres' (Compagnon, *La Seconde Main*, 302).

[117] 'Scepticism can best be conceived through the form of a question: "What do I know?"—*Que scay-je*, words inscribed on my emblem of a Balance' (Montaigne, 'An Apology of Raymond Sebond, *Essays*, II. 12, p. 591 ['Apologie de Raimond Sebond', *Essais*, II. xii, p. 508*b*]).

[118] See Richard H. Popkin, *The History of Scepticism from Erasmus to Descartes* (1961), 43–4.

[119] Montaigne, 'On Repenting', *Essays*, III. 2, p. 908; 'Du repentir', *Essais*, III. ii, p. 782*c*.

[120] Montaigne, 'On Repenting', *Essays*, III. 2, p. 908 ['Chaque homme porte la forme entiere de l'humaine condition', 'Du repentir', *Essais*, III. ii, p. 782*b*].

[121] See Good, *The Observing Self*, 8.

something universal.[122] Emphasis on particular knowledge as a 'universal particular' does not, therefore, 'imply a retreat into solipsism'.[123] On the other hand, the shift from the universal to the particular does imply the recognition that man's natural faculties, that his apprehension of reality through the senses which is now foregrounded, are limited. The very possibility of knowledge, in fact, is called into question; as Montaigne reflects: 'Man cannot avoid the fact that his senses are both the sovereign regents of his knowledge, and yet, in all circumstances, uncertain and fallible . . . then we are forced to conclude . . . that there is no such thing as knowledge.'[124] The fact that universal Truth has been replaced by individual truths, that is, by individual experience in particular places and at particular times, is the mark of an extreme relativization. The novelty and uniqueness of each experience does not only involve the different experiences of different individuals; it also suggests—as Montaigne makes perfectly clear in his *Essais*—that the truth is 'only valid for here and now',[125] and so not even valid from one moment to the next within the experience of any one individual. Paradoxically, then, the birth of the subject or consciousness which coincides with the rise of both novel and essay seems to be inextricably linked with a questioning of the knowing subject, with its discontinuity or dislocation. The fact that 'all thought is circumstantial', that there is 'no unconditional standpoint'—objective or subjective—from which reality can be apprehended explains why the essayist 'must continually reflect on the context or circumstances of his own discourse, and why in its very form the essay will bear traces of that contextuality'.[126] The very choice of the essay form (and of kindred forms like the dialogue, the meditation, or the aphorism) manifests philosophy's awareness of its time-bound, historical character, its recognition, in concrete terms, of the contingency of subject (writer or reader) and world upon discourse. As such, it marks the rejection, described by Berel Lang, of the ideal of a context-free or neutral medium characteristic of a philosophy which models itself upon scientific discourse. In the latter case, the reader is confronted with a ready-made truth, with the 'static or unified whole' of a philosophical system which 'intends to describe the world, not to change it, much less to be changed by it'. In literary terms, the author's position in systematic philosophy thus corresponds to the transcendental, universalist or 'authorial' point of view of the third (passive) person, and the space it ascribes to the reader is that, correspondingly, of an 'implied reader': one that 'embodies all those predispositions necessary for a literary work to exercise its

---

[122] Good, *The Observing Self*, 185.   [123] Ibid. 22.

[124] Montaigne, 'An Apology of Raymond Sebond', *Essays*, II. 12, p. 669 ['Il ne peut fuir que les sens ne soient les souverains maistres de la cognoissance; mais ils sont incertains et falsifiables à toutes circonstances . . . nous conclurrons . . . qu'il n'y a point de science', 'Apologie de Raimond Sebond', *Essais*, II. xii, p. 576c & b].

[125] Good, *The Observing Self*, 7.

[126] R. Lane Kauffmann, 'The Skewed Path: Essaying as Unmethodical Method', in Alexander J. Butrym (ed.), *Essays on the Essay: Redefining the Genre* (1989), 234 and 235.

effect' while precluding empirical interference.[127] The ideal of philosophical—as scientific—discourse is in fact the absence of point of view aimed at by pure exposition (what comes closest to drama), with no intrusion whatsoever of a narrative or interpretive voice.[128] The essay's resistance to this 'neutralist model' is illustrated by its interest in revealing the author's process of thinking unconstrained by any foregone conclusions. Instead of leading the passive reader 'step-by-step, in a logical and orderly manner, to an already established point of certainty and clarity', the essayist requires the reader's active participation in the form of a constantly renewed evaluation, deduction, and interpretation of the matter at hand.[129] In this 'interaction model'—to continue with Berel Lang's terminology—the reader, who is now empirical or contingent rather than transcendental or 'implied', must in other words be as actively involved as the speaker. 'Speech', Montaigne writes, 'belongs half to the speaker, half to the listener', as illustrated by his description of reader and writer on opposite sides of the tennis net.[130] In my earlier introduction to the relationship between the essay and Ian Watt's conception of modern philosophical realism, the 'common reader's' active involvement in the new manner of philosophizing was the result of the popularizing of, or a more empirical approach to ideas otherwise rigidly and abstractly handled in philosophical treatises and dissertations. It is now clear that this concession of the reader's leverage on the interpretation of the world, like that of the author's, also coincides with the recognition of his or her relative powerlessness. For the essaying of the writer and reader's ideas necessarily goes hand in hand with the essaying—and therefore with the continuous revision—of his understanding. 'If human reason knows anything at all, it must be its own essence and its own domicile'—Montaigne stipulates.[131] But the logic of this opinion leaves little room, it seems, for alternatives between the objective, unconditional standpoint of systematic philosophy which Montaigne rejects, and the contingency of subject upon discourse which, precisely because it is the expression of a felt inability to judge from the 'outside', leaves no possibility for writer and reader to break out of the vicious (hermeneutical) circle:

We register the appearance of objects; to judge them we need an instrument of judgement; to test the veracity of that instrument we need practical proof; to test that proof we need an

---

[127] See Berel Lang, *The Anatomy of Philosophical Style: Literary Philosophy and the Philosophy of Literature* (1990), 15–18. The 'implied reader' is a concept coined and defined by Wolfgang Iser in *The Implied Reader: Patterns of Communication in Prose Fiction from Bunyan to Beckett* (1974), and in *The Act of Reading: A Theory of Aesthetic Response* (1978), see esp. 34.

[128] Lang, *The Anatomy of Philosophical Style*, 35.

[129] Stanley Fish, *Self-Consuming Artifacts: The Experience of Seventeenth-Century Literature* (1974), 378.

[130] Montaigne, 'On Experience', *Essays*, III. 13, p. 1234 ['La parole est moitié à celuy qui parle, moitié à celuy qui l'escoute', 'De l'experience', *Essais*, III. xiii, p. 1066*b*]. See Cathleen M. Bauschatz, 'Montaigne's Conception of Reading in the Context of Renaissance Poetics and Modern Criticism', in Susan R. Suleiman and Inge Crossman (eds.), *The Reader in the Text: Essays on Audience and Interpretation* (1980), 264–5.

[131] Montaigne, 'An Apology of Raymond Sebond', *Essays*, II. 12, p. 608 ['Apologie de Raimond Sebond', *Essais*, II. xii, p. 523*a*].

instrument. We are going around in circles. . . . Our mental faculty of perception is never directly in touch with outside objects—which are perceived via the senses, and the senses do not embrace an outside object but only their own impressions of it; therefore the thought and the appearance are not properties of the object but only impressions and feelings of the senses.[132]

In short, the space ascribed to the active reader (as writer) ultimately bears out 'the experience of a prose that undermines certainty and moves away from clarity, complicating what had at first sight seemed perfectly simple, raising more problems than it solves'.[133] If answers are not only not provided in advance, but, more usually, not provided at all, this is because the reader's invitation to interpret is an invitation to the deeply 'unsettling' experience of having his conclusions then declared premature or invalid, and in the end of having 'the very possibility of understanding itself called into question'.[134]

At every level, then, the 'interaction model' implies 'dialogue' and 'polyphony' in the Bakhtinian sense already introduced above in the context of the essayistic novel. The *Essais* are intensely 'dialogic' or 'polyphonic' in that they juxtapose and confront a multiplicity of points of view or 'voices', none of which is subjected to a final, authorial control.[135] This relativization also accounts for the combination of literary modes (poetic, dramatic, and narrative) which is therefore not (only) to be presented, as it was in the first section of this chapter, as another feature of the essay's formlessness or a-genericness, but as a means which the *Essais*/essay deliberately exploits for the implementation of an alternative aesthetic and generic organization: Montaigne's choice of 'poetry' (literature) over 'philosophy' is in other words the choice of a form congruent with its content. Montaigne does not fail to express his allegiance to Plato, who seems to him to 'have quite knowingly chosen to treat philosophy in the form of dialogues', as he was thus 'better able to expound the diversity and variety of his concepts by putting them appropriately in the mouths of divers speakers'.[136] In fact, when applied to the essay the notion of 'dialogue' already partakes of the broader, Bakhtinian sense of 'dialogism', since the essayist's 'weighing' of his ideas from as many perspectives as there are voices or points of view is not 'exhausted in pragmatically motivated dialogues of characters'.[137] In this sense, both the structural function of the 'poem' and the 'story' in the essay can be said to contribute to its 'dialogic' mode. For poetry is associated

---

[132] Montaigne, 'An Apology of Raymond Sebond', *Essays*, II. 12, p. 679 ['Apologie de Raimond Sebond', *Essais*, II. xii, p. 585a].

[133] Fish, *Self-Consuming Artifacts*, 378.   [134] Ibid., abstract (unpaginated).

[135] Cf. Thomas E. Recchio, 'A Dialogic Approach to the Essay', in Alexander J. Butrym (ed.), *Essays on the Essay: Redefining the Genre* (1989).

[136] Montaigne, 'An Apology of Raymond Sebond', *Essays*, II. 12, p. 568 ['Platon me semble avoir aymé cette forme de philosopher par dialogues, à escient, pour loger plus decemment en diverses bouches la diversité et variation de ses propres fantasies', 'Apologie de Raimond Sebond', *Essais*, II. xii, pp. 489–90c].

[137] Mikhail Bakhtin, 'Discourse in the Novel', in *The Dialogic Imagination: Four Essays by M. M. Bakhtin*, ed. Michael Holquist (1990), 364.

with the disjunctive and associative structure which records the essayist's spontaneous thought-process, while narrative enables the essayist to 'try out' his ideas in time—in history—and this temporalization does justice to 'the living conditions in which thought is tangled': as opposed to 'dogmatic and conclusive speaking', narrative rather than teaching is also the mode of someone who 'speak[s] as one who questions and does not know'.[138] In Montaigne, the suspicion that human reason cannot achieve certainty in any area determines the rejection of totalizing modes of discourse and the idea that knowledge can only be relative, speculative, and hypothetical—in short a 'fiction', both in the radical sense of unlimited *différance* (with Montaigne and/as his discourse trying themselves out and never resolving themselves) and of the concretely fictional expressed by the aesthetic (quasi-novelistic) handling of object and subject. And this sceptical dimension of the essay's relation to fiction is not least directed against the assumption, promoted by the neutral, context-free or 'genre-less' ideal of philosophical discourse as scientific discourse, that language is a reliable or transparent medium of knowledge. Montaigne is acutely aware that language fails to coincide with what it represents, so that both the object and the subject of knowledge can only be grasped indirectly, analogically, metaphorically. This affords a more focused perspective on the familiar claim that the essayist, unlike the philosopher, exploits the 'poetic' function of language with an emphasis, usually, on ambiguity, word-play, and polysemy. With the incentive above all of the linguist Roman Jakobson's work, one has long since come to recognize this 'poetic function' as the dominant, determining function of art, one which promotes the 'palpability of signs'. When this function prevails, the communication is self-conscious or reflexive, oriented towards the message for its own sake, concerned above all to draw attention to its own nature. We have seen that the paratactic structure which the *Essais* are supposed to borrow from the poem relegate it to the 'not-yet-written'. Yet this alleged restriction to the 'not-yet-written', to neoteny and prematuration, is motivated by acute self-reflexivity: the conditions of meaning which are essayed rather than or before writing itself, betray a concern with nothing but writing, in the traditional and again in the post-structuralist sense: 'This phenomenon of neoteny and incompletion is analogous to what the French avant garde of yesterday called *signifiance*, production of the text, work of the signifier.'[139] Montaigne's choice of 'poetry' over 'philosophy' ultimately affiliates him to a great tradition of philosophers who understood that both were inextricably connected. The greatest philosophers of the past, as Montaigne reminds his reader, were themselves poets for the simple reason that poetry is philosophy's first and last 'authority': 'Certainly, philosophy is poetry adulterated by sophists. Where do all those Ancient authors get their authority from, if not from the poets? The original authorities were themselves poets; they treated

---

[138] Thomas Harrison, *Essayism: Conrad, Musil, Pirandello* (1992), 4; and Montaigne, 'On Repenting', *Essays*, III. 2, p. 909 ['Que je parle enquerant et ignorant . . . je n'enseigne poinct, je raconte', 'Du repentir', *Essais*, III. ii, p. 784*b*].

[139] Beaujour, *Poetics of the Literary Self-Portrait*, 119.

philosophy in terms of poetic art: Plato is a disjointed poet [*un poëte descousu*].'[140]
From this viewpoint, the 'imaginative re-creations' which the essay, like art, subjects reality to, are not so much an alternative as an indication of the extent to
which all representations are the result of speculation, invention—of how much
one reads into things. Hence Montaigne's description of philosophy as a work of
fiction:

Philosophy presents us 'not with what really is, nor even with what she believes to be true,
but with the best probabilities and elegancy she has wrought'.... Man is an object to be
seized and handled. Each philosopher, according to his fancy, has been left entirely free to
unstitch him, rearrange him, put him together again and furnish him out afresh.[141]

To conclude, the line between so-called 'philosophical realism' and scepticism
—between a more acute perception of reality's potential as an increased awareness of reality and as an increased awareness of reality's unreality—is a fine one.
Montaigne's *Essais* are in fact regarded as anticipating Descartes and a trend of
philosophical scepticism which originates with the Greeks (Pyrrho, Socrates) but
recognizably lies within the broader tradition of idealist philosophy represented by
Berkeley, Kant, Fichte, Schelling, Hegel.[142] Idealism is a doctrine that holds the
world to be essentially a mental vision: the *esse* (existence) of physical objects is
percipi (to be perceived), according to the eighteenth-century founder Berkeley.
Physical objects are only 'ideas', and thus have no existence apart from a mind that
is conscious of them, and this 'mainly on the ground that we cannot conceive as
existing in abstraction from our sense-experience any of the qualities we ascribe to
them'.[143] The typically 'superficial' or 'impressionistic' approach of many essays,
one which avoids delving deeper into the matter at hand, is already an acknowledgement of the necessary gap that exists between perceiver and perceived; taken
further, this acknowledgement results in the 'imaginative recreations' of a type of
criticism which is conscious that the best one can do, when talking 'about' a text
(or 'about' oneself), is to create another. Montaigne's *Essais* also recognizably
anticipate the spirit of free enquiry and experimentalism associated with men like
Bacon, Boyle, and Newton, which, together with the philosophies of Locke, Berkeley,
and Hume especially, launch the English tradition of essays. This English tradition
founded by Bacon, then, is not devoid of the sceptical elements discussed above,
elements which have been examined especially in relation to individual essayists
but which for obvious reasons remain associated above all with the Modernist

[140] Montaigne, 'An Apology of Raymond Sebond', *Essays*, II. 12, p. 602 ['Apologie de Raimond
Sebond', *Essais*, II. xii, p. 518c].
[141] Montaigne, 'An Apology of Raymond Sebond', *Essays*, II. 12, p. 603 ['Apologie de Raimond
Sebond', *Essais*, II. xii, p. 518a].
[142] Apart from Richard Popkin's *History of Scepticism from Erasmus to Descartes*, which devotes a
whole chapter to Montaigne and the 'New Pyrrhonists', see also Christopher Hookway, *Scepticism*
(1990); and Barry Stroud, *The Significance of Philosophical Scepticism* (1989).
[143] J. O. Urmson and Jonathan Rée (eds.), *The Concise Encyclopedia of Western Philosophy and Philosophers* (1989), 146.

essay. The affinities between the essays of Montaigne and, for example, Virginia Woolf, are plain to see. They include among other things the juxtaposition of viewpoints for the translation of limited angles of vision; the impressionistic approach to the subject-matter; the recognition of the role of time for the discontinuity and transformation of world and self. The two essayists also share a marked awareness of the problematic correspondence between words and reality, which is a reminder that nominalist scepticism is a fundamental element of the transition from Scholastic to modern realism as recounted by Ian Watt.[144] For all that, the English essay continues by and large to be perceived as belonging to a different, more 'aphoristic' tradition. Thus, choosing Montaigne as a model rather than Bacon initially goes with the common assumption of a clear-cut divergence between two respective types of essay, a divergence which, at its most extreme, would correspond to Carl Klaus's opposition between the 'meditative' and the 'argumentative' essay.[145] This opposition has, in fact, been interpreted in terms of the mode versus the genre, with the 'essayistic' as an attitude (the open-ended dimension of the form) attributed to Montaigne, and the essay itself as a closed form of art identified with Bacon.[146] In a sense, the English essay appears as a defendant of the 'thing-in-itself' rather than of the act of perception central to idealism: 'rather than' or 'as opposed to', for in an essayistic perspective, the essay comes to be regarded not only as an extrapolation, but as a distortion or perversion of the 'essayistic', to the point where 'the essayistic and the concrete (closed) form of the essay ultimately mutually exclude one another'.[147] Without going this far, the association of the English essay with the genre rather than with the mode is perhaps best seen as the subordination of the essayistic to the essay rather than the other way round, one in which the sceptical element does not lead so insistently to the renewed questioning of the genre as a genre. Doubtless, if 'the essay has been practiced most continuously in England, despite the fact that its founder was French', this is precisely because, as Graham Good points out, 'the empirical and individualistic quality of English culture and the early dominance of bourgeois values were obviously hospitable to the essay', that is, to the stabilization of the *genre*.[148] The more elusive essayistic mode or 'spirit' privileged by the etymological meaning of the word, on the other hand, remains more directly based on the 'Montaignian' essay than on the Baconian equivalent, independently of the fact

---

[144] See Watt, *The Rise of the Novel*, 30.   [145] Klaus, 'Essay', 24–5.

[146] See e.g. Ludwig Rohner, *Der deutsche Essay*, 60, which offers a description of Bacon's essay as the more rigorous, didactic, aphoristic, impersonal, and rhetorically conservative version of the genre.

[147] Bachmann, *Essay und Essayismus*, 195—a position which, although not applied to Montaigne and Bacon, underlies the conception of his book as a whole.

[148] Good, *The Observing Self*, p. viii (Good further situates the culmination of 'essayistic culture' in 1920 when 'originality, personality, individuality have become a kind of orthodoxy', p. 135). English hospitality to the essay as a genre is perhaps also consonant with the idea that French literature failed to produce a successor comparable with Montaigne—and hence a French essay tradition (another variant on the 'uniqueness' of Montaigne's *Essais*)—whereas 'England can claim all the great essayists of the world from Bacon to Lamb', as pointed out by H. V. Routh, 'The Origins of the Essay Compared in English and French Literature', *Modern Language Review*, 15 (1920), 33.

that Montaigne is the first practitioner and the first theorist of the genre. Further-more, as another critic observes: 'Though it was Walter Pater who rediscovered the essay as the "strictly appropriate form of our modern philosophical literature", it was central Europeans schooled in the German Idealist tradition [thinkers from Lessing to Adorno] who did most to justify this claim.'[149] So it is that in this study the Continental tradition which I identify with the so-called 'Montaignian essay' will prevail over its English counterpart, it being understood that in this choice only the focus, not the object itself, is determining.

1.4.2. The Montaignian Essay

If my brief overview of Montaigne's *Essais* is anything to go by, the Montaignian essay is likely to be an acutely reflexive form anachronistically hovering between mode and genre, process and product, a transitory form doomed to obsolescence or 'outmodedness'. On one level, this evidently confronts us with the paradox of having the specific features of the conjuncture characteristic of the Renaissance—the moment of the essay's birth—turned into the invariable elements of the essay's definition for ever after. Unless one continued to consider the revolutionary philo-sophical and literary innovations that took place in the Renaissance as simply the inauguration of 'the vast transformation of Western civilization since the Renais-sance'. This, however, would dismiss the idea of more stable spells of literary history during which a more controlled kind of essay regains the upper hand—as the idea of the more aphoristic or more argumentative essay associated with the English tradition implies. One might suggest, therefore, that within the overall continuity of a problematic 'modern' period which is seen formally to begin with the Renaissance and whose expected closure via the metaphor of the Book must always be postponed, one is perhaps simply led to recognize more marked periods of generic transitions and crises, periods when the peculiarities described in the previous section are more conspicuously reactivated or brought to the fore. Whether viewed as a continuity or as a 'resurgence', one such period or 'moment' in literary history is of course the period of early German Romanticism which theorizes concerns that equally apply to our own post-Romantic period or 'crisis'.[150] Not

---

[149] Kauffmann, 'The Skewed Path', 227.

[150] The idea of a continuity between these periods is defended by Michel Beaujour, in 'Genus Universum', 19: 'In the past, every major cultural-literary crisis has been bound up with a radical shift of the writer's position in the communicational and power networks, embodied in rhetoric and a symbolic system. There is no reason to think that the current, post-Romantic crisis is fundamentally different. Western writers have not yet come to terms with all the consequences of the Renaissance typographical–rhetorical revolution.' R. Lane Kauffmann, on the other hand, views the parallelism between essayistic periods in terms of renewal or 'resurgence'. He refers to romantic (and/or philo-sophical) essayism as one which 'was largely eclipsed by the positivistic turn in European thought in the second half of the 19th century'. By the turn of the present century, however, 'conditions allowed for the resurgence and fuller development of philosophical essayism' ('The Skewed Path', 227). This is also in keeping with Klaus Weissenberger's approach to the essay in 'Der Essay', in *Prosakunst ohne Erzählen*, which revolves around the idea of a fluctuation, in literary history, between the 'strengthen-ing' and 'stabilization' of the form, and its 'renewal' (pp. 110 and 115).

surprisingly, the most significant theorists of the essay to have identified the essayistic with the essence of the essay (Georg Lukács, Walter Benjamin, and Theodor W. Adorno) are themselves twentieth-century German theorists who explicitly draw on the works of Friedrich Schlegel, Novalis, and Jean Paul. Underlying their view that the genre is bound to rise and prosper in times of generic transitions and crises, which (always) makes evanescence and obsolescence a part of its very nature, is the connection they establish between the model of Montaigne's *Essais* and the early German Romantic theory of the fragment which thoroughly informs their conception of the genre.[151] The overall parallelism between the 'critical' periods of the Renaissance and of Romanticism—the fact that 'the German Romantic innovations can be perceived as a delayed replay of the Renaissance encyclopedia mutation'[152]—is itself implicit. But we know that the Romantic period is also a time of dismemberment and reconfiguration of the discursive system which leads to a reshuffling and displacement of generic boundaries, and to the intense reflexiveness this brings about.[153] Again in the Romantic period the subsequent tensions between fragmentary and totalizing modes of discourse go hand in hand with the dream of a virtual Book orienting the production of fragments. Like the Renaissance, Romanticism 'hates the taxonomic distribution of discourses and text into a hierarchical genre system' and thus favours 'the conceit of one Genre, of a literary absolute', of a *Genus Universum* described by Michel Beaujour as 'the whole of Culture, the sum of the arts and sciences in their essence—a flawless encyclopedia of knowledge'.[154]

In a Romantic perspective, the anachronistic wandering of the essay as a fragment between two systems is perceived as a transitory period between two 'golden ages' or utopias, those of antiquity and of a future, better time (a 'no longer' and a 'not yet'). The Greek period is a period of beauty, harmony, and order; its poetry the expression of the totality of being. The status of the essay as a precursor, on the other hand, is the mark of a problematic form—or rather, the essay is the typical response to a world which has become problematic. It is the typical expression of a lack of cultural unity, where man's faculties are exercised in isolation from one another. For the negativity of modern times which the essay embodies is characterized by a split between the 'I' and the world, between subject and object, between particular and universal, between art and philosophy, when all relationships are destroyed and reflected upon.[155] On the one hand, the negativity of this conjuncture has a positive dimension, since the essay also functions as a mediator

---

[151] The association of fragment and essay can also be found in Lacoue-Labarthe and Nancy, *L'Absolu littéraire*, 58 and 62.

[152] Beaujour, 'Genus Universum', 20.

[153] Cf. ibid. 'This sort of crisis is seen as a struggle in the course of which a new system of genres . . . supplants an obsolete institutionalized system. Such changeovers are accompanied by much theoretical and philosophical bluster.'

[154] Ibid. 20, 15, and 23.

[155] Cf. K. A. Horst quoted in Haas, *Studien zur Form des Essays*, 143. See 'Epochen der Dichtkunst', in *Gespräch über die Poesie*, in Rasch (ed.), *Friedrich Schlegel: Kritische Fragmente*.

between these oppositions and expresses the foreboding of their unification or synthesis. Romantic poetry is 'universal'; its aim, in Schlegel's view, is to 'reunite all the separate species of poetry and put poetry in touch with philosophy and rhetoric. It tries to and should mix and fuse poetry and prose, inspiration and criticism, the poetry of art and the poetry of nature.'[156] This corresponds to the essay's 'utopian' dimension, perceived as a nostalgia, both prospective and retro-spective, for a united world—which justifies descriptions of the essay as an 'anach-ronistic' form or a form written 'against the time'.[157] As well as this, though, Romantic philosophy also 'suspends' the teleological or systematic implications of this scheme by infinitely deferring the resolution of the parts into totality: 'The romantic kind of poetry is still in the state of becoming; that, in fact, is its real essence: that it should forever be becoming and never be perfected. It can be exhausted by no theory.... It alone is infinite.'[158] The essay thus reflects the Romantics' perception of the universe as 'a dynamic interplay of forces and polarities', as a 'ceaseless "productive activity" '.[159] As August Wiedmann reca-pitulates in his illuminating account of Romantic art theories, the 'static' and the 'generic' associated with the prevailing notions of atomism and mechanism of the time are 'replaced with the flexible models of organicism and universal dynamism', which brings about a shift of focus from 'permanence' to 'change', from 'product' to 'process', and from 'finished forms and seemingly unchanging timeless sub-stances' to 'dynamic fields of forces'. Hence the Romantic defence of the 'diffuse', the 'formless', the 'unfinished', and the 'incomplete', and the championing of unfinished literary forms that bear witness to the fact that 'there is no Being, only Becoming', only an 'open-ended, dynamically expanding process'.[160] Accordingly, Lukács, Adorno, and Benjamin emphasize the essay's postulation of a totality, but of a totality which is eternally suspended, never fulfilled, always yet to come. The essay is a form of 'desire', a 'longing' which 'drives it [infinitely] beyond itself',[161] 'exile' being again as in the Renaissance the 'condition of the dislocated *topos* eternally seeking reintegration', that is, the condition of a genre 'doomed to ever-lasting wandering and digression'.[162] So the Romantic notion of 'progressive, uni-versal poetry', which the essay as fragment embodies, confirms the paradoxical unity—or unity 'in excess'—of a genre beside itself, a genre which, consonantly with my above discussion of the paratext, is at once a detached piece [*Bruchstück*] and an autonomous whole. It is by 'expressing the expansion, the growth and process of life understood as a ceaseless becoming' (the 'progressive') that poetry

---

[156] Schlegel, *Athenäum Fragments*, 116, p. 46 [*Athenäums-Fragmente*, pp. 38–9].

[157] In Lukács, Adorno, and Bense. See Rohner, *Der deutsche Essay*, 331, 411, 647, and 784.

[158] Schlegel, *Athenäum Fragments*, 116, p. 47 ['Die romantische Dichtart ist noch im Werden; ja das ist ihr eigentliches Wesen, daß sie ewig nur werden, nie vollendet sein kann. Sie kann durch keine Theorie erschöpft werden ... Sie allein ist unendlich', *Athenäums-Fragmente*, p. 39].

[159] Friedrich Schelling quoted in August Wiedmann, *Romantic Art Theories* (1986), 5 and 8.

[160] Ibid. 8–9 and 55–6.

[161] Adorno, 'The Essay as Form', 161 ['Der Essay als Form', 30].

[162] Cave, *The Cornucopian Text*, 326.

can 'strive to embody within itself all the actual and possible modes of existence' (the 'universal'): 'it is equally fatal for the mind to have a system and to have none. It will simply have to decide to combine the two', writes Schlegel.[163] And this, in Romantic terms, is what is meant by 'irony', the paradox which juggles the radical contradiction and resolution of the individual and the universal. The 'self-conscious glance' of the Romantic artist—and thus of the essayist

recognizes both the representation in the artifact of a striving for the infinite, and the ultimate failure to reach that infinite. In this paradoxical recognition of the success in striving . . . with the simultaneous failure to reach the goal of the striving, irony reveals the creative tension of life and of thought in activity rather than in the stasis of a delusive finality.[164]

To become aware of one's own chaotic—modern—existence and to live it on a conscious, critical mode is to adopt an ironic attitude towards it which enables one to transcend and reverse the negativity and isolation it involves. At the same time, the 'critical' drive of this ironic attitude encompasses both the related senses of 'crisis' and 'critique'. The essay—like Romantic poetry in general—is the expression of a crisis in so far as it reflects the 'immanent loss of meaning of the world', but also of a critique of the ideal of the all-encompassing system—the traditional ideal of Western philosophy—'at a stage in history in which empirical life has itself become *refractory* to meaning and shuns all attempts at an independent, comprehensive, conceptual totalization'.[165]

The privileged German Romantic metaphors for the Book are the encyclopedia and the genre which gives its name to the movement, the novel itself [*Roman*]. In this respect, the exact nature of the relationship, in Schlegel's work, between the fragment—as absence of genre or 'matrix of all genericness'—and the novel—the genre supposed to unite all other genres 'beyond genre'—is not always clear. The novel apparently encompasses all the qualities previously ascribed to the fragment, and more: it is cast as the end-product of a process of reflection which seems to include the fragment as a necessary stage, and move beyond. The novel, therefore, is again the genre which the essay anticipates or 'looks forward to'. At the same time, fragment—or essay—and novel seem to continue to be interchangeable: 'what we now call the novel', writes Schlegel, is in fact simply a (Romantic) essay'.[166] This points again to the ambivalent position, discussed in the previous section, of the essay's diachronic and/or synchronic relation to the novel. The paradigm of the Romantic novel is the *Bildungsroman*, as represented especially by

---

[163] Schlegel, *Athenäum Fragments*, 53, p. 45 ['Es ist gleich tödlich für den Geist, ein System zu haben, und keins zu haben. Es wird sich also wohl entschließen müssen, beides zu verbinden', *Athenäums-Fragmente*, p. 31].

[164] Kathleen Wheeler (ed.), *German Aesthetic and Literary Criticism: The Romantic Ironists and Goethe* (1984), 21–2.

[165] Richard Wolin, 'The Essay as Mediation between Art and Philosophical Truth', in *Walter Benjamin: An Aesthetic of Redemption* (1982), 85.

[166] 'Der Roman, den wir jetzt so nennen, eigentlich nur ein (romantischer) essay', *Neue Fragmente*, ed. J. Korner, in *Die Neue Rundschau*, 36 (1925), 1300.

Goethe's *Wilhelm Meister*. And this is a type of essayistic novel which appears to take over the epistemological project of Montaigne's *Essais* in every way. Indeed, the German humanist concept of *Bildung* (the 'shaping', formation, or education of man) elaborated above all by Wilhelm von Humboldt, Schiller, and Goethe, revolves around the examination of the relationship between self and world with a view to discovering what one knows [*Que scay-je?*] and who one is and hence, through what Montaigne calls 'apprenticeship' and 'testing' [*apprentissage* and *espreuve*], to achieving self-realization.[167] The emphasis on self-cultivation and development makes of the *Bildungsroman* a kind of 'autobiography' or 'confession'; at the very least, its 'subjectivism' promotes 'a type of culture that might be called pietistic, given to autobiographical confession and deeply personal, one in which the world of the *objective*, the political world, is felt to be profane and is thrust aside with indifference'.[168] At the same time, subjectivity is posited as universality: in both the *Bildungsroman* and the essay it is man in his universality—the Renaissance *uomo universale*—who is at stake through the organic unfolding of the individual in all his complexity. The essay, I suggested at the beginning of this chapter, is an ambulatory form which develops around a number of topics that offer themselves along the way. In the *Bildungsroman*, the apprenticeship or 'self-essaying' of the main protagonist—in which self-control and stoicism also have a significant role to play[169]—occurs in the process of a concrete, geographical wandering from one 'place' ('locus') to another and from one 'trial' to another: Goethe's *Wilhelm Meister* itself consists of two parts, the *Years of Apprenticeship* [*Lehrjahre*] and the *Years of Travel* [*Wanderjahre*]. In both essay and *Bildungsroman*, in other words, 'erring' is the fundamental motor of the journey towards self-realization. It is the guarantor of an ongoing dissonance—discussed above in relation to the essayistic novel generally—between individual self and exterior world, between particular and universal, concrete and abstract, practice and theory, art and philosophy. In the *Bildungsroman*, the reconciliation or fusion of these various aspects is supposed to coincide with the self-achievement of the 'hero' at the end of his external and/or inward journey. In accordance with the endless postponement inherent in the Romantic concept of 'progressive universal poetry', however, even the most classical *Bildungsroman*—here Goethe's *Wilhelm Meister*—falls short of its totalizing impetus and remains above all the 'critical' (in the dual sense, again, of 'crisis' and 'critique') or 'ironic' reflection of a hiatus between various modes of knowledge which are no longer reconcilable. So the *Bildungsroman* is both hierarchically superior to the essay which it includes, and interchangeable with it as an equally problematic expression of modernity.

If the *Bildungsroman* 'occupies a central role in the philosophical investigations

---

[167] 'My soul is ever in its apprenticeship and being tested', Montaigne, 'On Repenting', *Essays*, III. 2, p. 908 ['Du repentir', *Essais*, III. ii, p. 782*b*].

[168] Lecture by Thomas Mann in 1923, quoted in W. H. Bruford, *The German Tradition of Self-Cultivation: 'Bildung' from Humboldt to Thomas Mann* (1975), p. vii.

[169] At least in the notion of *Bildung* as elaborated by von Humboldt. See 'Wilhelm von Humboldt in his Letters', in Bruford, *The German Tradition of Self-Cultivation*.

of the novel, from Hegel's *Aesthetics* to Dilthey to Lukács's *Theory of the Novel*'
and then to Mikhail Bakhtin's own work on the genre, to the extent that 'even
those novels that clearly are *not Bildungsromane* are perceived by us against this
conceptual horizon',[170] this is because, as suggested above, the *Bildungsroman* is not
so much a sub-species of the genre as its archetype. Its declared theme is the
awareness of the problematic relationship between subject and world—'the dilemna
coterminous with modern bourgeois civilization'—which determines the rise of
the novel generally.[171] But the *topos* of '*Bildung*' is crucial above all to the various
Idealist conceptions of (literary) history which German Romantic theories are
affiliated to and which culminate, after the Romantics, in a work often directly
compared to a *Bildungsroman*: Hegel's *Phenomenology of Spirit*. The Hegel of the
Phenomenology is a fundamental figure in the modern German theories of the
essay, one which clinches the relationship introduced in this and the previous
section between essay and *Bildungsroman*, that is, between essay and essayistic
novel and beyond, between the essay and the notion of literature *in potentia*. The
convergence between the *Bildungsroman* as a genre and as a metaphor for (literary)
history casts the essay as a part or stage in the latter's development: the
Bildungsroman, as we saw above, includes the essay. But since *Bildungsroman* and
essay are also interchangeable, the essay, aptly defined as 'the enactment of the
process of accommodation between the world and the "I"' and as 'consciousness
real-izing itself',[172] also offers a competing metaphor for the Idealist conception of
literary history as a whole. Hegel's *Phenomenology*, in which this conception culminates, has been described as 'the *Bildungsroman* of the *Weltgeist*, the story of its
development and education'.[173] In it history can be conceived as an 'odyssey'
where, 'in search for a homeland where it can dwell in peace, the human spirit is
shipwrecked again and again', or as an inland adventure in the more habitual
conception of history as 'the story of a wayfaring consciousness called Spirit,
travelling from what Hegel calls its "natural" state, along a road which, though it
passes through all sorts of deceptions and disappointments, leads ultimately to
"absolute knowledge".'[174] Whichever the itinerary, the 'plot' of the *Phenomenology*

[170] Franco Moretti, *The Way of the World: The 'Bildungsroman' in European Culture* (1987), 15.

[171] Ibid. Thus the novel itself could be regarded as a species of the *Bildungsroman* (Cervantes's *Don Quixote* has on occasions been described as the first great *Bildungsroman*).

[172] Hardison, 'Binding Proteus: An Essay on the Essay', 26.

[173] Walter Kaufmann, *Hegel: A Reinterpretation* (1978), 143. For Hegel's relation to previous idealist systems (Kant, Schelling, Fichte, etc.) and to major figures such as Goethe, Schiller, etc., see Wheeler (ed.), *German Aesthetic and Literary Criticism*; H. B. Nisbet (ed.), *German Aesthetic and Literary Criticism: Winckelmann, Lessing, Hamann, Herder, Schiller and Goethe* (1985); Simpson (ed.), *The Origins of Modern Critical Thought*; Israel Knox, *The Aesthetic Theories of Kant, Hegel, and Schopenhauer* (1958); and Juliet Sychrava, *Schiller to Derrida: Idealism in Aesthetics* (1989).

[174] Kaufmann, *Hegel: A Reinterpretation*, 143; and Jonathan Rée, *Philosophical Tales: An Essay on Philosophy and Literature* (1987), 63–4. In his preface [*Vorrede*], Hegel refers to knowledge as 'having to travel a long way and work its passage' (p. 15) ['einen langen Weg sich hindurch zu arbeiten', *Phänomenologie des Geistes*, ed. Johannes Hoffmeister (1952), p. 26], of 'the length of the path' (p. 17) [p. 27]; and in his introduction [*Einleitung*], 'the road can therefore be regarded as the pathway of doubt, or more precisely as the way of despair' (p. 49) ['der Weg des *Zweifels* . . . oder eigentlicher . . . der Weg der Verzweiflung', *Phänomenologie des Geistes*, p. 67].

thus reads like a 'journey of enlightenment' where the *Bildung* and self-realization of consciousness—which is also Everyman or 'the universal self'[175]—takes the form of a 'despairing passage through a world of illusions and errors' that also requires passing 'through every possible philosophical system on its way'.[176] Hegel's insistence that each philosophy 'contributes to the gradual refinement of knowledge'[177] is usually grasped (rightly or wrongly) in relation to his own alleged claim to have provided the ultimate System of all philosophical systems—hence the customary reference to his philosophy as master-system and/or as master-plot. Already, the particular relevance of Hegel's scheme to the genre of the essay appears to be twofold and paradoxical, since it implicates both the (dialectical) self-essaying of the System (the process) and the affirmation of the System itself to which the essay, as a fundamentally 'anti-systematic' form, must also always be accountable. The forms in Hegel's scheme are the various 'configurations' [*Gestaltungen*] which consciousness goes through in the course of its search for absolute knowledge or truth.[178] In so far as absolute knowledge—the end of the journey—coincides with the realization of consciousness as self-consciousness, the various configurations which consciousness goes through along the way will be a continuum of ever higher, more reflexive forms. Spirit [*Geist*] or the 'Idea' must in other words be submitted to its own immanent critique, the 'only possible approach to knowledge' being 'an examination of consciousness from the inside as it appears to itself'.[179] Within this itinerary, which begins with a simple form of consciousness that will develop into another, more complex form of consciousness which in turn will prove inadequate and so on, the forms of art, religion, and philosophy play a major role. They are the more articulate, reflexive forms in which the knowledge of the Absolute Spirit, which is supposed to be at work at every level of experience, comes to emergence.[180] Their relationship is hierarchical: the adequation of the Idea to itself at the end of history coincides with the self-transcendence of art and religion into philosophy as 'Science': 'The series of configurations which consciousness goes through along this road is, in reality, the detailed history of the *education* [*Bildung*] of consciousness itself to the standpoint of Science.'[181] The ultimate triumph of philosophy over art is a reminder of the ancestral opposition between the two modes of knowledge, where art is associated with imagination, sensibility, intuition, and with the particular or concrete, while philosophy is associated with logic, reason, the concept, universality, and abstraction.

---

[175] Hegel, *Phenomenology of Spirit* (1979), preface, p. 18 ('Knowing is the activity of the *universal self*') ['das allgemein Selbst', *Phänomenologie des Geistes*, p. 28].

[176] Rée, *Philosophical Tales*, 81 and 77.

[177] Walter Kaufmann, *Hegel: Text and Commentary* (1977), 10–11, on the preface of the *Phenomenology*.

[178] See Hegel, introduction [*Einleitung*] to *Phenomenology of Spirit*.

[179] Peter Singer, *Hegel* (1983), 51.

[180] See William Desmond, *Art and the Absolute: A Study of Hegel's Aesthetics* (1986), 66.

[181] Hegel, introduction to *Phenomenology of Spirit*, 50 ['Die Reihe seiner Gestaltungen, welche das Bewußtsein auf diesem Wege durchläuft, ist vielmehr die ausführliche Geschichte der *Bildung* des Bewußtseins selbst zur Wissenschaft', *Phänomenologie des Geistes*, p. 67].

Opposition, however, makes mediation possible: the philosophical concept, thought, or 'spirit' cannot for Hegel 'be entirely divorced from concrete experience';[182] it must be presented or externalized in sensuous form. This process in which the universal significance of the philosophical concept is concretized or particularized and thus acquires a sensuous form is none other than the process of the world in becoming, of time—of history:

There is no escape from our conditionedness, our rootedness in a certain time and place. On the other hand, the dimension of the unconditioned is not gainsaid; rather it is to be discerned as emergent within the conditions of time itself, as the eternal that is to be apprehended within time, immanent within the present itself.[183]

Ideally, then, the transcending of the individual poles of philosophy and art towards absolute knowledge takes the form of a sensuous presentation of the spirit which is also a spiritualization of the sensuous, of a dialectical whole which can be described as a 'concrete universal', as a 'temporal eternity' or alternatively an 'eternalization of the temporal'.[184]

From German theorists' point of view, the essay offers just such an ideal, mediating form. Its hybrid, marginal position between philosophy and art, far from discrediting it, is motivated by a search for wholeness intended to overcome the shortcomings of each mode of knowledge:

For (philosophical) knowledge proceeds to the universal directly, straight away; it is therefore unconcerned with the being of truth as embodied particularity—i.e. with the problem of the representation of truth as something concrete and individual. On the other hand, in and of itself art represents the moment of unmediated sensuousness or sheer particularity—i.e. truth in its merely inchoate form, as yet separated from the redemptive embrace of the universal.[185]

The criticism of individual works of art especially—which German theorists see as the proper vocation of the essay—enables the universal 'to unfold *from within the boundaries of the particular itself*':

Criticism seeks out the truth content of works of art—the moment of universality—as it exists immersed in the material content of the work; it thus attempts to redeem the latter from its immediate condition of speechless particularity by translating the nonconceptual language of art into the conceptual language of philosophical truth.[186]

On the other hand, the notion of mediation between philosophy and art in these terms implies an irreducible opposition between the two epistemological media which does not take into account the possibility of a kinship, of a dynamic interplay or continuity between them.[187] This continuity exists in the form of the

---

[182] See Hegel, *Phenomenology of Spirit*, preface, 28–9 [*Phänomenologie des Geistes*, p. 39]; Desmond, *Art and the Absolute*, p. xiii.

[183] Ibid. 74; see also p. 27.   [184] Ibid. 68–9.

[185] Wolin, 'The Essay as Mediation between Art and Philosophical Truth', 87.

[186] Ibid.   [187] See Desmond, *Art and the Absolute*, pp. xviii, 15–16, and 20.

aesthetical: the work of art itself already operates a mediation between the modes of knowledge, it already 'stands in the *middle*'—Hegel writes—'between immediate sensuousness and ideal thought'.[188] Because art is one of the privileged forms of experience in terms of man's relation to the Absolute, the work of art 'is only there in so far as it has taken its passage through the spirit', 'regardless of its existing independently as a sensuous object'.[189] In this respect, the analogy of portrait-painting already discussed in the context both of Lukács's essay and of Montaigne's *Essais* illustrates the function of the essay as art criticism which itself takes the form of a work of art. As a 'concrete universal' or a 'universal particular', the portrait epitomizes the activity of all art which can be variously described as one of self-articulation, self-recognition, self-knowledge, or self-consciousness. The representation of the artist's (and/or essayist's) own likeness alongside the likeness of the sitter, in Lukács's essay, is a result of the fact that 'man brings himself before himself by *practical* activity', 'producing' and 'recognizing' himself in 'whatever is present to him externally', so that 'In as much as man relates himself to things in accordance with his universality, it is his universal reason which strives to find itself in nature and thereby to re-establish that inner essence of things which sensuous existence, though that essence is its basis, cannot immediately display.'[190] The notion of 'aesthetic wholeness' (of art as a 'higher science')—i.e. the idea that 'in the aesthetic state we recognize ourselves as not only rational but also sensuous, and so we come to a full spiritual and moral understanding of ourselves as human'[191]—is fundamental to Romantic theories, to the related philosophies of Kant and Schelling, and to Schiller, whose *Letters on the Aesthetic Education of Man* express the conviction that 'there is no other way to make the man of the senses rational than to make him aesthetic first'.[192] This turns the *Bildungsroman*—and by extension Hegel's *Phenomenology*—into the proper vehicle of man's self-realization, since art determines both the form and the theme of the *Bildungsroman* when, as in Goethe's *Wilhelm Meister*, it typically recounts (within an art form) the artistic vocation (the 'becoming aesthetic') of its main protagonist.

The continuity between philosophy and art as 'distinct, though related modalities of meaning' is a reminder that the difference between philosophy and art is already a difference 'within', but also that Hegel's System is a dialectic, one which, like Plato's dialogues, involves conflict, antithesis, and opposition.[193] The 'True is whole', for Hegel,[194] but this is a dialectical whole, one which can be regarded as

---

[188] Hegel, *Aesthetics: Lectures on Fine Art*, i. 38 [*Vorlesungen über die Ästhetik*, 86].

[189] Ibid. i. 39 and 36 [87 and 82].   [190] Ibid. i. 37 [84].

[191] Sychrava, *Schiller to Derrida*, 25.

[192] Letter 23, quoted in Kaufmann, *Hegel: A Reinterpretation*, 23: see from p. 20 for the exact nature of Schiller's influence on Hegel; see also Nisbet (ed.), *German Aesthetic and Literary Criticism*, esp. p. 20; and Sychrava, *Schiller to Derrida*.

[193] See Desmond, *Art and the Absolute*, 32 and 91.

[194] Hegel, *Phenomenology of Spirit*, Preface, 11 ['Das Wahre ist das Ganze', *Phänomenologie des Geistes*, p. 21].

an 'essayistic totality', for it involves the 'holding together of the many opposites . . . not in any univocal unity . . . but in a complex unity immanently differentiated': 'For Hegel, everything is itself and also other. . . . Everything has some determinate identity. But this identity is complex and defined by an inherent process of differentiation. This process of differentiation makes it differ from itself as a simple identity, to become other than such.'[195] 'Spirit', writes Hegel, 'becomes object because it is just this movement of becoming an *other to itself*, i.e. becoming *an object to itself*' [*sich ein anderes, d.h. Gegenstand seines Selbst zu werden*]. The '*experience* [*Erfahrung*] which consciousness goes through' and which implies that 'in consciousness one thing exists for another' manifests 'the disparity [*ungleichheit*] between the "I" and its object . . . the disparity of the substance with itself'.[196] The role of temporal deferment in the process of essaying turns time into the essential factor of this sameness as otherness: the dialectic 'immediately situates us in a world of process or Becoming', a world where the 'nature of Being is posited as Becoming', so that 'a thing in time becomes *other* to its former shape'.[197] Hegel's conception of history as a continuum of ever higher, more reflexive forms in which consciousness attempts to assert itself corresponds to a process by which each form or 'configuration' claims to be absolute yet cannot but 'break up out of its own inherent tension or strain', 'deforming' or 'deconstructing itself under the relentless power of the "negative" '.[198] Hegel's dialectic thus incorporates 'the negative' and the 'thoroughgoing scepticism' [*vollbringender Skeptizismus*][199] practised by his Romantic predecessors and which anticipates Mikhail Bakhtin's 'dialogism'. However, this negativity is only one moment in Hegel's scheme, his aim being ultimately to transcend the Romantic position, to go beyond the ultimate emptiness and dissolution of the Romantic view in which time is a 'meaningless supersession of moments', an endless succession which is not overcome and so turns into a 'bad infinite' or an 'infinite absolute negativity'.[200] In order for history to become meaningful, that is, to come to a genuine realization of itself, the process of dissolving and negating must be counterbalanced by a 'positive' term so that 'the exposition of the untrue consciousness in its untruth is not merely a *negative* procedure'.[201] Spirit progresses according to the logic of the famous *Aufhebung* ('sublation') which ultimately posits 'the identity of identity and difference', a process in which 'what is cancelled is also preserved', in which 'each thing in time becomes other to its former shape while yet in this process of differentiation remaining itself'.[202]

---

[195] Desmond, *Art and the Absolute*, 95 and 92.

[196] Hegel, *Phenomenology of Spirit*, preface, 21 [32]; introduction, 53 [71]; and preface, 21 [32] respectively.

[197] Desmond, *Art and the Absolute*, 91 and 92.

[198] Ibid. 94. See Hegel, *Phenomenology of Spirit*, preface, 38–9, and introduction, 50–1 [*Phänomenologie des Geistes*, pp. 49, 68–9].

[199] Hegel, *Phenomenology of Spirit*, introduction, 50 [*Phänomenologie des Geistes*, p. 67].

[200] Desmond, *Art and the Absolute*, 100, 120, and 67.

[201] Hegel, *Phenomenology of Spirit*, introduction, 50 [*Phänomenologie des Geistes*, p. 68].

[202] Desmond, *Art and the Absolute*, 96 and 92.

The 'abstract . . . becomes alienated from itself and then returns to itself from this alienation' [*aus dieser Entfremdung zu sich zurückgeht*] when 'knowledge no longer needs to go beyond itself', when 'knowledge finds itself'.[203] It is by virtue of this progressive reconciliation or synthesis of opposites and differences that the dialectical relation of art and philosophy implied in the idea of 'aesthetic wholeness' must finally give way to the self-transcendence or consummation of art into philosophy (usually referred to as the 'death of art'): 'The work of art stands in the *middle* between immediate sensuousness and ideal thought. It is *not yet* pure thought, but, despite its sensuousness, is *no longer* a purely material existent either.'[204]

In part II of Hegel's *Aesthetics*, Romantic art represents the third and last stage of the itinerary, that is, the last form of art (after the Symbolic and the Classical) into which the Ideal develops. Within Romantic art, poetry itself (after painting and music) is the highest form, 'occupied' as it is 'with the universal element in art as such to a greater extent than is the case in any of the other ways of producing works of art'.[205] In terms of the Hegelian journey towards absolute knowledge, poetry, which 'can harbour the entire content of art and all the forms of art', thus 'runs the risk of losing itself in a transition from the region of sense into that of the spirit'.[206] In other words, 'poetry, as the highest art, has climbed to the threshold of the Idea, of philosophy', so that 'the triumph of poetry is the defeat of art'.[207] Only in the philosophical concept is the Idea fully immanent for Hegel, only 'as a realm of pure thinking unmarked by sensuous representation' can the emergence of Spirit occur: 'the substance of the universe is not material but conceptual'.[208] The transcendence of the Romantic position results in our defining the essayistic spirit as much against as in relation to Hegel. To approach the essay via the essayistic from the pre- and post-Hegelian perspective of German theorists is to subscribe to the 'negative dialectics' of the Hegelian scheme and to remain this side of the latter's ultimate view that 'the True is actual only as system'.[209] The inability to reduce otherness to sameness, non-identity to self-identity, and so to achieve a perfect fusion of practice and theory, being and thinking, art and philosophy remains inherent in both the *Bildungsroman* and the essay, as in both genres the acting out of the notion of self-realization (of man/humanity) is inextricably connected with a questioning of this very notion. In the periods of generic crises which are the focus of an 'essayistic' perspective, the acute reflexivity or

[203] Hegel, *Phenomenology of Spirit*, preface, 21 [32]; and introduction, 51 ['wo es nicht mehr über sich selbst hinauszugehen nötig hat, wo es sich selbst findet', *Phänomenologie des Geistes*, p. 69].

[204] Hegel, *Aesthetics: Lectures on Fine Art*, i. 38 [*Vorlesungen über die Ästhetik*, 86].

[205] Ibid. ii. 967.   [206] Ibid. ii. 968.

[207] Knox, *The Aesthetic Theories of Kant, Hegel, and Schopenhauer*, 96 and 94.

[208] Desmond, *Art and the Absolute*, 11; editor's (David Simpson's) introduction to Selections from Hegel, *Aesthetics: Lectures on Fine Art*, 356; and Knox, *The Aesthetic Theories of Kant, Hegel, and Schopenhauer*, 103–4.

[209] Hegel, *Phenomenology of Spirit*, Preface, 14 ['Daß das Wahre nur als system wirklich . . . ist', *Phänomenologie des Geistes*, p. 24].

self-consciousness which goes hand in hand with the crisis and critique of systems—of the System—entails the endless deferment of self-identity. My brief survey of Renaissance writing above suggests that the generalized essayism of such periods must turn all texts into the fragments, paratexts, or 'essays' of the endlessly deferred system: that essayism then becomes the transient and evanescent mode of all discourse. But it also suggests that the very distinction between 'classical' and 'modern' which the concept of 'generic crisis' relies on, is made redundant: within the logic of such periods texts will by definition always (at all times) be the fragments, paratexts, and essays of a work to come. This ambivalence, in fact, is at the heart of Friedrich Schlegel's speculations where Romantic poetry is a 'kind' of poetry which can be distinguished from other kinds, but also 'the only one that is more than a kind, that is, as it were, poetry itself', which prompts the conclusion that 'in a certain sense all poetry is or should be romantic'.[210]

In this Romantic conception of the text or book as fragment or essay, as literature *in potentia*, one recognizes the fundamentally 'modern' conception of literature[211] which connects the two main trends of Continental essayism. I have already referred to some of the exponents of the German trend (represented also by Nietzsche, Wittgenstein, and Bloch). The other main trend is of course French and mainly post-structuralist (Barthes, Lyotard, Foucault, Derrida), although it must be made to include the American branch of deconstructors (Geoffrey Hartman especially). Because of their pervasive influence on modern literary criticism, we know that both trends rebel against what has variously been referred to as 'the primacy of systems', 'absolute objectivity', the 'concept of method', 'totalizing modes of thought', 'metaphysical closures', 'theological motives', philosophies and 'principles of identity', etc., thus privileging instead fragmentation 'as an aesthetic and methodological principle' and 'proposing the methodological recognition of contingency'.[212] Both the German and the French exponents of Continental essayism and/or modern literary theory have a 'shared, tortuous, love–hate relation to Hegel'.[213] We know that Jacques Derrida ascribes to self-reflexiveness a role exactly opposed to that stipulated by Hegel. For the latter, 'it is reflection that makes the True a result';[214] for the former, reflection can never bring about self-mastery; on the contrary, it is the generator of infinite difference or *différance*: no part of the system can be made to assume a closural role over the other parts, either as origin or as finality, for the external, metalinguistic position from which this could be

---

[210] 'The romantic kind of poetry is the only one that is more than a kind, that is, as it were, poetry itself: for in a certain sense all poetry is or should be romantic' (Schlegel, *Athenäum Fragments*, 116, p. 47 ['Die romantische Dichtart ist die einzige, die mehr als Art und gleichsam die Dichtkunst selbst ist: denn in einem gewissen Sinn ist oder soll alle Poesie romantisch sein', *Athenäums-Fragmente*, p. 39].

[211] *L'Absolu littéraire* by Philippe Lacoue-Labarthe and Jean-Luc Nancy is an analysis, precisely, of the origins of modern notions of literature in German Romantic theory.

[212] Kauffmann, 'The Skewed Path', 232 and 234.

[213] Peter Dews, *Logics of Disintegration: Post-Structuralist Thought and the Claims of Critical Theory* (1988), 2.

[214] Hegel, *Phenomenology of Spirit*, Preface, 12 [['Die Reflexion] ist es, die das Wahre zum Resultate macht', *Phänomenologie des Geistes*, p. 21].

done does not exist. Or rather, to invert the proposition as Derrida himself does: 'if there were a definition of difference it would be precisely the limit, the interruption, the destruction of the Hegelian *Aufhebung* wherever it operates.'[215] With regard to the essay specifically, this is translated in Adorno's 'The Essay as Form' into the contention that 'the essay is more dialectical than the dialectic as it articulates itself', given that 'Hegelian philosophy, to be sure, remained trapped in the inconsistency that it criticized the abstract, over-arching concept, the mere "result", in the name of an internally discontinuous process, while at the same time, in the idealist tradition, speaking about dialectical method.'[216] One could say that in Adorno, the 'critique of the system' [*Die Kritik am System*[217]] effected by the essay is perceived as the 'stretching'—rather than as the 'interruption'—of the (Hegelian) limit. 'Philosophy'—Adorno recognizes—'has completed the fullest critique of definition from the most diverse perspectives, including those of Kant, Hegel and Nietzsche. But science has never adopted this critique'.[218] Hence the real target of the essay is a philosophy which identifies with 'scientific method' in the mode of Scholasticism.[219] Within the overall Hegelian framework, it is Descartes's concept of 'method' as the paradigm of a philosophy modelling itself on science (probably the greatest 'scholastic residue in modern thought'[220]) which for Adorno constitutes the immediate object of the essay's anti-systematic impulse. And as with Hegel and his dialectic, this association between the Montaignian essay and Descartes's method can be said to operate at the breaking-point. As mentioned in Section 1.2 of this chapter, Descartes is 'the first philosopher to ask, not just what the world is like, but how one can know what the world is like', thus starting—unlike previous philosophers—from the immediate data of consciousness and 'attempting to "work out" from them to an external world'.[221] In a sense, then, Descartes offers a systematization of the sceptical arguments provided only shortly beforehand by Montaigne. On the other hand, Cartesian philosophy also represents the 'limit' of Montaigne's thought, for it is by extending sceptical doubt as far as it can go—by embracing 'the deepest scepticism'—that Descartes proposes to '*overthrow*' it, that is, to 'find some foundation for knowledge which is resistant to such doubt' and to 'win through to certainty'.[222] He finds this in the *cogito*, in the conviction that, given the subject's divine origins, the immediate data of consciousness from which all philosophy must proceed are *indubitable*. This is roughly how Descartes's construction of a new dogmatic scientific theory by means of this individualist foundationalist approach inaugurates a philosophy of reflexivity that will reach its climax with Hegel, a philosophy where self-consciousness or

---

[215] Jacques Derrida, *Positions* (1981), 40–1.
[216] Adorno, 'The Essay as Form', 166 ['Der Essay als Form', 40].
[217] Ibid. 157 [21].   [218] Ibid. 159 [26].
[219] Ibid. 160 [27].   [220] Ibid. 159 [26].
[221] Urmson and Rée (eds.), *The Concise Encyclopedia of Western Philosophy and Philosophers*, 78.
[222] Hookway, 'Descartes: The Deepest Scepticism', in *Scepticism*, 41, 43, and 66. See also 'Descartes: Conqueror of Scepticism', in Popkin, *The History of Scepticism from Erasmus to Descartes*.

self-reflection becomes the first principle or 'ground of foundation and deduction for all systems of knowledge'.[223]

For Continental essayism at large, the rejection of self-reflection in those terms concerns not least the claim to linguistic transparency, to the transparence of the spoken or the oral made by a context-free, 'genre-less' philosophy which passes itself off as science. The 'movement' against 'scholastic residues in modern thought', which Adorno sees as beginning with Kant, 'replaces verbal definition with an understanding of concepts as part of the process in which they are temporally embodied', contrary to the 'individual sciences' which 'insist stubbornly on the pre-critical job of definition'.[224] This awareness of the intrinsic connection between the so-called 'metaphysics of identity' and discursive structures of domination is one which Adorno clearly shares with Derrida. Yet—perhaps on account of the distinction established by Richard Rorty between 'idealists' and 'textualists'[225]—it is in Derrida's work that the interrelation of language, writing, and 'différance' is most systematically explored. If, for Derrida, 'writing always leads to more writing, and more, and still more—just as history does not lead to Absolute Knowledge or to the Final Struggle, but to more history, and more, and still more',[226] this is because language, on account of its figural deviousness, never coincides with meaning. Hence 'the incompatibility, perhaps without recourse, between the appearance of language in its being and the self's consciousness in its identity',[227] an incompatibility which, as Michel Beaujour points out, Montaigne's *Essais* 'revealed . . . well before the formulation of the Cartesian *cogito*, that is, previous to the birth of the *subject* whose disappearance is sought or diagnosed by French modernism.'[228] In German essayism—Adorno's especially—this 'dehumanization' operates in what Graham Good describes as a 'curiously impersonal' treatment of 'the subjective component', namely in the construction 'of a subjectivized object in which the object is central and the subject simply refracts aspects of it'.[229] French post-structuralists, on the other hand, are known to 'extend the German post-Hegelian critiques of idealism' and 'eliminate all vestiges of Cartesianism and humanism from their thinking'. They act on the ultimate consequences of Montaignian scepticism, since 'the shift wrought by this negative dialectics first from God to man, and then from man to language itself'—that most basic of all indeterminacies—results in the completely autonomous operation of 'writing' or

---

[223] Rodolphe Gasché, *The Tain of the Mirror: Derrida and the Philosophy of Reflection* (1986), 19.

[224] Adorno, 'The Essay as Form', 159–60 ['Der Essay als Form', 26–7].

[225] Richard Rorty, 'Nineteenth-Century Idealism and Twentieth-Century Textualism', in *Consequences of Pragmatism: Essays: 1972–1980* (1982).

[226] Richard Rorty, 'Philosophy as a Kind of Writing: An Essay on Derrida', in *Consequences of Pragmatism*, 94.

[227] Michel Foucault ('La Pensée du dehors'), quoted in Beaujour, *Poetics of the Literary Self-Portrait*, 13.

[228] Ibid.

[229] Good, *The Observing Self*, 21 (the concept of 'dehumanization' is one which I borrow from the Spanish essayist José Ortega y Gasset's book *The Dehumanization of Art*).

'textuality' with no conscious subject in control, and so to the total abolition of the subjective principle.[230]

It may be noted that in our century, the self-essaying of philosophy and literature goes hand in hand with an intensive theorization and practice of margins which is consonant with the 'initial suspicion of the *Essais* with regard to the centralizing claims of writing'.[231] This can take the form of an interest in self-declared 'essays', as in the case of Lukács and Adorno. But it is more likely to take the form of an interest in paratexts generally. Lukács and Adorno's essays already appear in the form of paratexts: apart from the fact that Lukács's essay is a self-declared (albeit imaginary) letter while Adorno's essay is published among a collection of 'notes to literature', both texts function as prefaces or introductions to an overall volume of essays. French theoretical works on the paratext such as Genette's *Seuils* ('thresholds') or Antoine Compagnon's work on 'perigraphy' in *La Seconde Main, ou Le Travail de la citation* are the patent expression of this renewed interest in the frontiers of literature.[232] But the margins of philosophy remain the domain, above all, of Jacques Derrida: the footnote in 'Ousia and Gramme: Note on a Note from *Being and Time*' (in *Margins: Of philosophy*); the preface in 'Outwork' ['Hors-livre'] (on Hegel, in *Dissemination*); the title in 'Titre à préciser', (in *Parages*— literally 'vicinities'), etc. Yet, even further away from the genre of the essay, this essayistic focus on margins takes the form above all of an interest in paratextuality generally, that is, in the various, more diffuse ways in which the philosophical or literary text (consciously or unconsciously) foregrounds the question of its own writing. This focus on paratextuality (on the 'aspect of textuality' rather than the 'class of texts') will thus typically involve the internal and external borders of the text—its 'frame', and the question of self-reflexiveness or *mise en abyme*.[233] In the realm of literature narrative, structures are the privileged field of study while in the realm of philosophy, the relationship examined by Derrida between intention and form ('Form and Meaning: A Note on the Phenomenology of Language', and 'Signature, Event, Context'), between philosophy and metaphor ('White Mythology: Metaphor in the Text of Philosophy') or between philosophy and linguistics ('The Supplement of Copula: Philosophy before Linguistics') in *Margins: Of Philosophy*, and the study of 'The Parergon' in *Truth in Painting*, represent the various manners in which philosophy can be seen to question its own frame and closure. The frontier itself between literary or philosophical essayism as a theoretical object is of course artificial, since if anything characterizes these 'modern' periods, it is precisely that as a result of the eruption of explicit reflexiveness or self-criticism at the heart of literary and philosophical texts, neither can be wholly assigned to one

[230] Desmond, *Art and the Absolute*, 81; and Kauffmann, 'The Skewed Path', 233.

[231] See Rigolot, 'Montaigne et la poétique de la marge', 141.

[232] Research on the paratext also includes articles in recent volumes of *Poétique*, *L'Esprit Créateur*, and *Sub-Stance*; see also the final ch. of Laurence Lerner's *The Frontiers of Literature* (1988), entitled 'The Body of Literature'.

[233] The classic study of *mise en abyme* in literature remains Lucien Dällenbach's *The Mirror in the Text* (1989).

or the other category. To examine the question of framing and paratextuality in a philosophical context is to examine philosophy's relation to literature, philosophy as literature, as a 'kind of writing'.[234] Representation is the very theme of literature as of all art; and it is understood from the outset that the form of the literary text is likely to exceed to a greater or lesser extent its content or message, that the medium is not entirely transparent to its object, that a literary text does not necessarily mean what it says or say what it means. Literature, like all art, knows itself to be illusory. Yet like scientific or philosophical discourse, the literary text can foreground its message, play down its dominant poetic or aesthetic function and provide as good an illustration as the philosophical text of the so-called 'order of mimesis'.[235] In this case literature submits to philosophical demands; it 'yields from the outset to the constraints of its philosophical conceptualization' so that, like philosophy, it 'includes the project of effacing itself in the face of its signified content'.[236] The convergence of philosophy and literature, exemplified by Hegel's master-system as master-narrative, thus demonstrates the specificity they share of 'systematically curtailing the signifier'.[237] Essayism—whether philosophical or literary—therefore involves 'Literature' or the 'literary' with quotation-marks and/or capitals that indicate its subversive function with regard to both philosophy and literature in the narrow sense (in the sense of a literature 'under the dominion' of philosophy[238]). In this, one recognizes the asymmetry typical of critical periods when literature in the broad, capitalized sense of the literary absolute (of generalized or 'archi-literature') both includes and subverts the specific meaning of the word 'literature'and where the tension between individual genres in the empirical, historical sense is both maintained and transcended by the concept of Genre 'beyond genre'.[239]

One noticeable difference between theorists concerned with literary essayism or paratextuality (Genette or Compagnon) and theorists concerned (predominantly) with philosophical essayism or paratextuality (German and French) does remain, however, and materializes in the form in which their respective work is conducted. If we transfer our attention from the theorization to the practice of margins, we will note that the work of the first category of theorists (mainly structuralist, such as Genette and Compagnon) remains external and 'scientific' in its claims: it produces taxonomies of and theories 'about' essayism or paratextuality. The work of the (larger) second category of theorists (the Germans and post-structuralists),

---

[234] From the title of Richard Rorty's 'Philosophy as a Kind of Writing: An Essay on Derrida'. Adorno and Derrida—and, one might say, philosophical essayists in general—are as many 'edifying' or 'aphoristic' philosophers in Rorty's terminology: see his *Philosophy and the Mirror of Nature*, 3rd edn. (1986), 5–6 and 366–70.

[235] See Christopher Prendergast, *The Order of Mimesis: Balzac, Stendhal, Nerval, Flaubert* (1986).

[236] Gasché, *The Tain of the Mirror*, 256 (the last quotation is drawn from Derrida's *Of Grammatology*). See also Booth, *The Rhetoric of Fiction*.

[237] Gasché, *The Tain of the Mirror*, 256.   [238] Ibid. 259.

[239] See Jonathan Culler, *On Deconstruction: Theory and Criticism after Structuralism* (1983), 180–2 (as well, still, as *L'Absolu littéraire* by Lacoue-Labarthe and Nancy; and 'Genus Universum' by Beaujour).

on the other hand, is internal and reflexive: it is the work of essayists themselves for whom 'thought is inseparable from its mode of presentation'.[240] In this case, essayism and paratextuality can only be talked 'about' essayistically and paratextually. 'Aboutness' disappears for there is no 'unconditional standpoint', no external, objective, or metalinguistic perspective from which the essay and/or the paratext could be discussed. Philosophical essayism thus involves approaching the object on its own terms, 'reflexively' or 'immanently', in accordance with Schlegel's conception of 'poetic criticism' [*poetische Kritik*].[241] Moreover the essayist, as suggested when discussing Montaigne, 'must continually reflect on the context or circumstances of his own discourse',[242] so that the essaying of philosophy (and literature) in turn becomes the object of its own essaying. By judging the object 'reflexively' or 'immanently', philosophical essayists are able to examine their object without falling prey to those very conceptual procedures they denounce. As with Montaigne's *Essais*, then, the indirect, aesthetic treatment of the subject-matter corresponds to a sceptical *and* to a positive, counter-ideological response in which 'the philosophical essayist finds himself in strategic alliance with art against the imperial claims of theory'.[243] The paratactic, digressive, poetic logic of these essays makes their truth-content incommensurable with and thus not reducible to monologic scientific knowledge. And again as in Montaigne, the challenge to unity is conceived simultaneously as a challenge to immediate comprehensibility: the privileging of thought 'in progress' over ready-made truths calls for the active participation of a reader cast as a 'fellow labourer'. This dialogue between writer and reader which replaces scientific monologism implies that the reader is 'no longer a consumer, but a producer of the text', as Roland Barthes's famous definition of the 'writerly' [*scriptible*] text stipulates (in *S/Z*) in a way which hardly differs from Montaigne's conception of reader and writer on opposite sides of the tennis net.[244] In this respect again, the early German Romantics' promotion of an 'aesthetics of incomprehensibility' richly contributed to our modern conception of the reader as writer. The store which Friedrich Schlegel, Jean Paul, and Novalis set by 'incomprehensibility' corresponded to their belief that 'the author could not give a reader the truth, but only set him in the direction of the truth', for 'complete comprehensibility was a delusion, and indicated a major misconception of the nature of truth and communication, and a false expectation of what art or philosophy could offer.'[245]

---

[240] Kauffmann, 'The Skewed Path', 227.

[241] Schlegel's conception of criticism turns the internal construction of the work of art itself into the standard of aesthetic judgement as a 'medium of reflection'; see Wheeler (ed.), *German Aesthetic and Literary Criticism*, 25–6 and Schlegel, 'On Goethe's *Meister*', also in Wheeler (ed.) ['Über Goethes *Meister*', in W. Rasch (ed.), *Kritische Schriften*].

[242] Kauffmann, 'The Skewed Path', 234.   [243] Ibid. 235.

[244] See Bauschatz, 'Montaigne's Conception of Reading in the Context of Renaissance Poetics and Modern Criticism', 265.

[245] Kathleen Wheeler, 'Introduction' to Wheeler (ed.), *German Aesthetic and Literary Criticism*, 11. See Friedrich Schlegel, 'On Incomprehensibility', in Simpson (ed.), *The Origins of Modern Critical Thought*, 179–87; Jean Paul Richter, *School for Aesthetics* 1973; and Novalis, *Miscellaneous Writings* ['Über die Unverständlichkeit'], in Rasch (ed.), *Friedrich Schlegel: Kritische Schriften*.

The very concept of *Bildung* presupposes a slow and laborious journey of enlightenment for the reader who, at exactly the same pace as the individual represented in the text, must pass through the obstacles and trials that will ideally lead him to the standpoint of knowledge. Accordingly, the reader of Hegel's *Phenomenology* was later destined to 'pass through the formative stages of universal spirit' in the course of his reading, that is, to 'suffer through each position and to be changed as he proceed[ed] from one to the other'.[246] This justifies the significance, for Romantic essayists, of the fragment and of dialogue, both of which champion the use of paradox, self-contradiction, and indirection, thwarting the potential reader's easy, immediate comprehension, his 'passive acquiescing' and 'parroting' of other's labours and insights, and stimulating him instead to 'creative engagement'.[247] Ultimately, fragmentary utterances (all expressions of the Romantic love of 'preparatives' and 'propadeutics') are designed not only to stimulate the reader's power of imagination but to force him, as with the *Essais*, 'to grapple with thinking itself and with language as a vehicle of thought'.[248]

The essay's aesthetic treatment of its object as an alternative to the conceptual and totalizing approach of philosophy as science, motivates the displacement implied in the notion of 'philosophical essayism' from philosophy to philosophy of art (a philosophy concerned with representation, an 'aesthetics'), from philosophy of art to art or literary criticism, and finally to art or literary criticism as art or literature. So philosophical essayists—or 'new philosophic critics',[249] tend to be better known in the field of literature than in that of philosophy. As mentioned above, the 'superiority' of criticism over philosophy hinges on the fact that 'by taking the work of art as its point of departure, [the essay] can take into account the sensuous dimension of truth—the problem of *representation*—which the inherently abstract nature of the philosophical concept cannot help but suppress'.[250] On the other hand, in this 'immanent' and 'reflexive' literary criticism practised by (philosophical) essayists and which involves 'form[ing] once more what has already been formed', 'add[ing] to the work, restor[ing] it, shap[ing] it afresh' so that it 'represents the representation anew'—in Schlegel's terms[251]—the particular, literary object only acts as a starting-point or a pretext for an account of the general conditions of representation, of general aesthetic experience. From the perspective of Romantic aesthetics, the text as 'an autonomous entity' is of interest above all in so far as the underlying (subjective) process—the 'formal, shaping, creating,

---

[246] Kaufmann, *Hegel: A Reinterpretation*, 117.

[247] Wheeler, 'Introduction' to Wheeler (ed.), *German Aesthetic and Literary Criticism*, 8 and 13.

[248] Ibid. 9 and 8; see also pp. 10 and 11.

[249] As Geoffrey Hartman calls them in his 'Literary Commentary as Literature', in *Criticism in the Wilderness*, 190.

[250] Wolin, 'The Essay as Mediation between Art and Philosophical Truth', 87–8.

[251] Friedrich Schlegel, 'On Goethe's *Meister*', in Wheeler (ed.), *German Aesthetic and Literary Criticism*, 69 ['die Darstellung von neuem Darstellen, das schon Gebildete noch einmal bilden . . . das Werk ergänzen, verjüngen, gestalten', 'Über Goethes *Meister*', in W. Rasch (ed.), *Kritische Schriften*, 277].

processual aspects of literature—can be revealed.[252] In other words, the criticism characteristic of Continental essayism will 'not [be] interested in what the text means specifically, locally, historically, in a particular spatial and temporal context'; it will tend to 'emphasize the relative, self-referential, unstable, processual aspect of texts at the expense of the determinate, referential, stable, productive aspect, and . . . give no account of what is specific about a text, what it is about and what differentiates it from another'.[253]

To conclude, it appears that, from every angle, essayism functions as the paradigm of contemporary criticism, or conversely that the cutting edge of contemporary criticism has caught up with the essay. One form of post-structuralist criticism especially brings this out, a form which one could call 'paratextual criticism' for it literally develops as a footnote or gloss on the margins of a chosen philosophical or literary text. Derrida's 'Tympan', *Glas*, or 'Living On: Borderlines', which are the best specimens of this paratextual criticism, could be seen as extreme versions of Montaigne's *Essais* (and, by extension, of the Montaignian essay itself) which, as we know, also develop 'paratextually' as annotations in the margins of other texts. By staging the limit in this way, paratextual criticism dramatizes the 'crossing over' of criticism to literature,[254] or of 'critical' to 'poetic' intertextuality according to Schlegel's conception of interpretation as one which does not 'establish a final meaning that would close the book and relegate it to the past' but involves 'the infinite task of deciphering that relates the text to the future of the world and keeps it alive'.[255] The essayistic questioning of the notions of representation and mimesis initiated by Montaigne and amply rehearsed by the Romantics' renewed move away from imitation to creative reproduction, inevitably affects the traditional distinction and hierarchy between original and derived, central and peripheral, creation and commentary, primary and secondary, which govern traditional criticism: by visibly developing 'alongside' and on one level with the 'pre-text', the footnote or gloss enacts a situation where all texts are equally secondary, and therefore primary. The explicitly 'immanent' position of paratextual criticism between the inside and the outside of the work establishes a relationship of contamination whereby self-identity, determinacy, and closure are undermined on both sides of the margin. The adequation of parts and whole traditionally confirmed by an 'absolute', Hegelian reading thus becomes impossible both 'intratextually' and

---

[252] Sychrava, *Schiller to Derrida*, 43, 44, 45, and 51: 'Romantic aesthetics sustains a double perspective on to poetry. It is at once a *process* ("Romantic poetry is a progressive universal poetry . . . it is always becoming . . . it can never be completed") and a *product*, an organic whole ("an object of nature that wants to become an object of art")' (p. 51). See also Wiedmann, 'The Organic Theory of Art', in *Romantic Art Theories*.

[253] Sychrava, *Schiller to Derrida*, 163. Cf. also Jonathan Culler, *On Deconstruction*, 156: 'Deconstruction is never concerned only with signified content but especially with the conditions and assumptions of discourse.'

[254] Discussed in Geoffrey Hartman's 'Literary Commentary as Literature', in *Criticism in the Wilderness*.

[255] Ernst Behler, *German Romantic Litery Theory* (1993), 282.

intertextually: whether in the form of self-reflection or external reflection, 'difference' opens up every text, which, by definition, is always 'beside itself'.

1.5. ESSAYING THE ESSAY

Can the approach to a genre which is marginal be anything but marginal? The essay as a genre is neglected. Via the mode, on the other hand, one is able to draw attention to the possibility which the essay offers, precisely in its quality as a marginal genre, to move beyond the canonical oppositions of traditional generic studies and ultimately to confront 'literature' itself as a question, and so to catch up with the central concerns of modern literary theory and criticism. Yet to promote the essay to the centre of (modern) literary interests by foregrounding the essayistic—by stretching the genre to its limits and consciously adopting a decentred, 'excessive' approach, tackling the essay through what it is not—is in fact to redeem its initial marginalization by the orchestration, this time, of its total dispersal and definitive disappearance: the essence of a genre which is always 'in potentia' is by definition the essence of literature itself. However, the essay, far from being 'outmoded', remains very much alive throughout literary history, even in those neosceptical eras when generalized essayism is the prominent characteristic (or 'disease', as some would see it) of literature. The survival of the genre despite its apparent displacement by the mode points to the necessity of overcoming ideas about the mutual exclusion of essay and essayistic and the associated assumption that the essays of Montaigne and Bacon represent two contradictory versions of the genre. It is more pertinent to consider the two types of essay as two possible actualizations of the genre[256]—all the more so as the logic of those periods of generic crisis when the essayistic is foremost is itself founded on the irreducible paradox or self-contradiction of a Genre of genres (or of Literature) which, although it is beyond genre, still relies upon the individual genres which it simultaneously denies and transcends, and is therefore at once plural and singular. Even within the 'excessive' logic of the mode itself, in other words, the essay must be left to play on two levels simultaneously: the level of 'writing' where the particular text, the individual moment and situation opens on to the infinite to become the inexhaustible paradigm of the 'text' in general, but also the system of this particular work where the economy of individual genres which rules over the coded exchange of the different modes of enunciation, and by extension of the different modes of reception, still operates.

It is from the point of view of this dual perspective that the six chapters of this book—despite the 'essayistic' bias—must be read. Essayism marks a shift, already at the root of Montaigne's *Essais*, from the philosophical (the scientific) to the

---

[256] 'Two styles which have been influential in the development of the essay' (Rohner, *Der deutsche Essay*, 60); see also Good, *The Observing Self*, 43.

literary, and this shift will inform the trajectory of this book from Montaigne to Borges. It is in Borges's work that we find the implications of Montaignian scepticism fully actualized, that the essayistic explosion of the genre is most radical, since its fallout takes the form of as many paratextual permutations, all instances of the boundless work of Literature. Yet ending with Borges makes sense only in as much as in his work the outmost decentring of the genre also coincides with its innermost 'centring'. Conformably with Montaigne's *Essais*, which are one by being beside themselves (a unity in excess), the stretching of the essay to its outermost limits beyond genre also functions in Borges as a constant reaffirmation of the indispensability of generic boundaries, as a constant reminder of the power of these limits and of the power of all limits in the practical realm of the reader's confrontation with individual genres, texts, and authors. Between Montaigne and Borges, to whom I respectively devote my Chapters 2 and 6, the characteristics of German and French philosophical essayism already outlined in this chapter will be explored in more detail in Chapter 3, while Roland Barthes's own use of the essay(istic) will take up the whole of Chapter 4. In Barthes's work, the influence of both Montaigne and the Romantics is unmistakable, and it would be natural to relegate him to the philosophical essayism of the previous chapter, thus turning him, for example, into the exponent of an essayism more concerned with the manifestation of the System as narrative than as philosophy. On the other hand, his contribution to essay-writing is worth separate attention, as it conspicuously shuttles between an interpretation and exploitation of the essayistic as the radically literary or fictional (which culminates in 'deconstruction') and of the essayistic in the more limited sense of the concretely fictional. Barthes is indeed the prototype of the essayist as would-be or as failed novelist. He therefore provides a natural transition to the essayistic novelists—Proust, Broch, and Musil—of Chapter 5, a transition which signals both a (hierarchical) progression from essay to novel and a levelling of essay and novel as the traces (the 'novelistic' rather than the essayistic in Barthes's terms) of a (Romantic) Novel which can never materialize. In Borges, as a matter of fact, this tension between hierarchy and realignment is all the more blatant as the genre which he chooses for the 'novelistic' alongside the essay is the latter's fictional equivalent in size, the short story. Finally, the overall perspective of this book is one in which the essaying of the essay within the general context of literary history and within the work of any one individual author converge, although it will also be clear that the first three chapters are concerned predominantly with the former, while in the last three chapters more attention is paid to the latter.

The randomness and spontaneity associated with the idea of 'essaying' the essay is of course belied by the fact that my presentation of the genre in this chapter is necessarily already the result of the combination and selection of a fairly wide range of critical material. And this selection needs to be specially justified because of the striking lack of co-ordination that exists (i) within specialized studies on the essay and between them (both within one country and *a fortiori* between countries);

(ii) between studies on the essay and studies on particular essayists, and, overlapping with this; (iii) between studies on the essay, studies on genre, and literary criticism in general. In the first case, the lack of co-ordination takes the form of a lack of a sense of progress within the field of essay-scholarship also pointed out by Graham Good. Both intratextually (within studies) and intertextually (from one study to the next), one is overwhelmed with an accumulation of descriptive remarks which are seldom subordinated to an overall argument. As Graham Good formulates it, the singularly undisciplined body of studies which the essay has generated seems to rebel against the idea of an 'interpersonal body of knowledge' which would involve 'taking into account previous contributions to the topic', helping to 'cover the field' according to the temporal idea of progress, 'deriving general rules from specific instances, subordinating them through classification and hierarchical arrangement'.[257] For Graham Good, on the other hand, this resistance against the 'drive to unity' is due precisely to a respect for the methodological correspondence between the content (the essay as subject-matter) and the form of these studies:

The essay starts without preconceptions, and it is fitting that none of these writers offers a 'theory' of the essay, that is, a set of propositions capable of controlling or marshalling this last field. Instead, each puts forward an 'essay on the essay'. At first sight, this might seem weaker than a theory; but it is stronger in the sense that each is demonstrating or enacting the form while commenting on it.[258]

In actual fact, only essayists in their own right have managed to write 'essays on the essay', and this is the obvious reason for my choice of Lukács and Adorno.[259] To 'demonstrate or enact the form while commenting on it' presupposes the ability to write 'methodically unmethodically' (Adorno); it implies a high degree of reflexivity, a rigour (and a talent) which most other studies lack. The only way of remaining faithful to the project of these writers would indeed be to provide another essay on the essay, and Graham Good's book does not opt for this alternative any more than mine does.

A second manifestation of the lack of co-ordination mentioned above, is the striking disproportion between studies on particular essayists, and the relatively small number of studies on the genre itself. This disproportion is both quantitative and qualitative. I referred to the qualitative aspect in Section 1.3 when drawing attention to the fact that the genre remains paraliterary despite the evaluation of great essays as literary works. The quantitative aspect (which is related) involves the discrepancy between the attention given to any one essayist (Montaigne scholarship alone, for example, is enormous) and the number of existing studies on the essay in the essayist's country alone and everywhere else, and *a fortiori* between the

---

[257] See Good, *The Observing self,* 4–6.   [258] Ibid. 24.
[259] Walter Benjamin would have been another obvious choice—perhaps the most obvious, since, as Good remarks, he is 'the most consistently essayistic'; yet because his essays require a deeper understanding of Messianic religion, I have preferred to leave him out.

great number of prestigious essayists produced by any one country and the number of existing studies on the genre in that country and everywhere else. England, which has the longest, the most continuous, and the most profuse tradition in essay-writing, is a case in point. Apart from a few and mainly old home-based works, one must turn to Canadian or American theorists (of whom there are not many either) for a more updated examination of the genre.[260] It should be pointed out, however, that considering some essayists as the exponents of a particular literary trend (for example T. S. Eliot, Virginia Woolf, D. H. Lawrence, and English Modernism) also tends indirectly to lend them new theoretical or critical significance. French criticism similarly has remarkably less to offer on the essay as a genre than one might be led to expect. The fact that Montaigne is the founder of the genre and the object, to this day, of a staggering amount of secondary literature, and that in more recent times Roland Barthes has attracted almost as much attention, does seem to testify to a continuing fascination with a certain type of writing. But precisely the fact that the French essay tends to be acutely self-reflexive, obsessed with the question of its form, and that French essayists are therefore used to being at once masters and theorists of the essay, makes baffling the critical unawareness of the essay as a distinct genre from outside the essay, in French literary studies. Or is it perhaps simply that, on the contrary, the former makes the latter redundant? This, however, would disregard the case of the *Nouveau Roman*, for example, where the combination of theory and practice within the novel has encouraged rather than discouraged the proliferation of theory outside or 'around' it. Finally, Montaigne's *Essais* have benefited in recent years from a renewed and intensive critical interest in Renaissance literature generally, and similarly, the continuing success of Barthes's own work seems largely due to his being frequently considered as a representative first of structuralism, then of post-structuralism. Yet when it comes to applying insights extra-polated from the interpretation of these particular essayists to the study of the genre in general, the best works, apart from a couple of home-studies,[261] are again those produced from a much a more remote 'outside', as though the best insights into the essay as a distinct genre could only be produced from the margins.[262] As for Spain and Latin America, both have a strong tradition of essay-writing with a corresponding critical

---

[260] One section in 'A Puzzling Literary Genre: Comparative Views of the Essay' (*Comparative Literature Studies*, 20 (1983)) by Richard M. Chadbourne provides a good survey of the tradition of English and American essays, and specialized studies such as Laurence Stapleton's and Elbert N. S. Thompson (on the seventeenth-cent. English essay) are illuminating; but classic reference works on the English essay generally remain Hugh Walker, *The English Essay and Essayists* (1915) and Bonamy Dobrée, *English Essayists* (1946). As for Canadian and American works, they include above all Robert Scholes and Carl Klaus, 'Essay', in *Elements of the Essay* and the later *Elements of Literature*; *The Observing Self: Rediscovering the Essay* by Graham Good, which is without doubt the most interesting study on the essay (the English essay above all) to date, along with the essays of Hardison, Core, Recchio, Kauffmann, and Johnston referred to in this chapter and selected from *Essays on the Essays: Redefining the Genre* (ed. A. J. Butrym).

[261] Esp. *Pour une esthétique de l'essai* (1967) by Robert Champigny.

[262] See *Rhétorique de l'essai littéraire* (1977) by Jean Terrasse, and the special issue of the Canadian *Études Littéraires* devoted to the essay.

interest. Their shortcomings for the study of the essay as a genre have to do this time with the fact that they are more concerned with ways in which the content of essays reflects the history of ideas and the cultural identity of their countries than with the form itself. Thus, apart from a few old-fashioned attempts at a theory of the genre, the favoured type of study remains the 'history of the essay'.[263] The information about the essay which these histories provide is at best very indirect, for the continuity—and therefore the sense of tradition—which their projects seem to be founded on is reduced to chronology. Within this chronological frame, each essay is treated as a unique case and from a predominantly biographical and socio-cultural angle; and this completely overlooks the fact that such writers— however original—have chosen to express themselves in an already existing form. Again, this tendency does not seem to have been perturbed by the considerable and ever-growing secondary literature on Borges's work which, on the contrary, stresses the writer's purely formal, ahistorical use of the genre and his anticipation of all possible theoretical issues.

In general, then, the essay-scholarship of literatures I have chosen to focus on seems old-fashioned and even regressive in relation to literary criticism, except perhaps for the German contribution favoured throughout this chapter. Rich and extensive, it is concerned above all with form and with the essayistic (especially the essayistic novel). Even so, the most valuable German material on the essay—books and articles—dates back to the 1950s and 1960s (and even to 1910 in the case of Lukács's 'On the Nature and Form of the Essay') and has never been revised since.[264] Above all, the implications of considering the essayistic as the essence of the genre are not reflected upon anywhere.[265] On the other hand, the tradition of systematic aesthetics (marked out by Graham Good as one running 'from

---

[263] See Kurt L. Levy and Keith Ellis (eds.), *El ensayo y la crítica literaria en Iberoamérica* (1970); José-Luis Gómez-Martínez, *Teoría del ensayo* (1981); and Antonio Urello, *Verosimilitud y estrategia textual en el ensayo hispanoamericano* (1986); and for predominantly historical approaches, Donald W. Bleznick, *El ensayo español del siglo XVI al XX* (1964); José Emundo Clemente, *El ensayo* (1961); Peter G. Earle and Robert G. Mead, *Historia del ensayo hispanoamericano* (1973); Martin S. Stabb, *In Quest of Identity: Patterns in the Spanish-American Essay of Ideas, 1890–1960* (1967); Alberto zum Felde, *Índice crítico de la literatura hispanoamericana: Los ensayistas* (1954), and the review entitled *Los Ensayistas* (esp. the articles in the following issues: 1 (1976), 5 (1978), 10–11 (1981), and 14–15 (1983)).

[264] The books and articles which I have found most useful—apart from Georg von Lukács, 'On the Nature and Form of the Essay' ['Über Wesen und Form des Essays'] and Theodor W. Adorno, 'The Essay as Form' ['Der Essay als Form']—which I will discuss in detail in. Ch. 3—are: Bachmann, *Essay und Essayismus*; Max Bense, 'Über den Essay und seine Prosa', *Merkur*, 3 (1947), 414–24; Berger, *Der Essay; Form und Geschichte*; Richard Exner, 'Zum Problem einer Definition und einer Methodik des Essays als dichterischer Kunstform', *Neophilologus*, 46 (1962), 169–82; Haas, *Studien zur Form des Essays und zu seinen Vorformen im Roman*, and *Essay* (1969); Hamburger, 'Essay über den Essay'; Klaus Weissenberger, 'Der Essay', in *Prosakunst ohne Erzählen: Die Gattungen der nicht-fiktionalen Kunstprosa*; Bob Hullot-Kentor, 'Title Essay', *New German Critique*, 32 (1984), 141–50; and Rohner, *Der deutsche Essay: Materialien zur Geschichte und Ästhetik einer literarischen Gattung*, which is the most comprehensive work.

[265] Gerhard Haas, who in a first book is most willing to define the essay as a 'sum of its discreet features', is to the best of my knowledge the only theorist to voice the potential danger—though not the implications—of reducing the essay to the essayistic, in a section of his second book *Essay*, eloquently entitled 'Essayistisch—Essayismus—Essayifizierung' (p. 4).

Baumgarten in the mid-eighteenth century, through Kant and Hegel, down to
Emil Staiger's *Grundbegriffe der Poetik* in the mid-twentieth'[266]) which German
studies are recognizably affiliated to—and therein alone the immense and continuing resonance of Romantic aesthetics—places German studies at the heart of the
contemporary literary debate. In this respect, the notion of Montaignian essay as
I have described it in this chapter depends upon links between studies on the
essay, studies on genre, and literary criticism in general which are often far from
self-evident. German and French philosophical essayism have in recent years been
brought together under various guises: either in terms of a comparison between
the respective works of the two prominent figures of Adorno and Derrida; or
between Adorno's work and post-structuralist theories; or in the broader terms of
a comparison between the Frankfurt School and the 'school' of Deconstruction; or,
in even broader terms, between what Richard Rorty calls 'post-Kantian idealists'
and 'textualists'; or again, although more indirectly, via an itinerary which traces
the development of modern critical thought from Schiller through the Romantics
to post-structuralist thought.[267] And yet whether these affinities are presented
from the point of view of an anticipation of the French by the German or whether
they are seen to mask significant differences between them, the intermediary
between the German and the French is never referred to in terms of either
essayism or the essay.[268] The essay is in fact never mentioned in relation to the
post-structuralists themselves (except for Barthes who is not really one), probably
because it is (virtually) never referred to in any of their works[269] despite the fact
that our genre simultaneously thematizes all possible fashionable oppositions:
non-fiction and fiction, serious and frivolous, literal and metaphorical, whole and
fragment(ary), oral and written, discourse and narrative, criticism and literature,
literature and philosophy/science. And this is no doubt because of what the
irrecoverable 'dissemination' of the genre into the paradigm of all textuality—the
irrecoverable dissemination of the very concept of genre for that matter—leaves
out: the object, the subject, and the question of the reader's expectations which in

[266] Good, *The Observing Self*, 15.

[267] See e.g. Peter Dews, 'Derrida, Adorno and Heidegger', in id., *Logics of Disintegration*, and id.,
'Adorno, Post-Structuralism, and the Critique of Identity', in Andrew Benjamin, *The Problems of
Modernity: Adorno and Benjamin* (1989); Jochen Schulte-Sasse, 'Theory of Modernism versus Theory
of the Avant-Garde', foreword to Peter Bürger, *Theory of the Avant-Garde* (1984); Martin Jay, introduction to *Adorno* (1984); Rorty, 'Nineteenth-Century Idealism and Twentieth-Century Textualism',
in *Consequences of Pragmatism*; Kathleen Wheeler, *Romanticism, Pragmatism and Deconstruction* (1993);
the three vols. of the *German Aesthetic and Literary Criticism* anthology cited above; and Sychrava,
Schiller to Derrida.

[268] Except for Geoffrey Hartman in 'Literary Commentary as Literature', and R. Lane Kauffmann in
'The Skewed Path' who affirms that 'the work of French post-structuralists Derrida, Lyotard, Barthes,
Foucault constitutes the most significant development in Contemporary continental essayism' (p. 232),
and that despite differences between the German and the French, 'nevertheless, the French theorists
belong well within the tradition of philosophical essayism' (p. 233).

[269] Apart from the couple of references in Michel Foucault's *The Use of Pleasure* (1986) and Jean-
François Lyotard's *Économie libidinale* (1974) listed by R. Lane Kauffmann in 'The Skewed Path',
233–4

practice determines our shared perception of a genre's specificity. Graham Good's point that 'the essay's assumptions are both more subjective and more objective than textualism's, and that 'textualism, operating at the level of general laws (or anti-laws), would dismiss the essay's self and object as illusory textual "constructs"',[270] almost goes without saying. But it does not take into account the possibility of identifying post-structuralist practices with the genre of the essay, so to speak, *in absentia*, that is, with essayism or with a practice which from the outset has necessarily left the essay itself as an object behind. Or should a limit be imposed even on the correspondence between 'textualism' and 'essayism' on the grounds that, by a similar mechanism to that which enabled Descartes to 'work through' and overthrow Montaignian scepticism, 'textualism' stretches the essay's limits of indetermination to the point where indetermination merges into dogmatism? Both Good and Kauffmann are convincing on this issue, since both agree that the essay embodies 'the perennial dialectic between the individual thinker and established thought systems', but that 'it is skeptical precisely about general laws, even general laws of skepticism. Textualism, at least in its deconstructive form, is a universal, even dogmatic skepticism'.[271] 'The choice', Kauffmann further remarks, is not 'between unbridled subjectivity and the absolute system', given that both systems and anti-systems are 'preemptive, colonizing modes of thought'. The contemporary situation calls for a mode of response which is 'not governed by exclusive principles whether systematic or unsystematic in nature'. The situation of the modern essayist, Kauffmann concludes, is best captured by Friedrich Schlegel's above quoted aphorism: 'It is equally fatal for the mind to have a system and to have none. It will simply have to decide to combine the two'.[272]

Geoffrey Hartman himself—the only deconstructionist to relate post-structuralist criticism (in the form of Derrida's *Glas*) to the (Lukácsian definition of the) essay—appears, surprisingly enough, to reach a similar conclusion. For although the history of literature has had a tendency to 'view the critical essay too reductively', and although *Glas* testifies to the fact that 'literary commentary may cross the line and become as demanding as literature', it can be 'urged' against choosing a text like Derrida's *Glas* that 'bad cases make bad law', for it is questionable whether such an 'exceptional' work can 'represent criticism in any save an extreme contemporary form'.[273] Does what Hartman calls 'Criticism in the Wilderness' still respect the line which, in the Lukácsian essay, is ostentatiously transgressed: the 'line of exegesis', the limit of representation which safeguards the essay's fundamentally transitory nature between trends, genres, and epochs? This, after all, is what the paradox of the paratext, and of paratextual criticism, is about. Yet the essay is never explicitly considered as a paratext, not even in Gérard

---

[270] Good, *The Observing Self*, 180.

[271] Kauffmann, 'The Skewed Path', 236; and Good, *The Observing Self*, 180–1.

[272] Kauffmann, 'The Skewed Path', 237 (the translation I use is not Kauffmann's, but Kathleen Wheeler's, p. 45 [*Athenäums-Fragmente*, p. 31]).

[273] Hartman, 'Literary Commentary as Literature', 201 and 204.

Genette's inescapable taxonomies; and while Derrida 'naturally' conjoins criticism and the paratext but never mentions the essay, Hartman brings together essay and criticism for the illustration of the 'crossover' between commentary and literature without ever considering this intertextual crossover in the overtly paratextual terms that would refer Derrida's commentaries in notes back to the original form of Montaigne's own 'essaying' and laterally or forward to that of Barthes or Borges.

'Looking back', 'looking forward', 'beside itself': to counteract reductive conceptions of the essay, one is tempted to choose a more reflexive approach, ideally a vast mirror-effect that would hold the various facets of the essay together. The danger of this approach, however, is the unlimited power of the 'indirect angle' (backwards, forwards, sideways) to connect everything with everything else. Essaying the essay thus makes itself vulnerable to encyclopedic ambitions where the inexhaustible cross-connections would tend more and more avidly towards the utopia of a Book. Luckily this (typically essayistic) utopia is by definition unrealizable, if only because the scope of the questions which underlie this study is the scope of literature itself, which places this undertaking beyond the reach of any one answer and, in fact, of any answer whatsoever. What one can nevertheless do, hopefully, is draw attention to the potential of the essay, even if the manifestations of this potential are all to some extent hypotheses or even fictions of the genre. The essay being by definition 'always the expression of a possibility', it best lends itself to the kind of modern criticism which 'attempts to describe a few basic types of literature that *can* be written, not numerous kinds of work that *have* or, in the critic's view, *should* have been written'.[274]

---

[274] 'Der Essay is immer Möglichkeitsaussage' (Haas, *Studien zur Form des Essays*, 19); and Hernadi, *Beyond Genre*, 184.

Montaigne's Essais: A Poetics of the Margin

2.1. A 'PARA-DOXICAL' GENRE

The emergence of the *Essais* as a form which marks the transition between the reign of the universal and the particular is inextricably bound to the centrality of the practice of what we now call intertextuality. Indeed, in the Renaissance the text is seen as the principal instrument of human knowledge, and imitation is acknowledged as an indispensable prerequisite for literary production. Writing involves learning from one's predecessors, that is, from the wisdom and morality embodied in the texts of the antiquity. Samples of these sources capable of illustrating certain moral principles are compiled in a number of catalogue or inventory-like 'lesson'-books which are also used as formal, rhetorical models: compendia in which ideas, themes, quotations, words and phrases are put into storage and which constitute a collective memory. The 'topics'—the so-called *topoi* or *loci*—which the prospective author (or orator) of the time begins by assembling, are the mnemonic devices which enable him to repeat past discourse according to a given order. They form in effect the various stages of a mental itinerary or 'mnemonic architecture', in short an 'artificial memory' within which the order of the discourse is determined above all by relations of opposition, similitude, and contiguity. In the Renaissance, however, 'critical' is also synonymous with 'sceptical', since this is also a time of deep epistemological anxiety, a time when allegiance to the past is progressively overtaken by acute reflections regarding the problem of originality—the author's individual use of sources, his freedom of choice, and responsibility towards this past. As a result, '(Renaissance authors) make the source of their texts' authority the explicit subject-matter of their fictions: the way in which the text claims to produce its meaning is an inseparable, often central part of the meaning it produces.'[1] The *Essais* are paradigmatic of the transitory, paradoxical status of Renaissance books, for they embody these two opposite attitudes towards imitation, thus actualizing two seemingly incompatible modes of intertextuality. They are caught between the two eras or systems of the Middle Ages and the Classical age represented respectively by the medieval genre of the 'commentary' and the classical genre of 'criticism'. Concretely, this paradoxical position is expressed in the coexistence of two opposed positions or 'systems' of enunciation best accounted for by Antoine Compagnon in his examination of the strategic role of the *Essais* regarding the functional values of quotation in history. In the traditional mode of

---

[1] David Quint, *Origin and Originality in Renaissance Literature: Versions of the Source* (1983).

repetition or 'allegation' of past discourse—that of the commentary—only the quoted author and the quoting text are involved, to the detriment of the quoting author who 'disclaims all responsibility' with respect to his utterance, thus remaining 'absent' from the act of quotation. The relationship between text and intertext is characterized here by a movement from the inside of the text to the outside: the text delegates its authority to the intertext. On the other hand, the new type of intertextual relationship—what Compagnon calls 'citation'—involves the quoted text and the quoting author; it qualifies the quoting author himself who, in spite of repetition, is made to assume his own, proper enunciation and so emancipates himself from the status of compiler to that of individual judge and creator. 'Citation', then, marks the opposite orientation to 'allegation' as regards the relationship between text and intertext: the movement, this time, is from the outside to the inside as the intertext is 'summoned' and incorporated within the text's closure.[2]

The description of the essay as 'a kind of written discourse which allows the writer to think freely outside the constraints of established authority and traditional rhetorical forms'[3] could not be a more apt description of the *Essais*. For in so far as the latter exemplify the period's revolt against the orthodoxy of imitation, the paradoxicality of the *Essais* is perhaps above all to be taken literally as the questioning of the Renaissance *doxa*, of orthodoxy, common opinion, or the status quo. The *doxa*—a term much favoured by Roland Barthes—is a notion associated with a conception of mimesis as 'an essentially conservative and conserving force', one which 'participates in the production of a stable economy of signs and meanings through its perpetual recycling of the "ready-made"'.[4] By examining and questioning the hitherto undisputed authority of ancient sources, the *Essais* unmask the universal Truth which they are supposed to embody as simply the dominant world-view—the *doxa*—one which by definition is historically and culturally determined, since it comprises the 'norms through which a society constructs a general representation of its own reality'.[5] In as much as the secret aim of the *doxa* is to 'convince us of an enduring (human) Nature beyond the changing and heterogeneous forms of culture and history',[6] its 'demystification' will be achieved by displaying the interdependence of Truth and history, in other words, through a relativization or historicization. Meaning is no longer seen as transcending history:

---

[2] Antoine Compagnon, *La Seconde Main, ou Le Travail de la citation* (1979), 323, 327, 78–9, and 323. For the complex problem of writing in the Renaissance which I approach very perfunctorily here, see also Terence Cave, *The Cornucopian Text: Problems of Writing in the French Renaissance* (1979); Hugo Friedrich, *Montaigne* (1968); Michel Beaujour, 'Genus Universum', *Glyph*, 7 (1980), 15–31, and *Poetics of the Literary Self-Portrait* (1991); André Tournon, *Montaigne: La Glose et l'essai* (1983); François Rigolot, *Le Texte de la Renaissance: Des rhétoriqueurs à Montaigne* (1982); Rosalie Colie, *The Resources of Kind: Genre-Theory in the Renaissance* (1973); Michel Charles, *L'Arbre et la source* (1985); Floyd Gray and Marcel Tétel (eds.), *Textes et intertextes: Études sur le XVIéme siécle pour Alfred Glauser* (1979); and Quint, *Origin and Originality in Renaissance Literature*.

[3] Michael L. Hall, 'The Emergence of the Essay and the Idea of Discovery', in Alexander J. Butrym (ed.), *Essays on the Essay: Redefining the Genre* (1989), 78.

[4] Christopher Prendergast, *The Order of Mimesis: Balzac, Stendhal, Nerval, Flaubert* (1986), 12.

[5] Ibid. 51.   [6] Ibid. 2.

the authority of tradition is historically bound and must therefore be grasped in its historically, culturally limited context.[7] In the previous chapter we noted that 'to essay' is to be concerned with the foundations and criteria of truth (the 'how' rather than the 'what'), with conditions of meaning, with the question of representation or mimesis. The *Essais*'s confrontation with the authority or 'truth' of tradition is intimately linked to the examination and subversion of given discursive structures or forms. It consists in drawing attention to the dependence of the truth-content of past sources upon form, a form which is itself articulated on a socially accepted, ready-made master-discourse which has been 'uncritically circulated and repeated' and which society is conditioned to perceive as the 'mirror of nature' or reality.[8] Accordingly, the para-doxical criticism of the *Essais* anticipates what has been much discussed in contemporary literary theory under the notion of *vraisemblance* (literally 'vrai-semblance'[9])—and the related notions of 'naturalization', 'motivation', and 'recuperation'—namely that truth is a verbal illusion, a discursive, not a natural category, since 'what is passed off as the semblance of the real world is only ever the semblance of a socially accepted discourse about the real world', since in other words 'the "true" is a property not of the world, but of propositions about the world'.[10] In the Renaissance, to repeat past discourse is explicitly to repeat the rigidly codified rhetorical order of an (artificial) 'mnemonic architecture'. The deliberate disorder of Montaigne's *Essais*, which 'disregards both the accustomed procedures of topical invention and the decorum of composition', will thus be the product of a 'denaturalization' of the rhetorical strategies by which the intertext 'make[s] us believe that it is conforming to reality and not to its own (arbitrary) laws'.[11] This disorder stems from a situation where rhetoric —the traditional encyclopedia of commonplaces and the transformational rules allowing writers to turn those into completed, effective discourse—'turns itself inside out, questions its own cultural foundations, challenges the validity of its topics and tests the limits of its competency in a world of print'.[12]

The striking bulk of borrowed material (quotations, maxims, and *exempla*—the short narratives that function as particularizations or concretizations of the moral principles) in Montaigne's first essays forms the initial stratum, the starting-point for an intertextual relationship which presents all the characteristics of the traditional commentary. This has led critics usually to refer to these first essays as the more 'impersonal' essays. It is also clear, however, that the apparently traditional

---

[7] See Quint, *Origin and Originality*, esp. 7 and 16, and epilogue.

[8] Prendergast, *The Order of Mimesis*, 12.

[9] For the spelling out of the connection between *vrai* and *vrai-semblance*, see Julia Kristeva, 'La Productivité dite texte', in *Semiotikè: Recherches pour une sémanalyse* (1969), 151–2.

[10] Prendergast, *The Order of Mimesis*, 68. See also Kristeva, *Semiotikè*, 151; the whole of *Communications*, 11 (1968), on 'Le Vraisemblable'; 'Convention and Naturalization', in Jonathan Culler, *Structuralist Poetics: Structuralism, Linguistics, and the Study of Literature* (1974), esp. 137 and 139; and Gérard Genette, 'Vraisemblance et motivation', in *Figures*, ii (1969).

[11] Beaujour, 'Genus Universum', 28; and Tzvetan Todorov, quoted in Jonathan Culler, *Structuralist Poetics* (1974), 139. On *vraisemblance* and rhetoric, see Kristeva, *Semiotikè*, 152–4.

[12] Beaujour, 'Genus Universum', 29.

form of glossing which generates those first pieces already bears within it the more active confrontation commonly associated with the later, more 'mature' parts of Montaigne's book. In fact, a closer look at these introductory essays shows that behind their seemingly authoritative position, these borrowed sources are from the start 'weighed' rather than 'counted' ('I do not count my borrowings: I weigh them'[13]). The essayist's right to exercise his freedom of judgement is claimed in the face, above all, of the 'tyranny' of 'received opinion' such as Aristotle's 'first principles' which, like other sources, are passed on as a divine law rather than as 'merely human opinions':

Merely human opinions become accepted when derived from ancient beliefs, and are taken on authority and trust like religion or law! We parrot whatever opinions are commonly held, accepting them, as truths, with all the paraphernalia of supporting arguments and proofs, as though they were something firm and solid; nobody tries to shake them [*esbranler*]; nobody tries to refute them. . . . We do not doubt much, because commonly received opinions are assayed by nobody. We never try to find out whether the roots are sound. We argue about the branches. We do not ask whether any statement is true, but what it has been taken to mean. . . . It is understandable that this curb on our freedom of judgement and this tyranny over our beliefs should spread to include the universities and the sciences: Aristotle is the god of scholastic science: it is heresy to discuss his commandments. . . . What Aristotle taught is professed as law—yet like any other doctrine it may be false.[14]

As the particular illustration of the generally acknowledged Truth, the example (or rhetorical *exemplum*) plays a major role in the invariable and uncritical repetition of the *doxa*. Its iterability—the fact that it can be repeated indefinitely—guarantees the self-identical propagation of this Truth into all subsequent texts. Rather than compiling these examples as though their straightforward mediating role between past and present texts went without saying, Montaigne purports to examine the foundations of this notion of self-identity which is taken for granted. The emphasis, therefore, is going to be on differentiation and distinction.[15] And this first involves recognizing the arbitrariness, at any one period, of accepting one doctrine over another, an arbitrariness encapsulated by the contradiction in terms of the coexisting 'first principles' of different philosophers:

Where the first principles of Nature are concerned I cannot see why I should not accept, as soon as the opinions of Aristotle, the 'Ideas' of Plato, the atoms of Epicurus, the plenum and vacuum of Leucippus and Democritus, the water of Thales, the infinity of Nature of Anaximander, or the aether of Diogenes, the numbers and symmetry of Pythagoras, the infinity of Parmenides, the Unity of Musaeus, the fire and water of Apollodorus, the

---

[13] Montaigne, 'On Books', *Essays*, II. 10, p. 458 ['Des livres', *Essais*, II. x. p. 387*b*; in the *Essais*, 'to weigh' is formulated alternatively as *poiser* or *mettre à la balance*]. See Floyd Gray, *La Balance de Montaigne: Exagium/essai* (1982).

[14] Montaigne, 'An Apology of Raymond Sebond', *Essays*, II. 12, pp. 605–6 ['Apologie de Raimond Sebond', *Essais*, II. xii, pp. 520–1*a*].

[15] 'The most universal article of my own Logic is *Distinguo*', Montaigne, 'On the Inconstancy of our Actions', *Essays*, II. 1, p. 377 ['De l'inconstance de nos actions', *Essais*, II. i, p. 319*c*].

homogeneous particles of Anaxagoras, the discord and concord of Empedocles, the fire of Heraclitus, or any other opinion drawn from the boundless confusion of judgement and doctrines produced by our fine human reason, with all its certainty and perspicuity, when it turns its attention to anything whatever.[16]

Montaigne accordingly accumulates a mass of different examples from different classical authors to show that rather than unequivocally confirming one another, their confrontation with each other reveals ambiguities and contradictions: each particular embodiment of the Truth is shown to differ to a lesser or greater degree from the general, collective authority which it is supposed to represent. Having established that 'any human assumption, any rhetorical proposition, has just as much authority as any other, unless a difference can be established by reason',[17] a further stage of Montaigne's examination of received opinion will consist in breaking any one model into its component parts so as to expose the ambiguities and self-contradictions within. The *doxa* lays down the law as a closed, invariable model by means of a fixed and unquestioned interrelationship of meaning and form. Once the content is shown to vary according to the way in which it is formally embodied, the homology between truth as embodied particularity (the concrete example) and universal truth (the moral point, the maxim) is subverted or at least made problematic. Montaigne finds it strange and bewildering that 'men of understanding' should attempt to 'knit' man's deeds 'into one whole and to show them under one light'; that they should 'take such trouble to match up the pieces' or to 'weave us into one invariable and solid fabric',[18] given that 'everything has a hundred parts and a hundred faces' and that '[one] cannot see the whole of anything'.[19] Consequently, the examples or *exempla* used by Montaigne no longer fulfil their traditional paradigmatic role. However, they do not have a value of their own either. By being extracted from their context and raised to the status of example in a first instance, only to be subsequently deprived of their exemplariness in a second instance, they are stories which no longer represent the general under an exemplary form while also forming the constituents of a diversity and informative surplus which did not exist in the original context: 'Neither they (tacit *exempla*) nor my quotations serve always as examples, authorities or decorations: I do not only have regard for their usefulness to me: they often bear the seeds of a richer, bolder subject-matter'.[20]

Montaigne's 'weighing-procedure' has therefore turned the example into an instrument of doubt rather than conformity. By testing the paradigmatic function

---

[16] Montaigne, 'An Apology of Raymond Sebond', *Essays*, II. 12, p. 606 ['Apologie de Raimond Sebond', *Essais*, II. xii, p. 521*a*].

[17] Ibid. 607 [522*a*].

[18] Montaigne, 'On the Inconstancy of our Actions', *Essays*, II. 1, p. 375 ['De l'inconstance de nos actions', *Essais*, II. i, p. 315*a* and *b*].

[19] Montaigne, 'On Democritus and Heraclitus', *Essays*, I. 50, pp. 337–8 ['Je ne voy le tout de rien', 'De Democritus et Heraclitus', *Essais*, I. l, p. 289*c*].

[20] Montaigne, 'Reflections upon Cicero', *Essays*, I. 40, p. 281 ['Considerations sur Ciceron', *Essais*, I. xl, p. 245*c*]. See Karlheinz Stierle, 'L'Histoire comme exemple, l'exemple comme histoire: Contribution à la pragmatique et la poétique des textes narratifs', *Poétique*, 19 (1972), 192.

of the example as the particular instance of a generally acknowledged Truth, plurality has been introduced within the sealed unity of self-identity, and, with it, relativization. The abstract and timeless model is 'mobilized' (in the dynamic sense of the word) by its integration into a syntagmatic process in which the meaning it conveys is no longer given but grasped 'in progress':

I am unable to stabilize my subject: it staggers confusedly along with a natural drunkenness. I grasp it as it is now, at this moment when I am lingering over it. I am not portraying being but becoming [*Je ne peints pas l'estre. Je peints le passage*]: not the passage from one age to another . . . but from day to day, from minute to minute.[21]

Truth is contingent, ever-changing for the simple reason that 'time changes the nature of all things in the world', that 'there is nothing in Nature . . . which lasts or subsists in her, all things are either born, being born, or dying'.[22] And the temporal displacement or 'historicizing' of Truth as a fixed and timeless value is inseparable from the acknowledgement, in the *Essais*, of its relativization by each individual perception of it: 'When [Montaigne] express[es] [his] opinions it is so as to reveal the measure of [his] sight not the measure of the thing'.[23] We know that the epistemological project of the *Essais* ('What do I know?'[24]) is inseparable from the autobiographical project: since all knowledge is relative to one's own, limited, perception of the world, the question of whether knowledge is at all possible goes hand in hand with the possibility of knowing oneself. Thus, from the very beginning Montaigne warns that 'it is [his] own self that [he is] painting', that '[he himself] is the subject of [his] book'.[25] The idea of producing a self-portrait, of choosing oneself as the theme of one's book is presented on one level as the vain and idle activity of a man who lacks inspiration: 'Finding myself quite empty, with nothing to write about, I offered myself to myself as theme and subject-matter.'[26] On another level, however, the point of 'turning one's gaze inwards, planting it there and keeping it there', rather than 'gazing ahead' at what is 'confronting' one, as other people do, of being 'concerned with no one but [oneself]', of 'reflecting on [oneself] without ceasing',[27] denotes an intensity which seems hardly compatible with an arbitrary, accidental choice of subject-matter. The dependence of knowledge on self-knowledge as the only possible epistemological foundation of

[21] Montaigne, 'On Repenting', *Essays*, III. 2, pp. 907–8 ['Du repentir', *Essais*, III. ii, p. 782*b*]. See Jean Starobinski, *Montaigne en mouvement* (1982).

[22] Montaigne, 'An Apology of Raymond Sebond', *Essays*, II. 12, p. 681 ['Apologie de Raimond Sebond', *Essais*, II. xii, pp. 587 and 588*a*].

[23] Montaigne, 'On Books', *Essays*, II. 10, p. 460 ['Des livres', *Essais*, II. x, p. 389*a*].

[24] Montaigne, 'An Apology of Raymond Sebond', *Essays*, II. 12, p. 591 ['Apologie de Raimond Sebond', *Essais*, II. xii, p. 508*b*].

[25] In 'To the Reader' ['Au lecteur'].

[26] Montaigne, 'On the Affection of Fathers for their Children', *Essays*, II. 8, p. 433 ['De l'affection des peres aux enfans', *Essais*, II. viii, p. 364*a*]. See also the rest of the note 'To the Reader'.

[27] Montaigne, 'On Presumption', *Essays*, II. 17, p. 747 ['De la praesumption', *Essais*, II. xvii, p. 641*a*]; cf. also 'These are my own thoughts, by which I am striving to make known not matter but me', 'On Books', *Essays*, II. 10, p. 457 ['Des livres', *Essais*, II. x, p. 387*a*].

truth, the conviction that 'if human reason knows anything at all, it must be its own essence and its own domicile', is emphasized again and again.[28] Choosing oneself as a subject is therefore a sign of honesty, for one cannot claim to know anything other or at least better than oneself: 'Never did man treat a subject which he knew or understood better than I know and understand the subject which I have undertaken: in that subject I am the most learned man alive!'[29] Montaigne's essaying of the intertext will thus necessarily go hand in hand with a continual self-essaying which must be understood both as the essaying of his own book (its conditions of meaning, its own 'vraisemblance') and, since the book is 'of one substance with its author' [*livre consubstantiel à son autheur*[30]], as the essaying of the 'self'. But the mediation of truth by particular experience does not amount to the replacement of the transcendent Subject by the 'pure, abstract, Cartesian construction of the self'[31] of the coming classical era. For this would merely be to displace one position of authority for another. As a result of the historicization or relativization of collective tradition, the transcendent order of knowledge and the correspondingly transcendent knowing subject are reintegrated into the terms of history and society.[32] The fact that everything has 'a hundred parts and a hundred faces' implies that if the validity of any one truth changes from historical period to historical period, it already changes from moment to moment, not just from individual to individual, but for each moment of any one individual's life—which justifies already considering any one individual as a multiplicity of subjects and corresponding points of view:

We are entirely made up of bits and pieces, woven together so diversely and so shapelessly that each one of them pulls its own way at every moment.... And there is as much difference between us and ourselves as there is between us and other people.

Out of one subject we make a thousand and sink into Epicurus' infinitude of atoms by proliferation and subdivision. Never did two men ever judge identically about anything, and it is impossible to find two opinions which are exactly alike, not only in different men but in the same men at different times.[33]

The answer to the question 'What do I know?', if there is one, is therefore sceptical:

---

[28] Montaigne, 'An Apology of Raymond Sebond', *Essays*, II. 12, p. 608 ['Apologie de Raimond Sebond', *Essais*, II. xii, p. 523*a*].

[29] Montaigne, 'On Repenting', *Essays*, III. 2, p. 908 ['Du repentir', *Essais*, III. ii, p. 783*b*].

[30] Montaigne, 'On Giving the Lie', *Essays*, II. 18, p. 755 ['Du dementir', *Essais*, II. xviii, p. 648*c*]. See also 'On the Affection of Fathers for their Children', *Essays*, II. 8, p. 433 ['De l'affection des peres aux enfans', *Essais*, II. viii, p. 364*c* and *a*]. See Richard L. Regosin, *The Matter of my Book: Montaigne's 'Essais' as the Book of the Self* (1977), and Frederick Rider, *The Dialectic of Selfhood in Montaigne* (1973).

[31] Good, *The Observing Self*, 23.   [32] See Prendergast, *The Order of Mimesis*, 31.

[33] Montaigne, 'On the Inconstancy of our Actions', *Essays*, II. 1, p. 380 ['De l'inconstance de nos actions', *Essais* II. i, p. 321*a*]; and 'On Experience', *Essays*, III. 13, p. 1210 ['De l'experience', *Essais*, III. xiii, p. 1044*b*].

There is no permanent existence either in our being or in that of objects. We ourselves, our faculty of judgement and all mortal things are flowing and rolling ceaselessly: nothing certain can be established about one from the other, since both judged and judging are ever shifting and changing [*en continuelle mutation et branle*].[34]

The whole of the very long essay entitled 'An Apology of Raymond Sebond' from which this famous statement is drawn is in fact the most conspicuous embodiment of Montaigne's 'Pyrrhonian crisis'. In it he explores 'the extreme relativity of man's intellectual, cultural and social achievements' and comes to the conclusion that the only course of action, given the hopelessness of human knowledge, is 'doubt and suspense of judgement' [*la dubitation et surceance de jugement*].[35] However, the apparent negativity of this state of affairs is explicitly declared to be the positive justification and prerequisite for the very possibility of the essay form itself in the third book: 'If my soul could only find a footing I would not be assaying myself but resolving myself. But my soul is ever in its apprenticeship and being tested.'[36] In other words the act of essaying, as 'a reflection of and on the changing self in the changing world', depends upon the surplus of meaning which arises when knowledge is suspended and reflection takes over to become its own boundless object—when the 'pragmatic' gives way to the 'poetic'.[37]

The exploitation of this surplus of meaning can be traced back to Montaigne's reading habits, to the activity of annotation itself from which the *Essais* are generated.[38] Montaigne's acknowledgement that he does not 'study' books but 'dips into them', 'turning over the leaves of this book or that, a bit at a time without order or design',[39] already suggests that his reading involves the structural 'suspension' of parts from their overall context: 'Scattering broadcast a word here, a word there, examples ripped from their contexts, unusual ones, with no plan and no promises'.[40] Since 'it is impossible to put the pieces together if you do not have in your head the idea of the whole', since 'no man sketches out a definite plan for his life;

---

[34] Montaigne, 'An Apology of Raymond Sebond', *Essays*, II. 12, p. 680 ['Apologie de Raimond Sebond', *Essais*, II. xii, p. 586*a*].

[35] Richard H. Popkin, *The History of Scepticism from Erasmus to Descartes* (1961), 43–4; and Montaigne, 'An Apology of Raymond Sebond', *Essays*, II. 12, p. 561 ['Apologie de Raimond Sebond', *Essais*, II. xii, p. 483*a*].

[36] Montaigne, 'On Repenting', *Essays*, III. 2, p. 908 ['Du repentir', *Essais*, III. ii, p. 782*b*].

[37] Good, *The Observing Self*, 23. Cf. Karlheinz Stierle: 'L'essai est une action verbale à la fois pragmatique et poétique. En tant qu'action verbale pragmatique, il est une réflexion sur la possibilité de connaître "l'homme en général"; en tant qu'action verbale poétique, il transforme en objet cette réflexion elle-même dans l'imprévisibilité et le nécessaire inachèvement de son mouvement' ('L'Histoire comme exemple', 192).

[38] '(Books scribbled all over with my notes)—I have for some time now adopted the practice of adding at the end of each book . . . the date when I finished reading it and the general judgement I drew from it, in order to show me again at least the general idea and impression I had conceived of its author when reading it. I would like to transcribe here some of those annotations' (Montaigne, 'On Books', *Essays*, II. 10, p. 470 ['Des livres', *Essais*, II. x, p. 389*a*]).

[39] Montaigne, 'On Presumption', *Essays*, II. 17, p. 740 ['De la praesumption', *Essais*, II. xvii, p. 635*a*]; and 'On Three Kinds of Social Intercourse', *Essays*, III. 3, p. 933 ['De trois commerces', *Essais*, III. iii, p. 806*b*].

[40] Montaigne, 'On Democritus and Heraclitus', *Essays*, I. 50, p. 338 ['De Democritus et Heraclitus', *Essais*, I. l, p. 289*c*].

we only determine bits of it', it is fitting that among the texts in which he goes 'rummaging about' for 'sayings that please [him]'[41] he should favour those of Plutarch and Seneca. Indeed 'the knowledge that [he] seeks from them is treated in pieces not sewn together', so that he 'do[es] not need a great deal of preparation to get down to them and [he] can drop them whenever [he] like[s], for one part of them does not really lead to another'.[42] Whether examples are already 'ripped from their contexts . . . with no plans and no promises' or not, the 'unsewn' quality of Montaigne's reading is going to be reflected in his writing: 'I pronounce my sentences in disconnected clauses, as something which cannot be said at once and all in one piece [*en bloc*].'[43] To the imposition of the closed master-form of ready-made knowledge Montaigne ironically opposes a paratactic 'master-form' explicitly characterized by ignorance: 'I am under no obligation to make a good job of it [the example] nor even to stick to the subject myself without varying it should it please me; I can surrender to doubt and uncertainty and to my master-form, which is ignorance.'[44] 'Ignorance' conveys that no meaning is taken for granted, that nothing is presupposed. The order of elements is 'as it occurred *to me*', not 'as it usually occurs'.[45] In this sense, the act of weighing necessarily subverts the (rhetorical) 'order and logical succession' of the 'pre-text'.[46] Once the paradigm has been disarticulated and temporalized, there is no question of (re)organizing the parts towards the reconstruction of the original meaning—which would involve a syntagmatic totalization typical of traditional commentary. The order prompted by 'ignorance' is not the forward progression of hierarchical organizations, but an alternative development characterized by inversions or reversals—the paradoxical and so to speak 'intensive' growth of a 'pile' [*entassement*]. Elements are juxtaposed, assertions contradict one another, regression follows progression so that we are rooted to the spot:

My mind does not always move straight ahead but backwards too . . . (being as I am the sworn enemy of binding obligations, continuous toil and perseverance), nor that nothing is so foreign to my mode of writing than extended narration. I have to break off so often from shortness of wind that neither the structure of my works nor their development is worth anything at all.[47]

---

[41] Montaigne, 'On the Inconstancy of our Actions', *Essays*, II. 1, p. 379 ['De l'inconstance de nos actions', *Essais*, II. i, p. 320*a*]; and 'On Schoolmasters' Learning', *Essays*, I. 25, p. 154 ['Du pedantisme', *Essais*, I. xxv, p. 135*c*].

[42] Montaigne, 'On Books', *Essays*, II. 10, p. 463 ['Des livres', *Essais*, II. x, p. 392*a*].

[43] Montaigne, 'On Experience', *Essays*, III. 13, p. 1222 ['De l'experience', *Essais*, III. xiii, p. 1054*b*].

[44] Montaigne, 'On Democritus and Heraclitus', *Essays*, I. 50, p. 338 ['De Democritus et Heraclitus', *Essais*, I. l, pp. 289–90*c*].

[45] Good, *The Observing Self*, 8.

[46] 'I who am more concerned with the weight and usefulness of my writings than with their order and logical succession', Montaigne, 'On Cowardice, the Mother of Cruelty', *Essays*, II. 27, p. 793 ['Couardise mere de la cruauté', *Essais*, II. xxvii, p. 678*c*].

[47] Montaigne, 'On Vanity', *Essays*, III. 9, p. 1091 ['De la vanité', *Essais*, III. ix, p. 941*b*]; 'On the Power of Imagination', *Essays*, I. 21, p. 120 ['De la force de l'imagination', *Essais*, I. xxi, p. 105*c*]; and 'I am constantly making disclaimers', 'On Presumption', *Essays*, II. 17, p. 722 ['Je me desadvoue sans cesse', 'De la praesumption', *Essais*, II. xvii, p. 618*a*].

Given that discontinuity brings about simultaneity, the 'logical' relationship between the various parts of any one essay or of the *Essais* as a whole is encapsulated by the simultaneous and oxymoronic application of the conjunctions 'and' and 'or'. This enables the discourse of the essayist to deny itself, to take things back, and always to say 'otherwise'—to combine any one assertion with the simultaneous creation of an equally valid truth. What this juxtaposition of interchangeable elements recognizably exhibits, in the face of the *doxa*, is 'the infinite connectability of all things and the arbitrariness of most connections'.[48] The paradoxical 'progression' of the *Essais* ensures a type of articulation which always lends itself to interpolations—to the overrun and displacement of the whole by the addition of yet another part—and thus to the ongoing alteration of an illusory unity and closure. The many quotations from, and allusions to classical authors, together with the anecdotes from history and the examples which Montaigne draws from his own experience, are assembled as contradictory evidence 'in excess' of any one single thesis:

This is a register of varied and changing occurrences, of ideas which are unresolved and, when needs be, contradictory, either because I myself have become different or because I grasp hold of different attributes or aspects of my subjects. So I may happen to contradict myself but . . . I never contradict truth.[49]

To the 'repressive' nature of a *doxa* which effects a restriction of meaning that leaves nothing unaccounted for, no residue, the *Essais* oppose an impossibility to 'close' their discourse: a great number of endings are presented as interruptions or they are false endings which lead to the generation of yet more text. In this sense, the surplus of meaning of the anti-systematic discourse also appears as a deficiency of meaning. For the text gestures towards a closure which is postponed again and again, according to the critical 'obligation' which Montaigne claims he is under to 'half-state' matters [*ne dire qu'à demy*].[50] An 'obligation', because choosing 'superficiality' against the exhaustive treatment of subject-matters is a necessary consequence, for Montaigne, of his 'willingly acknowledging' the weakness and fallibility of his judgement which, like that of all men, can at best only 'give a just interpretation of such phenomena as its power of conception presents it with'.[51] So Montaigne 'keeps to that lower level because [he] is unable to conceive anything beyond the outer skin' and so to 'delve deeply' into things [*profonder, enfoncer plus avant*]; he is condemned to 'surface arguments', to 'outlines' [*les premiers lineaments*], to 'stopping at the outer rind and being unable to get right down to the bottom of things'. And this inability to do 'more than taste the outer crust of knowledge' accounts for the fact that his writings are ultimately 'a little about everything and

---

[48] Susan Stewart, *Nonsense: Aspects of Intertextuality in Folklore and Literature* (1979), 143. Stewart points out that the message 'this is play' always implies a discourse that denies itself (p. 72).

[49] Montaigne, 'On Repenting', *Essays*, III. 2, p. 908 ['De repentir', *Essais*, III. ii, p. 782*b*].

[50] Montaigne, 'On Vanity', *Essays*, III. 9, pp. 1126–7 ['De la vanité', *Essais*, III. ix, p. 974*c*].

[51] Montaigne, 'On Books', *Essays*, II. 10, p. 460 ['Des livres', *Essais*, II. x, pp. 389–90*a*].

nothing about anything, in the French style'.[52] The elliptical treatment of the subject may appear to function as a check to the potentially endless proliferation of the *Essais*: 'To make room for more, I merely pile up the heads of argument: if I were to develop them as well I would increase the size of this tome several times over.'[53] In fact, as Montaigne is well aware, ellipsis and excess are intrinsically connected: 'Anyone can see that I have set out on a road along which I shall travel without toil and without ceasing as long as the world has ink and paper.'[54]

The fundamental open-endedness of the form presupposes a subversive treatment of endings and beginnings so that the latter, like the former, tend to be false beginnings. The precedence, in the *Essais*, of the temporary and provisional over the universal precludes abstraction from the here and now both before and after, that is to say both as preconception or predetermination, and as universalization or systematization. As Graham Good puts it, since 'neither self nor world are pre-determined' but 'define each other in a temporary way', the essay's truths are 'particular, of the here and now' and 'only valid for here and now': they 'cannot be abstracted from particular circumstances of time and space, and made into a law'. The 'recognition of self and world' is 'not the result of applying a preconceived method, but is a spontaneous, unpredictable discovery'; there are no 'prejudg-ments', no 'prejudices'. In the same way, 'conclusions may arise, but they are not foregone conclusions'.[55] Montaigne resists the prescriptive character of rhetorical order with 'rhetorical arrangements which are free and undisciplined', a 'style' which he describes as 'a proceeding without definitions, subdivisions and conclu-sions, confused'[56] and which once more enables the essayistic discourse to deny or 'undo' itself again and again. This absence of definition, of articulation, of conclu-sion is emphasized by a proliferation, precisely, of articulations, of beginnings and ends, by a repetition of frames which could lead to a potentially infinite regression or digression. Nevertheless, the fact that Montaigne has 'no love for textures [*tissure*] where joins and seams all show', that he 'change[s] subject violently and chaotically', that '[his] pen and [his] mind both go a-roaming [*vagabondant*]'[57] does not imply that the thread which links these unsewn pieces no longer exists. It simply means that he is not willing to cater for the 'weak and inattentive ears' of those 'undiligent' readers 'who lose [his] subject'[58] because they expect the ready-made:

[52] Montaigne, 'On Presumption', *Essays*, II. 17, p. 725 ['De la praesumption', *Essais*, II. xvii, p. 621*a*]; 'On Books', *Essays*, II. 10, p. 460 ['Des livres', *Essais*, II. x, p. 389*a*]; and 'On Educating Children', *Essays*, I. 26, pp. 163–4 ['De l'institution des enfans', *Essais*, I. xxvi, p. 144*a* and *c*].

[53] Montaigne, 'Reflections upon Cicero', *Essays*, I. 40, p. 281 ['Consideration sur Ciceron', *Essais*, I. xl, p. 245*c*].

[54] Montaigne, 'On Vanity', *Essays*, III. 9, p. 1070 ['De la vanité', *Essais*, III. ix, p. 922*b*].

[55] Good, *The Observing Self*, 22 and 7.

[56] Montaigne, 'On Presumption', *Essays*, II. 17, p. 725 ['De la praesumption', *Essais*, II. xvii, pp. 621*a*, and 620*c*].

[57] Montaigne, 'On Educating Children', *Essays*, I. 26, p. 193 ['De l'institution des enfans', *Essais*, I. xxvi, p. 171*a*]; and 'On Vanity', *Essays*, III. 9, p. 1125 ['De la vanité', *Essais*, III. ix, p. 973*b* and *c*].

[58] Montaigne, 'On Vanity', *Essays*, III. 9, p. 1125 ['De la vanité', *Essais*, III. ix, p. 973*c*].

I intend my subject-matter to stand out on its own: it can show well enough where changes occur, where the beginnings are and the ends, and where it picks up again, without an intricate criss-cross of words, linking things and stitching them together for the benefit of weak and inattentive ears, and without glossing myself.[59]

What the reader must be able to grasp is a logic alternative to the conceptual logic of cause and effect, to 'dogmatic and conclusive speaking' [*le parler dogmatiste et resolutif*]: the logic of poetry whose 'gait' Montaigne loves precisely because it is 'all jumps and tumblings' [*à sauts et à gambades*].[60] The 'order' of poetry is a digressive one, one in which ideas are connected associatively, 'at a distance', 'obliquely' [*d'une veuë oblique*]. The essayist, like the poet, 'get[s] lost, but more from licence than carelessness'.[61] For like the poet, he is aware that:

Just as no event and no form completely resembles another, neither does any completely differ. . . . All things are connected by some similarity; yet every example limps and any correspondence which we draw from experience is always feeble and imperfect; we can nevertheless find some corner or other by which to link our comparisons.[62]

It is up to the reader to trace the key-words or topics which relate the digressions to one another and provide the 'oblique' connections. These pertinent words which are to be found 'in a corner somewhere' are referred to as *mots-bastants* ('sufficient' or 'adequate' words).[63] The role of these 'adequate words' is paradoxical. For inasmuch as they relate the fragments or chapters digressively, they function simultaneously as clarifying and complicating agents, and foreground the intrinsic link between the surplus and deficiency of meaning of the essayistic discourse. The reader who loses track of these 'adequate words' is one who has not realized that the generalized decentring by which the *Essais* expand, involves placing all items on one level in the process of relativization described earlier. As a result, no one item stands out to enjoy a position from which it could define the rest of the text from a privileged 'outside'. One could say that by turning themselves inside out in this way, the *Essais* consciously reveal their inner mechanism, the conditions of their own meaning along with the intertext's. And this display is inseparable from an emphasis on the peripheral, on the 'in-between' as either that which signifies too little or too much. Because of this levelling or 'flattening' of elements, those which are usually restricted—the insignificant, the ornamental, the accessory—tend to be blown up concomitantly with the flattening of 'main'

---

[59] Montaigne, 'On Vanity', *Essays*, III. 9, p. 1126 ['De la vanité', *Essais*, III. ix, p. 974*b*].

[60] Montaigne, 'An Apology of Raymond Sebond', *Essays*, II. 12, p. 569 ['Apologie de Raimond Sebond', *Essais*, II. xii, p. 490*c*]; and 'On Vanity', *Essays*, III. 9, p. 1125 ['De la vanité', *Essais*, III. ix, p. 973*b*].

[61] Ibid. 1124 [973*b*].

[62] Montaigne, 'On Experience', *Essays*, III. 13, p. 1213 ['De l'experience', *Essais*, III. xiii, p. 1047*b*].

[63] 'In a corner somewhere [*en un coing*] you can always find a word or two on my topic, adequate despite being squeezed in tight' (Montaigne, 'On Vanity', *Essays*, III. 9, p. 1125 ['De la vanité', *Essais*, III. ix, p. 973*c*]). See Mary B. McKinley, *Words in a Corner* (1981), and 'The Logic of the "Sufficient Word" in the Montaignian Essay', in Réda Bensmaïa, *The Barthes Effect: The Essay as Reflective Text* (1987).

elements.[64] On the whole, since all subjects are treated with equal right, 'indifferently'—as Montaigne puts it[65]—'central' themes or main points can only be found by accident, as in the works of Plutarch which Montaigne admires because the theme is 'forgotten' or 'treated only incidentally', 'entirely padded out' as it is 'with extraneous matter' [*tout estouffé en matiere estrangere*].[66] In this respect, the title of each essay is the most patent externalization of the paradoxical nature of the '*mot-bastant*'. It expresses Montaigne's own alleged difficulty in giving each action separately 'its proper designation from some dominant quality' given that 'they are so ambiguous, with colours interpenetrating each other in various lights'.[67] The title is by definition a fragment which visibly stands out, exhibiting its definitional, centralizing pretensions, subsuming the particular under the general. In the *Essais*, the apparent lack of connection between titles and contents until a more or less distant and thus seemingly 'accidental' link appears, is not random. The title ultimately turns out be one amongst the many features of the text which it was supposed to define, and its centralizing claim is ironically marginalized: 'The names of my chapters do not always encompass my subject-matter: often they merely indicate it by some token.'[68] So this mutually digressive relationship between the titles and their contents could not display more conspicuously the 'intensive' and fundamentally paradoxical progression of a text in which the hierarchy between centre and margin is played on and subverted. The beginnings and ends are already digressions, fragments metonymically connected to the rest of the 'pile'. Everything, from the start, is approached from an angle [*biais*], and more often than not—as Montaigne likes to think—from an unusual angle [*par quelque lustre inusité*].[69] The 'obligation' to 'half-state', never to treat a subject exhaustively, is therefore also to be approached from the point of view of obliquity. 'Sound[ing] out the ford from a safe distance' when one 'find[s] [one] would be out of [one's] depth', 'stick[ing] to the bank', is a result of 'our projects go[ing] *astray* because they are not addressed to a target';[70] thus the open-endedness of the *Essais* is synonymous with a text carried away by a proliferation of potentially infinite digressions at every level.

All the above justifies the idea of a genre 'beside itself'. The decentring of the text operates from the smallest meaningful unit—the name or concept—to the sentence, to the paragraph, to the chapter, and finally ends with the book itself. At one end of the spectrum, concepts and names—which are the most concise

---

[64] See Stewart, *Nonsense*, 200, 201, and 206. The more philosophical version of this whole argument can be found in *Logique du sens* (1969) by Gilles Deleuze.

[65] *Indifferemment* is in fact translated as 'without preconceptions' ('On Educating Children', *Essays*, I. 26, p. 164 ['De l'institution des enfans', *Essais*, I. xxvi, p. 145a]).

[66] Montaigne, 'On Vanity', *Essays*, III. 9, p. 1125 ['De la vanité', *Essais*, III. ix, p. 973c].

[67] Montaigne, 'On Experience', *Essays*, III. 13, p. 1222 ['De l'experience', *Essais*, III. xiii, p. 1054b].

[68] Montaigne, 'On Vanity', *Essays*, III. 9, p. 1125 ['De la vanité', *Essais*, III. ix, p. 973b].

[69] Montaigne, 'On Democritus and Heraclitus', *Essays*, I. 50, p. 338 ['De Democritus et Heraclitus', *Essais*, I. l, p. 289c].

[70] Ibid. 337 [289a]; and 'On the Inconstancy of our Actions', *Essays*, II. 1, p. 379 ['De l'inconstance de nos actions', *Essais*, II. i, p. 320a].

expression of general consensus—tend to be disarticulated: they are shown to be ambiguous, devious. They are examined from various (and often contradictory) angles or are coupled with contradictory adjectives or verbs via the recurrent use of the oxymoron, the paradoxical figure of speech which combines incongruous or contradictory elements. The decentring of concepts and names recognizably relates back to the already mentioned critique of language as a transparent epistemological medium which is at the core of the sceptical suspension of judgement in the form of a nominalist critique.[71] Like the relationship between signifier and signified which is not 'necessary'[72], that between the signified and the 'real' object which it represents is accidental. The unreliability of language naturally affects both the borrowed quotations—which, as Montaigne shows, say more than what they are meant to say—and the discourse of the *Essais* themselves. The word remains an arbitrary imposition upon a thing about which it can therefore never state anything certain: 'There are names and there are things. A name is a spoken sound which designates a thing and acts as a sign for it. The name is not part of that thing nor part of its substance: it is a foreign body attached to that thing; it is quite outside it [*c'est une piece estrangere joincte a la chose, et hors d'elle*].'[73] In this sense, the essay-titles, which obscure rather than clarify what they are supposed to define, are obvious examples for the ambiguous and approximate quality of the name. For Montaigne, the name can only express the object incompletely, with supplementary and thus unwanted connotations. The consensus which the name appeals to originally is a fiction based again on the repressive power of the *doxa*: the fiction of a common element which, on the basis of its repeatability and interchangeability, reduces unknown singularity to known generalities, thereby identifying what is not identifiable. At the opposite end of the scale, the frame of the Book as a whole is exceeded by the famous *alongeails* which visibly record its 'overrun': local additions to all three volumes, and perhaps most importantly, the imposing addition of the third volume itself.[74] The unifying body of the book is initially denied altogether ('I have not studied to write a book'). But this eventually gives way, in the third volume, to the explicit acknowledgement of the notion of paradoxical unity already partially quoted in Chapter 1, where the unity of the book is inseparable from 'a piece of badly joined marquetry', and from 'additional ornaments'.[75] In so far as they externalize this 'overweight' [*surpoids*] which is at the heart of the

---

[71] See Friedrich, *Montaigne*, 169–71; Compagnon, 'Nominalisme', in *La Seconde Main*, 288–9; and Hélène-Hédy Ehrlich, *Montaigne: La Critique et le langage* (1972).

[72] 'Reported words have both a different resonance and a different sense' (Montaigne, 'On Physiognomy', *Essays*, III. 12, p. 1205 ['Les paroles redictes ont, comme autre son, autre sens', 'De la phisionomie', *Essais*, III. xii, p. 1040*b*]).

[73] Montaigne, 'On Glory', *Essays*, II. 16, p. 702 ['De la gloire', *Essais*, II. xvi, p. 601*a*].

[74] See Tournon, *Montaigne: La Glose et l'essai*; and François Rigolot, *Les Métamorphoses de Montaigne* (1988).

[75] 'My book is ever one; except that, to avoid the purchaser's going away quite empty-handed when a new edition is brought out, I allow myself, since it is merely a piece of badly joined marquetry, to tack on some additional ornaments [*quelque embleme supernuméraire*]' ('On Vanity', *Essays*, III. 9, p. 1091 ['De la vanité', *Essais*, III. ix, p. 941*c*]).

essayistic discourse, the *alongeails* are definitely no additional ornaments or supplements to the text but the embodiment of its formal logic. They are the materializations of the temporal shifts, the ('final') challenge to the synchronic, to what is given '*en bloc*'. As self-annotation, they reinforce intratextually the intertextually paradoxical use of the gloss—its subordination to and/or emancipation from the text. The *alongeails* review the presuppositions on which the assertions of the given text found their authority, 'trying out' ideas in a way which visibly[76] enables the writer simultaneously to assert, criticize, and explore possible extensions simultaneously. Consequently, the reader is confronted with a 'final' display of the tension between actuality and virtuality which characterizes the strategies of suspension of a discourse not concerned with the imposition of one meaning, but with the very makings of sense. The changes of register between the concrete and the abstract, the particular and the general are prominent, as is the absence of a hierarchy between them or the fact that no more weight is granted to the one than to the other. Again, additions which Montaigne makes to a text already governed from the outset by supplementation are not to be taken as corrections—which would supersede earlier production and improve the overall structure of the text—any more than his internal re-marks:

All the various pieces of this faggot are being bundled together. . . . So it was assembled (at) intervals and at different periods, since I sometimes have occasion to be away from home for months on end. Moreover I never correct my first thoughts by second ones—well, except for the odd word, but to vary it, not to remove it [*pour diversifier, non pour oster*].[77]

And this lack of hierarchy favours the exploitation of a significant chronological confusion:

From this there can easily arise however some transposition of the chronological order, my tales finding their place not always by age but by opportuneness. My second reason is this: I fear that I will personally lose by the change. . . . I distrust my present thoughts hardly less than my past ones and my second or third thoughts hardly less than my first. We are often as stupid when correcting ourselves as others.[78]

What this preliminary examination of the *Essais* reveals, then, is an ever-renewed dramatization, at every level, of the dynamic tension between the singular and the plural, the noun and the verb, the genre and the process or 'mode' of essaying itself. I have attempted to show the interdependence of the intertextual

[76] 'Visibly', that is, if one is reading one of those modern edns. which indicate the different strata of the text by *a*, *b*, or *c* (see my page-references to the French version).

[77] Montaigne, 'On the Resemblance of Children to their Fathers', *Essays*, II. 37, p. 858 ['De la ressemblance des enfans aux peres', *Essais*, II. xxxvii, pp. 736–7*a* and *c*]. Cf. also 'J'adjouste, mais je ne corrige pas' ('De la vanité', *Essais*, III. ix, p. 941*c*). This refusal to correct can justify the generation of a whole new volume, as commented on in 'On Vanity', *Essays*, III. 9, p. 1092*b* ['De la vanité', *Essais*, III. ix, p. 942*b*]. See Rigolot, 'Montaigne et la poétique de la marge'; Beaujour, '"Considérations sur Ciceron" (I, XL)'. L'Alongeail comme marque générique: La Lettre et l'essai'; and Tournon, *Montaigne: La Glose et l'essai*, 203, 213–15, and 228.

[78] Montaigne, 'On Vanity', *Essays*, III. 9, p. 1091 ['De la vanité', *Essais*, III. ix, p. 941*c* and *b*].

and the intratextual: in both cases the suspension proper to the 'essaying' brings a paradoxical surplus of meaning by which the assumptions of past authority which no longer go without saying are relativized and decentred. This surplus is both an excess and a lack. One can see the multiplicity of viewpoints staged by the essayist as not reducible to the one authorized version of the *doxa*; or one can approach this juxtaposition of viewpoints—and the discontinuous, open-ended structure it induces—as the essayist's persisting challenge to remain this side of any one standpoint. In the latter perspective, the *Essais*'s rehearsal of the intertext's and their own conditions of meaning enables them, as it were, to 'write without writing', that is, to criticize the ideological structures of the *doxa* without falling prey to them themselves. On the other hand, this makes possible another, equally important—albeit contradictory—dimension of the essayistic project, to which we can now turn.

2.2. SECOND NATURE

The decentred structure of the *Essais* being the expression of a critical impulse, the 'unsewn' and digressive organization of the text is justified by both the impossibility and the refusal of the essayist to submit his discourse to the laws of ancient models. Montaigne's running commentary on his own discourse (the constant self-reflection) from which I extracted the quotations in the above section is in fact rife with phrases that express either this impossibility or this refusal. Because the essayist 'cannot see the whole of anything', it is 'impossible' for him to put the pieces together; he 'keeps to' the surface because he is 'unable to conceive anything beyond the outer skin'; his projects, like all projects, 'go astray because they are not addressed to a target'; not surprisingly, then, he has 'no love for textures where joins and seams all show', he is 'a sworn enemy of binding obligations', he 'intends his subject-matter to stand out on its own'—in short, like the poet, he 'gets lost, but more from licence than carelessness'. For all the essayist can do—like Socrates, to whom Montaigne pays tribute—is wisely to recognize 'ignorance' as 'the most certain faction in the school of the world'.[79] Nevertheless, expressions of this recognition are simultaneously coupled with a very insistent emphasis on the role of 'fortune' in the paratactic structure of the *Essais*. In the eighth chapter of the first book, Montaigne talks about his 'mind' bolting off like a 'runaway horse' [*un cheval eschappé*[80]]:

I have no sergeant-major to marshal my arguments other than Fortune. As my ravings present themselves, I pile them up . . .

To tell the truth, I 'toss a feather to the wind' (as the saying goes) and put myself at the mercy of Fortune. . . . The indecision of my judgement is so equally balanced in most

[79] Montaigne, 'On Experience', *Essays*, iii. 13, p. 1221 ['Le plus seur party de l'escole du monde', 'De l'experience', *Essais*, III. xiii, p. 1053*b*].

[80] Montaigne, 'On Idleness', *Essays*, I. 8, p. 31 ['De l'oisiveté', *Essais*, I. viii, p. 34*a*].

encounters that I would willingly have recourse to deciding by lots and by dice [*à la decision du sort et des dets*].[81]

'Ignorance' here, as the motto of the 'master-form', is taken literally; and the onset of arguments from an 'oblique' or unusual angle rather than from its expected beginning is now described as a coincidence rather than as a transgression, in accordance with the proceedings of what Montaigne calls his 'chance philosophy' [*impremeditée et fortuite*]:[82] 'I take the first subject Fortune offers: all are equally good for me.'[83] Along those lines, the reader is also told that this structure, which is governed by chance, is formless because it is natural—as natural as the pre-established conceptual order of the antique body of knowledge is artificial: 'I want people to see my natural ordinary stride, however much it wanders off the path [*ainsin detraqué qu'il est*]. I let myself go along as I find myself to be.'[84] Instead of emphasizing the idea of critical constraint or 'obligation' quoted earlier, this involves letting thought, imagination, phantasies develop unrestrained, to the rhythm of the moment's inspiration, in a natural way. Montaigne's love of poetry mentioned earlier, his adoption of the poetic 'gait' for 'concepts and judgement' that 'can only fumble their way forward, swaying, stumbling, tripping over', correspond to the 'essaying of his natural faculties'.[85] It is his 'natural, not at all [his] acquired abilities' which Montaigne modestly pits against the skill of 'master-craftsmen'. There is no question for the essayist of trying to compete with the latter: all he is putting to the test is himself.[86] In this sense, the 'natural' formlessness of his text which reflects the meanderings of his thoughts is closest to the formlessness of speech; it is the *parole vive* which Montaigne tries to capture, what he calls its 'naïvety' and 'simplicity':

Although my own bent leads me to imitate rather the spoken style of Seneca, I nevertheless esteem Plutarch's more highly. In doing as in writing, I simply follow my natural form: which perhaps explains why I am better at speaking than I am at writing.

I like the kind of speech [*le parler*] which is simple and natural, the same on paper as on the lip; speech which is rich in matter, sinewy, brief and short; not so much titivated and refined as forceful and brusque.[87]

---

[81] Montaigne, 'On Books', *Essays*, II. 10, p. 459 ['Des livres', *Essais*, II. x, p. 388*a*]; and 'On Presumption', *Essays*, II. 17, p. 743 ['De la praesumption', *Essais*, II. xvii, pp. 637–38*a*].

[82] 'A chance philosopher, not a premeditated one' (Montaigne, 'An Apology of Raymond Sebond', *Essays*, II. 12, p. 614 ['Apologie de Raimond Sebond', *Essais*, II. xii, p. 528*c*]).

[83] Montaigne, 'On Democritus and Heraclitus', *Essays*, I. 50, p. 337 ['De Democritus et Heraclitus', *Essais*, I. l, p. 289*a*].

[84] Montaigne, 'On Books', *Essays*, II. 10, p. 459 ['Des livres', *Essais*, II. x, p. 388*a*].

[85] Montaigne, 'On Educating Children', *Essays*, I. 26, p. 164 ['De l'institution des enfans', *Essais*, I. xxvi, p. 145*a*].

[86] Montaigne, 'On Books', *Essays*, II. 10, p. 457 ['Des livres', *Essais*, II. x, p. 387*a*].

[87] Montaigne, 'On Presumption', *Essays*, II. 17, p. 726 ['De la praesumption', *Essais*, II. xvii, pp. 621–2*a*]; and 'On Educating Children', *Essays*, I. 26, p. 193 ['De l'institution des enfans', *Essais*, I. xxvi, p. 171*a* and *c*]. Cf. also 'Meanwhile there is nothing fluent [*facile*] or polished [*poly*] about my language; it is tough and disdainful' ('On Presumption', *Essays*, II. 17, p. 725 ['De la praesumption', *Essais*, II. xvii, p. 621*a* and *c*]). On this whole question of nature and speech, see ch. 4 of Pt. I, 'Improvisation and Inspiration', and pp. 300–12 of the 'Montaigne' ch. in Cave, *The Cornucopian Text*.

This shift from the artifice of writing to the naturalness of speech is what guarantees the self-transparence of book and self, that is, the possibility for the book to be 'of one substance with its author'. 'Elsewhere', Montaigne writes, 'you can commend or condemn a work independently of its author; but not here: touch one and you touch the other.'[88] Through the self-presence of thought and 'natural' form as speech, the immediate record of ideas on paper allows both essayist and reader to witness the generation, the 'birth' of each fragment: 'I want to show my humours as they develop, revealing each element as it is born.'[89] And it is the immediate, self-present quality of Montaigne's writing as speech which ultimately makes the natural form—or formlessness—of his *Essais* the expression of his own, proper, self: 'For the firmest universal reasons that I have were, so to say, born in me. They are natural ones and entirely mine.'[90] Neither text nor subject predetermine each other but 'take a particular shape in conjunction, in configuration, with each other';[91] they emerge and develop their respective identity simultaneously, co-presently, 'consubstantially' with one another: 'I have not made my book any more than it has made me—a book of one substance with its author'.[92] In other words, the growth of the work through additions enables subject and book to remain contemporary to one another, from moment to moment and from year to year. It foregrounds the birth of an ever-actual subject concomitantly with the birth of an ever-actual text, only to be interrupted by Montaigne's death.

To follow (digressively, as always) this coexistent thread which links 'fortune' and 'nature' is thus simultaneously to discover another, equally valid and therefore apparently contradictory state of affairs to the one described in the previous section. There, the formlessness and digressiveness which the *Essais* opposed to the ready-made *doxa* manifested itself in excess beyond the margins of the intertext. Here, this is the formlessness of the not-yet-formed or not-yet-written, the excess also being a 'lack' which enables the essayist to operate this side of the intertextual margin of the *doxa*. Subsequently, the potential or hypothetical identity of subject and book is something which is metonymically gestured towards in a process which does justice to the etymological sense of the 'essay' as preview or rehearsal. Instead of the decentring of book and subject, we seem to be dealing with their recentring, from a position where originality can be claimed—both in the sense of the 'uniqueness' of Montaigne's style, and in the sense of what comes first. It is fitting that this other aspect of the paradoxical unity of the *Essais* should come out indirectly, 'obliquely', via the theme, here, of memory. Montaigne's insistence on his lack of memory runs throughout the *Essais*, in statements which range from the passing remark to ever-expanding digressions that threaten to take up entire

---

[88] Montaigne, 'On Repenting', *Essays*, III. 2, p. 908 ['Du repentir', *Essais*, III. ii, p. 783*b*].

[89] Montaigne, 'On the Resemblance of Children to their Fathers', *Essays*, II. 37, p. 858 ['Je veux representer le progrez de mes humeurs, et qu'on voye chaque piece en sa naissance', 'De la ressemblance des enfans aux peres', *Essais*, II. xxxvii, p. 737*c*].

[90] Montaigne, 'On Presumption', *Essays*, II. 17, p. 747 ['De la praesumption', *Essais*, II. xvii, p. 641*a*].

[91] Good, *The Observing Self*, 22–3.

[92] Montaigne, 'On Giving the Lie', *Essays*, II. 18, p. 755 ['Du dementir', *Essais*, II. xviii, p. 648*c*].

chapters. This is the first, apparently anodyne reference to memory in chapter IX of book I which functions as a pretext for a discussion on the act of 'lying': 'There is nobody less suited than I am to start talking about memory. I can hardly find a trace of it in myself; I doubt if there is any other memory in the world as grotesquely faulty as mine is! [*si monstrueuse en defaillance*]'.[93] In fact, not only is 'memory an instrument of wondrous service, without which judgement is hard put to do its duty'.[94] Montaigne constantly reminds the modern reader to what extent memory, in the Renaissance, is identified with intelligence and lack of memory with 'daftness' and 'stupidity'.[95] In this respect, Montaigne's annotations to the books which he reads, and from which the *Essais* are generated, both supplement his lack of memory and contribute to it. For the notes which Montaigne appends to the end of each book are 'the general judgement [he] draws from them in order to show [him] again at least the general idea and impression [he] had conceived of its author when reading it'.[96] What they help him remember is the impression this or that book, or this or that fragment or text made on him, to the detriment of the exact words or even of the context—including the author's name itself:

I do not study books, I dip into them: as for anything I do retain from them, I am no longer aware that it belongs to somebody else: it is quite simply that material from which my judgement has profited and the arguments and ideas in which it has been steeped: I straightaway forget the author, the source, the wording and the other particulars. . . . If anyone wanted to know the sources of the verse and *exempla* that I have accumulated here, I would be at a loss to tell him . . .

Myself, who am constantly unable to sort out my borrowings by my knowledge of where they came from.[97]

Still, although Montaigne's allegedly severe lack of memory is something he laments over and over again, the transcription of (often authorless) bits of discourse which may not be accurate can be excused, we are told, by the fact that these texts are 'all, except for very, very few, taken from names so famous and ancient that they seem to name themselves without help from [him]'.[98] But this is more than just an innocent whim. It marks the coexistence of two seemingly opposed attitudes with regard to the role of memory. On the one hand, Montaigne condemns his lack of memory because it hinders his faculties of understanding and judgement. On the other hand, memory is also presented as the enemy of judgement and consequently of the act of weighing which characterizes the essayistic procedure. To see 'no difference between memory and intelligence' is to 'do [him]

---

[93] Montaigne, 'On Liars', *Essays*, I. 9, p. 32 ['Des menteurs', *Essais*, I. ix, p. 34*a*].

[94] Montaigne, 'On Presumption', *Essays*, II. 17, p. 738 ['De la praesumption', *Essais*, II. xvii, p. 632*a*].

[95] Montaigne, 'On Liars', *Essays*, I. 9, p. 32 ['Des menteurs', *Essais*, I. ix, p. 35*b* and *c*].

[96] Montaigne, 'On Books', *Essays*, II. 10, p. 470 ['Des livres', *Essais*, ii. x, p. 398*a*].

[97] Montaigne, 'On Presumption', *Essays*, II. 17, p. 740 ['De la praesumption', *Essais*, II. xvii, p. 635*a* and *b*]; and 'On Books', *Essays*, II. 10, p. 458 ['Des livres', *Essais*, II. x, p. 388*c*].

[98] Ibid 458 [387*c*].

wrong'—Montaigne now claims. For 'experience shows us that it is almost the contrary: an outstanding memory is often associated with weak judgement', with most people's failure to exercise their own powers.[99] Memory, after all, is fundamentally negative in that it is connected with 'knowing off by heart', with the artificial knowledge of past sources which is radically opposed to real knowledge:

> They build them into our memory, panelling and all, as though they were oracles. . . . 'Knowing' something does not mean knowing it by heart; that simply means putting it in the larder of our memory. That which we rightly 'know' can be deployed without looking back at the model, without turning our eyes back towards the book. What a wretched ability it is which is purely and simply bookish! Book-learning should serve as an ornament not as a foundation.[100]

Those who exploit the artificial knowledge which memory provides, are 'pedants': they are only concerned with transcribing as many sources as 'might be useful for totting up and producing statements', just to 'show off', thus 'leaving the understanding and the sense of right and wrong empty'.[101] Schoolmasters and pupils (and, one surmises, Montaigne's potential readers) are both victims of this. The latter are compared with 'birds' that 'sometimes go in search of grain, carrying it in their beaks without tasting it to stuff it down the beaks of their young' so that their pupils 'are not nourished and fed by what they learn'.[102] Actually, schoolmasters and pupils use their own understanding and judgement in relation to what they repeat as much as 'parrots' would: 'We know how to say, "This is what Cicero said"; "This is morality for Plato"; "These are the *ipsissima vera* of Aristotle". But what have *we* got to say? What judgements do *we* make? What are *we* doing? A parrot could talk as well as we do [*Autant en diroit bien un perroquet*].'[103]

On the contrary, the emancipation involved in 'essaying' one's own judgement in the margins of other texts corresponds to a process of trans-formation (change of form) of the sources.[104] To the potential objection that he himself may appear, like those he condemns, 'merely [to have] gathered here a big bunch of other men's flowers' and to have 'furnished nothing of [his] own but the string to hold them together', Montaigne retorts that '[he] does not intend them to cover [him] up or to hide [him]' but to 'display nothing but [his] own—what is [his] by nature'.[105] Forgetting exact words and references which was acknowledged apologetically earlier on because of the 'alteration' and 'corruption' it brought about, is now a prerequisite rather than a hindrance to the act of essaying: Montaigne confesses to 'sometimes deliberately omit[ting] to give the author's name' 'in the case of those

---

[99] Montaigne, 'On Liars', *Essays*, I. 9, pp. 32 and 33 ['Des menteurs', *Essais*, I. ix, p. 35*b* and *c*].

[100] Montaigne, 'On Educating Children', *Essays*, I. 26, p. 171 ['De l'institution des enfans', *Essais*, I. xxvi, p. 151*a* and *c*].

[101] Montaigne, 'On Schoolmasters' Learning', *Essays*, I. 25, p. 154 ['Du pedantisme', *Essais*, I. xxv, pp. 136*a*, and 135*a* and *c*].

[102] Ibid. 154 [135 and 136*a*].   [103] Ibid. 154 [136*a*].

[104] Montaigne, 'On Physiognomy', *Essays*, III. 12, p. 1197 ['De la phisionomie', *Essais*, III. xii, p. 1034*c*].

[105] Ibid. 1196 [1033*b*].

reasonings and original ideas which [he] transplant[s] into [his] own soil and confound[s] with [his] own'.[106] The description of this necessary 'transplant' or 'corruption' of the original text into the new text, which is underscored time and again in the course of the three books, and which relies on a number of metaphors including that of raw and processed meat in the process of digestion,[107] of bees and honey,[108] of weaving and patching,[109] leaves no doubt as to the link between the 'natural', 'proper' discourse of the *Essais* and the 'appropriation' of the other discourse (its corruption or distortion) thanks to Montaigne's conveniently faltering memory—a link which Montaigne himself spells out:

> For if it is by his own reasoning that he adopts the opinions of Xenophon and Plato, they are no longer theirs: they are his. . . . He should not be learning their precepts but drinking in their humours. If he wants to, let him not be afraid to forget where he got them from, but let him be sure that he knows how to appropriate them. Truth and reason are common to all: they no more belong to the man who first put them into words than to him who last did so.[110]

What this statement also justifies is the inversion which is concomitant with the process of appropriation, the very 'inversion by which Montaigne's discourse can claim to be 'original' (imaginative and primary). Montaigne's repeated proclamation that he 'thieves' [*desrober*] others' discourse in order to 'decorate and support [his] own', to 'back up' and 'serve' his opinions [*assister* and *seconder*] 'long after they have taken shape',[111] to 'confirm and strengthen them', making his 'hold on them more secure', more than suggests that the pre-text has been displaced, 'naturalized', that it has become a secondary discourse, an accessory in the margins of Montaigne's own natural and primary discourse.[112] Montaigne goes even further in the exploitation of this inversion by introducing his discourse as 'raw' (as opposed to processed), and by expressing pleasant surprise when chancing upon examples which turn out to conform to the 'imaginations' that were 'born in him': 'If (as happens often) I chance to come across in excellent authors the very same topics I have undertaken to treat. . . . I do congratulate myself, however, that my opinions frequently coincide with theirs.'[113]

---

[106] Montaigne, 'On Books', *Essays*, II. 10, p. 458 ['Des livres', *Essais*, II. x, p. 387*c*].

[107] Montaigne, 'On Schoolmasters' Learning', *Essays*, I. 25, p. 155 ['Du pedantisme', *Essais* I. xxv, p. 136*a*]; and 'On Educating Children', *Essays*, I. 26, p. 169 ['De l'institution des enfans', *Essais*, I. xxvi, p. 150*a*; and 'Apologie de Raimond Sebond', *Essais*, I. xii, p. 527*a*].

[108] 'Bees ransack flowers here and flowers there: but then they make their own honey, which is entirely theirs and no longer thyme or marjoram', 'On Educating Children', *Essays*, I. 26, p. 171 ['De l'institution des enfans', *Essais*, I. xxvi, pp. 150–1*a*].

[109] 'I myself am more ready to distort a fine saying in order to patch it on to me [*pour la coudre sur moy*] than to distort the thread of my argument to go in search of one' (ibid. 192–3 [171*c*]).

[110] Ibid. 170 ['La vérité et la raison sont communes à un chacun, et ne sont plus à qui les a dites premierement, qu'à qui les dict après . . .', 150*a*].

[111] Montaigne, 'On Giving the Lie', *Essays*, II. 18, p. 756 ['Du dementir', *Essais*, II. xviii, pp. 648–9*c*].

[112] Montaigne, 'On Presumption', *Essays*, II. 17, p. 747 ['De la praesumption', *Essais*, II. xvii, pp. 641–2*a*]; 'On Books', *Essays* II. 10, p. 458 ['Des livres', *Essais*, II. x, p. 387*c*].

[113] Montaigne, 'On Educating Children', *Essays*, I. 26, pp. 164–5 ['De l'institution des enfans', *Essais*, I. xxvi, p. 145*a*].

The substance of the other discourse has been progressively appropriated, naturalized, so that it originates in and with the context of the present moment of enunciation, and one can now grasp the full sense in which the gloss or commentary by which the text of the *Essais* unfolds has become essentially a self-gloss, drawing upon and progressing from its own substance, in accordance with Montaigne's famous statement uttered in the first book that 'I only quote others the better to quote myself.'[114] By 'forgetting' the other text—the intertext of tradition with the prescribed rhetorical organization of discourse—and their own 'past' writings (which includes what has just been written), the *Essais* fold back upon themselves and acquire an autonomy founded on self-reference. The reading and writing of the other text has given way to the reading and writing of Montaigne's own text. As a result, the *Essais* have become a self-generating and self-validating construct. They use the reading of their own text as their sole source of knowledge, as their own origin. And this presupposes that Montaigne's lack of memory is the intratextual as much as the intertextual prerequisite for self-presence—that it applies to the reading and the writing of his own text as much as it initially applied to the reading and writing of other texts: 'I am so outstanding a forgetter that, along with all the rest, I forget even my own works and writings. . . . No wonder that my own book incurs the same fate as the others and that my memory lets go of what I write as of what I read [*si ma memoire desempare ce que j'escry*].'[115] Montaigne only remembers and thus only examines one feature of an overall argument, without considering the whole from which it is extracted; and his lack of memory justifies a similar short-sightedness with respect to the elaboration of his own text: any predetermination that would act as a constraint upon the present moment of enunciation is forgotten; hence the refusal to 'correct'.[116] The act of memorizing always induces an abstraction from the present moment, an 'inner distance'.[117] At its most abstract, memory is represented by the anonymous and artificial order of the traditional body of texts to which Montaigne opposes what is 'proper' to him at the time of enunciation. This favours the 'tabula rasa' situation from which the *Essais* can always create anew—both intertextually and intratextually —in the discontinuous and digressive fashion which ignores both what precedes and what follows. However, this is not to say that all internal means of regulation are done away with. What Montaigne shuns is a memory associated with 'orders, obligations and constraints', with 'prescribed command'—a memory which, 'as the storehouse of invention, does not belong to him *in his own right*' and 'depriv[es]

---

[114] Montaigne, 'On Educating Children', *Essays*, I. 26, p. 166 ['Je ne dis les autres, sinon pour d'autant plus me dire', 'De l'institution des enfans', *Essais*, I. xxvi, 146*c*].

[115] Montaigne, 'On Presumption', *Essays*, II. 17, p. 740 ['De la praesumption', *Essais*, II. xvii, p. 635*b* and *c*].

[116] Montaigne, 'On the Resemblance of Children to their Fathers', *Essays*, II. 37, p. 858 ['De la ressemblance des enfans aux peres', *Essais*, II. xxxvii, pp. 736–7*a* & *c*]; 'On Vanity', *Essays*, III. 9, p. 1091 ['De la vanité', *Essais*, III. ix, p. 941*b*]; and 'On some Lines of Virgil', *Essays*, III. 5, p. 989 ['Sur des vers de Virgile', *Essais*, III. v, p. 853*b*].

[117] Beaujour, *Poetics of the Literary Self-Portrait*, 109.

him and his utterance of their presence unto themselves in the very act of utter-
ing'.[118] As Michel Beaujour puts it, 'In voluntary remembrance (*a fortiori*, in the
recourse to artificial memory and methodical invention), my past, the discourses
I have made and retained, even my own previous writings, become as foreign to
me as the texts of other people.'[119] Memory, Montaigne writes, 'serves [him] best
when [he] takes it by surprise' or when he 'address[es] requests to it somewhat
indifferently' rather than forcing it.[120] So the associative configuration which
Montaigne elaborates in response to the logic of rhetoric, relies on a 'spontaneous'
memory that is made up of self-references, additions, and commentaries, and is
immanent in the text. This 'paper' memory which compensates for Montaigne's
alleged forgetfulness[121] enables the text to retrace its own steps and constantly
propose new alternatives. Since it promotes self-presence, this kind of 'memory
without memory' is no longer opposed to invention: on the contrary, it exhibits the
latter's inner mechanism. In other words, the foregrounding of this interdependence—retracing one's steps so as to say otherwise, so as to create anew—is as much
the invention of (a new) memory as it is the memory (the visible record) of
invention.[122]

We have now accounted for the *Essais'* progressive emergence from the space of
the suspended (mimetic) relationship between text and intertext, a relationship
which, because it no longer goes without saying, becomes an object of reflection.
The denaturalization of the intertext—the *doxa*—is concomitant with a process of
naturalization whereby the anonymous 'other' is appropriated and turned into the
substance of the *Essais*. The act of enunciation is increasingly seen to displace what
is enunciated—the pre-text itself—as the theme of the *Essais* 'folds back upon
itself' [*Mon theme se renverse en soy*] and the process of self-essaying (the essay
on the essay) takes over. The tension or conflict between intertext and 'intratext'
prompted by the fundamentally critical, sceptical impetus gives way to a utopian
moment which goes beyond the emancipation of the genre from critical to poetic
intertextuality, in that it seeks to implement the link between creation/originality
and the autobiographical project in terms of uniqueness and essence. In keeping
with the paradoxical logic which determines every aspect of the *Essais*, however,
the ideal of a subjective, natural, spontaneous, speech-like form which Montaigne
opposes to the false 'natural-ness' of the *doxa* (the lie of universality and pseudo-
objectivity) is no less problematic than the latter—and this is also reflected upon.
For in bridging the gap—intratextually this time—between 'other' (the intertext)
and same (the present moment of enunciation), the self-gloss or self-memorizing

---

[118] Ibid. 108 and 109.   [119] Ibid. 109.

[120] Montaigne, 'On Presumption', *Essays*, II. 17, p. 738 ['De la praesumption', *Essais*, II. xvii, p. 633a]; and 'On Vanity', *Essays*, III. 9, p. 1090 ['De la vanité', *Essais*, III. ix, p. 940b].

[121] 'Lacking a natural memory I forge one from paper: whenever some new feature occurs in my affliction, I jot it down' (Montaigne, 'On Experience', *Essays*, III. 13, p. 1240 'De l'experience', *Essais*, III. xiii, p. 1071c]).

[122] For this whole argument on the relationship between memory and invention, see 'Intratextual Memory', in Beaujour's *Poetics of the Literary Self-Portrait*.

betrays the inevitability of the process of abstraction which underlies that other, artificial memory rejected by Montaigne:

To the extent that, under the pretext of arriving at the authentic meaning, the gloss and commentary only widen the gap and strangeness separating the second text (the commentary) from the first (the commented text) and encourage a futile effort to remember meanings, they are subject to the same condemnation as memory; glosses proliferate without a center, fallen from self-presence. . . . Thus, the newest and most antirhetorical procedure used to produce the *Essays* seems condemned in its turn, because of its affinity with the procedures of recalling.[123]

The striving towards the invention of an authentic, natural 'I' in the course of the book's progress through gloss and self-gloss evidently (also) involves memorizing/ inventing oneself as another, consonantly with the idea that 'I have not made my book any more than it has made me'.[124] Self-possession involves fragmentation, dispersion, alienation, a shift from the self further and further away from self-presence and self-identity. In setting out to prove his identity in the face of the other text by constructing an alternative configuration (recentring by decentring first), Montaigne only renders explicit that this otherness is always already at the heart of the self-identity he is trying to assert.[125] In this respect, Montaigne's reflections upon the theme of gloss and self-gloss which accompany the glossing and self-glossing themselves are particularly revealing, as they maintain a subtle and essentially ironic mixture of 'blindness and insight'[126]—or rather of 'ignorance' and insight, since ignorance simultaneously encapsulates the idea of 'not knowing', and 'not wanting to know'—in the process of which the fiction of a not yet intertextually determined or 'mediated' space is alternately supported and undermined. When justifying his lack of memory in the face of the artificial memory he condemns, Montaigne prides himself on his ability to be concise and to get to the point, as opposed to the endless 'diversions' [*détournements*] connected with the effort of memorization: 'Then again I talk less; it is always easier to draw on the storehouse of memory than to find something original to say. If my memory had stood fast, I would have deafened my friends with my chatter.'[127] Memory, in the most anonymous and artificial sense of 'storage', is that which induces commentary upon commentary, an interpretative frenzy which Montaigne denounces as the 'natural sickness' not just of his peers but of man in general. Commenting promotes the illusion of a process of clarification eventually meant to lead to the discovery of

[123] Beaujour, *Poetics of the Literary Self-Portrait.* 117.

[124] Montaigne, 'On Giving the Lie', *Essays*, II. 18, p. 755 ['Du dementir', *Essais*, II. xviii, p. 648*c*].

[125] Despite the assertion towards the beginning of the third book that 'les raisons estrangeres peuvent servir à m'appuyer, mais peu à me destourner', Montaigne, 'Du repentir', *Essais*, III. ii, p. 792*c*].

[126] Borrowed from Paul de Man's *Blindness and Insight: Essays in the Rhetoric of Contemporary Criticism* (1983).

[127] Montaigne, 'On Liars', *Essays*, I. 9, p. 33 ['car le magasin de la memoire est volontiers plus fourny de matiere que n'est celuy de l'invention', 'Des menteurs', *Essais*, I. ix, p. 35*b* and *c*].

truth, whereas the proliferation of glosses only serves to obscure the original meaning:

Can anyone deny that glosses increase doubts and ignorance, when there can be found no book which men toil over in either divinity or the humanities whose difficulties have been exhausted by exegesis? The hundredth commentator dispatches it to his successor prickling with more difficulties than the first commentator of all had ever found in it. . . . Yet do we ever find an end to our need to interpret? Can we see any progress or advance towards serenity? . . . On the contrary we obscure and bury the meaning: we can no longer discern it except by courtesy of those many closures and palisades. Men fail to recognize the natural sickness of their mind which does nothing but range and ferret about, ceaselessly twisting and contriving and, like our silkworms, becoming entangled in its own works. . . . It thinks it can make out in the distance some appearance of light, of conceptual truth: but, while it is charging towards it, so many difficulties, so many obstacles and fresh diversions strew its path that they make it dizzy and it loses it way. . . . There is always room for a successor . . . and a different way to proceed. There is no end to our inquiries: our end is in the next world.[128]

As the 'natural sickness of man's mind', the activity of glossing is an ever-threatening obstacle to the immediate grasp of one's own, particular judgement which alone is the (albeit only transient) premiss from which truth can be approached; inevitably, commentaries become the author's enemy:

It is more of a business to interpret the interpretations than to interpret the texts, and there are more books on books than on any other subject: all we do is gloss each other [*nous ne faisons que nous entregloser*]. All is a-swarm with commentaries: of authors there is a dearth. Is not learning to understand the learned the chief and most celebrated thing that we learn nowadays! . . . Our opinions graft themselves on to each other. The first serves as stock for the second, the second for a third. And so we climb up, step by step. It thus transpires that the one who has climbed highest often has more honour than he deserves, since he has only climbed one speck higher on the shoulders of his predecessor.[129]

This sickness is in fact so 'natural', according to Montaigne, that it affects the works of many canonized authors who tend to 'overgloss' themselves, to indulge in the adjunction of unnecessary supplements—introductions, conclusions, and other definitions—that distract the reader's attention from the essence of their ideas. In Cicero's writings, for example, the core is said to be literally 'smothered' [*estouffé*] by the pre- (and post-)liminary apparatus [*apprets*]; and the very same sort of procrastination smothers the liveliness (in the literal sense of being close to life, spontaneous—*vif*) of Plato's *Dialogues:*

But to tell the truth boldly . . . his style of writing seems boring to me, and so do all similar styles. For his introductory passages, his definitions, his sub-divisions and his etymologies

---

[128] Montaigne, 'On Experience', *Essays*, III. 13, pp. 1210–11 ['De l'experience', *Essais*, III. xiii, pp. 1044–5*b*].

[129] Ibid. 1212 [1045–6*b* and *c*]. See '"Commentatio, commentitia"' and 'Commenter', pp. 236 and 162 in Compagnon, *La Seconde Main.*

eat up most of his work; what living marrow there is in him is smothered by the tedium of his preparations. If I spend an hour reading him . . . and then recall what pith and substance I have got out of him, most of the time I find nothing but wind, for he has not yet got to the material which serves my purposes and to the reasoning which actually touches on the core of what I am interested in.

Will the licence of our times excuse my audacious sacrilege in thinking that even Plato's *Dialogues* drag slowly along stifling his matter, and in lamenting the time spent on those long useless preparatory discussions by a man who had so many better things to say?[130]

Montaigne 'need[s] no sauce or appetizers', and 'instead of whetting [his] appetite with those preliminaries and preparations [*preparatoires et avant jeux*], they deaden it for [him] and dull it'.[131] In this critique of paratextual preliminaries we recognize an attack on the artifice of rhetoric, the artifice—quite simply—of 'art' which Montaigne equates with bluff, with 'turgidity' [*enflure*], and which is alien to nature and to life.[132] By refusing to indulge in pre- and post-liminary flourishes, in the 'marshallings of Aristotelian logic',[133] Montaigne rejects the rhetoric of the *beau discours* by which the Ciceronian orator catches the reader's sympathetic attention [*la benivolence du candide lecteur*].[134] He expresses the wish that 'arguments (should) drive home their first attack right into the strongest point of doubt', in other words, that authors—including himself—should refrain from such preliminaries and 'begin with their conclusion' [*je veux qu'on commence par le dernier poinct*] or at least *in media res*, with the most complex and most unexpected part of the argument.[135]

We will recall, however, that the act of 'hovering about the pot' [*languir autour du pot*] which Montaigne describes above as a situation where the main point is 'all smothered', was initially referred to in exactly the same terms via Plutarch as *praise*, and as a procedure which Montaigne considered to be 'central' to the elaboration of the *Essais*. In that context, 'losing the thread'—that is to say finding the main topic 'by accident'—was a positive feature. From the present angle, on the contrary, to tackle the subject-matter at 'the strongest point of doubt' as opposed to beginning with the beginning is to go straight to the point, to hit the nail on the head. In reality, the apparent contradiction between this centralizing motivation and the digressiveness and decentring to which it is associated in other parts of the *Essais*, is but another typically essayistic paradox. This is best grasped

[130] Montaigne, 'On Books', *Essays*, II. 10, p. 464 ['Des livres', *Essais*, II. x, p. 393*a*]; ibid. 465 [394*c*].
[131] Ibid. 465 [394*a*].
[132] Montaigne, 'On Educating Children', *Essays*, I. 26, p. 193 ['De l'institution des enfans', *Essais*, I. xxvi, p. 171*a, b, c*].
[133] Montaigne, 'On Books', *Essays*, II. 10, p. 464 ['Ces ordonnances logiciennes et Aristoteliques', 'Des livres', *Essais*, II. x, p. 393*a*]. See also 'On Vanity', *Essays*, III. 9, p. 1090 ['De la vanité', *Essais*, III. ix, pp. 940–1*b*].
[134] Montaigne, 'On Educating Children', *Essays* I. 26, p. 190 ['De l'institution des enfans', *Essais*, I. xxvi, p. 169*a*]. See Rigolot, *Les Métamorphoses de Montaigne*, 54 and 92.
[135] Montaigne, 'On Books', *Essays*, II. 10, p. 464 ['Des livres', *Essais*, II. x, p. 393*a*]; and 'On Presumption', *Essays*, II. 17, p. 725 ['De la praesumption', *Essais*, II. xvii, p. 621*a* and *c*].

when relating Montaigne's above reflections on the negative role of (self-)gloss (with regard to his predecessors and fellow-writers) to the function of this (self-)gloss in the *Essais*, and especially regarding Montaigne's treatment of beginnings and ends. For the spontaneous, disorderly beginnings and endings of the *Essais* which I referred to above as 'interpolations' turn out, in a large number, to be the result of successive (diachronic) rereadings and rewritings. In other words the 'unsewn' character of the incipits and excipits, their unusual angle, the 'artlessness' or natural quality of the *Essais*, rely upon those very processes of naturalization which Montaigne denounces in other texts.[136] In the *Essais*, the 'foreign-ness' of beginnings or ends is diminished or abolished by the addition, very often, of a personal touch: a personal anecdote appended to too general a reflection, for example. More 'natural' (less formal) incipits and excipits are created, or else their improvised character is simply 'strengthened', so to speak, by spontaneous reflections or afterthoughts including, for the effect of inconclusiveness, the frequent adjunction of ironic punchlines. This continuing rewriting of beginnings and endings, which sustains a 'fiction of formal flexibility', is more locatable in the first two volumes than in the third volume where the maximal degree of reflexiveness has been attained: where writing as rereading or rewriting has displaced everything else.[137] On the other hand, the effect of the book's presence unto itself is enhanced by editions which, conformably with Montaigne's project after all, do not indicate the successive additions. In these editions, the articulation of non-contemporary fragments, the temporal shifts within the sentence, the paragraph, or the chapter are not apparent to the reader as such, even though the reader is well aware that the apparent unity of the 'book' he or she is reading is the product of numerous revisions. Through this elaborate staging of the 'presence of the present',[138] the illusion of self-presence is thus at once created and destroyed. The essay commemorates its birth by beginning over and over again, but it can never recover this moment in itself; all it can do is to reflect this moment from the present and deferred point of enunciation of commentaries, additions, glosses. In this, we recognize the unequivocal symptoms of the 'natural sickness' of the gloss which Montaigne spends much time describing, and the irony behind the ambition that by keeping to 'invention' rather than 'memory', the *Essais* can remain as concise as possible, that they are able to avoid the dangerous accumulation of gloss and self-gloss and the artificial turgidity of the 'preparatory

[136] Except for remarks such as, 'If I were in that trade, just as they make nature artificial, I would make art natural', Montaigne, 'On Some Lines of Virgil', *Essays*, III. 5, p. 988 ['Si j'estois du mestier, je naturaliserois l'art autant comme ils artialisent la nature', 'Sur des vers de Virgile', *Essais*, III. v, p. 852c], and, in relation to the poetry of Plutarch: 'What beauty there is in such flights of fancy and in such variation, especially when they appear fortuitous and casual', 'On Vanity', *Essays*, III. 9, p. 1125 ['De la vanité', *Essais*, III. ix, p. 973c].

[137] See Rigolot, *Les Métamorphoses de Montaigne*, 124–7, and 145, and the whole of 'Défis à la Rhétorique (1): Entrées en matière', and 'Défis à la Rhétorique (2): Sorties de matière'; see also Tournon, *Montaigne: La Glose et l'essai*.

[138] Beaujour, *Poetics of the Literary Self-Portrait*, 113.

interlocutions' associated with the illusion that truth or absolute knowledge might ultimately be attained. The 'anti-memory' implemented in the *Essais* results in a sort of caricature, as it were, of this situation, a caricature which Montaigne is again perfectly aware of despite his 'ignorance'. In spite of his love of 'rhetorical arrangements which are free and undisciplined', '[he] fully realizes that [he] sometimes lets himself go (so) far in that direction, striving to avoid artificiality and affectation only to fall into them at the other extreme.'[139] This realization clearly involves his own use of borrowings, not accumulated, Montaigne had claimed, to 'show off' like everyone else; yet his 'rummaging about in books for sayings', in the end, 'pleases' not so much him—he admits—as the public:

Such foolishness fits my own case marvellously well. Am I for the most part not doing the same when assembling my material?

I have indeed made a concession to the taste of the public with these borrowed ornaments which accompany me.[140]

It therefore involves the connection between gloss and self-gloss:

[All we do is gloss each other . . . of authors there is a dearth.] How often and perhaps stupidly have I extended my book to make it talk about itself: stupidly, if only because I ought to have remembered what I say about other men who do the same. . . . For I am not sure that everyone will understand what entitles me to do so: that I must have more freedom in this than others do since I am specifically writing about myself and (as in the case of my other activities) about my writings.[141]

So Montaigne's own book becomes the worst case of 'scribbling' [*l'escrivaillerie*]— 'one of he symptoms of an age of excess' [*d'un siecle desbordé*]—and should therefore be the first to be banned.[142]

The process of addition, the simultaneous centralization and decentralization of the *Essais*, turns them from beginning to end into a fundamentally pre-liminary and post-liminary, an essentially supplementary discourse: Montaigne's text, like every text, is 'contaminated and pluralized, from the very outset, by its potential glosses'.[143] The emergence of the form of criticism represented by the *Essais* where 'invention takes incomparably higher precedence over quotation'[144] thus recognizably signals a shift between the traditional or closed conception of intertextuality characteristic of the genre of the commentary (and more broadly of so-called

[139] Montaigne, 'On Presumption', *Essays*, II. 17, p. 725 ['A force de vouloir eviter l'art et l'affectation, j'y retombe d'une autre part', 'De la praesumption', *Essais*, II. xvii, p. 621*a*].

[140] Montaigne, 'On Schoolmasters' Learning', *Essays*, I. 25, p. 154 ['Du pedantisme', *Essais*, I. xxv, p. 135*c*]; and 'On Physiognomy', *Essays*, III. 12, p. 1196 ['De la phisionomie', *Essais*, III. xii, p. 1033*b*].

[141] Montaigne, 'On Experience', *Essays*, III. 13, p. 1213 ['De l'experience', *Essais*, III. xiii, p. 1046*b* and *c*].

[142] Montaigne, 'On Vanity', *Essays*, III. 9, p. 1071 ['De la vanité', *Essais*, III. ix, p. 923*b*].

[143] Cave, *The Cornucopian Text*, 315.

[144] Montaigne, 'On Physiognomy', *Essays*, III. 12, p. 1197 ['Nous autres naturalistes estimons qu'il y aie grande et incomparable preferance de l'honneur de l'invention a l'honneur de l'allegation', 'De la phisionomie', *Essais*, III. xii, p. 1034*c*].

'critical' intertextuality), to the open or modern conception of intertextuality typical of the genre of 'criticism' (and more generally of so-called 'poetic' intertextuality). In the case of the traditional conception of intertextuality as typified by the genre of the commentary, the critical relationship implies the study of sources or at least the recognition of a diachronic filiation or chronological causality, since this goes hand in hand with the mimetic distinction between the original (the source) and the copy (the imitation), the primary and the secondary text. The modern, 'dialogic' conception of intertextuality which the *Essais* inaugurate, on the other hand, is one in which history is no longer considered in terms of diachronic filiation and chronological causality but rather as a circular and thus reversible space where all textual and discursive interactions are possible. The distinction between what is original and what is derived no longer holds: all is equally secondary and therefore primary. Because the author and his 'creation' are no longer seen as transcending their historical context, the text can be read not only in relation to its predecessors, but also in relation to coexisting and even future texts—hence the possibility, exploited by the *Essais*, of inversions: each text is a rewriting (a repetition, a transformation, a parody, an appropriation) of previous and future texts. This applies to the utopian externality of the 'I' with regard to language, to the favouring of 'speech' as a transparent, unmediated space outside history, culture, writing. At both ends of the universal and the particular, writing is prone to masking itself as speech, culture as nature. But the genre-less space of autobiography which Montaigne matches against the genre-less space of the *doxa* falls prey to the same fictional conventions by which the gesture towards 'reality' and 'truth' is made, for language/writing only begets more writing, further and further away from the object of knowledge—whether world or self. The recognition of this 'reciprocal exclusion between "I speak" and "I think"'[145] is at the heart of the paradoxical logic of the self-portrait—a genre which since the *Essais* has attracted much attention in literary theory. The self-portrait, we know, is opposed to autobiography in that it is organized topologically (according to a spatial logic) rather than chronologically, like all texts with a narrative dominant. Unlike the autobiography, it is fundamentally discontinuous and open-ended: it accumulates its material by cross-reference and addition, by (anachronistic) juxtapositions and correspondences between homologous elements. The self-portrait is a version of the *speculum*—the encyclopedic compilation of knowledge in the Middle Ages—which accounts for the fundamental significance of the 'mirror' as the master-metaphor of its topical organization, a 'mirror of the subject and a mirror of the world, a mirror of the "I" that seeks itself through the mirror of the universe'.[146] Indeed, the genre is conceived as the microcosm, 'written in the first person, of an encyclopedia', as 'the self-awareness of the attention "I" pay to the *things* (*res*)—the *loci* of ancient rhetoric—encountered in the process of scanning the encyclopedia'.[147] This

---

[145] Quoted from Michel Foucault ('La Pensée du dehors') in Beaujour, *Poetics of the Literary Self-Portrait*, 13.

[146] Ibid. 26–7.   [147] Ibid. 26; see also 27, 30, and 31.

relationship between microcosm and macrocosm, however—and with it the underlying metaphor of the mirror—is problematic from the outset, and this problem
takes the form of a paradox or of a 'dialectic' between the impersonal intertext
which pre-dates the subject and the autobiographical project which depends upon
the subject's self-affirmation in the margins of the intertext.[148] A 'dialectic' because
in a first instance, the affirmation of the 'I' is the product of the self-portraitist/
essayist's progressive diversion of these *topoi* which the self-portraitist gradually
adopts as his own. This diversion takes the form of a critical 'ambulation' from
topic to topic in a haphazard and no longer regulated way. The self-portraitist's
appropriation of the intertextual *topoi* points ahead to his 'qualification' as the
'quoting author', to his 'assuming his own, proper enunciation'. But the writer's
attempt to describe or find out who he is relies upon a collective and thus impersonal store of ideas and knowledge organized according to impersonal patterns
(those of ancient rhetoric) which necessarily overruns the individual in his singularity, thereby inducing a deflection or refraction of the subject. The impersonal
intertext 'disappropriates' the individual self-portraitist in the very instance of this
appropriation:

As a metamorphosis of the encyclopedic mirror, the self-portrait obliquely and obstinately
questions itself about the writing subject's own identity with himself. The subject tells
himself only through what surpasses, goes through, and denies him. As a result, the diverse
self-portraits set up a network of mirrors of our culture, of this ill-centered macrocosm that
expropriates the writer and delivers him to all that he is not, a plural, polymorphous and
polygraphic *we*, where one reads the destiny of Western culture undermined by its Other:
savagery, exoticism, strangeness, what contests but yet fails to elude its sway or to set up at
its center in a position of mastery.[149]

So the dialectic of the self-portrait requires this unresolvable tension between
singularity and collectivity or 'otherness'. The self-gloss, in as much as it enables
the essayist to stage the desired self-presence of his enunciation, simultaneously
affirms the unbridgeable rift which separates the idealized subject from the multiple
postures of enunciation (personae) of which the subject is made, along the inherently and endlessly intertextual chain of language. The self-portraitist's diversion
of the impersonal intertext is concomitant with his own displacement or *deflection*
(plurality rather than self-identity) by the impersonal intertext which, from his
marginal position, he can never completely take in his own name.

   This brings us finally to the 1580 foreword 'To the Reader' ['*Au Lecteur*']—the
longest and most tangible self-gloss of the book. As a frame within the frame of the
book, it could be said to function as a kind of 'mirror' or *mise en abyme* to the

---

[148] 'La dialectique entre le discours d'autrui et l'expression de soi est au coeur même de la poétique
des *Essais*. Elle pose le problème de la coexistence de l'*intertexte*, impersonnel et antérieur au moi, et du
projet autobiographique dont l'essence même est de s'affirmer en marge de la parole intertextuelle'
(Rigolot, 'Poétique de la marge', 146).
[149] Beaujour, *Poetics of the Literary Self-Portrait*, 35 (see also 32, 33, 34).

extent that by substituting and representing the book on a smaller scale, it is a 'microcosm' which 'increases the reader's ability to grasp the pattern of meaning as a whole' and therefore strengthens closure. The paratext, and especially the preliminary paratext, is above all the space of a pragmatic strategy: the space where the writer indicates how his text should be read (what he means, here, by the overall title *'Essais'*), the space, ultimately, of a generic contract.[150] The foreword is supposed to close the text, lending it a final degree of meaningfulness; it is the space where the text most perceptibly folds back upon itself in a gesture which re-unites the disparate fragments of the book and guarantees self-identity. The fore-word (re-)establishes the connection between the particular example of the text, and the generic norm to which this text must be affiliated. In the case of the *Essais*, which question and subvert this very connection, the note 'To the Reader' is bound to be the most conspicuous space of confrontation between otherness and self-identity, and of the paradoxical 'unity in excess' of the book as a whole. It is not only the fragment with the greatest claim to autonomy within a book in which the parts have been shown already to exceed their (internal and external) frame. Its pre-textual or extratextual autonomy and the pragmatic transaction which it effects with the reader are reinforced by the speech-like quality of a dialogue in which Montaigne, claiming authenticity and 'good faith' ('you have here, Reader, a book whose faith can be trusted' [*C'est icy un livre de bonne foy, lecteur*]) gives the reader his 'word'. The 'shifters' which determine the illocutionary force of the message, here, are more than simple marks of enunciation or 'utterance' [*énonciation*]; they seem to be the direct expression of an intention where the pragmatic sense of 'giving one's word' is to be taken in the literal sense of the spoken rather than the written word.[151] More assertively than in terms of authorial control—which im-plies the subordination of the text to its author—'To the Reader' seals the self-identity of the author and his discourse in accordance with Montaigne's idea of his *Essais* as 'a book of one substance with its author'. However, 'To the Reader' is unquestionably a 'preparatory interlocution' which, like those of Cicero, sets out to 'catch the reader's sympathetic attention'—a strategy which, in the course of the *Essais*, will be denounced because it is concerned with verisimilitude [*vraisemblance*] rather than truth. Indeed, the extratextual position of the paratext as a detached commentary highlights the metalinguistic function of the frame as a guarantor for the work's verisimilitude. It happens to be the ultimate self-commentary or addi-tion [*alongeail*], the rewriting which most conspicuously presents itself as a spon-taneous beginning. So it is also the fragment least able to impose its authority from a vantage-point outside the writing of the *Essais*, giving them their law, for it

---

[150] Genette, *Palimpsestes*, 9. See also his *Seuils*, 13, 15, and 16.

[151] The shift from what the linguist Émile Benveniste calls *énoncé* ('statement') to *énonciation* ('utter-ance') is characterized by the use of *deixis* and the presence of 'shifters': first- and second-person pronouns, adverbs like 'now', 'then', 'here', as well as the use of the present tense (see Émile Benveniste, *Problèmes de linguistique générale*, vol. i, ch. 21 ('De la subjectivité dans le langage'), and ii. 82–3). For 'illocutionary acts', which include 'stating, questioning, commanding, promising', see chs. 2 and 3 of John R. Searle, *Speech Acts: An Essay in the Philosophy of Language* (1969).

denies the unity of the book at the very moment in which it affirms it. 'To the Reader' is a reminder of both the welding and the splitting force of the *mise en abyme*, conformably with the classical distinction between 'mirrors which assimilate diversity' and 'mirrors which dislocate uniqueness/unity'. The *mise en abyme* is both metaphorically and metonymically connected with the book. But the book cannot repeat itself at one and the same time. A temporal shift or discordance—an anachronism or 'anachrony'—arises between it and the part which reduplicates it, which adds to it as an 'analogon' that opens up what it was supposed to close, thus 'unhinging' both author and text.[152] 'To the Reader', which is the space where the author can speak in his own name, is a textual supplement in the same way that the author is. Accordingly, it is in this preliminary paratext that the full implications of Montaigne's nominalist views can come to light. For the arbitrariness which characterizes the relationship between names and the objects which they designate does not spare the relationship between the proper name and its bearer nor that, by extension, between discourse and subject. We have seen that the writing of the *Essais* inevitably remains external to the subject, to his mind and to his thought.[153] Hence Montaigne's allegation, alongside the persisting affirmation of the identity of author and book, that 'I have no name which is sufficiently my own' [*Je n'ay point de nom qui soit assez mien*].[154] This recognizably goes hand in hand with the 'game of hide and seek' generated by the ongoing oscillation between the authorial 'absence' of 'allegation' and the authorial 'presence' of 'citation', in short by the essayist's hybrid intertextual and intratextual position, since Montaigne simultaneously assumes and denies authorial responsibility both in relation to the other discourse and to his own.[155] 'Good faith', then, is perhaps to be found in this double strategy which is 'rehearsed' (almost) simultaneously in the short paragraph of the foreword where the essayist entreats the reader to trust ('a book whose faith can be trusted') and not to trust the presumptive authority of the work ('I have not been concerned to serve you nor my reputation: my powers are inadequate for such a design. . . . It is not reasonable that you should employ your leisure on a topic so frivolous and so vain'). There can be no constant, responsible author outside the text, only a multiplicity of heterogeneous textual subjects which change from minute to minute according to the context of enunciation. All the paratext of 'To the Reader' does, is to rehearse the paradoxical relationship of the *Essais* themselves as fragment (microcosm and analogon), as *parergon* in the margins of a work to come. And given the logic—at both periods—of the potentially endless

[152] Compagnon, *La Seconde Main*, 327. See Jean Ricardou, *Pour une théorie du nouveau roman* (1971), 262; Dällenbach, *The Mirror in the Text*, where *mise en abyme* can function as simple duplication, infinite duplication, or aporetic duplication; and Genette's discussion of 'anachrony', in *Figures*, iii. 78–9.

[153] See Friedrich, *Montaigne*, pp. 170–1.

[154] Montaigne 'On Glory', *Essays*, ii. 16. p. 712 ['De la gloire', *Essais*, ii. xvi. p. 610a].

[155] For a proper (and therefore much more complex) account of this idea, see Compagnon, *La Seconde Main*, 288–9, 295, and 302.

deferment of the fragment beyond mere anachronism, it is appropriate that 'To the Reader' should rehearse or 'essay' a discourse which itself is but the rehearsal of its virtual, potential form: that nothing should follow from this false beginning—nothing, or rather, 'only essays'.[156]

By exposing the coincidence of nature and naturalization, unwritten and rewritten, reading and writing, production and reproduction, invention and memory, the form of the *Essais* is shown to hinge upon a paradox which, by being exploited as a paradox, is never reducible to either one or the other of its component parts. In so far as it embodies a particularly acute awareness of the interdependence of derivation and originality, the form of the *Essais* can simultaneously acknowledge itself as secondary (derived), and as primary (original), in a tension which is never resolved. Since the *Essais* are 'by nature' intertextually determined, derived, the only 'nature' their discourse can really offer is a surrogate which mimes the potentially endless repetition of their own beginning and originality.[157] The *Essais*, as I suggested in the introduction, embody what David Quint describes as a dialectical relationship between 'the idea of a single, timeless, originary truth' and 'the growing and anxious Renaissance awareness of historical multiplicity and proliferation of human meaning'.[158] Out of this tension arises a historical relativism whereby the artist 'deprives' his own work, like that of the ancients, of 'absolute priority with respect to subsequent imitation', a shift which Quint defines as one from 'origin to originality'.[159] Only through historical relativism can the notions of individual originality and creativity emerge, an originality which 'can only be fully defined in historical terms', which is contingent rather than absolute. By foregrounding the idea that all texts are equally original for the very reason that they are all equally secondary, derived and belated,[160] the *Essais* can ultimately be said to demonstrate the positive, creative role of this 'anxiety of influence'. Indeed, by never losing sight of the intrinsic connection between primary and secondary, the *Essais* are free not only to accept derivation as 'second' nature (the natural sickness of the gloss), but to present themselves as second 'nature': the essayist

---

[156] See John O'Neill, 'To the Reader', in *Essaying Montaigne: A Study of the Renaissance Institution of Writing and Reading* (1982).

[157] Cf. 'Nature can clearly only become visible, then, through the lattices of art; or, more strictly, "real" nature is always absent, so that discourse can only offer its replica or surrogate' (Cave, *The Cornucopian Text*, 302; see also 300–1).

[158] Quint, *Origin and Originality*, 23.   [159] Ibid. 5.

[160] Cf. 'Truth and reason are common to all: they no more belong to the man who first put them into words than to him who last did so', 'On Educating Children', *Essays*, I. 26, p. 170 ['De l'institution des enfans', *Essais*, I. xxvi, p. 150*a*]; and 'Off I go, rummaging about in books for sayings which please me—not so as to store them up . . . but so as to carry them back to this book, where they are no more mine then they were in their original place', 'On Schoolmasters' Learning', *Essays*, I. 25, p. 154 ['où elles (les sentences) ne sont plus miennes qu'en leur premiere place', 'Du pedantisme', *Essais*, I. xxv, p. 135*c*]. This, of course, is first and foremost a result of printing: 'when a man has mortgaged his book to the world I find it reasonable that he should no longer have any rights over it', 'On Vanity', *Essays*, III. 9, p. 1091 ['De la vanité', *Essais*, III. ix, p. 941*b*: 'par ce que celuy qui a hypothecqué au monde son ouvrage, je trouve apparence qu'il n'y aye plus de droict'].

assumes his own, proper enunciation despite repetition (or thanks to the acknowl-edgement of repetition as repetition) and justifies his claim to originality despite/thanks to secondariness.[161]

---

[161] 'Rewriting is contaminated by, and at the same time flourishes on, difference. The only chance of rewriting . . . nature, is to accept deviation as a second nature' (Cave, *The Cornucopian Text*, 309). For the notion of 'contingent originality' to which I will come back to in my last ch., see Edward Said, 'On Originality', in *The World, the Text, and the Critic* (1984).

3
Philosophical Essayism

As suggested in Chapter 1, Lukács and Adorno's complementary approaches to the essay(istic) in 'On the Nature and Form of the Essay' and 'The Essay as Form' provide an appropriate link between Montaigne's *Essais* and the Montaignian essay. The affinities and differences between Lukács and Adorno's aesthetics have been explored at length; but in so far as the essays which concern us here were written in the margins, as by-products of a 'main'—or at least better-known—work, one can argue that they are 'separate, self-contained pieces'[1] which do not require an understanding of the respective philosophies. Or rather—in accordance with the relationship between fragment or paratext and whole discussed previously—these separate, self-contained pieces already 'represent' or make present in some degree the philosophies on the margins of which they develop. Thus the famous Lukács–Adorno debate will necessarily appear somewhere beneath the surface, although this debate is usually made to involve the relationship between Adorno and the later, Hegelian-Marxist Lukács rather than the early Lukács of *Soul and Form* (published in 1911). As Eva Corredor points out, Lukács's essay on the essay is still the expression of his 'highly idealistic', pre-Marxist phase in which he views literary genres predominantly as transcendental or atemporal forms, 'independent from time and history'.[2] The shift from man's (the human soul's) 'struggle toward the absolute' to 'man's relationship to the world in its historical and material reality', and thus 'the definition of forms dictated by an awareness of historical and sociological ties between art, history and society rather than purely subjective idealism', will occur a few years later in his *Theory of the Novel*.[3] In contradistinction, the awareness of these ties determines every aspect of Adorno's essay on the essay: the essentially critical quality of the genre is inseparable from its counter-ideological motivation, that is, from its challenge of the status quo and of the *doxa* as examined in the context of Montaigne's *Essais*. Nevertheless, Adorno's comments on Lukács's essay in his own 'The Essay as Form' show that he reads the latter's piece to a large extent in terms of what it anticipates, so that the real divergence between the two essays does implicate, or at least point to, the later Lukács. This divergence, simplified to the extreme, involves the 'extorted

[1] Good, *The Observing Self*, 15.
[2] Eva L. Corredor, 'The Essay as Nostalgia for Form', 52, and 'The Problematic Elements of the Novel', 73, in *György Lukács and the Literary Pretext* (1987).
[3] Corredor, 'The Problematic Elements of the Novel', 81 and 73.

reconciliation' [*erpresste Versöhnung*] of Hegelian Marxism defended by Lukács and which prescribes the necessary overcoming of the dissonance, typical of modern times, between subject and object, particular and general, art and philosophy, etc., which both thinkers see the essay as mediating. Like Walter Benjamin, 'Adorno holds fewer illusions about the intrinsic capacities of a philosophical aesthetic to restore the lost totality of fulfilled life, in keeping with the fundamentally "negative theological" impulses of his eschatological horizon.'[4]

However, Lukács's essay cannot only be seen for what it anticipates, and its affinities with Adorno's own approach to the genre remain uppermost. Above all, both texts are proper essays on the essay, a reflection on the genre and an 'enactment'. Despite the fact that Lukács's title connotes 'aboutness' ('*Über*', in the tradition of the Montaignian 'de' . . .) in a way that Adorno's precisely does not, the claim of Adorno's titles, that 'the work they contain is the presentation of the object itself' equally applies to Lukács.[5] Each piece is not so much 'a study on the essay as a presentation of its form'—or rather both these things simultaneously.[6] Both 'theorists' respect the congruence between the form and the content of the genre and choose the internal and reflexive approach already discussed in my introductory chapter, whereby the essaying of philosophical systems goes hand in hand with a further essaying of the very vehicle—the essay—in which this essaying is performed. And in this reflexive interdependence of the essaying of the intertext and self-essaying, one recognizes the strategy central to the development of the *Essais*. The essay is always its own object; only in the case of our German theorists, the 'self' of this 'self-essaying' is no longer an autobiographical self or a self intent on portraying itself. In every other respect, the choice of the essay as the only fitting approach to a genre which rejects monologic scientific totalizations foregrounds the aesthetic and/or 'dialogic' dimension of philosophical essayism. Dialogue, in fact, can already be said to operate in the relationship between the two essays which, although chronologically related, cannot be arranged hierarchically in terms of the argument. Adorno's essay is a sort of extension of Lukács's, which he explicitly uses as a starting-point. Yet to grant Adorno the last word would be to ignore a complementarity by which not only the former is essential to the understanding of the latter, but the latter considerably contributes to the understanding of the former. When focusing on the essay's kinship with art, Lukács stipulates that 'two essays can never contradict one another: each creates a different world'.[7] Rather than in a method of correction and progress implied in the idea

[4] Richard Wolin, 'The Essay as Mediation between Art and Philosophical Truth', in *Walter Benjamin: An Aesthetics of Redemption* (1982), 88. See also 'The Debate between Adorno and Lukács', in Peter Bürger, *Theory of the Avant-Garde* (1984); 'Lukács and Adorno', in Lambert Zuidervaart, *Adorno's Aesthetic Theory: The Redemption of Illusion* (1991); and Fredric Jameson, *Marxism and Form: Twentieth-Century Dialectical Theories of Literature* (1971).

[5] Bob Hullot-Kentor, 'Title Essay', in *New German Critique*, 32 (1984), 141. This text can be read as an introduction to Adorno's essay (or rather to Hullot-Kentor's trans. of it).

[6] Hullot-Kentor, 'Title Essay', 142.

[7] Georg Lukács, 'On the Nature and Form of the Essay', in *Soul and Form: Essays* (1974), 11 ['Über Wesen und Form des Essays', in *Die Seele und die Formen: Essays* (1911), 25].

of 'contradiction', the essayistic process typically consists in a superimposition or juxtaposition of elements—a 'mosaic-like' relation [*mosaikhaft*]—in Adorno's words —'whether in the essay's proper progress [*Fortgang*] or in its . . . relation to other essays'.[8] So both essays are 'dialogic' in the sense that they visibly evolve as a 'trying out' of ideas characteristic of the unveiling of thought 'in progress': each idea which, by definition, claims authority on the basis of its ability to exclude others, is put into dialogue with another. Hegelian dialectic is the recognizable backcloth against which both essays develop, even though Lukács's essay is often thought to be more immediately 'neo-Kantian' than Hegelian. Accordingly, both essayists include themselves and their potential reader into the dialogue, the reader being required to participate actively if he or she wants to follow the wanderings of the author's thoughts. Admittedly, the dialogism of Lukács's text is more conspicuous than Adorno's since his essay is cast in the form of a letter. For this enables him constantly to stage questions and answers in the manner of Plato's *Dialogues*, which he happens to consider the greatest essays ever written. More-over, Lukács's heavy symbolism throughout the text, which exploits to an extreme the genre's tendency to illustrate its concepts through images, marks its aspiration to be a 'poem'—albeit an 'intellectual poem', to quote a formula which the essayist borrows from Schlegel for the definition of the essay. And this would appear to be congruent with the fact that Lukács's text tackles the question of the essay's generic identity emphatically from the point of view of art. On the other hand, the predominantly philosophical angle from which Adorno argues, together with the fact that his essay is more politically involved, less idealistic, and that its language is less figurative, allegedly makes his essay more 'intellectual'. As a matter of fact, this difference between the two has encouraged some critics to see Adorno's essay as the 'monologic' form of a tract, and so, ultimately, as an 'anti-essay'.[9] This view, however (and independently of the ironic fact that Adorno sets himself from the start against the future 'system' of Lukács's work), disregards the aesthetic or poetic style of Adorno's philosophical writing, a style which, in its paratactic subversion of discursive logic, has also appropriately been described as 'atonal', consonantly with the compositional techniques of the Schoenberg school of music which influenced it. As well as his collections of essays on musical and literary themes of which his 'notes' on literature are the most obvious illustration, Adorno's work includes other essayistic aggregates such as *Minima Moralia: Reflections from Damaged Life*, which is a series of one hundred and fifty-three aphorisms, or *Prisms: Cultural Criticism and Society*, the title of which is self-explanatory. And even the later *Negative Dialectics*, which is usually considered as Adorno's most

[8] Theodor W. Adorno, 'The Essay as Form', *New German Critique*, 32 (1984), 164 ['Der Essay als Form', in *Noten zur Literatur*, i (1958), 36].

[9] See e.g. Ludwig Rohner, *Der deutsche Essay: Materialien zur Geschichte und Ästhetik einer literarischen Gattung* (1966), 128; and R. Lane Kauffmann, who argues that 'Adorno's practice is diametrically opposed to that of Montaigne', in 'The Skewed Path: Essaying as Unmethodical Method', in Alexander J. Butrym (ed.), *Essays on the Essay: Redefining the Genre* (1989), 231.

systematic and dogmatic piece, remains 'essentially essayistic in spirit'.[10] Neverthe-less, if both Adorno and Lukács's essays want to reflect the genre they purport to describe, philosophical and aesthetic knowledge must counter-balance each other to compose not just a poem but an intellectual poem. This is best expressed by the paradoxical, oxymoronic project of Adorno's paradigmatic 'Aesthetic Theory' which denotes neither a 'direct intellectualizing of art' nor a 'straightforward aestheticizing of theory', but 'a philosophy in which neither art *nor* philosophy is lacking'.[11]

3.1.1. Lukács

3.1.1.1. Introducing the Essay

The first paragraph of Lukács's letter to Leo Popper immediately announces the question which preoccupies him (and ourselves), namely how the essay can be related to and distinguished from the realm of art. In as much as the letter functions as an overall introduction to *Soul and Form*, this question relates to the volume of essays as a whole. Indeed, the problem for Lukács is whether the works published in that volume 'can give rise to a new unity'. By 'unity', Lukács is not referring to the content of these essays—as he hastens to add—not, that is, to 'what these essays can offer as studies in literary history' but to the possibility of a 'new form of its own' which would imply the recognition of a 'principle' that would be 'the same in each one'.[12] Our attention is thus drawn from the outset to the relationship between the theoretical speculation of the essay on the essay, and the individual essays themselves as pretexts for this speculation. On the one hand, the inclusion of this particular collection of essays into one 'book' is what overtly prompts the question of a possible generic unity: each essay becomes an example or illustration that concretely grounds a reflection which is therefore not merely speculative. On the other hand, the need to find a conceptual unity tran-scends the continuity of this particular collection of essays (and indeed of the essays, in general, of this particular essayist) to encompass all writings which in the history of literature have called themselves or have been called (the one does not necessarily entail the other) 'essays':

because it is not I nor my book that should be the subject under discussion here. The question before us is a more important, more general one. It is the question whether such a unity is possible. To what extent have the really great writings which belong to this category been given literary form, and to what extent is this form of theirs an independent one [*selbständig*].[13]

By combining the pragmatic dimension of an introduction with that, more ab-stract, of a theory, Lukács's letter-cum-preface thus appears to move beyond those limitations most typical of the majority of works on the genre. Above all, Lukács's

[10] See ch. 2 of Martin Jay, *Adorno* (1984): 'Atonal Philosophy'.
[11] Zuidervaart, *Adorno's Aesthetic Theory*, 63 and 143 (see also 133).
[12] Lukács, 'On the Nature and Form of the Essay', 1 ['Über Wesen und Form des Essays', 1].
[13] Ibid.

interest in the essay seems initially to be triggered by the problematic relationship, discussed in Chapter 1, between the literary form retrospectively ascribed to the writings of great essayists—here Plato's *Dialogues*, the texts of the mystics, Montaigne's *Essais*, Kierkegaard's imaginary diaries and short stories, the work of Nietzsche—and the artistic or literary value of the genre from an absolute, 'ontological' point of view. Hence the connection between the notions of literary status and independence, both of which establish the foundations of this introduction's central issue expressed in the form of the following proposition: 'I want to try and define the essay as strictly as is possible, precisely by describing it as an art-form.'[14] The independence which Lukács grants the essay, then, is the independence—the autonomy—of an art-form. And since the essay is synonymous with criticism in Lukács, this amounts to granting criticism the autonomy of art: 'Criticism, the essay—call it provisionally what you will—as a work of art, a genre?'[15]

Lukács backs up his suggestion that through its form the essay acquires the status of a work of art by referring to 'a truth that was already known to the German Romantics'.[16] In fact, as the beginning of the letter makes clear, Lukács uses the notion of 'independence' to convey two different messages. Speculating about the essay as an independent art-form not only involves the essay 'as' an independent art-form, but also (or rather) the essay as an art-form independent 'from' other art-forms. And this accounts for the above idea that the search for the generic unity of these essays should or might consist in the search for 'something in them that makes them a new form *of its own*' (emphasis added).[17] Lukács's claim that he wants 'to try and define the essay as strictly as is possible, precisely by describing it as an art-form' can therefore only make sense when the initial part of the statement has been reckoned with: 'But if I speak here of criticism as a form of art, I do so . . . solely on the strength of my feeling that the essay has a form which separates it, with the rigour of a law, from all other art forms.'[18] On the one hand, the point is to discover 'to what extent' the essay has 'a form of its own', one that removes it from the domain of positive knowledge or that 'lifts it out of the sphere of science and places it at the side of the arts', yet 'without blurring the frontiers of either'.[19] Despite Lukács's initial equation of the essay—as criticism—

---

[14] Ibid. 2 ['Ich versuche den Essay so scharf wie überhaupt möglich zu isolieren eben dadurch, daß ich ihn jetzt als Kunstform bezeichne', 5].

[15] Ibid. 1 ['Also: die Kritik, der Essay—oder nenne es vorläufig wie Du willst—als Kunstwerk, als Kunstgattung?', 'Über Wesen und Form des Essays', 4].

[16] Ibid. As I mentioned in Ch. 1, the influence of English impressionist criticism on Lukács's essay is just as unmistakable as that of German Romantic theories; but I will adopt Geoffrey Hartman's idea that the former acts more as a 'filter' for the latter (see 'Literary Commetary as Literature', in *Criticism in the Wilderness*) and therefore confine myself to the latter.

[17] Lukács, 'On the Nature and Form of the Essay', 1 ['. . . wodurch sie zu einer neuen, eigenen Form werden', 'Über Wesen und Form des Essays', 1].

[18] Ibid. 2 ['. . . nur aus der Empfindung heraus, daß er eine Form hat, die ihn mit endgültiger Gesetzesstrenge von allen anderen Kunstformen trennt', 5].

[19] Lukács, 'On the Nature and Form of the Essay', 1 ['Inwiefern die Art der Anschauung und ihr Gestalten das Werk aus dem Bereich der Wissenschaften herausheben, es neben die Kunst stellen, ohne aber beider Grenzen zu verwischen?', 1–2].

with the work of art, the overall purpose, therefore, is not going to be to 'speak of the essay's similarities with works of literary imagination, but of what divides it from them', and to let any resemblance 'serve here merely as a background against which the differences stand out all the more sharply'.[20]

3.1.1.2. *The Essay as an Art-Form*

In order to establish the nature of these similarities and of these differences so as to confront 'the essence of the real question: what *is* an essay? What is its intended form of expression, and what are the ways and means whereby this expression is accomplished?',[21] Lukács focuses on an initial distinction between two forms of writing—the scientific and the artistic—two polar means of expression that provide the familiar background against which the essay can then be compared with and differentiated from art. 'Science' [*Wissenschaft*], he asserts, 'affects us by its contents', whereas 'art [*Kunst*] affects us by its forms'; or again, 'science offers us facts and the relationships between facts, but art offers us souls and destinies'.[22] This corresponds, further on in the text, to a fundamental distinction between two 'separate means of expression', between 'image' and 'significance'. For the 'image-creating' [*Bilder-schaffend*] principle, there 'exist only things', whereas for the 'significance-supposing' one [*Bedeutung-setzend*], 'only the relationships between them, only concepts and values' exist. Since you 'do not address questions to pure things, only to their relationships', 'poetry' (in the broad sense of the word *Dichtung*), 'knows no questions', unlike criticism, for which 'there is no life of things, no image, only transparence, only something that no image would·be capable of expressing (completely)'.[23] It is on the basis of these oppositions that Lukács initially situates the essay and by extension criticism as a predominantly scientific type of writing which, by virtue of its conceptual form of expression and its concern with significance, can unambiguously be distinguished from 'poetry'.

The argument shifts, however, as this distinction between 'the two poles of possible verbal expression' elsewhere turns out to be a distinction between the two poles of literary expression, between—as Lukács puts it—the 'two types of reality of the soul'.[24] What is involved now, is the 'practical, palpable proof of the inner divorce of forms', of art-forms that is, for in an art-form, both poles 'are equally effective but they cannot be effective at the same time', and 'something that is viable in one art-form is dead in another'.[25] Nevertheless, once the distinction between the two poles of writing (science/criticism versus art/literature) has been shown to be operational within the one category of art itself, the validity of the distinction itself as distinction is questioned; for in the end, are not his poet and

---

[20] Ibid. 2 [5].

[21] Ibid. 1–2 ['. . . der Frage, was der Essay sei, was sein beabsichtigter Ausdruck und welche die Mittel und Wege dieses Ausdrucks seien', 4].

[22] Ibid. 3 [6–7].   [23] Ibid. 5 [11].

[24] Ibid. 6 and 4 ['die beiden Pole der schriftlichen Ausdrucksmöglichkeit', 13 and 10]. We saw earlier that 'souls and destinies' characterize art as opposed to science.

[25] Ibid. 6 [13–14].

his critic 'empty abstractions'? The answer is that they are ('but not, perhaps, quite empty ones'), because 'even Socrates must speak in images of his "world without form"', and even the notion of '"imagelessness" is a metaphor'. The critic is necessarily also a poet—and vice versa—for the simple reason that 'the separation of image and significance is itself an abstraction', that 'significance is always wrapped in images and the reflection of a glow from beyond the image shines through every image'.[26] Rather than offering souls and destinies, on the one hand, and relationships, concepts, and values, on the other, 'all writings represent the world in the symbolic terms of a destiny-relationship', and 'this unity, this coexistence is so strong that neither element ever occurs without the other'. Lukács's initial discrimination between the 'two poles of possible verbal expression' in their 'naked purity' thus only holds as a theoretical necessity. In practice, it turns out to be merely a 'shift of emphasis' [*ein Unterschied der Betonung*].[27] So this transition from the opposition between art and science/philosophy to the opposition between the artistic and scientific within art corresponds to a transition between the conception of art in the narrow, exclusive sense of the word, to Art as the unity of sense and reason, the sensuous and the conceptual. In parallel, Lukács's speculations switch from the acknowledgement of (traditional) art criticism as a 'science of the arts' ('there is, then, a science of the arts [*Kunstwissenschaft*]') to the observation that 'there is also an entirely different kind of expression which usually takes the form of writing about the arts'—a science which, as an art, would do justice to 'intellectuality, conceptuality as sensed experience, as immediate reality, as spontaneous principle of existence'.[28] I have already discussed the dialectic relativization of the universality of scientific and philosophical knowledge ('intellectuality', 'conceptuality') by the particularity of the 'immediate reality' of 'sensed experience', in the context of Hegel's *Phenomenology*. In Lukács, the opposition between art and science is translated into that between life (or soul) and form. 'Life' views the ordering principles of 'form' as a restriction, and form, for its part, views life as inherently unordered or chaotic. The essay succeeds simultaneously in providing form with life (without which it remains an empty shell, pure abstraction) and life with form (without which it remains inarticulate, inchoate immediacy). Elsewhere in his letter, Lukács deplores the fact that the essay is only ever compared to imaginative writing on the basis of superficial stylistic features (above all that of being 'well written'), when the similarity is in fact much more essential.[29] This has to do with the same 'gesture' or 'attitude' by which both the essay and the literary or artistic work 'address their questions to life', as I described it in Chapter 1 via the central metaphor, borrowed from Lukács's essay, of portrait-painting.[30]

---

[26] Ibid. 5 [12].   [27] Ibid. 7 [16].

[28] Ibid. 3 and 7 ['Intellektualität, Begrifflichkeit . . . als sentimentales Erlebnis, als unmittelbare Wirklichkeit, als spontanes Daseinsprinzip', 7 and 15].

[29] Ibid. 2 ['das Gutgechriebensein', 4]. Hence the title 'Über Wesen und Form des Essays'.

[30] Lukács, 'On the Nature and Form of the Essay', 18 ['(Der Essay) steht dem Leben mit der gleichen Gebärde gegenüber wie das Kunstwerk', 39].

Indeed, if the transitions which lead from the essay to imaginative writing are 'almost imperceptible',[31] this is because the essayist's attitude towards life enables him, like the artist, to reorder and thus 'reshape it'. Even in its 'abstract conceptuality', form for the critic/essayist is that through which he 'glimpses destiny', it is 'immediate reality', the 'image-element', the 'living-content' of his writings. It 'acquires a life of its own through the power of that experience', and becomes a 'world-view' from which reality can be 'created anew'.[32] The capacity of the essay's 'creative' response with regard to its object is such, that although essays usually take the form of writing about the arts, many of them (and especially 'the writings of the greatest essayists: Plato, Montaigne, Kierkegaard') do not need this kind of mediation in order to pursue their essential aim of 'addressing questions directly to life itself'. In this respect, 'literature and art are the typical, natural subject-matter of criticism'[33] not in so far as they remove the essay from life, but, on the contrary, in as much as they provide a pretext—a 'starting-point' or 'springboard'— for its concern with 'the ultimate questions of life'.[34] In other words, and as reported in Chapter 1, the essay as criticism 'enables the universal to unfold from within the boundaries of the particular itself':[35] truth as embodied particularity enables the problem of representation to be taken into account, and this is done by 'representing the representation' (in the vocabulary which Lukács appropriates from Schlegel[36]) in a way that conversely operates a universalization of the particular. Thus the essayist, Lukács observes, only uses texts or pictures as pretexts, forgetting all that is 'concretely incidental' about them. And therein lies for him the first dimension of the essay's fundamental irony: 'And the irony I mean consists in the critic always speaking about the ultimate problems of life, but in a tone which implies that he is only discussing pictures and books, only the inessential and pretty ornaments of real life.'[37] It is precisely this tendency to speak about the ultimate problems of real life as though one were simply concerned with paintings or books, with life's 'inessential and pretty ornaments', which must have characterized Montaigne's attitude as an essayist in Lukács's view—Montaigne who used the 'simple modesty' of the title '*Essais*' as an 'arrogant courtesy', 'dismissing his own proud hopes which sometimes lead him to believe that he has come close to the ultimate' by claiming that 'after all, he has no more to offer than explanations of the poems of others, or at best of his own ideas'.[38] The same applies to that other 'great essayist', Plato, for whom 'criticism, like everything else, was

---

[31] Ibid. 3 ['Eine unendliche Reihe kaum faßbar feiner Übergänge führt von hier zur Dichtung', 8].

[32] Ibid. 8 ['eine Möglichkeit, es selbst umzuformen und neu zu schaffen', 17].

[33] Ibid. 8 ['daß Literatur und Kunst die typischen natürlichen Stoffe der Kritik sind', 18].

[34] Ibid. 16 [32].

[35] Wolin, 'The Essay as Mediation between Art and Philosophical Truth', 87.

[36] From Schlegel, 'On Goethe's *Meister*', in Wheeler (ed.), 69 ['Über Goethes *Meister*', in W. Rasch (ed.), 277].

[37] Lukács, 'On the Nature and Form of the Essay', 9 ['Über Wesen und Form des Essays', 20].

[38] Ibid. 9 [21].

only an occasion, an ironic means of expressing himself'.[39] As with portrait-painting, what counts ultimately is the force of 'vision' of the essayist's work, its 'incarnation' of life, so that like a piece of literature or a painting, 'each essay creates a different world'. This is why, like two works of art, 'two essays can never contradict one another'.[40]

3.1.1.3. The Essay Not (Yet) as Art-Form, or as Parergon

As announced in my introduction to Lukács's essay, the first part of Lukács's initial question, namely 'to what extent do the standpoint of such a work and the form given to this standpoint lift it out of the sphere of science and place it at the side of the arts', which I have attempted to substantiate in the previous section, is developed alongside, or 'weighed against' a second part which stipulates that despite the central notion of 'conceptuality *as* sensed experience', the frontiers of science and art should on no account be blurred. Lukács maintains the distinction on the basis of an equally 'essential' difference, a difference in nature, as an early comment makes clear: 'if I speak here of criticism as a form of art, I do so . . . purely symbolically and non-essentially [*rein symbolisch und uneigentlich*]'.[41] What differentiates the essay from art is that 'it faces life with the same gesture as the work of art, but only the gesture, the sovereignty of its attitude is the same; otherwise there is no correspondence between them [*sonst gibt es zwischen ihnen keine Berührung*].[42] As a matter of fact, the essayist's aim to transcend his pretext (whether painting or book) by shaping it anew makes his dependence upon that object all the more ostensible. 'Of course there is a science of the art', Lukács concedes, 'there has to be one', and what is more, those 'greatest essayists' earlier praised for their ability to achieve their aim without mediation 'are precisely those who can least well do without it: what they create must be science, even when their vision of life has transcended the sphere of science'.[43] Because the essayist 'orders things anew' rather than 'forming something new out of formlessness, he is bound to them and must always speak the "truth" about them, must find expression for their essential nature', 'whereas the poet is not obliged to tell the truth about his subject-matter'.[44] Irony, therefore, does not only lurk behind most people's need to believe 'that the writings of the essayists are produced only in order to explain books and pictures, to facilitate their understanding'. Irony prevails in the fact that as well as being accidental, inessential, this relationship between the essay and its object is also 'profound and necessary' (all the essayist can do is to 'ironically adapt himself to this smallness, and even emphasize it with ironic modesty'[45]). And 'it is precisely the indivisible and organic quality of this mixture of being-accidental and being-

---

[39] Ibid. 15 [32].   [40] Ibid. 11 [25].   [41] Ibid. 2; [5].   [42] Ibid. 18 [39].
[43] Ibid. 13 ['was sie schaffen, muß auch Wissenschaft sein, wenn ihre Lebensvision einmal den Umkreis der Wissenschaft überschritten hat', 28].
[44] Ibid. 10 [23].   [45] Ibid. 9–10 [21].

necessary [*Zufällig- und Notwendig-Sein*] which is at the root of that humour and that irony which we find in the writings of every truly great essayist.'[46]

In the end, the full implications of this 'irony' which Lukács recognizably inherits from his Romantic predecessors points to a difference between essay/criticism and art which is above all temporal, since it involves the identification of the essay with the (Romantic) fragment, and places at the end of history the reconciliation of science, poetry and philosophy, the particular and universal, 'life' and 'form' discussed above. The essay—criticism—at its 'truest and most profound' is 'occasioned by' something already created and which reveals what Lukács now in overtly idealist fashion calls its 'idea'. It is through the 'life-forming force' of judgement of the idea he has glimpsed that the essayist is 'delivered from the relative, the inessential'. However, this transcendence of the object which likens the essayist to the artist is also what turns the 'possibility of his existence' into a 'profoundly problematic' one. For the criteria of the essayist's judgement are 'indeed created within him', yet in the end 'it is not he who awakens them to life and action' but the 'great value-definer of aesthetics' who is still to come: 'The essay form has not yet, today, travelled the road to independence which its sister, poetry, covered long ago—the road of development from a primitive, undifferentiated unity with science, ethics and art.'[47] In so far as it anticipates rather than embodies the 'idea', the essay can only ever be the 'pure type of the precursor' [*der reine Typus des Vorläufers*]; and this is in turn intrinsically connected with its quality as 'fragment' or parergon, as Lukács's final reference to Schopenhauer (an idealist in the Kantian tradition whose theory carried considerable romantic appeal) makes clear. 'Parergon' means by-product, supplement, example [*Bei-Spiel*]. The essayist, we are told, is 'a Schopenhauer who writes his *Parerga* while waiting for the arrival of his own (or another's) *The World as Will and Idea*'.[48] And because the parergon only exists in relation to the *ergon*, its 'results cannot be justified (from) purely within themselves'. The existence of the essay, in other words, is only justified 'as a necessary means to the ultimate end, the penultimate step in the hierarchy'; its 'most vigorous accomplishment becomes powerless once the great aesthetic comes', which denies it any independent value of its own ('no independent value can be attached to it'), making it 'merely provisional and occasional'.[49] Identifying the essay with the 'penultimate step in the hierarchy' suggests looking forward to a final reconciliation, to a world which will be made whole once more; it suggests that the 'longing' (the Romantic *Sehnsucht*) which the essay embodies will be 'fulfilled within the great redeeming system'. On the other hand, the 'great value-definer of aesthetics' which must necessarily make

---

[46] Lukács, 'On the Nature and Form of the Essay', 9 [20].

[47] Ibid. 13 [29].

[48] Ibid. 17 and 16 ['Der Essayist ist ein Schopenhauer, der die Parerga schreibt auf die Ankunft seiner (oder eines anderen) "Welt als Wille und Vorstellung" wartend', 36 and 35].

[49] Ibid. 17 [37].

the essay redundant, is also for Lukács 'the one who is always about to arrive', yet who is 'never quite there' [*der immer Kommende, der noch nie Angelagte*],[50] in keeping with the Romantic notion of 'progressive universal poetry'. This is what turns the essay into a '*pure* precursor' (emphasis added), thus making it doubly problematic:

And if that other [*The World as Will and Idea*] does not come—is not the essayist without justification? And if the other does come, is he not made superfluous thereby? . . . He is the pure type of the precursor, and it seems highly questionable whether, left entirely to himself—i.e. independent from the fate of that other of whom he is the herald—he could lay claim to any value or validity.[51]

For the deployment, in diachronic terms, of the full measure of Romantic 'irony', which can be defined as 'the form of an absolute striving accompanied by a recognition of its merely relative means',[52] Lukács does not fail also to implicate a past figure central to the speculations of early German Romanticism: Socrates. It is Socrates's life or destiny which Lukács sees as a paradigm of the destiny—or the 'becoming destiny'—of the essay form. Form in the essay only ever gestures towards or '*becomes* destiny'[53] rather than offering destiny itself like 'poetry', which places approximation and process at the heart of its logic: 'The essay is a judgement, but the essential, the value-determining thing about it is not the verdict (as is the case with the system) but the process of judging.'[54] It is fitting that a form which emphasizes process (such as the essay and/or the Socratic dialogues) should favour questions over answers. The form of the essay has been described above as 'the voice with which it addresses its *questions* to life' (emphasis added),[55] and in so far as the problems which the essay confronts are 'raised as a question only', it can be distinguished both from art and from science/philosophy, in the narrow sense. From art because, as we saw in the first part of Lukács's text, 'you do not address questions to pure things, only to their relationships'; from science—or, 'at purer heights', philosophy—for 'the answer, here, does not supply a "solution" '.[56] In this sense, the life of Socrates, who 'always lived in the ultimate questions', is 'the typical life for the essay-form',[57] precisely because of this paradoxical mixture of the 'ultimate' and of the 'questions'. In both cases, 'only the end gives meaning, sense and form to the whole', yet 'it is precisely the end which is always arbitrary and ironic here' for 'a question is thrown up and extended so far in depth that it becomes the question of all questions, but after that everything remains open'. This arbitrary and ironic ending is an 'interruption' which 'can only be viewed

---

[50] Ibid. 16 [35].
[51] Ibid. 16–17 ['Und wenn jener kommt—ist er dann nicht ohne Berechtigung? Und wenn jener erscheint—ist er dadurch nicht überflüssig geworden?', 36].
[52] Thomas Harrison, *Essayism: Conrad, Musil and Pirandello* (1992), 3.
[53] Lukács, 'On the Nature and Form of the Essay', 7 ['Über Wesen und Form des Essays', 16].
[54] Ibid. 18 ['Der Essay ist ein Gericht, doch nicht das Urteil ist das Wesentliche und Wertenscheidende an ihm (wie im System) sondern der Prozeß des Richtens', 38].
[55] Ibid. 8 [18].   [56] Ibid. 5 and 7 [11 and 15].   [57] Ibid. 13 [29–30].

humoristically', though 'it is also a profound life-symbol—and, for that reason, still more profoundly humorous—that the essential is always interrupted by such things in such a way'.[58] The corollary of this infinite deferment of the system (the 'verdict', the 'answer'), on the other hand, is also that the essayist's 'longing for value and form, for measure and order and purpose, does not simply lead to an end that must be reached so that it may be cancelled out and become a presumptuous tautology'. For 'in the system of values yet to be found, the longing we spoke of would be satisfied and therefore abolished [*erfüllt und aufgehoben*]; but this longing is more than just something waiting for fulfillment, it is a fact of the soul with a value and existence of its own.'[59] In accordance with the paradoxical logic of the fragment as a detached piece and as an autonomous whole (a self-sufficient totality), as an 'analogon' and a 'microcosm', the essay also exists alongside the work which it only ever strives towards (and defers) yet always already actualizes (represents, exemplifies, embodies). Again, the 'para' of the parergon's relation to the 'ergon' is most apt to translate the paradox of a form that 'lives off a desire that has an in-itself, that is more than something merely waiting to be completed, and removed, by absolute knowledge'.[60]

Think again of the example of the *Parerga*: whether they occurred before or after the system is not a matter simply of a time-sequence; the time-historical difference is only a symbol of the difference between their two natures. The *Parerga* written before the system create their preconditions from within themselves, create the whole world out of their longing for the system, so that—it seems—they can give an example, a hint; immanently and inexpressibly, they contain the system.[61]

The justification of the essay's existence 'as a necessary means to the ultimate end, the penultimate step in the hierarchy' which denies it 'any independent value of its own' is 'only the value', Lukács adds, 'of what it *does*': 'the fact of what it *is* has yet another, more independent value'.[62] In the end therefore, the status of the essay as 'literature *in potentia*'—a potential which connotes both the pre-literary and the other-than-literary, as suggested in the first chapter—is aptly translated into a pair of verbs, one dynamic ('does' [*Leistung*]) and one static ('is' [*Existenz*]). The combination of the two enables Lukács simultaneously to take into account 'process' and 'product', correspondingly again with the Romantic conception of the poem as organism. 'Only now', Lukács can conclude, 'would it not be contradictory,

---

[58] Lukács, 'On the Nature and Form of the Essay', 14 [31].   [59] Ibid. 17 [37–8].

[60] Hartman, 'Literary Commentary as Literature', 195.

[61] Lukács, 'On the Nature and Form of the Essay', 17–18 ['Denkt an jenes Beispiel der Parerga! Es ist kein bloß zeitlicher Unterschied, ob sie vor oder nach dem System stehen: diese zeitlich-historische Differenz ist nur ein Symbol der Trennung ihrer Arten. Die Parerga vor dem System schaffen aus Eigenem ihre Voraussetzungen, erschaffen aus der Sehnsucht nach dem System die ganze Welt, um— scheinbar—ein Beispiel, einen Hinweis zu gestalten, sie enthalten immanent und unaussprechbar das System', 'Über Wesen und Form des Essays', 38].

[62] Ibid. 17 ['Dies aber ist nur der Wert seiner Leistung, die Tatsache seiner Existenz hat noch einen anderen, selbständigeren Wert', 37].

ambiguous and false to call it a work of art and yet insist on emphasizing the thing that differentiates it from art'.[63] The essay is an art-form as well as not (yet) being an art-form; and this continues to grant it an 'independent value', a 'unity' despite its fundamentally transient, evanescent, and anachronistic position in the margins of art.

Having come full circle to Lukács's opening proposition, the paradox of which is at the core of his essay, what remains briefly to be seen is how this proposition is translated structurally, given that the text is both 'about' something (the essay) and that something itself. One could say that it is at the level of the form of Lukács's 'intellectual poem' that the predominantly (and often excessively) symbolic if not mystical dimension of Lukács's speculations on the essay is most effectively translated into concrete, structural terms. The fact that intertextually the essay as a fragment is not (as yet[64]) to be foreclosed by any system is reflected intratextually by the fragmentariness or parataxis by which each part (of the definition) exceeds or suspends the whole. A first reading of the essay shows that there is no logical argument to hold on to, only an accumulation of points or themes mysteriously related to the generic concept of 'unity' which is introduced as a pretext for the discussion of the essay as a whole. Nevertheless, I have constructed my own presentation of the content (what is said about the essay) around the introductory part of the text because there the concept of 'unity' prompts an initial proposition or definition ('The essay is an independent art-form') which presents itself as the core or outline, precisely, of an argument. This is not meant to suggest, however, that one part of the essay (the introductory part) is logically organized while the other (the elaboration) is not. For although the concept of 'unity' is posited at the level of content, and although it is apparently made to cover the unity not only of the genre, but of the argument itself by which the genre is also to be formally displayed, it is in fact suspended from the start by the very form—the essayistic form—in which it appears. Indeed, the proposition or definition ('The essay is an independent art-form') which clarifies what is understood by 'unity' is immediately specified as meaning: 'the essay is, yet is not an art-form'. Rather than having the logical core of an argument, we thus have a central contradiction, a paradox, which is in fact the condensed version, structurally as well as in content, of the whole text. The central formula 'is, yet is not' is what I would describe as the first type of suspension or 'weighing'. As was so typical in Montaigne's *Essais*, each assertion is followed or 'suspended' by its contradiction, each example by its counterexample.[65] This is manifest at the level of the text's main articulations

---

[63] Ibid. 18 [39].

[64] 'Not as yet' also in the progression of Lukács's own work, since from Adorno's and other thinkers' point of view Lukács later falls into the trap of this very system.

[65] This is not to say that the contradiction necessarily appears immediately after the assertion, for it would lend the essay-structure a systematic organization which it does not have. The counterargument is in fact found elsewhere when you are least expecting it, and when you are likely to have 'digested' the initial argument.

(the change of paragraphs) where these 'weighing-procedures' are literally 'voiced' by Lukács's enactment of the imaginary dialogue he is having with his reader and which includes potential objections. But the weighing-procedures are not confined to the main articulations; they pervade every single level of the text. The 'is, yet is not'-pattern operates between the sentences, but in a much less clear-cut fashion, since the 'yet' which provided the intelligible link between the assertion and its negation is usually done away with at this level, thus leaving the reader without transitions. Because regression tends to follow progression, this first type of suspension gives the static impression of being rooted to the spot. In contradistinction, the second type of suspension which prevails in this essay is essentially dynamic. I am now referring to the 'questioning' as gesture 'towards': before being translated into the paradox of the 'is, yet is not', the generic concept of unity is posited and asserted (paradoxically again) through questions. Lukács's own remarks on the significance of 'questioning' in the essay, which function as an ongoing confirmation of his allegiance to the dialogism of his favourite essayist Plato, make clear that the last word on the problem of unity can only be raised as a question rather than as an answer, and that one question can only lead to another. The fact that the accumulation of points presented in the preliminary part of this preliminary text should be a 'pure' succession of questions, is not accidental. For the goal of Lukács's essay is 'What is this unity—if unity there is?', to which he immediately adds, 'I make no attempt to formulate it. . . . The question before us is a more important, more general one. It is the question whether such a unity is possible.'[66]

Both strategies of suspension (assertion with negation and assertion through question) characterize a 'theory' which can only remain a speculation about the possibility of a concept (the unity of the genre) accordingly 'tried out' or 'essayed'. In fact, the two stages of the 'is', yet 'is not' (the mutual cancellation of which rules out an answer, taking us back to initial questions) is 'sublated' in a third dialectical stage which does not exhaust either possibility. The question ultimately displaces or defers the 'is' and the 'is not'—both of which are temporarily fixed—into the third dynamic (dialectical) and irreducible movement of the 'is not *yet*' which is introduced at the end of Lukács's essay. This 'not *yet*' thus becomes the concrete expression of the 'gesturing towards' which characterizes the form of the essay as a whole. It defers the potentially static quality of the initial 'alongside' (the essay alongside art) which despite its paradoxical and hence dynamic connotation ('is, yet is not') threatened (because of the independent, 'abstracted' development of each aspect) to find itself neatly reduced to two equally assertive answers: 'is' on the one hand, and 'is not' on the other. Explicitly presented as a temporal shift, this third term effects not a synthesis but rather a final opening which defers the possibility of generic unity while pointing to this deferment as that unity itself.

[66] Lukács, 'On the Nature and Form of the Essay', 1 ['Über Wesen und Form des Essays', 1].

3.1.2. *Adorno*

3.1.2.1. *Essaying the Pre-Text*

Adorno's preliminary investigation into the form which he has chosen to adopt for his *Noten zur Literatur* is prompted by the need to justify writing in a genre whose status has, in recent times, become discredited. This discredit is primarily a consequence of the essay's hybrid status between science and art [*Mischprodukt*], of the fact that it neither 'achieves something scientifically', nor 'creates something artistically', but 'catches fire, without scruple on what others have already done' instead—a strategy which can be considered as both 'idle' and 'childish'.[67] The beginning of Adorno's essay explicitly presents itself as a dialogue with Lukács's own essay, as a 'trying out' of his predecessor's ideas which he 'weighs' (accepts and rejects) in typically essayistic fashion, from contradictory or opposite angles. In Lukács, it was the critical impetus of the essay that bound it to scientific requirements while also giving it access to the realm of art. Adorno fully endorses the critical motivation of the essay which he immediately defines as a 'speculative investigation of specific, culturally predetermined objects'.[68] But unlike Lukács, he gives immediate prevalence to the constraining aspect of this critical inclination which from the outset fundamentally distinguishes the essay from art. What prevails—and he quotes directly from Lukács in a footnote—is that the essay, in so far as it is 'always concerned with something already formed' and 'only gives a new order to such things as once lived', must therefore 'always speak "the truth" about them'.[69] Through 'the compatibility of the interpretation with the text and with itself and its power to release the object's expression in the unity of its elements', the essay does 'acquire an aesthetic autonomy that is easily criticized as simply borrowed from art'. It remains true, nevertheless, that the essay 'distinguishes itself from art through its conceptual character and its claim to truth free from aesthetic semblance', that 'on account of the concepts which appear in it and which import not only their meaning but also their theoretical aspects, the essay is necessarily related to theory'.[70] The parallel implication of Lukács's description of the essay as an independent art-form in the sense of 'as independent *from* other art-forms', which reinstates the conceptual character and bind to truth stressed by Adorno, does nothing to sway him, for this independence is the temporary independence of the 'not-yet' (not yet art) that looks ahead to the possibility of a concrete reunion between science and art, of the essay's 'undifferentiated unity

---

[67] Adorno, 'The Essay as Form', 152 ['Anstatt wissenschaftlich etwas zu leisten oder künstlerisch etwas zu schaffen', 'Der Essay als Form', 11]. For Adorno, this discredit also involves the position of the modern essay trapped between the stifling academic disciplines, on the one hand, and the frivolity of vulgarized mass-culture, on the other.

[68] Ibid. 1 ['Spekulation über spezifische, kulturell bereits Vorgeformte Gegenstände', 10].

[69] Lukács, 'On the Nature and Form of the Essay', 10 ['Über Wesen und Form des Essays', 22].

[70] Adorno, 'The Essay as Form', 153 ['Durch diese ähnelt der Essay einer ästhetischen Selbständigkeit, die leicht als der Kunst bloß entlehnt angeklagt wird, von der er gleichwohl durch sein Medium, die Begriffe, sich unterscheidet und durch seinen Anspruch auf Wahrheit bar des ästhetischen Scheins', 'Der Essay als Form', 12–13]; and ibid. 165 [38].

with science, ethics, and art', which Adorno finds unacceptable. For him the separation of knowledge from art is 'irreversible', and 'a consciousness in which perception and concept, image and sign would be one is not, if it ever existed, to be recreated with a wave of the wand'. What would happen, in the event of a 'restitution' would be 'a return to chaos'—according to an idea more fully elaborated in other writings—since by cancelling the distinction between subject and object, the restoration of this unity would mean a disastrous loss of capacity for reflection.[71] Hence the belief stated here that the wish for such a reunion is the mark of a 'utopianism' which only 'naïvety' can bring about and which at best can only result in 'pseudo-art' or 'pseudo-knowledge'.[72]

On the other hand, Adorno also warns that 'although art and science have separated from each other in history, their opposition is not to be hypostatized':

In all their necessity these divisions simply attest institutionally to the renunciation of the whole truth [*Verzicht auf die Ganze Wahrheit*]. The ideals of purity and cleanliness bear the marks of a repressive order; these ideals are shared by the bustle of authentic philosophy aiming at eternal values, a sealed and flawlessly organized science, and by a conceptless, intuitive art.[73]

Adorno suspends the conviction that 'internal boundaries between art and science will not be obviated by good will or over-arching planning' by drawing attention to the (equally naïve) presupposition that knowledge can only be identified with organized science.[74] To let this presupposition inform the question of knowledge, is to 'renounce the whole truth' by ignoring the epistemological dimension of art, that is, by ignoring that art provides a form of knowledge which cannot, precisely, be converted into scientific knowledge.[75] After Kant, Hegel, and Nietzsche, the last great essayist to have realized and acted upon this, in Adorno's view, is Proust.[76] And with this reference to a writer who is at once an art critic and a great artist, Adorno is able simultaneously to 'rescue aesthetic experience from those who would render it inferior to science, religion or philosophy',[77] and to establish an essential connection between the essay, art criticism, and art. After all 'only the essence of (the essay's) content, not the manner of its presentation, is commensurable with logical criteria'; for a science or philosophy of the arts cannot hold in good faith that 'what is written about art may claim nothing of art's mode of presentation, nothing, that is, of its autonomy of form': 'It is scarcely possible to speak of the aesthetic unaesthetically, stripped of any similarity with its object, without becoming narrow-minded and a priori losing touch with the aesthetic

[71] Adorno, 'The Essay as Form', 154 ['Der Essay als Form', 16]. See Jay, *Adorno*, 63–4.

[72] Ibid. 154–5 [16 and 17].

[73] Ibid. 156 ['einer hieb, und stichfesten, lückenlos durchorganisierten Wissenschaft und einer begriffslos anschaulichen Kunst', 18].

[74] Ibid. 157 [21].

[75] Ibid. 156 ['daß alle Erkenntnis potentiell in Wissenschaft sich umsetzen lasse', 19].

[76] Ibid. 156 [19].   [77] Jay, *Adorno*, 76.

object.'[78] Lukács's definition of 'the essay—criticism as an art-form, as a work of art', which Adorno takes issue with at first, must therefore be weighed against the 'positivistic' tendency of a scientific mind which, by virtue of the 'rigid divorce' it promotes between form and content, 'approaches the stupidly dogmatic mind'.[79] The seemingly opposite stands of the two essayists thus eventually meet in the middle ground where the science of the arts gives way to that alternative form of writing about the arts which Lukács defined as 'intellectuality, conceptuality as sensed experience', and where the mixture of the cognitive and the aesthetic which the essay provides, far from discrediting it, turns out to be its greatest resource. So, having tackled the genre from the point of view of its conceptual, theoretical dimension—from the point of view of its content—Adorno devotes the best part of his investigation to the question of the essay's form or 'manner of presentation'. For Adorno, the paratactic structure of the essay must from the outset be interpreted as a resistance to the system, as the genre's endemically sceptical rejection of 'scientific procedure and its philosophic grounding as method' embodied by 'philosophies of identity' and its 'scholastic residues in modern thought'. This 'critique of the system' from which the essay 'draws the fullest consequences' takes the form of an 'aesthetic struggle' [*sich ästhetisch sträuben*[80]] against systematic 'claims of totality and continuity', against 'any reduction to one principle', thereby 'doing justice to the concept of non-identity [*Nichtidentität*]'.[81] At the same time, this 'accentuation of the fragmentary, the partial rather than the total', is not equivalent to an absence of order but to an alternative order which Adorno summarizes in his famous oxymoronic formula of the essay as 'unmethodical method' [*methodisch unmethodisch*[82]].

3.1.2.2. Essaying as 'Unmethodical Method'

As announced in my first chapter, the paradigm used by Adorno for the concrete and detailed exploration of the essay's anti-systematic impulse, of its 'suspension' of 'the traditional concept of method'[83] is a work whose systematic elaboration of the concept of philosophical method has exerted a fundamental influence on modern Western thought—Descartes's *Discourse on Method*. The essay, Adorno writes, is 'a protest against the four rules that Descartes's *Discourse on Method* sets up at the beginning of modern Western science and its theory'.[84] The second and fourth of these rules are the most appropriate ones to begin with regarding my

---

[78] Adorno, 'The Essay as Form', 153 ['wie denn überhaupt von Ästhetischem unästhetisch, bar aller Ähnlichkeit mit der Sache kaum sich reden ließe', 'Der Essay als Form', 13].

[79] Ibid. [13–14].   [80] Ibid. 164 [35].

[81] Ibid. 157 ['Im Verhältnis zur wissenschaftlichen Prozedur und ihrer philosophischen Grundlegung als Methode zieht der Essay, der Idee nach, die volle Konsequenz aus der Kritik am System'; and 'in der Enthaltung von aller Reduktion auf ein Prinzip, im Akzentuieren des Partiellen gegenüber der Totale, im Stückhaften', 21–2].

[82] Ibid. 161 [29].

[83] Ibid. 159 ['Damit suspendiert er (der Essay) zugleich den traditionellen Begriff von Methode', 25].

[84] Ibid. 161 [30].

introduction to Adorno's essay, since they respectively stipulate the 'decomposition of the object into "as many parts as possible and as might be necessary for its adequate solution"', and command that 'one should in every case institute such exhaustive enumerations and such general survey' that one is 'sure of leaving nothing out'.[85] This fourth rule, introduced by Adorno as 'the ultimate principle of systematic thought [*das eigentlich systematische Prinzip*]', is a reminder that the exhaustive enumeration of the individual elements is only possible 'if it is determined in advance that the object in question can be fully grasped by the concepts which treat it', which presupposes that 'the object can be presented in an airtight deductive system'.[86] In both cases, the precepts of exhaustiveness, totality, and continuity are at stake, all of which the essay subverts by accentuating the part over the whole, by breaking off wherever it wants to while combining its parts in such a way that it could always go on adding elements to the discussion, and by 'shrinking back from an overarching concept [*Oberbegriff*]' which would subordinate individual concepts: 'self-relativization is immanent in its form'.[87] Exactly how this subversion operates is further specificied in the last part of Adorno's text, where the essay is said to 'coordinate elements, rather than subordinating them', so that its transitions 'disavow rigid deduction in favour of internal cross-connections, something for which discursive logic has no use'.[88] Non-identity implies 'association' and 'neglect of logical synthesis', the combination of which presents the various aspects of the argument as the 'interweaving of a carpet' rather than a continuum or progression of thought in a single direction.[89] Concepts are 'neither deduced from any first principle, nor do they come full circle and arrive at a final principle': they are introduced 'directly', 'immediately' [*unmittelbar, umstandslos*], in a process in which they are only 'temporarily embodied' rather than defined:

Its concepts receive the light from a *terminus ad quem* hidden in the essay itself, and not from an obvious *terminus a quo*. . . . All its concepts are presentable in such a way that they support one another, that each one articulates itself according to the configuration that it forms with the others.[90]

The rejection of the third Cartesian rule—'to conduct my thoughts in such an order that, by commencing with the simplest and easiest I know, I might ascend

---

[85] Adorno, 'The Essay as Form', 161 and 163 ['Der Essay als Form', 30 and 33].

[86] Ibid. 163 ['daß der Gegenstand in lückenlosem Deduktionszusammenhang sich darstellen lasse', 34].

[87] Ibid. 164 ['scheut er zurück vor dem Oberbegriff, dem sie [die Begriffe] gemeinsam unterzuordnen wären'; and 'Seiner Form ist deren eigene Relativierung immanent: er muß so sich fügen als ob er immer und stets abbrechen könnte', 35].

[88] Ibid. 170 and 169 ['Er koordiniert die Elemente, anstatt sie zu subordinieren'; and 'Seine Übergänge desavouieren die bündige Ableitung zugunsten von Querverbindungen der Elemente, für welche die diskursive Logik keinen Raum hat', 47 and 46].

[89] Ibid. 160 ['In ihr [geistige Erfahrung] bilden jene [Konzepte] kein Kontinuum der Operationen, der Gedanke schreitet nicht einsinnig fort, sondern die Momente verflechten sich teppichartig', 28].

[90] Ibid. 160–1 ['daß ein jeglicher (Begriff) sich artikuliert je nach den Konfigurationen mit anderen', 27 and 30].

little by little, step by step, to the knowledge of the more complex' thus almost goes without saying, since in opposition to 'the notion of truth as network of cause and effects', the essay 'begins with the most complex, not the most simple, which is in every instance the habitual'.[91]

The essayistic structure, then, is like the 'stringent and yet aconceptual art of transition' of (atonal) music.[92] Still, the essay, like (atonal) music, is not unlogical. It simply develops according to a logic different to that of discursive logic, 'thematically'—that is—rather than 'conceptually':

For the essay is not situated in simple opposition to discursive procedure. It is not unlogical; rather it obeys logical criteria in so far as the totality of its sentences must fit together coherently [*stimmig*]. Mere contradictions may not remain, unless they are grounded in the object itself. It is just that the essay develops thoughts differently from discursive logic.[93]

In the essay, the fragmentary and the partial are accentuated over totality, but 'neither are the specific elements to be developed purely out of the whole, nor vice versa':[94] 'The essay must let the totality light up in one of its chosen or haphazard features but without asserting that the whole is present.'[95] The irreducibility of fragment to whole turns the totality of the essay-form into the paradoxical 'totality of a non-totality' by which Adorno refers the essay back to the 'negative' dimension of Hegelian dialectic, the 'logic' of which the essay 'takes at its word', for 'neither may the truth of totality be played off immediately against individual judgments, nor may truth be reduced to individual judgments', but by being 'more dialectical than the dialectic as it articulates itself'.[96] And this 'totality of a non-totality' affiliates the genre to the Romantic conception of the fragment as 'an artifact which is not complete in itself but openly striding into infinity by way of self-reflection'.[97] Like the fragment, the essay gains its unity 'only by moving through the gaps, not by smoothing them over', and the paradoxical totality which it effects is always a set of 'tensions' or a 'conflict' 'brought (temporarily) to a standstill'. This fundamental tension between the dynamic and the static is never resolved, for the apparently static quality of the essay as a 'constructed juxtaposition of elements' is in reality a 'force field'.[98] By describing the paratactical form of

---

[91] Ibid. 162 ['insofern als [die Essayform] vom Komplexesten ausgeht, nicht vom Einfachsten, allemal vorweg Gewohnten', 32].

[92] Ibid. 169 ['Auch darin streift der Essay die musikalische Logik, die stringente und doch begriffslose Kunst des Übergangs', 46].

[93] Ibid. 169 ['Denn der Essay befindet sich nicht im einfachen Gegensatz zum diskursiven Verfahren.... Nur entwickelt er die Gedanken anders als nach der diskursiven Logik', 46–7].

[94] Ibid. 162 ['Weder sind die Momente rein aus dem Ganzen zu entwickeln noch umgekehrt', 31].

[95] Ibid. 164 ['Der Essay muß an einem ausgewählten oder getroffenen partiellen Zug die Totalität aufleuchten lassen, ohne daß diese als gegenwärtig behauptet würde', 36].

[96] Ibid. 166 ['Darum ist der Essay dialektischer als die Dialektik dort, wo sie selbst sich vorträgt', 40].

[97] Ibid. 164 ['Die romantische Konzeption des Fragments als eines nicht vollständigen sondern durch selbstreflexion ins Unendliche weiterschreitenden Gebildes', 35].

[98] Ibid. 170 and 161 ['nur daß jene Statik selber eine von gewissermaßen stillgestellten Spannungsverhältnissen ist'; and 'als Konfiguration aber kristallisieren sich die Elemente durch ihre Bewegung. Jene ist ein Kraftfeld', 47 and 30].

the essay in terms of a logic alternative to discursive logic, a logic that proceeds 'methodically unmethodically', Adorno's presentation of the essay counter-balances the arbitrariness and 'slovenliness' [*Schlamperei*[99]] the genre is often accused of with a rigour and precision that 'forces it to a greater intensity than discursive thought can offer' and ultimately likens it to a work of art; so that finally:

The essay is both more open and more closed than traditional thought would like. It is more open insofar as, through its inner nature, it negates anything systematic. . . . On the other hand, the essay is more closed in that it labors emphatically on the form of its presentation [*weil er an der Form der Darstellung emphatisch arbeitet*]. The consciousness of the non-identity between presentation and presented materials forces the form to make unlimited efforts.[100]

For Adorno, the question of representation, the conditions of meaning and truth which it is in the nature of the essay to examine, is inextricably connected with (bourgeois) ideology, with the *doxa*. The essay's revolt against the system is described as 'a permanent revolt against orthodoxy and ideology of any kind' and in so far as the essay is 'the critical form par excellence', it is 'the critique of ideology'.[101] The Cartesian method chosen by Adorno as a paradigm of the System thus tacitly becomes the prototype of the 'order of mimesis' discussed in the previous chapter.

3.1.2.3 The Critique of Ideology

The essay, we are told, 'shakes off the illusion of a simple, basically logical world that so perfectly suits the defence of the status quo'.[102] The Cartesian method is an ideal example of the interrelation between the *doxa* and discursive structures. Its scientific claims arc a prerequisite for the arbitrary foundations of the *doxa* to be passed off as the universal and timeless categories of rationality and logic.[103] Hence, to essay or unmask the 'rules' which the *Discourse on Method* hinges upon is to denaturalize the rhetorical strategies by which it occults the arbitrariness of its choices and guarantees its verisimilitude or *vraisemblance*. Among these rules, which stipulate exhaustiveness, hierarchy, induction and deduction, one recognizes the related strategies of 'recuperation' and 'motivation' that testify to the fundamentally 'repressive' nature of the *doxa*. 'Repressive', because it applies the laws of teleological necessity: the 'desire to leave no chaff, to let nothing escape the

---

[99] Adorno, 'The Essay as Form', 169 ['Der Essay als Form', 46].

[100] Ibid. 165 ['Das Bewußtsein der Nichtidentität von Darstellung und Sache nötigt jene zur unbeschränkten Anstrengung', 38]. Cf. also: 'The essay takes the matter of presentation more seriously. . . . The *how* of expression [*Das Wie des Ausdrucks*] should rescue, in precision, what the refusal to outline sacrifices' (ibid. 160 [28]).

[101] 'The essay remains what it always was, the critical form par excellence . . . it is the critique of ideology' (ibid. 166 ['Er ist, was er von Beginn war, die kritische Form par excellence; und zwar . . . Ideologiekritik', 39]).

[102] Ibid. 163 ['so schüttelt der Essay die Illusion einer einfachen, im Grunde selber logischen Welt ab, die zur Verteidigung des bloß Seienden so gut sich schickt', 33].

[103] See Christopher Prendergast, *The Order of Mimesis: Balzac, Stendhal, Nerval, Flaubert* (1986), 50 and 54.

process of assimilation'; the assertion of the text's 'organic unity' and 'the contribution of all its parts to its meanings or effects'; the retrospective 'concealment' of the arbitrariness of the various parts' positions in the work 'behind a mask of causal determination' for the relationship between the particular and the general to be perceived 'as one of implication and explanation'.[104] The first step in this critique of ideology is the relativization or 'historicization' of philosophical Truth which Adorno justifies from the perspective of a continuity with the Renaissance conjuncture, when he asserts that 'the intellectual process which canonizes a distinction between the temporal and the timeless is losing its authority'.[105] Philosophy is of course an obvious repository for a set of ideas which reflects the dominant political, social, and cultural beliefs of its time under the guise of a timeless and ever-valid truth about the world. In the previous chapter, the *Essais* were shown to oppose the epistemological claims of a universal and speculative philosophy, a knowledge based on individual experience, a practical philosophy or a philosophy 'in action', the findings of which 'do not lend themselves readily to scientific generalization'.[106] Again, the essayistic 'suspension' of the totalizing or 'overarching' concept of Descartes's discourse takes the form of a relativization of abstract, objective Truth by particular, subjective truths, or of the polarization of truth as a temporal concept versus Truth as a timeless concept. By foregrounding the essential role of individual perception, the essay subverts the implications of a transcendent order of knowledge dependent upon a transcendent knowing subject, and, by extension, the presupposition that truth and time must remain external to each other—indeed that they are incompatible:

The essay shys away from the violence of dogma, from the notion that the result of abstraction, the temporally invariable concept indifferent to the individual phenomenon grasped by it, deserves ontological dignity.

If truth has in fact a temporal core, then the full historical content becomes an integral moment in truth; the *a posteriori* becomes concretely the *a priori*. Therefore the essay is not intimidated by the depraved profundity which claims that 'truth and history are incompatible'. . . . It [the essay] does not insist stubbornly on a realm transcending all mediations . . . rather the essay seeks truth contents as being historical in themselves.[107]

It is precisely because truths are particular and 'only valid for here and now' that, as described in the previous section, concepts are 'neither deduced from any first principle, nor do they come full circle and arrive at a final principle'; that they are introduced 'directly', 'immediately', in a process in which they are only 'temporarily embodied' rather than defined: 'all levels of the mediated are immediate to the essay before its reflection begins'.[108] The recognition of contingence and

---

[104] Jonathan Culler, *Structuralist Poetics: Structuralism, Linguistics, and the Study of Literature* (1974), 137–8; and Gérard Genette, 'Vraisemblance et motivation', in *Figures*, ii (1969), 74–5 and 94–7.

[105] Adorno, 'The Essay as Form', 158 ['Der Essay als Form', 24].

[106] See ibid. 156–7 [20].   [107] Ibid. 158 [23–4].

[108] Ibid. 159 ['Alle Stufen des Vermittelten sind dem Essay unmittelbar, ehe er zu reflektieren sich anschickt', 26].

circumstantiality against the universal validity of conceptual thought, means that the essay 'becomes true in its progress, which drives it beyond itself' and which is determined above all by 'its mobility, its lack of solidity which science demands'.[109] As reviewed in relation to both Hegel and Montaigne, the relativization of the temporally invariable concept by individual phenomena does not entail the substitution of a general Truth by a particular truth—that of 'the pure, abstract, Cartesian construction of the self'.[110] This emphasis on individual experience, Adorno points out, marks a departure from both rationalist and empiricist trends in so far as the latter, though 'granting priority to open, unanticipated experience over firm conceptual ordering, remain systematic to the extent that they investigate what they hold to be more or less constant preconditions of knowledge and develop them in as continuous a context as possible'; no less than rationalism, they are therefore also a 'method'.[111] If the essay revolts first of all 'against the doctrine—deeply rooted since Plato—that the changing and ephemeral is unworthy of philosophy', it also makes clear that its desire 'is not to seek and filter the eternal out of the transitory [*das Ewige im Vergänglichen aufsuchen und abdestilieren*]; it wants, rather, to make the transitory eternal [*des Vergängliche verewigen*]'.[112] In the context of a structure in which neither part nor whole can be completely deduced from each other, the truth 'in progress' of the essay is to be sought in the ever-shifting ground of a to-ing and fro-ing between constantly changing selves and constantly changing worlds, subjective experience being 'the all-encompassing experience of historical humanity'.[113]

Society, on the other hand, 'ultimately tolerates nothing indicative of its own omnipresence and necessarily cites, as its ideological complement, that nature which its own praxis eliminates'.[114] This turns the 'interrelation of nature and culture' into the 'proper theme' of the essay [*sein eigentliches Thema*]. In investigating 'culturally predetermined objects', what the essay demystifies is the 'myth' of the 'natural' which 'perpetuates itself in culture', and according to which 'culture is some epiphenomenon superimposed on being' rather than that which properly underlies nature: 'The more energetically the essay suspends the concept of some first principle, the more it refuses to spin culture out of nature, the more fundamentally it recognizes the unremittingly natural essence of culture itself.'[115] If

---

[109] Adorno, 'The Essay as Form', 161 ['Wahr wird er in seinem Fortgang, der ihn über sich hinausstrebt', 'Der Essay als Form', 30]; and ibid. 168 [43].

[110] Good, *The Observing Self*, 23.

[111] Adorno, 'The Essay as Form', 157 ['Empirismus nicht weniger als Rationalismus war ... "Methode" ', 'Der Essay als Form', 21–2].

[112] Ibid. 158 and 159 [23 and 25].

[113] Ibid. 158 ['die bloß individuelle Erfahrung, mit welcher das Bewußtsein als mit dem ihr nächsten anhebt, ist selber vermittelt durch die übergreifende der historischen Menschheit', 24].

[114] Ibid. 159 ['und notwendig als ideologisches Komplement jene Natur herbeizitiert, von der ihre Praxis nichts übrig läßt', 25–6].

[115] Ibid. 167 ['Je energischer er aber den Begriff eines Ersten suspendiert und sich weigert, Kultur aus Natur herausspinnen, um so gründlicher erkennt er das naturwüchsige Wesen von Kultur selber', 41].

'truth' is inescapably historical, then there is no first principle, no origin from which philosophy may proceed, for 'there is no salvaging the distinction of a first philosophy (or 'philosophy of origins') from a mere philosophy of culture that assumes the former and builds on it'.[116] The paratactic style of the essay, its refusal to establish a hierarchy between its parts is the obvious expression of this 'suspension' of first principles. By resisting 'something all-embracing, the totality of which would resemble creation [*Schöpfung*]', the essayist conspicuously 'uses the relationship to its object as a weapon against the spell of beginnings [*wider den Bann des Anfangs*]'.[117] It demystifies the requirement of the image of the *tabula rasa*—the beginning [*Anfang, Erste*], the origin [*Ursprung*], of the 'primal' [*Urgegebenheit*]— by which science 'secures its claim to domination'.[118] Its very form 'follows the critical thought that man is no creator, that nothing human is creation': 'nature', the 'primal' is always derivative. It can have no priority over culture, the 'mediated', since 'primacy itself is an object of reflection, something negative'.[119] What the essay 'transgresses', in the end, is the assumption, which underlies the 'orthodoxy of thought', of an unhindered, transparent correspondence between thought and the external world, as though thought could 'break out of *thesis* into *physis*, out of culture into nature' when the fact is that it 'can only hold true to the idea of immediacy by way of the mediated'.[120] This is what evidently motivates the characteristic essayistic 'play' [*Spiel*] with concepts described above, which consisted in 'temporarily embodying' rather than 'defining' concepts, 'examining the meaning of a word in constantly changing contexts', exploiting the 'nuances which the context establishes in every individual case',[121] for:

it is mere superstition of a science exclusively concerned with the appropriation of raw materials to believe that concepts are in themselves undetermined, that they are first determined by their definition. . . . In actual fact, all concepts are already implicitly concretized through the language in which they stand.[122]

To establish—however playfully—that the meaning of a concept changes according to the context in which it appears, as Montaigne does, is to demonstrate that

---

[116] Ibid. 158 ['Die Unterscheidung einer ersten von einer bloßen Kulturphilosophie . . . ist nicht zu retten', 24].

[117] Ibid. 165–6 ['Er sträubt sich gegen die Idee des Hauptwerks, welche selber die von Schöpfung und Totalität widerspiegelt', 37 and 39].

[118] Ibid. 167 and 160 ['Der Vorstellung des Begriffs als einer tabula rasa bedarf die Wissenschaft, um ihren Herrschaftsanspruch zu festigen', 40–1 and 27].

[119] Ibid. 165 and 167 ['Seine Form kommt dem kritischen Gedanken nach, daß der Mensch kein Schöpfer, daß nichts Menschliches Schopfung sei'; and 'weil ihm die Ursprünglichkeit selber Gegenstand der Reflexion, ein Negatives ist', 37 and 42].

[120] Ibid. 171, 159, and 167 ['Weil nach Hegel's Diktum nichts ist was nicht vermittelt wäre, hält der Gedanke der Idee von Unmittelbarkeit Treue nur durchs Vermittelte hindurch', 49, 26, 42].

[121] Ibid. 161 ['gegenüber den unverwechselbaren Nuancen, die der Kontext in jedem einzelnen Fall stiftet', 29].

[122] Ibid. 160 ['Denn es ist bloß Aberglaube der aufbereitenden Wissenschaft, die Begriffe wären an sich unbestimmt, würden bestimmt erst durch ihre Definition. In Wahrheit sind alle Begriffe implizit schon konkretisiert durch die Sprache, in der sie stehen', 27].

language is fundamentally ambiguous, devious, that there is no natural invariable sense, no zero-degree of meaning, no *tabula rasa*. Cultural predetermination begins with language, and so, too, does arbitrariness: since the link between signifier, signified, and referent is not necessary, signs refer to more signs away from an external, metalinguistic position—either intratextual or intertextual—which could give us direct access to reality.

It follows that the essay's counter-ideological impulse which is at the heart of its critical motivation, does not allow it to criticize the master-work—the concrete philosophical or literary object—from a separate, neutral (ideological) vantage-point. Instead, it approaches the work on the work's own terms, thus performing an immanent critique which comes to 'measuring the underlying logic of the norms and structures under investigation by the same criteria of unity and coherence they already espouse',[123] confronting every text with 'its own emphatic concept' or with 'the truth that each text intends even in spite of itself':[124]

The essay remains what it always was, the critical form par excellence; specifically, it constructs the immanent criticism of cultural artifacts, and it confronts that which such artifacts are with their concept; it is the critique of ideology.[125]

Because of its refusal to approach its object from an external vantage-point, the essay has been accused of 'lacking a standpoint' [*Standspunktlosigkeit*], yet this is simply congruent with its opposition to 'mere standpoint philosophy'.[126] As shown in Montaigne, the subversion of the order of mimesis is concomitant with a transition from one type of criticism to another, from what Adorno calls the 'theological' to the 'critical'. For this lack of standpoint marks an attitude which is 'no longer naive and dependent on the prominence of its objects'.[127] The essay 'settles itself into texts as though they were simply there and had authority': but instead of naïvety, 'cunning' [*List*] prevails, and the genre's impulse is reported to be 'the exact opposite of the theological; it is critical'.[128] Adorno's identification of the essay with a move away from theological exegesis where notions of 'origin', 'creation', 'first principle' referred to above are at their strongest is a reminder of the genre's emergence as a critique of scholastic philosophy and theology in the Renaissance. It corresponds to a move away from the typical subservience of the traditional (medieval) commentary to its master-text where the characteristically self-effacing gesture of the former is meant to (re)affirm the latter's closure—its overall meaning. Yet if a text cannot, for reasons recalled above, reflect or be 'about' an external

---

[123] Harrison, *Essayism: Conrad, Musil, Pirandello*, 10.

[124] Adorno, 'The Essay as Form', 168 ['durch Konfrontation der Texte mit ihrem eigenen emphatischen Begriff, mit der Wahrheit, die ein jeder meint, auch wenn er sie nicht meinen will', 'Der Essay als Form', 42–3].

[125] Ibid. 166 [39].   [126] Ibid. [40].

[127] Ibid. ['nicht länger naiv und der Prominenz ihrer Gegenstände hörig', 39].

[128] Ibid. 167–8 ['Listig macht der Essay sich fest in die Texte, als wären sie schlechterdings da und hätten Autorität', 42].

'original' reality, the relationship between a 'primary', 'original' textual object and a 'secondary' or 'derived' critical essay does not hold either. The 'lack of standpoint' which some critics reproach the essay, then, has to do with the lack of this mimetic 'aboutness' in the relationship between 'primary' and 'secondary' text, the lack of a proper confrontation between two clearly distinguishable texts by which the second discourse undertakes to reaffirm the authority and closure of the 'original'. Once the concept of 'representation' has been shown to be an illusion, as suggested in the context of the *Essais*, all discourses turn out to be equally secondary and therefore equally primary.

In this respect, Adorno is also aware of the essay's 'utopian' tendency previously illustrated by the *Essais*. He is aware of the potential danger involved in rejecting the conception of truth as something 'ready-made' so that 'all levels of the mediated are immediate until its reflection begins'. For the 'immediate' integration of concepts which 'articulate themselves with the configuration they form with others', 'defining each other in a temporary way', turns the essay into a self-generating, self-validating construct. And the truth 'in progress' by which the essay denaturalizes the pre-determined totality of the mimetic discourse can also appear as an alternative way of promoting those very concepts of 'nature', 'immediacy', 'tabula rasa', 'originality', 'creation' which it denounces as myths. We know that in the *Essais*, this 'immediate' integration of concepts which are suspended from their initial context allows them to become 'proper' to the essay as the internal 'cross-connections' multiply (the 'interweaving of the carpet'), so that the process of denaturalization associated with the idea of 'truth in progress' seems to go hand in hand with a parallel process of naturalization. This is one way of understanding Adorno's remark that the truth of the essay (the truth 'in progress') is also its 'untruth', one which 'resides in the essay's basic form, in its relation to what is culturally preformed and derived as though it [the latter] were something in-itself'.[129] However, one recognizes in this conditional 'as though' the essay's critical procedure which consists in consciously passing off as 'immediate' or unmediated what is already necessarily and patently mediated—or, in Adorno's words, of 'immersing itself in cultural phenomena as in a second nature, a second immediacy'—only 'in order through persistence to remove the illusion of immediacy'.[130] In so far as it is presented as a process, naturalization is simultaneously enacted and suspended, and reflexivity plays a major role in the essaying of the essay's own truth. So the first counter-ideological response, which consists in approaching the work aesthetically, is complemented by a second strategy in which the essay applies reflexiveness to itself, constantly reflecting upon the context of its enunciation, deconstructing itself as it deconstructs the intertext. 'Arbitrariness' is taken 'reflectively into the essay's own procedure' instead of being 'masked as spontaneity':

[129] Ibid. 166–7 ['in seiner bloßen Form, der Beziehung auf kulturell Vorgeformtes, Abgeleitetes, als wäre es an sich', 41].

[130] Ibid. 167 ['Nicht umsonst versenkt er . . . sich in Kulturphänomene als in zweite Natur, zweite Unmittelbarkeit, um durch Beharrlichkeit deren Illusion aufzuheben', 41].

'the essay, unlike discursive thought, does not proceed blindly, automatically, but at every moment it must reflect on itself'.[131] Not only are the concepts which the essay appropriates 'implicitly concretized through the language in which they stand', so that the essay 'begins with such meanings and forces them on farther [*und treibt sie weiter*]';[132] the essay is presented from the outset (that is, at the level of its title already) as an intertext, as secondary rather than as primary material. As was the case in the *Essais*, it is on the basis of the ostensibly mediated nature of a genre which is explicitly 'about' something, according to the terms of a contract with the reader which stipulates that the essay 'always directed towards artifacts [*stets bezogen auf schon Geschaffenes*], does not present itself as a creation',[133] that all it can do, to use Lukács's terms, is to 'order things anew', to re-frame what is already framed. From that position, the essay can effectively abstract the appropriated from the 'proper', the culturally derived from the 'natural', the mediated from the 'immediate', and so unmask the immediate as mediated, the proper as appropriated, the natural as derived. The 'irony' by which the recognition of this interrelation allows the genre to present itself simultaneously as a secondary and as a primary form is described as follows: 'The essay abandons the main road to the origins, the road leading to the most derivative, to being, the ideology that simply doubles that which already exists; at the same time the essay does not allow the idea of immediacy, postulated by the very concept of mediation, to disappear entirely.'[134] Behind the ongoing process of relativization of the natural by the cultural, the maintenance of the tension ensures that the 'myth' of the immediate, the original, is reinforced as well as removed, not just as a critical strategy but as the uncircumventable sign of a 'naïvety' which Adorno describes as the essay's 'utopian intention' [*die utopische Intention*].[135] In other words, it is thanks to—as well as in spite of—the awareness of its own derived and secondary status that the essay can ultimately afford not only to exploit immediacy reflexively, as an idea, but also to act it out. The genre continues to hover between its creative, emancipated quality and the critical (conceptual) dimension which counteracts this creative quality, between criticism as art and criticism as commentary—or simply between what I have referred to as commentary and criticism. Yet in reverse, it is also by fully assuming its declared status as commentary, as secondary, as intertextually bound, that the essay can also fully assume its creative and emancipative potential.

---

[131] Adorno, 'The Essay as Form', 166 ['Er (der Essay) möchte den Gedanken von seiner Willkür heilen, indem er sie reflektierend ins eigene Verfahren hineinnimmt, anstatt sie als Unmittelbarkeit zu maskieren', 'Der Essay als Form', 40]; and ibid. 170 ['Weil der Essay nicht gleich diesem (dem diskursiven Gedanken) blind, automatisiert verfährt, sondern in jedem Augenblick auf sich selber reflektieren muß', 47].

[132] Ibid. 160 [27].   [133] Ibid. 165 [37].

[134] Ibid. 159 ['Er verläßt die Heerstraße zu den Ursprünglichen, die bloß zu dem Abgeleiteten, dem Sein führt, der verdoppelnden Ideologie dessen, was ohnehin ist, ohne dass doch die Idee von Unmittelbarkeit ganz verschwände, die der Sinn von Vermittlung selbst postuliert', 26].

[135] 'The essay becomes true in its progress. . . . In this the very method of the essay expresses the utopian intention' (ibid. 161 [30]).

And in the end, this self-consciousness is the measure of the authenticity which, if it cannot claim the 'good faith' of Montaigne's 'word' to the reader, still guards it against the bad faith of ideology.

3.2. THE LOGIC OF THE PARERGON

Both my previous chapter on Montaigne and the first section of this chapter seem to demonstrate that it is virtually impossible to talk about the so-called 'order of mimesis'—about questions of closure or open-endedness, of play with boundaries or strategies of naturalization—without resorting to the findings and jargon of narratology. It is not surprising, therefore, that the anti-systematic thrust of the essay, which can be approached either from a philosophical or from a literary angle, is often described in terms of a play with frames. In both pictorial and verbal terms, the frame is the borderline or zone of transition between 'the internal world of the representation and the world external to the representation'.[136] The frame involves the whole demarcative apparatus of a text, that is to say both its external and internal borders, whether implicit (blanks) or explicit (paratexts).[137] The preconception of the text which the question of the frame brings into play, tends to be typically 'structuralist'. It is the preconception of a systematic and homogeneous construct founded on a 'parallel compositional organization of the whole and its relatively self-contained parts' which are held together by an 'overarching concept'—whether this is called 'intentionality' or 'transcendental signified'.[138] As an order of hierarchically related equivalences which assigns a particular function to each one of its parts, the (systematic) text necessarily relies on the use of metalanguage. The frame, that is, is nothing other than the space where 'an implicit or explicit metalinguistic discourse tends to develop, of the text about itself', framing-devices being 'operators of equivalence, of translation, of paraphrase, in short of rewriting'.[139] The level of framing with the greatest degree of metalinguistic determination is of course the 'closure' itself which encompasses both the end and the beginning of the text and lends it its final degree of meaningfulness. As its name suggests, it is the repressive space of a final restriction of meaning which must leave nothing unaccounted for, no residue. In the case of the

---

[136] See Boris Uspensky, 'The Structural Isomorphism of Verbal and Visual Art', in *A Poetics of Composition: The Structure of the Artistic Text and Typology of a Compositional Form* (1973), 143. See also Erving Goffman, *Frame Analysis: An Essay on the Organization of Experience* (1974); Dieter Metzing (ed.), *Frame Conceptions and Text Understanding* (1980); Philippe Hamon, 'Clausules' and 'Texte littéraire et métalangage', *Poétique*, 24 (1975) and 31 (1977); and Susan Stewart, *Nonsense: Aspects of Intertextuality in Folklore and Literature* (1979).

[137] Hamon, 'Clausules', 496, and 'Texte littéraire et métalangage', 266.

[138] Uspensky, *A Poetics of Composition*, 152. See also A. J. Greimas, *Structuralist Semantics: An Attempt at Method* (1983) and *On Meaning: Selected Writings in Semiotic Theory* (1987).

[139] Hamon, 'Texte littéraire et métalangage', 263; see also 265.

Essais where supposedly 'the concept of the "book" has priority for Montaigne over the individual "essay" as the essential organizational unit',[140] the framing-devices which most noticeably 'stand out' are the paratexts (or 'perigraphy') of the essay-titles (which function as so many chapter-headings), and the preliminary note 'To the Reader'. They link the various parts or fragments of Montaigne's discourse together into an identifiable whole. The paratext is meant to be subordinated to the text; it is a textual 'auxiliary' or 'accessory', a transparent mediator between the text and what lies outside it.[141] Given that the preface is the most 'over-determined' zone of authorial control[142] and the space of generic contracts—as established in relation to 'To the Reader', it is only to be expected that the paradoxical use of the paratext as an *emblème supernuméraire* in the *Essais* should be the most obvious manifestation of their overall sceptical determination and of the play with boundaries by which they 'elude all system'.

In Antoine Compagnon's history of intertextuality, in which the *Essais* play a fundamental, pivotal role, the question of the frame is a convincing justification for the notion of 'Montaignian essay' or—as one could also choose to call it—of the 'modern essay'. In so far as the subversive use of the frame, as illustrated for example in Adorno's essay via the Cartesian method, equals a subversion of self-representation or self-reflection as self-identity—and therefore of the self-certainty of the thinking subject which defines Cartesian self-consciousness—the bringing together of *Essais* and essay in Compagnon coincides with the bringing together of the pre- and post-Cartesian periods. If the *Essais*, between two systems of enunciation, are 'fundamentally paradoxical' or even 'impossible', as Compagnon suggests, this is because they mark the 'advent of modern quotation', that is, the transitory stage between the 'ephemeral and subversive sign characteristic of the XVIth Century' (the *emblem*) and the reconstruction of the book from its frame (its paratext or 'perigraphy') characteristic of the 'classical economy of writing'.[143] Montaigne's paradoxical use of the frame, then, is justified by the fact that the classical economy of writing which the advent of perigraphy exemplifies has not yet occurred. The paratextual overrun of the *Essais*, which leads both subject and text to 'come off their hinges',[144] is about to be framed by the introduction of the paratext (perigraphy)

---

[140] Good, *The Observing Self*, 27.

[141] The aim, usually, is to establish a final relation of implication and explanation between the particular case of the text and the ever valid, universal maxim or rule of the *doxa*: 'Le texte met en relief sa clausule en la faisant assumer par un énoncé autonome et suffisant, souvent en position détachée, affirmation universelle ou maxime péremptoire qui fonctionne à la fois comme le résumé, la conclusion, la morale, et la "légende" de l'énoncé (au sens cartographique: la clé qui permet de lire ou relire l'ensemble)' (Hamon, 'Clausules', 519–20).

[142] Cf. 'La périgraphie situe le texte, le met en place dans l'intertexte, *elle témoigne du contrôle que l'auteur exerce sur lui*. C'est une scénographie qui met le texte en perspective, *et l'auteur en est le centre*' (Compagnon, *La Seconde Main*, 328); and 'Frange toujours porteuse d'un commentaire auctoriale, ou plus ou moins légitimé par l'auteur' (Genette, *Seuils*, 8).

[143] Characterized, as we saw in Ch. 2, by the genre of 'criticism'. Compagnon, *La Seconde Main*, 11.

[144] 'des ajouts qui mettent le sujet hors de lui et le texte hors de ses gonds' (Compagnon, *La Seconde Main*, 327).

as a system of authorial regulation. Correspondingly with Compagnon's description of the classical economy of writing which the *Essais* tend towards but have not
yet reached, perigraphy thus coincides with the 'centering of Descartes's own
method around the *ego* that will systematize and normalize Montaigne's sceptical
invention of a subjective method'.[145] Hence the exact symmetry between the subversive situation of the paratext in the *Essais* and the kind of quotation—or
intertextual relationship—which characterizes contemporary (or at least 'modernist') literature, and which also derives its paradoxicality from the simultaneous
implementation of two contradictory values of quotation.[146] On the one hand,
therefore, we seem to be dealing with an overrun of the paratextual which ante-
dates the institutionalization of the paratext as authorial control and regulation of
the text. On the other, the overrun of the paratextual postdates the paratext in its
capacity as authorial control and regulation. This identical perversion of the paratext
(this side and beyond its regulating capacity) which is illustrated by the liberation
of the quotation from the regulating frame of its quotation-marks or by a playing
or 'cheating' with the rule, prompts Compagnon to bring Montaigne and Borges
together.[147] But the latter is referred to not so much in his capacity as essayist,
as in his capacity as writer of fictions. For the subversive use of the frame which
prompts the excess of genre by mode, product by process, characterizes not only
the genre of the essay but all texts which, in the periods of generic crises we are
concerned with here, function like essays: in periods of generic crises all texts are
fundamentally paradoxical or even 'impossible', all texts seem to be essays, paratexts,
or parerga that develop in the margins of a (Mallarmean) Book which is endlessly
deferred.

In Genette's study of the literary paratext,[148] in fact, the subversive use of the
frame expressly characterizes periods of generic instability or 'modernist' periods.
It is a deviation from the normal subordination of the paratext to the text at work
in more stable periods, the paratext being *by definition* the paradigm of the classical
economy of writing. What is at stake, Genette claims, is 'bad' versus 'good' literary
use: 'literary' because the paratext is not only 'a class of texts' but also 'an aspect
of textuality' and '*a fortiori* an aspect of literariness'.[149] 'Self-representation', he
points out, is endemic to the literary act even though all works or texts, whether
aesthetic or not, require a paratext.[150] And the function of the paratext is to reduce
the potential difference between the invariable work and any reading of it at any

---

[145] Beaujour, 'Genus Universum', 27.   [146] Compagnon, *La Seconde Main*, 11.

[147] Borges's use of intertextuality is described as 'Everything that cheats or plays with the rule of the
game, and which existed in Montaigne before this rule was formalized' (Compagnon, *La Seconde Main*,
363).

[148] In *Seuils* ('Thresholds').

[149] Genette, *Palimsestes: La Littérature au second degré* (1982), 15.

[150] Genette, *Seuils*, 269 and 9 (including n. 1). This is echoed by Philippe Hamon who underlines
the fact that framing-devices are central to all written texts because of decontextualization (see 'Texte
littéraire et métalangage', 264 and 270).

one period and at different periods in history, thus guaranteeing the 'fate' of the text 'in keeping with the author's intention'.[151] What happens at times of generic instability or crisis, is that the paratext exploits its liminal position, usurps its role as mediator between text and 'extratext', and so becomes an obstacle to the literary work's self-identity. A bad use of the paratext equals an abusive use of self-reflexiveness, that is, the foregrounding of the 'aspect of textuality' or 'literariness' typical of modernist writing. At its worst, this 'subversive' form of paratextuality creates the danger of trading the already vain fetish of the Closed Text for that, even more vain, of the Paratext: the complete paratextual destabilization of closure could result in a situation where '*all* would be paratext'.[152] As an antidote, Genette therefore warns, it is imperative that both writers and readers 'beware of the paratext', as do those authors 'most attached to classical dignity and/or realist transparency'.[153] In other words, Genette's belief in the possibility of keeping the potentially perverse effects of paratextuality at bay relies on a fundamental 'exteriority' of the two related features of the paratext (the 'class of texts' and the 'aspect of textuality'), an exteriority which enables him to separate good from bad literary practice and to keep apart the invariable self-identity of the text and the empirical, socio-historical reality of its reception. For the actualization of the potential paratextual overrun at certain periods of literary history does not alter the fact that the paratext is in other respects not only a class of texts but also a genre.[154] So its liminal position does not stop it from having its own well-defined territory; it does not threaten the acknowledgement of the boundary between inside and outside by which the notion of closure can be questioned but not made inoperative.[155] In this sense, the exteriority which Genette insists on maintaining between the invariable self-identity of the text and the empirical reality of its reception converges with the more renowned distinction between 'meaning' and 'significance' which E. D. Hirsch appropriates from Gottlob Frege:

Meaning is that which is represented by a text; it is what the author meant by his use of a particular sign sequence. . . . *Significance*, on the other hand, names a relationship between that meaning and a person, or a conception, or a situation. . . . Significance always implies a relationship, and one constant, unchanging pole of that relationship is what the text means.[156]

---

[151] 'Le paratexte ménage entre l'identité idéale, et relativement immuable du texte, et la réalité empirique (sociohistorique) de son public' (Genette, *Seuils*, 374) (this, of course, includes the 'constant modifications to the text's presentation', both by the author—during his lifetime—and by the 'more or less competent' posthumous editors', p. 375); and 'Le paratexte n'a pas pour principal enjeu de "faire joli" autour du texte, mais de lui assurer un sort conforme au dessein de l'auteur' (ibid. 374).

[152] Ibid. 376 and 374

[153] Ibid. 347, 376, and 269.   [154] Genette, *Palimpsestes*, 15.

[155] 'Le caractère indécis des limites n'empêche pas le paratexte d'avoir en son centre un territoire propre et incontestable où se manifestent clairement ses "propriétés" ' (Genette, *Seuils*, 374).

[156] E. D. Hirsch, Jr., *Validity in Interpretation* (1967), 8.

Hence Hirsch's belief in a so-called 'intrinsic genre', this side of distinctions between literature and non-literature, fiction and non-fiction, and of the different genres signalled by different paratextual apparatuses within either category:[157]

What can we properly mean when we speak of the philosophical interpretation of philosophy or the literary interpretation of literature? I suggest that we cannot properly mean that there is one particular set of categories and canons appropriate for each of the families of texts that we happen to call literary, philosophical, legal or sacred. To be more blunt, there is no such thing as the philosophical interpretation of philosophy or the literary interpretation of literature, but there emphatically is such a thing as the intrinsic interpretation of a text.[158]

The 'intrinsic genre' is the self-identical entity determined by the boundaries of the author's meaning or intention which guarantees the original meaning.[159] The status of the intrinsic genre, for Hirsch, is that of speech: writing is radically indeterminate and must therefore be excluded from authorial intention if meaning is to be determinate and sharable. For even though the process of speech is also necessarily temporal, it is controlled by 'some kind of overarching notion'—a fundamentally spatial or structural metaphor which frees both self and meaning from the dynamism of time.[160] Thus, according to Hirsch, 'purpose is the most important unifying and discriminating principle in genres', and 'all valid interpretation of every sort is founded on the re-cognition of what an author meant': 'All valid interpretation is intrinsic interpretation: whatever one may do with a literary text *after* it has been understood on its own terms achieves validity only because that preliminary task has been performed.'[161] From this point of view, the paratext—and especially the (family of the) preface which Genette singles out as the most typical paratext and therefore as the most typical of all literary practices 'in the best, or sometimes worst sense of the word'[162]—is not only the space of generic contracts in the broad, 'extrinsic' sense of the word. The proximity of Genette's conception of the frame to Hirsch's suggests that for the former also, the decision to honour or to subvert a generic contract always involves first and foremost the 'intrinsic genre', the author's *parole* (Montaigne's 'word') and hence the notion that every text, like the *Essais*, is 'the only one of its kind' [*unique en son genre*].[163]

One need not know very much about Derridean post-structuralism to surmise that, contrary to the views of Compagnon and Genette, the 're-mark' of framing, which is 'ever possible for every text, for every corpus of traces' but which 'is

---

[157] Cf. 'Each genre, as a distinct and institutionalized horizon of thematic and formal expectation, is characterized by its own system of framing-devices, that is, by its own special *vraisemblance*' (Culler, *Structuralist Poetics*, 147); and Hamon, 'Clausules', 500: 'Chaque genre développe ses propres clausules, qui lui servent d'indicatif, de leitmotiv signalétique', and 'On pourrait envisager de classer les genres selon leur manière de *distribuer* et d'*expliciter* un certain nomre de signaux démarcatifs à des endroits prédeterminés.'

[158] Hirsch, *Validity in Interpretation*, 115.   [159] Hirsch, 'Intrinsic Genres', in ibid. 78–89.

[160] Ibid. 78.   [161] Ibid. 100, 126, and 113.   [162] Genette, *Seuils*, 270.

[163] On framing-devices and 'utterance', see also Hamon, 'Clausules', 501 and 513.

absolutely necessary for and constitutive of what we call art, poetry or literature',
is inherently subversive.[164] Derrida considers the paradox of the paratext and of the
frame generally already to be inherent in its liminal position on the margins of any
text at any point in time. This 'absolute' paradox has to do with self-reflexivity or
self-presentation, with *mise en abyme*, with the fact, more specifically, that a part
detaches itself to frame a whole to which it belongs. The consequence of this view
for the notion of the 'Montaignian essay' is indisputable. If there is something
about the frame or the act of framing which is inherently paradoxical, then the
modal excess which drives the *Essais* beyond themselves is no longer made to apply
simply to the modern essay, or to the other texts or genres of the periods under
consideration on the basis that they tend to present all the characteristic features
of the essay (as implied in Compagnon and Genette's positions). It concerns all
texts or genres without exception. In Derrida's work, the mechanism which underlies this whole question of the paradox of the frame, of the paratext, and finally of
genre—since framing and paratextuality ultimately have to do with genre—is that
of the parergon, the very parergon with which Lukács identifies the essay at the
end of his 'On the Nature and Form of the Essay'. In Lukács, the parergon is
expressly associated with Schopenhauer; yet, as Derrida's own essay testifies, the
parergon is a fundamental notion in the work of that other philosopher whose
influence is felt at every level of Lukács's text (and of German writings on the
essay generally)—Kant himself, and especially the Kant of the *Critique of Judgment*. This third 'Critique' is the text which most directly tackles the question of
the unity of aesthetic experience. In it Kant attempts to delimit or 'frame' aesthetic
from cognitive judgements, and—as Derrida himself recapitulates—'identifies in
art . . . one of the middle terms [*Mitten*] for resolving [*auflösen*] the "opposition"
between mind and nature, internal and external phenomena, the inside and the
outside, etc.'.[165] Nevertheless, according to Hegel via whom Derrida launches his
discussion, this attempted reconciliation 'still suffer[s] from a lacuna, a "lack" '
which Hegel sees as his task to 'supplement' with his own *Lectures on Aesthetics*.
Derrida, who proposes to examine this lack, presents the problem as the 'question
of the immense abyss [*abîme*] which separates the two worlds [nature and mind]'
and of the possibility or impossibility of 'throwing a bridge from one shore to
the other'.[166] One assumes that 'there must surely be an analogy between two
absolutely heterogeneous worlds, a third term to cross the abyss, to heal over the
gaping wound and think the gap' [*un tiers pour passer l'abîme, cicatriser la béance et
penser l'écart*].[167] Yet 'thinking the gap', precisely, is problematic; for where is one
supposed to 'think' it from: what, in other words, is the status of a philosophical

---

[164] 'What interests me is that this re-mark—ever possible for every text, for every corpus of traces—
is absolutely necessary for and constitutive of what we call art, poetry or literature' (Jacques Derrida,
'The Law of Genre', *Glyph*, 7 (1980), 211 ['La Loi du genre', in *Parages* (1986), 263]).
[165] Jacques Derrida, 'The Parergon', Part I, in *The Truth in Painting* (1987), 35 ['Le Parergon', in *La
Vérité en peinture* (1978), 42].
[166] Ibid. 36 [43].   [167] Ibid.

discourse on art, given the role ascribed here to art? For Derrida, the paradox which operates here as everywhere is that of reflexivity, of self-representation or *mise en abyme* (the 'abyss'), the fact that 'philosophy, which in this book has to think art through . . . as a part of its field or of its edifice, is here *representing itself* as a part of its part'. It is the paradox which arises when something (a painting,[168] a discourse) 'detaches from itself a proxy, a part of itself beside itself in order to think the whole, to saturate or heal over the whole that suffers from detachment'.[169] Given that the entire analysis of aesthetic judgement presupposes that one be permanently able rigorously to distinguish what is intrinsic from what is extrinsic, 'where', Derrida asks, 'does the frame take place. Does it take place? Where does it begin? Where does it end? What is its internal limit? Its external limit?'. The answer, already anticipated in these questions, is that this delimitation is impossible, for the frame is itself relative to what it defines. The cognitive is only articulated with respect to the aesthetic: thus in Kant 'the philosophy of art presupposes an art of philosophizing'.[170] Against Formalist and Jakobsonian views also endorsed by Genette, framing or the self-referential nature of poetic language are anything but an effective means of differentiating literature and keeping it 'outside' philosophy and vice versa. The frame perfectly illustrates the logic of the parergon; it is a parergon,[171] if one respects the definition of the majority of dictionaries which, according to Derrida, 'most often give "hors-d'œuvre", which is the strictest translation, but also "accessory", "foreign or secondary object", "supplement", "aside", "remainder" ' [*supplément, à-côté, reste*]. Contrary to what the French word *hors-d'œuvre* denotes, the parergon 'does not simply stand outside the work' but 'also act[s] alongside it, right up against the work' or *ergon*: 'A parergon comes against, beside, and in addition to the *ergon*, the work done [*fait*], the fact [*le fait*], the work, but it does not fall to one side, it touches and cooperates within the operation, from a certain outside.'[172] The parergon 'inscribes something which comes as an extra' which is 'exterior to the proper field'; but it is essential to see that this 'transcendent exteriority', which 'comes to play, abut onto, brush against, rub, press against the limit itself', 'intervenes in the inside only to the extent that the inside is lacking', that 'it is lacking *in* something and it is lacking *from itself*'.[173] In other words,

---

[168] Kant's speculations on picture-frames and ornaments (the link between garment and statues, column and building) in art in his *Critique of Judgment* take up the best part of Derrida's essay.

[169] Derrida, 'The Parergon', Part II, 41 ['détache d'elle-même un mandataire, une partie d'elle-même auprès d'elle-même pour penser le tout, saturer ou cicatriser le tout qui souffre de détachement', 'Le Parergon', 48].

[170] Ibid. ['La philosophie de l'art suppose un art de philosopher', 'Le Parergon', 48].

[171] Ibid. 60 ['Le cadre: *parergon* comme les autres', 'Le Parergon', 71].

[172] Ibid. 54 ['Un *parergon* vient contre, à côté et en plus de l'*ergon*, du travail fait, du fait, de l'œuvre, mais il ne tombe pas à côté, il touche et coopère, depuis un certain dehors, au-dedans de l'opération', 'Le Parergon', 63].

[173] Ibid. 56 ['dont l'extériorité transcendante ne vient jouer, jouxter, frôler, frotter, presser la limite elle-même et intervenir dans le dedans que dans la mesure où le dedans manque. Il manque *de* quelque chose et *se* manque à lui-même', 65].

what constitutes them as *parerga* is not simply their exteriority as a surplus, it is the internal structural link which rivets them to the lack in the interior of the *ergon*. And this lack would be constitutive of the very unity of the *ergon*. Without this lack, the *ergon* would have no need of a *parergon*.[174]

The frame 'labors' or 'gives' [*travaille*]. It is a 'place of labor', a 'structurally bordered origin of surplus value, i.e., overflowed on these two borders by what it overflows'. Thus the frame inevitably dislocates and overruns what it frames. As a result, '*there is* frame, but the frame does not exist' [*Il y a du cadre, mais le cadre n'existe pas*].[175]

So Derrida's logic of parergonality destroys the mutual exteriority which Genette and Compagnon hold on to and turns the 'aspect of textuality' or the 'paratextual' (literariness in the 'worst' sense) into the supplement which always already determines and undermines the paratext from within. The paratext is the 'external' manifestation of an internal and intrinsic overrun—the difference of the text from itself—which is constitutive of all texts. Every text, like Montaigne's *Essais*, is 'contaminated and pluralized, from the very outset, by its potential glosses', for 'every text has a reserve of additional meaning that overflows any reading of it, and permits its use in a variety of contexts'.[176] The paratext, then, is always the *emblème supernuméraire* that it was in Montaigne, since self-reflexivity is endemically incompatible with the self-identity and above all with the self-presence to which it aspires, with the aim to 'present the text in order to make it present' [*présenter le texte, pour le rendre présent*].[177] It is fitting, therefore, that Derrida's essay 'Outwork' ['Hors-livre'] on the most representative paratext of the preface, which is itself supposed to function as the preface to the book *Dissemination*, should begin with a denial both of the book and of the beginning ('This (therefore) will not have been a book'). The preface is the parergon most readily associated with intention, unification, totalization, and mastery; yet, as shown in the *Essais*, it has 'always incribed itself in a strange warp of both time and space':[178]

From the viewpoint of the fore-word, which recreates an intention-to-say after the fact, the text exists as something written—a past—which, under the false appearance of a present, a hidden omnipotent author (in full mastery of his product) is presented to the reader as his future. . . . The *pre* of the preface makes the future present, represents it, draws it closer,

[174] Derrida, 'The Parergon', Part II, 59–60 ['Le Parergon', 69].

[175] Ibid. 75 and 81 ['Le cadre travaille en effet. Lieu de travail, origine structurellement bordée du plus de valeur, c'est-à-dire débordée sur ces deux bords par ce qu'elle déborde, il travaille en effet. Comme le bois. Il craque, se détraque, se disloque alors même qu'il coopère à la production du produit, le déborde et s'en déduit', 87 and 93].

[176] Terence Cave, *The Cornucopian Text: Problems of Writing in the French Renaissance* (1979), 315; and Steven Rendall, 'In Disjointed Parts/*Par articles decousus*', in Laurence Kritzman (ed.), *Fragments: Incompletion and Discontinuity* (1981), 82.

[177] Genette, *Seuils*, 7.

[178] Introductory note to the English translation of *Dissemination* (1981) by Barbara Johnson, 'Outwork, or Disseminating Prefacing', p. xxxii.

breathes it in, and in going ahead of it puts it ahead. The *pre* reduces the future to the form of manifest presence.[179]

The attempt, then, is to 'cancel out the textual displacement which is at work "here" '.[180] But since—as Antoine Compagnon also points out—the preface can only be 'in the conditional' ('this is what I would like to have said'), since the 'real preface would have to be the rewriting of the book', the preface (and by extension the paratext in general) 'is a fiction':[181]

Prefaces, along with forewords, introductions, preludes, preliminaries, preambles, prologues and prolegomena, have always been written, it seems, in view of their own self-effacement. Upon reaching the end of the *pre-* (. . .), the route which has been covered must cancel itself out [*le trajet doit en son terme s'annuler*].[182]

Predictably, however, 'this subtraction leaves a mark of erasure, a *remainder* which is added to the subsequent text and which cannot be completely summed up within it'. In so far as it 'preced[es] what ought to be able to present itself on its own', the preface 'falls like an empty husk, a piece of formal refuse, a moment of dryness or loquacity, sometimes both at once'.[183] For Derrida, the philosophical preface is a case in point since 'philosophical exposition has as its essence the capacity and even the duty to do without a preface'. In this respect, his own exploitation of the space of the preface to discuss the *impossibility* of the (philosophical) preface reflects the practice of that master among masters of philosophical exposition—Hegel—whose relationship to prefaces constitutes the main focus of Derrida's essay. In his famous *Introduction [Einleitung]* to the *Phenomenology of Spirit* already referred to in Chapter 1 (and which is itself supposed to function as a preface introducing the *Logic*, in turn to become one part of the *Encyclopedia of Philosophical Sciences*), Hegel states that if the preface is 'an explanation of the author's aim', then 'in the case of a philosophical work, such an explanation seems not only superfluous but, in view of the subject-matter, even inappropriate and misleading'.[184] As a matter of fact, 'for a philosophical text as such, a preface is neither useful nor even possible', for it is 'the site of a kind of chit-chat external to the very thing it appears to be talking about': the preface is in other words 'left high and dry by the philosophical process which acts for itself as its own *presentation*'; in remaining external to the self-movement of truth, it can only be 'both

---

[179] Derrida, 'Outwork', *Dissemination*, 7 ['Le *pré* de la préface rend présent l'avenir, le représente, le rapproche, l'aspire et en le devançant le met devant. Il le réduit à la forme de la présence manifeste', 'Hors-livre', 13].

[180] Ibid. 7 [13].

[181] 'Le conditionnel est inhérent au genre car la seule vraie préface, dont toute préface tient lieu, serait la récriture du livre. La préface, telle que Descartes en posa les termes, est un genre impossible ('Voici ce que j'aurais voulu dire')' (Compagnon, *La Seconde Main*, 344); and Derrida, 'Outwork', 36 ['Hors-livre', 42].

[182] Ibid. 9 [14].

[183] Ibid. ['elle tombe comme une écorce vide et un déchet formel, moment de la sécheresse et du bavardage, parfois l'un et l'autre ensemble', 14 and 15].

[184] Ibid. 9–10 [15].

negated and internalized in the presentation of philosophy by itself, in the self-production and self-determination of the concept'.[185] The work's identity-to-itself is undermined in so far as its 'liminal space' is 'opened up by an inadequation between the form and the content of discourse or by an incommensurability between the signifier and the signified'.[186] For Derrida, this incommensurability—the introduction of 'excess' [*débord*] which results here in a philosophy 'beside itself'—only demonstrates that 'semantic saturation is impossible', that 'the gap between the empty "form", and the fullness of "meaning" is structurally irremediable'.[187] This said, the logic itself which governs the simultaneous impossibility and necessity of the preface in Hegel's work—and especially in relation to the *Phenomenology of Spirit*—cannot simply be dismissed; for 'Hegel, too, allows for the insistence of a certain gap between the form and content', that is, 'between what he calls certainty and what he calls truth'.[188] The *Phenomenology of Spirit*, as I recapitulated it in Chapter 1, is in fact the very history of this inadequation between signifier and signified, of the negative struggle involved in the concept's difference from itself, in the 'certain spacing between concept and existence', between 'thought and time'.[189] The indispensability of the foreword, the 'necessity of prefaces', Derrida reminds us, stems from the fact that 'culture must be fought, or rather "formed" [*gebildet*] better'; that it 'belongs to the *Bildung*'.[190] In other words,

> this struggle appears to be external to philosophy since it takes place rather in a didactic setting than within the self-presentation of a concept. But it is internal to philosophy to the extent that, as the Preface also says, the exteriority of the negative (falsehood, evil, death) still belongs to the process of truth and must leave its trace upon it.[191]

Self-essaying—and the preface is the most conspicuous site of this self-essaying—is inherent in Hegel's speculative philosophy, a philosophy which 'proscribes the preface as empty form and as signifying precipitation' but 'prescribes it, on the other hand, insofar as it is in the preface that meaning *announces itself*, philosophy being always already engaged in the Book'.[192] We know that speculative dialectic must overcome 'the opposition between form and content', the 'discrepancy between production and exposition', the 'anteriority or belatedness of form', the 'exteriority of content', so that 'tautology and heterology would be coupled together in the

---

[185] Derrida, 'Outwork', 11, 10, and 11 respectively ['A un texte philosophique en tant que tel une préface n'est ni utile ni même possible'; 'C'est le lieu d'une causerie extérieure à cela même dont elle entend parler'; 'Reste-t-elle en rade du procès philosophique qui est à lui-même sa propre *présentation?*', 'Hors-livre', 16; and 'à la fois niée et interiorisée dans la présentation de la philosophie par elle-même, dans l'auto-production et l'auto-détermination du concept', 'Hors-livre', 16–17].

[186] Ibid. 18 ['L'espace liminaire est donc ouvert par une inadéquation entre la forme et le contenu du discours ou par une incommensurabilité du signifiant au signifié', 25].

[187] Ibid. 20–1 [27].   [188] Ibid. 21 [28].   [189] Ibid. 12 [18].

[190] Ibid. 11–12 [17].   [191] Ibid. 12 [17].

[192] Ibid. 28–9 ['La philosophie spéculative proscrit donc la préface en tant que forme vide et précipitation signifiante; elle la prescrit pour autant que le sens s'y *annonce*, qu'elle est toujours déjà engagée dans le Livre', 35].

speculative proposition' and the 'analytic procedure and the synthetic procedure would mutually envelop each other'. Only then will the concept present itself 'in its own words, in its own voice, in its logos'.[193] But for Derrida, of course, the *Phenomenology*—and the whole of Hegel's enterprise—can only ever remain the narrative or tale (and 'recital') of 'an infinite preface'.[194] Art, historically, is only supposed to be a propaedeutic to a metaphysical Dialectic, or a dialectical Metaphysic, yet nothing can ever check the self-essaying, the 'chatter' of Writing or Literature, the movement of *différance* described as a 'productive', conflictual movement which cannot be preceded by any identity, any unity, or any original simplicity; which cannot be 'relieved', 'resolved', or 'appeased' by any philosophical dialectic.[195] What Derrida's 'disseminating prefacing' underscores, ultimately, is that self-reflection is endemically alien to self-identity, that 'all theoretical discourse—including [Derrida's] own—forever remains both belated and precipitous with respect to the textual practice it attempts to comprehend'.[196]

The paradigmatic paratext of the preface brings out the inability of the text—*any* text—to account for itself, thus proving the 'a-genericity' of all texts, an idea developed in 'The Law of Genre' ['La loi du genre'],[197] in which Derrida takes the logic of the parergon ('the overflow of a re-mark'[198]) to its expected conclusion. The impossibility of the preface as a genre—the genre associated with generic contracts—marks the impossibility of the paratext as a genre, and must ultimately reflect the impossibility of the concept of genre itself. Derrida's 'The Law of Genre' takes up the question raised in relation to the preface in 'Outwork': 'What is the *status* of a text when it *itself* carries itself away and marks itself down [*se démarque lui-même*]?'—this time with reference to Blanchot's narrative *La folie du jour*. The question of genre is the clearest instance of the paradox elaborated previously, of what Derrida variously calls 'participation without belonging' or 'membership', the 'law of excess' [*La loi de débordement*] or the 'law of impurity', the 'principle of contamination', all features of a 'parasitical economy' [*une économie du parasite*].[199] Given the 'excess of the re-mark', that which asserts or manifests class membership is not itself a member of that class. As a result, though it always participates in genre, a text belongs to no genre, because the frame or trait that marks its belonging does not itself belong. The 'topos' of genre again 'gathers together the corpus and, at the same time, in the same blinking of an eye, keeps it from closing, from identifying itself with itself'. In a nutshell: 'Making genre its mark, a text demarcates itself' [*En se marquant de genre, un texte s'en démarque*]: there is 'genre'

---

[193] Ibid. 22, 30–1 [28 and 37].
[194] Ibid. 21 ['Le récit d'une préface infinie', 28, which is translated as 'recital', the disadvantage being that this does away with the idea of narrative, central to the *Phenomenology*].
[195] Ibid. 6–7 [12].
[196] Johnson, 'Outwork, or Disseminating Prefacing', p. xxxiii.
[197] In *Glyph*, 7 (1980), 202–29, and in *Parages*.
[198] Derrida, 'Outwork', 21 ['L'excès d'une re-marque', 'Hors-livre', 28].
[199] Derrida, 'The Law of Genre', 206 and 210 ['La Loi du genre', 256 and 262].

or 'genres' [*du genre* and *des genres*] rather than a genre, in the same way that there is 'framing' [*du cadre*] rather than a frame.[200] German Romanticism, and German idealist aesthetics more generally, are particularly central *topoi* to Derrida's exposition of the absolute paradox of the paratext 'beyond genre'. The 'law of impurity' or the 'principle of contamination' discussed above is identified with a generic excess which is simultaneously a 'mixture of genres' and a generic 'dissolution':

Romanticism, if something of the sort can be thus identified, is also the general repetition of all the folds that in themselves gather, couple, divide *physis* as well as *genos* through the genre, and through all the genres of genre, through the mixing of genre that is 'more than a genre', through the excess of genre in relation to itself, as to its abounding movement and its general assemblage which coincides, too, with its dissolution.[201]

'Modernist' philosophical and literary texts which in one way or another foreground the question of their frame, or of the relationship between text and genre[202] (as in Kant, Hegel, Rousseau, Nietzsche, Heidegger, or Mallarmé, Blanchot, Ponge, and Leiris), are favoured. And in typically Romantic vein, Derrida turns those texts which most explicitly partake of the paradoxical 'Genre of genres' or the 'Genre of Literature' ('It is possible to have several genres, an intermixing of genres or a total genre, the genre "genre" or the poetic or literary genre as genre of genres'[203]) into a symptom of the a-genericity of all texts, in the same way that after historically distinguishing Romantic from classical texts, the German Romantics end up applying the definition of Romantic literature to all literature.[204] Correspondingly, the theory of the fragment which embodies the conceptualization of a-genericity also becomes in Derrida the generalized theory of all 'Literature' or 'Writing'. All texts without exception are by definition fragments, paratexts, parerga, 'essays'; they are all 'open-ended, neotenous texts which are the disconnected entries and prospective fragments of a Book-yet-to-come'. All literature is 'potential literature', whereby the notion of 'potentiality' recognizably becomes the mark of Literature itself, since it bears within it the infinite deferment of *différance*. All texts are

---

[200] Derrida, 'The Law of Genre', 212 ['Il rassemble le corpus et du même coup, du même clin d'oeil, il l'empêche de s'identifier à lui-même'; and 'Un texte ne saurait *appartenir* à aucun genre. Tout genre *participe* d'un ou de plusieurs genres, il n'y a pas de texte sans genre, il y a toujours du genre et des genres', 'La loi du genre', 264–5].

[201] Ibid. 208 ['tous les genres du genre, le mélange du genre qui est "plus qu'un genre", l'excès de genre, l'excès du genre par rapport à lui-même, son débordement, son rassemblement général à la fois et sa dissolution', 259].

[202] See Jean-Marie Schaeffer, 'Du texte au genre: Notes sur la problématique générique', *Poétique*, 53 (1983), 3–18.

[203] Derrida, 'The Law of Genre', 211 ['Il peut s'agir de plusieurs genres, d'un mélange de genres ou du genre total, du genre "genre" ou du genre poétique ou littéraire comme genre des genres', 'La Loi du genre', 263].

[204] 'In a certain sense all poetry is or should be romantic', Friedrich Schlegel, *Athenäum Fragments*, 116, p. 47 ['denn in einem gewissen Sinn ist oder soll alle Poesie romantisch sein', *Athenäums-Fragmente*, p. 39].

rewritings of other texts caught up in the process of the endless 'interglossing' [*entreglose*] described by Montaigne.[205]

3.3. POSTSCRIPT: PARATEXTUAL CRITICISM

If the inherently paradoxical logic of the frame summarized above is so familiar, this is because it pervades modern literary criticism and has turned, ironically, into its underlying *doxa*. Vincent Leitch's schematization of the situation is an accurate report of how things are perceived in the field:

There are two texts: the old and the new. The old 'text' possesses a title, margins, signature (author), a beginning, an end, overall unity, and limited content. Outside its frame lies a 'referential realm'. . . . All these boundaries, frames, divisions, limits—*borders*—mark out and enclose the old 'text', making it a very special and highly differentiated entity and object. Since the late 1960s, however, a new *text* has come to our attention. It touches and tampers with—it changes and spoils—all the old boundaries, frames, divisions, and limits. The identity of 'text' alters. The overrun of all the old borders forces us to rethink the 'text'.[206]

In short, our post-structuralist age is one in which the world has become 'an infinite, borderless text'.[207] The difference itself between the structuralist and post-structuralist positions on 'thresholds' is not so much an opposition—as it first appears—as a difference in emphasis. In actual fact, the exteriority which Genette and Compagnon seem to be able to maintain between 'class of text' and 'aspect of textuality', between the ideal transparency of the literary work and the perverse

---

[205] Useful secondary criticism and further reading for this (superficial) discussion of Derrida as a whole includes: Jonathan Culler, *On Deconstruction: Theory and Criticism after Structuralism* (1983); Christopher Norris, *Deconstruction: Theory and Practice* (1982); Vincent Leitch, *Deconstructive Criticism: An Advanced Introduction* (1983); Harold Bloom *et al.* (eds.), *Deconstruction and Criticism* (1979); Mark Krupnick (ed.), *Displacement: Derrida and After* (1983); John Llewelyn, *Derrida on the Threshold of Sense* (1986); David Carroll, *Paraesthetics: Foucault, Lyotard, Derrida* (1987); Juliet Sychrava, *Schiller to Derrida: Idealism in Aesthetics* (1989); Hilary Lawson, *Reflexivity: The Post-Modern Predicament* (1985); Rodolphe Gasché, *The Tain of the Mirror: Derrida and the Philosophy of Reflection* (1986); David Wood, *Philosophy at the Limit* (1990); Barbara Johnson, *The Critical Difference: Essays in the Contemporary Rhetoric of Reading* (1980); Stephen W. Melville, *Philosophy Beside Itself* (1986); Berel Lang, *The Anatomy of Philosophical Style: Literary Philosophy and the Philosophy of Literature* (1990); (as well as works by Geoffrey Hartman, Paul de Man, Jean-Jacques Lecercle, Michel de Certeau, François Laruelle, Jean-Louis Galay, Sören Gosvig Olesen, Christopher Butler, Eugene Goodheart, see Bibliography). Articles or essays include: Richard Rorty, 'Philosophy as a Kind of Writing: An Essay on Derrida', in *Consequences of Pragmatism: Essays: 1972–1980* (1982); Jean-Luc Nancy, 'Logodaedalus (Kant écrivain)', *Poétique*, 21 (1975), 24–52; Philippe Lacoue-Labarthe, 'La Fable', *Poétique*, 1 (1970), 51–63; 'Le Détour (Nietzsche et la rhétorique)', *Poétique*, 5 (1971), 53–76; and 'L'Imprésentable' *Poétique*, 21 (1975), 53–95; Denis Kambouchner, 'Le Labyrinthe de la présentation' *Critique*, 368 (1978), 41–62; Jean-Marie Schaeffer, 'Note sur la préface philosophique', *Poétique*, 69 (1987), 35–44; and collections of essays such as Josué V. Harari, *Textual Strategies: Perspectives in Post-Structuralist Criticism* (1979) or Robert Young, *Untying the Text: A Post-Structuralist Reader* (1981).

[206] Leitch, *Deconstructive Criticism*, 118–19.   [207] Ibid. 118.

effects of paratextuality characteristic of realist versus modernist periods, is not so clear-cut, if only because the paratext is presented as both these things simultaneously. Genette's approach to the paratext in *Seuils* is mainly taxonomic; it aims at a synchronic definition, not at a history of the paratext, as he himself declares at the end of his introduction.[208] It is out of this synchronic definition and articulation of the field of the paratext, however, that the acknowledgement of its inherently paradoxical status as a class of text and an aspect of textuality emerges, which is then said to be determined by the historical perspective itself. So it is as though the historical actualization of the paratextual overrun exemplified by Montaigne's *Essais* were turned into the retrospective justification for a (potential) paradox which Genette presents synchronically. Compagnon's parallel presentation of the paradox of the paratext in terms of a historical perspective, that is to say from a certain 'outside', is equally ambiguous, as we find out when confronting the question, again, of the relationship between diachronic and synchronic approach in the book. This time, the diachronic (the chronological survey of the second part entitled '*Généalogie*' and '*Tératologie*') is supposed to have priority over the synchronic (the typology of quotation of the first part—'*Phénoménologie*' and '*Sémiologie*'). In the foreword, we are told that the purpose is not to analyse quotation in itself but to explore the various discourses [*entregloses*] in which it is exposed;[209] and this justifies the chronological surveys [*sondages*] of which not only Montaigne's *Essais*, but also Borges's work as a whole, are a very significant instance. For 'the whole of Borges's work is a game which systematically perverts the classical economy of writing': 'each one of his texts actualizes one particular perigraphical anomaly' and conversely, 'there must be a Borgesian tale that illustrates every possible anomaly'.[210] But the prevalence of the empirical over the formal undertaking has earlier been sustained by Compagnon's 'confession' that it is Borges's exploration of the 'perversions of quotation', in fact, which underlies his (Compagnon's) entire project of looking for—and even inventing—the structure of 'normal' quotation.[211] And to confirm this, the whole first part of the book is a theoretical description of the force of displacement which all quotation, as repetition, necessarily involves; hence the subtitle of the book '*le travail de la citation*'.[212] Because of this 'labour', or force of displacement, a quotation is presented from the outset as always inducing the very 'excess' or perversion of the 'paratextual' (the essayistic). A quotation cannot be abstracted from the 'overrun' implied in the act of quoting itself: this overrun is simply more or less noticeable depending on the 'value' which is foregrounded.[213] So the centring of the text by the paratext is but the foregrounding of the class of text over the aspect of

---

[208] Genette, *Seuils*, 18.   [209] Compagnon, *La Seconde Main*, 11.

[210] Ibid. 370.   [211] Ibid. 364.

[212] Cf. the first page of the foreword: 'le produit de la force qui saisit la citation par le déplacement qu'elle lui fait subir' (ibid. 9).

[213] Thus the full regulating and closing role of the paratext, of which the author is the centre, coincides with the *priority* of the iconic value: 'L'auteur est le *denotatum* de la périgraphie, du titre et de la citation, dès lors qu'il ont une valeur prioritaire de signes iconiques' (ibid. 331).

textuality which always underlies and somehow undermines it.[214] Montaigne's famous phrase 'all we do is gloss each other' is itself quoted on the first page of the foreword, to illustrate this idea of 'displacement', of the 'labour' or 'give' of quotation within the synchronic perspective, with the comment that 'all writing is gloss and intergloss [*glose et entreglose*], all utterance [*énonciation*] repeats'.[215] The distinction which Genette and Compagnon try to hold onto between 'class of texts' (the main function of the paratext) and 'aspect of textuality' (its peripheral aspect) succumbs in other words to the perverse effects of the logic of parergonality which they strive to keep 'outside'.

Whether from a post-structuralist or a structuralist perspective, then, the interest in the paratext as a distinct genre which upgrades it from the periphery to the centre of literary studies (and which also goes hand in hand with the typically essayistic concern with marginal texts, genres, or authors) paradoxically leads to a repeated emphasis on its lack of specificity: the distinctiveness of the paratext—the fact that it stands out—is of interest only in so far as it is shown to be the concrete embodiment or manifestation of an internal, textual lack. None the less in the difference between structuralist and post-structuralist priorities still suffices to justify a difference in methodology. Genette and Compagnon's choice to believe in the possibility of a metalinguistic paratext allows them to write about or 'frame' the paratext from an external vantage-point, and so to avoid the philosophical essayists's highly self-conscious approach which Genette rates as 'paratextual coquetry [*coquetterie paratextuelle*[216]]'. This applies notably to the form of post-structuralist criticism which I introduced in my first chapter as 'paratextual criticism' and which includes especially Derrida's 'Tympan', *Glas*, and 'Living On: Borderlines', all of which are commentaries in the form of a marginal gloss or footnotes. In the case of 'Tympan' and *Glas*, two discourses appear side by side on the same page, whereas in 'Survivre', one discourse runs beneath the other. Geoffrey Hartman, one of the main exponents of Yale deconstruction, sees in Derrida's *Glas* (which confronts Hegel and Genet) the appropriate illustration and continuity of Lukács's conception of the essay.[217] As I suggested in Chapter 1, one can in fact take this further and see these texts as variants and/or extreme versions of Montaigne's *Essais*. The conspicuous 'staging' of the 'line of exegesis' in Derrida's *Glas* points first of all to the space where criticism or the essay is seen to 'cross over' to literature. Geoffrey Hartman justifies the link which he establishes between Lukács's conception of the essay and what he calls 'philosophical criticism' with the remark that, if it is 'not entirely new', the 'fusion of creation with criticism' which he sees as occurring in the writings of contemporary critics, 'is now methodically pursued'. And those critics who pursue it (above all Derrida, Adorno, or Benjamin) are 'not creative writers in the accepted sense of that phrase', that is, neither poets nor novelists; yet their work nevertheless 'stands in a complex and even crossover

[214] Cf. 'La périgraphie met un terme au débat, au délire quant à l'utilisation du déjà dit' (ibid. 349).
[215] Ibid. 9.   [216] Genette, *Seuils*, 218.
[217] In his 'Literary Commentary as Literature', in *Criticism in the Wilderness*.

relation to both art and philosophy'.[218] Hartman cónfesses to being struck by the remarkable anticipation, in Lukács's essay on the essay, of the questions raised by Derrida and other 'philosophic critics' with regard to 'the proper relations between "critical" and "creative" activities, or between "primary" and "secondary" texts'. Before and like them, Lukács 'does not accept subordination as a defining characteristic of the essay' and explores 'the uneasy coexistence, in essays, of their referential function as commentary with their ambition to *be* literature and not only about it'.[219] Like them, Lukács is concerned with the question as to 'whether any critic has value who is only a critic: who does not put us in the presence of "critical fictions" or make us aware of them in the writings of others'.[220] Hartman's further remark that 'though the irony described by Lukács may formally subdue the essay to a given work, a reversal must be possible whereby this "secondary" piece of writing turns out to be "primary"'',[221] is a reminder that irony, in Lukács, also underlies this very reversal: 'there is no mysticism'—Hartman writes in his conclusion—'only irony, in the fact that literary commentary today is creating texts—a literature—of its own'.[222] On the whole, then, Hartman sees literary commentary as 'an unpredictable or unstable genre that cannot be subordinated, a priori, to its referential or commentating function':

the perspectival power of criticism, its strength of recontextualization, must be such that the critical essay should not be considered a supplement to something else . . . the 'speculative instruments' of criticism 'are now exercising their own textual powers rather than performing, explaining, or reifying existing texts'.[223]

The paratext being an 'uncertain zone between inside and outside, a zone without a rigorous limit either towards the inside (the text) or towards the outside (the world's discourse on the text)',[224] the essay as paratextual criticism conspicuously develops between the outside and the inside of the work which it comments upon. In Hartman's terms, 'criticism as commentary *de linea* . . . crosses the line and changes to one *trans lineam*', so that the commentator's discourse 'cannot be neatly or methodically separated from that of the author: the relation is contaminated and chiastic; source text and secondary text, though separable, enter into a mutually supportive, mutually dominating relation.'[225] The way in which the logic of the parergon (the paradoxical 'para') or what Derrida calls 'parasitical economy' operates in a specifically critical context has been spelt out most clearly by another deconstructionist 'on the wild side', J. Hillis Miller, in his now classic 'The Critic as Host'.[226] By exploiting the etymology of the 'para' of 'parasite', Hillis Miller shows how the meanings of allegedly opposed concepts (e.g. the critic, on one side

[218] Hartman, 'Literary Commentary as Literature', 190 and 191.
[219] Ibid. 189, 191, and 196.   [220] Ibid. 201.   [221] Ibid.
[222] Ibid. 213 (final sentence of the text).   [223] Ibid. 201–2.   [224] Genette, *Seuils*, 8.
[225] Hartman, 'Literary Commentary as Literature', 206.
[226] In Bloom *et al.* (eds.), *Deconstruction and Criticism*. See Christopher Norris, 'Deconstruction "on the wild side": Geoffrey Hartman and J. Hillis Miller', in *Deconstruction: Theory and Practice* (1982), 92.

of the dividing line, and the host on the other) overlap with one another, each calling up their apparent opposite.[227] If the 'para' involves at once proximity and distance, similarity and difference, interiority and exteriority, something equivalent in status and also subsidiary, the relation between the critical text and the literary text 'cannot be encompassed by the ordinary logic of polar opposition'.[228] Both texts are 'each parasite and host for the other, each feeding on the other and feeding it, destroying and being destroyed by it'.[229] It is in the intrinsic property of the word 'para' that it is already 'fissured within itself', that this 'uncanny antithetical relation exists not only between pairs of words in this system, host and parasite, but within each word in itself': 'Each word in itself becomes divided by the strange logic of the 'para', membrane which divides inside from outside and yet joins them.'[230] The parergonal status of the critical text which is visibly situated between the inside and the outside of the text it comments upon rather than confronting it 'metalinguistically' from the 'outside', raises again the problem of totalization and self-identity central to the paradoxical logic of framing and paratextuality. Since according to Derrida 'there is nothing outside the text', given that one cannot reach outside the discursive framework under examination, the critical discourse, by operating 'paratextually' on its margin, demonstrates the impossibility of closing the text. For Derrida, 'the very possibility of reflexivity is also the subversion of its own source':[231] no absolute reading of a Hegelian kind is conceivable; if anything characterizes the text, and especially language, it is sheer indeterminacy or *différance*—on both sides, therefore, of the margin. The paratext is the visible space of the text's difference from itself, for the difference between the two sides of the critical relationship is the re-enactment of a difference within.[232] Because of the parergonal logic of the text which folds back upon itself like an 'invaginated pocket' so that the inside is granted a position of exteriority—so that, in other words, the external authority is shown to derive from a place inside—the critical discourse (the external gloss) cannot account for the text any more than the discourse of the text (the internal self-gloss) can account for itself. The point of 'immanent' or 'reflexive criticism', then, is that the 'primary' text, which is read ('deconstructed') in its own terms or 'turned back on itself', is seen to fall by its own criteria. By being reflexively applied to themselves, the original standards, definitions, or distinctions which ensure the coherence of the text find themselves 'unsettled' and 'shattered'.[233]

Hartman's reading of *Glas* illustrates the workings of the 'parasitical economy' described in Hillis Miller by showing that the recontextualisation of *Glas*—which deals reflexively with Genet's *Journal du voleur*—is 'a thievish book in essence'

[227] Hillis Miller, 'The Critic as Host', in Bloom *et al.* (eds.), *Deconstruction and Criticism* (1979), 219.
[228] Ibid. 224.   [229] Ibid. 249.   [230] Ibid. 221.
[231] Gasché, *The Tain of the Mirror*, 102.
[232] For this difference between as difference within, see also Barbara Johnson, *The Critical Difference: Essays in the Contemporary Rhetoric of Reading* (1980).
[233] See 'Reflexivity—as Critique', in the 'Derrida' ch. of Hilary Lawson, *Reflexivity: The Post-Modern Predicament* (1985), 93.

('*Glas*, then, is Derrida's own Journal du voleur'[234]), involving as it does the questioning of all properties, including, of course, the proper noun itself: 'Property, even in the form of the *nom propre*, is *non-propre*, and writing is an act of crossing the line of the text, of making it indeterminate.'[235] The mutual transgression and contamination of the discourses subvert the constructs associated with framing—origin, self, author, book, as well as the respective identities of 'criticism', 'philosophy' or 'literature':

It is not only hard to say whether *Glas* is 'criticism' or 'philosophy' or 'literature', it is hard to affirm it is a book. *Glas* raises the specter of texts so tangled, contaminated, displaced, deceptive that the idea of a single or original author fades . . . into the charged Joycean phrase: 'Jungfraud's messonge book'.[236]

In the post-structuralist jargon, this transgression and contamination of discourses by which 'the presence of Genet is not (even on the first page) restricted to one column' but 'crosses the line into the commentary on Hegel' thus 'quietly pervading the Hegel column',[237] is also encompassed by the metaphor of the 'graft' which consists in inserting one discourse into another, or intervening in the discourse one is interpreting.[238] It presents the reader with an extreme case of the essayistic strategies of interpolation and extrapolation described in relation to Montaigne. The particular typographical parade of the play with frames makes the destabilization (or suspension) of any one (type of) discourse immediately visible both intertextually and intratextually, the respective columns being divided not only vertically, but also horizontally by typographical cuts (changes of typeface) which convert the frames within the frames into as many 'rectangles within rectangles'.[239] Hartman's remark that

the critical essay today, to qualify as such, must contain some close-ups: it tends to proceed, in fact, by shifts of perspective (as in some kinds of sequential art or concrete poetry) that expose the non-homogeneity of the fact at hand, the arbitrariness of the knots that bind the work into a semblance of unity. The close-ups are not there merely to illustrate or reinforce a suppositious unity but to show what simplifications, or institutional processes, are necessary for achieving any kind of unitary, consensual view of the artifact[240]

is a reminder of the logic which also motivates what I described in the previous chapter as Montaigne's 'short-sighted' readings. Only here, the 'close-ups' are such that at every level, the (apparently random) disarticulation of the text, the playing of fragments against one another, the relentless 'grafting' of quotations, is

[234] Hartman, 'Literary Commentary as Literature', 205.
[235] Ibid. See also 'How to Reap a Page', in Hartmen, *Saving the Text: Literature/Derrida/Philosophy* (1981), 93.
[236] Hartman, 'Literary Commentary as Literature', 204.   [237] Ibid. 207.
[238] See 'Grafts and Graft', in Culler, *On Deconstruction*.
[239] See Hartman, 'How to Reap a Page', 85.
[240] Hartman, 'Literary Commentary as Literature', 196–7.

phrenetic. As in the *Essais*, the process of appropriation and disappropriation proves to be central to the recontextualization in *Glas*. But Derrida's radical use of 'contagion' and of 'the infinite circulation of general equivalence'[241] makes it virtually impossible to identify the exact nature of the interferences (echoes of all kinds) at work between the frames. The interrelationship of excess and lack of meaning observed in the *Essais* tends here towards 'zero signification', and displays therefore a drastic version of Montaignian scepticism. By dint of 'oversignifying', 'primary' and 'secondary' texts no longer signify anything at all: 'Here, of course'—Hartman writes—'the notion of transgression (of limits) and indeterminacy (of endlessly approaching the limit we call meaning) seem to merge'.[242] Hartman talks about 'difficult critics'; but the essayistic 'aesthetics of incomprehensibility' appears to be total.[243] The essayistic 'play', and the 'wandering' which is at the etymological roots of the genre, have turned into 'free play' and an 'errancy' which cannot, at any point, be gathered back. The exploration of the border between sense (the logic of conceptual discourse) and nonsense (the arbitrary 'play' of language), the play with hierarchy and direction that involves the reversals or denials typical of a 'discourse under erasure', leads in *Glas* to an exploitation of nonsense over sense which goes beyond the mere display of mutual dependency. Derrida's remark, towards the beginning of *Margins: Of Philosophy*, that 'such a play—*différance*—is no longer simply a concept, but the possibility itself of conceptuality, of the conceptual process and system generally',[244] is acted upon so 'literally' in *Glas*, that the associative, metaphorical (tropological) transgression of the conceptual order of discourse results in apparent delirium. The 'methodical pursuit'—described by Hartman elsewhere as the 'methodical madness of the cutting-up and agglutination against all decorum'[245]—is one obvious feature of this delirium. Everything in *Glas* is 'systematically' contaminated by equivocation, and the never-ending resonances and cross-wording create a dismemberment or 'dissemination' of parts of texts or language more appropriately referred to as 'stumps' [*moignons*] than as 'fragments'.[246]

In the end, Hartman's initial assumption that 'the perspectival power of criticism, its strength of recontextualization, must be such that the critical essay should not be considered a supplement to something else',[247] is ambivalent. For what the paratextual presentation of this 'crossing over' of literary commentary to literature shows, is that the 'power of recontextualisation', which makes a 'reversal' between

---

[241] See ibid. 207.   [242] Ibid.

[243] Cf. 'It may well be that some of the difficult critics of whom I speak (whether Adorno or Blackmur or Derrida)' (ibid. 198). For the recapitulation of the Romantic aesthetics of incomprehensibility, see my Ch. 1, Section 1.4.2.

[244] *Margins: Of Philosophy* (1982), 11 ['Un tel jeu, la différance, n'est plus alors simplement un concept mais la possibilité de la conceptualité, du procès et du système conceptuel en général', 'La Différance', *Marges: De la philosophie* (1972), 11].

[245] Hartman, 'How to Reap a Page', 72.   [246] See ibid. 79 and 85.

[247] Hartman, 'Literary Commentary as Literature', 202.

primary and secondary discourse possible,[248] is clearly (also) dependent upon this supplementariness. *Glas*, Hartman writes, 'reveals the vol-onto-theology of writing. Writing is always theft or bricolage in the logos. The theft redistributes the logos by a new principle of equity, as unreferable to laws of property, boundary etc.'[249] What the essay in this openly paratextual form acts out, more than ever, is the transition from a closed to an open-ended conception of intertextuality in which literary history is regarded as a series of 'footnotes' in the margins of already existing and future texts. Each text is a 'rehearsal' of other texts, in both the senses of the French 'repetition'. Each text, like Derrida's 'criticism', rewrites the text on either side of its margins, so that the 'interglossing' of essayism takes the form of notes simultaneously 'about' and 'towards' a text which is always 'in progress'. The 'reading-as-writing' involved in the act of essaying is therefore always but one of the actualizations of the potentially infinite number of virtual glosses which overrun the boundaries of each and every text. On the other hand, the staging of the limit in this way also warrants the claim to an 'originality' defined by Edward Said as a 'displacement'—illustrated literally here—'from inscription to parallel script' or from 'descendence' to 'adjacency', an originality which depends upon the 'anguish and self-scrutiny' of 'creative critics' or 'frustrated poets' who know, like Montaigne, that culture 'progresses by *contamination*'.[250] Hartman ultimately considers *Glas* as 'a creative testing and illumination of *limits*: the limits of what Hegel called "absolute knowledge" . . .'.[251] These limits are displaced indefinitely since, as *Glas* purports to show, 'there is no absolute knowledge but rather a textual infinite, an interminable web of texts and interpretations'.[252] Thus Derrida, whose allegiance to the German Romantics Hartman does not fail to point out, produces a 'counterencyclopedia', that is, 'a synthesis of *poetry* and *philosophy*' which can only take a fragmentary form'—a 'text', not a 'book'.[253] And for Hartman this counterencyclopedia is precisely what is meant by the notion of 'essayistic totality': 'the word *text* . . . means something quite specific: historically viewed, it is a development of the Romantic fragment, a sustained fragment as it were, or—seen from the Hegelian system of absolute knowledge—an essayistic totality.'[254] All the same, conceding that 'literary commentary may cross the line and become as demanding as literature' and that 'it is an unpredictable or unstable genre that cannot be subordinated, a priori, to its referential or commentating function', does not alter the fact, for Hartman, that 'commentary certainly remains one of the defining features (of the essay), for it is hardly useful to describe as "criticism" an essay that does not review in some way an existing book or other work'.[255] With *Glas*, however, one seems to be dealing with a text completely freed from any contextual commitment, as implied in the notion of 'criticism in the wilderness' which it is intended to exemplify. So it is questionable whether one can still talk about an 'essayistic totality' when, as in deconstruction, the negative effects of reflexivity are taken to

---

[248] Hartman, 'Literary Commentary as Literature', 201.   [249] Ibid. 205.
[250] Ibid. 198.   [251] Ibid. 202.   [252] Ibid.
[253] Ibid. 205, 211, and 212.   [254] Ibid. 212.   [255] Ibid. 201.

their limits. Indeed, the paradox inherent in the notion of 'essayistic totality' hardly seems able to survive when the tension between the 'strength of re-contextualization' of criticism and its 'referential' function—between what the essay 'does' and what it 'is', in Lukács's terms—is no longer relevant and the essay, stretched to its outermost limits, is made to represent the 'matrix of all generic possibilities'. For a less 'excessive' practice of essayism, one would therefore do well to turn to Roland Barthes's own (late) 'critical fictions' which, perhaps by virtue of their intermediate position between a structuralist and a post-structuralist approach, are clearly made to operate both at the level of writing and textuality, and within the economy of particular genres. In his work, the substitution of the encyclopedia for the novel anticipated by Schlegel[256] follows the Romantic usage of the encyclopedia as a 'system in fragments', that is, as a form that 'rejects the metaphysical-ontological implications of any type of absolute systematization on the one hand, but without altogether denying notions of totality and coherence on the other'.[257] Thus in his writings, which Réda Bensmaïa introduces as 'engaging in a sort of *generalized repetition* [*répétition générale*] of the movement that, from Montaigne's *Essays* to Maurice Blanchot's *L'Entretien infini* by way of the German Romantics, had sedulously contested the validity of reigning theories of genres',[258] the essay's difference from itself mobilizes both levels of the 'potentially Literary' and of the 'potentially literary'; it mobilizes fiction as the disseminating force of Derrida's *écriture* but it also involves the 'concretely' literary and fictional that still relies upon an opposition between the fictional and the non-fictional, and between the corresponding modes of enunciation and reception.

[256] 'In der nächsten Generation wird an die Stelle der Encyklopädie ein Roman treten', *Kritische Friedrich Schlegel Ausgabe*, ed. Ernst Behler, 35 vols. (Schöningh, 1958–), xviii. 364.
[257] See Behler 'The Early Romantic Notion of Encyclopedia', in *German Romantic Literary Theory*, 282–3.
[258] Réda Bensmaïa, *The Barthes Effect: The Essay as Reflective Text* (1987), p. xxvi.

4

The Glosses of Roland Barthes:
The Encyclopedic and the Novelistic

4.1. PLAYING WITH SYSTEMS

Although Barthes has produced several volumes of self-declared 'critical essays', critics tend to hesitate to refer to him as an essayist and prefer labels such as 'critic', 'mythologist', and perhaps above all 'semiologist'—as well, less flatteringly (but typically when categorizing essayists), as 'dandy' or 'minor writer'.[1] In practice, his texts are mostly referred to as 'essays' when their unclassifiability is emphasized. And this unclassifiability has to do both with form and with content, given the wide range of Barthes's concerns which include food, wrestling, toys, advertising, fashion, paintings, foreign countries, etc., as well as books. If these concerns have anything to do with essayism, however, this is above all in so far as they provide the various myths of mass culture for Barthes's counter-ideological pursuit. In this respect, the project of *Mythologies* is probably most representative of Barthes's enterprise as a whole, since in it Barthes purports to 'account *in detail* for the mystification which transforms petit-bourgeois culture into a universal nature', a transformation which he refers to as a 'mythic inversion'.[2] As an instrument of bourgeois ideology, 'myth' is a notion which for Barthes perfectly encapsulates the 'falsely obvious', what contributes to making 'innocent' the culture of the time, to 'purifying' it, to founding it as nature, 'suggesting and miming a universal economy' by subtracting it from all historical responsibility.[3] Myth has the task of 'making contingency appear eternal', so the role of the essayist is again to emphasize the need to historicize, to reinscribe myth in time, to 'interrogate historically, i.e. *relatively*, objects supposed to be most natural'.[4] As expected, the examination or 'trial' of the conditions of meaning of these myths involves unmasking the arbitrary techniques which legitimate and naturalize them, according to the idea that if ideology impregnates human life through and through, language

[1] Barthes often refers to himself as an essayist, and as a semiologist: 'pour ma part, je garderai le mot de "sémiologie", sans esprit de particularité et pour dénoter commodément l'ensemble d'un travail théorique varié' ('Avant-Propos' (1971) of Barthes *Essais Critiques*, 7).

[2] Roland Barthes, *Mythologies*, preface to the 1970 edn., 9 ['Rendre compte *en détail* de la mystification qui transforme la culture petite-bourgeoise en nature universelle', *Mythologies*, 7]; and Barthes, *The Rustle of Language* (1989), 65 [*Le Bruissement de la langue*, 79].

[3] See Barthes, *Mythologies*, 11, 141, 142, 143 [*Mythologies*, 8–9 and 230–1].

[4] Ibid. 142 [229]; and *Roland Barthes by Roland Barthes*, 'The Ethnological Temptation', 84 ['La Tentation ethnologique', 87].

is the least innocent category of all. Myth is a language, a 'type of speech chosen by history', and this justifies the fact that 'while concerning [himself] with phenomena apparently most unlike literature (a wrestling match, an elaborate dish, a plastics exhibition)', Barthes does not feel he is leaving the literary aspect of earlier essays behind.[5] Myth is 'a mode of signification, a form'; it can be described as 'a semiological system', semiology being a science of forms, the study of how language articulates and constructs the world.[6] Barthes's focus on 'the structure which society imposes, by writing it, upon a reality which it already structures by fabricating it', also justifies his combining the semiological enterprise with a revival of the interest in rhetoric, a field which seemed to have fallen by the wayside since the Renaissance.[7] 'It is through their rhetoric', Barthes points out, 'that bourgeois myths outline the general project of this *pseudo-physis* which defines the dream of the contemporary bourgeois world.'[8] Examining 'the rhetorical forms of bourgeois myth'[9]—the ways in which it articulates and mentally cuts up of the world—provides an obvious link between the miscellaneous objects of a work like *Mythologies*, and the logic of narrative (the 'rhetoric of fiction') which over the years constitutes a major focus for the anti-systematic motivation of Barthes's essays. *S/Z* and *Roland Barthes by Roland Barthes* (henceforth referred to simply as *Roland Barthes*) which will concern us here, both develop against narrative sequence: that of Balzac's short story *Sarrasine* for the former, and of the 'classical' autobiographical project for the latter. Narrative, as suggested in the previous chapters, is the most pertinent area for the examination of the mechanisms of the *doxa* ('the cultural (or discursive) mediation through which power speaks'[10]) and of verisimilitude already explored in the context of Montaigne's *Essais*, for narrative logic 'is nothing other than the development of the Aristotelian *probable* (common opinion and not scientific truth)'.[11] Narrative logic is the clearest expression of the scientific or philosophical claims of literature illustrated by Hegel's conception of history as a 'plot'. Art in general represents man's effort to make sense of his world, to make history meaningful by gathering an otherwise meaningless supersession of moments into a unity or a whole. The role of art, therefore, is to eliminate anguish; it corresponds to man's need for 'the sense of an ending': 'Men, like poets, rush "into the middest", *in medias res*, when they are born; they also die *in mediis rebus*, and to make sense of their span they need fictive concords with origins and ends, such as give

[5] Barthes, *Mythologies* 11 [*Mythologies*, 8–9].   [6] Ibid. 109 and 111 [193, 196].

[7] Barthes, *The Semiotic Challenge* (1988), 166 ['La langue est le domaine des *articulations*, et le sens est avant tout découpage. Il s'ensuit que la tâche future de la sémiologie est beaucoup moins d'établir des lexiques d'objets que de retrouver les articulations que les hommes font subir au réel', *L'Aventure sémiologique*, 53].

[8] Barthes, *Mythologies*, 150 [*Mythologies*, 238].   [9] Ibid.

[10] Barthes, *The Rustle of Language*, 120 [*Le Bruissement de la langue*, 122].

[11] Barthes, *The Semiotic Challenge*, 144 ['La logique narrative, il faut le reconnaître, n'est rien d'autre que le développement du *probable* aristotélicien (opinion commune et non verité scientifique); il est donc normal que, lorsqu'on a voulu légaliser cette logique (sous forme de contraintes et de valeurs esthétiques), ce soit encore une notion aristotélicienne que les premiers théoriciens classique du récit ont mise en avant: celle de *vraisemblable*', *L'Aventure sémiologique*, 214].

meaning to lives and to poems.'[12] Time becomes historically meaningful when through recollection—*Erinnerung* for Hegel—man 'thoughtfully gathers his past to his present, in a manner which gives the past a meaningful place in the formation of the present, and which gives the present a measure of ballast and articulation in order to make a meaningful future possible'.[13] By assimilating the world to the (pseudo-)logical rules of narrative, man fills in the gaps and links up meaning to give the illusion of a homogeneity or plenitude without residue of the world, and thus of a fully mastered and organized reality.

The essaying or 'trying out' of narrative fiction in Barthes entails the examination of the underlying principles of narrative structures, first through the identification of their constituents, and then through the exposure of the implicit rules and conventions that betray their dependence upon cultural and ideological codes. Thus, the reading of *Sarrasine* in *S/Z* consists in cataloguing and classifying every one of the short story's elements in order then to refer them to the 'encyclopedia' of 'anonymous knowledge' or 'received opinions' of the *doxa*. Every aspect of Barthes's work, in fact, seems to have an encyclopedic orientation, for the systematic demystification of a text like *Sarrasine* ostensibly participates in the overall project of giving a '*detailed*' account of so-called 'mythical inversions'. Correspondingly, the heterogeneity of Barthes's subject-matter or examples from the most serious to the apparently most trivial, which could easily be put down to the characteristic 'sloppiness' of the essayist, serves above all to show that nothing escapes culture: 'from garment to book, from food to image . . . from end to end of the social scale': culture is an object '*without remainder*'.[14] Far from being sloppy or haphazard, then, Barthes's work resembles an exhaustive repertoire, a sort of encyclopedia of cultural myths. However, by following the implications of counter-ideological criticism to their conclusion, doesn't one end up turning the essay into the natural vehicle for the kind of 'poetics' generally favoured by French structuralists (if a 'poetics' can be said to reconstruct rather than interpret a message[15]), or even for the 'grammar' of narrative which narratologists took over from the Russian Formalist Vladimir Propp's initial work on folktales? The thrust of semiology itself is systematic and encyclopedic, since it purports to be a science of signs. What, then, becomes of the essayistic spirit? In a sense, the evolution of Barthes's work is an answer to this question in as much as it records his increasing awareness that semiology's scientific ambition manifests an unwillingness to confront the aporia inherent in its counter-ideological project: how to refuse language as the principal instrument of perpetuation of the *doxa* by means of language; how to defend an objective, extraterritorial position from which language and rhetoric could be assessed given the conviction that language permeates the whole of

[12] Frank Kermode, *The Sense of an Ending: Studies in the Theory of Fiction* (1967), 7.
[13] William Desmond, *Art and the Absolute: A Study of Hegel's Aesthetics* (1986), 67.
[14] Barthes, *The Rustle of Language*, 100 [*Le Bruissement de la langue*, 107].
[15] Cf. Barthes, *Critical Essays*, 214: 'The goal of all structuralist activity . . . is to reconstruct an "object" in such a way as to manifest thereby the rules of functioning (the "functions") of this object.'

reality.[16] It is because of Barthes's acute 'essayistic' awareness that the semiologist's position is immersed in language and cannot appeal to a metalanguage which history will soon replace with another anyway, that he (also) purports to turn semiology into the most 'un-scientific' of sciences.[17] The problem of 'disengaging science from ideology' concerns all human sciences; yet for Barthes, 'if there is a discourse that encompasses the discourse of ideology, it is indeed semiology, which, being a science of signs, can advance only by the criticism of signs, and therefore of its own language':

It is the responsibility of semiology, and perhaps of semiology alone of all the human sciences today, to question its own discourse: as a science of language, of languages, it cannot accept its own language as a datum, a tranparency, a tool, in short as a meta-language . . . it interrogates itself as to *the place from which it speaks*, an interrogation without which any science and any ideological criticism is ridiculous.[18]

From the moment semiology becomes an established field, an orthodoxy that rigidly sets in its own jargon and no longer 'plays' with its objects, Barthes increasingly operates on its margins. From its periphery he can defend his rejection of a 'simple' or 'positivist' science and act out his idea of a semiology that constantly tries itself out.[19] In this sense, Barthes's exploitation of the genre of the essay carries on semiology's initial and/or ideal anti-scientific gesture through an ongoing 'mobilization' of its operations in perpetually renewed forms. Only by persistently 'putting into question [its] own type of utterance, [its] own mode of discourse' reflexively, can semiology be 'homogeneous with the theory it enunciates'.[20] And to continually reflect on the context and circumstances of his discourse, 'interrogating [himself] from the place from which [he] speaks' is what the essayist does by definition. Since criticism must be reflexive—regardless of the cultural object—the (critical) essay is the only possible form of criticism, the only form that avoids the 'capital sin' of 'good conscience' or 'bad faith':[21]

All criticism must include in its discourse (even if it is in the most indirect and modest manner imaginable) an implicit reflection on itself. Every criticism is a criticism of the work *and* self-criticism; for criticism is knowledge of the other and knowledge of oneself to the

---

[16] 'There is no place without language: one cannot contrast language, what is verbal, with some pure and dignified space of reality and truth, a space outside language. Everything is language, or more precisely, language is everywhere. It permeates the whole of reality; there is nothing real without language' (Barthes, *The Grain of the Voice: Interviews 1962–1980* (1991), 162 [*Le Grain de la voix: Entretiens 1962–1980* (1981), 153]).

[17] See Barthes, *The Rustle of Language*, 178 [*Le Bruissement de la langue*, 207].

[18] Barthes, *The Grain of the Voice*, 132 [*Le Grain de la voix*, 125]; and Barthes, *The Semiotic Challenge*, 8 ['Il appartient à la sémiologie, et peut-être, de toutes les sciences humaines aujourdhui, à la sémiologie seule, de mettre en cause son propre discours . . . elle s'interroge sur *le lieu d'où elle parle*, interrogation sans laquelle toute science et toute critique idéologique sont dérisoires,' *L'Aventure sémiologique*, 14].

[19] 'Nor do I desire . . . that Semiology should be a simple science, a positivist science' (ibid.).

[20] Barthes, *The Grain of the Voice*, 212 [*Le Grain de la voix*, 200]; and id., *The Rustle of Language*, 169 [*Le Bruissement de la langue*, 198].

[21] Barthes, *Critical Essays*, 257 [*Essais critiques*, 254].

world. In other words, criticism . . . is a series of intellectual acts profoundly committed to the historical and subjective existence (they are the same thing) of the man who performs them.[22]

All criticism is self-criticism (*'con-naître'*—'to know'—meaning literally 'to be born with'); yet as in Montaigne, self-knowledge—let alone knowledge of the other—can only be viewed sceptically: the self is indeterminate and plural. Hence the constant displacement or 'drifting' of Barthes's position [*un sujet anachronique, en dérive*[23]] between determined intellectual *loci*, a 'suspension' which goes hand in hand with the multiplicity of heterogeneous subjects and postures of enunciation, and thus recognizably rehearses or repeats the 'atopia' of the *Essais*'s own author.

Because one cannot accede to a supposedly neutral language, 'the only possible subversion in language is to displace things'.[24] So, from the margins of all the different theoretical fields or 'sciences' his work draws on over the years, Barthes produces a 'counter-encyclopedia' which both exploits and questions the various manifestations of the *doxa*. If Barthes's essays can be seen as a replay of the *Essais*, this is not least because they rehearse the transition, discussed in relation to Montaigne, between the old encyclopedia and a new encyclopedia 'in progress' which diverts the former's taxonomy. The link between *Roland Barthes* and the encyclopedia is familiar thanks to Michel Beaujour's study on the poetics of the self-portrait as an 'encyclopedic *speculum*' or as a 'metamorphosis of the encyclopedic mirror'[25] referred to in my discussion of the *Essais*. In his book, Beaujour draws attention to the surprising lack of evolution between Montaigne and Barthes's use of the self-portrait. 'While "genres" have been evolving in the course of the modern period', Beaujour notes, 'the self-portrait stagnates: one would be hard put to say what *formally, fundamentally* differentiates Montaigne's *Essays* from . . . *Roland Barthes*'.[26] Like Montaigne, 'Barthes uses a series of places *(loci,* topoi) likely to be treated according to the dialectic method familiar to all Renaissance schoolboys and the ensemble of which constitutes an encyclopedia . . . then a second movement tends to dislocate, exorcize, erase, blur these places.'[27] In this chapter, we will see that Barthes applies this dual movement of the setting up and transgression of topological frameworks not only to *Roland Barthes* but also to *S/Z*, assuming that the equivalence of criticism with self-criticism turns the more straightforwardly critical *S/Z* into the natural extension of the predominantly autobiographical *Roland Barthes*. So it is in relation to both texts that Barthes can be said to implement the idea of an 'anti-structural criticism' tentatively described in his self-portrait:

I can imagine an antistructural criticism; it would not look for the work's order but its disorder; for this it would suffice to consider any work as an *encyclopedia*: cannot each text

---

[22] Barthes, *Critical Essays*, 257 ['Toute critique est critique de l'œuvre et critique de soi-même . . . elle est connaissance de l'autre et co-naissance de soi-même au monde', 254–5].

[23] Barthes, *Le Plaisir du texte*, (1973), 99 [*The Pleasure of the Text* (1990), 63].

[24] Barthes, *The Grain of the Voice*, 162 [*Le Grain de la voix*, 153].

[25] Beaujour, *Poetics of the Literary Self-Portrait*, 35.

[26] Ibid. 7.   [27] Ibid. 20.

be defined by the number of disparate objects (of knowledge, of sensuality) which it brings into view with the help of simple figures of contiguity (metonymies and asyndetons)? Like the encyclopedia, the work exhausts a list of heterogeneous objects, and this list is the work's antistructure, its obscure and irrational polygraphy.[28]

Already, one surmises that this 'anti-structural criticism' is likely to revert the pre-text (and itself) back to its initial state as a 'list of heteroclitic objects', the better to play the fragments against the whole. The modern conception of the encyclopedia which is both a Renaissance and a Romantic metaphor of the Book-to-come is founded on a conflict between order and disorder, forces of totalization and forces of fragmentation. Barthes's use of the encyclopedia as counter-encyclopedia is justified precisely by the fact that the encyclopedia is a fundamentally 'paradoxical' discourse in the literal sense in which he likes to highlight this adjective.[29] The encyclopedia is the repository of the *doxa*; it thus 'changes according to the ideologies in fashion'.[30] Its ambition to be the timeless, scientific receptacle of all knowledge is necessarily dependent upon historical progress, upon the rhetorical, ideological mechanism by which the dominant social forces 'mentally cut up', classify, and appropriate the world. The encyclopedia's ambition is to master reality in its totality by systematizing knowledge. But this systematization is itself reliant on fragmentation, on the juxtaposition of heterogeneous items, upon a list. As Walter Moser's work on the structure of the Romantic encyclopedia makes clear, the systematic impulse of the encyclopedia is questioned by the presence within it of two conflicting discourses or modes of representation—the System (associated with closure) and the Dictionary (associated with open-endedness).[31] The cumulative method of the Dictionary corresponds to Barthes's 'list of heteroclitic objects'; it compiles and juxtaposes its constituents and makes up the main body of the encyclopedia, thereby incurring constant interruptions between the elements of the Book. What the System represents, in contradistinction, is the homogeneous and continuous philosophical or scientific discourse that elaborates a unifying principle behind the disparate material accumulated in the Dictionary, supplementing the fragmentation through cross-references by drawing the network of all connections for a coherent and structured whole. The striving of the systematic method towards the construction of an architectonic whole is further displayed by a third element, the Map, which compresses it in a synoptic table and presents a

[28] *Roland Barthes*, 'The Work as Polygraphy', 148 ['J'imagine une critique antistructurale; elle ne rechercherait pas l'ordre, mais le désordre de l'œuvre; il lui suffirait pour cela de considérer toute œuvre comme une encyclopédie: chaque texte ne peut-il se définir par le nombre des objets disparates qu'il met en scène à l'aide de simple figures de contiguïté (métonymies et asyndètes). Comme l'encyclopédie, l'œuvre exténue une liste d'objets hétéroclites et cette liste est l'antistructure de l'œuvre, son obscure et folle polygraphie', 'L'œuvre comme polygraphie', 151].

[29] The dictionary as a 'perfectly paradoxical object', Barthes, *The Grain of the Voice*, 99 [*Le Grain de la voix*, 96].

[30] Beaujour, *Poetics of the Literary Self-Portrait*, 21.

[31] Walter Moser, 'L'Encyclopédie romantique: Le Brouillon de Novalis', in *Le Genre/Die Gattung/ Genre* (Colloque International de Strasbourg, 1979), and 'Fragment and Encyclopedia: From Borges to Novalis', in Laurence Kritzman (ed.), *Fragments: Incompletion and Discontinuity*, (1981).

visual synopsis of its totality through the simultaneous juxtaposition of its materials.[32] However, the conceptual, universalizing ambition of the encyclopedia depends upon the open-ended, arbitrary structure of language. For the encyclopedia's ambition to master reality is not least founded on the extralinguistic and thus 'direct' access to reality which it claims to enjoy. It is distinguished from the language dictionary in that, unlike the latter where the entries (the words of the nomenclature) are considered and approached as (linguistic) signs, the encyclopedia relates to its entries as contents. In other words, the encyclopedia's didactic enterprise theoretically benefits from the use of a neutral descriptive and analytical language, from the possibility of describing the world from an extratextual vantage-point. Yet its nomenclature, like that of the dictionary, offers only words. And the distinction between words that designate things and words that designate words only contributes to bowing to the evidence that the encyclopedia cannot elude the syntactic and semantic structures of the language it uses to reconstruct a world which it claims to reflect like a mirror (or 'speculum'). The arbitrary relationship between signifier and signified belies the idea of a closed and natural (if not divine) structure; each signified must in turn occupy the position of a signifier, of another entry, so that the 'cycle' of the en-cyclo-pedia, rather than guaranteeing closure, denotes the potentially infinite regression of the 'vicious circle' away from the 'last word' of the completed System. The dictionary, Barthes writes, is an 'infinite decentered structure': 'A dictionary is composed of signifiers, i.e., words printed in bold type, each one of them furnished with a definition serving as its signified. Now these signifieds, these dictionary definitions, are themselves made up of other words, and so on forever.'[33] The use of the encyclopedia will therefore ensure that both the pre-text and the critical discourse are released again and again from their temptations towards 'exteriority' and 'totality': since 'nothing exists outside the text, there is never a *whole* of the text'.[34] To foreground the work's anti-structure (its difference from itself) by treating it like an encyclopedia (here *Sarrasine* and the story of the self) will involve playing the work's 'dictionary' against its 'system' (the narrative system), forces of fragmentation against forces of totalization, process against product. Via the encyclopedia, the examination of 'how' the text means will intensify the suspension of parts from whole, of signifiers from signified; and the confusion promoted by the mimetic text between consequence (the logical connections of cause and effect) and sequence (what simply comes 'before' and 'after')

[32] Therefore it belongs in Walter Moser's view to another semiotic register, the pictorial: see his 'L'Encyclopédie romantique: Le Brouillon de Novalis', 501, 503–4; and 'Fragment and Encyclopedia: From Borges to Novalis', 116–17.

[33] Barthes, *The Grain of the Voice*, 99 ['Un dictionnaire est composé de signifiants, c'est-à-dire de mots vedettes imprimés en corps gras, et chacun de ces mots est nanti d'une définition qui a valeur de signifié. Or ces signifiés, ces définitions du dictionnaire, sont constitués eux-mêmes d'autres mots, et cela à l'infini', *Le Grain de la voix*, 96].

[34] Barthes, *S/Z*, II, 'Interpretation', 6 ['En même temps que rien n'existe en dehors du texte, il n'y a jamais un *tout* du texte (. . .): il faut à la fois dégager le texte de son extérieur et de sa totalité', 'L'Interprétation', 12].

will be particularly flagrant. To play the dictionary against the system is ultimately to foreground the poetic dimension of the encyclopedia, of the essay, of language in general: the organization of the fragments is aesthetic rather than conceptual. In fact, the encyclopedia shows more clearly than any essay that the logic of discourse (whether autobiographical or critical) depends upon linguistic associations which are epitomized by the alphabet as the system of classification of the list.

So the production of a counter-encyclopedia (or simply of a new encyclopedia) is an emphatic response to scientific 'bad faith'—the 'bad faith' attached to supposedly neutral language, to a language unaware of its own existence: it is an obvious step in the movement, repeatedly prescribed by Barthes, 'from science to literature'.[35] In order to subvert scientific 'meta-language', science must 'write itself': the structuralist, linguist, or semiologist must become a writer, for the writer, unlike the scientist, does not say but writes what he knows.[36] Correspondingly, the 'science of literature' as Barthes practises it in relation to *Sarrasine* involves the 'discovery' of 'how [the text] was written' by 'writing—or rewriting—the text [one] is reading'.[37] And we will see that in Barthes, this 'writing' is also explicitly conceived in terms of a second, competing metaphor for the Book-to-come—that of the novel. At the same time, the paradox which Barthes borrows from the encyclopedia (or from the dictionary which he describes as 'a perfectly paradoxical object, both structured and indefinite'[38]) requires that science continue 'to conceive itself at once and contradictorily as science and as writing'.[39] This Barthes emphasizes by adopting not only the structure of the list, but also every feature of the typographical apparatus that goes with it and which reinforces the impression of a 'powerful metalinguistic drive'.[40] *S/Z* and *Roland Barthes* are paradigmatic of the predominantly tabular rather than linear logic of a good many of his texts which combine extreme fragmentation with nominal articulations (headings that seem to function like Montaignian *topoi*) and graphical articulations: different typefaces (bold, italics, capitals, etc.) preceded by letters (in *Roland Barthes*) or numbers (Roman and Arabic, in *S/Z*), blanks, and the extensive use of punctuation. Such a striking paratextual relief cannot but prompt the question as to whether the systematic use of the fragment can really aim at a 'typographical discontinuity that interrupts the plenitude of the discourse', or whether it might on the contrary set up 'a configuration that frames and regulates discursive discontinuity'—an internal system of control destined to check and finally master the generalized disruption of the text.[41] The answer, of course, is undecidable. As Montaignian essays, Barthes's texts paradoxically position themselves between old and new encyclopedia and exhibit the mobilization, the 'processing' of the system and the systematization

---

[35] The title of an essay in Barthes, *The Rustle of Language*.   [36] Ibid. 10 [20].

[37] Barthes, *The Grain of the Voice*, 189 [*Le Grain de la voix*, 180].   [38] Ibid. 99 [96].

[39] Barthes, *The Rustle of Language*, 169 [*Le Bruissement de la langue*, 198].

[40] Culler, *On Deconstruction*, 26.

[41] See Ginette Michaud, 'Fragment et dictionnaire: Autour de l'écriture abécédaire de Barthes', *Études françaises*, 18 (1983), 76 and 80; and Marie-Christine Barillaud's 'Roland Barthes: Les Fragments, langue équivoque', *Revue Romane*, 16 (1981), 32.

itself of the process—the system as process for which Barthes coins the appropriately dynamic term of the 'systematics':

Is not the characteristic of reality to be *unmasterable*? And is it not the characteristic of any system to *master* it? What then, confronting reality, can one do who rejects mastery? Get rid of the system as apparatus, accept *systematics* as writing (as Fourier did).

Systematics is the play of the system; it is language that is open, infinite, free from any referential illusion (pretension).[42]

To 'accept systematics as writing' involves liberating the signifier from the signified, or asymmetrically favouring the dynamic concepts of structuration over structure, production over product, process over judgement, etc.—all of which are connected with the reader/critic's active participation in the production and writing of the text. To examine the underlying conditions of meaning of a literary work—of a narrative text like *Sarrasine*—by 'breaking [it] down into its constituents, naming and classifying in a rationalist or scientific spirit' becomes the means by which 'rather than treat the text as the product or manifestation of an underlying system, [Barthes] will explore its difference from itself'.[43] Yet privileging the infinite surplus of Writing—the so-called 'writerly' [*scriptible*] or 'Text' as opposed to the 'readerly' [*lisible*] or 'work'—requires the theoretical maintenance of all these opposites. What Barthes labels 'limit-' or borderline works [*œuvre-limite*] are therefore bound to be the favourite targets of his 'anti-structural' or (counter-) encyclopedic criticism, since they flaunt the transgressive power of classical or 'readerly' texts. Among them (*Dom Juan, La vie de Rancé, Bouvard et Pécuchet*), Balzac's *Sarrasine* stands out as 'one of these texts which, in the work of a great writer, represent the very strange temptations by which it can be made to anticipate or preempt modernity'.[44] *Sarrasine* is indeed first and foremost a borderline work in that, as well as representing narrative order and being the work of one of the greatest representatives of the 'classical' text, it is a marginal piece in the writer's overall work and a marginal fictional genre (a short story rather than a novel). The typically essayistic choice of a marginal text and genre (but also of marginal authors and figures) with regard to the accepted canon reflects here again the essayist's concern with a historical 'responsibility of forms': to choose a

---

[42] *Roland Barthes*, 'System/Systematics', 172 ['Le propre du réel ne serait-il pas d'être *immaîtrisable*? Et le propre du système ne serait-il pas de le *maîtriser*? Que peut donc faire, face au réel, celui qui refuse la maîtrise? Econduire le système comme appareil accepter le systèmatique comme écriture', *Roland Barthes*, 'Système/systématique', 174–5; 'System/Systematics', 110]; and *Sade, Fourier, Loyola* (1971) ['Le systématique est le jeu du système; c'est du langage ouvert, infini, dégagé de toute illusion (prétention) référentielle', *Sade, Fourier, Loyola*, 114–15]. See Réda Bensmaïa, 'The Problem of the Essayistic Text's "Constitution"', in *The Barthes Effect: The Essay as Reflective Text* (1987).

[43] Culler, *On Deconstruction*, 26.

[44] ['Un de ces textes qui dans l'œuvre d'un grand écrivain, représentent des tentations très étranges qui lui font en quelque sorte prévoir la modernité'], interview quoted in Stephen Heath, *Vertige du déplacement: Lecture de Barthes* (1974), 104.

marginal text is to raise the question of the 'essence' of a literature which accredits the notion that it is eternal or 'natural', that it 'goes without saying'.[45] Ways in which *Sarrasine* is 'borderline' in so far as its story is itself about generic excess have been overglossed. It will suffice to mention that *Sarrasine* is about the imposture of a castrato (La Zambinella) who appears to the hero (Sarrasine) as a woman, but who is in fact neither man nor woman and yet both (a living oxymoron), something 'in-between', something unnamable, unlocatable [*irrepérable*]: the very embodiment of the figure of paradox or transgression. For Barthes, *Sarrasine* therefore blatantly functions as a metaphor for the breakdown or 'confusion of representation' [*le trouble de la représentation*]:

It is then no longer possible regularly to contrast opposites, sexes, possessions; it is no longer possible to safeguard an order of just equivalence; in a word, it is no longer possible to *represent*, to make things *representative*, individuated, separate, assigned; *Sarrasine* represents the very confusion of representation, the unbridled (pandemic) circulation of signs, of sexes, of fortunes.[46]

Like all Montaignian essays, Barthes's texts are the expression of a crisis, of a transition, of the transgression of established generic boundaries. So, one might say that *Sarrasine* is a particularly good pretext for the staging of the moments of 'semantic scandal' which characterize Barthes's essayistic interest. By turning Balzac's story into the story of the breakdown of mimesis, Barthes also makes it thematize the breakdown of the mimetic relationship between primary text and criticism: the impossibility of saying anything 'about' *Sarrasine* reflects the impossibility of saying anything about oneself, despite the apparently equally mimetic programme of the *Roland Barthes 'by' Roland Barthes* (my quotation marks). The essayist, like the castrato, is always somewhere 'in-between'; and one cannot but be conscious, when reading Barthes, of the fundamental connection between the act of writing and his own sexual 'marginality' or 'a-genericness'. We will begin, in Section 4.2, with an examination of how Barthes's essayistic or 'anti-structural criticism' operates in *S/Z*, in order then to explore, in Section 4.3, the extension of this notion to the essayist himself in the context of an autobiographical project in many ways reminiscent of Montaigne's self-portrait. This will lead, in Section 4.4, to our finally focusing on the excess or overflow generated by this anti-structural criticism as *novelistic* excess.[47]

---

[45] Barthes, *Critical Essays*, 250 ['Refuser de s'interroger sur l'être de la littérature, c'est du même coup accréditer l'idée que cet être est éternel, ou si l'on préfère, naturel, bref, que la littérature *va de soi*', *Essais critiques*, 247].

[46] Barthes, *S/Z*, XCII, 'The Three Points of Entry', 216 ['Il n'est plus possible de sauvegarder un ordre de la juste équivalence; en un mot il n'est plus possible de *représenter*, de donner aux choses des *représentants*, individués, séparés, distribués: *Sarrasine* représente le trouble même de la représentation', 'Les Trois Entrées', 221–2].

[47] For this survey of *S/Z* and *Roland Barthes*, I am indebted above all to Barbara Johnson, *The Critical Difference: Essays in the Contemporary Rhetoric of Reading* (1980); Jonathan Culler, *Barthes* (1983); Heath, *Vertige du déplacement*; Vincent Jouve, *La Littérature selon R. Barthes* (1986); Steffen

4.2. THE ORDER OF DISORDER

Barthes's commentary of Balzac's short story *Sarrasine* in *S/Z* seems to correspond in every way to the essayist's 'idea' of an 'anti-structural criticism' which consists, as explained above, in looking at the work as a (counter-)encyclopedia, as a 'list of heteroclitic objects'. It is presented as an interlinear gloss which proceeds directly from the breaking up of *Sarrasine* into a dictionary, as it were, of the story, every element of which is made to function as a numbered 'entry' (in bold characters). This first type of gloss—which decomposes the whole of *Sarrasine* into five hundred and sixty-one 'lexias' or lexical units and assigns every item or 'entry' to one or more cultural codes—immediately testifies to the systematic nature of the demystification at work. In the same way that nothing—no area of life—escapes these codes in the extremely varied corpus of Barthes's work as a whole, no item of the text can claim to be 'natural'. Each element or 'lexical unit' of *Sarrasine* is cast as a quotation (in bold type) of the 'ready-made and already read' *doxa* also described as the anonymous encyclopedic knowledge of a sort of Flaubertian *dictionnaire d'idées reçues* shared by both reader and writer. Each item of the classical text can therefore be affiliated to one or more of the five 'codes' identified and named by Barthes (listed p. 28 and signalled this time by the use of capital letters), and whose structuring of the work amounts to 'creating a kind of network, a topos through which the entire text passes' (*S/Z*):

All the cultural codes, taken up from citation to citation, together form an oddly joined miniature version of encyclopedic knowledge [*un petit savoir encyclopédique bizarrement cousu*], a farrago: this farrago forms the everyday 'reality' in relation to which the subject adapts himself, lives.

These citations are extracted from a body of knowledge, from an anonymous Book. . . . On the one hand, this anterior Book is both a book of science . . . and a book of wisdom. . . . Although entirely derived from books, these codes, by a swivel characteristic of bourgeois ideology, which turns culture into nature, appear to establish reality, 'Life'. 'Life' then, in the classic text, becomes a nauseating mixture of common opinions, a smothering layer of received ideas.[48]

In revealing the work's conditions of meaning, Barthes denounces the work's ambition 'innocently' to present culture as nature. The reality or truth which the work claims to denote 'outside' or beyond itself as a text is none other than the

Nordahl Lund, *L'Aventure du signifiant: Une lecture de Barthes* (1981); Donald Rice and Peter Schofer, '*S/Z*: Rhetoric and Open Reading', in *L'Esprit Créateur* (1982); Philippe Roger, *Roland Barthes, Roman* (1986); Susan Sontag, *L'Écriture même: À propos de Roland Barthes* (1982); Michel Charles, *L'Arbre et la source* (1985); Steven Ungar, *Roland Barthes: The Professor of Desire* (1983); Bensmaïa, *The Barthes Effect*; Paul Jay, *Being in the Text: Self-Representation from Wordsworth to R. Barthes* (1984); and Bernard Comment, *Roland Barthes, Vers le neutre* (1991), as well as the volumes of *Communications, Critique, Poétique, Tel Quel, Textuel*, and *Studies in 20th Century Literature* dedicated to Barthes.

[48] Barthes, *S/Z*, LXXVIII, 'To Die of Ignorance', 184–5 ['Mourir d'ignorance', 190]; and *S/Z*, LXXXVII, 'The Voice of Science', 205–6 ['Voix de la science', 211].

underlying encyclopedic intertext of the *doxa*. *Sarrasine* does not depict or represent: it repeats or quotes the written text of so-called 'reality', since 'realism . . . consists not in copying the real but in copying a (depicted) copy of the real'.[49] For all that, the apparently encyclopedic inventory of the work's affiliation to the encyclopedic intertext is not to be taken at face value. Despite the fact that the compilation of glosses is supplemented by cross-references, the random, unsystematic nature of these cross-references together with the local and elliptical affiliations of each lexical unit to the codes do not add up to the expected hierarchical organization of the network which is intended to cover all the entries of the text. Given that the code is expressly affiliated to the topos (the stock topic—basic theme or concept—of ancient rhetoric), one can expect topological transgressions. In his discussion of codes in the second type of gloss which one could describe as a topical itinerary, Barthes in fact not only warns against the 'attempt to structure any one of them [the codes], or the five in relation to each other'. Rather than paradigms, he writes, the codes are a 'mirage of structures'; they do not function as anything more than a 'perspective of quotations' the origin of which is lost:

Thus, if we make no effort to structure each code, or the five codes among themselves, we do so deliberately, in order to assume the multivalence of the text. . . . Hence we use *Code* here not in the sense of a list, a paradigm that must be reconstituted. The code is a perspective of quotations, a mirage of structures.[50]

In providing a dictionary of the text, turning every item into an 'entry' signalled by its bold type, it is not so much the text as quotation (in quotation-marks) which Barthes has in mind as the general citationality of the text (without quotation-marks), its unlocatable, irrecoverable [*irrepérable*] 'difference', what articulates it upon 'the infinity of texts, of languages, of systems'.[51] To essay the narrative system is again to affirm its participation in the 'vast "dissolve" [*fading*], which permits both overlapping and loss of messages',[52] that is, in the infinite circulation of Montaigne's 'interglossing'. The demystification of the narrative system, which emphasizes by extension how literary meaning like all meaning depends upon cultural or ideological codes, thus acts as a reminder that all literary work, by virtue of being literature, prefigures this excess; that all good narrative exceeds its codes in the same way that the encyclopedia includes within it its own anti-structure.

Methodologically, the commentary is the critical approach to *Sarrasine* which makes possible this paradoxical use of codes, for it enables the essayist to 'make the code skid while seeming to respect it'.[53] As with Montaigne's *Essais* and the

---

[49] Barthes, *S/Z*, XXIII, 'Painting as a Model', 55 ['Ainsi le réalisme . . . consiste non à copier le réel, mais à copier une copie du réel', 'Le modèle de la peinture', 61]; and 'Lexia 25', ibid. 39: 'the realist author spends his time referring back to books: reality is what has been written' ['Léxie 25', 46].

[50] Barthes, *S/Z*, XII, 'The Weaving of Voices', 20 ['Le Tissu des voix', 27].

[51] Barthes, *S/Z*, I, 'Evaluation', 3. ['L'Évaluation', 9].

[52] Barthes, *S/Z*, XII, 'The Weaving of Voices', 20 ['Le Tissu des voix', 27].

[53] Barthes, *The Rustle of Language*, 175 ['faire déraper le code tout en ayant l'air de le respecter', *Le Bruissement de la langue*, 204].

paratextual criticism discussed in the previous chapter, it is the position of the gloss in the margins of the intertext, between inside and outside, which determines the ambiguity of the relationship between primary and secondary discourse. Only here, this ambiguity is heightened by the fact that the gloss—traditionally understood as the interlinear or marginal comment, in difficult texts, of a word or phrase—is systematized into the discourse of a dictionary. The aim of the dictionary, which does historically originate in the gloss, is indeed to break language up into a systematic list so as to ascertain every single meaning.[54] The application of this procedure to the whole of *Sarrasine* suggests that Barthes appropriates not only the tabular structure of the list from the dictionary but its totalizing, 'exhaustive' purpose ('Like the encyclopedia, the work *exhausts* a list of heterogeneous objects' (emphasis added)).[55] By supplementing the list, the numerical system of *S/Z* appears to function from the start as the guarantor of this exhaustiveness: its sequentiality lends the 'heteroclitic' order of the list its greatest possible degree of verisimilitude over and above the 'juxtaposition' of its elements. No residue seems to escape the commentary which purports to be as systematic as the inventory is exhaustive. As a direct extension of the text, or expansion in the text's margin, the commentary gives every appearance of being concerned only with justifying or disambiguating the original context. It does not exist for its own sake, but only in so far as it makes the text intelligible—here by assigning to every unit a number of corresponding codes. The integral quotation of the short story appears to provide the unmovable frame (entry and exit) within which the commentary develops, a guarantee of mutual dependence, so that the constant citational coming and going is ultimately framed by, or subordinated to, a return to the text. In other words, the gloss necessarily induces a process of fragmentation which makes the story momentarily less intelligible, since each quotation finds itself extracted from its narrative context. But the discourse which settles into the space of this disarticulation is immediately supposed to compensate for this by a piecing together, a reconstruction which strengthens the original context and collaborates in the 'mastery of meaning'.

It is by flaunting all the expected trappings of the conventional commentary (its theological dimension[56]), however, that Barthes's play or 'mobilization' of the

---

[54] The repertoire of classified head-words with their respective rubrics called 'articles' is the result of an increasing systematization of the method of clarification and classification, and seems to have emerged after recurrent stages of confused taxonomic procedures. This progress eventually leads to the production of 'glossaries' themselves: alphabetic lists of unfamiliar or difficult words and phrases, sometimes appended to the edn. of the particular text, sometimes published as a separate volume. See e.g. B. Quemada, 'Du glossaire au dictionnaire: Deux aspects de l'élaboration des énoncés lexicographiques dans les grands répertoires du XVIIe siècle', *Cahiers de Lexicologie*, 20 (1972).

[55] *Roland Barthes*, 'The Work as Polygraphy', 148 ['Comme l'encyclopédie, l'œuvre *exténue* une liste hétéroclite d'objects', 'L'œuvre comme polygraphie', 151].

[56] Whereas 'the *author* is always supposed to go from signified to signifier, from content to form, from idea to text', the '*critic* goes in the other direction [*refait le chemin inverse*], works back from signifiers to signified . . . the *author* is a god . . . as for the critic, he is the priest whose task is to decipher the Writing of the god', *S/Z*, LXXIV, 'The Mastery of Meaning', 174 ['La Maîtrise du sens', 180]). See also *S/Z*, XXXIX, 'This is Not an "Explication de Texte"'.

systematic intent both of the 'tutor text' and of criticism as commentary is most effective. Like Montaigne, Barthes indulges in his taste for 'disjointed reading'[57] by breaking the model into its component parts, taking stock of its borders by interpolating and 'temporalizing' so as to examine the unquestioned relationship between form and content not as a 'given' but 'in progress', and thus to liberate the force of transgression of the intertext. Barthes can in fact be said to intensify the 'disrespectful' tendency of Montaigne's 'short-sighted' readings ('I do not see the whole of anything') by systematizing the 'micro-readings'[58] of the primary text to such an extent that the decontextualization of each part from its overall frame is radical: the text is presented as a list of pure interruptions or *hors-textes*. This 'step by step' [*pas à pas*] method which prompts a disarticulation of the narrative in 'slow-motion' enables the essayist to 'avoid structuring the text *excessively*, it avoids giving it that additional structure which would come from a dissertation and would close it'. Instead, the text is 'starred' [*étoilé*] in such a way that the essay— which elsewhere Barthes explicitly opposes to the dissertation [*l'essai sans la dissertation*]—can systematically play on digression.[59] The additional perigraphical system of the numbering greatly contributes to this 'systematic play'. For behind the semblance of a logical order which it grants the items of the list, it radicalizes the essayistic strategy by exacerbating the effect of 'disjointed articles' [*piece descousue*], the abstraction of the individual parts from each other and from the overall organization of the story. The interruption or interpolation effected by the essay stages each fragment as a surplus or 'excursion' that subverts the hierarchy and direction—the intention—of the narrative. As in the *Essais*, the fragment is a 'departure' [*départ*], the 'mark, the sign of a virtual digression toward the remainder of a catalogue'.[60] Thus, the apparent 'verisimilitude' which the numerical system, in its sequentiality, lends the heteroclite order of the list, is a fiction. What the numbering does, on the contrary, is to reinforce the arbitrary order of the list by systematizing this arbitrariness. Its verisimilitude is the result of a confusion which Barthes fights relentlessly in his work: that between sequence (what comes before and after), and consequence (the logic of cause and effect) since in the mimetically ordered text what comes 'after' is given as what is 'caused by': 'This is the narrative fabric: seemingly subject to the discontinuity of message, each of which, when it comes into play, is received as a useless supplement . . . but is in fact saturated with pseudo-logical links, relays.'[61] Behind its 'pseudo-logical' façade, numbering is a purely arbitrary, purely meaningless order, which can only contribute

[57] Cf. 'I'm unable, unwilling, to sum up a book . . . but on the contrary, I'm quite ready to pick out certain sentences, certain characteristics of the book, to ingest them as discontinuous fragments' (Barthes, *The Grain of the Voice*, 221 [*Le Grain de la voix*, 208]).

[58] A term borrowed from Jean-Pierre Richard, *Micro-lectures* (1979).

[59] Barthes, *S/Z*, VI, 'Step by Step', 12 and 13 ['Pas à pas', 19 and 20]. Cf. 'I created a slow-motion image of *Sarrasine*, like a film director who de-composes a sequence, showing it at a slower speed' (*The Grain of the Voice*, 88 [*Le Grain de la voix*, 87]).

[60] Barthes, *S/Z*, XII, 'The Weaving of Voices', 20 ['Le Tissu des voix', 27].

[61] Barthes, *S/Z*, LXXVII, 'The Readerly II: Determined/Determinant', 182 ['Le Lisible II: déterminé/déterminant', 187–8].

to releasing and flaunting 'the work's antistructure, its obscure and irrational [*folle*] polygraphy'. The sequence of numbering subverts the very notion of hierarchy from the outset, emphasizing the fact that the list (the items of the story) can be extended indefinitely by the addition of elements, as in a dictionary: 'There is no entrance language or exit language for the textual dictionary, since it is not the dictionary's (closed) definitional power that the text possesses, but its infinite structure.'[62] All the parts of the story are 'flattened' to one level; all are granted equal value, all are interchangeable—main and peripheral, significant and less significant, opaque and transparent.[63] The numbering helps flaunt the 'infinite connectability of all things, and the arbitrariness of most connections'[64] which underlies the 'motivated' order of the fragments in the narrative. Hence the unexpected cutting up of *Sarrasine* into an arbitrary chain of signifiers or 'reading units', regardless of the text's 'natural' divisions. These units do not necessarily consist of words or sentences, that is, of what the reader might see as meaningful units, but often of something 'in-between'. Nouns, verbs, and complements tend for example to be separated as a result of apparently random choices of beginnings and ends:

The commentary, based on the affirmation of the plural, cannot therefore work with 'respect' to the text; the tutor text will ceaselessly be broken, interrupted without any regard for its natural divisions (syntactical, rhetorical, anecdotic); inventory, explanation, and digression may deter any observation of suspense, may even separate verb and complement, noun and attribute; the work of the commentary, once it is separated from any ideology of totality, consists precisely in *manhandling* [*malmener*] the text, *interrupting* it [*lui couper la parole*].[65]

The 'step by step' approach, reinforced by the numbering, undermines the notion of a privileged access—entry or exit—to the text, and on the contrary releases the 'reversibility of structures from which the text is woven' like a 'network with a thousand of entrances' [*un reseau à mille entrées*].[66] And finally, the flattening of all levels extends to the origin and ultimate guarantor of the work—Balzac himself—who 'is not an innocent subject, anterior to the text' but 'a plurality of other texts, of codes which are infinite, or, more precisely, lost (whose origin is lost)'.[67] The author, like his characters, is a 'figure of paper', a text like any other text which

---

[62] Barthes, *S/Z*, LIII, 'Euphemism', 120 ['Il n'y a pour le dictionnaire textuel ni langue d'entrée, ni langue de sortie, car le texte a, du dictionnaire, non le pouvoir définitionnel (clos) mais la structure infinie', 'L'Euphémisme', 127].

[63] On the 'list', see Susan Stewart, *Nonsense: Aspects of Intertextuality in Folklore and Literature* (1979), 135–7.

[64] Ibid. 143.

[65] Barthes, *S/Z*, VIII, 'The Broken Text', 15 ['Le Texte brisé', 21–2].

[66] Barthes, *S/Z*, VI, 'Step by Step', 13 and 12 ['Pas à pas', 19]; cf. also *S/Z*,-II, 'Interpretation', 5: 'This text is a galaxy of signifiers, not a structure of signifieds; it has no beginning; it is reversible; we gain access to it by several entrances, none of which can be authoritatively declared to be the main one' ['L'Interprétation', 12].

[67] Barthes, *S/Z*, V, 'Reading, Forgetting', 10 ['Le Lecture, l'oubli', 16].

again adds itself (a 'connection' rather than a 'filiation') to the rest of the text rather than enjoying the privilege of an extratextual vantage point:

The Author himself—that somewhat decrepit deity of the old criticism—can or could some day become a text like any other: he has only to avoid making his person the subject, the impulse, the origin, the authority, the Father, whence his work would proceed, by a channel of *expression*; he has only to see himself as a being on paper and his life as a *bio-graphy* (in the etymological sense of the word), a writing without referent, substance of a *connection* and not of a *filiation*.[68]

The numbering, then, is a system which represses all notion of origin and telos. Yet in accordance with the subversion of rhetorical taxonomy as a mnemonic device, Barthes foregrounds this repression as 'amnesia', acknowledging like Montaigne (but less insistently) that 'it is precisely because [he] forget[s] that [he] read[s]'.[69] The mnemonic function of the number is turned on its head and becomes the memory, as it were, of Barthes's lack of memory.[70] And this 'amnesic' step by step approach by which the model or paradigm is diverted from its ultimate Signified enables Barthes, like Montaigne, to claim his right to use the example or 'primary' text as a pretext—a right which Barthes sees as the prerogative of every critic given the dialogism or 'multilingualism' of forms:

In fact, the meaning of a text can be nothing but the plurality of its systems, its infinite (circular) 'transcribability': one system transcribes another, but reciprocally as well: with regard to the text, there is no 'primary', 'natural', 'national', 'mother' critical language: from the outset, as it is created, the text is multilingual [*le texte est d'emblée, en naissant, multilingue*].[71]

Turning the 'model' around, or upside down, or inside out, going through it, displacing it, is a veritable hobby of Barthes's.[72] To deny the text ownership is to remove the sign 'no trespass', and so to allow the trespasser to possess the text. The displacement of the model by the critical text illustrated in the previous chapters by inversion, appropriation, and theft, is again staged rather theatrically in *S/Z* through the coexistence, within the essay, of the interlinear gloss (its

---

[68] Barthes, *S/Z*, XC, 'The Balzacian Text', 211 ['Le Texte balzacien', 217]. See also *S/Z*, XXVIII, 'Character and Figure', ['Personnage et figure'], *S/Z*, XLI, 'The Proper Name' ['Le Nom propre'], and *S/Z*, LXXVI, 'Character and Discourse', ['Le personnage et le discours'].

[69] Barthes, *S/Z*, V, 'Reading, Forgetting', 11 ['La Lecture, l'oubli', 18].

[70] This is expressed in relation to the use of the alphabet in *Roland Barthes*, 'The Order I No Longer Remember', 148: 'In the course of what classification, of what succession? He no longer remembers. The alphabetical order erases everything, banishes every origin' [L'ordre alphabétique efface tout, refoule toute origine', 'L'Ordre dont je ne me souviens plus', 151].

[71] Barthes, *S/Z*, LIII, 'Euphemism', 120 ['L'Euphémisme', 126–7]. Cf. also 'We know that a text consists not of a line of words, releasing a single "theological" meaning (the "message" of the Author-God), but of a multi-dimensional space in which are married and contested several writings, none of which is original: the text is a fabric of quotations, resulting from a thousand sources of culture', Barthes, *The Rustle of Language*, 52–3 [*Le Bruissement de la langue*, 65].

[72] ['Les modèles, ce qui m'amuse au fond, c'est de passer a travers, de les tourner, de les retourner, de les renverser, de les déplacer, d'en faire autre chose et par là même d'une certaine façon j'ai besoin qu'ils existent', Interview quoted in Comment, *Roland Barthes, Vers le neutre*, 22].

regimentation through numbers) and the relegation of Balzac's story (quoted as a whole) to the periphery of the book. This visibly turns the retrospective position of the essay into a prospective one. Nevertheless, this 'reversability of structures' does not entail the reversal of the hierarchy between primary and secondary text, but the redefinition of intertextuality as rewriting in the space of a 'perpetual present': 'The writerly text is a perpetual present, upon which no *consequent* language (which would inevitably make it past) can be superimposed; the writerly text is *ourselves writing* [*le texte scriptible, c'est nous en train d'écrire*].'[73]

In this 'perpetual present' in which the essay interpolates into the text, adding itself to it like another element of the list, one recognizes the dimension within which the whole of Barthes's fragmentary work develops, and the 'tabular' presentation of our two books comes closest to presenting the discourse of criticism, like that of narrative, as a 'heteroclitic list of objects' or a set of 'pure interruptions'. By exploiting parataxis within each essay (articles etc.) and between essays, his work, which looks like a heterogeneous accumulation of notes, refuses to constitute itself into a totalizing *œuvre*. The purposeful, strategic choice of a type of writing where the whole is constantly exceeded by its parts is underlined time and again in Barthes's work:

I have long had a taste for discontinuous writing. . . . Rereading my books and articles . . . I noticed that my mode of writing was never lengthy, always proceeding by fragments, miniatures, paragraphs with titles, or articles . . . It's this taste for the short form that is now becoming systematic. The implication from the point of view of an ideology or a counter-ideology of form is that the fragment breaks up what I would call the smooth finish, the composition, discourse constructed to give a final meaning to what one says, which is the general rule of all past rhetoric. In relation to the smooth finish of constructed discourse, the fragment is a spoilsport, discontinuous, establishing a kind of pulverization of sentences, images, thoughts, none of which 'takes' definitively.[74]

Again the anti-systematic motivation of the essay does not simply take the form of an opposition between fragment and whole, which for the essayist would still mean operating within the logic he has rejected. In the same way that in *S/Z* 'the only novations consist not in destroying the story, the anecdote, but in *deviating* it', 'rupture' goes hand in hand with 'heterology', with 'skidding' [*dérapage*], with 'deviation';[75] as in Montaigne the fragments develop 'around the centre', they deviate and 'warp' the whole by 'taking tangents':

[73] Barthes, *S/Z*, II, 'Interpretation', 5 ['L'Interprétation', 11].

[74] Barthes, *The Grain of the Voice*, 209–10 [*Le Grain de la voix*, 198]. Cf. also: 'Liking to find, to write *beginnings*, he tends to multiply this pleasure: that is why he writes fragments: so many fragments, so many beginnings, so many pleasures (but he doesn't like the ends: the risk of the rhetorical clausule is too great: the fear of not being able to resist the *last word*' (*Roland Barthes*, 'The Circle of Fragments', 94 ['Le Cercle des fragments', 98]). See also ibid. 93 [97], and the 1971 foreword of the *Critical Essays* ['L'assemblage en est rhapsodique: dès le départ, aucune volonté de sens général, aucune envie d'assumer un "destin" intellectuel: seulement les éclats d'un travail progressif, souvent obscur à lui-même'].

[75] Barthes, *The Rustle of Language*, 175 [*Le Bruissement de la langue*, 204].

To write by fragments: the fragments are then so many stones on the perimeter of a circle: I spread myself around: my whole little universe in crumbs; at the center, what?

We skirt, we avoid, we dodge such values: *we take tangents*: strictly speaking, this is not a change of course; the fear is that we fall into opposition, aggression, i.e., into meaning.[76]

And for this alternative logic which Adorno described as the 'stringent and aconceptual art of music', Barthes adopts the analogy of the 'rhapsody' and the (Romantic) song cycle.[77] Yet Barthes is also constantly aware that despite their 'insignificant' order, even lists have the insidious tendency to succumb to the 'temptation of meaning' or even just to the 'effects of meaning' potential in a compilation or enumeration—the risk of the aggregate assuming a certain order towards something, a system.[78] So, as well as fragmenting his critical discourse, Barthes chooses to 'subjugate the series of figures (inevitable as any series is, since the book is by its status obliged to *progress*), to a pair of arbitrary factors: that of nomination and that of the alphabet':

I shall not explicate this text; I shall merely produce a number of fragments which will be, in a sense, *outcomes* of the text [*les sorties du texte*]. These fragments will be in a more or less emphatic state of severance with each other: I shall not attempt to link, to organize these 'outcomes'; and in order to be sure of frustrating any liaison (any systematizing of the commentary), in order to avoid any rhetoric of 'development', of the developed subject, I have titled each of these fragments, and I have put these titles in alphabetical order—which is, of course, both an order and a disorder [*un ordre et un désordre*], an order stripped of meaning [*un ordre privé de sens*], the degree zero of order [*le degré zéro de l'ordre*]. It will be a kind of dictionary . . . which will deal obliquely with the sustaining text.[79]

Along with the numbering, which, as I have shown, also promotes this 'order of disorder' in *S/Z*, these factors and the typographical features of both essays at first encourage the reader to distinguish different types of metalinguistic structure— three in the former and two in the latter—which appear in fact to provide different levels of critical or theoretical definition. I devoted the previous section to the first, which is properly intertextual. Both *S/Z* and *Roland Barthes* share the second type

[76] *Roland Barthes*, 'The Circle of Fragments', 92–3 ['Écrire par fragments: les fragments sont alors des pierres sur le pourtour du cercle: je m'étale en rond: tout mon petit univers en miettes; au centre, quoi?, 'Le Cercle des fragments', 97]; and *Roland Barthes*, 'Paradoxa', 140 ['Paradoxa', 143]. See also *Roland Barthes*, 'Plural, Difference, Conflict', 69 ['Il ne s'agit pas de retrouver dans la lecture du monde et du sujet des oppositions mais des débordements, des fuites, des glissements, des dérapages', 'Pluriel, différence, conflit', 74].

[77] *Roland Barthes*, 'The Circle of Fragments', 94 ['Le Cercle des fragments', 98].

[78] In *S/Z*, LI, 'The Blazon', 114: 'that a *complete* inventory can reproduce a *total* body, as if the extremity of enumeration could devise a new category, that of totality' ['Le Blason', 121]; and *Roland Barthes*, 'The Alphabet', 148: 'This order [of the glossary], however, can be mischievous: it sometimes produces effects of meaning' ['L'Alphabet', 151]. See Michaud, 'Fragment et dictionnaire', 62; Barillaud, 'Roland Barthes: Les fragments, langue équivoque', 33; and Alain Coulange, 'L'Étrange mode de l'alphabet', *Courrier du Centre International d'Études Poétiques*, 121–2 (1977).

[79] Barthes, *The Rustle of Language*, 238 [*Le Bruissement de la langue*, 271]. See also Introduction to *A Lover's Discourse: Fragments*, 8: 'to discourage the temptation of meaning, it was necessary to choose an *absolutely insignificant* order' [*Fragments d'un discours amoureux*, 10 and 11].

of gloss presented this time as a topical itinerary. In *S/Z*, this is constituted by ninety-three short rubrics or articles that develop around topics presented in a different typeface to the entries of the story, all of which are now preceded by Roman rather than Arabic numbers. The topical rubrics of this second type of discourse are intercalated in the interlinear gloss which they interrupt and take over at given points. Because the headings or topics themselves are often concepts preceded by a definite article, this layout easily gives one the impression that these sections act as points of synthesis, subordinating the disparate and heterogeneous material by recapitulating and/or anticipating its content. The coherent, continuous critical discourse which they seem to oppose to the commentary is all the more plausible as in *S/Z*, the book opens with a preliminary aggregate of ten of these sections. And this bloc seems to be granted the position of a general introduction to the overall critical enterprise of *S/Z*, the sort of role assumed by a preface in relation to a network of footnotes.[80] The topical rubrics appear to provide a systematization—and thus a higher degree of reflection—of the elliptical, partial, and very specialized 'micro-readings' of the commentary. The topical itinerary of *Roland Barthes* itself, which is ordered alphabetically instead of numerically, is in fact even more likely to be thought of as metalinguistically superior, since it is a text written later and which *includes* references to *S/Z*. What is more, the alphabetical system is finite rather than infinite, which promotes the idea of necessary closure. In both texts, finally, internal fragmentation calls for the ultimate metalinguistic level of tables and indexes. Through the synchronic juxta-position of the disjointed materials of the text, the tables at the end of the book seem to master the scattered network of the text's disjunctions via yet another taxonomic system, turning it once and for all into a clear, structural figure, a sort of *mise en abyme* which can be grasped at first glance. The tables are the final framing-device which seem to supply the 'legend', 'key', or 'map' for the text as a whole.[81] However, the 'subjugation of figures' to nomination, alphabet, and numbering turns the centralizing ambition of criticism and autobiography on its head. What the combination of nomination, alphabet, numbering (and typography) contributes to essays which are already presented as a series of *hors-textes* or as a 'pure series of interruptions',[82] is an additional support to the strategy of interruption and interpolation by which the essayist tackles his object again and again 'from a different angle': 'It is in order to halt, to deflect, to divide this descent of discourse toward a destiny of the subject, that at certain moments the alphabet calls you to order (to disorder) and says: *Cut! Resume the story in another way* [*Coupez! Reprenez l'histoire d'une autre manière*].'[83] This imperative to 'Cut! Resume the story in another way' which also

---

[80] Footnotes are usually seen as constituting a set of landmarks, or a 'network of junctions' for prefaces and conclusions (see Antoine Compagnon, *La Seconde Main, ou Le Travail de la citation*, (1979), 339).

[81] Philippe Hamon, 'Clausules', *Poétique*, 24 (1975), 519–20.

[82] *Roland Barthes*, 'The Circle of Fragments', 94 ['L'œuvre n'est faite que de hors-texte', and 'Que veut dire une suite pure d'interruptions?' 'Le Cercle des fragments', 98].

[83] *Roland Barthes*, 'The Order I No Longer Remember', 148 ['L'Ordre dont je ne me souviens plus', 151].

rules over the fragmentary progression of the *Essais*, recognizably informs the digressive logic of Barthes's entire work, one that links pre-text and commentary, · commentary and critical (or topical) sections, the topics or headings of the critical sections and their 'development', the critical sections to each other and to the tables, and finally the different essays themselves to each other. At all levels, the essay's potential 'rhetoric of development' is thwarted by the addition 'in a corner' (as Montaigne would put it) of the different parts to each other:

Not only is the fragment cut off from its neighbors, but even within each fragment parataxis reigns. This is clear if you make an index of these little pieces; for each of them, the assemblage of referents is heteroclite; it is like a parlor game: 'Take the words: *fragment, circle, Gide, wrestling match, asyndeton, painting, discourse, Zen, intermezzo*; make up a discourse which can link them together'.[84]

This force of 'ex-centricity', which promotes the impression of accidental and arbitrary rather than logical and necessary connections—the impression of 'insignificance'—is again in keeping with the essayist's refusal 'to separate the act of thinking from that of writing', with his obligation to criticize from a standpoint which is not ideologically suspect. Through temporal and spatial relativizations, constantly modified points of view and changed levels of perception—all features of what Barthes also calls 'the neutral'[85]—indirection secures the repetition of the same as other in opposition to the 'bad' repetition of the *doxa*, of 'current opinion, meaning repeated *as if nothing had happened*' [*comme si de rien n'était*].[86] It thus favours the oxymoronic logic of the and/or (as opposed to the either/or) characteristic of the Montaignian essay.

What Barthes emphatically sets up in all its possible forms and in order the better to violate it, is the 'spectacle of meaning' itself which is founded upon paradigmatic divisions, upon binary structures, upon the 'paradigmatic slash mark' which separates 'reasonably' and founds the 'power to legally substitute'.[87] We know that structuralist thought is fascinated with the rhetorical figure of antithesis, the role of which is 'to consecrate (and domesticate) by a name, by a metalinguistic object, the division between opposites and the very irreducibility of this division' described as the irreducibility between 'two plenitudes'.[88] Barthes himself—who devotes two topical sections to the taxonomic and rhetorical significance of antithesis in *S/Z* confesses in *Roland Barthes* to being very drawn to binary oppositions under the form, notably, of paired concepts:

Being the figure of opposition, the exasperated form of binarism, Antithesis is the very spectacle of meaning [*le spectacle même du sens*]. . . . He himself likes to resort to Antithesis.

[84] *Roland Barthes*, 'The Circle of Fragments', 93 ['Le Cercle des fragments', 97].
[85] See *Roland Barthes*, 'The Neutral' ['Le Neutre'].
[86] *Roland Barthes*, 'Medusa', 122 ['Méduse', 126]; see also ibid., 'The Wrong Object' ['Le Mauvais Objet'].
[87] Barthes, *S/Z*, Lexia 54, p. 48 ['La barre paradigmatique qui sépare raisonnablement', 55]; and *S/Z*, XCII, 'The Three Points of Entry', 216 ['Les Trois Entrées', 221].
[88] *S/Z*, XIV, 'Antithesis I: The Supplement', 26–7 ['L'Antithèse I: Le Supplément', 33 and 34].

. . . My discourse contains many coupled notions (*denotation/connotation, readerly/writerly*).[89]

But what he likes to do above all, is to use these rhetorical figures or 'conceptual procedures' without 'honouring' them, to set up paradigms in order to 'divert and alter them'.[90] And what happens when the division of opposites is no longer mastered is described in relation to the title 'S/Z', that is, to the *abyme* of the antithetical slash between the 'natural' opposites (plenitudes) of Sarrasine and la Zambinella, S and Z: the work succumbs to a 'generalized collapse of economies' which takes the form of 'frantic metonymy', since the 'power to legally substitute' is destroyed. The 'transgression' of a third, 'excentric' element occurs within the paradigm, adding itself unlawfully to rhetorical closure under the name of 'paradoxism', a third term which is not one of synthesis but of difference or *déport* which brings about the infinitely (scattering) effects of 'supplementariness'.[91] This third transgressive term of temporal deferment and spatial displacement which, as in the *Essais*, takes the form of topological transgressions, reflect here the topological transgressions of the castrato's sexual identity.[92] The supplementariness is at once a surplus and a lack of meaning, in the same way that the castrato of Balzac's story is both a woman and a man, and neither: '*more* and *less* can be generically placed in the same class, that of excess, what is *beyond* no longer differs from what is *short* of a limit . . . the two transgressions are united.'[93] Either way, the topic or headings's definitional function is ironized: it becomes a site of transition and dislocation, as the *hors-texte* is made to cover two conflicting senses which are constantly played against one another. In effect, the metalinguistic, extratextual claim of the numbered or alphabetically ordered heading is underlined and undermined by these ever-renewed 'departures of meaning' which also 'exit' out of meaning [*hors-sens*], that is, out of the meaning of the ideological mastertext of the *doxa*. Initially, the topics in both our texts denote the mastery of meaning associated with the naming activity of reading/criticizing. The specificity of the readerly text,

---

[89] *Roland Barthes*, 'Antithesis', 138 ['L'Antithèse', 142], and 'Forgeries', ibid. 92 ['Forgeries', 95].

[90] Ibid. [96].

[91] *S/Z*, XLVII, 'S/Z', 107 ['S/Z', 113]; *S/Z*, XIV, 'Antithesis I: The Supplement', 27 and 28, and *S/Z*, XXVII, 'Antithesis II. The Marriage', 65–6 ['L'Antithèse I: Le Supplément', 34 and 35, and 'L'Antithèse' II: Le Mariage', 72: 'Lorsqu'un corps supplémentaire est produit qui vient s'ajouter à la distribution déjà accomplie des contraires, ce supplément . . . est maudit: le *trop* éclate: le rassemblement se retourne en éparpillement']. *Roland Barthes*, 'Dialectics', 69: 'The binary dialectic (*Doxa* and its paradox) is the dialectic of meaning itself. . . . In him, another dialectic appears . . . the contradiction of the terms yields in his eyes by the discovery of a third term, which is not a synthesis but a *translation*' ['Dialectiques', 73].

[92] '*Sarrasine* recounts the topological transgressions of this body' (Barthes, *S/Z*, XCII, 'The Three Points of Entry', 215 ['Les Trois entrées', 220]). The body of the text is constantly exhibited, its physical characteristics flaunted everywhere by a multitude of organic and geographical metaphors (*tissu, tresse, L'Arbre, Pas à pas, Le Camp de la castration, Au-delà et en-deçà, Derrière, plus loin, Les Lignes de destination, Les Trois entrées*, etc.).

[93] Barthes, *S/Z*, XXX, 'Beyond and Short', 71–2 ['Le plus et le moins peuvent être rangés génériquement dans une même classe, celle de l'excès, ce qui est au-delà ne diffère plus de ce qui est en-deçà . . . les deux transgressions se confondent', 'Au-delà et en-deçà', 78].

Barthes writes, is that which 'names, signs, closes it off': 'to read is to find meanings, and to find meanings is to name them', to 'subject the sentences of the text to a semantic transformation', for 'to name is to subject, and the more generic the nomination, the stronger the subjection'.[94] However, narratology has shown the reading of all classical narrative to involve a 'suspension' of this final appropriation by the name—a suspension of the 'answer'; all narrative hinges on the deferral of the metaphoric resolution by the metonymic wandering and error inherent in its 'dilatory' structure.[95] Thus the 'named meanings are swept toward other names', for 'to read (to perceive the *readerly* aspect of the text) is to proceed from name to name, from fold to fold' in a metonymic approximation towards 'the generic word it continually attempts to join'.[96] In *S/Z*, this process is encapsulated by the idea of an 'expanding nomination' or nomination in progress summarized as follows: 'I name, I unname, I rename: so the text passes: it is a nomination in the course of becoming, a tireless approximation, a metonymic labor.'[97] Progression, then, also means regression: to confront the classical text is to regress or to *retreat* from name to name, starting from the signifying thrust' [*reculer de nom en nom à partir de la butée signifiante*].[98] But in the case of the narrative or generic scandal staged in *Sarrasine* where the 'generic word' must 'always' be gestured towards, never grasped, the approximation of this nomination in progress turns into infinite regression, regulated metonymy gives way to 'frantic metonymy': the name, rather than ultimately fixing and classifying meaning creates an 'excess of information', the disorder of a supplementarity which is 'what is forever added on without solving anything, without finishing anything'.[99]

Barthes's appeal to the 'infinite structure of the dictionary rather than its definitional power' stresses the fact that the 'scattering' induced by the addition of the third element—the generic 'scandal' of his essayistic work as a whole—is the scattering of meaning toward the infinite of language.[100] The very essence of the

[94] Barthes, *S/Z*, V, 'Reading and Forgetting', 11 ['La Lecture, l'oubli', 17]; *S/Z*, XL, 'The Birth of Thematics', 92 ['Naissance du thématique', 98–9]; and *S/Z*, LVI, 'The Tree', 129–30 ['Le sens est une force: nommer, c'est assujettir, et plus la nomination est générique, plus l'assujettissement est fort', 'L'Arbre', 136].

[95] 'To narrate (in the classic fashion) is to raise the question as if it were a subject which one delays predicating' (*S/Z*, XXXII, 'Delay', 76 ['Raconter à la façon classique, c'est poser la question comme un sujet que l'on tarde à prédiquer', 'Le Retard', 83]); and *S/Z*, XXXIII, 'And/or', 77: 'a suspension of the answer, required by the dilatory structure of narrative' ['Suspension de réponse obligée par la structure dilatoire du récit', 'Et/ou', 83].

[96] Barthes, *S/Z*, V, 'Reading, Forgetting', 11 ['La Lecture, l'oubli', 17]; and *S/Z*, XXXVI, 'Folding, Unfolding', 82–3 ['Le Pli, le dépli', 89]; *S/Z*, XL, 'The Birth of Thematics', 92 ['le mot générique qu'il essaye toujours de rejoindre', 'Naissance du thématique', 99].

[97] Barthes, *S/Z*, V, 'Reading, Forgetting', 11 ['Je nomme, je dénomme, je renomme: ainsi passe le texte: c'est une nomination en devenir, une approximation inlassable, un travail métonymique', 'La Lecture, l'oubli', 17–18].

[98] Barthes, *S/Z*, XL, 'The Birth of Thematics', 93 ['Naissance du thématique', 100].

[99] As opposed to truth which is 'what completes, what closes', Barthes, *S/Z*, XXXII, 'Delay', 76 ['Le Retard', 82].

[100] Barthes, *S/Z*, LXXVII, 'The Readerly II: Determined/Determinant', 182 ['L'éparpillement perdu des sens vers l'infini du langage', 'Le Lisible: déterminé/déterminant', 188]. Cf. also 'If the

dictionary is definitional, founded as it is on paradigmatic divisions which are signalled by a wide-ranging use of perigraphy (headings, blanks, colons, numbering, alphabet), all manifestations of the 'paradigmatic slash'. The structure of the dictionary relies on well circumscribed fragments both within and between articles. Its task is to disambiguate a word or sequence by explicating it, literally unfolding it in a process which is based upon a visible separation of entry and predication, signifier and signified, on the one hand, and between the various signifieds on the others, so that the principle of non-contradiction is respected.[101] What is essential to the whole didactic process of the definition, in other words, is that the frontiers should be very clearly set up, and the various levels of the definition kept under control: the main/usual meanings of a word and its peripheral or less common meanings, the proper and the figurative sense, the latter being recorded as a kind of deviation from the rule. In this way, the reader takes in the multiple aspects of a word while retaining a clear sense of what is included in and excluded from the centre of any one definition, which forces him or her to choose between one meaning and the other.[102] According to Barthes, to read classical narrative—that is, to 'follow certain synonymic chains' and to 'yield to an expanding nomination'—equals 'leaving the dictionary behind' [*sortir du dictionnaire*].[103] This is bound to be all the more true of *Sarrasine* in which: 'the fundamental crime or disaster ('Monster'!) is in fact to interrupt the circulation of (aesthetic and biological) copies, to disturb the controlled permeability of meanings, their *concatenation* [*enchaînement*], which is classification and repetition, as with language.'[104] In reality, rather than 'leaving the dictionary behind', this 'disaster' simply reveals the conditions of meaning of the dictionary in which each signified is in turn a signifier, and hence a part or fragment of what it is claiming to define or frame from a metalinguistic position—and *a fortiori* since these metalinguistic fragments constitute the discourse of the dictionary through and through. The structure of the dictionary thus already implies a potentially infinite regression away from the 'last word'. The false exteriority of headings and key-words ('tutor-words' and 'mana-words' rather than Montaigne's 'adequate words') in the topical sections of both *S/Z* and *Roland Barthes*, is a clear illustration of this:

study of language has taken on such importance nowadays, it's because language offers us the image of a structured and decentered ensemble, or set. . . . The dictionary, I repeat, is the concrete object that best accounts for this contradictory quality of language. A dictionary refers to a structure of language, but it is at the same time without a center (working on decentered structures)' (Barthes, *The Grain of the Voice*, 170–1 [*Le Grain de la voix*, 163]).

[101] The distribution of the lexical units themselves in alphabetical order, and the distribution of the various fragments for each unit, i.e. within each 'article' via an elaborate system of numbering which, by landmarking the typographical articulations, reinforces the article's metalinguistic content. See Alain Rey, 'Les Dictionnaires: Forme et contenu', *Cahiers de Lexicologie*, 7 (1965), 65 and 67.

[102] See Alain Rey, 'A propos de la définition lexicographique', *Cahiers de Lexicologie*, 6 (1965), 67–80; and Josette Rey-Debove, 'La Définition lexicographique: Recherches sur l'équation sémique', *Cahiers de Lexicologie*, 8 (1966), 71–94.

[103] Barthes, *S/Z*, XL, 'The Birth of Thematics', 93 ['Naissance du thématique', 99].

[104] Barthes, *S/Z*, LXXXV, 'Interrupted Replication', 202 ['La Réplique ininterrompue', 207–8].

In an author's lexicon, will there not always be a word-as-mana, a word whose ardent, complex, ineffable, and somehow sacred signification gives the illusion that by this word one might answer for everything? Such a word is neither eccentric nor central; it is motionless and carried, floating, never *pigeon-holed*, always atopic (escaping any topic), at once remainder and supplement, a signifier taking up the place of every signified.[105]

As in the *Essais*, the discrepancy between the accessory, peripheral nature of the key-words which are made to 'stand out' either as 'mana-words' or as headings, and the metalinguistic role which they are expected to play, reflects the nature of the problematic de-finition. Under the guise of straightforward predication (see for example the multiplicity of colons) and/or of a 'new departure', each one of these words is in fact a substitution, a 'translation', a 'synonym' which 'adds to its neighbor some new trait' (the same as other, the and/or of the oxymoron), a feature, 'at once remainder and supplement' of what precedes and follows it, a 'connection' rather than a 'filiation'.[106] Hence the impression one has of dealing with an inversion of the 'normal' dictionary definition: 'It does not define a word, it names a fragment; it does precisely the converse of the dictionary; the word emerges from the utterance, rather than the utterance proceeding from the word.'[107] The topics or headings are already the result of an indirect interpretation of the text; more often than not in *S/Z*, they are metaphors for the problems of representation which the text illustrates, metaphors which in turn indirectly reflect the essayist's own activity. The overlap or mutual inclusion of concepts constantly challenges and short-circuits the impermeability between main and secondary elements, but also between opposed elements (antonyms). The transgression of non-contradiction inherent in the essayistic 'weighing' is flagrant in the preliminary critical section of *S/Z*, for example, where, again with the assistance of numbers, opposed sections corresponding to opposed values (e.g. III. 'Connotation: Against'; IV. 'Connotation: For, Even So') are put into dialogue with one another in a way that does not give precedence to either and results therefore in a surplus of meaning which cannot be reduced to either term.

So one may describe the blurred taxonomy which Barthes produces as a syntagmatic overcoming of the frontiers of the sign in the course of it definitional unfolding: the intermediate, approximate, or peripheral elements—the various synonyms that represent the features of the entry—operate at one level with the key-word, spilling over diachronically in a process of usurpation that leads further

---

[105] *Roland Barthes*, 'Mana-word', 129 ['Ce mot n'est ni excentrique ni central; il est immobile et porté, en dérive, jamais *casé*, toujours *atopique* (échappant à toute topique), à la fois reste et supplément, signifiant occupant la place de tout signifié', *Roland Barthes*, 'Mot-mana', 133]. See 'From the sufficient word to the mana-word', in Bensmaïa, *The Barthes Effect*.

[106] Barthes, *S/Z*, XL, 'The Birth of Thematics', 92 ['la lecture est ainsi absorbée dans une sorte de glissement métonymique, chaque synonyme ajoutant à son voisin quelque trait, quelque départ nouveau', 'Naissance du thématique', 99].

[107] *Roland Barthes*, 'The Alphabet', 148 ['Il ne définit pas un mot, il nomme un fragment; il fait l'inverse même du dictionnaire: le mot sort de l'énoncé, au lieu que l'énoncé dérive du mot', 'L'Alphabet', 151].

and further away from a reassimilation of these features into the head-word.[108] For all that, the proliferation of new predicates is still contained within the boundaries of the article, that is, ultimately, by the head-word itself which acts as both entry and exit. The internal subversion thus takes the form of a recomposition of the head-word from the elements of its decomposition. Since the new semantic combinations operate progressive shifts within the frame of the definition, so that the act of defining finds itself merged with the (re)constitution of the word to which it was typographically opposed, the overrun of the name is synchronic as well as diachronic: on the one hand, the different signifieds are visibly disaggregated as they are in the dictionary article, while on the other, each one of these key-terms is itself the nexus of all the externalized shifts which have generated it, and which it in turn generates:

Each word *turns*, either like milk, spoiled in the disintegrated space of phraseology. . . . Other words, finally, are cruisers [*dragueurs*]: they follow what they meet up with . . .

the first (system) breaks down the title (noun or verb) according to its constituents moments. . . . The second system attaches contingent actions to a guide word. . . . These systems, one analytical, the other catalytical, one definitional, the other metonymical.[109]

The subversion of the name by its constituent, peripheral meanings, is also necessarily a subversion from within, the key-word being the point of fusion of all the carefully separated levels of signifieds in the dictionary article. Each topic is shown paradoxically to include its contradictory others, correspondingly with the essayist's taste for 'actualizing amphibologies'. 'In general'—writes Barthes—'the context forces us to choose one of the two meanings and to forget the other', whereas 'each time he encounters one of these double words, R.B., on the contrary, insists on keeping both meanings . . . so that *one and the same word*, in *one and the same sentence*, means *at one and the same time* two different things, and so that one delights, semantically, in the one by the other.'[110] The semantic potential of each name is unlimited, for its etymology or origin no longer acts as a check to the potentially endless regression of the definition, as it does in the dictionary: 'by dint of combinations made within one and the same name, nothing is left of the *origin*'.[111] 'Cutting the word at the root' turns the word, and by extension the entire discourse, into a palimpsest: 'His discourse is full of words he cuts off, so to speak,

[108] Cf. 'Each synonym adding to its neighbor some new trait, some new departure' (*S/Z*, XL, 'The Birth of Thematics', 92) and 'to fold the text according to one name and then to unfold it along the new folds of this name' (*S/Z*, XXXVI, 'Folding, Unfolding', 83 ['Naissance du thématique', 99; and 'Plier sous un nom puis déplier le texte selon les nouveaux plis de ce nom', 'Le Pli, le dépli', 89]). These shifts often involve a change of grammatical category: transitions from noun to verb or to adjective, which goes against the dictionary definition of one item by another item of the same category.

[109] *Roland Barthes*, 'Limpness of Important Words', 126 ['Mollesse des grands mots', 129]. *S/Z*, XXXVI, 'Folding, Unfolding', 82 ['Le premier décompose le titre (nom ou verbe) selon ses moments constitutifs. . . . Le second accroche au mot-tuteur des actions voisines. Ces systèmes, l'un analytique, l'autre catalytique, l'un définitionnel, l'autre métonymique', 'Le Pli, le dépli', 88–9].

[110] *Roland Barthes*, 'Amphibologies', 72 ['Amphibologies', 76].

[111] *Roland Barthes*, 'The Ship *Argo*', 46 ['Le Vaisseau Argo', 50].

at the root. Yet in etymology it is not the truth or the origin of the word which pleases him but rather the *effect of overdetermination* [*l'effet de surimpression*] which it authorizes: the word is seen as a palimpsest.'[112] In the dictionary, this 'effect of overdetermination' is proscribed by the abstraction of sign and meaning where signs—entries—are physically demarcated as though they did not mean anything prior to their definition, conformably with Adorno's description of the way in which the essay tackles its concepts.[113] The alphabet, as Barthes notes in an essay on Erté's 'letters', 'achieves a kind of Adamic state of language: it is language before the Fall, because it is language before discourse, language before the syntagm'.[114] Without necessarily stretching the concept of 'innocence' this far, the fragment itself of the entry, which is given out of context, is doubtless identified with a 'natural' meaning which is in fact simply that of a 'memorized linguistic consciousness'—the *status quo* or *doxa* of the time.[115] In the case of the encyclopedia, this 'exteriority' involves not least the claim to an extralinguistic neutrality, since linguistic facts are only considered as indirect means for the description of the world, in contradistinction to the dictionary. In both cases, however, the fragments which are made to stand 'out' in this way are as many quotations, the products of prior and future textual displacements. As the cutting up of *Sarrasine* has shown, the detached, abstracted fragment is always already reinscribed in a multiplicity of other contexts. In this sense, Barthes's reference to 'the possibility of the word, the word pregnant with its possibilities'[116] perfectly encapsulates the zero degree of the paratextual fragment's position, its 'suspended' status between the discourse from which it has been extracted and the discourse of the definition in which it is to be reintegrated. The space of this suspension is in fact nothing other than the space of its (infinite) intertextual potential:

Denotation is not the first meaning but pretends to be so; under this illusion, it is ultimately no more than the *last* of the connotations (the one which seems both to establish and to close the reading), the superior myth by which the text pretends to return to the nature of language, to language as nature . . .

Denotation is not the truth of discourse: denotation is not outside structures, it has a structural function on a par with others: that of *justifying* structure [*innocenter la structure*].[117]

Like Montaigne, Barthes emphasizes the precedence of connotation (of the metaphorical, the poetic, the 'oniric') over denotation by 'subjecting' his 'objects of knowledge and discussion . . . no longer to an instance of truth, but to a considera-

---

[112] *Roland Barthes*, 'Etymologies', 85 ['Etymologies', 88].

[113] See my Chapter 3, 3.1.2.2., 'Essaying as "Unmethodical Method"'.

[114] Barthes, *The Responsibility of Forms: Critical Essays on Music, Art, and Representation* (1991), 120 [*L'Obvie et l'obtus* (1982), 113].

[115] See Josette Rey-Debove, 'Autonymie et métalangue', *Cahiers de Lexicologie*, 2 (1967), 22.

[116] Barthes, *S/Z*, XXXVI, 'Folding, Unfolding', 82 ['la possibilité du nom, le nom gros de ses possibles', 'Le Pli, le dépli', 89].

[117] Barthes, *S/Z*, IV, 'Connotation: For, Even So', 9 ['Pour la connotation, tout de même', 16]; and *S/Z*, LV, 'Language as Nature', 128 ['Le Langage comme nature', 134].

tion of *effects*' [*une pensée des effets*].[118] As in the *Essais*, the argument is not just
supplemented by images because 'it is a good thing . . . that out of consideration
for the reader, there should pass through the essay's discourse, from time to time,
a sensual object.'[119] Rather, 'argumentation' is replaced by 'the unfolding of an
image' [*dépliement d'une image*] and 'reasoning' by a 'series of metaphors' [*un
enchaînement de métaphores*]. So the 'intellectual object' is neither 'invented' nor
'combined', but 'translated' in a movement which, in keeping with a 'successful
metaphor', affords no hierarchy between its terms and 'removes all hindrances
from the polysemic chain'.[120] Barthes's description of this 'leverage upon the
signifier' [*pesée sur le signifiant*] as originating in the creation of a 'magical word' or
'*word-thought* [*pensée-mot*] . . . which will ferret through all [his] language' as in an
'echo chamber', underlines the fact that in all discourse, it is the word that leads
the idea and not the other way round.[121] To 'have ideas *on the level of language*' is
'quite simply: to write' and 'to enjoy *deporting* the object, by a kind of imagination
which is [ultimately] more homologic than metaphoric'.[122] The pseudo-logical
system of the numbering in *S/Z* already renders conspicuous the dependence of
the conceptual upon a-logical and associative progression. But the use of the
alphabet in *Roland Barthes* spells out the associative process of the dictionary even
more directly. The alphabet, which orders the nomenclature in the dictionary, is
not only sequential; it is finite and also verbal and is therefore an even more
powerful means than the number to unmask the arbitrariness and meaninglessness
(the 'verisimilitude') of the order of language from within (or by means of) language. Above all, the alphabet 'decrees that Law in whose name every extravagance can be reduced' while on the other hand 'tirelessly releas[ing] a profusion of
symbols', thus combining like no other system 'censorship' and 'bliss' [*jouissance*]:
'On the one hand, [the letter] "keeps" language, the whole written language,
within the yoke of its twenty-six characters . . . but on the other hand, it releases
an imagery vast as a cosmography; on the one hand, it signifies the most extreme
censorship (. . .), on the other, the most extreme bliss.'[123] In its quality as a 'signifying chain' that operates within the realm of the sign yet 'outside' (or on the edge
of) the realm of meaning or meaningfulness ('A letter, at the same time, *means* and
means nothing'; 'it is a signifying chain, a syntagm outside meaning but not outside

---

[118] *Roland Barthes*, 'Fiction', 90 ['La Fiction', 94].

[119] *Roland Barthes*, 'Movements of Objects into Discourse', 135 ['Passage des objets dans le discours',
138].

[120] *Roland Barthes*, 'Which reasoning?', 152 ['Quel raisonnement?', 155]; *Roland Barthes*, 'Comparison is Motive', 58 ['Comparaison est raison', 62]; and *S/Z*, XXXIII, 'And/Or', 77 ['Et/ou', 84].

[121] *Roland Barthes*, 'Movement of Objects into Discourse', 134, and 134–5 ['Passage des objets dans
le discours', 138]; *Roland Barthes*, 'The Transitional Word', 130 ['Le Mot transitionnel']; and 'Which
Reasoning', 152 ['Quel raisonnement?', 155].

[122] *Roland Barthes*, 'Etymologies', 85 ['avoir des idées *à même la langue*', 'Etymologies', 88]; 'Comparison is Motive', 58 ['Comparaison est raison', 62].

[123] Barthes, *The Responsibility of Forms*, 98–9 (NB The translator uses 'pleasure' for *jouissance* rather
than 'bliss' which, given Barthes's famous distinction between the two words, seems to me to be
mistaken) [*L'Obvie et l'obtus*, 95].

of the sign'[124]), the alphabet epitomizes the conflict between signifying and meaningful order, between the conceptual foundation of the encyclopedia's totalizing, epistemological project and its dependency upon the nonsensical—in the proper sense of the idea of *folle polygraphie*. The way in which the order of the dictionary overrides the logic of the encyclopedic project can in fact be described as a complete conceptual aberration, since rather than concerning itself 'semantically' with its corpus, that is to say with meaningful units or 'first articulations', it is only concerned with the transcription of units of secondary articulation (distinctive rather than meaningful units[125]). More simply, the overdetermined signifying system of the encyclopedia—its 'writerly' dimension—is its 'poetic' dimension. The poetic, Barthes writes, 'is, very exactly, a form's symbolic capacity; and this capacity has value only if it permits the form to "depart" in many directions and thereby potentially to manifest the infinite advance of the symbol': 'All poetry—the whole of the unconscious—is a return to the letter.'[126]

The tables at the end of both *S/Z* and *Roland Barthes* are the last and most eloquent instance of the paradoxical logic which governs the 'systematics' of both essays. In them the essayist's 'leverage upon the signifier' occurs most conspicuously within a strikingly regimented structure. In both essays, the tables and indexes seem at first sight to compensate for the internal fragmentation of the autobiographical discourse in *Roland Barthes*, and of the constant mutual interruption of gloss and theoretical sections in *S/Z* which makes it difficult for the reader to follow the progression of either one and/or the contribution of the one to the other. In terms of the modern encyclopedia, the table can be identified with the third mode of representation beside the Dictionary and the System: the Map. The table is a reduced model, a tabular synopsis of the System—the continuous, cohesive philosophical or scientific discourse which forms the underlying network of relations between the scattered, heterogeneous elements of the dictionary.[127] As an intersection between 'compilation and order',[128] it provides a final regulation for the text's heteroclite accumulation of fragments, a 'reasoned' check to its 'irrational polygraphy'. In *S/Z* the final 'Table', which one expects to encompass the book as a whole, is in fact a third table, one which is thus supposed to frame not only the book, but the two previous tables of the *Appendices* ('Appendice 2' and 'Appendice 3') which it includes in its listing. The presence of not just one but three tables is already a contradiction in terms in relation to the totalizing aim of the 'closure', unless perhaps one assumes a complementary function of, and hierarchy between, the different tables. There is no reason why not, for the first table (entitled

[124] Barthes, *The Responsibility of Forms*, 116 and 99 ['Car une lettre, tout à la fois, veut dire et ne veut rien dire', *L'Obvie et l'obtus*, 110, and 'C'est une chaîne signifiante, un syntagme hors du sens, mais non hors du signe', *L'Obvie et l'obtus*, 96].

[125] See Rey: 'Les dictionnaires: Forme et contenu', 81–2; and Oswald Ducrot and Tzvetan Todorov, *Dictionnaire encyclopédique des sciences du langage* (1972), 73–4.

[126] Barthes, *The Responsibility of Forms*, 124 and 99.

[127] Moser, 'L'Encyclopédie romantique', 503–4, and 'Fragment and Encyclopedia', 116–17.

[128] Michaud, 'Fragment et dictionnaire', 74.

'Sequence of Actions') has to do with the gloss (it refers to the bulk of the lexical units from the angle of the code of actions, the 'frame of the readerly text', p. 259), and the third table (the 'key') with the topical sections. The most authoritative table appears to be the second, so-called *Table raisonnée* (translated simply as 'summary of contents') which could then be seen as occupying a significant pivotal or dialectical position between the other two. But hierarchy—and the related search for the 'last word'—cannot be recovered this way either, for what this 'summary of contents' does, is simply repeat the already tabular structure of the text 'otherwise'. In it a new system of articulations operates, whereby the Roman numerical ordering is broken up into the Arabic which is in turn subdivided alphabetically. The meta-headings of the *Table raisonnée* themselves turn out to be but the result of a reshuffling between main and peripheral areas of the text. They relegate the new definitional terms to seemingly less decisive levels of the inventory where compilation prevails over order. And this interchangeability of levels clearly constitutes a final demonstration of the arbitrariness of any one organization of fragments, the *Table raisonnée* being denied the right to represent anything but another, equally valid reading of the text. Rather than representing the final mastery of critical discourse, the table 'indexes' the most radical scattering of that discourse into its peripheral elements and enacts once again the differential character of the structure. In the encyclopedia itself after all, the Map, which duplicates the System, is redundant or supplementary.[129] The tables, in short, are the last example of the 'third' dialectical term not of synthesis but of 'deport' which adds itself 'transgressively' to a part of the text it is supposed to frame, and which is itself already explicitly 'added' to the book as a whole—as the word *Appendices* ('Annexe') makes clear. In *Roland Barthes*, which can be regarded as metalinguistically 'superior' to *S/Z*, the two tables entitled *Repères* (an index) and *Table* have a slightly different way of putting the same point across; but again the transgressive mechanism of the text is magnified. This time, the first table—the index—functions as a *Table raisonnée* in relation to the second which simply lists all the topical sections of the essay with corresponding page numbers. In this second table, the alphabetical ordering of fragments which Barthes uses to interrupt the sequence of fragments and their temptation to 'mean' is itself shown to be undermined by an inconsistent and erratic use. The pseudo-logical order of the alphabet is itself discouraged—warped or deviated—when for example the word (the topic) which begins with the right letter is not the main word in the syntagm but a peripheral one (*Au tableau noir*, for example, comes before *Le vaisseau Argo*). The *Table* also reveals that the essayistic strategy of indirection can lead to the intervention of a complete outsider within the alphabetical ordering of fragments: *Noms propres*, for example, follows *La baladeuse* and *Quand je jouais aux barres*. In

---

[129] Moser, 'L'Encyclopédie romantique', 503–4. As the unifying and cohesive principle, the System not only complements the Dictionary but, since it only constitutes a small part (usually preliminary) of the overall textual volume of the Book, frames the Book. And in the same way the Map duplicates the System, thereby providing a second level of framing.

fact, these outsiders do not undermine the alphabetical system so much as draw attention to it. They can be considered as fragments which are inserted either too early or too late, and their presence seen either as reinforcing the arbitrariness of the alphabet, or on the contrary as breaking this arbitrariness for consequence (concepts) to win over sequence. Whatever the case may be, the very oblique (if not totally digressive) approach of the *Table* fully warrants the existence of a methodical index (of 'landmarks' or so-called *Repères*): thanks to the page numbers attributed to each one, a proper continuity in the essayist's treatment of each key-word or topic can be re-established over and above the interruptions and digressions. The index, as Michel Beaujour reminds us, is meant to be the 'method', the 'reason (the reasoned table or synoptic chart) of what is delirious in the fragmentation of the encyclopedic text'.[130] But of course the choice itself of key-words in Barthes's index is random. The index is not exhaustive: some of the more important (or recurrent) key-words of Barthes's text are not listed, while other peripheral topics (including topics which appear in parenthesis in the text—for example the adjective, p. 176) are given first choice in the index. This reflects again the lack of coincidence, in the text, between the topics listed and the subject-matter of these topical sections. The reshuffling of boundaries by which fragments constitute themselves according to yet another order confuses the reader once and for all: the encyclopedic taxonomy is blurred and the logical connections forgotten or repressed. As in *S/Z*, then, the more exhaustive the final recognition of the work's identity attempts to be, the more radically it needs to disarticulate the text, applying to it most extreme possible coercive system of nominal and graphic demarcations which, rather than checking the mad paratextual proliferation, releases one last frenzy of unrestrained 'polygraphy'. Thus, if the index appears, like the other tables, to 'rationalize' the fragmentation of the encyclopedic text, it is also the point at which reason—the 'rationality of discourse'—breaks down: 'The index of a text is not only an instrument of reference; it is itself a text, a second text which is the *relief* (remainder and asperity) of the first: what is wandering (interrupted) in the rationality of the sentences.'[131]

4.3. 'THIS IS NOT YOUR PLACE'

The open-endedness of both essays made definitive by the subversion of this final paratext of the table corrupts the ultimate controlling instance of the text—the

---

[130] Beaujour, *Poetics of the Literary Self-Portrait* ['L'index est la raison (la table raisonnée, le tableau synoptique) de ce qu'il y a de délirant (de sauvage et d'antique) dans la fragmentation du texte encyclopédique. C'est la *méthode* du texte, qui le transforme en répertoires de lieux communs', *Miroirs d'encre*, 223]. See also Michaud, 'Fragment et dictionnaire', 74.

[131] *Roland Barthes*, 'The Circle of Fragments', 93 ['L'index d'un texte n'est pas seulement un instrument de référence; il est lui-même un texte, un second texte qui est le *relief* (reste et aspérité) du premier: ce qu'il y a de délirant (d'interrompu) dans la raison des phrases', 'Le Cercle des fragments', 97].

essayist himself—since 'by decomposing, [the essayist] agree[s] to accompany such decomposition, to decompose [himself] as well, in the process'.[132] In the context of the paratextual cutting up of *Sarrasine*, the author was shown to be 'a text like any other' (or rather a 'plurality of other texts'), one which added itself without closing, like Barthes's 'appendices'; he was a 'being on paper', a 'writing without referent', the 'substance of a *connection* and not of a *filiation*': in other words not 'the subject, the impulse, the origin, the authority, the Father, whence [the] work would proceed'.[133] *Sarrasine*, which is a 'classically plural' text between the classic ('haunted by the appropriation of speech') and the modern text ('where language speaks, nothing more') represents for Barthes the perfect example of a discourse in which 'the voice gets lost' and the reader/critic is invited to:

listen to the text as an iridescent exchange carried on by multiple voices, on different wavelengths and subject from time to time to a sudden *dissolve*, leaving a gap which enables the utterance to shift from one point of view to another, without warning: the writing is set up across this tonal instability (which in the modern text becomes atonality), which makes it a glistening texture of ephemeral origins.[134]

In this sense, the enunciatory position of the author of the classically plural text evidently applies (albeit indirectly) to the essayist's relation to his own discourse. The essayist's subjectivity, like the realist author's, is 'a plenary image, with which [he] may be thought to encumber the text, but whose deceptive plenitude is merely the wake of all the codes which constitute [him]'.[135] Like Montaigne, Barthes acts upon this 'deceptive plenitude'—the 'gap' left by the 'dissolve of voices' which prompts the reader to ask 'who is speaking?'. Both his essays become this 'iridescent exchange carried on by multiple voices' which 'enables the utterance to shift from one point of view to another, without warning'. Again, the 'vacancy' of the essayist's enunciatory position does not correspond so much to his absence (as in the modern text where no one speaks) as to the 'unlocatability' or 'irretrievability' which Barthes associates with the 'principle of drifting':

I am not hidden within the text, I am simply irrecoverable [*irrepérable*] from it: my task is to move, to shift systems whose perspective ends neither at the text nor at the 'I' . . .

. . . the vacancy of the 'person', if not annulled at least rendered irretrievable—absence of *imago*—the suspension of judgment, of due process—displacement—the refusal 'to keep

---

[132] *Roland Barthes*, 'Decompose/Destroy', 63 ['En décomposant, j'accepte d'accompagner cette décomposition, de me décomposer moi-même, au fur et à mesure: Je dérape, accroche et entraîne', Décomposer/détruire', 68].

[133] Barthes, *S/Z*, XC, 'The Balzacian Text', 211 ['Le Texte balzacien', 217].

[134] Barthes, *S/Z*, XX, 'The Dissolve of Voices: Who is Speaking?', 41–2 ['Le Fading des voix: 'Qui parle?', 48 and 49].

[135] Barthes, *S/Z*, V, 'Reading, Forgetting', 10 ['La subjectivité est une image pleine, dont on suppose que j'encombre le texte, mais dont la plénitude, truquée, n'est que le sillage de tous les codes qui me font . . .', 'La Lecture, l'oubli', 17].

oneself in countenance' (the refusal of any countenance whatever)—the principle of delicacy—drifting [*la dérive*].[136]

The emptiness or 'vacancy' of the person which makes possible this 'drifting' of the essayist between multiple postures of enunciation—what Barthes calls his 'atopia'—is the logical consequence, as in Montaigne, of the recognition of the subject's 'inconsistency' and therefore of the impossibility of self-expression: the text as the 'expression' of a subject anterior to it is a fiction, and so, therefore, is 'lyricism': 'Writing subjects me to a severe exclusion . . . because it forbids me to "express myself": *whom* could it express? Exposing the inconsistency of the subject, his atopia, dispersing the enticements of the imaginary, it makes all lyricism untenable (as the utterance of a central 'emotion').'[137] The text is not that by which the author/essayist describes or defines himself with a view to 'restoring' his authentic being. Rather the author/essayist is a product of the text, the result of a retrospective 'connection'. We saw in the topical sections of both essays that Barthes 'does not define a word, [he] names a fragment; [he] does precisely the converse of the dictionary; the word emerges from the utterance, rather than the utterance proceeding from the word'. Concurrently, the essayist '[does] not say: "I am going to describe myself" but: "I am writing a text, and I call it R.B."', in the case of *Roland Barthes*.[138] It is precisely because 'the subject is merely an effect of language' that it can occupy multiple postures of enunciation and 'wrap [itself] in the mist of an enunciatory situation', via the 'shifters' ('I', 'here', 'now', 'tomorrow') which by definition favour 'leaks of interlocution', since they are 'mobile' and 'empty' signs which can be appropriated by any locutor.[139] The emptiness of the shifters thus allows shifts of points of view whereby the 'I' who speaks is never the same.

In the application of this 'atopia' to the self-critical discourse of the essayist, one recognizes the mechanism of the self-portrait already discussed in Montaigne. In this respect, the title *Roland Barthes* can simply be said to turn the self-essaying—which always goes hand in hand with the process of essaying—into a more straightforwardly autobiographical process than *S/Z* does. Arguably the difference between the two types of self-essaying is marginal, since not only the declared self-portraitist but the (Montaignian) essayist in general 'tells himself only through what surpasses,

---

[136] Barthes, *S/Z*, V, 'Reading, Forgetting', 10 ['La Lecture, l'oubli', 17]; and *Roland Barthes*, 'The Neutral', 132 ['Le Neutre', 136]. Cf. also 'It is a *diffraction* which is intended, a dispersion of energy in which there remains neither a central core nor a structure of meaning: I am not contradictory, I am dispersed', 'The person divided?', 143 ['je ne suis pas contradictoire, je suis dispersé', 'La Personne divisée?', 146]. ·

[137] *Roland Barthes*, 'Celine and Flora', 86 ['Mettant à vif l'inconsistance du sujet, son atopie . . . elle rend intenable tout lyrisme', 'Céline et Flora', 89].

[138] *Roland Barthes*, 'The Alphabet', 148 ['L'Alphabet', 151]; and *Roland Barthes*, 'Coincidence', 56 ['Coïncidence', 60].

[139] *Roland Barthes*, 'New Subject, New Science', 79 ['Nouveau sujet, nouvelle science', 82]; and *Roland Barthes*, 'The Shifter as Utopia', 166 ['je parle, mais je m'enveloppe dans la brume d'une situation énonciatrice qui vous est inconnue; je ménage dans mon discours des fuites d'*interlocution*', 'Le Shifter comme utopie', 168].

goes through, and denies him': in both cases the 'dispersion' or 'diffraction' of the subject occurs via a confrontation with an intertext.[140] The essay has been defined as 'a characterization of its object (a place, a work, a person), but also of its maker; a *reciprocal* characterization', which emphasizes the fact that 'selfhood cannot be grasped independently', that it 'can only be configured with an object'.[141] Barthes's confession to the pleasure he takes in 'reversing' and appropriating models unmistakably echoes the self-affirmation of the (Montaignian) essayist in the margins of the encyclopedia or intertext: for him writers like Proust, Blanchot, Kafka, Artaud act as 'mediators of desire', not the 'desire to write *on* these authors (not even . . . *like* them), but to *write*'. Similarly, Barthes considers his essays as 'a gathering of materials [*un recueil de matériaux*], a "repertory" of critical themes', an 'instrument of study' intended for the 'virtual creator' in every reader.[142] But conversely, this notion of 'pretext' implies that the essayist's affirmation in the margins of the intertext—past and future—does not take place without the decentring of his position of enunciation by both existing and virtual writers. In both essays, then, the questioning of the writing subject's own identity with himself is inseparable from the recognition of a necessarily indirect, oblique approach: the 'I' can only be grasped as another and via the other, analogically, metaphorically, in an act of (self-)translation. So, one might say, *Sarrasine*, Balzac, and the numerous other texts (including Barthes's own), authors, characters, rhetorical figures, theories, systems of knowledge, etc. referred to in Barthes's work all function as the necessary pre-texts for the essayist's (self-)expression, that is, as the objects in which the essayist (mis-)recognizes himself:

It is clear in the *Critical Essays* how the subject of the writing 'evolves' . . . he evolves according to the authors he treats, in order. The inducing object, however, is not the author I am talking about but rather *what he leads me to say about him*: I influence myself *with his permission*: what I say about him forces me to think as much about myself (or not to think as much), etc.

Can one—or at least could one ever—begin to write without taking oneself for another? For the history of sources we should substitute the history of figures: the origin of the work is not the first influence, it is the first posture: one copies a role, then, by metonymy, an art: I begin producing by reproducing the person I want to be. This first want (I desire and I pledge myself) establishes a secret system of fantasies which persist from age to age, often independently of the writings of the desired author.[143]

We will recall that by definition the self-portrait 'mediates' 'between the individual and his culture'; that it is the space of a dialectic between the impersonal intertext

[140] Beaujour, *Poetics of the Literary Self-Portrait*, 35.   [141] Good, *The Observing Self*, 22.
[142] Barthes, *The Rustle of Language*, 40–1 [*Le Bruissement de la langue*, 45]; and Barthes, *The Grain of the Voice*, 26 [*Le Grain de la voix*, 31].
[143] *Roland Barthes*, 'What is Influence?', 106 ['Qu'est-ce que l'influence?', 110]; and *Roland Barthes*, 'Abgrund', 99 ['Abgrund', 103]; cf. also *Roland Barthes*, 'Phases': '(1) The intertext is not necessarily a field of influences; rather it is a music of figures, metaphors, thought-words . . .', 145 ['Phases', 148].

which pre-dates the subject and the autobiographical project, whereby the 'empirical individual . . . matters much less . . . than the unstable *places* of an impersonal memory always exceeding with its "wild polygraphy" the memories of an individual'.[144] In Barthes's own words:

Once I produce, once I write, it is the Text itself which (fortunately) dispossesses me of my narrative continuity. The Text can recount nothing; it takes my body elsewhere, far from my imaginary person, toward a kind of memoryless speech which is already the speech of the People, of the non-subjective mass (or of the generalized subject), even if I am still separated from it by my way of writing.

A kind of collective 'id' replaces the image I thought I had of myself, and that 'id' is me.[145]

If Barthes's 'obscure *speculum* is an encyclopedia with a scrambled taxonomy', this is because 'the encyclopedia is not the self-portrait's manifest structure but rather its nontotalizing antistructure, the "last word" of which eludes the self-portrayer'.[146] By exploiting the 'nontotalizing antistructure' of the encyclopedia—the topical dispersions, the dislocated agencies of enunciation, 'atopia'—Barthes consciously escapes the fate of being 'pigeonholed' [*fiché*], of being 'assigned to an (intellectual) site' [*assigné à un lieu (intellectuel)*], to 'residence in a caste (if not in a class)'.[147] The essayist's conception of identity as an arbitrary collection of features or as 'a delicately proportioned and henceforth absolutely original combination of tiny characteristics organized in fugitive scenes, from day to day',[148] incites him constantly to stage the creation or writing of the self as other, from a different angle or point of view:

Any classification you read provokes a desire in you to put yourself into it somewhere: where is your place? At first you think you have found it: but gradually, like a disintegrating statue or an eroding relief, its shape blurs and fades . . . you are no longer classifiable . . . you unite in yourself supposedly distinctive features which henceforth no longer distinguish anything; you discover that you are at one and the same time (or alternately) obsessive, hysterical, paranoiac, and perverse to the last degree . . . or that you sum up all the decadent philosophies: Epicureanism, eudaemonism, Asianism, Manichaeism, Pyrrhonism.[149]

And this 'you'—another example of Barthes's versatile use of shifters—is of course also the 'you' of the reader who, in putting himself in the place of the essayist is never allowed to find the resting-place of self-recognition either, nor to get behind

---

[144] Beaujour, *Poetics of the Literary Self-Portrait*, 35 and 34.
[145] *Roland Barthes*, 3 (in italics) [6]; and *Roland Barthes*, caption: 'Structuralist Fashions', 146 ['Une sorte de çà collectif se substitue à l'image que je croyais avoir de moi, et c'est moi, "çà"', 'La Mode structuraliste', 149].
[146] Beaujour, *Poetics of the Literary Self-Portrait*, 31–2.
[147] *Roland Barthes*, 'Atopia', 49 ['L'Atopie', 53].
[148] *Roland Barthes*, 'Friends', 64 ['une combinaison délicatement dosée . . . de menus traits réunis dans des scènes fugitives, au jour le jour', 'Les Amis', 69].
[149] *Roland Barthes*, 'The Person Divided?', 143–4 ['La Personne divisée?', 146–7].

the various masks of the essayist's 'impostures'.[150] The topics by which Barthes essays himself in the very act of essaying the intertext are caught in a process of self-commentary or self-gloss whereby, like Montaigne, Barthes '[has] no other solution than to *rewrite* [himself]—at a distance, at a great distance—here and now'. And consonantly with the 'translation' and 'deporting' of topics examined above, this 'self-translation' consists in 'add[ing] to the books, to the themes, to the texts, another utterance, without [the essayist] ever knowing whether it is about [his] past or [his] present that [he] [is] speaking'.[151] In *S/Z*, writing as 'rereading' 'alone saves the text from repetition' and 'draws the text out of its internal chronology'.[152] This promotion of chronological confusions already at work in the *Essais* enables the essayist to escape the metalinguistic trap of rewriting as correction, allegedly out of modesty or sense of decency ('self-commentary? What a bore'[153]), but more convincingly because the essayist '[does] not strive to put [his] present expression in the service of [his] previous truth', in the name of an 'authenticity' ('the exhausting pursuit of an old piece of [himself]') in which he does not believe: 'The modern *scriptor* is born *at the same time* as his text; he is not furnished with a being which precedes or exceeds his writing, he is not the subject of which his book is the predicate; there is no time other than that of the speech-act, and every text is written eternally *here* and *now*.'[154] Thus, as with the various phases of elaboration of the *Essais*, it is inevitable that in Barthes's work, 'between the periods, obviously, there are overlappings [*chevauchements*], returns, affinities, leftovers'.[155] By 'translating himself', 'doubling one phrase by another', it is 'as if, striving to epitomize himself, [Barthes] could not get it over with, heaped summary on top of summary, unable to decide which is best'.[156] In reality, this 'indecision' is the consequence of a decision to make each 'phase' 'reactive': 'the author reacts either to the discourse which surrounds him, or to his own discourse, if one and the other begin to have too much consistency, too much stability; one nail

---

[150] This self-translation—the translation of the same as other—by which Barthes demarcates himself from existing systems or schools of thoughts and simultaneously adopts the multiple postures or masks referred to at the beginning of this chapter (as a writer, a critic, a semiologist, etc.) is of course also the mark, here, of the essayist's impostures. Cf. *Roland Barthes*, 'The Imago's Impossible Graph', 61–2 ['La Courbe folle de l'imago', 66].

[151] *Roland Barthes*, 'Patchwork', 142 ['Je n'avais d'autre solution que de me *ré-écrire*—de loin, de très loin—de maintenant: ajouter aux livres, aux thèmes, aux souvenirs, aux textes, une autre énonciation, sans que je sache jamais si c'est de mon passé ou de mon présent que je parle', 'Patch-work', 145].

[152] Barthes, *S/Z*, IX, 'How Many Readings?', 16 ['Combien de lectures?', 22 and 23].

[153] *Roland Barthes*, 'Patchwork', 142 ['Me commenter? Quel ennui!', 'Patch-work', 145].

[154] *Roland Barthes*, 'Coincidence', 56 ['La Coïncidence', 60]; and Barthes, *The Rustle of Language*, 52 [*Le Bruissement de la langue*, 64].

[155] *Roland Barthes*, 'Phases', 145 ['Phases', 148]; cf. also *Roland Barthes*, 'Misunderstood Ideas', 103: 'We see one and the same critical idea . . . nourish one book (On Racine) . . . and reappear much later in another (*S/Z*). So there are recurrent ideas [*des idées qui reviennent*]' ['Les Idées méconnues', 107].

[156] *Roland Barthes*, 'Comparison is Motive', 58 ['Lui-même se traduit parfois, redouble une phrase par une autre phrase. . . . C'est comme si, voulant se résumer, il ne s'en sortait pas, entassait résumé sur résumé, faute de savoir lequel est le meilleur', 'Comparaison est raison', 62].

drives out another'.[157] We know that the essay is a genre which from the outset emerges as a 'reaction' to the 'bad' repetition of the *doxa* referred to in Barthes in terms of 'stability', 'consistency', 'solidification', 'paralysis'.[158] For all that, the 'para-doxical' discourse of the essayist (the repetition of the same as other) runs the risk, at every moment, of constituting itself into a new *doxa*. The 'banalities', 'stereotypes, 'received opinions' which the essayist must react against are also his own. Hence Barthes's book 'is not the book of his "ideas"', but 'the book of [his] resistances to his [own] ideas': a *'recessive* book'.[159] Both intertextually and intratextually, the essayist, 'like a watchful cook', must make sure that meaning 'does not permit itself to be caught', that it 'remains fluid'; that 'language does not thicken, that it does not *stick*'.[160] And as in the *Essais*, this ongoing 'mobilization' of meaning which must ultimately guarantee that 'what [Barthes] writes about [himself] is never *the last word*', that 'the latter is nothing but a *further* text, the last of the series, not the ultimate in meaning',[161] is achieved mainly through reflexivity. Reflexivity precludes self-coincidence and promotes the non-identity of the same as other: 'as soon as it *thinks itself*, language becomes corrosive', Barthes reflects at yet one more remove, and the fact that the essayist has a tendency to be 'a maniac of the second degree' opens 'the way to endless detachment'.[162]

4.4. 'ALMOST A NOVEL'

By exploiting the excessive or eccentric ('ex-centric') dimension of the dictionary/ encyclopedia in relation to its totalizing structure, Barthes foregrounds the power of dis-location of his essays and their ever-renewed alertness to 'be one by being beside themselves'. Via the metalinguistic apparatus of the dictionary/encyclope-dia, the scene of meaning is constantly set up and transgressed in ways that enables the essayist always to secure the possibility of saying otherwise. In Barthes, the particular theatricality of this encyclopedic 'spectacle' of meaning more than ever

[157] *Roland Barthes*, 'Phases', 145 ['Phases', 148].

[158] *Roland Barthes*, 'Ideology and Aesthetic', 104 ['l'idéologie: ce qui se répète et consiste', 'Idéologie et esthétique', 108].

[159] *Roland Barthes*, 'Doxa/Paradoxa', 71 ['mais de nouveau le Texte risque de se figer: il se répète. . . . Où aller?', 'Doxa/paradoxa', 75]; *Roland Barthes*, '"As We Know"', 137 ['Réagir contre une banalité: bien souvent, pas celle de l'opinion courante, mais la sienne propre', 'On le sait', 140–1]; and *Roland Barthes*, 'The Book of the Self', 119 ['livre de mes résistances à mes propres idées; c'est un livre *récessif* (qui recule, mais aussi, peut-être, qui prend du recul)', 'Le Livre du moi', 123].

[160] *Roland Barthes*, 'The Thrill of Meaning', 97–8 ['Frisson du sens', 101]; and *Roland Barthes*, 'Sed Contra', 162 ['Telle une cuisinière vigilante, il s'affaire, veille à ce que le langage ne s'épaississe pas, à ce qu'il n'*attache* pas', 'Sed contra', 166].

[161] *Roland Barthes*, 'Lucidity', 120 ['mes textes se déboitent, aucun ne coiffe l'autre; celui-ci n'est rien d'autre qu'un texte *en plus*, le dernier de la série non l'ultime du sens', 'Lucidité', 124]. See also *Roland Barthes*, 'Deaf to One's Own Language' ['La Surdité à son propre langage'].

[162] *Roland Barthes*, 'The Second Degree and the Others', 66 ['si j'ôte le cran d'arrêt (. . .), si je mets l'énonciation *en roue libre*, j'ouvre alors la voie d'une déprise sans fin', 'Le Second Degré et les autres', 71].

turns 'meaning', 'truth' into values which are both 'desired' and 'avoided'—or rather into values which are avoided precisely because they are the objects of an impossible desire:

The connotative signified is literally an *index*: it points but does not tell; what it points to is the name, the truth as name; it is both the temptation to name and the impotence to name. . . . Thus, with its designating, silent movement, a pointing finger always accompanies the classic text: the truth is thereby long desired and avoided, kept in a kind of pregnancy for its full term, a pregnancy whose end, both liberating and catastrophic, will bring about the utter end of the discourse.[163]

Not just the topics and key-words, but the whole essayistic discourse becomes a 'transitional' text which 'stages a kind of absence of object, of meaning'.[164] In this sense, the striking reinforcement of the discursive paratext (headings, index) by the graphic paratext (blanks, different typefaces, underlining, numbers/letters) considerably contributes to this self-demarcation, since the graphic paratext is the most blatant way for truth to be 'pointed to without being named'. The doubling of the paratext's didactic strategy by the non-discursive paratext supplements a discourse already 'under erasure': the recurrent use of italics and other means of 'bringing out' or accentuating usually connected with 'making a point' ironically underlines the shift from signified to signifier. More emphatically than ever, the counter-ideological strategy of the essayist who, in his refusal to 'stick' to any position constantly denies himself or takes things back, reduces truth or meaning 'to a simple appearance' and operates 'as though' he had something to affirm: 'It is the reader who is concerned that the truth be simultaneously named and evaded, an ambiguity which the discourse nicely creates by *as though*, which indicates the truth and yet reduces it declaratively to a mere appearance.'[165] This 'as though' enables the essayist 'to devote [himself] to the totally ritual and totally arbitrary preparation of meaning'.[166] It enables him to 'invoke', to 'rehearse' or to allude to notions (actualizing more than one meaning by simply 'letting them be understood'[167]) and thus, like Montaigne, to avoid 'reaching the core, depth, profundity', by 'remain[ing] on the surface' or 'superficial':

He is not very good at getting to the heart of things [*approfondir*]. A word, a figure of thought, a metaphor, in short, a form fastens upon him for several years, he repeats it, uses it everywhere . . . but he makes no effort to reflect further as to what he means by such

[163] Barthes, *S/Z*, XXVI, 'Signified and Truth', 62 ['Signifié et vérité', 69].

[164] *Roland Barthes*, 'The Transitional Word', 130 ['C'est au fond une sorte d'absence de l'objet, du sens, qu'ils mettent en scène', 'Le Mot transitionnel', 134].

[165] Barthes, *S/Z*, LXIV, 'The Voice of the Reader', 151 ['le *comme* du discours, puisqu'il indexe la vérité et cependant la réduit déclarativement à une simple apparence', 'La Voix du lecteur', 157].

[166] *Roland Barthes*, 'The Soothsayer's Gesture' (on the topic of *S/Z*), 47 ['s'adonner à la préparation totalement rituelle et totalement arbitraire d'un sens', 'Le Geste de l'aruspice', 52].

[167] *Roland Barthes*, 'The Echo Chamber', 74 ['La Chambre d'échos', 78]; and *Roland Barthes*, 'Amphibologies', 72 ['Amphibologies', 76].

words or such figures . . . you cannot get to the heart of a refrain; you can only substitute another one for it.[168]

This substitution (the movement of metaphor examined above) which character-izes the 'recessive' discourse of an essayist who is forced to remain this side of any commitment clearly marks the radical fictionalization of the essayistic 'play' with systems. But in Barthes, the 'is/yet is not', the 'is not really here and now' and the 'is not really true' (the 'as though') of concrete fiction is also at stake.[169] For him, everything that 'comes back' as 'translation' rather than as 'synthesis' comes back 'as Fiction' or as 'aesthetic discourse' which might in a sense be the remainder and supplement of all political, religious, or scientific utterances.[170] Brecht, this time, is the pretext for the essayist's endorsement of an 'ideological critique' which 'is not made *directly*' but 'passes through aesthetic relays—in short for a 'counter-ideology' which 'creeps in by means of a fiction'.[171] The aesthetic 'protection' or 'distancing' which Barthes opposes to the 'dissertative' style is indeed an obvious relay in the use of his own pronominal shifts from the 'I' (where 'the "I" might not be "me"') to the 'you' ('I can say to myself "you" as Sade did, in order to detach within myself the worker, the fabricator, the producer of writing, from the subject of the work {the Author}'), and to the epic 'he':

on the other hand, not to speak of oneself can mean: *I am He who does not speak about himself*; and to speak about oneself by saying 'he' can mean: *I am speaking about myself as though I were more or less dead* . . . or again: I am speaking about myself in the manner of the Brechtian actor who must distance his character . . . (Brecht recommended that the actor think out his entire role in the third person). Possible affinity of paranoia and distancing, by the intermediary of narrative: the 'he' is epic. . . . Here is a series of outdated propositions: *I would be nothing if I didn't write. Yet I am elsewhere than where I am when I write. I am worth more than what I write.*[172]

---

[168] *Roland Barthes*, 'Patchwork', 142 ['Patch-work', 145]; and *Roland Barthes*, 'Fashion-Word', 127 ['Mot-mode', 131]; and *Roland Barthes*, 'Movement of Objects into Discourse', 134–5: 'I can create a kind of *word-thought* for myself which will ferret through all my language. This word-object is both *vested* (desired) and *superficial* (employed, not explored)', ['Mot-objet à la fois *investi* (désiré) et *superficiel* (on en use, on ne l'approfondit pas)', 'Passage des objets dans le discours', 138].

[169] Cf. Stewart, *Nonsense*, 36 and 100: 'The surplus of meaning which characterizes "play" is not only potential, but intrinsic, to any fictive text', and 'both works of play and fiction involve the same reframing of messages or manipulation of context, both make the matter of the "dimensions" of discourse "problematic", threatening the reader with an "unlimited amount of significance" that con-tradicts the balance of significance and insignificance typical of commonsense and "realism" '.

[170] *Roland Barthes*, 'Dialectics', 69 ['toute chose revient, mais elle revient comme Fiction', 'Dialectiques', 73]; and *Roland Barthes*, 'Aesthetic Discourse', 84 ['Le Discours esthétique', 87] Cf. also *Roland Barthes*, 'Fiction', 90 'Why should science not grant itself the right to have visions? . . . Could not science become fictional?' ['Fiction', 94]; and 'Linguistic Allegories', 124: 'concepts come to constitute allegories, a second language, whose abstraction is diverted to fictive ends' ['dérivée à des fins romanesques', 'Les Allégories linguistiques', 127].

[171] *Roland Barthes*: 'Ideology and Aesthetic', 104 ['La critique idéologique chez Brecht ne se fait pas *directement*; elle passe par des relais esthétiques; la contre-idéologie se glisse sous une fiction. C'est peut-être là le rôle de l'esthétique dans notre société: fournir les régles d'un discours indirect et transitif', 'Idéologie et esthétique', 108].

[172] *Roland Barthes*, 'Myself, I', 168–9 ['Moi, je', 171–2].

The appearance of this 'he' as the most notable translation of the essayist's sense of 'exclusion', of 'detachment', of the fact that he is 'forever assigned the place of the *witness* . . . never *lyrical*, never homogeneous with the pathos outside of which he must seek his place',[173] enforces the preliminary and hand-written paratext of *Roland Barthes* which stipulates that 'it must all be considered as if spoken by a character in a novel' [*Tout ceci doit être considéré comme dit par un personnage de roman*]. The full version of this injunction, which is to be found (by chance) in one of the fragments of the self-portrait, reads as follows:

All this must be considered as if spoken by a character in a novel—or rather by several characters. For the image-repertoire, fatal substance of the novel, and the labyrinth of levels in which anyone who speaks about himself gets lost—the image-repertoire is taken over by several masks (*personae*) . . . (and yet *no one*—*personne*, as we say in French—is behind them). . . . nothing is more a matter of the image-system, of the imaginary, than (self-) criticism [*Pas de plus pur imaginaire que la critique (de soi)*]. The substance of this book, ultimately, is therefore totally fictive [*romanesque*]. The intrusion, into the discourse of the essay, of a third person who nonetheless refers to no fictive creature, marks the necessity of remodeling the genres: let the essay avow itself *almost* a novel: a novel without proper names.[174]

In a sense, then, the posture of the novelist is the final, uncircumventable expression of the essayist's 'impostures', of the essayist's recognition that he cannot be represented without quotation-marks. On the other hand, and according to the logic by which Barthes's 'anti-structural criticism' illustrated above is only referred to speculatively, as a fantasy ('I imagine an antistructural criticism . . . it would . . .'), the novel only operates on the mode of the 'as if' ('all this must be considered as if spoken by') and of the 'almost' ('let the essay avow itself almost a novel'): a proper counter-ideological critique implies that no posture is tenable, not even a fictional one. Thus, the essayistic surplus is encompassed by what Barthes calls the 'novelistic' rather than the novel; 'The writerly is the novelistic without the novel, poetry without the poem, the essay without the dissertation . . . production without product, structuration without structure.'[175] In *S/Z*, the essayist's 'returning' of the author into an 'irretrievable, irresponsible figure' must also be read as the returning of a 'documentary figure' into a 'novelistic figure'.[176] The 'novelistic' exceeds both the novel and the short story by virtue of the fact that, as discussed in Section 4.1, all good narrative displaces and exceeds its codes. The novelistic, in other words, is associated with the destabilizing, 'dialogic' power of the literary

---

[173] *Roland Barthes*, 'Exclusion', 86 ['Il se sentait plus qu'exclu: *détaché*: toujours renvoyé à la place du *témoin* . . . jamais *lyrique*, jamais homogène au pathos en dehors dequel il doit chercher sa place', 'L'Exclusion', 89].

[174] *Roland Barthes*, 'The Book of the Self', 119–20 ['L'intrusion, dans le discours de l'essai, d'une troisième personne qui ne renvoie cependant à une créature fictive, marque la nécessité de remodeler les genres: que l'essai s'avoue *presque* un roman: un roman sans noms propres', 'Le Livre du moi', 123–4].

[175] Barthes, *S/Z*, II, 'Interpretation', 5 ['Le scriptible, c'est le romanesque sans le roman, la poésie sans le poème, l'essai sans la dissertation', 'L'Interprétation', 11].

[176] Barthes, *S/Z*, XC, 'The Balzacian Text', 211–12 ['*retourner* la figure documentaire de l'auteur en figure romanesque, irrepérable, irresponsable', 'Le Texte balzacien', 217].

text (or of the signifier). This accounts for the fact that the increasingly 'writerly' dimension of Barthes's work parallels his growing 'desire' for a 'novel' in the Romantic sense, 'beyond genre'.[177] To 'produce the novelistic without the novel' is equivalent for Barthes to 'fantasizing' in both the psychoanalytical and the German Romantic ('Schubertian or Schumannian') sense of *Fantasieren*, of 'a pure *wandering*' [*une errance pure*].[178] All of Barthes's work is in a sense 'prefatory', it 'defines or imagines aims, horizons; it is a writing made primarily of projects':

> These projects [*annonces*], generally heralding a summative, excessive [*démesuré*] book, parodic of the great monument of knowledge, can only be simple acts of discourse (prolepses indeed); they belong to the category of the dilatory. . . . The Annunciation of the Book (the *Prospectus*) is one of those dilatory maneuvers which control our internal utopia. I imagine, I fantasize, I embellish, and I polish the great book of which I am incapable: it is a book of learning and of writing, at once a perfect system and the mockery of all system [*à la fois système parfait et dérision de tout système*].[179]

As expected, these projects (the 'splinters of a progressive work' [*éclats d'un travail progressif*]) are the expression of impotence or scepticism (either way the project cannot be realized) and of the utopianism characteristic of essayism. The 'dilatory' is the 'denial of reality (of the realizable)'; the quest is 'haunted by its own impossibility'; the 'Text . . . is a utopia', the 'semantic function' of which is 'to make the present literature, art, language signify, insofar as they are declared *impossible*'.[180] At the same time, this 'untenable, impossible, purely *novelistic* instant' defines the 'pleasure of the text' in the form of the 'thrill of a future praxis, something like an *appetite*'; it fascinates the essayist 'because of the notion that [*he*] *is going to do something with it*', because 'what is posited, outlined, advanced by the utterance remains as *the availability of the meaning*'.[181] 'One cannot at one and the same time desire a word and take it to its conclusion', Barthes writes, and adds that 'in him, the desire for the word prevails'.[182] However, as he well knows, the logic

---

[177] Cf. 'The necessity of entering completely into the signifier, i.e., of disconnecting myself from the ideological instance as signified' which Barthes describes as 'an entrance, not into the novel, but into the novelistic: i.e., the signifier and the retreat of the signified' (Barthes, *The Grain of the Voice*, 84 [*Le Grain de la voix*, 83]); 'the novelistic . . . is merely the circulatory space of subtle, flexible desires' (Barthes, *The Rustle of Language*, 333 [*Le Bruissement de la langue*, 370]); and 'the Novel (I still mean by the Novel that uncertain, quite uncanonical Form, insofar as I do not conceive it but only remember or desire it)' (ibid. 289 [324]).

[178] Barthes, 'The Romantic Song', *The Responsibility of Forms*, 291 [*L'Obvie et l'obtus*, 257].

[179] *Roland Barthes*, 'Later', 173 ['Plus tard', 175 and 76]. And, at the beginning of the page: 'He has a certain foible of providing "introductions", "sketches", "elements", postponing the "real" book till later. This foible has a rhetorical name: *prolepsis*' ['Plus tard', 175].

[180] Ibid. ['dénégation du réel (du réalisable)', 175]; *Roland Barthes*, 'What is Utopia for?', 76–7 ['A quoi sert l'utopie', 80].

[181] Barthes, *The Pleasure of the Text*, 15 ['le plaisir du texte est semblable à cet instant intenable, impossible, purement *romanesque*', *Le Plaisir du texte*, 15; *Roland Barthes*, 'Color Word', 129 ['Mot-couleur', 133]; and *Roland Barthes*, 'The Theme', 178 ['ce qui est posé, découpé, avancé par l'énonciation et reste comme *la disponibilité du sens*', 'Le Thème', 181].

[182] *Roland Barthes*, 'The Echo Chamber', 74 ['On ne peut en même temps approfondir et désirer un mot: chez lui, le désir du mot l'emporte', 'La Chambre des échos', 78].

of the Romantic fragment has it that the alleged 'impotence' or 'potentiality' of the not (yet) written is (also) the embodiment or essence of 'writing' or 'Literature' itself:

Now let us reverse all this: these dilatory maneuvers, these endlessly receding projects may be writing itself. First of all, the work is never anything but the meta-book (the temporary commentary) of a work to come which, *not being written* [*ne se faisant pas*], becomes this work itself: Proust, Fourier never wrote anything but such a 'Prospectus'.

. . . a fragment of writing is still an essence of writing. This is why, willy-nilly, every fragment is finished, from the moment it is written; this is why, too, we cannot compare a broken work [*une œuvre brisée*] to a sustained one [*une œuvre suivie*]; this is why, lastly, no one can deny the greatness of fragmentary works: the greatness not of ruin or of promise, but the greatness of the silence which follows any fulfillment.[183]

What the essayist, as 'someone who wants to write',[184] leaves behind, is a 'fragment' (made up of a set of fragments), but this fragment is a work of literature in its own right ('at once a perfect system and the mockery of all system'). By announcing that he is going to write in order not—or no longer—to have to do so ('It is important for me to act *as if* I were to write this utopian novel'[185]), the essayist partakes in the fundamentally 'modern' conception of literature: in keeping with the notion of literature *in potentia*, 'modernity is tried' or essayed [*la modernité est essayée*]; but this 'trying out'—this potentiality (the 'almost', the 'as if')—is also the very definition of modernity.[186] The novelistic thus not only turns the essayist into a writer [*écrivain*] by virtue of the fact that, unlike the 'scriptor' [*écrivant*] who uses language as an instrument, transitively, the writer uses it 'intransitively' and so embarks on something radically 'new' (or 'novel') in relation to the essayistic mode of his past discourse.[187] It turns the essayist into a fundamentally 'modern' writer, of which Proust—the essayistic novelist *par excellence*— is the supreme model. Proust, that is, 'has given modern writing its epic', for in his *Remembrance of Things Past* 'he makes the narrator . . . not the one who writes, but the one who *is going to write*—wants to write but cannot':[188]

---

[183] *Roland Barthes*, 'Later', 174–5 ['Plus tard', 177]; and Barthes, *The Rustle of Language*, 223 [*Le Bruissement de la langue*, 255].

[184] Barthes, *The Rustle of Language*, 288 ['Celui qui veut écrire', *Le Bruissement de la langue*, 324].

[185] Ibid. 289 ['Ce Roman utopique, il m'importe de faire *comme* si je devais l'écrire', 325].

[186] *Roland Barthes*, 'The Echo Chamber', 74 ['La Chambre des échos', 78].

[187] 'Nous voulons *écrire quelque chose*, et en même temps nous *écrivons* tout court' (Barthes, *Essais critiques*, 153). See also 'To Write: An Intransitive Verb?' ['Écrire, verbe intransitif'], in *The Rustle of Language*. To write 'within "the novelistic without the novel"' amounts to producing 'new "mythologies" . . . less involved in the signified' (Barthes, *The Grain of the Voice*, 130 [*Le Grain de la voix*, 124]). And on novelty: 'And then a time also comes (the same time) when what you have done, worked, written, appears doomed to repetition: What! Until my death, to be writing articles, giving courses, lectures, on "subjects" which alone will vary, and so little! (It's that "on" which bothers me). This feeling is a cruel one; for it confronts me with the foreclosure of anything New or even of any Adventure' (Barthes, *The Rustle of Language*, 285 [*Le Bruissement de la langue*, 321]); and ibid. 288 [325].

[188] Ibid. 51 [63].

The critic is the man who is going to write and who, like the Proustian narrator, satisfies this expectation with a supplementary work, who creates himself by seeking himself and whose function is to accomplish his project of writing even while eluding it. The critic is a writer, but a writer postponed.[189]

Hence the anachronistic position of the essay between a 'bad' lost unity and a prospective, utopian unity in Barthes also manifests a 'nostalgia' or 'fantasy of fusion' inherent in Romanticism. As in the *Essais*, parataxis, the exploitation of ellipsis, of the (poetic) 'instant', of beginnings and the logic—in general—of a 'recessive' work, as well as being the marks of heterology and detour, tend towards essence and self-presence. The 'departures of meaning' or exits out of meaning [*hors-sens*] by which Barthes resists linguistic structures of domination, are also a realm supposed to escape the mediation of meaning. They are the decontextualized sphere of immediate and pure presence, of the unification of subject and object prior to the disseminating effects of language and therefore to man's inscription in society. The merging of paradigms (the permeability of boundaries) in an a- or pre-social and pre-linguistic world therefore also corresponds to the negation of sexual (generic) duality, as the motive of the androgyne and/or of the super-sex in *S/Z* suggests.[190]

Yet this utopian essayistic dimension in which the fragment embodies the synthesis which it infinitely defers beyond or this side of genre, never removes the essay from its concretely pre-generic status: if the 'novel is always the critic's horizon',[191] this is because for Barthes 'to write' also implies a complement of object, the desire for an attainable generic form which is represented by the novel in the concrete sense. The potentially literary status of the essay (the 'almost') casts the fragment with which it is identified as both the essence of writing and the detached 'epitextual' piece waiting to be reintegrated into a system. Thus Barthes's essays are the various entries 'in progress' of a novel which he is preparing or rehearsing, and which he has simply 'not yet' begun to write. Transitivity continues to coexist with intransitivity, and therefore with the hierarchy between scriptor/critic and writer, primary and secondary text. In other words, the virtuality of a project which, in accordance with the Romantic conception of literature, cannot be realized

---

[189] Roland Barthes, preface to the *Critical Essays*, p. xxi ['Le critique est *celui qui va écrire*, et qui, semblable au Narrateur proustien, emplit cette attente d'une œuvre *de surcroît*, qui se fait en se cherchant et dont la fonction est d'accomplir son projet d'écrire tout en l'éludant. Le critique est un écrivain, mais un écrivain en sursis', *Essais critiques*, 18].

[190] Cf. 'Order of the signifier, the Text participates in its way in a social utopia; before History (supposing that History does not choose barbarism), the Text fulfills if not the transparency of social relations at least the transparency of language relations: it is the space in which no language prevails over any other (Barthes, *The Rustle of Language*, 64 [*le Bruissement de la langue*, 77]). And 'The fact that we cannot manage to achieve more than an unstable grasp of reality doubtless gives the measure of our present alienation. . . . It would seem that we are condemned for some time yet always to speak *excessively* about reality . . . this is what we must seek: a reconciliation between reality and men, between description and explanation, between object and knowledge' (end of *Mythologies*, 159 [*Mythologies*, 247]). See Bernard Comment, 'Un fantasme de fusion', in *Roland Barthes: Vers le neutre*.

[191] Barthes, *Critical Essays*, Preface, p. xxi ['Le roman est toujours l'horizon du critique', *Essais critiques*, 18].

does not only exonerate the essayist and turn him into a writer. Producing 'fictitious' fictions rather than 'real' fictions expresses the recognition of the impossible project but also of the essayist's incapacity and inferiority with regard to the writer or novelist. From this point of view, Barthes's writings on the preparation of the novel and the novel itself are incompatible: the preparation is a sort of stopgap for the novel the essayist is unable to write, and conversely, the actual writing of a novel would have precluded such dedicated reflections on its preparation. The impotence of the essayist in relation to the novelist has here to do with the former's inaptitude (and not only with his unwillingness) to construct a narrative sequence and to 'fabulate'. Barthes is tempted by a 'great continuous work' (as well as a 'great fragmentary work') but cannot 'see [himself] composing a story, an anecdote, with characters who have names, in short, a novel'.[192] Apart from his inability to master narrative continuity, Barthes confesses to being incapable of 'inventing a lie', of 'feigning', of 'fictionalizing'. In contradistinction to the novelist's imagination which is powerful enough to 'create the Other', his own faculty of fantasizing remains above all 'narcissistic'; at best it enables him to 'pick up' or 'tap' the novelistic [*capter du romanesque*] but not to produce a novel.[193] Consequently, Barthes resigns himself to the fact that '[he] [is] an essayist', that '[He] [has] written neither novels nor plays: [he] [has] never created fictional characters. In certain essays, of course, [he] [has] approached the fictive, but only as a category.'[194] Compared with the novelist, the essayist ultimately remains doomed to a certain truth and to a certain authenticity:

Doom of the essay, compared to the novel: doomed to *authenticity*—to the preclusion of quotation marks.

. . . like the writer, he wants to be believed less because of what he writes than because of his decision to write it; but unlike the writer, he cannot *sign* that desire; he remains condemned to error—truth.[195]

---

[192] 'J'ai maintenant la tentation très forte de faire une grande œuvre continue et non pas fragmentaire. (. . .). Ce que j'appelle le "roman" ou "faire un roman", j'en ai envie non pas dans un sens commercial mais pour accéder à un genre d'écriture qui ne soit plus fragmentaire' (interview quoted in Comment, *Roland Barthes, Vers le neutre*, 209). See also Barthes, *The Grain of the Voice*, 203, and 222–3 [*Le Grain de la voix*, 192 and 210].

[193] Barthes, *The Grain of the Voice*, 203 [*Le Grain de la voix*, 192]. A novel is 'un mensonge qui fait mousse; la fabulation; la mythomanie. Alors pourquoi est-ce que je ne peux produire que des écrits qui, certes, ne sont pas dans la vérité, mais qui témoignent d'une inaptitude à mentir, c'est-a-dire à feindre, à fictionner . . . je sens cette impuissance comme une pauvreté, car l'imagination fabulatrice du romancier est une puissance généreuse, elle revient à . . . savoir créer l'Autre . . . je dirai qu'il me semble que personnellement j'ai une imagination fantasmatique non fabulatrice et donc une imagination narcissique dans la mesure où elle est fantasmatique, et c'est en cela qu'elle n'est pas romanesque . . . la grande imagination, le grand mensonge du romancier me manque' (*Le Bruissement de la langue*, 324–5).

[194] Barthes, *The Grain of the Voice*, 319 [*Le Grain de la voix*, 297].

[195] *Roland Barthes*, 'Fatigue and Freshness', 89 ['Fatalité de l'essai, face au roman: condamné à l'*authenticité*—à la forclusion des guillemets', 'La Fatigue et la fraîcheur', 93]; and Barthes, *Critical Essays*, Preface, p. xxi ['comme l'écrivain, (le critique) voudrait bien que l'on croie moins à ce qu'il écrit qu'à la décision qu'il a prise d'écrire; mais à l'inverse de l'écrivain, il ne peut *signer* ce souhait: il reste condamné à l'erreur—à la vérité', *Essais Critiques*, 18].

This reinstatement of the distinction between essayist and novelist seems in fact to follow logically from the distinction, in the reading of the classically plural text of *Sarrasine*, between its modernist and its realist dimension, between the 'writerly' or dialogic excess of literature and the readability and monologism of classical narrative. As with the essay, the short story's 'anticipation of modernity' converts it, in a sense, into the most modern of texts; yet this 'anticipation' is also what literally makes it 'fall short of' modernity: in the end, the dialogism of forms in the inexhaustible, intertextual sense is checked by the monologism of classical narrative's realistic or 'readerly' aim. Correspondingly, the 'spectacle of meaning' which is so emphatically set up in both essays via the paratextual apparatus of the encyclopedia, is not only a simulacrum: the fragments—the set of *hors-textes* or 'pure interruptions'—also 'ensure the reterritorialization of the drifting text'.[196] What the 'pure interruptions' of the numbered or lettered fragments also interrupt, in both essays, is the potentially infinite unfolding of the metonymic shifts, the externalization of the head-word being indeed—as in the dictionary—both the condition for this 'mobilization' and the repeated possibility for the discourse generated by that word to begin all over again from a zero degree of order and meaning ('Each synonym adding to its neighbor some new trait, some new departure') and to elaborate a constant form: 'To thematize is, on the one hand, to leave the dictionary behind, to follow certain synonymic chains . . . to yield to an expanding nomination . . . and, on the other, to return to these various substantive stations in order to create some constant form (*'which doesn't take'*) [*ce qui ne prend pas*].'[197] The idea of an 'expanding nomination' illustrated in *S/Z* and condensed in the phrase 'I name, I unname, I rename' also perfectly conveys the process of disjunction by which the 'exteriority' of the concept is secured, and maintains the illusion that the latter does not exist prior to its definition. And as in Montaigne, 'amnesia', which constitutes the essayist's excuse for wandering away from the all-inclusive mnemonic system of the encyclopedia ('The order I no longer remember'), also makes possible the reappropriation of a certain taxonomy: to 'unname' is at once to undo and to define, to delimit from an outside, to resort to an external instance in order to mark a new beginning ('the alphabet calls you to order (to disorder) and says: '*Cut! Resume the story in another way*'[198]). Thanks to a faltering memory by which the essayist has conveniently forgotten that 'there is nothing outside the (inter-)text', denotation can be exploited 'innocently'.[199] The 'substantive stations' which are created are the mark of the intertext's 'coded' regression or 'retreat' from signifier to signifier and of the 'critical levels' of the essay which, even though they may be the arbitrary result of a 'throw of dice', temporarily

[196] Barillaud, 'Roland Barthes: Les fragments, langue équivoque', 34.

[197] Barthes, *S/Z*, XL, 'The Birth of Thematics', 93 ['Naissance du thématique', 99].

[198] *Roland Barthes*, 'The Order I No Longer Remember', 148 ['L'Ordre dont je ne me souviens plus', 151].

[199] Cf. 'This is why, if we want to go along with the classic text, we must keep denotation, the old deity, watchful, cunning, theatrical, foreordained to *represent* the collective innocence of language' (*S/Z*, IV, 'Connotation, For, Even So', 9 ['Pour la connotation tout de même', 16]).

'arrest and fix the skid of names' and enable the essayist to do justice to the tension between 'endless nomination' (the 'enduring character of language' [*le caractère perpétuel du langage*]) and the list of reading's products [*la table de ses produits*].[200] What the cutting up of the classical text into lexical units liberates, ultimately, is a 'restrained dissemination', that is, 'the namable, computable trace of a *certain* plural' of the 'only polysemic' classical text.[201] The exploration of the text's difference from itself releases digressions—virtualities—that are at once infinite, but nevertheless 'controlled, attested to by a systematic reading'.[202] For the truly plural text, 'there cannot be a narrative structure, a grammar, or a logic': it is precisely because we are dealing with 'parsimoniously' or 'incompletely plural texts' that such structures can be generated at all.[203] The 'reterritorialization' effected by the fragment, also puts a check to the endless drifting of the subject between 'bliss' and 'pleasure':[204]

I have the illusion to suppose that by breaking up my discourse [*en brisant mon discours*] I cease to discourse in terms of the imaginary about myself [*je cesse de discourir imaginairement sur moi-même*], attenuating the risk of transcendence; but since the fragment . . . is *finally* a rhetorical genre and since rhetoric is that layer of language which best presents itself to interpretation, by supposing I disperse myself [*en croyant me disperser*] I merely return, quite docilely, to the bed of the imaginary.[205]

Coming to terms with the 'illusory' nature of desire goes hand in hand for Barthes with gradually 'recognizing in [himself] a growing desire for readability', of '[want[ing] the texts [he] write[s] to be "readable"': a sentence 'can *tend* toward a certain obscurity by a certain use of *ellipsis*', yet 'ellipses must be restrained [*dosées*]; metaphors, too', for 'a continuously metaphorical writing exhausts [him]'.[206] Like the classical text, both *S/Z* and *Roland Barthes* are plural, but within certain limits, and these limits are their readability, their articulation as a literature of the Signified, their affiliation with a musical score which remains 'tonal':[207] 'my text is

---

[200] Barthes, *S/Z*, XL, 'The Birth of Thematics', 93 ['Ce recul est évidemment codé: lorsque le déboîtement nominal s'arrête, un niveau critique est créé, l'œuvre se ferme, le langage par lequel on termine la transformation sémantique devient nature, vérité, secret de l'œuvre'; 'Seule une thématique infinie, proie d'une nomination sans fin, pourrait respecter le caractère perpétuel du langage, la production de la lecture, et non plus la table de ses produits'; 'Dans le texte classique, fatalité du coup de dés qui arrête et fixe le glissement des noms: c'est la thématique', 'Naissance du thématique', 100].

[201] Barthes, *S/Z*, IV, 'Connotation: For, Even So', 8 ['la trace nommable, computable, d'un *certain* pluriel du texte', 'Pour la connotation, tout de même', 14].

[202] Barthes, *S/Z*, VII, 'The Starred Text', 14 ['une banquette de sens possibles (mais réglés, attestés par une lecture systématique', 'Le Texte étoilé', 21].

[203] Barthes, *S/Z*, II, 'Interpretation', 6 ['Pour le texte pluriel, il ne peut y avoir de structure narrative, de grammaire ou de logique du récit; si donc les unes et les autres s'y laissent parfois approcher, *c'est dans la mesure . . . où l'on a affaire à des textes incomplètement pluriels, des textes dont le pluriel est plus ou moins parcimonieux*', 'L'Interprétation', 12].

[204] 'He enjoys the consistency of his selfhood (that is his pleasure) and seeks its loss (that is his bliss [*jouissance*])', *The Pleasure of the Text*, 14 [*Le Plaisir du texte*, 26].

[205] *Roland Barthes*, 'The Fragment as Illusion', 95 ['Le Fragment comme illusion', 99].

[206] Barthes, *The Rustle of Language*, 352 [*Le Bruissement de la langue*, 391].

[207] 'The area of the (readerly) text is comparable at every point to a (classical) musical score. . . . The readerly text is a *tonal* text' (*S/Z*, XV, 'The Full Score', 28 and 30 ['La Partition', 35 and 37]).

in fact *readerly*: I am on the side of structure, of the sentence, of the sentenced text . . . *I write classic.*'[208]

A conclusion on Barthes's use of essayism, if there is one, must inevitably take the form of a third dialectical term which will not be of synthesis but of 'translation'. For Barthes's essays simultaneously actualize both senses of the 'potentially literary', allowing the essay both to be and not (yet) to be a novel. From a synchronic point of view, the essay evolves alongside the novel; it is 'almost a novel' in that it shares features with it, yet must be differentiated from it. From a diachronic point of view, this 'almost' records the temporal difference which separates the essay from its final development into a novel. Thus the essay develops 'against' the novel—against narrative fiction—in the dual sense of opposition and contiguity also connoted by the prefix 'para' of paraliterature: narrative fiction is that against which and in relation to which the essay is positioned. In this sense, reading the essay 'as if' it were a novel both makes the leap and underlines the fact that the effectiveness of this leap—the verisimilitude behind the idea of reading the essay as a novel—depends on the acknowledgement of the distinct if not opposed conventions or 'pacts' of fiction and non-fiction respectively. What is at stake again is the tension, inherent in the essay, between its (aesthetic) form and its (conceptual) content: for the 'writer-scriptor', to choose the essay is precisely to adopt a third paradoxical form which is neither the preparation of the novel nor that novel itself, but something that anachronistically hovers in-between:

I will probably never write a 'novel', a story fitted out with characters and events; but if it's so easy for me to deprive myself of this activity (after all, it really must be quite enjoyable to write a novel), it's doubtless because my writings are already full of the novelistic (which is the novel minus the characters); and it's true that at present, looking ahead to a new phase of my work as straightforwardly as possible, what I would like to do is to *try out* novelistic forms, to essay them, in such a way that none of them would be called a 'novel' but each one would keep, and if possible renew, the title 'essay'.[209]

It is the choice of this third paradoxical form which for Barthes entitles him to 'set Proust and [himself] on one and the same line' or to 'identify [himself] with him'. This 'association', he hastens to add, is one 'of practice, not of value': he does not identify himself 'with the prestigious author of a monumental work', but with the 'now tormented, now exalted, in any case modest' 'worker' at a 'crucial period of hesitation' in his life when he 'seems to be at the intersection of two paths, two genres, torn between two "ways" he does not yet know could converge . . . the way of the Essay (of Criticism) and the way of the Novel'. The hesitation between the two 'ways'—which reflect the two 'ways' [*côtés*] of the *Search* (Swann's way and the Guermantes' way)—corresponds to the structural alternation formulated by

[208] *Roland Barthes*, 'Forgeries', 92 ['mon texte est en effet *lisible*: je suis du côté de la structure, de la phrase, du texte phrasé . . . j'écris classique', 'Forgeries', 96].
[209] Barthes, *The Grain of the Voice*, 176 ['ce dont j'ai envie, c'est d'*essayer* des formes romanesques, dont aucune ne prendrait le nom de "roman", mais dont chacune garderait, si possible en le renouvelant, celui d'"essai" ', *Le Grain de la voix*, 168–9].

Jakobson, between Metaphor ('What does it mean?') and Metonymy ('What can follow what I say?'):

Proust is a divided subject: he knows that each incident in life can give rise either to a commentary (an interpretation) or to an affabulation which produces or imagines the narrative *before* and *after*: to interpret is to take the Critical path, to argue theory (siding against Sainte-Beuve); to think incidents and impressions, to describe their developments, is on the contrary to weave a Narrative, however loosely, however gradually.[210]

Proust's indecision, like Barthes's, is of course both tormenting and 'cherished', as their shared admiration for 'certain writers who have also practiced a certain indecision of genres' testifies.[211] All the same, the production of the 'third', 'rhapsodic' form which will be 'neither Essay nor Novel' yet both, since it 'abolishes the contradiction between them',[212] will be called a 'novel' in Proust rather than an 'essay'. Hence our move to the (essayistic) novels of the next chapter provides a further opportunity to explore the essay from the 'novelistic' angle. But this 'entrance into the novelistic' also marks the final stage of my announced *progression* from essay to novel.

---

[210] Barthes, *The Rustle of Language*, 277–8, and 279 [*Le Bruissement de la langue*, 313–14, and 314–15].

[211] Ibid. 279 [315].   [212] Ibid. 281, 283–4 [317 and 319].

5

Novels 'Without Qualities'

To illustrate the transition from essay to novel as rehearsed and theorized in the writings of Roland Barthes, we now turn to novelists who are not only known to have begun their career as essayists, but whose more famous novels are supposed to have developed directly from essayistic material (in the wider, 'epitextual' sense of notebooks, journals, aphorisms, letters, diaries, articles, etc.), and even from specific essays. Proust's *Remembrance of Things Past*, which Barthes refers to time and again, is representative, for it is the reworking of a number of pieces which include essays, notebooks, sketches, translations, articles, pastiches, and, more particularly, the development of one essay begun around 1908, the fragments of which are subsequently published under the title *Against Sainte-Beuve* [*Contre Sainte-Beuve*]. In this essay, Proust presents his ideas on literature by way of a critique of Sainte-Beuve's method which champions the understanding of the work of art through the personal knowledge of the writer as a man. The 'invasion' of the essay by narrative fragments supposed to back up its ideas, in the context of a fictive dialogue between himself and his mother, is noticeable. And it is Proust's desire to illustrate the essay's propositions and a number of philosophical and psychological views already voiced in his early writings, that eventually induces him to launch into a fully-fledged novel.[1] The essay thus clearly functions from the outset as an intermediary between theory and art. In the case of Robert Musil's *The Man Without Qualities* [*Der Mann ohne Eigenschaften*] (1930) and Hermann Broch's *The Sleepwalkers* [*Die Schlafwandler: Eine Romantrilogie*] (1931–2), the essay also mediates between the human sciences (philosophy, psychology, sociology, history, art criticism) and art. Both writers incorporate into their novels already existing essays on psychology (the treatise on the psychology of feeling in Musil) and epistemology (the 'Disintegration of Values' in Broch); and some of their essays on current, cultural topics and on the question of art and literature recognizably function as the by-products, commentaries, or complements of their fiction. Only here, the mediating role of the essay is all the more noteworthy as the 'theoretical' also encompasses the more abstract realms of mathematics, physics, and engineering which in fact constitute the initial (and continuing) areas of

---

[1] For Proust's 'experiments', see J. M. Cocking, *Proust: Collected Essays on the Writer and his Art* (1982); Anthony R. Pugh, *The Birth of 'À La Recherche du Temps Perdu'* (1987); Robert Vigneron, 'Creative Agony', in René Girard (ed.), *Proust: A Collection of Critical Essays* (1977); and Luc Fraisse, *Le Processus de la création chez Marcel Proust: Le Fragment expérimental* (1988).

interest of both writers.[2] In a sense, the range of Musil and Broch's essayistic objects is an illustration of how extensively the span between the cognitive and the aesthetic inherent in the essay can be exploited. Actually, this range tends to be seen rather as the measure of these writers' progress from the theoretical or scientific to the literary, especially as, like Proust, they do not turn to the novel until fairly late in their career as writers. There is no doubt but that the long and laborious transition from essay(ism) to narrative fiction and the fact that these novels are subsequently hailed as some of the greatest this century, prompts one doubly to associate the novel with 'maturity' and to relegate the essays to the status of experiments for the (belated) outburst of literary talent.

The temptation, discussed in detail in my first chapter, to view the relationship between essay and fiction diachronically and hierarchically, arises no doubt from the long-standing belief, shared by literary criticism and public opinion that narrative fiction is superior to abstract formulation, 'depicting' or 'showing' to 'telling'. We are used to defending the notion that 'the interest in ideas and theoretical statements' is 'alien to the genius of the novel proper, where the technical problem is to dissolve all theory into personal relationships'.[3] The novelist who 'cannot get along without ideas' or who 'has not the patience to digest them'[4] is therefore not likely to be praised. So the fact that, as well as concretely moving from essay to novel, Proust, Broch, and Musil eventually produce a third form which is both essay and novel, and neither—an 'essayistic novel'—implies that three of the great exemplars of the novel's 'genius' have somehow managed to get away with doing exactly what a good novel should never do. The term 'essayistic novel' calls into question the idea of progression; it suggests that the (initial) essayistic material has not been 'dissolved' into the fabric of the novel after all, but plainly stands out of the narrative strand. The offence is not so terrible when the essayistic reflections are 'motivated': in most novels, the essayistic appears in the form of reflections or digressions which are taken over by the characters. For example, Proust's speculations on the conditions of the work of art elaborated in *Against Sainte-Beuve* are presented as the narrator's thoughts in the last part of *Remembrance of Things Past*, 'Time Regained'. And although a glance at the table of contents of Musil's *The Man Without Qualities* indicates a clear (albeit asymmetrical) alternation between fictional narrative chapters and essays, the abstraction between the two poles is also relativized by the fact that the theoretical reflections are assumed to a large extent by the main character Ulrich (albeit often retrospectively and indirectly), or, to a lesser extent, by the other characters with whom he engages in endless dialogues. As in Proust, passing off entire sections of abstract reflection as the potential interior monologue of the character is a procedure which is vindicated by the acceptability or plausibility of the associative rather than straightforwardly disruptive

---

[2] See Dieter Bachmann, 'Die essayistischen Schriften', in both his Musil and his Broch chs., in *Essay und Essayismus* (1969); and, for Musil, Annie Reniers-Servranckx, 'Pläne und Unvollendetes', in *Robert Musil: Konstanz und Entwicklung von Themen, Motiven und Strukturen in den Dichtungen* (1972).

[3] Northrop Frye, *The Anatomy of Criticism: Four Essays* (1957), 308.

[4] Ibid.

relationship it bears to the narrative sequence. Yet this is the procedure which Broch, precisely, rejects. His contempt for the choice of the intellectual hero as mouth-piece for authorial justifications is unreserved: he regards this strategy as 'conversational padding' and 'absolute kitsch', and accuses not only Musil, but also Gide, Mann, Huxley of indulging in it.[5] As with *The Man Without Qualities*, the table of contents of *The Sleepwalkers* also indicates a clear separation between the narrative fiction and essay—here two types of essayistic texts: the bulk of diary-entries (entitled 'Story of the Salvation Army Girl in Berlin' [*Geschichte des Heilsarmeemädchens in Berlin*]) of which about half is cast in the form of poems, and the essay-sections of the 'Disintegration of Values' [*Zerfall der Werte*] grouped in the third novel as separate chapters or excursus which alternate with the fiction. This dual structure of 'fictional' versus 'conceptual' already operates at the level of each novel-title, *Pasenow the Romantic* [*Pasenow oder die Romantik*], *Esch the Anarchist* [*Esch oder die Anarchie*], and *Huguenau the Realist* [*Huguenau oder die Sachlichkeit*]. Only in *The Sleepwalkers*, the essayistic passages are abstracted from the fiction, and this abstraction never stops increasing in the course of the trilogy. In the first two novels, essayistic digressions (marked by blanks and a switch to the present tense) interrupt the narrative. The last novel, on the other hand, is broken into a series of numbered sections where fiction and essay alternate. The fragmentation is such, that towards the end of the novel one essay-section of the 'Disintegration of Values' is itself broken up into fragments.[6] Broch's text can thus pass as the most radical of the three novels, the one which most blatantly transgresses the law of the novel's 'genius'. But *The Sleepwalkers* can also be regarded as the most purely essayistic work. Indeed, German theorists who have focused on the interaction of essay and novel question the legitimacy of 'already' or 'still' talking about 'essays' when everything is done to merge the essayistic material into the plot.[7] Some argue that a clear distinction, or even a complete abstraction, between the two poles of theory and fiction, is the prerequisite for what must not be perceived so much as the failure to write a 'proper' novel than as the mastery of a specific type of novel—one which, as we will see, largely coincides with the German Romantic conception of the genre.

---

[5] ['Nun wäre nur noch dazu zu sagen, daß das Wissenschaftliche eben nicht als Gesprächsfüllsel verwendet wird, sondern als oberste rationale Schicht mitschwimmt and mitschwingt'; and 'Eine "gebildete" Gesellschaftsschicht zum Romanträger zu erheben, ist eine absolute Verkitschung', Hermann Broch, letter to Dr Brody, 5 Aug. 1931, in *Hermann Broch: Kommentierte Werkausgabe*, ed. Paul Michael Lützeler, vol. 13/1 (Frankfurt, 1981), 151; cited below as *KW*.]

[6] Hermann Broch, 'Disintegration of Values' (8), in *The Sleepwalkers* (1986), 523.

[7] Adolf Frisé, 'Roman und Essay: Gedanken u.a. zu Hermann Broch, Thomas Mann und Robert Musil', in *Plädoyer für Robert Musil* (1987), 82–3; Gerhard Haas, 'Essay und Roman', in *Essay* (1969), 71–2; in the section 'Romanform und Essay' of his other book, *Studien zur Form des Essays und zu seinen Vorformen im Roman* (1966), 135–6, Haas locates the proper area of the essayistic between complete fusion and the kind of abstraction exemplified by Broch's *Sleepwalkers*, and chooses Jean Paul's *Titan* or Immermann's *Münchhausen*, which exploit paratextual digressions (footnotes and letters), as typical examples. The partisan of complete abstraction is Bachmann, *Essay und Essayismus*, 180 ['Nun macht ein denkender Mensch einen Roman allein noch nicht unbedingt essayistisch. Essayistisch wird ein Roman erst, wenn ganze Partien nur noch abstrakte, allgemeine Reflexion enthalten, den Gang der Erzählung verlassen, aus dem Kontext herausfallen'].

Among critics of Proust, Broch, or Musil's—and similar—novels, the deliberate abstraction of theory and fiction has often strengthened the idea that one only needs to extract the theoretical propositions from their narrative fictional context (the logical concepts from the human relations) to ascertain the meaning of the work at hand. The more abstracted the essayistic parts, the easier this extraction: one simply 'goes back' from the fiction to the essay and from the narrator to the author within and outside the novel, the fiction being then considered simply as the narrative transposition or indirect communication of a thought which can (and has) been expressed directly. The prior and hence independent existence of a large part of the essayistic material subsequently incorporated in Proust, Musil, and Broch's novels greatly encourages this approach. For it confirms that the essayistic reflections have not been added retrospectively to the narrative fiction in order to bring out its meaning. Rather, the opposite seems to be the case. What is more, the illustrative and thus to some extent secondary role ascribed to narrative fiction is substantiated by Proust, Musil, and Broch's avowed fear that their ideas might be degraded or debased by literature. Our writers' esteem for literature and the form of the novel more specifically is in fact coupled with a resistance to literature which seems to play a significant role in their hesitation to 'move on' to the novel, and to justify the difficulty they then encounter in surrendering or dissolving the essayistic dimension of their work. In many ways, all three writers are, like Broch, 'writers against their will':[8] they dread entrusting their philosophical convictions to the pernicious prosaism or even vulgarity of plot and to the irresponsible mode of fiction, both of which signal a kind of betrayal of their ideals and commitments if not intellectual facility and/or impotence. In his *Remembrance of Things Past*, Proust's narrator frequently refers to his 'demonstration'; he never stops promising 'mysterious truths' and 'great laws'; in 'Timed Regained' especially, he feels 'jostling each other within [him] a whole host of truths concerning human passions and character and conduct'.[9] We know that although the essay gives way to the novel, the novel itself culminates in the enormous essayistic epilogue, the significance of which is underlined by Proust himself in a letter written at the time when the provisional title of the book is still *Contre Sainte-Beuve, Souvenir d'une matinée*. In this famous letter, Proust voices the hope that 'once people have finished the book they will see (. . .) that the whole novel is simply the implementation of the artistic principles expressed in this final part, a sort of preface if you like placed at the end'.[10] This resistance to literature is even stronger in the case of our Austrian

---

[8] Term used by Hannah Arendt and Egon Vietta.

[9] Marcel Proust, *Remembrance of Things Past*, 'Time Regained' (1981), 935 ['Je sentais se presser en moi une foule de vérités relatives aux passions, aux caractères, aux moeurs', *À la recherche du temps perdu*, 261].

[10] ['Je termine un livre qui malgré son titre provisoire: *Contre Sainte-Beuve, Souvenir d'une matinée* est un véritable roman. . . . Le nom de Sainte-Beuve ne vient pas par hasard. Le livre finit bien par une longue conversation sur Sainte-Beuve et sur l'esthétique . . . et quand on aura fini le livre, on verra (je le voudrais) que tout le roman n'est que la mise en œuvre des principes d'art émis dans cette dernière partie, sorte de préface, si vous voulez, mise à la fin', Proust, Letter to Alfred Valette, in *Selected Letters*, ii. *1904–1909* (1989)].

novelists who are more concerned with what Barthes or Adorno see as 'the responsibility of forms'. Musil's feeling that 'narrated episodes can be allowed to be secondary, even superfluous . . . not ideas', accounts for the fact that despite his apparent use of character as a vehicle for these ideas, his novel will not take the form of the biography or *Bildungsroman* of a character—which Musil regards as one obvious type of novel available—but of the biography or '*Bildungsroman* of an idea', which he considers to be the novel *par excellence*.[11] This choice nevertheless impels him to ask himself whether in the end he has not written a novel because he lacks the courage to assume responsibility for his thoughts in a philosophical or scientific form. As a matter of fact, the above-mentioned tendency of critics to consider the essayistic novel as the indirect communication of a thought that could be expressed directly, and thus to ignore aesthetic protection or distancing, is endorsed all the more unreservedly by Musil as for him, this protection or distancing equals a betrayal: in his view 'what is better expressed rationally—indeed what *can* at all be expressed rationally—*should not* be expressed poetically' (emphasis added).[12] Broch, who also agrees that 'what can be expressed discursively belongs to the scientific, not to the literary realm', emphatically refers to his essay 'Disintegration of Values' as the key to his trilogy, and, despite incorporating it into his novel (which ends with the last part of the essay), reinforces its right to an independent, 'scientific' status by resolutely subscribing to the appearance of the essay's English translation in a periodical.[13] Against his editor's concern that the essay as it stands might make the novel too esoteric for the reader, he gives rent to his contempt for the 'belletristic', and points out that his *Sleepwalkers* is no train-station reading anyway.[14] Above all, story-telling, which Broch pejoratively associates with the anecdotal or with the journalistic [*Geschichtel erzählen*] is the mark of a certain 'epic naïvety' and the refusal to assume one's responsibilities in

[11] ['Ich erinnere mich, schon sehr früh das Eindruck erhalten zu haben, daß die theoretisch-essayistische Äußerung in unserer Zeit wertvoller ist als die Künstlerische', in Robert Musil, *Tagebücher, Aphorismen, Essays und Reden* (1955) (henceforth referred to as *TAER*), 282; 'Meine Meinung ist, daß erzählte Episoden überflüssig sein dürfen und nur um ihrer selbst willen vorhanden, Gedanken aber nicht', Musil, *TAER*, 298; 'Bilder kommen in zweiter Linie, in erster der Gedanke!!!!', in Musil, *Prosa, Dramen, Späte Briefe* (1957) (henceforth referred to as *PDB*), 716; '"Überflüssige", "langschweifige" Erörterungen: das ist ein Vorwurf, den man mir oft gemacht hat, wobei man vielleicht gnädig zugab, daß ich erzählen "konnte". Daß mir diese Erörterungen die Hauptsache sind!' (quoted in Alan Holmes, 'Ulrich—Theory and Reflection', in *Robert Musil, 'Der Mann ohne Eigenschaften': An Examination of the Relationship between Author, Narrator and Protagonist* (1978), 123); 'Ich bleibe in der Mühe des Denkens befangen und lege kein Gewicht mehr auf die Anwendung', Musil, *TAER*, 453; 'Ausgewählte Kapitel aus meinem Leben. Hauptsache: eine Art *Biographie meiner Ideen*', Musil, *TAER*, 298; and 'Der Bildungsroman einer Person, das ist ein Typus des Romans. Der Bildungsroman einer Idee, das ist der Roman schlechtweg', *Briefe 1901–1942*, p. 956].

[12] ['Müsste nicht gesagt werden, daß ich einfach nicht den Mut habe, was mich philosophisch beschäftigt hat, denkerisch und wissenschaftlich darzustellen, und daß es darum hintenherum in meine Erzählungen eindringt und diese unmöglich macht?', Musil, *TAER*, 458; and 'Was man rational besser ausdrückt, ja überhaupt so ausdrücken kann, soll man nicht dichten', Musil, *TAER*, 458].

[13] ['Was diskursiv ausgedrückt werden kann, gehört in den wissenschaftlichen, nicht in den dichterischen Bereich', Broch, letter to Willa Muir, 3 Aug. 1931, *KW* 13/1: 158. Letter to Edwin Muir, 24 Oct. 1931, *KW* 13/1: 158.

[14] Broch, letter to Dr Brody, 23 Sept. 1931, *KW* 13/1: 154–5.

an age when the novel is no longer entitled to entertain.[15] Finally, Broch insists that his literary production is not the culmination of his career as a writer and thinker but an intermediate stage, a springboard for his further and exclusive devotion to epistemological books (above all books on the history of philosophy).[16] Ironically, his theories—such as the lengthy and ponderous *Die Massenwahntheorie*—have never raised much interest except in so far as they retrospectively illuminate aspects of his fiction; and for this the ideas developed (more succinctly) within the fiction are usually deemed to be more than sufficient.

In keeping with the standard definition of the essay as a 'short, non-fictional prose form', the other significant aspect of the essay's 'resistance' to the novel, which results in the production of an 'essayistic' novel, involves the relationship between fragment and whole discussed in Chapter 1. The presence of essayistic excerpts in the fiction inevitably induces a mutual interruption of theory and fiction which makes for a conspicuously fragmentary novel. And what this fragmentation manifests above all, is an opposition to narrative continuity and totalization—or to what I referred to in Chapter 1 as the conceptual or 'philosophical' claims of narrative. So the role of essayism in the novel appears from the start to be dual and contradictory: in relation to narrative *fiction*, the essay (perceived as a genre) is identified with ideas, with theory or philosophy; in relation to *narrative* fiction, on the other hand, the essay effects a rejection—and to some extent a 'fictionalization'—of the (narrative or philosophical) system, this time in the etymological, modal sense of 'to essay'. Whether around or within the novels of Proust, Broch, or Musil, essaying visibly competes with and hinders the possibility of narrating or of lending experience a definite meaning, and this materializes as a disintegration of both the narrative syntagm and the unified (Cartesian) subject. The modern world is no longer thought to offer us a coherent Hegelian narrative, with a beginning, a middle, and an end. Man's effort to make sense of his world, to make history meaningful by 'informing' an otherwise arbitrary series of events, is vain. Hence the tendency to associate essayism with the idea of a novel 'in crisis', a tendency registered not only among critics, but among the writers themselves. The vast essayistic workshop (essays, diaries, letters) that surrounds *The Man Without Qualities*, for example, is riddled with Musil's laments that he is incapable of writing, that his work is paralysed, all the more paralysed as the essayistic notes and reflections (including those which record this paralysis) multiply and threaten to occupy the entire space initially allotted to the novel.[17] However, a novel in crisis plays on the dual meaning of the term 'critical', and the inability to 'write' also underscores the refusal to indulge in what is precisely

---

[15] ['Wenn ich Romane schreibe, habe ich das Gefühl der Verantwortungslosigkeit', Broch, KW13/3: 412; and 'Wir müssen uns ja darüber klar sein, daß die Zeit für den Schriftsteller vorüber ist, weil die Zeit eben mit Kunst nichts mehr zu tun hat', letter to Willa Muir, 19 Mar. 1932, *KW* 13/1: 182.

[16] See Richard Thieberger, 'Hermann Brochs Zweifel am Roman', in Michael Kessler and Paul Michael Lützeler (eds.), *Hermann Broch: Das dichterische Werk* (1987), 116–17.

[17] ['Ich weiß nicht, warum es mir nicht gelingt zu schreiben', Musil, *TAER*, 525; 'Immer wieder in der Arbeit erlahmend', *TAER*, 526; 'Ich bin zu abstrakt geworden, und würde mich gerne . . . zum Erzählen zurückziehen', *TAER*, 308].

perceived as the naïve complacency, the irresponsibility, or the ideological bad faith of the epic narrator who, to use one of Musil's images, is like a nanny reading to a child. The intense self-reflection one finds in all three essayistic novels cannot therefore be identified with the naïve or awkward product of a writer who has not yet learnt 'maturely' to translate his message into artistic form—as implied in the hierarchy between 'telling' and 'showing', essayist and novelist. Nor can it be mistaken for the kind of essayistic control at work in the classical narrative of a Balzac. Rather one is dealing with what, like Foucault, one could call the conscious 'folding back' of literature 'on the enigma of its origin' which becomes the 'anxious and infinite quest of is own source',[18] a folding back by which our essayistic novels, despite their tremendous size, are presented as fragments. Indeed, in all three examples, the end of the volume we are reading does not coincide with the end of a book which is only interrupted. In Broch's novel, the epilogue conveys the sleepwalkers' continuing (and never-ending) journey ahead. Musil's novel, begun in the 1920s and which occupies him all the rest of his life, remains literally unfinished, with the last intended part in notes and drafts usually provided at the end of the volume (at least in German editions) along with the multiplicity of variants of a number of chapters. Proust's enormous novel, which also absorbs the author to the end of his life, is of course the paradigm of this paradox, since the ending is less a conclusion than the scaffolding of the book Marcel is about to begin writing, the novel's 'rehearsal' being the very theme of the 'search' [*Recherche*]. In this sense, these are works which, for all their encyclopedic intent, 'centrifugally' 'revert to the fragments of which [they] [are] composed' to form what could be described as vast essays.[19]

The above already more than justifies the fact that in German criticism, 'essayistic novels' tend to be discussed from the point of view of Romantic theories of the novel, when they are not referred to directly as Romantic or 'post-Romantic' novels.[20] The predominantly intellectual and epistemological dimension of such works alone, with their strong emphasis on 'ideas', warrants this affiliation. So, undeniably, does the notion of the whole (here a novel) as fragment. We know that the essence of Romantic poetry is that it is 'progressive', i.e. 'eternally evolving, never completed', for it strives for an unattainable infinity.[21] We also know that

---

[18] Michel Foucault, *The Order of Things: An Archeology of the Human Sciences* (1973), 300.

[19] Terence Cave, *The Cornucopian Text: Problems of Writing in the French Renaissance* (1979), 332, quoted in relation to Renaissance literature in Ch. 1. See also Gerda Blumenthal, 'Beyond the Text', in *Thresholds: A Study of Proust* (1984); and Fraisse, *Le Processus de la création chez Marcel Proust*.

[20] See Haas, 'Essay und Roman', in *Essay*, and 'Romanform und Essay', in *Studien zur Form des Essays*; Ludwig Rohner, 'Essay und Roman', in *Der deutsche Essay: Materialien zur Geschichte und Ästhetik einer literarischen Gattung*; Bruno Berger, 'Der Essayistische Stil im Roman', in *Der Essay: Form und Geschichte* (1966); Frisé, 'Roman und Essay'; Bachmann, *Essay und Essayismus*; Jürgen Schramke, 'Der Erkenntnisanspruch des modernen Romans: Reflexion und Essayismus', and 'Die hypothetische Darstellungsweise', in *Die Theorie des modernen Romans* (1974); E. Boa and J. H. Reid, 'Essayism', in *Critical Strategies: German Fiction in the 20th Century* (1972); and John McCormick, *Fiction as Knowledge: The Modern Post-Romantic Novel* (1975).

[21] Friedrich Schlegel, *Athenäum Fragments*, 116, p. 47 ['daß sie (die romantische Dichtart) ewig nur werden, nie vollendet kann', *Athenäums-Fragmente*, p. 39, in W. Rasch (ed.), *Friedrich Schlegel: Kritische Schriften* (1970)].

what makes it 'progressive' also makes it 'universal', in the sense of 'striving to embody within itself all the actual and possible modes of existence'.[22] And this, as shown in the previous chapter, is what turns the essay or novel 'in potentia' into the essence of the Romantic novel, the difference being, of course, that unlike Barthes's essays the texts we are dealing with here are self-declared novels. Above all, our novels' affiliation to the Romantic tradition has to do with the ambivalent attitude they share towards 'reason' and 'feeling' respectively, Romanticism being 'a creative tension between a uniquely self-conscious intellect and an equally self-conscious anti-intellectualism'.[23] Proust, Musil, and Broch's numerous reflections on art, literature, and the novel reveal that despite their misgivings, their choice to incorporate essayistic material into a novel is motivated by the awareness that the abstract force of theory (reason, the intellect) must be relativized, concretized by the senses, by feeling. For Broch and Musil, the growing tendency of the modern world towards abstraction due to scientific and technological development requires art and especially the novel 'to swallow those areas of philosophy that are seen today as unscientific or mystical'—the 'soul' (Musil), the 'irrational', or what Broch also calls the 'metaphysical remainder' of philosophy.[24] Alongside their acute intellectualism, the Romantics' attack on the mechanization and materialism characteristic of the Enlightenment, on the alleged inferiority of imaginative truth (the truth of the heart and of the senses) in relation to the truth of reason, their very distrust of reason or the intellectual faculty itself, scarcely needs stressing.[25] But art—and especially the novel with its ability to mix and combine all genres— is also the mode within which the cognitive and the aesthetic can be transcended into a third, dialectical form. Novalis's conviction that poetry and poetry alone is 'absolutely and genuinely real', that 'the more poetic, the more true', does not simply involve the 'superiority of the unconscious over conscious recollection and conscious observation', of instinct and the senses over the intellect and ideas.[26] It records above all the ambition to create a wholeness or unity in which reason, associated first and foremost with the 'dividing or dissecting gaze of science'[27] and thus initially opposed to feeling, also has a part to play in the reconciliation of this very division. For poetry to be capable of synthesizing those particulars generated

---

[22] August Wiedmann, *Romantic Art Theories* (1986), 19.   [23] Ibid. 11.

[24] ['Sie kennen meine Theorie, daß der Roman und die neue Romanform die Aufgabe übernommen haben, jene Teile der Philosophie zu schlucken, die zwar metaphysischen Bedürfnissen entsprechen, gemäß dem derzeitigen Stande der Forschung aber heute als "unwissenschaftlich" oder . . . als "mystisch" zu gelten haben. *Die Zeit des Polyhistorischen Romans ist angebrochen*', Broch, letter to Dr Brody, 5 Aug. 1931, *KW* 13/1: 150–1; see also 'Dichtung und Mythos', *KW* 9/2 (1976); and 'Der ungeheure metaphysische Rest, . . . seine Fragen und Probleme sind vorhanden, sind sogar drängender als eh und je, nur ihre Beweisbasis muß anderwärts gesucht werden—und die ist bloß im Irrationalen, im Dichterischen zu finden', Broch, letter to Frank Thiess, 6 Apr. 1932, *KW* 13/1: 186.]

[25] August Wiedmann's *Romantic Art Theories* provides an excellent recapitulation.

[26] Novalis (*Schriften*), quoted and trans. in Wiedmann, *Romantic Art Theories*, 76; and Proust, *Remembrance of Things Past*, 'Time Regained', 913 [*À la recherche du temps perdu*, 237–8].

[27] Wiedmann, *Romantic Art Theories*, 7; cf. Schlegel: 'Whereas reason can only comprise each object separately, feeling can perceive all in all at one and the same time', quoted ibid. 11.

by 'life's increasing fragmentation and dissolution into discrete parts—social, political, scientific, philosophical, religious', reason must be 'animated by imagination, imagination find place for rationality': the 'sciences', Novalis urged, 'must all
be made poetic' and once 'poeticized' become part of a still more comprehensive
or 'higher science' which incorporates all forms of knowledge, including poetry
and painting, philosophy and religion.[28] Art and art alone, for Schelling also,
comprises the unique meeting-ground of the subjective and the objective, of the
ideal and the real, of freedom (the conscious realm of mind) and necessity (the
unconscious domain of nature), where 'nature becomes spirit and spirit an en-
nobled and redeemed nature'.[29] In *Remembrance of Things Past*, the fact that involun-
tary memory (a knowledge of the world dominated by the senses) is only meant to
be the support of a novel that has other, more essential philosophical purposes,
paradoxically coexists with the narrator's energetic denunciation of theory or what
he regards as the crass intrusion of ideology, as a 'gross impropriety', voiced in his
famous formulation that 'a work in which there are theories is like an object which
still has its price-tag on it'.[30] According to the narrator of 'Timed Regained', the
writer's 'temptation to write intellectual works', which results in the narrative
being merely 'the bankruptcy of the author's intentions', is stimulated mainly by
critical theorists who are not able to recognize intellectual and moral merit from
the quality of the writer's language or the beauty of his images, but 'only when
they see it directly expressed'.[31] And yet 'the truths which the intellect apprehends
directly in the world of full and unimpeded light have something less profound,
less necessary than those which life communicates to us against our will in an
impression which is material because it enters us through the senses.'[32] The 'ideas
formed by pure intelligence'—the narrator resumes a little further—'have no
more than a logical, a possible truth, they are arbitrarily chosen'; so 'only the
impression . . . is a criterion of truth'.[33] Nevertheless, reason must not—cannot—
be eliminated from the creative act. As expounded in the essay of 'Time Regained',
the superiority of what enters through the senses—of the material—has yet 'a
spiritual meaning' which it is the writer's task to 'extract'. Sensations which are the

---

[28] Ibid. 1 and 9, and Novalis, letter to A. W. Schlegel, quoted ibid. 7.

[29] Friedrich Schelling, quoted ibid. 75.

[30] Proust, *Remembrance of Things Past*, 'Time Regained', 916 ['D'où la grossière tentation pour
l'écrivain d'écrire des œuvres intellectuelles. Grande indélicatesse. Une œuvre où il y a des théories est
comme un object sur lequel on laisse la marque du prix', *À la recherche du temps perdu*, 241].

[31] Ibid. ['Je déteste tellement les ouvrages idéologiques où le récit n'est tout le temps qu'une faillite
des intentions de l'auteur', 239]; and ibid. 916 ['cette qualité du langage dont croient pouvoir se passer
les théoriciens, ceux qui admirent les théoriciens croient facilement qu'elle ne prouve pas une grande
valeur intellectuelle, valeur qu'ils ont besoin, pour la discerner, de voir exprimée directement et qu'ils
n'induisent pas de la beauté d'une image', 241].

[32] Ibid. 912 ['Car les vérités que l'intelligence saisit directement à claire-voie dans le monde de la
pleine lumière ont quelque chose de moins profond, de moins nécessaire que celles que la vie nous a
malgré nous communiquées en une impression, matérielle parce qu'elle est entrée par nos sens', 237].

[33] Ibid. 914 ['Les idées formées par l'intelligence pure n'ont qu'une vérité logique, une vérité
possible, leur élection est arbitraire. . . . Seule l'impression, si chétive qu'en semble la matière, si
insaisissable la trace, est un critérium de vérité', 238 and 239].

'signs' of the many 'laws' and 'ideas', must be 'drawn from the shadow', 'interpreted', 'converted' into a 'spiritual equivalent'; for 'until one has brought [one's feelings] within range of the intellect one does not know what they represent'.[34] Only when the impression is made to 'pass through all the successive states which will culminate in its fixation, its expression', can the 'depth' of (experience) be 'recreated'.[35] And in this interrelation of the subjective and objective, of feeling and analysis, of revelation and 'intellectualization', lies the creation of a work of art.[36] So the essayistic novel is founded on an asymmetry, already discussed in the previous chapters, where the aesthetic mode of knowledge is made to include what it is also opposed to: art is perceived in opposition to science (reason), but also as the force capable of reconciling and transcending the opposed poles of the cognitive and the aesthetic.

The essayistic novel is entitled to claim its supreme status in Romantic poetry in so far as 'in all its descriptions, this poetry should describe itself, and always be simultaneously poetry and the poetry of poetry'.[37] The early Romantic predilection for the novel derives in other words as much from the genre's poetic potential as from its constituent capacity for self-reflection. A writer must reflect or philosophize about his art, and so the novel must include a philosophy of the novel: this is a philosophy which has transferred its interest in the individual work towards the principles of aesthetic experience which inform it, a theory of the novel which must itself 'represent the representation' and become a novel.[38] Thus, the inseparability of the question of truth from the question of truth in art stresses the mistaken nature of a critical method which consists in 'going back' from narrative fiction to essay and ascribing to the latter an independent or 'extratextual' status. Of course, the writers themselves seem to do everything they can to encourage this tendency; but they do so alongside a continuing emphasis on the effort of literary construction. The 'vision' of Proust's novel, we know, must be sought in its 'style'. More immediately, one only needs to look at Proust's delight, expressed in one of his famous letters, at having 'at last . . . found a reader who has hit upon [*qui devine*] the fact that [his] book is a dogmatic work and a construction' and his related complaint that 'people fail only too often to realize that [his] books form a

---

[34] Proust, *Remembrance of Things Past*, 'Time Regained', 912 and 933 [*À la recherche du temps perdu*, 236, 237, 239, and 259].

[35] Ibid. 916 and 935 [261].

[36] 'And this method, which seemed to me the sole method, what was it but the creation of a work of art?' (ibid. 912 [237]).

[37] Schlegel, *Athenäum Fragments*, 238, p. 49 ['in jeder ihrer Darstellungen sich selbst mit darstellen, und überall zugleich Poesie und Poesie der Poesie sein', *Athenäums-Fragmente*, p. 53]; and *Critical Fragments*, 117, 'Poetry can be criticized only by way of poetry', p. 44 ['Poesie kann nur durch Poesie kritisiert werden', *Kritische Fragmente*, p. 22].

[38] Schlegel, 'then the poet will have to philosophize about his art', *Athenäum Fragments*, 255, p. 50 ['so muß der Dichter über seine Kunst philosophieren', *Athenäums-Fragmente*, p. 57]; and 'such a theory of the novel would have to be itself a novel', in 'Letter about the Novel', in Wheeler (ed.), 79 ['Eine solche Theorie des Romans würde selbst ein Roman sein müssen', 'Brief über den Roman', in W. Rasch (ed.), 516].

construction . . . a rigorous structure to which [he] has subordinated everything'.[39] Similarly, Musil warns that despite his own description of his novel as the '*Bildungsroman* of an idea', ideas must not be allowed to stand in their own right in a novel, as though they were stated by a thinker; that they must be part of a total structure or pattern [*Gestalt*].[40] In the course of his long and laborious work on *The Man Without Qualities*, this warning will be heard all the more urgently as Musil feels to have become the victim of an invasion or 'overweight' of self-reflection and theory which he says he is no longer able to control. The result, he fears, is a novel that is too abstract, a stilted and lifeless piece.[41] As for Broch's trilogy, its essayistic 'purity' simply makes the author more rather than less aware of the demands of literary integration. Broch's letters reveal that when he decides to incorporate his existing essay, 'Disintegration of Values', he intends to place it at the very end of the book, as a 'historical and philosophical commentary' supposed to illuminate the narrative like a long footnote. His later decision to insert those chapters together with the diary into the plot of the last novel after all, is motivated by the overwhelming impression of an unliterary [*undichterisch*] construction. A concession to the readers is not alien to this alteration; but in all of Broch's essayistic writings, his deference for Goethe's sense of universality, his great admiration for the 'architectonic' construction of Joyce's *Ulysses* and his own ambition to create a 'contrapuntual unity' are equally strong. The great pains he goes to to incorporate the essayistic material into his third novel is aimed precisely at achieving the desired balance between feeling and reason—although like Musil (albeit to a lesser extent), Broch worries that this balance might be impaired by essayistic excess.[42]

[39] Marcel Proust, letter to Jacques Rivière, Feb. 1914, quoted in René Girard (ed.), *Proust: A Collection of Critical Essays* (1977), 104 and 105.

[40] ['Gedanken dürfen nicht um ihrer selbst willen in einem Roman stehen. Sie können darin . . . auch nicht ausgeführt werden, wie es ein Denker täte; sie sind Teile einer Gestalt', Musil, *Der Mann ohne Eigenschaften*, quoted in Holmes, *Robert Musil, 'Der Mann ohne Eigenschaften*, 125. In this structure, the essayistic material is supposed to be counterbalanced by 'lively scenes' and 'passion of a fantastic kind': 'zweitens habe ich meiner Meinung nach allem Essayistischen gegenüber ein Gegengewicht in der Herausarbeitung lebendiger Szenen, phantastischer Leidenschaftlichkeit', interview quoted in Rohner, *Der deutsche Essay*, 567; and 'Ich bin kein Philosoph, ich bin nicht einmal ein Essayist, sondern ich bin ein Dichter', Musil, *TAER* 288].

[41] 'Ich mußte gestern rasch die Korrekturen von 300 Seiten überprüfen und war ganz niedergeschlagen von der Überladenheit des Romans mit Essayistischem, das zerfließt und nicht haften bleibt' ibid. 340–1; 'Der Hauptfehler lag in der Überschätzung der Theorie', quoted in Holmes, *Robert Musil, 'Der Mann ohne Eigenschaften*', 126; 'Ich bin zu abstrakt geworden, und würde mich gerne . . . zum Erzählen zurückerziehen', Musil, *TAER*, 308; 'Ich sehe meine Arbeit an. Sie ist bewegungslos; wie aus Stein. Nicht bedeutungslos, aber die Sätze rühren sich nicht', ibid. 163.

[42] For the work of art as an epistemological totality—from the most irrational to the most rational—or as an epistemological short-cut which he refers to as an 'impatience to know' [*die Ungeduld der Erkenntnis*], see Broch's essay, 'James Joyce und die Gegenwart', 65, 75, 85, and 86 in *KW* 9/1, ed. Paul Michael Lützeler (1976). On the failure to achieve the right balance because of essayistic excess, see his Letter to Frank Thiess of 6 April 1932 ['Und weil Sie der ideale Leser sind, gibt es etwas in Ihrem Brief, das mich schmerzlich berührt hat: nämlich, daß die gefühlsmäßige Spannung nicht durchhielt. Denn ich hatte die Hoffnung, daß der rein gefühlige, also romanhafte Inhalt des Huguenau noch stark genug sein würde, die rationalen Einschube und Bremsungen zu überwinden, sie sozusagen mitzuschemmen. Mir ist natürlich während des Schreibens die Gefahr einer rationalen Überwucherung

So, parallel to what I quoted from him above, Broch also insists that the creation of this artistic totality 'excludes' the possibility of considering the 'scientific' dimension of his novel as a separate block alongside it, because from beginning to end the essay 'emerges *from* the novel'.[43] Hence his refusal to have the 'Disintegration of Values' appear in italics in the novel, the chapters which the essay is divided into being 'regular novel chapters' which should not be made to 'stand out' too noticeably.[44] In a sense, then, problems of construction and integration in the so-called essayistic novel are a reminder, applicable to all literature, that:

the reduction of a work of art to a doctrinal statement—or, even worse, the isolation of passages—is disastrous to understanding the uniqueness of a work: it disintegrates its structure and imposes alien criteria of value

and that:

Poetry cannot be judged according to the degree of insight which it shows into the philosophy it adopts . . . [for] poetry is not substitute-philosophy; it has its own justification and aim. . . . It must not be judged by the value of the material but by its degree of integration and artistic intensity.[45]

In the present, and particularly 'marked' context of the essayistic novel—and especially of a type of essayistic novel which appropriates already existing material—one would certainly need to provide a comparative reading of the essays or essayistic reflections outside and within the fiction. And this would probably show—as Vincent Descombes has done in his reading of Proust—not only that the novel is in no way a simple transposition or translation of the essay, but that in such cases, the novel offers a philosophy of its own which is in the end superior to the philosophy of the (initial) essay.[46] An analysis of this kind would require an entire chapter, and lies beyond the purpose of this study. But we will see that the carefully preserved abstraction, within the essayistic novel, of essay and fiction, enables one to tackle the question of the fiction's contribution to the essay in much the same way.

To conclude with this introduction, the type of novel which, in my title, I have chosen to call a novel 'without qualities' is a fundamentally ambivalent product. And as will be shown in my brief survey of Musil's novel from which I draw this expression, ambivalence—the faculty of being at once one thing and another—is precisely what this lack of qualities denotes. The first way to account for this ambivalence is to present the two dimensions of the essayistic novel—the 'essayistic'

aufgedämmert, und dem ursprünglichen Plan gemäß hätte der "Zerfall der Werte" einen viel geringeren Platz einnehmen sollen', *KW* 13/1: 185].

[43] See Broch's letters to Frank Thiess 6 Apr. 1930, *KW* 13/1: 83, to Dr Brody, 5 Aug. 1931, *KW* 13/1: 152, and to Edwin Muir, 24 Oct. 1931, *KW* 13/1: 158–9.

[44] Broch, letter to Dr Brody, 23 Sep. 1931, *KW* 13/1: 154–5.

[45] René Wellek and Austin Warren, *Theory of Literature*, 3rd edn. (1982), 110, 114, and 124.

[46] See Vincent Descombes, *Proust: Philosophie du roman* (1987), 15, 18–19. Hermann Krapoth does the same in relation to Broch in *Dichtung und Philosophie: Eine Studie zum Werk Hermann Brochs* (1971).

(as theory) and the 'fiction' (as narrative fiction)—as mutually exclusive modes of knowledge which can therefore complement each óther within a third form. Yet in doing so, it soon becomes obvious that the difference between categories is also a difference within: both the novel and the essay are a combination of, or intermediary between, the cognitive and the aesthetic. What I described above as Broch, Musil, or Proust's reasons for opting to be novelists seems to coincide exactly with reasons recounted previously for deciding to be essayists. We will recall that, if for Adorno, Proust represents the last great essayist—or if his work exemplifies the essayistic project at its best—this is because it fruitfully combines the particular and the universal, individual experience and abstract knowledge in a way that enables the universal to develop from within the boundaries of the particular in an attempt to transcend the limitations of both scientific and artistic knowledge respectively, and capture what Hegel calls 'the whole truth'.[47] Thus, the idea of diachronic progression constantly gives way to a synchronic overlap which appears to make both genres more or less interchangeable, and which clarifies the tendency, within German studies, to list essayistic novels as typical manifestations of the essay. Schlegel himself, as we know, describes the novel as a 'Romantic essay'.[48] I will begin with a brief examination of *The Sleepwalkers* (Broch) and *The Man Without Qualities* (Musil), both perceived as typical examples of the essayistic novel. Like Proust's novel, these texts are the outcome of a hesitation between two forms, a dilemma which Proust himself does not know whether to ascribe to laziness, doubt, or impotence, but which comes down to a question which the other two writers could equally well have formulated: 'Must I turn this into a novel, a philosophical study, am I a novelist?'[49] The answer is the production of a form which is neither one nor the other, and the creation of a narrator or character who has to bear the weight of the author's dilemma. Marcel constantly postpones the writing of something which might or might not be a novel. The split personality of Broch's narrator enables him to sway between a philosophical and a poetic mode of expression, but he remains unable to justify the legitimacy of either. In *The Man Without Qualities*, the predicament which Ulrich experiences is formulated as follows: 'a man who is after the truth sets out to be a man of learning; a man who wants to give free play to his subjectivity sets out, perhaps, to be a writer. But what is a man to do who is after something that lies between?'[50] and it takes on such proportions that the predominantly artistic entirely gives way to the

---

[47] Adorno, 'The Essay as Form', 156; Hegel, *Phenomenology of Spirit*, 11 [*Phänom.* 21].

[48] 'Der Roman, den wir jetzt so nennen, eigentlich nur ein (romantischer) essay' (*Neue Fragmente*, ed. J. Körner, in *Die Neue Rundschau*, 36 (1925), 1300'.

[49] ['La paresse ou le doute ou l'impuissance se réfugiant dans l'incertitude sur la forme d'art. Faut-il en faire un roman, une étude philosophique, suis-je romancier?', Proust *Le Carnet de 1908* (1976), 61].

[50] Musil, *The Man Without Qualities*, i., ch. 62, 'The earth too, but Ulrich in particular, pays homage to the Utopian idea of Essayism', 302 ['Ein Mann, der die Wahrheit will, wird Gelehrter; ein Mann, der seine Subjektivität spielen lassen will, wird vielleicht Schriftsteller; was aber soll ein Mann tun, der etwas will, das dazwischen liegt?', *Der Mann ohne Eigenschaften*, 254].

existential. In all three cases, the autobiographical component is unmistakable, although in the act of writing, the essayist—faithful to Lukács's injunction—has created himself as another, as one whose intense reflection on the conditions of representation and/or of his life has led him temporarily to withdraw from 'action'. This is a withdrawal of both the artist and the essayist together and respectively. Life and experience—as opposed to literature, to the pseudo-life of the artist—are what is meant by 'action'. At a further remove, however, 'action' is associated with writing, with producing a work of literature—here a narrative—as opposed to simply thinking or speculating about it 'essayistically'. Finally, the essayism of these novels will have to be tested in relation to the specific categories of the *Bildungsroman* (where, traditionally, the hero is an artist-to-be) and of the 'polyphonic' novel to which they have been affiliated, and for which I will rely on the work of German Romantics, of Lukács, of modern theorists of the German *Bildungsroman*, and of Bakhtin. In contradistinction to the mainly essay-oriented approach of my reading of Broch and Musil's texts, this involves a more novel-oriented perspective, if only because the essay does not feature as a point of reference in the theories of either type of novel. Nevertheless, this perspective will reinforce my initial hypothesis that the essayistic novel enhances the attributes of the essay to the extent, both of confronting the reader with the equivalent of blown-up essays, and of blowing up the essay out of all generic shape.

5.2. 'MONSTROUS ESSAYS'

5.2.1. *Sleepwalkers and Men Without Qualities*

Broch's trilogy *The Sleepwalkers*, which includes *Pasenow the Romantic* [*Pasenow oder die Romantik*], *Esch the Anarchist* [*Esch oder die Anarchie*], and *Huguenau the Realist* [*Huguenau oder die Sachlichkeit*], traces the disintegration of objective values in the course of three historical periods: the Romantic dissolution of the old world around 1888; the anarchic confusion of the pre-war period around 1903; and generalized nihilism around 1918. Each strand is meant to illustrate the problematic relation of the individual to his age.[51] This disintegration of values coincides with the dissolution of a unified image of the world which, in the essay entitled 'Disintegration of Values' of the third novel, is associated with the Middle Ages, when the world is 'founded on being' rather than 'becoming'.[52] In the 'criminal and rebellious age' of the Renaissance, the 'seeds of the modern world' are 'planted', and 'values are no longer determined by a central authority'.[53] There begins an 'unreal' period where man 'stand[s] mutely between what has been and what is not

---

[51] ['Das Buch besteht aus einer Reihe von Geschichten, die alle das gleiche Thema abwandeln, nämlich die Rückverweisung des Menschen auf die Einsamkeit—eine Rückverweisung, die durch den Zerfall der Werte bedingt ist', Broch, letter to Frau Brody, 23 July 1931, *KW* 13/1: 144.

[52] Broch, *Huguenau the Realist*, 'Disintegration of Values' (6), 447 ['Eine Welt, die sich durchaus im Sein, nicht im Werden begründete', 497].

[53] Ibid. (7), *Historical Excursus*, 480 and 483 [*Historischer Exkurs*, 533 and 536].

yet';[54] and the modern individual's state of suspension between two ethical systems or cycles of reality is precisely what is encompassed by the notion of 'sleepwalking' [*schlafwandeln*]. In the German word for 'walking' in 'sleepwalking' [*wandeln*] one finds both the ideas of 'wandering' and of 'transformation' crucial to the Romantics, and to the conceptualization of times of transition generally. Certainly, the travel theme and all the related themes of 'nostalgia', of 'longing', of 'yearning' [*Sehnsucht, Traum, Erlösung, Heimat, Ferne, Fremde, Angst, Hoffnung*] are rife in the trilogy. In Broch, however, the 'sleepwalker' is distinguished from the merely 'Romantic man' who 'shrinks away from knowledge' in that he 'seeks in the past [the Middle Ages] the completeness he longs for'.[55] The sleepwalker is a man turned towards the future, a man in a 'state . . . hovering between knowledge not yet grasped and knowledge grasped', a man about to awaken to the 'rebirth of humanity', to 'freedom'.[56] Nevertheless, the isolation and disorientation he finds himself in in the mean time, makes him vulnerable to a similar kind of regression; it justifies his being overcome by child-like impulses, such as extreme eroticism or extreme irrationality. The sleepwalker is a child who 'wanders out alone into the world', and for whom experience has lost its ability to mean beyond the particularity and arbitrariness of each event. Value-systems are 'thrown back on themselves'; they have 'separated from one another, now run parallel to each other, and, since they can no longer combine in the service of a supreme value, claim equality one with the other'.[57] The 'final indivisible unit' in the disintegration of values is 'the human individual':

the less that individual partakes in some authoritative system, and the more he is left to his own empiric autonomy—in that respect, too, the heir of the Renaissance and of the individualism that it heralded—the narrower and more modest does his 'private theology' become, the more incapable it is of comprehending any values beyond its immediate and most personal environment. . . . The man who is thus outside the confines of every value-combination, and has become the exclusive representative of an individual value, is metaphysically an outcast, for his autonomy presupposes the resolution and disintegration of all system into its individual elements; such a man is liberated from values and from style, and can be influenced only by the irrational.[58]

The drama, for both characters and readers, is that 'we know too well that we are ourselves split and riven, and yet we cannot account for it';[59] for man

[54] Ibid. (10), *Epilogue*, 640 ['Sie stehen ohne Sprache zwischen dem Noch-nicht und dem Nicht-mehr', 707].
[55] Ibid. (6), 446 ['wer die Erkenntnis fürchtet . . . und der das ersehnte Bild in der Vergangenheit sucht', 496].
[56] Ibid. 'Story of the Salvation Army Girl in Berlin', 575 ['eine Art Schwebezustand zwischen Nocht-nicht-Wissen und Schon-Wissen', 635]; and 'Disintegration of Values' (10), 643 ['Die ewige Erneuerung des Humanen', 710].
[57] Ibid. 591 ['Ein achtjähriges Kind, das die Absicht hat, allein in die Welt hinauszuwandern', 653], and 'Disintegration of Values' (6), 448 [498].
[58] Ibid. (10), *Epilogue*, 628–9 ['desto unfähiger wird diese, irgendwelche Werte außerhalb ihres engsten individuellen Bereichs zu erfassen. . . . der metaphysisch "ausgestoßene" Mensch', 692 and 693].
[59] Ibid. (1), 375 [421].

never knows anything about the irrationality that informs his worldless actions; he knows nothing of 'the invasion from below' to which he is subject, he cannot know anything about it, since at every moment he is ruled by some system of values that has no other aim but to conceal and control all the irrationality on which his earth-bound empirical life is based.[60]

Hence the 'longing for a leader', for a man 'in whom all the events of our time [would take] significant shape', a man who would 'provide us with the motivation for events that in his absence we can characterize only as insane'.[61] From the point of view of the novel's form, this seems to justify the fact that the general or universal value which each event or 'action'—the experience of each character—no longer represents, must be complemented by the interpretations (the rationalization) of a narrator who appropriately turns out to be one Dr Bertrand Müller, philosopher. Characters suffer from 'unreality', they are unable to see the 'point' of their lives, they cannot 'tell whether [they] [have] lived that life or whether it [is] a tale someone [has] told [them]'.[62] In this sense, the titles of the three novels are reassuring, for they denote a balanced complementation of narrative and interpretation both at the level of each novel, and at the level of the trilogy as a whole in relation to the overall commentary of the final essay, 'Disintegration of Values', in the third novel. In the first and second novels, the comments which accompany the narrative appear in other words to reinforce and to anticipate the function and content of the final essay. Moreover, the latter's radical abstraction from the narrative, the fact that it forms a separate (and, as we saw, already existing) text, encourages the reader to attribute its authority to the author himself rather than simply to the philosopher/narrator. Thus the switch from narrative fiction to essay appears to call for a switch from fictional to non-fictional, from particular to general—and so from partial to total knowledge.

Correspondingly with the negative dialectic of the third term which we have consistently encountered in previous chapters, however, the last novel of the trilogy, which is the most radically essayistic, thwarts the above expectations. Formally, the anticipation of the final, totalizing comment induces a progressive imbalance between narrative and essay, whereby the essayistic insertions which start as mere remarks lengthen visibly and end up by providing increasingly detailed interpretations of facts which conversely lose their significance until they seem to be reduced to pretexts. The individual, particular occurrence is given less and less space as the contiguous justification follows more and more rapidly. And if this expansion of essayistic fragments does anticipate the final essayistic bulk, this is in so far as the latter effects not a totalizing interpretation but an ultimate disintegration both at the level of form and at the level of content. Ironically, in other words, the essayistic material emphasizes that the desired totalization which

---

[60] Broch, *Huguenau the Realist*, 'Disintegration of Values' (10), *Epilogue*, 625 [689–90].

[61] Ibid. (1), 375 ['Deshalb wohl sehnen wir uns nach dem "Führer", damit er uns die Motivation zu einem Geschehen liefere, das wir ohne ihn bloß wahnsinnig nennen können', 421].

[62] Ibid. (10), *Epilogue*, 633 ['und schließlich wußte er nicht mehr, ob er jenes Leben gelebt hatte oder ob es ihm erzählt worden war', 698].

it purports to bring about with regard to the plot is inevitably dependent upon the very fragmentation it is supposed to counteract. This simultaneous process of totalization and disintegration of meaning is after all the very subject-matter of the trilogy. The desired synthesis into a higher unity—here embodied by the third and most technically ambitious part of the trilogy—necessarily fails, since it is intended to supply both the explanation and the illustration of a disintegration of values which is predicted from the outset.[63] Having inserted the 'Disintegration of Values' in the last novel to exemplify what Broch describes as 'adapting the presentation and the style to the content', it is inevitable that this essay should be both a totalizing comment upon the disintegration of values, and the motor of this very disintegration which it can no longer control from a safe, external or neutral vantage-point. Broch feels he has successfully applied the 'Theory of Relativity' which, like so many other novelists, he borrows from the empirical sciences, and the related principle of the 'observer's intervention in the field of observation' [*der Beobachter im Beobachtungsfeld*], whereby both the observed and the act of observation, the object of representation and the technique of representation must be part of the representation's content.[64] In *The Sleepwalkers*, in effect, the philosopher's 'intervention in the field of observation' results in his becoming a victim of the crisis he is attempting 'rationally' to account for. This is more than hinted at from the beginning of the third novel, where the question of the 'unreality' of modern life, of the 'non-meaning of a non-existence' which the characters of the first two novels have been seen to suffer from, is raised with new urgency—both in the 'scientific' essay of the 'Disintegration of Values', and in the opposite type of essayistic material, the diary or so-called 'Story of the Salvation Army Girl in Berlin'.[65] Along with other clues which critics have picked out, the quasi-identical formulation of the problem of unreality in both types of essay confirms that the two seemingly independent series of digressive chapters which interrupt the narrative are related by one and the same narrator: the philosopher Bertrand Müller turns out to be the diarist and poet of the 'Story of the Salvation Army Girl in Berlin'. For one thing, this merging of the two opposite poles of essayism (the

---

[63] Apart from the mutual interruption of essay and fiction, 'Disintegration of Values' (8), 523 [578] and ch. LXV, 539 [595] are a series of fragments.

[64] 'Methodologically regarded, to define a thing as the "product of a product" [*die Setzung der Setzung*] is nothing else than to introduce the ideal observer into the field of observation, as has been already done long since by the empirical sciences (by physics, for example, in the Theory of Relativity)', *Huguenau the Realist*, 'Disintegration of Values' (9), *Epistemological Excursus*, 563 [623]. See also Broch, 'James Joyce und die Gegenwart', 77.

[65] 'Is this distorted life of ours still real? Is this cancerous reality still alive? . . . It is as if the monstrous reality of the war had blotted out the reality of the world. Fantasy has become logical reality, but reality evolves the most a-logical phantasmagoria' (*Huguenau the Realist*, 'Disintegration of Values' (1), 373 ['Hat dieses verzerrte Leben noch Wirklichkeit?', 418]); and: 'Can this age be said still to have reality? Does it possess any real value in which the meaning of its existence is preserved? Is there a reality for the non-meaning of a non-existence?' (ibid. (9), *Epistemological Excursus*, 559 ['Gibt es Wirklichkeit für den Nicht-Sinns eines Nicht-Lebens?', 618]); and finally: 'Can this age, this disintegrating life, be said still to have reality?' (ibid. 'Story of the Salvation Army Girl in Berlin' (13), 557 ['Hat diese Zeit, hat dieses Zerfallende Leben noch Wirklichkeit?', 615]).

objective and the subjective) points to the relativization of absolute knowledge by the perceiving subject or individual experience. It draws attention to the inseparability of the quest for truth and the knowledge of oneself to the world (the essayistic 'what do I know?') in a way that installs not only the autobiographical but the lyrical at the heart of all epistemological motivation. But the philosopher— as the reader soon finds out from one of the 'confessions' in the diary—also suffers from the unreality and meaninglessness of his own existence. He too feels his 'life . . . darkening behind [him]', and 'do[es] not know if [he] [has] lived or if [his] life was a tale told to [him]'.[66] Initially, the very fact that 'on all sides he encounters unreality' together with his resulting 'passivity' (which he describes as 'increas[ing] from day to day') are the prerequisites for the 'sole real activity' which is 'the contemplative activity of philosophizing'.[67] Yet even philosophizing must fail in a 'world without Being':

I try to philosophize—but where is the dignity of knowledge to be found today? Is it not long defunct? Has Philosophy itself not disintegrated into mere phrases in face of the disintegration of its object? . . . Is there any resignation deeper than that of an age which is denied the capacity to philosophize?[68]

'Philosophy', the philosopher/poet laments, 'has become an aesthetic pastime'.[69] The convergence of reason and feeling, philosophy and poetry, essay and fiction betrays a desire for the synthesis of absolute knowledge. But what it really does is to underline the essay's ambition to lend the fiction a transcendental meaning and thus close it 'extratextually', and acknowledge—because the essay is now part of the fictional (novelistic) frame—that this closure is impossible. The essayistic fragments, which express a series of speculations or hypotheses no longer validated by a transcendent authority, remain 'phrases' [*Worte*], 'fictions', in a world where nothing can be ascertained. Both Broch's incorporation of his philosophy into a novel and the ambivalent status of the philosopher/poet in the text thus concur to express the incapacity of any philosophical claim—and, by extension, of any transcendental authorial position—to escape the realm of fiction. The reassuring 'or' of Broch's chapter-titles (in the original, e.g. 'Pasenow *or* Romanticism') recognizably signals the oxymoronic 'and/or' typical of essayistic dialogism. The philosopher/ poet's inability to make sense of the characters'—and his own—lives parallels his

---

[66] Broch, *Huguenau the Realist*, 'Story of the Salvation Army Girl in Berlin' (13), 558 ['mein Leben verdämmert hinter mir, und ich weiß nicht, ob ich gelebt habe, oder ob es mir erzählt worden ist', 617].

[67] Ibid. 557 ['die einzig wahre Aktivität . . . die kontemplative Aktivität des Philosophierens', 615].

[68] Ibid. ['Ich versuche zu philosophieren—doch wo ist die Würde der Erkenntnis geblieben? ist sie nich längst erstorben, ist die Philosophie angesichts des Zerfalls ihres Objektes nicht selber zu bloßen Worten zerfallen? Diese Welt ohne Sein', 615].

[69] Ibid. ['Selbst das Philosophieren ist zu einem ästhetischen Spiel geworden', 616]. Cf. also 'Andererseits kennen sie meine These von den heutigen Zustand der Philosophie: die philosophie als solche, soweit sie nicht mathematisiert, kann nichts mehr "beweisen"—wozu sie als "Wissenschaft" verpflichtet wäre. . . . Der metaphysische Rest . . . im Dichterischen zu finden', Letter to Frank Thiess, 6 Apr. 1932, *KW* 13/1: 186.

inability to make sense of historical events, of historical unity: neither story nor history can be given a definitive meaning, since 'truth is just a value among other values'.[70] So narrative and commentary are each cast as competing, alternative discourses or perspectives, neither of which can account for the other. In this respect, *The Sleepwalkers* can be said to take over the problematic translation between particular and general, (narrative) example and general maxim already discussed in the context of Montaigne's *Essais*. In the *Essais*, the story is the medium by which the example—which implies the moral principle—explicitates itself: as at once a form of expansion and a form of reduction, the example is the narrative unit which refers back to the systematic unit, reflecting it as faithfully as possible.[71] The story is supposed to concretize or actualize the otherwise ungrounded generality of the reflections. But we saw that its paradigmatic value as example is precisely what is questioned: both syntagmatic and paradigmatic poles lose their respective exemplariness, thereby producing a residue which always remains to be interpreted or embodied by yet another example. The 'sleepwalker', in other words, is doomed to go on wandering in an essayistic no-man's-land where there is no definitive answer, no last word—be it God's or Hegel's:

The lines of inquiry no longer converge on this idea of God (they no longer converge on any point, one may say, but run parallel to each other), cosmogony no longer bases itself on God but on the eternal continuance of inquiry, on the consciousness that there is no point at which one can stop, that questions can for ever be advanced and must therefore be advanced . . . that every solution is merely a temporary solution, and that nothing remains but the act of questioning in itself . . .

Hegel called history 'the path to the liberation of spiritual substance', the path leading to the self-liberation of the spirit, and it has become the path leading to the self-destruction of all values. . . . Hegel's values are not absolutes, but only finite postulates. Does this mean that all values are made relative? That one must abandon all hope of the logical Absolute ever manifesting itself in reality through the unifying of thought and being? that one must abandon all hope of ever even drawing near to the path that leads to the self-liberation of the spirit and of humanity?[72]

---

[70] 'What is a historical event? What is historical unity? or, to go still further: what is an event at all [*was ist ein Ereignis überhaupt*]? what principle of selection must be followed to weld single occurences into the unity of an event?' (*Huguenau the Realist*, 'Disintegration of Values' (9), *Epistemological Excursus*, 560 [618–19]); and ibid. (4), 415 ['daß die Wahrheit ein Wert unter allen anderen Werten ist', 462].

[71] See Karlheinz Stierle, 'L'Histoire comme exemple, l'exemple comme histoire: Contribution à la pragmatique et à la poétique des textes narratifs', *Poétique*, 10 (1972), 182 and 184.

[72] Broch, *Huguenau the Realist*, 'Disintegration of Values' (5), *Logical Excursus*, 426 ['Die Frageketten münden nicht mehr in dieser Gottesidee, sondern laufen tatsächlich in die Unendlichkeit (sie streben sozusagen nicht mehr nach einem Punkt, sondern haben sich parallelisiert), die Kosmogonie ruht nicht mehr auf Gott, sondern auf der ewigen Fortsetzbarkeit der Frage, auf dem Bewußtsein, daß nirgends ein Ruhepunkt gegeben ist, daß immer weiter gefragt werden kann . . . daß jede Lösung bloß als eine Zwischenlösung gilt, und daß nichts übrig bleibt als der Akt des Fragens als solcher', 474–5]; Broch, *Huguenau the Realist*, 'Disintegration of Values' (9), *Epistemological Excursus*, 559, 561, and 562 [618, 620, and 'Bedeutet dies Relativierung aller Werte? . . . Aufgabe der Hoffnung, daß der weg zur Selbstbefreiung des Geistes und der Humanität jemals auch nur annäherungsweise beschritten werden

In the end, the 'uncertainty of an ever-questioning logic whose point of plausibility has vanished into the infinite'[73] can itself only be discussed by way of a question. And with the oxymoronic exploitation of non-contradiction referred to above, this use of questioning is the strategy of 'suspension'—already described in the context of Lukács's essay—with which one could come to a (tentative) conclusion as to the function of the essayistic in *The Sleepwalkers*. This is a paradoxical function, since the essayistic is at once the prerequisite for, and obstacle to, the achievement of total knowledge or to the fulfilment of what Broch calls 'the impatience to know' [*die Ungeduld der Erkenntnis*].[74] We have seen that the apparent opposition between essay (as a distinct genre) and narrative fiction is taken over by a generalized essayism or essayistic attitude (the mode) which ultimately permeates the entire novel. With regard to the way in which I situated essay and novel in relation to each other in Chapter 1, this 'attitude' underscores the philosophical perspective which determines the emergence of both genres. *The Sleepwalkers* illustrate the ambition, through particular experience, to provide universal knowledge, since 'every man bears the whole Form of human condition'.[75] Yet the historical transition from the universalism of the 'Scholastic' to the particularism of 'modern realism' also implies a recognition that man's apprehension of reality through the senses is limited, and the very possibility of knowledge is called into question. Characters in *The Sleepwalkers* incarnate the extreme relativization involved in the replacement of universal Truth by individual experience in particular places and at particular times, and where the reality of each experience is only valid for here and now. Not surprisingly, the questioning of the knowing subject, his discontinuity and dislocation finally affect the one being capable of extrapolating the universal from the particular   the narrator/author himself. His position in *The Sleepwalkers* reflects the fact that all thought is circumstantial, that there is no unconditional standpoint from which reality can be apprehended. Despite seeming to adopt the ideal of a context-free or neutral medium characteristic of a philosophy which models itself upon scientific discourse, the narrator's position—which is after all that of a character—expresses a flagrant rejection of this ideal. It manifests philosophy's awareness of its time-bound, historical character, its recognition, in

---

könne?', 621]. Cf . also 'Irrealizable my yearning, unattainable the Promised Land, invisible the ever-brightening but constantly receding radiance. . . . lost as I am in ever-increasing strangeness, blind in ever-increasing blindness, failing and falling asunder in yearning remembrance of the night of home . . .', *Huguenau the Realist*, 'Story of the Salvaltion Army Girl in Berlin' (14), 558 ['unerfüllbar die Sehnsucht, unerreichbar das gelobte Land, unsichtbare die immer größere, niemals erreichbare Helligkeit . . . fremd in stets zunehmender Blindheit, vergehend und zerfallend im Erinnern an die Nacht der Heimat . . .', 617]; and 'Irretrievably lost is our home, inaccessibly stretches the distance before us . . .', *Huguenau the Realist*, 'Story of the Salvation Army Girl in Berlin' (14), 577 ['Unwiederbringlich ist die Heimat verloren, uneinbringlich liegt die Ferne vor uns', 638].

[73] Broch, *Huguenau the Realist*, 'Disintegration of Values' (9), *Epistemological Excursus*, 559 [618].

[74] ['Man mag diesen Erkenntniswillen des Dichterischen . . . eine Ungeduld der Erkenntnis nennen . . . die bloß schrittweise und niemals sie erreichend zu solcher Totalität vordringt', Broch, 'James Joyce und die Gegenwart', 86]. Hence Broch's fascination with Joyce's 'work in progress'.

[75] Montaigne, 'On Repenting', *Essays*, III. 2, p. 908 ['Du repentir', *Essais*, III. ii, p. 782*b*].

concrete terms, of the contingency of subject (writer or reader) and world upon discourse. Thus, the narrator's thoughts are also a continuous revision of his understanding—a revision to which the different generic perspectives offered in *The Sleepwalkers* (narrative, poetry, and drama[76]) also contribute. Knowledge, as in the *Essais*, is shown to be speculative and hypothetical—a 'fiction', both in the radical sense of unlimited *différance* (the discourse never resolves itself) and of the concretely fictional expressed by the aesthetic—here novelistic—handling of object and subject. Like the *Essais*, however, *The Sleepwalkers* does not posit the fictitious foundations of knowledge from the outset. Recognizing the omnipotence of essayism is the result of a (mental) journey and progression which, despite and with the complicity of the overall novelistic frame, depends upon the tension between essay and fiction, cognitive and aesthetic required by the essayistic novel.[77]

Musil's *The Man Without Qualities* initially appears as less 'pure' an example of essayistic novel, since, as mentioned above, he seems to prefer the motivation of his reflections to their complete abstraction from the narrative context. In reality, one could say that the type of essayism he adopts is even more undiluted, for in *The Man Without Qualities*, the confrontation between essay and fiction immediately gives way to a generalized essayism, the novel we are reading being the product of a narrative crisis which forbids the story even to begin. The first chapter significantly entitled 'Which, remarkably enough, does not get anyone anywhere' [*Woraus bemerkenswerterweise nichts hervorgeht*] and which opens a first book itself entitled 'A Sort of Introduction' [*Eine Art Einleitung*], provides a parodically precise description of the geographical context of the 'action'—a road accident. From the outset, the irony of the essayistic comments which are at first assumed by a narrator is unmistakable, as they lend the event and its description not the expected credibility but, on the contrary, the exact measure of its implausibility. The impossibility of ascertaining the identity of the characters at hand is a first step in this direction:

The two people who were walking up a wide, busy thoroughfare . . . knew who they were and that they were in their proper place in a capital city that was also an imperial residence.

---

[76] Drama is represented by 'The Symposium or Dialogue on Redemption', Broch, *Huguenau the Realist*, 497.

[77] For this brief survey of *The Sleepwalkers* and of Broch's work generally, see the sections on the essayistic novel by Haas, Berger, Rohner, Bachmann, Frisé, Boa and Reid, already listed in n. 20, and Hermann Krapoth, *Dichtung und Philosophie: Eine Studie zum Werk Hermann Brochs* (1971); Paul Michael Lützeler, *Hermann Broch: Ethik und Politik. Studien zum Frühwerk und zur Romantrilogie 'Die Schlafwandler'* (1973); Michael Kessler and Paul Michael Lützeler (eds.), *Hermann Broch: Das dichterische Werk* (1987); Manfred Durzak (ed.), *Hermann Broch: Perspektiven der Forschung* (1972); Hartmut Steinecke, *Das Schlafwandeln: Zur Deutung des Motivs in Hermann Brochs Trilogie* (1978); Karl Robert Mandelkow, *Hermann Broch's Romantrilogie 'Die Schlafwandler': Gestalt und Reflexion im modernen deutschen Roman* (1962); Dorrit Cohn, *The Sleepwalkers: Elucidations of Hermann Broch's Trilogy* (1966); Theodore Ziolkowski, *Dimensions of the Modern Novel* (1969) (ch. 5); 'Hermann Broch', in John McCormick, *Fiction as Knowledge: The Modern Post-Romantic Novel* (1975); Maurice Blanchot, '"Les Somnambules": Le Vertige logique', in *Le Livre à venir* (1959); and *Europe*, 741–2 (1991), 'Robert Musil/Hermann Broch'.

Let us assume that their names were Arnheim and Ermelinde Tuzzi—but no, that would be a mistake, for Frau Tuzzi was spending this August in Bad Aussee. . . . So we are confronted with the enigma of who they were.[78]

The function of such speculations is in turn justified in the first properly essayistic chapter (chapter 4), 'If there is such a thing as a sense of reality, there must also be a sense of possibility' [*Wenn es Wirklichkeitssinn gibt, muß es auch Möglichkeitssinn geben*] which follows indirect preliminary approaches to the main character Ulrich (via his abode, and via his father) who is progressively made to assume the essayistic reflections. In this chapter, the link between being able to 'summon up [a] sense of reality' and the 'possession of qualities' is established, and from that link follows the recognition that the hero is devoid of both—a 'man without qualities'. Only here, this recognition is presented as a self-recognition: our hero, who is subjected to the same disintegration or breakdown of reality as Broch's characters, is no 'sleepwalker'.[79] In the same way that the characters in the first chapter cannot be unequivocally defined, the attempt to provide a 'biography' of Ulrich, also at the beginning of the novel, must fail. Instead, the narrator's description of Ulrich is replaced by three 'attempts' (corresponding to chapters 9, 10, and 11) at 'becoming a man of importance', respectively entitled 'First of three attempts at becoming a man of importance'; 'The second attempt. First developments in the moral philosophy of being a Man Without Qualities'; and 'The most important attempt of all'.[80] These chapters feature Ulrich as successively a cavalry officer, a civil engineer, and a mathematician, all of which must be abandoned: Ulrich, the typical bourgeois hero, is devoid of unity and of a unified story. His successive experiences only accentuate the unbridgeable gap between himself and the world or society which he tries to integrate, thus reinforcing the subjective, introspective quality of his life until again 'there [is] only philosophy left for him to turn to'.[81] The 'story', then, will prove—as in Montaigne's *Essais*—to be mainly the adventure of the character's thoughts.[82] It begins 'properly' when the 'hero', retreating into the abstract realm of reflection, renounces all action and decides to take a year's 'holiday from life' in order to 'seek an appropriate way of using his

---

[78] Robert Musil, *The Man Without Qualities*, i. 4–5 [*Der Mann ohne Eigenschaften*, 10].

[79] Ibid. i. 14 ['Und da der Besitz von Eigenschaften eine gewisse Freude an ihrer Wirklichkeit voraussetzt, erlaubt das den Ausblick darauf, wie es jemand, der auch sich selbst gegenüber keinen Wirklichkeitssinn aufbringt, unversehens widerfahren kann, daß er sich eines Tages als ein Mann ohne Eigenschaften vorkommt', 18].

[80] ['Erster von drei Versuchen, ein bedeutender Mann zu werden'; 'Der Zweite Versuch. Ansätze zu einer Moral des Mannes ohne Eigenschaften'; 'Der wichtigste Versuch'].

[81] Musil, *The Man Without Qualities*, i. 49 ['Ein geniales Rennpferd reift die Erkenntnis, ein Mann ohne Eigenschaften zu sein', 47].

[82] Cf. 'Montaigne understood that in an essay, the track of a person's thoughts struggling to achieve some understanding of a problem *is* the plot, is the adventure', quoted in Thomas E. Recchio, 'A Dialogic Approach to the Essay', in Alexander J. Butrym (ed.), *Essays on the Essay: Redefining the Genre* (1989), 273.

abilities'.[83] However, this introspective withdrawal which collapses the distinction between thought and action into thought in action or 'in progress', will only confirm the rift between the hero's abilities and their application; for the problematic modern world is a world where, as Marcel also discovers in *Remembrance of Things Past*, individuals are subject to general laws; or rather, events are experienced but no one is there to experience them:

In earlier times one could be an individual with a better conscience than one can today. Today . . . responsibility's point of gravity lies not in the individual but in the relation between things. Has one not noticed that experiences have made themselves independent of man? . . . There has arisen a world of qualities without a man to them, of experiences without anyone to experience them, and it almost looks as though under ideal conditions man would no longer experience anything at all privately and the comforting weight of personal responsibility would dissolve into a system of formulae for potential meanings.[84]

The only remaining 'action' in *The Man Without Qualities* seems to take place in the subsidiary plots of the so-called 'Collateral Campaign' [*Parallelaktion*] and of the trial of the murderer Moosbrugger. The Collateral Campaign is an organization meant to prepare for a nation-wide festival to celebrate the Austrian Emperor's Jubilee, but really generated from the desire to overcome the fragmentation of the modern world through the elaboration of a total System, an infallible order supposed to reinstate the lost harmony of the Middle Ages. The project of this cultural and epistemological synthesis, which depends upon the revelation of an ultimate value that would mark the fusion of the cognitive and the aesthetic (of 'thought' and 'soul'), is expected to occur thanks to the bringing together of moral forces represented by the most prestigious scientific and artistic minds of the period. Ulrich's retirement from life or from the world of 'action' is to be read in contrast to the naïvely enthusiastic efforts of the *Parallelaktion* to do something about the disillusionment which underlies this decision. But the book's 'progress' will show that this 'action', as the ironic emphasis on the very word 'action' already anticipates, leads nowhere. The bringing together of men with the greatest 'qualities' turns out to be powerless: the perspectives remain literally 'parallel' or essayistically

---

[83] 'He saw wonderfully clearly that—with the exception of that necessary for earning a living, which he did not need—he had in himself all the abilities and qualities favoured by the time in which he lived; but he had somehow lost the capacity to apply them [*Die Möglichkeit ihrer Anwendung war ihm abhanden gekommen*]. And since, after all, when even footballers and horses have genius, it is only the use one makes of it that can still save one's individuality, he decided to take a year's leave from life in order to seek an appropriate way of using his abilities' (Musil, *The Man Without Qualities*, i. 49 [*Der Mann ohne Eigenschaften*, 47]).

[84] Ibid. 'A Man Without Qualities Consists of Qualities Without a Man', i. 174–5 ['Heute dagegen hat die Verantwortung ihren Schwerpunkt nicht im Menschen, sondern in den Sachzusammenhängen. Hat man nicht bemerkt, daß sich die Erlebnisse vom Menschen unabhängig gemacht haben? . . . Es ist eine Welt von Eigenschaften ohne Mann entstanden, von Erlebnissen ohne den, der sie erlebt, und es sieht beinahe aus, als ob im Idealfall der Mensch überhaupt nichts mehr privat erleben werde und die freundliche Schwere der persönlichen Verantwortung sich in ein Formelsystem von möglichen Bedeutungen auflösen solle', 'Ein Mann ohne Eigenschaften besteht aus Eigenschaften ohne Mann', 150].

juxtaposed. If the Collateral Campaign is collateral to anything, if it 'parallels' anything at all, it is the generalized absence of standard or objective values by which a crime such as Moosbrugger's (Broch's 'irrational from below') can be measured, and as a result of which his case drags on without getting anywhere, in the same way that the 'summing up' of Ulrich via the minimum number of qualities required for the identification of a novel's main protagonist or 'hero' proves to be impossible.

The intrinsic connection between the breakdown of narrative and the loss of the subject's identity or essence is explicitly seen from the point of view of the 'epic', it being understood that in the epic, the character is deduced from action. The time of 'deductive living', when individual action was derived from 'certain definite assumptions' or universal absolutes is past; 'nowadays', Ulrich ponders, 'we live without any guiding idea, but also without any method of conscious induction. We go on trying things as haphazardly as an ape does!'[85] In the following chapter, which appropriately records the thread of Ulrich's further speculations on this issue in the course of his 'wander' back home ('The way home' [*Heimweg*]), it occurs to him that 'the law of life, for which one yearns . . . dreaming of simplicity' is 'none other than that of *narrative order*', the 'simple order' that enables the 'lucky' man to be able to say 'when', 'before', and 'after'.[86] And if 'in their basic relation to themselves most people are narrators', if they crave for the 'orderly sequence of facts', for the 'unidimensional' and the 'chronological', this is because it 'has the look of a necessity' and gives them the 'impression that their life has a "course" [*Lauf*]', thus making them 'feel somehow sheltered in the midst of chaos'.[87] Art plays a major role in fulfilling this need, Ulrich and/or the narrator knows, and not least the novel which 'has artificially turned [this] to account'.[88] In this respect, Ulrich's painful awareness that he has 'lost this elementary narrative element to which private life still holds fast, although in public life everything has now become non-narrative, no longer following a "thread", but spreading out as an infinitely interwoven surface', clearly reflects Musil's own impossibility of coming up with a plot, his inability to narrate being—as he writes in a letter—at once his own stylistic problem and the existential problem of his character.[89] I have already

---

[85] Musil, *The Man Without Qualities*, 'Talking Man to Man', ii. 418 ['Früher hat man gleichsam deduktiv empfunden, von bestimmten Voraussetzungen ausgehend, und diese Zeit ist vorbei; heute lebt man ohne leitende Idee', 'Die Aussprache', 636].

[86] Ibid., 'The Way Home', ii. 435–6 ['Es fiel ihm ein, daß das Gesetz dieses Lebens, nach dem ich, überlastet und von Einfalt träumend, sehnt, kein anderes sei, als das der erzählerischen Ordnung! Jener einfachen Ordnung, die darin bestent, daß man sagen kann: "als das geschehen war, hat sich jenes ereignet!"', 'Heimweg', 650]. At the end of ch. 83 ('The like of it happens, or, why does one not invent history'), Ulrich's mental digressions [*Abschweifungen*] lead him to his geographically losing his way.

[87] Ibid. ii. 436 [650].

[88] Ibid. ii ['Das ist es, was sich der Roman künstlich zunutze gemacht hat', 650].

[89] Ibid. ii ['Und Ulrich bemerkte nun, daß ihm dieses primitive Epische abhanden gekommen sei, woran das private Leben noch festhält, obgleich offentlich alles schon unerzählerisch geworden ist und nicht einem "Faden" mehr folgt, sondern sich in einer unendlich verwobenen Fläche ausbreitet', 650; and 'Das Problem, wie komme ich zum Erzählen, ist sowohl mein stilistisches wie das Lebensproblem der Hauptfigur', in *PDB*, 726].

referred to the vast workshop which surrounds *The Man Without Qualities* and verbalizes—as well as exposes—Musil's 'inability' to write, due to the growing invasion of self-reflection or theory.[90] Within *The Man Without Qualities*, the translation of this 'paralysis' into the generalized essayistic spirit of the novel is already expressed in the titles 'Sort of Introduction', 'The Like of It Now Happens', 'First of three attempts'. These headings signal the expected features of an essayistic structure: the oxymoronic logic of 'The Like of It Now Happens' suggests that narrative has given way to a competition of conflicting hypotheses—propositions or versions which are given as equally valid. The individual who has retired from the world, from 'action' in order to speculate on its meaning comes to the realization, like Montaigne or Marcel (in Proust), that he is a 'sequence of juxtaposed but distinct "I's", that no sign refers unequivocally to a fixed signified, but to several signifieds, all contradictory.[91] And as noted in the *Essais*, the relativization of all levels promotes the impression of being rooted to the spot or even of regressing rather than progressing—of beginning again and again, or of not being able to begin at all. The logic of 'The Like of It Now Happens' thus goes hand in hand with 'attempts' ('First of Three Attempts'), with 'sorts of introduction' ('A Sort of Introduction'), with a pervasive sense of 'rehearsal'.

At the same time, the loss of the 'elementary narrative element' so lucidly acknowledged by Ulrich, is also clearly defiant—a protest against the idea of history (and by extension the story) as 'that of a billiard-ball, which, once it had been hit, ran along a definite course', against the refusal to accept that 'there was inherent in the course of history a certain element of going off the course'.[92] For narrative order is after all the 'everlasting epic device by means of which nannies soothe their little charges'—the quintessentially naïve, a 'tried and tested "intellectual foreshortening"' also exploited by philosophers.[93] Hence, the impulse which underlies Ulrich's dedication to the abstract realm of reflection may be philosophical, but he refuses to be identified with philosophy:

He was no philosopher. Philosophers are violent and aggressive persons who, having no army at their disposal, bring the world into subjection to themselves by means of locking it up in a system,

---

[90] See n. 17.

[91] Cf. Proust: 'When I recapitulated the disappointments of my life as a lived life, disappointments which made me believe that its reality must reside elsewhere than in action . . . our inherent powerlessness to realise ourselves in material enjoyment or in effective action', *Remembrance of Things Past*, 'Time Regained', 911 [*À la recherche du temps perdu*, 235]; and cf. Musil, in *TAER*, 303: 'Wie muß man sich aber stellen, um mit einer Welt fertig zu werden, die keinen festen Punkt hat?'

[92] Musil, *The Man Without Qualities*, 'The Like of It Happens, or, Why does One not Invent History?', i. 70 ['Der Weg der Geschichte ist also nicht der eines Billiardballs, der, einmal abgestoßen, eine bestimmte Bahn durchläuft, sondern er ähnelt dem Weg der Wolken, ähnelt dem Weg eines durch die Gassen Streichenden, der . . . abgelenkt wird und schließlich an eine Stelle gerät, die er weder gekannt hat, noch erreichen wollte', 'Seinesgleichen geschieht oder warum erfindet man nicht Geschichte', 361].

[93] Ibid. 'The Way Home', ii. 436 ['Dieser ewige Kunstgriff der Epik, mit dem schon die Kinderfrauen ihre Kleinen beruhigen'; and 'perspektivistische Verkürzung des Verstandes', 650].

whereas

there was something in Ulrich's nature that worked in a haphazard, paralysing, disarming manner against logical systematization, against the one-track will, against the definitely directed urges of ambition; and it was also connected with his chosen expression, 'Essayism'.[94]

Ulrich's 'lack of qualities' and 'active passivism' [*aktiver Passivismus*[95]] are the prerequisite for an experience of the world and of himself which is both negative and positive, consonantly with what Musil calls the 'utopia of essayism'. The essayistic reluctance to reduce both world and subject to unequivocal definitions which no longer do justice to the complexity and many-sidedness of either, becomes a creative disposition to handle the world alternatively and thus the condition of freedom for both character and writer. By refusing to favour one discourse at the expense of another, always dealing exhaustively with the object of his thoughts (the essay is defined as a fusion of exactitude and indetermination), Ulrich confronts a negatively experienced reality—old forms of being—with a world of possibilities. In this respect, Musil's hero is not only, like Proust's, a man of the possible whose fragmented narrative is an association of possible stories. He is cast as the very embodiment of the essayistic spirit:

It was approximately in the way that an essay, in the sequence of its paragraphs, takes a thing from many sides without comprehending it wholly—for a thing wholly comprehended instantly loses its bulk and melts down into a concept—that he believed he could best survey and handle the world and his own life.[96]

The negative a priori of Ulrich's 'lack of qualities' and the related fact that he is 'far from logically consistent' [*von Folgerichtigkeit noch weit entfernt*][97] is already counteracted, in the first essay-chapter, by the narrator's unmistakably favourable approach to the 'sense of the possible' [*Möglichkeitssinn*] as opposed to the 'sense of reality':

Anyone possessing it [a sense of possibility] does not say, for instance: Here this or that has happened, will happen, must happen. He uses his imagination and says: Here such and such might, should or ought to happen. And if he is told that something *is* the way it is, then he thinks: Well, it could probably just as easily be some other way. So the sense of possibility

---

[94] Musil, *The Man Without Qualities*, 'The Earth too, but Ulrich in particular, Pays Homage to the Utopian Idea of Essayism', i. 300 ['Er war kein Philosoph. Philosophen sind Gewalttäter, die keine Armee zur Verfügung haben und sich deshalb die Welt in der Weise unterwerfen, daß sie sie in ein System sperren'; and 'Es gab etwas in Ulrichs Wesen, das in einer zerstreuten, lahmenden, entwaffnenden Weise gegen das logische Ordnen, gegen den eindeutigen Willen, gegen die bestimmt gerichteten Antriebe des Ehrgeizes wirkte, und auch das hing mit dem seinerzeit von ihm gewählten Namen Essayismus zusammen', 'Auch die Erde, namentlich aber Ulrich, huldigt der Utopie des Essayismus', 253].

[95] Ibid. 'The Assertion that even Ordinary Life is of Utopian Nature', i. 79 ['die Behauptung, daß auch das gewöhnliche Leben von utopischer Natur ist', 368].

[96] Ibid. 'A Man Without Qualities Consists of Qualities Without a Man', i. 297 ['Ungefähr wie ein Essay in der Folge seiner Abschnitte ein Ding von vielen Seiten nimmt, ohne es ganz zu erfassen,— denn ein ganz erfaßtes Ding verliert mit einem Male seinen Umfang und schmilzt zu einem Begriff ein—glaubte er, Welt und eigenes Leben am Richtigsten ansehen und behandeln zu können', 250].

[97] Ibid. 'If There is such a Thing as a Sense of Reality, There Must also be a Sense of Possibility', i. 13 [16].

might be defined outright as the capacity to think how everything could 'just as easily' be, and to attach no more importance to what is than to what is not.[98]

From the 'sense of the possible', which Ulrich is supposed to have developed from a tender age, to the notion of 'living hypothetically' [*hypothetisch leben*, p. 249] there is but one step. Already in the 'earliest times of the first self-confidence of youth', Ulrich has 'a vague intuitive feeling' that:

this order of things is not as solid as it pretends to be; nothing, no ego, no form, no principle, is safe, everything, is in a process of invisible but never-ceasing transformation, there is more of the future in the unsolid than in the solid, and the present is nothing but a hypothesis that one has not finished with.[99]

In a school essay, he further speculates that God himself must also be an essayist, since 'even [He] probably prefer[s] to speak of His world in the subjunctive potentiality (. . .), for God made the world and while doing so thinks that it could just as easily be some other way.'[100] So by later choosing to 'hold aloof from the world', his hesitation 'to become anything', a 'character, a profession, a definite mode of existence', Ulrich simply acts on his initial intuition.[101] To live hypothetically, 'conjunctively', is to retain one's freedom with regard to the world, to refuse to adopt a fixed personality, to refuse to be identified with the false values and mediocre compromises of dominant social codes. In not realizing himself or his ideas concretely, 'sensibly', Ulrich remains 'the unwritten poem of his own existence' and, by extension, a 'potential man', the 'quintessence of human possibilities'.[102]

What applies to Ulrich—as the embodiment of the essayistic spirit—applies to

---

[98] Ibid. i. 12 ['Wer ihn besitzt, sagt beispielsweise nicht: Hier ist dies oder das geschehen, wird geschehen, muß geschehen; sondern er erfindet: Hier könnte, sollte oder müsste geschehen; und wenn man ihm von irgend etwas erklärt, daß es so sei, wie es sei, dann denkt er: Nun, es könnte wahrscheinlich auch anders sein', 16].

[99] Ibid. 'The Earth too, but Ulrich in particular, Pays Homage to the Utopian Idea of Essayism', i. 296–7 [249; and 'diese Ordnung ist nicht so fest, wie sie sich gibt; kein Ding, kein Ich, keine Form, kein Grundsatz sind sicher, alles ist in einer unsichtbaren, aber niemals ruhenden Wandlung begriffen, im Unfesten liegt mehr von der Zukunft als im Festen, und die Gegenwart ist nichts als eine Hypothese, über die man noch nicht hinausgekommen ist', 250].

[100] Ibid. 'Ulrich', i. 15 ['daß wahrscheinlich auch Gott von seiner Welt am liebsten im Conjunctivus potentialis spreche (. . .), denn Gott macht die Welt und denkt dabei, es könnte ebensogut anders sein', 19].

[101] Ibid. 'The Earth too, but Ulrich in particular, Pays Homage to the Utopian Idea of Essayim', i. 97 ['Darum zögert er, aus sich etwas zu machen, ein charakter, Beruf, eine feste Wesensart', 250].

[102] Ibid. i 298 ['der Mensch als Inbegriff seiner Möglichkeiten, der potentielle Mensch, das ungeschriebene Gedicht seines Daseins', 251]. Apart from the above-mentioned sections on the essayistic novel by Bachmann, Haas, Rohner, Berger, Schramke, Boa and Reid, useful studies on Musil include: Ulf Schramm, *Fiktion und Reflektion: Überlegungen zu Musil und Beckett* (1967); Joseph P. Strelka, *Kafka, Musil, Broch und die Entwicklung des modernen Romans* (1959); P. Zima, *L'Ambilence romanesque: Proust, Kafka, Musil* (1980), and 'Zu Robert Musil's *Der Mann ohne Eigenschaften*', in *Textsoziologie: Eine kritische Einführung* (1980); Adolf Frisé, *Plädoyer fur Robert Musil* (1987); Anne Longuet-Marx, *Proust, Musil: Partage d'écritures* (1986); Alan Holmes, *Robert Musil, The Man Without Qualities: An Examination of the Relationship between Author, Narrator and Protagonist* (1978); Thomas Harrison, *Essayism: Conrad, Musil, Pirandello* (1992); Peter Bürger, *Prosa der Moderne* (1988); Lothar Huber and John J. White (eds.), *Musil in Focus: Papers from a Centenary Symposium* (1982); David Luft, *Robert Musil and the Crisis of European Culture 1880–1942* (1980); Jean-Pierre Cornetti, *Robert Musil, ou L'Alternative romanesque* (1985); and *Europe*, 741–2 (1991), 'Robert Musil/Hermann Broch'.

the novel, which could also be described as the 'unwritten poem of [its] own existence' and as the 'quintessence of [novelistic] possibilities'. The disintegration of narrative syntax into the coexistence of several parallel narrative strands favours the paradigmatic or 'poetic' structure typical of the Montaignian essay. And in relation to prose—and *a fortiori* to narrative sequence—this paradigmatic, poetic structure, which juxtaposes rather than subordinates its elements, has the quality of the 'unwritten' or of the 'not yet written'. This is a structure which, like the *Essais*, one can add to again and again; it is not checked by the arbitrary contours of the published book. Over the years, the enormous workshop which surrounds Musil's work in progress (a work which, like Proust's, is always 'beside itself') constitutes the vast reserve of notes and variants by which the writer secures the right to modify and interpolate, and so to pursue what looks like a huge montage. In the space of the 'utopia of essayism' also exploited by Barthes, time provides the possibility of rewritings no longer subordinated to the logic of chronology, or to (self-)correction, or to narrative causality and hierarchy. Moreover, the hypothetical constructions made possible by the renewed recontextualisations of essayistic narrative do emphasize the fact that reality as we perceive it is only one possible realization among others. The present, in the essayistic novel, is 'nothing but a hypothesis that one has not finished with', the result—as Adorno puts it—of a 'conflict *temporarily* brought to a standstill'.[103] By remaining closest to the ideal of the fragment, of the not-yet-written, this side of any one realization, the essayistic novel sustains the Romantic fantasy of a 'universal' poetry which 'embodies within itself all the actual and possible modes of existence'.[104] We know that the Romantics' acute sense of the finite, of the passing of time, their despair at having to choose one moment (itself pregnant with possibilities) rather than another and therefore to exclude other options, betrays the intense desire to be able to live several lives at once, and to unite all contraries in an impossible fusion that would remove the need to choose: 'It is equally fatal for the mind to have a system and to have none', Schlegel writes; 'It will simply have to decide to combine the two'.[105] The essayistic disintegration of narrative syntax, with the resulting prevalence of what Broch calls the *Nebeneinander* (literally the 'alongside-one-another' suggested by the paradigmatic structure) over the *Nacheinander* (the syntagmatic 'after-one-another' of narrative sequence), manifests the longing to grasp the essence of things—infinity—in one instant.[106] It creates the conditions for an absolute

---

[103] Cf. 'Ein erstarrter Einzelfall seiner Möglichkeiten' in *The Man Without Qualities*, ch. 62; and Adorno, 'The Essay as Form', 170.

[104] Wiedmann, *Romantic Art Theories*, 19.

[105] Schlegel, *Athenäum Fragments*, 53, p. 45 ['Es ist gleich tödlich für den Geist, ein System zu haben, und keins zu haben. Es wird sich also wohl entschließen müssen, beides zu verbinden', *Athenäums-Fragmente*, p. 31].

[106] [Cf. Broch: 'Immer geht es um die Simultaneität, um die Gleichzeitigkeit der unendlichen Facettierungsmöglichkeit des Symbolhaften, überall spürt man das Bestreben, die Unendlichkeit des Unerfaßlichen, in dem die Welt ruht und die ihre Realität ist, mit Symbolketten einzufangen und zu umranken, die möglichst gleichzeitig zum Ausdruck gebracht werden sollen; und wenn auch dieses Streben nach Simultaneität (. . .) nicht den Zwang durchbrechen kann, daß das Nebeneinander und

experience—a moment of what Proust calls 'ecstasy'—which, as we also saw in relation to Barthes's self-portrait, is supposed to escape the contingencies of time.[107] Our novels' absence of 'qualities' and the non-contradiction which it promotes reflects the Romantic craving for union and fusion, for 'infinite unity' (Schlegel) or 'inner total fusion' (Novalis) with the world, with the idea that each part could participate again in the totality from which it has been excluded and satisfy the 'solitary soul's' yearning to 'melt into the boundless whole'.[108] This, as August Wiedmann recapitulates, involves a 'wholehearted surrender to nature and the universe, in a selfless participation in all modes of being', a 'submerging' of the 'ego in the reality of the non-ego, in a universal oneness of which the self [is] a subservient element or part', and thus a monistic state of mind whereby 'the All as One and the One as All'.[109] In Musil, this absolute experience, called 'the Other State' [*Der andere Zustand*] and which pertains to the realm of the unconscious (and therefore of necessary rather than arbitrary truths) seems closest to Barthes's, since it takes the form of an androgynous fusion between Ulrich and his sister, of a generic *coincidentia oppositorum*; but all three writers are to some extent visionaries or mystics. The essayist's creative disposition, we are told in *The Man Without Qualities*, is 'remarkable'. For like God (or Ulrich's creator), he must have 'made the world and while doing so [thought] that it could just as easily be some other way'; and since 'something real means no more than something imagined', his 'constructive will . . . treats [reality] . . . as a mission and an invention': he 'awakens new possibilities' and is free to 'invent' history.[110] In all three novels in fact, the essayist becomes no less than a 'prophet', conformably with the Romantic conception of the artist as the one chosen to proclaim the coming of the Spirit, whether this is called the 'messiah', the 'Promised Land' (Broch), 'redemption' (Broch), 'home', the Golden Age (Novalis), or the Millennium (Musil).[111]

Ineinander durch ein Nacheinander ausgedrückt werde . . . so bleibt die Forderung nach Simultaneität trotzdem das eigentliche Ziel alles Epischen, ja alles Dichterischen: das Nacheinander der Eindrücke und des Erlebens zur Einheit zu bringen, den Ablauf zur Einheit des Simultanen zurückzuzwingen, das Zeitbedingte auf das Zeitlose der Monade zu verweisen, mit einem Wort die Überzeitlichkeit des Kunstwerks im begriff der unteilbaren Einigkeit herzustellen', 'James Joyce und die Gegenwart', 72–3].

[107] 'Ecstasy: Fragments of Existence Withdrawn from Time', Proust, *Remembrance of Things Past*, 'Time Regained', 908 ['Le Temps retrouvé', 233].

[108] From Goethe's 'How yearns the solitary soul to melt into the boundless whole', Wiedmann, *Romantic Art Theories*, 2.

[109] Ibid. 53, 103, and 102.

[110] Musil, *The Man Without Qualities*, 'If There is such a Thing as a Sense of Reality, There must also be a Sense of Possibility', i. 12 and 13 [*Der Mann ohne Eigenschaften*, 19]; and 'The Like of It Happens, or, Why does One not Invent History?', i. 70 [362].

[111] Cf. Friedrich Schlegel's insistence that art 'aims for the last Messiah', for the millennium in sight, discussed by August Wiedmann in 'Mythopoetic Imagination: Prophecy, Millenarianism, and Eschatology', in *Romantic Art Theories*. As Wiedmann points out, this corresponds to a craving (particularly noticeable in Broch's work) for 'a community of faith and worship and, with mounting urgency, for a community of state . . . a politically united and regenerated people' (ibid. 4). Musil's third volume (after Volumes I and II entitled 'The Like of It Now Happens', is entitled 'Into the Millennium (The Criminals)'; at one stage, he thought of calling his novel 'The Redeemer' [*Der Erlöser*].

The sense in which the essayistic novel can be described as an 'unwritten poem' and the 'quintessence of [novelistic] possibilities' recognizably pertains to the logic, already discussed in Barthes, by which the novel 'in potentia' is perceived as the essence of the novel and of literature generally. The path from Broch to Musil is one which leads to a novel with fewer and fewer 'qualities', to a 'monstrous' essay—as Musil describes his own novel[112]—and therefore to an increasingly 'failed' novel in the accepted sense. In Romantic terms, however, it is precisely the novel's affinity with the essay that makes it 'essentially' a novel: the greater the resistance to the novel, the purer (the more modern) the novelist. The novel as 'search', as rehearsal, as 'idea' of the novel is 'the accomplishment of perfection' rather than the mark of failure; it is incomplete because incompletable—what Maurice Blanchot calls a 'monument admirably in ruins'.[113] Through their tendency to exploit the universal, encyclopedic character of the novel, our novels declare their ambition to become the ultimate, total book, the Book of all books which is by definition a 'Book-to-come', since the Book is only ever 'affirmed in its becoming' (the existence of the Book would of course put an end to all literature). If the essayistic novelist, like the essayist, is 'ceaselessly postponing literature by declaring that [he] is going to write and by turning this declaration into literature itself',[114] this is because the Book is identified with its announcement and expectation, it has 'no other content than the presence of its endlessly problematic future', it is 'always before it can be, always separated and divided finally to become this very separation and division'.[115] From an idealist (and predominantly German) point of view, this 'radical intransitivity' accounted for in Barthes concerns above all the 'idea' of the novel; for the textualist (and predominantly French) point of view, this is the intransitivity of language or writing. The modern literary text, which Michel Foucault situates at the beginning of the nineteenth century, 'curves back in a perpetual return upon itself, as if its discourse could have no other content than the expression of its own form', and 'seeks to re-apprehend the essence of all literature in the movement that brought it into being'.[116] And so it ignores the diversity of forms or the division of genres; only the Book counts, away from genres in relation to which it refuses to be categorized and to be granted a place or form: 'A book no longer belongs to a genre, it partakes in literature only', for the essence of literature paradoxically 'evades any form of essential determination that might stabilize or even realize it'.[117] Thus for Genette, the essayistic characteristics of Proust's *Remembrance of Things Past*—the 'invasion of story by [psychological,

---

[112] For Musil, it is 'überhaupt kein Roman, sondern ein Essay von ungeheuren Dimensionen', quoted in Lothar Köhn, *Entwicklungs-und Bildungsroman: Ein Forschungsbericht* (1969), 77; and for Boa and Reid, '*Der Mann ohne Eigenschaften*, to a greater degree than that of any of the other novels discussed, is one protracted essay', 'Essayism', 175.

[113] Blanchot, *Le Livre à venir*, 220 and 198.

[114] Barthes, *Critical Essays*, 98 [*Essais critiques*, 106].

[115] Blanchot, *Le Livre à venir*, 343.   [116] Foucault, *The Order of Things*, 300.

[117] ['Un livre n'appartient plus à un genre, tout livre relève de la seule littérature', Blanchot, *Le Livre à venir*, 293].

historical, esthetic, metaphysical] commentary, novel by essay, narrative by dis-course'—are not only answerable for the fact that this novel 'is experienced by everyone as being "not completely a novel any more"'; for him this is 'the work which . . . concludes the history of the genre (of the genres) and, along with some others, inaugurates the limitless and indefinite space of modern *literature*'.[118] Whether perceived as moving beyond, or as remaining this side of the novel, the essayistic novel becomes the point of convergence of the sub-literary and the supra-literary, of a-genericness and the 'matrix of all generic possibilities' discussed in Chapter 1 in relation to the essay. In other words, the essayistic novel becomes the 'Other that generates all (other) genres', while conversely genres become the '"fallout", the historically determined actualizations of what is potentially woven into the [essayistic novel]'.[119] On the other hand, the essayistic novel, even more resolutely than the *Essais* because of its greater subjection to the constraints of narrative, confirms that time and language cannot be transcended for a total representation of the world. Expressing the unconscious or the 'other state' in a novel which, what is more, constantly stresses the role of 'reason' or of the 'intellect', must itself remain a self-consciously paradoxical or aporetical project.[120]

5.2.2. *Essay,* Bildungsroman, *and Polyphonic Novel*

When Musil describes his novel as a 'monstrous essay', he is referring to its already enormous and ever-expanding size. In my reading of Broch and Musil's texts, I have attempted to show that if the essayistic novel looks like a 'monstrous essay', this is above all because it literally 'magnifies' those characteristics which I had so far ascribed to the essay—and size is certainly not alien to this effect. But since the path we have chosen has led 'from essay to essayistic novel', this could well be an optical illusion due to our tackling the essayistic novel from the limited angle of the essay. From the time of their appearance, the novels of Proust, Musil, and Broch have recurrently been listed under the category of the *Bildungsroman* (the para-digm of the German Romantic novel) or of the 'polyphonic' novel, both obvious manifestations of the essayistic novel even though neither has been theorized in relation to the essay. The investigations not only of the early German Romantics, of Lukács and of Bakhtin, but of theorists of the *Bildungsroman* (for example Martin Swales or Franco Moretti) and of the polyphonic novel (for example Julia Kristeva and Peter Zima) since then, have stressed the fact that these are forms which include within them the possibility (in the case of the *Bildungsroman*) or the compulsion (for the polyphonic novel) of their own excess. Again, this excess is measured in relation to the Hegelian master-plot: both Lukács and Bakhtin con-flate literary history with the history of consciousness and interpret literary history

---

[118] Gérard Genette, *Narrative Discourse: An Essay in Method* (1980), 259.

[119] Réda Bensmaïa, *The Barthes Effect: The Essay as Reflective Text* (1987), 91–2.

[120] See Anne Longuet-Marx, 'Le Distemps ou l'impossible de la langue', in *Proust, Musil: Partage d'écritures* (1986).

itself as a kind of *Bildungsroman* that records the journey from the undifferentiated, child-like world of the epic to the fraught but mature world of the novel.[121]

Despite the absence of the essay in both theories of the novel, the overwhelming parallels between the type of novel Lukács describes in his *Theory of the Novel* and the essay are of course all the easier to bring out as he wrote and published on both genres at a few years' interval (1911 and 1916). A brief comparison between the two works reveals that both forms are regarded as fundamentally 'problematic' forms of writing: the novel, like the essay, is the historical and philosophical expression of a godforsaken world in which man's relation to the absolute—or rather 'society', since this is a more Hegelian–Marxist reading—has become decidedly problematic. Lukács's Romantic and Hegelian interpretation of the transition from epic to novel is more or less identical to Broch's in *The Sleepwalkers*, or vice versa. The epic is the genre of the great Greek era; its theme is 'not a personal destiny but the destiny of the community', for the 'value system which determines the epic cosmos' is too 'round', 'complete', 'too organic for any part of it to become so enclosed within itself'.[122] This time of universal harmony vanishes with classical Greece, when men become aware of an 'unbridgeable chasm between cognition and action, soul and created structure, self and world', and thus come to philosophize: 'all substantiality has to be dispersed in reflexivity'.[123] The epic gives way to the novel, which, like all other art forms, 'carr[ies] the fragmentary nature of the world's structure into the world of forms'.[124] Like the essay, then, the novel is 'the epic of an age in which the extensive totality of life is no longer directly given, in which the immanence of meaning in life has become a problem'; it is 'an expression of . . . transcendental homelessness'.[125] Like the essay, however, the novel 'still thinks in terms of totality', one which is no longer found in the present world, as a concrete entity, and which must therefore be created in abstract terms.[126] The result is a dialectical movement between the two extremes of what is (reality, or 'being') and what should be (the ideal, desired world—or 'becoming'). The 'inner form' of the novel, like that of the essay, is 'the process of the problematic individual's journeying towards himself', the 'story of the soul that goes to find itself, that seeks adventures in order to be proved and tested by them, and, by proving itself, to find its own essence'.[127] Through the feeling of constant homelessness and nostalgia for utopian perfection on the one hand, and the awareness of hopeless existential imperfection on the other, the novelist and the novel's hero

---

[121] See Hegel, *Aesthetics*, 1037–62, on the 'world situation' of the Epic.

[122] Lukács, *Theory of the Novel*, 66 [*Die Theorie des Romans*, 57].

[123] Ibid. 34 [26].   [124] Ibid. 39 [30].

[125] Ibid. 56 and 41 [47, and 'die Form des Romans ist, wie keine Andere, ein Ausdruck der transzendentalen Obdachlosigkeit', 32].

[126] Ibid. 56 and 70 [47 and 60].

[127] Ibid. 80 and 89 ['die Wanderung des problematischen Individuums zu sich selbst'; and 'sein Inhalt ist die Geschichte der Seele, die da auszieht, um sich kennenzulernen, die die Abendteuer aufsucht, um an ihnen geprüft zu werden, um an ihnen sich bewährend ihre eigene Wesenheit zu finden', 70 and 78].

experience within themselves the duality which governs the inner structure of the novel as it governs that of the essay. Again, the journey takes place, but it never reaches its aim ('The voyage is completed: the way begins"[128]). Hence the life or biography of the hero which structures and limits the novel externally is exceeded by the infinite deferment of the hero's inward quest, a deferment also inherent in the autobiographical (and therefore never-ending) project of the essay. In Lukács's novel too, it is the 'process' that counts, not the verdict, for 'the novel, in contrast to other genres where the existence resides within the finished form, appears as something in the process of becoming'.[129] At the same time, the hero's estrangement from the world expressed by self-reflection ('the need for reflection is the deepest melancholy of every great and genuine novel',[130]) is the positive condition for self-transcendence, as in the essay. The novel's 'homelessness' or alienation confer upon it a certain independence and maturity which enable it to recognize its imperfections (the imperfection of its age) and thus to arrive at a partial self-abolition of its subjectivity and at a certain amount of objectivity. In this sense, not only does the novel, like the essay, mark a decisive stage in the critical consciousness of the subject; it is the 'art form of virile maturity, in contrast to the childlikeness of the epic'.[131] As expected, this maturity is associated with Romantic 'irony' which, in his essay on the essay, Lukács already traces back to Socrates and Montaigne via Friedrich Schlegel, but without elaborating it as fully as he does in his *Theory of the Novel*. Irony, for which I previously used the definition of 'the form of an absolute striving, accompanied by a recognition of its merely relative means',[132] is in Lukács's reformulation of Schlegel 'a negative mysticism to be found in times without a god', 'an attitude of *docta ignorantia* towards meaning', the 'self-surmounting of a subjectivity that has gone as far as it was possible to go' and hence 'the objectivity of the novel'.[133] Irony, in other words, is 'the self-recognition and, with it, [the] self-abolition of subjectivity'; in becoming its/his own object, the novel/subject's awareness of the metaphysical dissonance of which it/he is part, of the rupture between 'inside' and 'outside', is a condition both for this rupture and its transcendence, that is, the possibility of participating, despite everything, in the harmony that is historically denied it/him and thus of declaring the negative situation to be transitory. At the same time, 'this reflection in turn becomes an object for reflection etc.':[134] the desired unity depends upon the reflection of reflection of reflection ad infinitum, with an interval always needing to be

[128] Ibid. 73 ['begonnen ist der Weg, vollendet die Reise', 63].

[129] Ibid. 72–3 ['So erscheint der Roman im Gegensatz zu dem in der Fertigen Form ruhenden Sein anderer Gattungen als etwas Werdendes, als ein Prozeß', 62].

[130] Ibid. 85 ['Dieses Reflektierenmüssen ist die tiefste Melancholie jedes echten und großen Romans', 74].

[131] Ibid. 71 ['Der Roman ist die Form der gereiften Männlichkeit im Gegensatz zur normativen Kindlichkeit der Epopöe', 61].

[132] Harrison, *Essayism: Conrad, Musil, Pirandello*, 3.

[133] Lukács, *Theory of the Novel*, 90, 93, and 90, respectively [*Die Theorie des Romans*, 79, 82, and 79].

[134] Ibid. 74 and 85 [64, and 'Diese Reflexion wird aber nochmals zum Gegenstand des Nachdenkens', 74].

breached. Irony, in Schlegel's words, is the 'form of paradox', the 'infinite plenitude of chaos'; it is the sign both of radical contradiction and of its resolution, of negation and affirmation, of self-annihilation and self-creation, of the Individual and the Universal;[135] it is, in Lukács's recapitulation,

a subjectivity which sees through the abstract and, therefore, limited nature of the mutually alien worlds of subject and object, understands these worlds by seeing their limitations as necessary conditions of their existence and, by thus seeing through them, allows the duality of the world to subsist. At the same time the creative subjectivity glimpses a unified world in the mutual relativity of elements essentially alien to one another, and gives form to this world. Yet this glimpsed unified world is nevertheless purely formal; the antagonistic nature of the inner and outer worlds is not abolished but only recognised as necessary.[136]

In the typology of the various novel forms (all based on the problematic hero's soul in its relationship to the existing world) which constitutes the second part of his book, Lukács, like the early German Romantics before him, chooses the *Bildungsroman*, epitomized by Goethe's *Wilhelm Meister* novel, as the most representative example of the above paradoxa, that is, for its skilful use of ironic detachment. As suggested in Chapter 1, the fact that the *Bildungsroman* should feature so prominently among examples of so-called essayistic novels[137] has to do with the fundamental significance of the humanist ideal of *Bildung* for the genre of the essay. Lukács's definition of the novel as the 'story of the soul that goes to find itself, that seeks adventures in order to be proved and tested by them, and, by proving itself, to find its own essence', perfectly captures this significance. It highlights the epistemological project of the *Essais* which also consists in the examination of the relationship between self and world with a view, through what Montaigne calls 'apprenticeship' and 'testing', to achieving self-realization. The *Bildungsroman* is the 'sublimation and rendering inward of the novel of adventures'—according to Thomas Mann's equally famous definition.[138] In the essay similarly, the subject's education and self-discovery through his confrontation with the world (the discourse of the self versus the discourse of others) involves an inward journey, the different stages of which record the different stages of the subject's necessary 'erring'. And this 'erring' guarantees the continuing tension and interaction between theory and practice, general and particular, mind (or idea)

[135] See Schlegel, *Critical Fragments*, 42, pp. 41–2, in Wheeler (ed.) [*Kritische Fragmente*, pp. 10–11]; *Critical Fragments*, 48, p. 42 ['Ironie ist die Form des Paradoxen', p. 12]; *Critical Fragments*, 108, p. 43 [*Kritische Fragmente*, p. 20]; and *Ideas* 69, p. 198 in David Simpson (ed.), *The Origins of Modern Critical Thought* [*Ideen*, p. 97, in W. Rasch (ed.)]. See also 'Irony and Fragment', pp. 141–53, in Ernst Behler, *German Romantic Literary Theory*.

[136] Lukács, *Theory of the Novel*, 74–5 [*Die Theorie des Romans*, 64].

[137] Including Wieland's *Agathon*, Moritz's *Anton Reiser*, Jean Paul's *Titan*, Immermann's *Münchhausen*, Gottfried Keller's *Der grüner Heinrich*, and novels by later writers such as Thomas Mann, Alfred Döblin, Hermann Hesse, Stefan Zweig, Max Frisch, etc. See the studies listed above on the essayistic novel.

[138] Quoted in Martin Swales, *The German Bildungsroman from Wieland to Hesse* (1978), 23.

and story, fragment and whole which underlies both genres, and which, in both genres, records both a (past) estrangement and the hope for a future reconciliation or fusion when all errors will have been transcended. Reader participation is crucial for the production of this higher unity which both essay and essayistic novel aspire to. In the *Bildungsroman*, this participation explicitly consists in 'leading the individual from his uneducated standpoint to knowledge', whereby the individual 'must also pass through the formative stages of universal spirit': the reader, like the author, 'is meant to suffer through each position and to be changed as he proceeds from one to the other'.[139] Where the artist 'educates himself and develops his "transcendental self", his spirit, through creating works of art', the reader, who is also invited to educate and improve himself through self-criticism and awareness of his present limitations, does so by 'recreating these works of art in his "uniquely personal (but not merely subjective) way"'.[140] In the wake of Hegel, theorists of the *Bildungsroman* agree that the reconciliation between the 'I' and the 'world', which tends to be above all a reconciliation between the 'I' and society, involves in principle a 'coincidence without rifts' between 'one's formation as an individual in and for oneself' and 'one's social integration as a simple *part of a whole*'.[141] If man is truly himself only in as much as he exists for the whole, each moment of the 'plot of his life' must 'strengthen [his] *sense of belonging* to a wider community'.[142] Hence, the conclusion of the *Bildung* (the 'marriage of Truth and the Whole'[143]) coincides theoretically with the end of the story (the plot sequence), when the youth has 'passed into maturity' and 'merged with his new world'.[144] The happy ending, in this sense, is the clearest expression of the 'triumph of meaning over time',[145] in keeping with Hegel's notion of self-consummation: 'The true is the whole. But the whole is nothing else than the essence consummating itself through its development. Of the Absolute, it must be said that it is essentially a *result*, that only in the *end* is it what it truly is.'[146] The self-realization of protagonist and novel (and reader) thus depends upon the perfect adequation of idea and story, theory and fiction, between what Swales (like Broch), calls the '*Nebeneinander* (the "one-alongside-another") of possible selves within the hero and the *Nacheinander* (the "one-after-another") of linear time and practical activity', that is, 'between

---

[139] Hegel, *Phenomenology of Spirit*, Preface, 16 [*Phänom.* 26] (cf. 'The *length* of this path has to be endured, because, for one thing, each moment is necessary.... Since the substance of the individual, the World-Spirit itself, has had the patience to pass through these shapes over the long passage of time, and to take upon itself the enormous labour of world-history ... and since it could not have attained consciousness of itself by any lesser effort, the individual certainly cannot by the nature of the case comprehend his own substance more easily', ibid. 17 [*Phänom.* 27–8]); and Walter Kaufmann, *Hegel: A Reinterpretation* (1978), 117.

[140] Kathleen Wheeler, 'Irony and Self-Criticism', in id. (ed.), *German Aesthetic and Literary Criticism: The Romantic Ironists and Goethe* (1984), 17, 15, and 17, respectively.

[141] Franco Moretti, *The Way of The World: The 'Bildungsroman' in European Culture* (1987), 16.

[142] Ibid. 19.   [143] Ibid. 60.   [144] Ibid. 26.   [145] Ibid. 55.

[146] Hegel, *Phenomenology of Spirit*, Preface, 11. ['Das Wahre ist das Ganze. Das Ganze aber ist nur das durch seine Entwicklung sich vollendende Wesen. Es ist von dem Absoluten zu sagen, daß es wesentlich *Resultat*, daß es erst am Ende das ist, was es in Wahrheit ist', *Phänomonologie des Geistes*, Vorrede, 21].

potentiality and actuality'.[147] Although the concept of *Bildung* is 'tried out' in the process of becoming [*Werden*] or life of an individual, in a sense 'actualities' are only esteemed 'insofar as they are validated and underwritten by the hero's inwardness' or 'potentialities': 'trying out' the idea is tantamount to composing the story 'according to some idea of how the world *ought* to evolve', so that 'the subjective yearning for "meaning" is entirely satisfied by, and subsumed under the objective legislation of "causality"'.[148]

On the other hand, the very fact that the plot of the *Bildungsroman* 'is enacted within the finite realm of social practicality' and 'also partakes of the infinite realm of his inwardness'[149] indicates from the outset that the genre includes within it the possibility of its own excess. As noted in my Chapters 1 and 3, the self-identity of Hegel's own *Bildungsroman*, the *Phenomenology of Spirit*, is undermined in so far as this is a work which 'allows for the insistence of a certain gap' or incommensurability between form and content, signifier and signified: the *Phenomenology* is the very history of the inadequation or negative struggle involved in the concept's difference from itself, in the certain 'spacing' between 'thought and time'.[150] 'The essay', writes Gerhard Haas, 'is always the expression of a possibility.'[151] In this sense, 'practical reality' (marriage, family, career) which is a 'necessary dimension' of the hero's self-realization is also regarded as 'delimiting' or 'constraining' the complexity of individual potentiality.[152] To accept reality and society, the idealistic hero inevitably has to compromise on his dreams, desires, fantasies, in the same way that the necessary concretization of the philosophical concept or Idea in Hegel's own plot also entails to some extent a debasement of this concept—as our essayistic novelists proved to be well aware. Defying this compromise in *The Man Without Qualities*, and so favouring the 'idea' of both character and novel over its realization, induces the narrator to conceive character and novel as the 'unwritten poem[s] of [their] own existence', correspondingly with the relationship between what Hegel calls 'the poetry of the heart and resisting prose of circumstances'.[153] In both cases, philosophy and poetry are placed on one level as they are in the *Essais*, which is a reminder that the essayistic simultaneously stands for theory, for the fragment (the epitext and the 'not-yet-written'), and for the 'poetic' (when the paratactic structure, the use of associations, images, metaphors is conceived as an alternative to logically ordered discourse). The most discernable echo to Hegel's 'poetry of the heart' and 'resisting prose of circumstances', before Montaigne, is Aristotle's famous assertion that poetry is more philosophical (more essential and necessary) than history because it discloses a universal meaning that is purified of the insignificant contingencies which history tends to be cluttered with.[154]

[147] Swales, *The German Bildungsroman*, 29.
[148] Ibid. 157, 23, and 17—my emphasis on 'ought'—and Moretti, *The Way of the World*, 69.
[149] Swales, *The German Bildungsroman*, 17.   [150] Derrida, 'Outwork', in *Dissemination*, 12.
[151] ['Der Essay ist immer Möglichkeitsaussage', Haas, *Studien zur Form des Essays*, 19].
[152] See Swales, *The German Bildungsroman*, 29.
[153] Hegel, 'Vorlesungen über die Ästhetik', 983.   [154] Desmond, *Art and the Absolute*, 61.

Similarly, Hegel refers to historical truths as 'concerned with a particular exist-ence, with the contingent and arbitrary aspects [*Zufälligkeit und Willkür*] of a given content, which have no necessity' or, even more strongly, with 'relative circum-stances, clustered with accidents, and sullied by arbitrariness'.[155] Poetry in Hegel plays a privileged role among art forms, for it 'is occupied with the universal element in art as such to a greater extent than is the case in any of the other ways of producing works of art'.[156] Unlike prose, the 'proper subject-matter of poetry is spiritual interests'; poetry 'is the original presentation of the truth, a knowing which does not yet separate the universal from its living existence in the individual . . . but which grasps the one only in and through the other'.[157] The 'prosaic mind', on the other hand, 'treats the vast field of actuality in accordance with the restricted thinking of *understanding* and its categories, such as cause and effect, means and end'; it 'persists in separating the particular existent from the universal law in merely relating them together'.[158] Thus, where historians are limited to 'report[ing] the facts', the poet, like the philosopher, is capable of 'penetrat[ing] below them to their underlying substance and moving force'.[159] In relation to the *Bildungsroman*, this implies that the 'prosaic facticity of the given social world' is 'redeemed' through its relation to the inner potentiality of the hero which transcends any simple translation of virtuality into actuality.[160] In fact, the *Bildungsroman*, which is 'essentially an epic of inwardness', 'celebrates the imagi-nation of the hero as the faculty which allows him to transcend the limitations of everyday practicality'.[161] At its best, then, the *Bildungsroman* ultimately embodies a healthy 'skepticism about the law of linear experience': 'The *Bildungsroman* is able to offer a critique of those cherished human presuppositions explored by Kermode in *The Sense of an Ending*. It allows the novel to concern itself with a definition of experience which precludes any simple sense of finality, of "over and done with".'[162] The outcome is the ironic predicament described above, of novels which 'inhabit the awkward middle ground'—the essayist's no-man's-land—'between wholeness and constriction, between possibility (creative transcendence) and actuality'.[163]

---

[155] Hegel, *Phenomenology*, Preface, 23 [*Phänomonologie des Geistes*, 35], and *Aesthetics*, ii. 993 ('In historiography the prosaic element lay especially in the fact that . . . its actual form had to appear accompanied in many ways by relative circumstances, clustered with accidents, and sullied by arbitrari-ness').

[156] Hegel, *Aesthetics*, ii. 967.

[157] Ibid., 'The Poetic Work of Art as distinguished from a Prose Work of Art', ii. 972 and 973.

[158] Ibid. ii. 971 ('The sort of conception characteristic of the Understanding therefore gets no further than particular laws for phenomena; it persists in separating the particular existent from the universal law in merely relating them together').

[159] See Kaufmann's footnote, in Hegel, *Aesthetics*, 993: 'In Hegel's view, historians must report the facts, but the philosopher penetrates below them to their underlying substance and moving force—i.e. the accomplishment of the Will of God. In the sphere of art, the poet can do this too.' Cf. poetry as philosophy's ultimate authority in Montaigne (discussed in my Ch. 1): 'the original authorities [are] themselves poets; they treat philosophy in terms of poetic art: Plato is a disjointed poet', Montaigne, 'An Apology of Raymond Sebond', *Essays*, II. 12, p. 602.

[160] Swales, *The German Bildungsroman*, 23.   [161] Ibid. 29.   [162] Ibid. 30 and 33.

[163] Ibid. 157. See also Moretti, *The Way of the World*, 5, 6, 16, and 69.

In his preface Lukács claims to have written 'the first work belonging to the *Geisteswissenschaften* in which the findings of Hegelian philosophy are concretely applied to aesthetic problems'.[164] The dialectical method of analysis which he inherits from Hegel turns the *Bildungsroman—Wilhelm Meister—*into the third term of a so-called 'attempted synthesis' in a typology in which it 'steers a middle course between abstract idealism, which concentrates on pure action, and Romanticism, which interiorises action and reduces it to contemplation'.[165] This indicates that although Lukács selects the *Bildungsroman* precisely because of its anachronistic, paradoxical position, his predominantly Hegelian viewpoint finally champions the transcendence of the negative dialectic and emphasizes self-identity. Despite the tentativeness connoted by the word 'attempt', 'synthesis' remains the key-word for his evaluation of *Wilhelm Meister*. This may well be encouraged by the relationship between the two volumes of the novel itself. Generally, the first volume (*Wilhelm Meister's Years of Apprenticeship* [*Lehrjahre*]) is regarded as the text which remains closest to von Humboldt's conception of *Bildung*, and therefore to the Romantic ideal of self-expression. The second and final volume (*Wilhelm Meister's Travels* [*Wanderjahre*]), on the other hand, is 'less concerned with the development of individual personalities than with that of man in society',[166] and one knows how the Romantics—for all their praise of this novel—hate its ending.[167] Wilhelm Meister's evolution from one volume to the next seems to correspond to Lukács's growing belief in the individual's ability to 'find responses to the innermost demands of his soul in the structures of society'.[168] The very choice of a 'theory' rather than an 'essay' on the novel seems to testify to this conviction. Thus, and despite the obvious parallels between Lukács's 'Nature and Form of the Essay' and his *Theory of the Novel*, the latter ultimately veers away from—or transcends—the essayistic spirit. If in his essay on the essay, forms are viewed a-temporally and from the angle of a purely subjective idealism, and Lukács is 'resigned to the impossibility of human fulfilment and the burden of eternal *Sehnsucht*', in the *Theory of the Novel* the idealist hero's longing or nostalgia is a 'historically conditioned homelessness' which does not eliminate the possibility of the problematic hero's future fulfilment.[169] Lukács's later work on the novel is well-known definitively to move away from his early conception of the essay, since in it modernism's increasing awareness of the 'inner formlessness of existence' is

---

[164] See the preface to the *Theory of the Novel*, 15 [*Theorie des Romans*, 9] (Lukács also acknowledges his indebtedness to Goethe, Schiller, and Solger).

[165] Ibid. 135 [117]. The book includes readings of *Don Quixote* and French nineteenth-cent. novels by Balzac and Flaubert.

[166] See W. H. Bruford, *The German Tradition of Self-Cultivation: 'Bildung' from Humboldt to Thomas Mann* (1975), 57 and 98.

[167] See Schlegel, 'On Goethe's *Meister*' and 'Letter about the Novel'; and 'Goethe's *Wilhelm Meister* and the Early Romantic Theory of the Novel', 165–80, in Ernst Behler, *German Romantic Literary Theory*. Some theorists of the *Bildungsroman* like Franco Moretti establish a (relative) distinction between the classical *Bildungsroman* (as exemplified by *Wilhelm Meister*) and the modern.

[168] Lukács, *Theory of the Novel*, 133 [*Die Theorie des Romans*, 118].

[169] Corredor, 'The Problematic Elements of the Novel', 73 and 81. See my introduction to Lukács in Ch. 3.

perceived as wrongly encouraging its novels to lose faith in the possibility of an epic totality and gratuitously to indulge in fragmentation. By such standards, Broch, Musil, or Proust's novels, which theorists have categorized either as borderline *Bildungsromane* or as anti-*Bildungsromane*, no doubt go too far. The 'journey' which they represent is not one from a lesser to a greater adaptation of subject and world, but the progressive confirmation of an irreversible disintegration of all relationships. In Proust, the price to pay for maturity seems to be the definitive loss of the initial, symbiotic relation of the child to the world typical of the epic. In Broch, the increasing disintegration which reflects the journey from the unified world of the epic to the decomposed world of the novel is indissociable from the regression of his protagonists to a child-like state which, since one is dealing with adults, connotes alienation.[170] In both cases, the quest does not so much involve the felicitous or hindered unfolding of the characters' potentiality— of experience with its trials and errors—as the conditions and possibilities of individual personality and experience, which goes together with more than a 'healthy scepticism' regarding plot. In *The Man Without Qualities* in fact, the essayistic rendering of the hero's quest has from the outset all but replaced the plot. Musil's description of his novel as not only a 'spiritual adventure' (in keeping with Thomas Mann's definition of the *Bildungsroman* as the 'sublimation and rendering inward of the novel of adventures') but the '*Bildungsroman* of an idea', appears from the beginning to have given up the notion of a possible or impossible concretization or particularization of the idea, that is, of the 'translation' of idea into plot. Ulrich and the novel remain 'a reservoir of unrealized potentiality rather than a finite sum of knowable actualities'.[171] In this sense, the 'utopia of essayism' embodies a risk, inherent in the project of the *Bildungsroman*, of 'promising' the 'realization of human wholeness' at the 'unacceptable price of stasis, bloodlessness, death', the story being 'the guarantor that one is living'—as Musil himself is of course well aware.[172] At the same time, the essaying of narrative which results in it not beginning and/or in it beginning again and again, flagrant above all in Musil and Proust, foregrounds the typically essayistic interdependence of the 'excess' of ideas and the 'excess' of plot. One knows that in Proust's *Remembrance of Things Past*, the role of time as the return of 'the same as other' is the essential compon-ent of the perpectivism or relativism which makes possible the narrator's ever-changing perception of characters.[173] Rid of its telos, narrative effects the essayistic

---

[170] Broch sees in *Wilhelm Meister's Travels* the model of the polyhistorical novel: 'Und es ist jene Totalität des Daseins, die ihn zu ganz neuen Ausdrucksformen drängte, und die in den "Wanderjahren" den Grundstein der neuen Dichtung, des neuen Roman, legte' 'James Joyce und die Gegenwart', 87; and 'Wenn der Zerfall eine neue Romanform inauguriert (N.B. nicht einmal ganz neu, denn der "Wilhelm Meister" zeight ähnliche Ansätze!)', Broch, letter to Dr Brody, 23 Sept. 1931, *KW* 13/1: 154–5.

[171] Swales, *The German Bildungsroman*, 31.   [172] Ibid. 33.

[173] 'I had seen people present various aspects according to the idea that I or others possessed of them, a single individual being several different people for different observers (. . .) or even for the same observer at different periods over the years', Proust, *Remembrance of Things Past*, 'Time Regained', 950 [*À la recherche du temps perdu*, 278].

temporalization or mobilization of meaning at work in Montaigne and which is translated into an endless supersession of aspects—what Hegel regards as a 'bad infinite'. This, too, is inherent in the logic of the *Bildungsroman*, in which the centrality of 'process', the process of the hero's 'becoming' [*werden*] potentially exceeds 'the celebration of any goal which can thereby be attained'.[174] So, rather than acting as a mediator between the 'idea' and its narrative concretization, the essayism of our novels emphasizes and deepens the very rift, warned against by Hegel, between a 'wrong absence of history' and a 'wrong excess of history': with the former, the 'approach is so atemporal that it can offer no real point of insertion into the concrete world'; with the latter one 'staggers rudderless from relativity to relativity'.[175] One can therefore understand critics describing Broch, Musil, and Proust's novels both as anti-*Bildungsromane* and as extreme (in the sense of 'borderline') versions of the *Bildungsroman*. In many ways, these novels 'make clear that traditional *Bildung*-stories are no longer possible'.[176] And yet, since this awareness—which is more or less acute depending on the epistemological climate —is also endemic to the *Bildungsroman*, these novels can be said simply to remain 'on the borders of tradition'.[177]

In Bakhtin also, the *Bildungsroman*, which he sees as originating with Fielding and Sterne, and as represented Continentally by Goethe, Blanckenburg, Wieland, Wezel, Hippel, and Jean Paul,[178] plays a major part in the evolution of epic to novel. Rising as it does 'on the border between two epochs', the *Bildungsroman* reflects with particular clarity the emergence of a new ideological and artistic awareness of time as a 'process of becoming', 'where there is no first word (no ideal word), and the final word has not yet been spoken'.[179] It shows how 'time is

---

[174] Swales, *The German Bildungsroman*, 19.   [175] Desmond, *Art and the Absolute*, 58–9.

[176] Jürgen Jacobs and Markus Krause, *Der deutsche Bildungsroman: Gattungsgeschichte vom 18. bis zum 20. Jahrhundert* (1989), 207, and Swales, 'Musil's conclusions go far beyond those of the major Bildungsroman novelists in that he withdraws, both in philosophical and aesthetic terms, any allegiance to plot, to those specifics through which the self realizes itself in activity', *The German Bildungsroman*, 31.

[177] Cf. Swales, 'Nonetheless, the questions raised by [even Musil's] novel are also urgent intimations from the Bildungsroman tradition', *The German Bildungsroman*, 31; Longuet-Marx, *Proust, Musil: Partage d'écritures*, 8; and Schrader, in *Mimesis und Poiesis*, who compares Wieland's *Agathon* with Musil's *The Man Without Qualities* as two *Bildungsromane*. See also Jürgen Jacobs and Markus Krause, *Der deutsche Bildungsroman: Gattungsgeschichte vom 18. bis zum 20. Jahrhundert* (1989), 200; Köhn, *Entwicklungs-und Bildungsroman*, 77. On Proust and the *Bildungsroman*, see McCormick, *Fiction as Knowledge*, esp. 24 and 33, who stresses the centrality of the element of *Bildung* in Proust's novel, and Genette, in *Narrative Discourse*, who emphasizes the fact that although the 'Story of a vocation' is the avowed subject of the Proustian narrative (p. 226), 'the *Recherche* parts company with the *Bildungsroman* tradition and approaches certain forms of religious literature, like Saint-Augustine's *Confessions*: the narrator does not approach with a gradual and continuous movement, but quite to the contrary, despite the omens and notices that have here and there preceded it, rushes in on him at the very moment when in a certain way he feels himself more distant than ever from it' (p. 253); Blanchot, in *The Siren's Song*, 70–1, puts this divergence down to the treatment, above all, of time.

[178] Mikhail Bakhtin, 'Discourse in the Novel', in Michael Holquist (ed.), *The Dialogic Imagination: Four Essays by M. M. Bakhtin* (1990), 393.

[179] Bakhtin, 'The Bildungsroman and Its Significance in the History of Realism (Toward a Historical Typology of the Novel)', in Emerson and Holquist (eds.), *Bakhtin: Speech Genres and Other Late Essays*, 23 and 19; and 'Epic and Novel; in *The Dialogic Imagination*, 30.

introduced into man, enters into his very image, changing in a fundamental way the significance of all aspects of his destiny and life', so that the 'testing' is not that of a 'ready-made', preformed or predetermined, 'unchanging' hero characterized by 'permanence' and 'self-identity', but of a 'dynamic unity'.[180] Man 'cease[s] to coincide with himself, and consequently men ceas[e] to be exhausted entirely by the plots that contain them';[181] so neither man's identity nor history (the story) are seen as simply unfolding or revealing what was somehow present all along. Rather, this unfolding is a process of genuine growth: context is no mere background; it shapes the events themselves.[182] For Bakhtin, then, the *Bildungsroman* is the paradigmatic expression of a world which has 'lost [its] absolute, God-given, eternal structure' and is now determined by the 'historical multi-temporality' characteristic of 'the contradictions of contemporary life'.[183] However, Bakhtin—unlike Hegel and Lukács—looks upon this change as irreversible. His conception of history does not take the form of a constant 'upward-moving surge of progressive consciousness that we find in Hegel and Lukács'; rather the course of history is conceived more along early German Romantic lines, as having 'no necessary telos built into it':[184] 'instead of a teleology whose course is a movement from one unitary state to another, Bakhtin's historical masterplot opens with a deluded perception of unity and goes on to a growing knowledge of ever-increasing difference and variety that cannot be overcome in any uniting synthesis.'[185] Thus, the *Bildungsroman* is an important step in the development of the 'polyphonic' (or 'heteroglot') novel, a genre instituted by Dostoyevsky and characterized by its confrontation of a multiplicity of 'voices', none of which is subjected to a final, authorial control. As such, the *Bildungsroman* partakes of the 'dialogic' rather than the 'monologic', the latter being for Bakhtin an impulse 'typical of societies in which diversity and change either go unrecognized or are actively suppressed'.[186] In fact, as well as the 'growing knowledge of ever-increasing difference and variety', history involves a '*constant* struggle' between the two 'impulses' of the monologic (associated with the epic) and the dialogic (associated with the novel), the epic not being 'a genre confined to a moment in the distant past' but an 'always-still-available possibility'.[187] It follows that focusing on the polyphonic novel will mean focusing on periods when dialogism is uppermost: periods of intense criticism when dominant ideologies

---

[180] Bakhtin, 'The *Bildungsroman* and Its Significance', 20–1.
[181] Bakhtin, 'Epic and Novel', 35.
[182] See Gary Saul Morson and Caryl Emerson, *Mikhail Bakhtin: Creation of a Prosaics* (1990), 405.
[183] Bakhtin, 'The *Bildungsroman* and Its Significance', 26. Cf. 'The time of epic is not chronological. . . . It is impossible to change, to rethink, or to reevaluate anything in epic time, for it is finished, conclusive, and immutable. It exists in a world without relativity or any gradual, purely temporal progression that might connect it with the present where people constantly rethink, change and reevaluate', Clark and Holquist, *Mikhail Bakhtin*, 287–8.
[184] Holquist, *Dialogism: Bakhtin and his World*, 75.
[185] Ibid. 76. See also Peter V. Zima, 'Bakhtin's Young Hegelian Aesthetics', in *The Bakhtin Circle Today, Critical Studies*, 1/2 (1989), ed. Myriam Diaz-Diocaretz.
[186] Holquist, *Dialogism: Bakhtin and his World*, 77.   [187] Ibid.

come under scrutiny, that is, key periods of essayism such as the Renaissance and the (second half of the) eighteenth century.

The (Montaignian) essay naturally lends itself to a dialogic approach. Hence in the course of this work I have already introduced a number of features pertaining to Bakhtinian dialogism, in the vague, approximative way in which literary theorists have appropriated this term. What rightly comes out of everyone's use of the word, though, is that dialogism 'can never be exhausted in pragmatically motivated dialogues of characters', even though the dialogue—in particular Plato's—determines the concept.[188] Dialogism is a principle which Michael Holquist neatly encapsulates as stipulating that 'nothing can be perceived except against the perspective of something else'.[189] Hegelian dialectic, in the 'negative' sense, is an obvious expression of the dialogic mechanism. It highlights the interdependence stressed above of time and plurality, for in time—as in Hegel's system—'everything is itself and also other'. In William Desmond's account in Chapter 1, the recognition of time as a process immediately situated us in a world where the 'nature of Being [was] posited as Becoming'.[190] Identity in Hegel was defined by 'an inherent process of differentiation'; and temporal deferment, which enables the Idea to be 'tried out' or 'essayed', was 'the essential factor of this sameness as otherness'. For Bakhtin, all is dialogic—and for a start, language and self. 'Language', Bakhtin writes, 'is not a neutral medium that passes freely and easily into the private property of the speaker's intentions; it is populated—overpopulated—with the intention of others'.[191] Every word, text, or literary structure is 'half someone else's';[192] it is generated in relation to other words, texts, or structures. As Kristeva's much quoted reformulation of Bakhtin goes: 'Each word (text) is an intersection of words (texts) where at least one other word (text) can be read. . . . Any text is constructed as a mosaic of quotations; any text is the absorption and transformation of another.'[193] We have seen that Montaigne's *Essais* overtly confront the word of an individual—a personal opinion—with the authoritative voice of tradition. And this confrontation, which records the transition from a closed, hierarchical conception of literary history or intertextuality to an open conception of intertextuality, necessarily results in the relativization of both so-called 'objective' and subjective discourse. The *Essais* are indeed 'constructed as a mosaic of quotations' where source-texts, which are put into 'dialogue' with one another, are juxtaposed in a way that 'confirms, complicates, contradicts' their respective substance and style,[194] thus constantly shifting and relativizing any one authority—including that of the essayist himself. The typically early Romantic rejection of

---

[188] Bakhtin, 'Discourse in the Novel', 364.

[189] Holquist, *Dialogism: Bakhtin and his World*, 21–2.

[190] Desmond, *Art and the Absolute*, 91.   [191] Bakhtin, 'Discourse in the Novel', 294.

[192] 'Language, for the individual consciousness, lies on the borderline between oneself and the other. The word in language is half someone else's', Bakhtin, 'Discourse in the Novel', 293.

[193] Julia Kristeva, 'Word, Dialogue and Novel', in Toril Moi (ed.), *The Kristeva Reader* (1986), 37.

[194] Recchio, 'A Dialogic Approach to the Essay', 282.

notions of stylistic and generic purity, of unity or originality, in favour of mixtures, of aggregates, of shared (and often unidentified) authorship and even plagiarism, which expresses the belief that 'all literature, indeed all language and experience, is fragmentary and incomplete in part because of limited perspective and point of view involved in all gestures',[195] also recognizably participates in the dialogic élan. In Bakhtin, the essayistic or 'dialogic' element of the polyphonic novel is characterized by a constant confrontation with and 'mobilization' of other works, genres and 'belief systems' in its own structure, which is the typical way in which it keeps relativizing and criticizing its own and other discourses in their claim 'faithfully [to] reflect' or 'transpose' reality. The polyphonic novel 'is skeptical of all languages that assume they are the only voice of truth'.[196] This scepticism, central to the Platonic dialogue, typically takes the form of a parody of canonized genres and styles or, as in Rabelais, of a 'parodic attitude toward almost all forms of ideological discourse—philosophical, moral, scholarly, rhetorical, poetic and in particular the pathos-charged forms of discourse', to the point where 'it [becomes] a parody of the very act of conceptualizing anything in language'.[197] Hence the polyphonic novel's inclusion of and 'special relationship with extraliterary genres', with 'ideological genres' such as the 'rhetorical genres of letters, diaries, confessions', etc. (which are also the novel's many constituents or precursor forms), and with the 'genres of everyday life'.[198] The centrality of speech and of the vernacular examined in the context of the *Essais* is fundamental to the polyphonic novel's attack on 'refined', monologizing languages. By being put into dialogue in a way that guarantees the fullest range of 'voices', the various levels of discourses evolve in 'non-exclusive opposition', oxymoronically, in order to stress—as in the *Essais*— that each element is grasped in its diversity or in its 'difference', that everything (language, plot, character) is simultaneously one thing and another.[199] And this inevitably includes the 'level' identified with the authorial point of view: the novelist 'turns up on the field of representation' as yet another element of the dialogue, and for Bakhtin 'this new positioning of the author must be considered one of the most important results of surmounting epic (hierarchical) distance'.[200] The fact that the self is dialogic, a 'relation', implies that the writer of the polyphonic novel, like that of the essay, is his own 'interlocutor'. It suggests that he is the constant reader of his own discourse as though of another, 're-reading himself as [he] rewrites himself', eternally 're-thinking', 're-evaluating' and thus distancing himself not only from the ready-made truths of past discourse in general, but from his own past writings:[201]

---

[195] Bakhtin, 'Discourse in the Novel', 365.   [196] Clark and Holquist, *Mikhail Bakhtin*, 292.
[197] Bakhtin, 'Discourse in the Novel', 309.   [198] Bakhtin, 'Epic and Novel', 33.
[199] For a recapitulation of this logic of the 'double' in the Bakhtinian perpective, see also Julia Kristeva, 'Word, Dialogue and Novel', and 'From Symbol to Sign', in Moi (ed.), *The Kristeva Reader*. See also Zima, *L'Ambivalence romanesque: Proust, Kafka, Musil*, and *Textsoziologie*.
[200] Bakhtin, 'Epic and Novel', 27 and 28.
[201] Kristeva, 'World, Dialogue, and Novel', 56; and Bakhtin, 'Epic and Novel', 31.

In the monologic work, only the author, as 'the ultimate semantic authority', retains the power to express a truth directly. The truth of the work is his or her truth, and all other truths are merely 'represented'. . . . By this, Bakhtin means that in a monologic work each character's truth must be measured against the author's own ideology, because authorial ideology dominates the work and creates its unity. . . . However complex, ambiguous, or fraught with contradictions and doubt the author's truth may be, it never treats the truths of other consciousnesses as equals. . . . By contrast, in a polyphonic work, the form-shaping ideology itself *demands* that the author cease to exercise monologic control. . . . Polyphony demands a work in which several consciousnesses meet as equals and engage in a dialogue that is in principle unfinalizable.[202]

So in the polyphonic novel, the author occupies the same status as the characters he has created; his truths lie on the same plane as theirs: all is uttered with quotation-marks. The endlessness of the dialogue turns the polyphonic novel into a genre which, under the essayistic influence and like the essay, 'has no canon of its own', no generic identity; a genre 'that continues to develop, that is as yet uncompleted'.[203]

5.3. ESSAY(ISTIC) OR NOVEL(ISTIC)?

Theories of the novel concerned with the *Bildungsroman* or the polyphonic novel reinforce what the brief survey of particular examples of essayistic novels already reveal, which is that essayism confers to the novel characteristics that are inherent in the (Montaignian) essay: under the essayistic influence, the novel becomes fragmentary, heterogeneous ('multi-voiced, multistyled, and often multi-languaged'[204]), open-ended, and intensely self-reflexive. At the same time, the essayistic novel not only reproduces, but contributes to and enhances the essayistic spirit. As mentioned at the beginning of this chapter, our essayists tend to perceive the idea of working their philosophy into fiction as a concession to the reader or as a compromise. Nevertheless, this integration also corresponds to the type of 'philosophy' the essayist has to offer, a philosophy which is aware that it 'presents us "not with what really is, nor even with what she believes to be true, but with the best probabilities and elegancy she has wrought"';[205] or, more pessimistically, a philosophy which is aware that today, philosophizing is no longer possible, or only possible as 'poetry'. In this sense, not only is the novel neither antagonistic nor external to the essay: I pointed out in Chapter 1 that some theorists go so far as to

---

[202] Morson and Emerson, 'Polyphony and the New Position of the Author', in *Mikhail Bakhtin: Creation of a Prosaics*, 238–9. See also Clark and Holquist on authorship and point of view, *Mikhail Bakhtin*, 245.

[203] Bakhtin, 'Epic and Novel', 3.

[204] Bakhtin, 'From the Prehistory of Novelistic Discourse', In *The Dialogic Imagination*, 265.

[205] Montaigne, 'An Apology of Raymond Sebond', *Essays*, II. 12, p. 603 ['comme aussi au reste la philosophie nous presente non pas ce qui est, ou ce qu'elle croit, mais ce qu'elle forge ayant plus d'apparence et de gentillesse', 'Apologie de Raimond Sebond', *Essais* II. xii, p. 518a].

consider essayism—the 'modal' exploitation of the essay in the novel—as the very essence of the essay. This amounts to defending that 'ultimately the essayistic and the concrete (closed) form of the essay mutually exclude each other', and that the essay is not just an extrapolation but a distortion or perversion of the essayistic.[206] Dieter Bachmann, who is the main defendant of this proposition in keeping with Musil's own view that 'the "pure essay" is an abstraction for which there are hardly any examples', regards Musil and Broch's separate essays as monologic if not dogmatic; in his opinion, they are closer to the tractate, not playful, and therefore alien to the essayistic spirit.[207] Since neither writer 'really cultivates the *form* of the essay', still according to Bachmann, their novels provide the only possibility for the essay to safeguard the experimental and 'dialogic' dimension usually assumed by the genre's aesthetic treatment of its object.[208] Therefore, it is not simply ironic that despite Broch's philosophical ambitions, his theories should only have gained recognition in the context of their indirect novelistic expression —or rather, this irony is not alien to the essayist's ambitions. The complete abstraction between essay and fiction within the novel which, for Bachmann also, is a prerequisite for the novel to be called 'essayistic', can be said to stage the 'dialogization' of the falsely independent essay in a way that reproduces the tension between (aesthetic) form and (conceptual) content within the essay. Only here, narrative operates on a much bigger scale, and fiction is self-declared. We know that in the *Essais*, narrative appears first of all in the form of *exempla* (the short narratives drawn from the stock of ancient rhetoric), which increasingly give way to the 'stories' drawn from Montaigne's own experience, and to the creation of hypothetical characters in hypothetical contexts designed to substantiate the essayist's speculations on the physical and spiritual charateristics of man in general. The role of concrete illustration played by these examples is itself encompassed by Montaigne's more general inclination to narrate rather than to teach [*Je n'enseigne point, je raconte*[209]], whereby the essayist's process of thinking is revealed step by step, unconstrained by any foregone conclusion. So narrative in the novel becomes the fundamental agent of the pragmatic 'trying out' or translation of ideas and arguments; it effects the necessary temporalization or mobilization which allows the essayist to 'portray the living conditions in which thought is tangled',[210] that is, rather than to analyse it abstractly, to 're-create' and 'breathe life into it'.[211] In this sense, the philosophy of the novel may well be 'superior' to the philosophy of the

---

[206] See Haas, in *Studien zur Form des Essays*, 39–40; Berger, *Der Essay: Form und Geschichte*, 189; Michael Hamburger asserts that 'the essay is a style rather than a form' in 'Essay über den Essay', 291; and above all, Bachmann, *Essay und Essayismus*, 195.

[207] ' "Der reine Essay" ist eine Abstraktion, für die es beinahe keine Beispiele gibt', Musil *TAER*, 147]; and Bachmann, *Essay und Essayismus*, 154, 158, and 195. Cf. the title of his conclusion, 'Essayismus und die Zerstörung der Form' ('Essayism and the destruction of form').

[208] Ibid. 139–40, and 158, and 193–6.

[209] Montaigne, 'On Repenting', *Essay*, III. 2, p. 909 ['Du repentir', *Essais*, III. ii, p. 784*b*].

[210] Harrison, *Essayism: Conrad, Musil, Pirandello*, 4.

[211] Cf. Proust: 'Cette évolution d'une pensée, je n'ai pas voulu l'analyser abstraitement, mais la recréer, la faire vivre.'

essay, more 'sophisticated' and more 'advanced'; for in 'submitting his ideas to novelistic analysis' the essayist ensures that rather than 'reducing' the 'scene of action' to 'the mind of a thinking subject', he approaches every event from as many angles as there are characters.[212] In Chapter 1, I explored the ways in which this 'trying out' of ideas can be said to come close to the 'as if' of fiction: truth, for the essayist, must be sought in the imaginative re-creation of his object—whatever the latter may be; it depends not on the accuracy of description but on what Lukács called the 'intensity of vision'.[213] We know that the line between the aesthetic or literary treatment of the subject-matter—which already transforms the essayist into the quasi-narrator of quasi-fictional compositions—and the fully fictional narrators and texts, say, of English periodicals of the eighteenth and nineteenth century, is a fine one. And crossing that line—also discussed in Chapter 1— testifies as much to the awareness of reality's 'unreality' as to the perception of reality's potential. What I can now confirm, is that with its questioning of character and plot-making, the essayistic novel doubly underlines the self-declared fictional dimension of its text in a way that makes its use of narrative fiction not only the accomplice but the expression of the essay's essence.

And yet this proposition could just as easily be reversed, and essayism made to express the novel's own essence—all the more easily so as these texts are too long, in the end, to be seriously considered as even 'vast' essays,[214] and especially since they announce themselves as 'novels'. From this point of view, the so-called essayistic novel is not a type or sub-category of the novel, but a typical example of 'the' novel, as Lukács and Bakhtin's theories of 'the' novel imply. German theorists have time and again identified the essayistic novel with a novel 'in crisis', a crisis which they see as particularly acute in the twentieth century.[215] Conversely, they perceive our 'critical' age as a typically 'essayistic age', and this is made pejoratively to record the fact that the essay is 'thriving on the crisis of the generic triad', that its 'infiltration' and 'usurpation' is everywhere to be found, and above all in the novel. For them, 'the striking increase of reflection and theory in the modern novel', or the growing 'intellectualization of the novel', goes together with 'the appearance, in the twentieth century, of the essayistic as a new species'.[216] Rather than simply producing a 'type' of novel, this usurpation of the essayistic prompts nothing less than a 'degeneration', or a 'pathology' of the novel which results in the proliferation of so-called 'anti-novels'.[217] At the very least, the essayistic novel with its 'invasion of the story by the commentary, of the novel by the essay,

---

[212] Descombes, *Proust: Philosophie du roman*, 19, and his Introduction as a whole.

[213] Lukács, *Soul and Form*, 11.

[214] See ' "Der Mann ohne Eigenschaften" ein Essay?', in Bachmann, *Essay und Essayismus*, 190–2.

[215] See Haas, 'Essay und Roman', in *Essay*, 74; Berger, *Der Essay: Form und Geschichte*, 128; Rohner, 'Essay und Roman', in *Der deutsche Essay*, 566–7; the whole of 'Essay und Roman' by Adolf Frisé; Jacobs and Krause, 'Die Krise des Romans', in *Der deutsche Bildungsroman*, 198–201; 'Essayism', 170, in Boa and Reid, *Critical Strategies*; Zima, *L'Ambivalence romanesque*, and 'Die Krise des Romans', in *Textsoziologie*; Schramke, 'Der Erkenntnisanspruch des modernen Romans: Reflexion und Essayismus', *Die Theorie des modernen Romans*.

[216] Boa and Reid, 'Essayism', 175.

[217] See Haas, *Essay*, 74, and Rohner, *Der deutsche Essay*, 567.

of the narrative by its own discourse', is considered responsible for 'the strongest shock given . . . to the traditional equilibrium of novelistic form'—Genette writes of Proust's *Remembrance of Things Past* which, as we recall, he also describes as being 'not completely a novel any more' but 'the work which, at its level, concludes the history of the genre (of the genres) and, along with some others, inaugurates the limitless and indefinite space of modern *literature*'.[218] However, histories of the novel—including Ian Watt's *The Rise of the Novel* discussed in Chapter 1—show how easily this argument can be countered; how the essayistic novel—which after all one only calls 'essayistic' in theory—is the prototype of the modern novel, or rather, since these are redundant terms, simply of the novel itself as the expression of 'modernity'. All novels are to some extent anti-novels. If essayism connotes self-reflection and open-endedness, then the novel is without a doubt the most essayistic of genres: the most heterogeneous—with a capacity to combine the narrative, the lyric, and the dramatic, and to include entire essays—the most open-ended, the most reflexive or self-critical.[219] The novel, not a certain 'type' of novel, is 'ever sceptical' and 'experimental'. It is the genre 'least secure (or most self-conscious) about its own status as a genre', the genre 'most at pains to establish its generic identity', the genre which 'has no canon of its own', 'the sole genre that continues to develop, that is as yet uncompleted'—a 'homeless', 'rootless', 'wandering' genre, an 'epistemological outlaw'.[220] In other words, the focus on key periods and a certain number of privileged authors corresponds to the modernist revival of possibilities which Cervantes (*Don Quixote*) 'does not merely anticipate', but 'fully realizes'.[221] Rather than a degeneration, the essayistic novel becomes the purest expression of what was always implicitly present in the novel.

[218] Genette, *Narrative Discourse*, 259.

[219] Self-criticism is 'one of the primary distinguishing features of the novel as a genre', Bakhtin, 'Discourse in the Novel', 412; and 'This ability of the novel to criticize itself is a remarkable feature of this ever-developing genre', Bakhtin, 'Epic and Novel', 6. See also Robert Alter, *Partial Magic: The Novel as a Self-Conscious Genre* (1975), 12–13, and 158; 'Commentary in Literary Texts', in Ross Chambers, *Meaning and Meaningfulness: Studies in the Interpretation of Texts* (1979); Geoffrey Bennington, *Sententiousness and the Novel: Laying Down the Law in Eighteenth-Century French Fiction* (1985); David Richter, *Fable's End: Completeness and Closure in Rhetorical Fiction* (1974); and Susan R. Suleiman, 'Le Récit exemplaire: Parabole, fable, roman à thèse', *Poétique*, 32 (1977), 468–89.

[220] Holquist, *Dialogism: Bakhtin and his World*, 72; Morson and Emerson, *Mikhail Bakhtin: Creation of a Prosaics*, 352; and Clark and Holquist, *Mikhail Bakhtin*, 276.

[221] Alter, *Partial Magic*, 29; cf. 'In [*Don Quixote*], the novelistic genre becomes what it really is, it unfolds in its fullest potential' (Bakhtin, 'Discourse in the Novel', 409); and Swales, 'the work which inaugurates the modern novel in all its resonance is Goethe's *Meister*' (*The German Bildungsroman*, 13), and 'It is important to stress that the discursiveness, the intellectual debate which is so much a feature of the *Bildungsroman* has by now become acceptable, even commonplace within the novel form. Many twentieth-cent. novels operate with a kind of 'essayism' which allows us to see the *Bildungsroman* not as a German aberration but as a tradition which anticipates modern developements' (p. 157); and 'the self-reflective discursiveness . . . has long been a feature of the novel tradition as a whole' (p. 148). Franco Moretti describes the Bildungsroman as 'the form which will dominate, or more precisely, make possible the Golden Century of Western narrative' (*The Way of the World*, 3), or simply as the 'dominant genre of Western narrative' (p. 10). See also Marthe Robert, *Roman des origines, et origines du roman* (1972); Ralph-Rainer Wüthenow, *Im Buch die Bücher oder Der Held als Leser* (1986); Hans Blumenberg, *Die Lesbarkeit der Welt* (1983); and Gabriel Josipovici, *The World and the Book: A Study of Modern Fiction* (1979).

Beyond the novel, the essayistic arguably encompasses the characteristics of narrative fiction generally, as illustrated by Genette's approach to the paratext in Chapter 3, and by Barthes's reading of the short story *Sarrasine* in the previous chapter. The essayistic covers the ways in which narrative draws attention to the essential role of its 'frontiers'—whether in the form of specific paratexts, or in the more elusive form of what I have called 'paratextuality'. Above all, the essayistic embodies the transgression of narrative fiction by what Genette, prior to his specific concern with the paratext, sees as the 'most important and most significant' narrative frontier, that of 'discourse'.[222] Genette's distinction between narrative and discourse is modelled on a more or less similar distinction in Benveniste who, we will recall, shows that

certain grammatical forms, like the pronoun 'I' (and its implicit reference 'you'), the pronominal (certain demonstratives), or adverbial indicators (like 'here', 'now', 'yesterday', 'today', 'tomorrow' etc.) and (at least in French) certain tenses of the verb, like the present, the present anterior, or the future, are confined to discourse, whereas narrative in its strict form is marked by the exclusive use of the third person and such forms as the aorist (past definite) and the pluperfect.[223]

The relationship between the two is first introduced by Genette as a straightforward opposition 'between the objectivity of narrative and the subjectivity of discourse'.[224] The exteriority of 'discourse' in relation to narrative appears as the 'asymmetrical contamination' of narrative and 'discourse' by one another:

It is obvious that narrative does not integrate these discursive enclaves (rightly called by Georges Blin 'authorial intrusions'), as easily as discourse receives the narrative 'enclaves': narrative inserted into discourse is transformed into an element of discourse, discourse inserted into narrative remains discourse and forms a sort of cyst that is easy to recognize and to locate. The purity of narrative, one might say, is more manifest than that of discourse.[225]

'Discourse' thus seems an unwelcome interpolation in narrative, a disruption of context. This is all the more perceptible in the case of essayistic fictions, where the structure is characterized by a set of detached fragments which not only induce a visible recontextualization or 'internal rewriting', but abstract themselves from the narrative sequence to the extent that they can be read independently of it.[226] In the case of 'epitextual' (letters, diaries) and 'peritextual' (prefaces, footnotes) excursions (as with the novels of Jean Paul or Sterne), one is dealing not just with 'easily locatable cysts', but with autonomous classes of discursive texts or genres which, despite their citational relation to the narrative, function according to a logic of their own. In so far as essayistic digressions take the asymmetrical or anachronistic

---

[222] Genette, 'Frontiers of Narrative', in *Figures of Literary Discourse*, 137.

[223] Ibid. 138.   [224] Ibid. 138.   [225] Ibid. 141.

[226] Cf. Bachmann, *Essay und Essayismus*, 180: 'Essayistisch wird ein Roman erst, wenn ganze Partien nur noch abstrakte, allgemeine Reflexion enthalten, den Gang der Erzählung verlassen, aus dem Kontext herausfallen.'

function of 'discourse' to its limits, that is to say beyond its role as a 'negative frontier', it may be justified, therefore, to consider it as a dimension properly external to narrative fiction.[227] On the other hand, Genette also draws attention, via Benveniste, to the fact that 'such objectivity and subjectivity are defined by criteria of a strictly linguistic order:

'subjective' discourse is that in which, explicitly or not, the presence of (or reference to) 'I' is marked, but this is not defined in any other way except as the person who is speaking this discourse; just as the present, which is the tense *par excellence* of the discursive mode, is not defined other than as the moment when the discourse is being spoken, its use marking 'the coincidence of the event described with the instance of discourse that describes it'.[228]

In our novels, the extreme abstraction between narrative and discursive planes just tends to make the interdependence between them the more evident. 'Discourse' may act as a means of controlling the meaning(s) of the text from an 'outside', but the meaningfulness which it seeks to establish is itself only a part of the text it pretends to control—indeed not only a part, in the case of my examples, but the greatest portion of the text. In reality, these 'essences of narrative and discourse', as Genette also points out, 'are almost never found in their pure state in any text: there is almost always a certain amount of narrative in discourse, a certain amount of discourse in narrative'.[229] Narrative cannot break away from the order of 'discourse', from the act of enunciation and interpretation which underlies it implicitly if not explicitly. The absence of narrator, the impression one gets that 'no one speaks here', that 'the events seem to narrate themselves', only corresponds to the 'rigorous expunging of any reference to the instance of discourse that constitutes it'.[230] So the essayistic stages what is at work in all narrative fiction, demystifying the 'idea or feeling that narrative *tells itself*, that nothing is more natural than to tell a story or to put together a set of actions in a myth, a tale, an epic, or a novel'.[231] As a manifestation of the 'evolution of literary consciousness', one could say that the essayistic 'draws our attention to the singular, artificial, and problematic aspect of the narrative act' and compels us to 'recognize the negative limits of narrative, to consider the principal sets of oppositions through which narrative is defined, and constitutes itself over and against the various forms of the non-narrative'.[232] Ultimately—and 'for better or for worse'—the essayistic rehearses the modern tendency of discourse to absorb narrative, 'as if it had exhausted or overflowed the resources of its representative mode, and wanted to fold back into the indefinite murmur of its own discourse'.[233] As with the novel, then, the essayistic can be said

---

[227] 'Anachrony' is the term which Genette uses to characterize the 'different forms of discrepancy between the order of narrative and the order of discourse'. See the whole section on 'Order', in his *Narrative Discourse*.

[228] Genette, 'Frontiers of Narrative', 138–9; see Benveniste, *Problèmes de linguistique générale*, i. 262 and 254.

[229] Genette, 'Frontiers of Narrative', 140.   [230] Ibid. 139.

[231] Ibid. 127.   [232] Ibid. 127 and 128.   [233] Ibid. 143.

to be the mark of modern narrative fiction, but only in so far as 'modern' narrative fiction externalizes the qualities inherent in all narrative fiction. Following the ambivalent logic—examined in Chapter 3—of Genette's discourse on narrative frames which oscillates between a historical interpretation and an a priori interpretation, the essayistic foregrounds the self-consciousness of narrative fiction to the extent that it is both specific to 'modern' narrative fiction and inherent in narrative fiction generally.[234]

Whether as novels, novellas, or short stories, the dominant of 'modern' fiction is epistemological; it deploys strategies which engage questions as to how the world can be interpreted, by whom, and with what degree of certainty—hence the foregrounding of the process and subject of writing and the corresponding shift of emphasis from 'showing' to 'telling', from 'utterance' [*énoncé*] to 'enunciation' [*énonciation*] (Benveniste). It challenges the very basis of knowledge, 'suspending judgement' and flaunting the fact that objective orders are only human constructs, not natural, given entities; that reality and truth are only accessible through the highly unreliable medium of language. This epistemological uncertainty and the subsequent emphasis, in modern fiction, on the relativity of all interpretation, is formally dramatized by the questioning of totalizing systems, which promotes the marginal and the 'ex-centric' under the various labels of discontinuity, dislocation, heterogeneity, decentring, and provisionality explored in relation to the essay(istic). The self-essaying of narrative (in the form of self-gloss, internal rewritings or *mises en abyme*) draws attention to the strategies which make narrative meaningful or which on the contrary question its meaningfulness—to the poetics of fiction. Essayistic digressions are an essential part of narrative economy: they are the essence of narrative transformation and 'desire'—the 'digressive' or 'dilatory' space

---

[234] Accordingly, 'pinpointing and measuring these narrative *anachronies* . . . implicitly assumes the existence of a kind of zero degree that would be a condition of perfect temporal correspondence between narrative and story. This point of reference is more hypothetical than real. . . . We will thus not be so foolish as to claim that anachrony is either a rarity or a modern invention. On the contrary, it is one of the traditional resources of literary narrative' (Genette, *Narrative Discourse*, 35–6). Apart from studies listed in Ch. 3 in the context of frames, indispensable works on narrative include: Peter Brooks, *Reading for the Plot: Design and Intention in Narrative* (1984); Paul Ricoeur, *Temps et récit*, i, ii (*La Configuration du temps dans le récit de fiction*), and iii (*Le Temps raconté*); Claude Brémond, *Logique du récit* (1973); Tzvetan Todorov, *Poétique de la prose, suivi de Nouvelles recherches sur le récit* (1971); *Poétique du récit*, ed. R. Barthes, W. Kayser, W. C. Booth, and Ph. Hamon; A. J. Greimas and J. Courtès, 'The Cognitive Dimension of Narrative Discourse' *New Literary History*, 7 (1976), 433–47; Shlomith Rimmon-Kenan, *Narrative Fiction: Contemporary Poetics* (1983); Seymour Chatman, *Story and Discourse: Narrative Structure in Fiction and Film* (1978); Mieke Bal, *Narratologie: Essais sur la signification narrative dans quatre romans modernes* (1977); W. J. T. Mitchell (ed.), *On Narrative* (1981); Robert Scholes and Robert Kellogg, *The Nature of Narrative* (1966); J Hillis Miller, *Fiction and Repetition* (1982); Ross Chambers, *Story and Situation: Narrative Seduction and the Power of Fiction* (1984); Christopher Prendergast, *The Order of Mimesis: Balzac, Stendhal, Nerval, Flaubert* (1986); Frank Kermode, *The Genesis of Secrecy: On the Interpretation of Narrative* (1979); Jeremy Hawthorn (ed.), *Narrative: From Malory to Motion Pictures* (1985); the volume entitled *Narrative Analysis and Interpretation* (1982); Ann Jefferson, *The Nouveau Roman and the Poetics of Fiction* (1980); Elizabeth Dipple, *The Unresolvable Plot: Reading Contemporary Fiction* (1988); Wladimir Krysinski, *Carrefours des signes: Essais sur le roman moderne* (1981); Brian McHale, *Postmodernist Fiction* (1987); Linda Hutcheon, *A Poetics of Postmodernism: History, Theory, Fiction* (1988).

of 'postponement', 'deviance', and 'error'; of 'wandering' and 'misinterpretation'.[235] The favouring of process over product and the questioning of narrative causality and hierarchy turn essayism into the rhetorical 'suspension' or 'suspense' of narrative, as corroborated by Barthes's description of the 'classical' text in *S/Z*.[236] Hence the correlation between the essayistic and the organization of so many fictions as 'quests' if not straightforwardly as detective stories or novels, the detective story being considered as the epistemological genre *par excellence* and the paradigm of all narrative,[237] with its implications of withheld or obliquely presented information, problems of accessibility and reliability—all encapsulated by the now commonplace metaphors of the 'labyrinth' or the 'maze'. The foregrounding of narrative 'desire' and 'suspense' also goes hand in hand with the utopian sense of the 'possible' initially associated with essayism. The possibility of saying 'otherwise', thanks to a rhetoric of rupture—of juxtapositions and interpolations—lays the foundations for the creation of narratives and 'worlds under erasure'.[238] The strategies of embedding, circularity, and infinite regress which flout narrative causality and hierarchy are ways in which narrative displays the conditions of its meaning or mechanism, as Borges himself confirms when appropriating these strategies for the conception of a classical Chinese novel in which all the possible bifurcations of a system or story are simultaneously actualized. Indeed, in 'The Garden of Forking Paths', the increasingly limited choice implied by narrative actualization is confronted with the infinity of potential choices faced by the narrative agent—each of which is equally valid.[239] Perhaps more clearly than any other example, Borges's analysis of narrative into a system of branchings (which curiously resembles the procedures of French structuralists) partakes of what is *essentially* involved in all plot and fiction-making, thus rendering the very notion of the 'essayistic'—the garden of forking paths of all fictions—wholly superfluous.

Considering the essayistic novel as a novel rather than as an essay seems to have confirmed what I put forward in Chapter 1, namely that everything about the overlap between essay and novel points to the 'outmodedness' of the former. The essayistic not only reveals the essence of the novel; it reveals the essence of all literature or 'writing', as foregrounded by (self-conscious) philosophical or literary texts. But the prevailing connection (especially in German theories) between essayism

---

[235] Peter Brooks, *Reading for the Plot*, 96 and 139. Cf. Fernand Ouellette on 'errancy', 'desire', and the essay: 'Mon essayiste est un être qui accepte fondamentalement l'*errance*', and 'L'essai apparaît comme l'une des formes privilégiées du désir et de l'inespéré. Il est mû davantage par "l'imagination du désir", par le possible, que par la volonté d'élaborer une synthèse, par le saisissement de ce qui est' ('L'Essai', *Études Littéraires*, 5 (1972), 12 and 9). Cf. also Paul Ricoeur: 'Le facteur d'écart, de retardement, lequel temporalise proprement l'épreuve, est *essentiel* au récit' (*La Narrativité*, 39).

[236] For the rhetorical figure of 'suspension', see Pierre Fontanier, *Les Figures du discours* (1977), 364–6.

[237] See e.g. 'Typologie du roman policier', in Todorov, *Poétique de la prose*.

[238] An expression used by McHale, *Postmodernist Fiction*, 45.

[239] 'In all fiction, when a man is faced with alternatives, he chooses one of them at the expense of the others. In the unfathomable Ts'ui Pên, he chooses—simultaneously—all of them' (Borges, *Fictions*, 89).

and the novel also affects my initial suggestion that in times of epistemological anxiety and generic crises, all texts tend to be 'like' essays, and that the domination of the essay is indissociable from the generalization of the essayistic mode. For in view of the above, one might just as well say that all texts are like novels, and that the novelistic (in Barthes's sense of the 'romanesque', without the novel, or of Bakhtin's 'novelness') rather than the essayistic, is the generalized mode of all discourse in such periods, and/or the repressed 'other' of all discourse at all times. In Bakhtin, the novel is intrinsically connected with 'reconceptualization' in European thought, 'when relativity dominates physics and cosmology and thus when *non-coincidence* of one kind or another—of sign to its referent, of the subject to itself—raises troubling new questions about the very existence of mind'.[240] It is the genre which marks the most decisive stage in the history of consciousness or perception: the fact that it is 'constituted by openness to change' and that it 'seeks variety' makes it the 'accomplice and the witness of all that which, today, fixes and displaces the limits of reason'.[241] In other words, the novel is the genre which by definition externalizes the privileged moments of the becoming 'polyphonic' of the world, the super-genre 'in which all the fundamental principles of dialogism come most clearly to light'.[242] Hence the novel manifests to the highest degree what is not confined to it as a genre; in effect, the novel is not so much a literary genre as a special kind of impulse or force ('novel ness'), the 'body of utterances that is least reductive of variety', that 'least restricts the world's possible meanings'.[243] Identically to what I described initially as the 'usurpation' or 'infiltration' of the essay in all other discourse, 'in an era when the novel reigns supreme, almost all the remaining genres are to a greater or lesser extent "novelized"'.[244] The predominance of the novel in periods of generic crises goes together with a generalization of the 'novelistic spirit' or with a 'novelization' of all texts and genres. And since the novel, like the essay, is a progressive, boundless, non-canonic genre, the 'salient features' of this novelization are the 'freedom' and 'flexibility' which these texts and genres acquire: they 'become dialogized, permeated with laughter, irony, humor, elements of self-parody', thus participating in an extensive kind of 'generic criticism'; above all, they are 'caught up in the process of "becoming"', for the novel 'inserts into these other genres an indeterminacy, a certain semantic openendedness, a living contact with the unfinished, still-evolving contemporary reality (the open-ended present)'.[245] Given that Bakhtin 'assigns the term "novel" to whatever form of expression within a specific literary system reveals the limits

---

[240] Holquist, *Dialogism: Bakhtin and his World*, 17.

[241] Kristeva, 'From Symbol to Sign', 72 [Kristeva, *Le Texte du roman*, 52] Cf. Bakhtin, 'Epic and Novel', 15: 'When the novel becomes the dominant genre, epistemology becomes the dominant discipline.'

[242] Cf. 'The potential for such dialogue is one of the fundamental privileges of novelistic discourse, a privilege available neither to dramatic nor purely poetic genres' (Bakhtin, 'Discourse in the Novel', 320).

[243] Holquist, *Dialogism: Bakhtin and his World*, 84.   [244] Bakhtin, 'Epic and Novel', 5.

[245] Ibid. 6–7 and 39.

of that system as inadequate, imposed, or arbitrary',[246] forms which influence novel-istic prose are perceived not so much as precursor-forms of the novel as novels themselves: 'pre-novels' become 'early novels' or simply 'novels'. In this respect, not only are Plato's Socratic dialogues (which foreground the importance of self-consciousness and self-criticism ['Know thyself!'], of speech, popular language and irony) an 'essential step in the evolution of the novel'[247]; they are, as Bakhtin affirms by standing Schlegel's famous aphorism on its head, 'the novels of our time'.[248] Similarly, Rabelais, 'whose influence on all novelistic prose . . . was very great'[249] because he turns away from the artificial language of the official culture of his day and makes extensive use of the changeable kinds of language to be found in carnival', is also a novelist.[250] The interchangeability of essayistic and novelistic or 'novelness' in the history of consciousness, takes much the same form in the context of Romantic theories of the novel. What the adjective 'Romantic' [*romantisch*] denotes first of all, is the essentially modern—as opposed to the classical—the novel [*Roman*] being not just the dominant genre in modern periods, but the very embodiment of modernity.[251] As Behler notes, it then tends to 'lose its chronologi-cal, historical character of designation and enters an anthropological, transcenden-tal, absolute realm' to become 'synonymous with the poetic' and so to be made to encompass the characteristics common to all great art.[252] Like Bakhtin's novel-ness, 'Romanticism' is a way of thinking about the world, a state of mind rather than a genre. 'The Romantic', Schlegel writes in his famous 'Letter about the Novel', 'is not so much a literary genre as an element of poetry which may be more or less dominant or recessive, but never entirely absent . . . I postulate that all poetry should be Romantic and . . . I detest the novel as far as it wants to be a separate genre.'[253] In other words, 'Roman' does not signify 'novel', and Goethe's *Wilhelm Meister*, which provides a starting-point for early Romantic theories of the novel, must imperatively be transcended. Nor does *Roman* indicate a preference for prose over poetry, but rather 'a tendency of modern literature away from classical styles and towards prose of an intensely poetic kind, embracing a wide

---

[246] Clark and Holquist, *Mikhail Bakhtin*, 276.   [247] See Bakhtin, 'Epic and Novel', 22–5.

[248] Ibid. 22 ('Novels are the Socratic dialogues of our time', Schlegel, *Critical Fragments*, 26 p. 40 ['Die Romane sind die sokratischen Dialoge unserer Zeit', p. 71].

[249] Bakhtin, 'Discourse in the Novel', 309.

[250] Bakhtin, 'And there arrived on the scene, at last, the great Renaissance novel—the novels of Rabelais and Cervantes' ('From the Prehistory of Novelistic Discourse', 80).

[251] 'Romantic also includes Romance and related prose narratives; the adjective Roman (as in Roman civilization); Romanze (medieval romances and ballads), and Romantic (love, sentimental, exotic, fan-tastic)' (Wheeler, Introduction, *German Aesthetic and Literary Criticism*, 3). See also 'The Words "Romantic" and "Romanticism"', pp. 24–32 of the chapter entitled 'Formation and Main Representa-tives' in Ernst Behler, *German Romantic Literary Theory*.

[252] Ernst Behler, *German Romantic Literary Theory*, 28.

[253] Schlegel, 'Letter about the Novel', 43 ['daß das Romantische nicht sowohl eine Gattung ist also ein Element der Poesie, das mehr oder minder herrschen und zurücktreten, aber nie ganz fehlen darf. Es muß Ihnen nach meiner Ansicht einleuchtend sein, daß und warum ich fordre, alle Poesie solle romantisch sein, den Roman aber, insofern er eine besondre Gattung sein will, verabscheue', 'Brief über den Roman', *Friedrich Schlegel: Kritische Fragmente*, 515].

range of content and styles as well as genres', consonantly with the notion of *Mischgedicht*.[254] Thus, beyond its limits, the (Romantic) novel, when dominant in 'modern' periods, also determines the other genres to which it lends its generic tone in a way that relativizes or ignores generic differences and reinforces the 'adjectivization' of the concept of genre.[255] If in Bakhtin the role of the novel is assumed by such forms as the confession, the utopia, or the Menippean satire, the paradigms of Romantic literature—of 'novel ness'—include not only novels and novellas, or any text relating directly to literature springing from the romance, but any 'Romance-like' literature such as the writings of Dante, Tasso, Cervantes, and Shakespeare in whom Schlegel would like to fix . . . the core of the Romantic imagination.[256] In every respect, then, the novelistic has well and truly replaced the essayistic and made both the genre and the mode definitively redundant.

---

[254] Wheeler, Introduction, 4.

[255] See also Peter Szondi, *Poésie et poétique de l'idéalisme allemand* (1975), 134.

[256] See Ernst Behler, *German Romantic Literary Theory*, 24–5, Kathleen Wheeler, Introduction, 7, and Friedrich Schlegel, 'Letter about the Novel', 77: 'and then think of Shakespeare, in whom I would like to fix . . . the core of the Romantic imagination. This is where I look for and find the Romantic— in the older moderns, in Shakespeare, Cervantes, in Italian poetry, in that age of knights, love, and fairytales in which the thing itself and the word for it originated' ['. . . und erinnern sich dann an Shakespeare, in den ich das eigentliche Zentrum, den Kern der romantischen Phantasie setzen möchte', 'Brief über den Roman', 514].

6

Postscript: Borges, or the Essayistic Spirit

6.1. THE ESSAYIST AS MASTER OF MODERN FICTION

Borges, a writer of poems, essays, and short stories continues after his death to be hailed as one of the greatest masters of modern fiction; yet in relation to his production of poems and essays, the short stories form a relatively small part of his work. Moreover, the short story, far from being the genre of 'modern fiction', has conventionally been considered as a rather archaic or at least 'minor' genre, especially when conspicuously deriving from the traditional (folk-)tale, as it does in Borges. In contradistinction, the scarce attention paid to the essay in the already vast and ever-growing corpus of critical studies on Borges is striking, given the crucial role it plays in the writer's career. One could say that this neglect is motivated or compensated for by a massive and generalized emphasis on the various manifestations, in Borges's work, of the essayistic mode—even though the latter is not recognized as such. Again, attention to the mode eclipses the genre, but in a way that promotes the genre from a marginal to a central status: it is the implicitly essayistic quality of Borges's work which (paradoxically) justifies the author's supreme ranking as the master of modern fiction. One reason why the essay as such is disregarded is that critics tend to be more interested in the intertextual relationships between the writer's work and the rest of literature— the 'universal intertext' so insistently thematized in Borges's stories—than in the intratextual relationship between Borges's own texts. What is more, in order to pay attention to the relationship between essay and fiction within Borges's work, one must be willing to consider the essay as an intertext in its own right. Yet even those critics who propose to remedy the widespread perception of the Borgesian essays as by-products or supplements to the fiction (as adjuncts or residues which, having played their part, can be discarded) consider the essay from the point of view of the fiction. Jaime Alazraki, who is the author of two articles on Borges's essays, 'Tres formas del ensayo contemporaneo: Borges, Paz, Cortázar', and 'Estructura oximorónica en los ensayos de Borges',[1] is a case in point. He advocates against the tendency to consider the essays for their content only, as explanatory complements to the stories. Instead, one should evaluate the author's 'contribution to the genre' by concretely examining the ways in which the Borgesian essays 'renovate' or even 'innovate' the genre. Both Alazraki's articles converge on the

---

[1] Included in Jaime Alazraki, *La prosa narrativa de Jorge Luis Borges: Temas, Estilo* (1983), and published previously, in typically Borgesian manner, under the name of 'Una nueva técnica ensayística'.

idea that Borges 'renews' the essay by applying to it the techniques of narrative fiction. Of these techniques, the paradoxical handling of themes expressed by a prevalence of the 'oxymoronic structure' is of particular importance to Alazraki: not only is it a 'reminder of the texture of the stories', but the most striking evidence of the essay's acquisition of a narrative fictional texture.[2] Thus, the Borgesian essay deserves to be treated in its own right in so far as it 'acquires', 'explores', and 'develops' towards 'new forms', for ultimately, Borges is 'just as inventive and innovative in his best essays as he is in his fictions' ('Tres formas'). Alazraki's argument is ambivalent: his indistinct use either of 'renovation' and 'renewal', or of 'innovation' and 'invention', points to the recognition that not only Borges's best essays but the essay at its best is one which skilfully exploits the techniques of fiction and literature generally. Conversely, the oxymoronic structure which the Borgesian essay is supposed to 'acquire' from narrative fiction is already an essential feature of Montaigne's *Essais*, and therefore not a very convincing proof of 'innovation' or 'invention'. Under the pretext of doing the essay justice, Alazraki energetically encourages the genre to be examined 'retrospectively', from the point of view of the narrative fiction which it prefigures. He contributes therefore to the pervasive conception of a diachronic progression from essay to short story in Borges's work, despite the fact that Borges's career as an essayist begins with the publication of *Inquisiciones* (1925) and continues until the publication of *El Hacedor* in 1960;[3] that, in other words, Borges pursues his essay-writing after what is usually regarded as the culmination of his creative writing—*Fictions*; and that most critics (including Alazraki) consider the collection of essays he writes after *Fictions*—*Otras Inquisiciones*—as his most representative volume of essays. The titles of some articles, such as 'Del ensayo a la ficción narrativa'[4] immediately betray critics' utter confidence in the validity of this diachronic conception. Others, like Ronald Christ, found entire books on this a priori—although in his celebrated study Ronald Christ does not see the 'progress' of the essay towards fiction in terms of 'acquisition' and 'innovation', but in the much more convincing terms of 'potential', which suggests that the difference 'between' essay and fiction is grasped above all as a difference 'within'.

For Ronald Christ, the relationship between essay and fiction can be described as an itinerary from 'conception' to 'development' and finally to 'embodiment', a progression which in his view has less to do with different types of writing than with different stages of expression. As expected, the difference in potential concerns plot and character above all, Borges's essays being prose elaborations without plot or character of a situation 'which could in conventional ways be worked into

---

[2] For the examination of the oxymoronic structure in (some of) the essays, see also Edelweiss Serra, 'La Estrategia del Lenguaje en *Historia Universal de la Infamia*', in *Revista Iberoamericana*, 43 (1977), 275–84.

[3] *Elogio de la sombra* (pub. 1969), also contains some essayistic prose alongside the poems.

[4] Alba Omil de Pierola, 'Jorge Luis Borges: Del ensayo a la ficción narrativa', in Kurt L. Levy and Keith Ellis (eds.), *El ensayo y la crítica literaria en Iberoamérica* (1970).

a story'.[5] So if Borges's essays are potential literature waiting to be actualized, his fiction conversely 'develops ultimately from metaphysical notions which are described in nearly pure abstraction in the essays'.[6] Given this sharp distinction between the two opposed poles of expression, the first 'stage' of the journey towards fiction corresponds to an almost naked idea or '*donnée*', which by degrees becomes 'thoroughly homogenized with the narrative form' until, in some instances, 'the inspiring notion is entirely implicit in the words or deed of the character'.[7] Thought of in this way, the progress from essay to fiction is the 'progress from the conception of a possible plot expressing metaphysical ideas and a discussion of its values, to the development of a possible character and place expressing certain metaphysical-literary notions, to the embodiment of a metaphysical notion, a character, and a place in a genuine narrative'.[8] The evolution of Borges's work from 'conception' to 'embodiment' does not only involve the relationship between essay to fiction but, within the fiction, between the predominantly 'essayistic' stories and the fully developed narratives. Christ accordingly classifies Borges's tales into the three categories corresponding to the stages described above. The first category comprises those stories which take their form predominantly from the essay; the second, those stories which are 'half-way houses' between essay and fiction; and the third, those which have little or no essayistic quality.[9]

From this point of view, the case of the 'half-way house between essay and fiction' is particularly revealing, as Christ demonstrates in his reading of 'The Approach to Al-Mu'tasim' [*El acercamiento a Almotásim*], henceforth referred to as 'The Approach'. 'The Approach'—third text in the compilation of Borges's *Fictions* but which first appears in *Historia de la Eternidad* published in 1936—is the story of a novel itself called *The Approach to Al-Mu'tasim* by one Mir Bahadur Ali. It is the obvious case of a writing both 'about' and 'of' a story, that is, of the 'emergence' of fiction in a form where the writing of a story has not yet been divorced from the writing about a story. Christ derives his use of the adjective 'essayistic' from the main volume-titles of Borges's essays—*Discusión* ('Discussion'), and above all *Inquisiciones* ('Inquisitions') and *Otras Inquisiciones* ('Other Inquisitions')—which he sees as epitomizing the structure of Borges's most typical essays, and which cast the essayist in the role of the 'scholar detective'.[10] Thus, the 'skeletal structure' of 'The Approach' 'conforms' to the 'inquisitive' or 'questing' pattern of the essay which Christ schematically divides into four parts, with the last part (a footnote, incidentally) reflecting the suspended ending typical of the Montaignian essay:

I. Background
  (1) Criticism
  (2) Bibliography

---

[5] Ronald Christ, *The Narrow Act: Borges's Art of Allusion* (1969), 101.
[6] Ibid.   [7] Ibid.   [8] Ibid.   [9] Ibid. 100.   [10] Ibid. 118 and 130.

II. Summary
III. Judgement
    (1) Criteria
    (2) Evaluation
IV. Analogues
    (1) Possible sources
    (2) Underlying myth.[11]

This schematic representation is supposed to confirm the impression one has, upon reading the 'story', that the essayistic structure is not only predominant, but 'virtually precludes narrative'.[12] The plot-summary section itself of the novel *The Approach to Al-Mu'tasim* is extremely perfunctory, showing 'how little is devoted even to the *re*telling of the story'. It would appear, in short, that 'we do not have the presentation of a story but the dissection of one'.[13] As an alien and therefore easily identifiable structure, the 'inquisitional' pattern of the essay appears in other words to have an unmistakable effect on the development of the story. And this is above all disruptive, since the essay 'virtually precludes narrative'. 'The Approach' being a 'half-way' house between essay and fiction, however, Christ is also intent on showing that the essay provides Borges with a means of 'telling a story, a method of implementing the basic modes of his (Borges's) thought in narrative'.[14] Finally, it is understood that the implementation of these basic modes of thought in narrative is also—or simply—that 'of a detective story', as 'for [Borges], the mechanism of the detective story and the mechanism of the essay are identical'.[15] The detective work of Borges's own 'approach' parallels and reflects the original plot of Mir Bahahur Ali's novel *The Approach to Al-Mu'tasim*, a version of the second edition significantly subtitled 'A Game of Shifting Mirrors' which recounts the 'insatiable search for a soul through the subtle reflections which the soul has left in others'.[16] This search is triggered off by a murder and marked by a multiplicity of encounters with various men ('a dizzy pullulation of *dramatis personae*'[17]) who, as the 'reflections' or 'mirrors' of that soul, represent the turns, trials, and errors [*las peripecias*] of the quest towards a revelation which is only alluded to, since the novel ends at precisely that point.[18] The various essayistic parts identified by Ronald Christ thus constitute the obvious strategies of the story's self-essaying (the 'shifting mirrors') towards a final interpretation which is denied, the absent revelation of Al-Mu'tasim (which, one suspects, is the reflection of the protagonist's own soul) being the suspended ending to which most modern fiction subjects the traditional detective story. The essayistic structure, then, is not alien to the nature of narrative but on the contrary its most appropriate vehicle: it 'contributes'

---

[11] Ronald Christ, *The Narrow Act*, 99.   [12] Ibid. 93.   [13] Ibid. 99 and 100.

[14] Ibid. 119.   [15] Ibid. 118 and 120.

[16] Jorge Luis Borges, *Fictions* (1985), 38 [*Ficciones*, 9th edn. (1980), 41].

[17] Ibid. 37 [40].

[18] 'Bahadur's burdened novel is an ascending progression, whose final end is the presentiment of a "man called Al-Mu'tasim"' (ibid. 38 [42]).

to the story by foregrounding a structure which is paradigmatic of narrative and literally—as is the case here—its 'core'.

So much for showing that 'while the lasting value of the essay may well be largely in the light they throw on the mind of the artist who created the stories, they are nevertheless of considerable interest in themselves'.[19] But Borges himself, after all, promotes the supremacy of narrative fiction in his work, firstly by describing the essays of his first volume, *Discusión* (1932), as 'resigned exercises of anachronism' [*resignados ejercicios de anacronismo*], and then in the two successive prologues of his following volume *Historia Universal de la Infamia* written respectively in 1935 and 1954, as 'exercises of narrative prose' [*ejercicios de prosa narrativa*]. The intermediate status of *Historia Universal de la Infamia* is unmistakable, for it recounts the lives of real and fictitious criminals—some ascribed also to fictitious authors, and mark the real beginning of Borges's continuing investigation into the relationship of fiction, truth, and identity. The two prologues of these volumes include the famous statements in which Borges introduces himself as 'someone who does not have any more right to (some of) them than would a translator or a reader' (1935),[20] and then evokes in third-person narration a 'timid' man's tentative peregrination from the composition of essays to that of fictions:

These pages are the irresponsible game of a timorous man who could not bring himself to write stories and whose entertainment was to distort and misrepresent other people's tales. From these ambiguous practices he came round to the laborious composition of a proper narrative.[21]

This would confirm the intermediate status of 'The Approach' between the irresponsible game of a man who, disclaiming all responsibility, is not bold enough to assume his own enunciation, and the creation of the 'direct' tales of *Fictions*. On the other hand, it so happens that 'The Approach' is initially published as a 'note' in the predominantly essayistic *Historia de la Eternidad* (1936), and again identically (i.e. word for word) as a 'fiction' in the volume of *Fictions*. In the latter, the 'fiction' is thus presented 'as' an essay, or 'as though' it were an essay. From the narrative outlines of *Historia Universal de la Infamia*, Borges does in fact learn to 'progress' to the 'direct' tales of *Fictions*—as he himself ironically suggests in the prologue—in so far as his elliptical essayistic exercises have taught him to master a kind of narrative economy which preserves the essayist's alleged 'shyness' at all costs, and enables him to ascribe to all his texts the status of 'exercises'.[22] The

[19] Thomas R. Hart, 'The Literary Criticism of Jorge Luis Borges', *Modern Language Notes*, 78 (1963), 499.

[20] ['En cuanto a los ejemplos de magia que cierran el volumen, no tengo otro derecho sobre ellos que los de traductor y lector', Jorge Luis Borges, *Obras Completas: 1923–1972* (1974), 289].

[21] '(Estas páginas) son el irresponsable juego de un tímido que no se animó a escribir cuentos y que se distrajo en falsear y tergiversar (sin justificación estética alguna vez) ajenas historias. De estos ambiguos ejercicios pasó a la trabajosa composición de un cuento directo', Prologue to the second edition of *Historia Universal de la Infamia* (1954), Borges, *Obras Completas*, 291.

[22] Including the poems of the first and third book, *Fervor de Buenos Aires* (1923) and *Cuaderno de San Martin*, which are referred to in their respective prologues as 'estos ejercicios' and 'los ejercicios de este volumen'.

choice of another minor genre—the short story, rather than the novel—makes possible this complete identity of 'essay' and 'fiction', with the short story appearing as the 'natural' fictional equivalent of the essay. In the previous chapter, placing essay and essayistic novel on one level posed the problem of scope and size (except from an essentialist perspective), the essayistic novel being what is more a particularly enormous version of the novel. It led critics finally to reject the option of the essayistic novel as a 'vast essay' without even taking the pragmatic aspect into account. The famous prologue to *Fictions* justifies Borges's choice of the short story as a reaction against the 'laborious' and 'impoverishing' composition of 'vast books'.[23] Given Borges's well-known aversion to psychology and biographism which a short, elliptic form of narrative is bound to reduce to a minimum, one cannot help but see the novel, precisely, as the main target of this prologue. For if in Borges's work the novel is studiously avoided as a form, it is nevertheless recurrently thematized. The novel is at the centre of the plot of 'The Approach', and even more so in 'The Garden of the Forking Paths'—referred to at the end of the previous chapter—where the writing itself of a novel (the hero's ancestor's) is the enigma, the object of the quest. 'Tlön, Uqbar, Orbis Tertius', of which I will provide a reading in this chapter, begins with a lengthy discussion 'about a great scheme for writing a novel in the first person, using a narrator who omitted or corrupted what happened and who ran into various contradictions';[24] and we know that 'Pierre Ménard, Author of Don Quixote'—probably Borges's best-known story—revolves around the whole enterprise of copying or rather rewriting a fragment of Cervantes's famous novel. In a sense, then, the hegemony of the novel is made conspicuous through its absence—in keeping with Barthes's definition of the 'novelistic' and Mikhail Bakhtin's 'novelness'. The size of the short story is not, in fact, incompatible with the adaptation of those essayistic features (reflexiveness, inclusion of extra-literary genres) which characterized our previous novels. On the contrary, the condensed nature of the short story makes these features all the more pronounced. The essayistic qualities which determine the striking 'modernity' of the otherwise rather archaic—or at least very ancient—genre of the tale to which Borges's short stories are affiliated, can in fact be said to be the signs of the (Bakhtinian) 'novelization' of that genre. Through its complex treatment of narrative processes and temporal representation, and its capacity to comment upon its own devices by confronting within its frame different texts or genres, the Borgesian short story becomes a 'stylistic re-creation' of the traditional tale, one which has absorbed elements of all subsequent genres and especially the novel.[25]

---

[23] Borges, *Fictions*, 13 [*Ficciones*, 12].

[24] Ibid. 17 ['una vasta polémica sobre la ejecución de una novela en primera persona, cuyo narrador omitiera o desfigurara los hechos', *Ficciones*, 13].

[25] Alberto Julián Pérez, *Poética de la prosa de J. L. Borges: Hacia una crítica Bakhtiniana de la literatura* (1986), 48 and 252. See also Dario Puccini, 'Borges como crítico literario y el problema de la novela', in Kurt L. Levy and Keith Ellis (eds.), *El ensayo y la crítica literaria en Iberoamérica* (1970), 148–9.

Borges's use of the short story, then, appears as both an alternative to the novel and a way of remaining this side of the latter's ambitions, as a sort of 'rehearsal' which nevertheless affirms the self-sufficiency of a constituted genre. As the prologue of *Fictions* further suggests, Borges escapes the 'laborious' composition of 'vast books', books of 'five hundred pages', by operating 'as though' these books 'already existed' and by 'offering a summary or a commentary'.[26] Indeed, for Borges the best short story is one which alludes to, invokes, stages the conditions of, or 'mimes' a narrative rather than writing it out, thus 'reducing the plot to its most rudimentary outline' and ultimately resorbing both the novel and itself into a pure formal possibility.[27] By presenting the short story as 'summary' or 'commentary', essaying the absent book, Borges is able, like Montaigne and Barthes, to avoid 'reaching the core, depth, profundity', to 'remain on the surface' or 'superficial': 'Why—Borges asks—go on for five-hundred pages developing an idea whose perfect oral exposition is possible in a few minutes'?[28] The speech-like quality of Borges's stories is not limited to parataxis and the outline; it is also reinforced by the oral origin of the folktale from which the short story descends. Like Barthes, Borges 'announces' that he is going to write in order not—or no longer—to have to do it ('It is important for me to act *as if* I were to write this utopian novel'—writes Barthes). Only this 'as if' is the 'is/yet is not', the 'is not really here and now' and the 'is not really true' of fiction itself—of the short story, of a fiction which, as we will see, constantly reminds the reader of its fictitious character. The 'as if' of Barthes's injunction that his self-portrait 'must be considered as if spoken by a character in a novel—or rather by several characters' indicated that for the essayist, no posture was tenable, not even a fictional one. In Borges, the paratextual structure of his stories is the essential feature of this untenability even of the fictional posture; it is the guarantor that the fictions remain 'essays of fiction'.

In this sense, Borges's description of his short stories as 'summaries' or 'commentaries' is a timid—or modest—account of the systematic exploitation of the hypertextual, metatextual, and paratextual which they display in all its possible and impossible forms. 'Possible' because of their actualization of all kinds of second-hand practices: copy, allusion, plagiarism, parody, pastiche, translation, review, commentary, explanation, correction, summary, preface, compilation, etc. But 'impossible' in so far as Borges's vertiginous use of paratextuality also includes all those citational practices which he refers to and uses as the subject-matter of his stories, without trying them out: even in the indirect realm of the paratextual

[26] 'A better course of procedure is to pretend that these books already exist, and then to offer a résumé, a commentary' (Borges, *Fictions*, 13 ['Mejor procedimiento es simular que esos libros ya existen y ofrecer un resumen, un comentario', *Ficciones*, 12]).
[27] Christ, *The Narrow Act*, 106; and Raphaël Lellouche, *Borges, ou L'Hypothèse de l'auteur* (1989), 163.
[28] Borges, *Fictions*, 13 ['Desvarío laborioso y empobrecedor el de componer vastos libros; el de explayar en quinientas páginas una idea cuya perfecta exposición oral cabe en pocos minutos', *Ficciones*, 12].

'as if', 'staging' or 'saying' tends to prevail over 'doing'.[29] The fallible or porous memory of Borges's narrators (except for Funes—but he confirms the rule), and/ or the often insurmountable difficulty of directly acceeding to original documents or sources of information, warrants the supremacy of the paratext and greatly contributes to Borges's famous art of allusion. In both cases, the stories 'epitomize and suggest rather than exhaust and detail' by being duly filtered and abbreviated.[30] The act of narration itself is always questioned, since a defective memory precludes abstraction from the here and now, the construction of causal links—in short, of narrative continuity, which relies on both preconception or predetermination, and universalization or systematization. Instead, the essayistic utopia of an 'eternally evolving, never completed' succession of textual states which 'strives to embody within itself all the actual and possible modes of existence'[31]—like the narrative of 'The Garden of Forking Paths' which tells several narratives simultaneously and is itself the story in which we find a story (Ts'-ui-Pên's novel) which structurally contains several others—is promoted both intertextually and intratextually. As with Montaigne, Barthes, and the essayistic novelists, the oxymoronic logic of the 'and/or' goes together with the paratextual development of the text, but to the extent, here, that the text is constituted by nothing but paratexts: introductions, notes, and above all the self-declared postscripts which usually take care of the essays' or stories' 'suspended' endings. The reduction of each text and of the work as a whole to a fragment, to its outline, and Borges's cultivated 'shyness', which results in his never presuming to place himself on one level with creation, are a constant reminder of his conception of the text as both the rehearsal and the repetition of the universal intertext. Not for one minute is one allowed to forget that Borges's life is that of a 'non-writer' and of a 'rewriter' simultaneously, not only because he literally learns to write by translating and imitating other writers, but by virtue of the fact that every text is by definition a rewriting—a repetition, a transformation, a parody, an appropriation—of previous and future texts. Since 'all we do'—according to Montaigne's famous formulation—'is gloss each other',[32] any text that does not signal itself as a footnote in the margins of literature smacks of superfluity, vanity, and self-indulgence. Probably no writer since the Renaissance has shown more acute symptoms of Bloom's famous 'anxiety of influence', expressed here in the revival of the Renaissance situation where the text is seen as the principal instrument of human knowledge, and imitation is acknowledged as an indispensable prerequisite for literary production; few writers have made the source of their texts' authority the more explicit subject-matter of their fictions;[33] few have shown a greater awareness of the inseparability of the nature of 'originality' from the notions and strategies of duplication, of the fact

---

[29] Michel Lafon, *Borges ou La Réécriture* (1990), 108.   [30] Christ, *The Narrow Act*, 6.

[31] August Wiedmann, *Romantic Art Theories* (1986), 19.

[32] Montaigne, 'On Experience', *Essays*, III. 13, p. 1212.

[33] 'Renaissance authors make the source of their texts' authority the explicit subject-matter of their fictions', David Quint, *Origin and Originality in Renaissance Literature: Versions of the Source* (1983), 31.

that literature is 'an eccentric order of repetition'.[34] Given his sense of 'literary exhaustion',[35] how could the author possibly claim rights other than those of a translator and reader, both with regard to other people's texts and to the corpus of his own writings? The return of the same as other and of the other as the same (the oxymoronic 'and/or'), which necessarily induces a generalized mirror-effect between texts, genres, styles, rhetorical figures, characters, themes, writers, etc., fosters a repetitious sense of going round in circles. At its most pessimistic, this vision of literature not only vindicates the idea that there is nothing much left to say except for a few footnotes; it also imposes the ultimate inevitability (resignation) of identically repeating the already-said, as Borges himself does when publishing the same text in two different volumes: 'The Approach', and of course Ménard—Borges's best-known character—whose most ambitious writing project consists in reproducing word for word a fragment of Cervantes's *Don Quixote*. The disease of 'interglossing' seems to have reached such proportions in Borges, that it is unlikely for him to think one could ever recover. All he does, in fact, is modestly apologize for what he calls the 'essential monotony' of his work which, like literature (and history in general) is a variation on a few metaphors, which does nothing to pacify critics, who, in the course of his career, increasingly accuse him of vacuity and reductivism. On the other hand, the cage of rewriting, as other critics have been quicker to point out, is a golden one, and the originality with which Borges exploits his despairing belatedness continues to astonish most readers. Under the cover of modesty and apology, Borges's recognition that one is doomed to 'going around in circles' is a superior knowledge, one which betrays the fantasy of a literary utopia also recurrently thematized in his stories, the utopia of bringing everything together. By methodically varying the point of view so as fictively to actualize the greatest possible number of simultaneous interpretations in a single elliptical and ambiguous text, the secret affinities and symmetries between all things can be unmasked, and Borges is able to participate in the dream of a perfect synthesis and absolute knowledge represented above all by the 'circular' structure of the encyclopedia.

It is the pre-existence of all books in Borges's famous metaphor of the Library of Babel which justifies operating 'as though' these books already existed and offering a commentary. And this is what also turns 'essays of fictions' into 'fictions of essays'. The imaginative potential of Borges's essays is already expressed in the titles ('El espejo de las enigmas', 'La muralla y los libros'; 'El sueño de Coleridge'; 'Formas de una leyenda', etc.), which resemble to the point of confusion those of his short stories. In the case of 'The Approach', the imperceptible 'transition' from the 'essay' to the 'fiction' externalizes the already inherently fictional essence—rather than potential—of an essay which reviews a non-existing text: Mir Bahadur Ali's novel, *The Approach to Al-Mu'tasim*, is an imaginary book. What we have,

---

[34] Edward W. Said, *Beginnings: Intention and Method* (1975), 12.

[35] Cf. John Stark, *The Literature of Exhaustion: Borges, Nabokov, and Barth* (1974), which includes a comparison between Nabokov's *Pale Fire* and 'Tlön, Uqbar, Orbis Tertius'.

therefore, is 'neither a legitimate investigation nor actual story, but ... a *fiction*, literally, a *feigning* on both sides'.[36] According to the rules of citational practices, the authenticity of the reviewer depends upon the authenticity of his quotations— of their reference.[37] We have observed the essayist's inclination to quote inaccurately, that is, to exploit his lack of memory and/or the unverifiability of his sources in order unfaithfully to emancipate himself from the mimetic constraints of criticism. Borges, as mentioned above, makes plentiful use of his essayist/narrators' whims and adds his own twist to them: in most cases, the line between a lost source and an invented source, is a very fine one. Do not critics 'falsify' and 'distort' other people's stories because, like Kinbote in Nabokov's *Pale Fire*, they read into a text whatever they wish to read, to the point of producing another text which is a pure product of their imagination? In fact, Borges's well-known epistemological convictions cast 'The Approach', like the majority of his other texts, as a metaphor for knowledge in general, since it communicates the understanding that our access to reality (and to ourselves) is inevitably 'filtered' or distorted primarily by language, by texts, and because Borges regards fiction as the only appropriate or even possible medium for expressing the tentative formulations of the mind.[38] This is no doubt why the *Fictions* are perceived as the yardstick against which Borges's entire work must be measured. Fiction-making is the sole and proper exercise of thought; hence the systematic tendency, expounded and typically understated in the epilogue to the volume of essays *Otras Inquisiciones* (1952), to 'assess religious and philosophical ideas according to their esthetic value and even for what they contain of the singular and the marvellous', which 'may be the indice of an essential scepticism'.[39] This 'essential scepticism' is what makes Borges an inhabitant of the world of Tlön, where metaphysics is considered a branch of fantastic literature and metaphysicians seek not 'truth' but 'a kind of amazement'. Tlön is the imaginary world described in the first story of the volume of *Fictions* ('Tlön, Uqbar, Orbis Tertius'), a typically essayistic 'utopia' in which men live strictly according to the principles of philosophical idealism (Berkeley's mainly). In Tlön, reality is a mental act, and the existence of an 'external' reality is only one possible order of the world, one element of the series of conceivable figures. Since

---

[36] Christ, *The Narrow Act*, 100.

[37] Cf. Antoine Compagnon on authentic quotation, authenticity, and authorship: 'Le denotatum d'une citation ... est une preuve de fidélité, d'exactitude, de sincérité (la qualité d'une énonciation, d'une répétition, d'être authentique ou controuvée, certifiée conforme ou apocryphe)', and 'La citation, preuve de sa référence à l'appui, authentifie un individu par son énonciation, elle le consacre auteur. L'auteur n'est tel, il n'est authentique, que si les citations qu'il fait le sont' (*La Seconde Main, ou Le Travail de la citation* (1979), 341).

[38] Cf. Michel Lafon, who asserts that Borges's *Fictions* can be seen as 'the point of departure of all Borgesian production: at once hypertext of previous writings, hypertext and hypotext of itself, and hypotext of texts to come' (*Borges ou La Réécriture*, 107).

[39] ['Dos tendencias he descubierto, al corregir las pruebas, en los misceláneos trabajos de este volumen. Una, a estimar las ideas religiosas o filosóficas por su valor estétio y aun por lo que encierran de singular y de maravilloso. Esto es, quizá, indicio de un escepticismo esencial', Borges, *Obras Completas*, 775].

there is 'no classification of the universe that is not arbitrary and conjectural', philosophical systems are dialectical games, philosophies of 'As If'.[40] In other words, this is a world 'without qualities' where the 'capacity to think how everything could "just as easily" be, and to attach no more importance to what is than to what is not',[41] prevails; where men, like Ulrich, live according to the idea that 'this order of things is not as solid as it pretends to be; nothing, no ego, no form, no principle, is safe, everything is in a process of invisible but never-ceasing transformation, there is more of the future in the unsolid than in the solid, and the present is nothing but a hypothesis that one has not finished with.'[42] In such a world, notions of objectivity and identity are replaced by a series of endless approximations which correspond to the incessant activity or 'game' of a mind refuting and commenting upon itself, and—because thought cannot dissociate itself from language in Tlön—of the empty 'play' of language, of signifiers emancipated from all referent: a game, as in 'The Approach', of 'shifting mirrors'. Accordingly, the Tlönian conception of literature—which is 'tried out' in more detail in 'Pierre Ménard, Author of Don Quixote'—is that of a single plot which is subjected to every possible permutation. In fact, the shift from a closed to an open-ended conception of intertextuality exemplified by the works of our previous essayists, and following Montaigne's observation that 'all is a-swarm with commentaries: of authors there is a dearth',[43] is radicalized to the point where all books are the work of one single writer who is timeless and anonymous, which does away with the notion of plagiarism altogether.

Critics, like Borges, are forever searching for the one book or text that will contain all others. Given the circular structure of Borges's work, it is not surprising that each one of the 'best' fictions should have been made to play that role. For our own purpose, the choice (or sacralization) of 'Tlön, Uqbar, Orbis Tertius' and 'Pierre Ménard, Author of Don Quixote' as the essential, cardinal texts towards which all other texts converge, is imperative.[44] In Borges's work, (narrative) fiction is engendered by the 'trying out' or essaying of philosophical pretexts, or by the failure or aporias of these pretexts as 'theories'.[45] And one could say that the principles of Tlön are the philosophical pretext from which all his texts are derived. In 'Tlön, Uqbar, Orbis Tertius' as elsewhere, the formal translation of such principles results in a narrative in which the essayistic or paratextual structure prevails, one which confronts or juxtaposes contradictory interpretations in a way that totally eliminates the object's claim to an independent, objective existence (i.e.

---

[40] Borges, *Fictions*, 24 [*Ficciones*, 23].   [41] Musil, *The Man Without Qualities*, i. 12.

[42] Ibid. i. 296–7.   [43] Montaigne, 'On Experience', *Essays*, III. 13, p. 1212.

[44] 'Pierre Ménard' is Borges's first real fiction, not in the ordering of the book, but chronologically (before it Borges had only written the short stories of 'Hombre de la Esquina Rosada' and 'El acercamiento'), which also contributes to ascribing to it the status of a founding text.

[45] Cf. Jaime Alazraki, 'Estructura oximorónica en los ensayos de Borges', id., *La prosa narrativa de Jorge Luis Borges* (1983), 326, and 'Philosophical aporia translates into narrative creation: this is its positive aspect' (Walter Moser, 'Fragment and Encyclopedia: From Borges to Novalis', in L. Kritzman (ed.), *Fragments: Incompletion and Discontinuity* (1981), 116).

to an existence independent of our perception of it). But 'Tlön, Uqbar, Orbis Tertius', which describes the emergence and progressive invasion of an imaginary world into the 'real' world of the narrative, is particularly exemplary in that the translation of the 'idea' (mediated by the text of an encyclopedia) also happens to be its theme, what the story is 'about'. In this sense, 'Tlön, Uqbar, Orbis Tertius's' display of its construction 'in progress' provides a reflection on the conditions not only of its own writing, but on the conditions of writing of all the other stories. Staging the emergence of Tlön into the world of the story relies on a tension between conception (virtuality) and embodiment (narrative actualization), between the pseudo-actualizations of all narrative structures and the choice of one narrative sequence, all of which can also be perceived as a progression from the one (the essay) to the other (the fiction). This is what makes of 'Tlön, Uqbar, Orbis Tertius' a predominantly essayistic type of story, while at the same time, it is the tale's essayistic qualities which implicitly contribute to its being considered as especially representative of Borges's short stories according to the criteria described in the previous chapter.

In 'Tlön, Uqbar, Orbis Tertius', the materialization of the imaginary world of Tlön depends upon the discovery of fragments of a fake encyclopedia. As expected from my discussion of Barthes, the encyclopedia—which offers an abbreviation (microcosm and analogon) of the world—has a fundamental role to play in the foregrounding of the above-mentioned tensions and ambivalences, if only because Borges more than any other modern author is supposed to have dealt with 'virtually all the themes of totalization by developing them in conflict with the forces of fragmentation': his *Fictions* have been described as constituting a sort of 'encyclopedia of the thematic, tropological, and narrative fantasies of representational totalization that our culture has accumulated over the centuries'.[46] In 'Tlön, Uqbar, Orbis Tertius', the encyclopedia is more than a simple mediation: it becomes (is) the world, and conversely, Tlön is a world made of a purely bookish reality. This involves acknowledging first of all that despite its claim (discussed in Barthes) to reflect or mirror the world (the 'speculum') by virtue of the fact that it deals with concepts rather than words, the encyclopedia is made of language, and of nothing but language. By making the emergence of the new world hinge on the discovery of an encyclopedia, Borges makes clear that language does not reflect 'the' world so much as create 'a' world which, like the one we hold to be our own, is imaginary, a projection of our minds. Borges liked to claim that encyclopedias really were the starting-point in his exploration of books for the simple reason that reference books could be found on open shelves, and thus spared him the struggle—too great for a notoriously shy man—of asking for 'real' books (literature) at the desk. This anecdote also contributes to the perception of the reference book as 'not(-yet)-written' and which thus functions here as a sort of metaphor for Borges's life prior to writing, or for his production of predominantly 'essayistic' stories—if

[46] Moser, 'Fragment and Encyclopedia', 11 and 112.

one identifies the paratextual presentation of the story with the paratactic, 'vertical' structure of the encyclopedia. The totalizing ambitions of the genre are represented by the gradual invasion by the planet Tlön of our world. At the same time, the encyclopedia is used to underscore the opposition, central to all of Borges's texts, between the conventionally real and the conventionally fictional. The encyclopedia is a reference book which, what is more here, is introduced as *The Anglo-American Cyclopedia*, a literal reprint of the renowned *Encyclopedia Britannica*. Besides, since the tale—like so many of Borges's tales—takes the form of a detective scholarly work, the encyclopedia is the object of an erudite exploration undertaken by a number of 'real' and well-known writers, including Bioy Casares whom one knows to be a real collaborator and friend of Borges's. This turns the 'real' Borges himself into the supposed subject of the first-person narration. But of course, *The Anglo-American Cyclopedia* is 'an inadequate reprint' of the *Encyclopedia Britannica*, a clone, the critical enterprise thus amounting, as in 'The Approach', to 'notes upon an imaginary book', to a 'fiction'.[47] The invasion of 'fiction' by 'reality' becomes that of 'reality' by 'fiction', and the result is a journey into the 'fantastic' (Bioy Casares, like Borges, is a 'real' writer of fantastic fictions). In this sense, the inherently fantastic or 'magical' dimension of the encyclopedia exploited to a lesser degree by Barthes, greatly contributes to 'assess[ing] philosophical and religious ideas according to their esthetic value and even for what they contain of the singular and the marvellous'. Through its magical dimension, the encyclopedia becomes an essential link within the fantastic tradition of the Romantic and philosophical tale from which Borges's short stories derive and which has shown its continuing fascination with the hostile forces of chaos, the undecided frontiers between life and death, the theme of the double, fantastic travel and the description of utopias, etc.[48] Borges's conception of the encyclopedia's magical power is summed up in his famous reference, in his essay 'El idioma analítico de John Wilkins', to a fictive Chinese encyclopedia in which the blanks themselves between the incongrous elements accumulated in a taxonomy of rupture (of interpolations and cross-connections) become the mysterious or even 'monstrous' generating space of fantastic combinations. Similarly, the 'utopia' (literally the 'no place') of Tlön, is created from the juxtaposition of items in the a-topia of the encyclopedic structure of our text—an 'infinitely decentred' structure which, as we saw in Barthes, magnifies the 'no place' or 'nowhere' (the forever quested and forever absent origin) of language or writing: 'Where', Foucault asks, 'could [these items] ever meet, except in the immaterial sound of the voice pronouncing their enumeration, or on the page transcribing it? Where else could they be juxtaposed except in the non-place of language? Yet, though language can

---

[47] Cf. prologue to *Fictions*: 'More reasonable, more inept, more indolent, I have preferred to write notes upon imaginary books. Such as "Tlön"', 13 ['Más razonable, mas inepto, mas haragán, he preferido la escritura de notas sobre libros imaginarios', *Ficciones*, 12].

[48] See Lellouche, *Borges ou L'Hypothèse de l'auteur*, 271–2.

spread them before us, it can do so only in an unthinkable space.'[49] It is to the 'unthinkable' space of Tlön that we now turn, before concerning ourselves with two of its most famous inhabitants, Ménard and Borges.[50]

6.2. THE WORLD AS TLÖN

6.2.1.   A Game of Shifting Mirrors

Bioy Casares's discovery of the article on Uqbar which the first part of 'Tlön, Uqbar, Orbis Tertius' (henceforth referred to as 'Tlön') revolves around, constitutes the initial link between real and fictional texts, since *The Anglo-American Cyclopedia* is a bogus encyclopedia, a 'literal yet belated reprint' (1917) of the *Encyclopedia Britannica* of 1902. But to make things more complicated, there are two distinct copies of the *Anglo-American Cyclopedia*, of which only one—Bioy Casares's own copy—contains the entry and article on the land of Uqbar, even

---

[49] Foucault, *The Order of Things: An Archeology of the Human Sciences*, 6 ['Où pourraient-elles jamais se rencontrer, sauf dans la voix immatérielle qui prononce leur énumeration, sauf sur la page qui les transcrit? Où peuvent-elles se juxtaposer sinon dans le non-lieu du langage? Mais celui-ci, en les déployant, n'ouvre jamais qu'un espace impensable', *Les Mots et les choses*, p. 8, Introduction]. Foucault's whole book is supposed to have been inspired by Borges's 'monstrosities'.

[50] For secondary work on Borges, apart from Alazraki, *La prosa narrativa de Borges: Temas, Estilo*; Christ, *The Narrow Act*; Lafon, *Borges ou La Réécriture*; Lellouche, *Borges ou L'Hypothèse de l'auteur*; Pérez, *Poética de la prosa de J. L. Borges*, and the articles referred to in this introduction, see also: Jaime Alazraki (ed.), *Jorge Luis Borges: El escritor y la crítica* (1984), which includes articles by Paul de Man, Gérard Genette, Maurice Blanchot, George Steiner, etc.; Jaime Alazraki, *Versiones, inversiones, reversiones: El Espejo como modelo estructural del relato en los cuentos de Borges* (1977); Kurt Levy and Keith Ellis (eds.), *El ensayo y la critica literaria en Iberoamerica* (1970), which includes articles by Rodriguez Monegal, Peter G. Earle, etc.; Sylvia Molloy, *Las letras de Borges* (1979); Carter Wheelock, *The Mythmaker: A Study of Motif and Symbol in the Short Stories of J. L. Borges* (1969); Jaime Rest, *El laberinto del universo: Borges y el pensamiento nominalista* (1976); John Sturrock, *Paper Tigers: The Ideal Fictions of Jorge Luis Borges* (1977); Tony Tanner, *City of Words: American Fiction 1950–1970* (1971); Martin S. Stabb, *Jorge Luis Borges* (1970); Arturo Echavarría, *Lengua y literatura de Borges* (1983); Anna María Barrenechea, *La Expresión de la irrealidad en la obra de Borges* (1967); Juan García Ponce, *La errancia sin fin: Musil, Borges, Klossowski* (1981); Rosa Pellicer, *Borges: El estilo de la eternidad* (1986); Jean-Pierre Mourey, *Jorge Luis Borges: Verité et univers fictionnels* (1988); Juan Nuño Montes, *La filosofia de Borges* (1986); Gabriela Massuh, *Borges: Una estética del silencio* (1980); Emil Volek, *Cuatro claves para la modernidad: Análisis semiótico de textos hispánicos (Aleixandre, Borges, Carpentier, Cabrera Infante)* (1984); Alberto C. Pérez, *Realidad y suprarealidad en los cuentos fantásticos de J. L. Borges* (1971); John Dominic Crossan, *Raid on the Articulate: Comic Eschatology in Jesus and Borges* (1976); Elizabeth Dipple, 'Borges: The Old Master', in *The Unresolvable Plot: Reading Contemporary Fiction* (1988); Sylvia Molloy, ' "Dios Acecha en los Intervalos": Simulacro y causalidad textual en la ficción de Borges', *Revista Iberoamericana*, 43 (1977); Alfred J. MacAdam, 'Translation as Metaphor: Three Versions of Borges', *Modern Language Notes*, 90 (1975), and 'Lenguaje y Estética en *Inquisiciones*', *Revista Iberoamericana*, 43 (1977); Peter G. Earle, 'El ensayo hispanoamericano: Del modernismo a la modernidad', *Revista Iberoamericana*, 48 (1982); Emil Volek, ' "Aquiles y la Tortuga": Arte, Imaginación, y la Realidad según Borges', *Revista Iberoamericana*, 43 (1977); David W. Foster, 'Para una Caracterización de la *Escritura* en los Relatos de Borges', *Revista Iberoamericana*, 43/100–1 (1977); Nicolas Bratosevich, 'El Desplazamiento Como Metáfora en Tres Textos de Jorge Luis Borges', *Revista Iberoamericana*, 100–1 (1977).

though the general index does not list that entry. The article, which the narrator (the supposed Borges) himself eventually gets to read and describe, provides 'vague' points of reference[51] as to its frontiers; nevertheless, a few 'memorable' features draw the narrator's attention, among which the fact that 'its epics and legends never referred to reality, but to the two imaginary regions of Mlejnas and Tlön'.[52] This is the first, indirect reference to Tlön, and leads eventually in part II to the narrator's accidental discovery of the Volume XI of *A First Encyclopedia of Tlön* in which a friend of his father, H. Ashe (a man who 'suffers from a sense of unreality'[53]), has had a hand. Only the one Volume XI which the narrator chances upon is known to exist, although it is reportedly one of a set of forty volumes. After an apparently marginal description—Tlön is so far the imaginary region of an imaginary land—the reader is intrigued to hear that not only the narrator, but other well-known writers and critics (Nestor Ibarra, Drieu La Rochelle, Alfonso Reyes), have been puzzling over it for some time, desperately trying to find the preceding and following volumes. The failure of this attempt prompts Alfonso Reyes to propose that they themselves reconstruct the other volumes from the evidence of Volume XI, which bears the mysterious inscription of *Orbis Tertius* on the front page and is evidently the 'substantial fragment of the complete history of an unknown planet'.[54] The narrator then quotes from this volume the most significant parts of the exhaustive description he finds of its world which happens to be the embodiment of a certain school of idealist philosophy.

The third and final part of the text is introduced as a postscript [*postdata*] and describes the discovery of someone's letter in one of H. Ashe's books which at last 'clears up entirely the mystery of Tlön'.[55] The planet of Tlön, the reader is told, was invented in the seventeenth century by a secret society whose subsequent generations of collaborators progressively produced the forty volumes of the *First Encyclopedia of Tlön* completed in 1914, and which was to be the basis for another work written in one of the languages of Tlön provisionally called *Orbis Tertius*. For the reader, Orbis Tertius has so far been a world described in the language of an imaginary planet which in turn is the region of a non-existent country. In the second part, *Orbis Tertius* figures on the first page of the 'Tlön' volume, and thus only appears as a part of 'Tlön'. In this third part, the concept of *Orbis Tertius* becomes more and more autonomous—and not surprisingly. For this part is the summary (as the narrator puts it) of the history of the planet's intrusion into our world, and the prediction of its total usurpation of reality ('The world will be Tlön'[56]) after the discovery and divulgation of its encyclopedia.

It is in the explicitly named 'Postscript', in fact, that the reader is informed that he has been reading a story and not just a set of disconnected notes with a few oblique connections in common ('Here I conclude the personal part of my

---

[51] Borges, *Fictions*, 19 [*Ficciones*, 16].   [52] Ibid.   [53] Ibid. 20 [17].
[54] Ibid. 21 ['Un vasto fragmento metódico de la historia total de un planeta desconocido', 19].
[55] Ibid. 30 [31].   [56] Ibid. 33 ['El mundo será Tlön', 36].

narrative'[57]), which retrospectively converts the three described parts into three chronologically ordered narrative cycles (1935–1940–1947) that mark the progressive contact with the fantastic. In reality, the 'action' of the story, its diachronic unfolding is shown to be above all a folding 'within', a process of in- and outgrowth by internal mirroring which is intertextual and above all intratextual. The narrator or annotator, and with him the reader, only ever has access to little bits of texts, second-hand material of a totality which remains to be (re)constructed; the annotator himself is only one (and probably not the last) amongst the many readers involved in making sense at different historical stages of the various encyclopedic fragments which are discovered. So the story is presented as an intricate juxtaposition of frames which correspond to the supplementary versions, fake duplicates of one another and of an absent whole. The various bogus copies which 'reflect' the original contain both more and less than the original, and are the many misreadings or supplements by which the story both emerges and 'progresses'. One can expect little else, admittedly, after the first sentence of the story—'I owe the discovery of Uqbar to the conjunction of a mirror and an encyclopedia'[58]—and the whole introduction to the discovery of Uqbar which continues to be punctuated by very emphatic remarks on the presence of mirrors. The narrator recounts that while dining with his friend Bioy Casares, 'the unnerving mirror hung at the end of a corridor', adding further that 'from the far end of the corridor, the mirror was watching us', which leads to the 'discovery' that 'mirrors have something monstrous about them'.[59] The pretext for the discovery of Uqbar turns out to be a phrase allegedly uttered by an Uqbar heresiarch, which Bioy Casares quotes after speculating on the monstrosity of mirrors: 'Mirrors and copulation are abominable, since they both multiply the numbers of men.'[60] Having awakened the narrator's curiosity as well as his suspicion that the quotation is just a fiction invented by Bioy Casares to justify a phrase, the latter checks his article at home and finds that he has misquoted the 'original' which says 'Mirrors and fatherhood are abominable because they multiply it (the visible universe) and extend it.'[61] Since the relationship between the annotation of the rules which govern the world of Tlön in the second part and its gradual intrusion into and as the formal reality of the text 'Tlön' partakes of that same mirror-effect, we now move on to the account of the principles which govern the planet of Tlön with a view to taking a closer look at the 'translation' of these principles into the story 'Tlön'.

6.2.2. Tlön and 'Tlön'

After a number of preliminary remarks, the narrator begs for a 'few minutes' in order to expound Tlön's conception of the universe, its corresponding rules and

---

[57] Borges, *Fictions*, 32 ['Aquí doy término a la parte personal de mi narración', *Ficciones*, 34].

[58] Ibid. 17 ['Debo a la conjunción de un espejo y una enciclopedia el descubrimiento de Uqbar', 13].

[59] Ibid. ['Descubrimos que los espejos tienen algo monstruoso', 13 and 14: NB the translator's choice of 'grotesque' for 'monstruoso' seems wholly inadequate].

[60] Ibid. [14].   [61] Ibid. 18 [15].

maxims. Despite Hume's dismissal of Berkeley's idealist notions on the ground that they are inapplicable, Tlön is a planet constructed upon the very logic of idealism. What this means, above all, is that objective reality is denied; it only exists as 'a heterogeneous series of independent mental acts' unfolding in time but not in space: 'For them, the world is not a concurrence of objects in space, but a heterogeneous series of independent acts. The men of that planet conceive of the universe as a series of mental processes, whose unfolding is to be understood only as a time sequence.'[62] Tlönians have no conception of objects in space, so our notion of causality is non-existent: the perception of smoke on the horizon, and then of the countryside on fire, and finally of the half-extinguished cigar which caused the fire, would be considered an example of the association of ideas.[63] This clearly invalidates our notion of science, for 'to explain or to judge an event is to identify or unite it with another one'; and in Tlön, 'this connection is a later stage in the mind of the observer, which can in no way affect or illuminate the earlier stage'.[64] Science and rational thought as we conceive them disappear, therefore, and give way to a multiplicity of individual games.

Similarly, metaphysics is considered a 'branch of fantastic literature', and philosophy presented from the outset as a 'dialectical game', a 'philosophy des Als Ob'.[65] Events are either brought into contact or opposed according to similarities and differences, and they only exist in the temporary present of perception: future and past have no other reality than that of 'present hope' [*esperanza presente*] or 'present memory' [*recuerdo presente*].[66] With no cause and effect, all events—as individual mental perceptions—are equally real and can be combined endlessly. Things thus duplicate themselves in Tlön. In literature, for example, books are all the 'imaginable permutations' of one book, and a 'book which does not include its opposite, or "counterbook" is considered incomplete'.[67] Objects, in Tlön, are concretizations of ideas, sensations, thoughts, hopes, or imagination with no other frontiers than those of their own possibilities: in the same way that they are duplicated when remembered, they cease to exist when forgotten. The typical 'secondary' objects produced by suggestion or hope are the 'Hrönir' and the 'Ur', all duplicates of duplicates which may exist in an infinite series.[68] Likewise, literary works are also objects, 'poetic objects'[69] which are summoned and dismissed according to the poetic needs of the moment.

Finally and most importantly, since idealists deny matter or external referents,

---

[62] Ibid. 22 and 24 ['El mundo para ellos . . . es una serie heterogénea de actos independentes', 21 and 23].

[63] Ibid. 24 [23].   [64] Ibid.

[65] Ibid. [23–4]. Cf. *The Philosophy of As-If: A System of the Theoretical, Practical and Religious Fictions of Mankind* by the German philosopher Hans Vaihinger, published in 1911.

[66] Borges, *Fictions*, 25 [*Ficciones*, 24].

[67] Ibid. 28 ['También son distintos los libros. Los de ficción abarcan un solo argumento, con todas las permutaciones imaginables . . . Un libro que no encierra su contralibro es considerado incompleto', 28].

[68] Ibid. 28 and 29 [28–30].   [69] Ibid. 23 [22].

all Tlönian disciplines are determined by—or rather are the derivations of— language.[70] As an actualization of idealism, Tlön is a planet exclusively constituted by language, and this comes out in two connected ways. Because there is no objective reality, there are no nouns in the 'hypothetical *Ursprache* of Tlön'. In one hemisphere, nouns are replaced by 'impersonal verbs qualified by monosyllabic suffixes or prefixes which have the force of adverbs'. The verb overtly marks action in language: it is thought in movement. On the other hemisphere of Tlön, reality is set in motion by a primary cell which is no longer the verb but the monosyllabic adjective: the noun, this time, is translated into an aggregate of adjectives which approximate it.[71] The linguistic substance thus obeys the same rules as the above-mentioned 'poetic objects' which are temporary stages of fixation in the linguistic continuum. The avoidance of direct naming and the exploitation of deviations or ambiguous meanings generate the potentially infinite multiplicity mentioned above. Signs are permuted and combined according to inherent rules and not as a mere transcription of some prior, non-verbal reality.

The formal implications of the rules which govern Tlön are reflected by the paratextual 'unfolding' of the story in which these rules are described, and to which these rules are applied. The narrator's report marks the coincidence between the accumulation of fragmentary evidence towards the totalization of the story—the progressive integration of the fragments into the whole—with the progressive disintegration which this integration also entails, for 'contact with Tlön and the ways of Tlön have disintegrated this world'.[72] Hence a structure determined by parataxis and which constantly mobilizes its material and secures the coexistence of simultaneous potentialities in a process that moves away from notions of identity and objectivity. The disjunction of the structure is not just graphical (the blank between the three parts); it holds throughout the reading of the three parts which are presented as heterogeneous acts with no explicit transition of cause and effect between them. Instead, figures of contiguity characterize the accumulative, rather than hierarchical growth of the fragmentary information which constitutes the story. The links between the parts are links of similarity and difference which, to the reader, look accidental, not necessary. This addition and substitution of one part by the other corresponds to the process of revision which prevails in Tlön, and to the process of rewriting (and decentring) by which the piecemeal information on Tlön accumulates. As in Tlön, the discovery of the encyclopedic fragments by which the story progresses hinges on the 'permutations' of one (unattainable) book, so that main and peripheral, original and fake texts and/or meanings which are confronted in the story are granted equal status. In this respect, the 'Philosophy of As-If' which rules over Tlön recognizably corresponds to the sceptical relativization and suspension of Musil's 'The Like of It Now Happens'. Until the end of the story, for example, the account of Tlön

---

[70] Borges, *Fictions*, 22 [*Ficciones*, 21].   [71] Ibid. 23 [21–2].

[72] Ibid. 33 ['El contacto y el hábito de Tlön han desintegrado este mundo', 35].

always appears as a marginal, contingent description; and conversely, what seems to be the most important part of the story—the final announcement and description of Tlön's usurpation of our world—is only added to the rest in the form of a postscript. Similarly, the beginnings of parts II and III appear as digressions from part I which already plunges the clueless reader into the middle of the 'action'. From I to II, the reader leaps from the mystery of Uqbar to a description, seven years later, of a so-called friend of the narrator's father, H. Ashe, with the notification of his death—which proves only after a while to be indirectly related to the discovery of the Tlön encyclopedia (itself only indirectly related to the content of part I). As for the leap from II to III, it is even more extreme, for the first sentence of the postscript bluntly contradicts what the reader had been given to understand in the second part: part II was supposed to be an outline of the principles described in Volume XI of *A First Encyclopedia of Tlön*, while part III now states that the former was the more or less faithful reproduction of an article published in the *Anthology of Fantastic Literature*. More confusing even is the abrupt return to the discussion of Tlön which follows, without the slightest hint as to how things are correlated. These constant interpolations and modifications are of course a reminder that in Tlön, there is no system of thought or belief which does not contain within itself its own refutation ('A book which does not include its opposite, or "counterbook", is considered incomplete'[73]). And this includes typical operations of 'unnaming' (to interpolate was to unname at a structural level): since both Tlön and the essayistic structure are in the process of becoming, nouns in the narrator's report are also set in motion or 'mobilized' by being coupled with contradictory adjectives, oxymoronically, or with pairs of contradictory adjectives separated by disjunctions such as 'and' or 'or'. Tlön itself, we are told on the first page, is the story of 'an atrocious or banal reality'. The striking increase of metaphors which parallels the gradual intrusion of Tlön (in which all is necessarily metaphorical) until the final stage of the usurpation of 'objects' which are themselves solidified metaphors, constitutes the other essential type of displacement. In fine, disjunctions decentre the structure of the text at all levels and favour the multiplication of peripheral parts, approximations and obliquities. Events or objects are never described directly, but only via quotations, allusions, references, letters, and more remotely still, via the memory of this already fragmentary second-hand evidence, the story being triggered off by the memory of a quotation. Likewise, the 'end' of the story—Tlön's invasion of the whole of reality—is only alluded to in the 'postscript', and given the form of a projection of the reader's 'hopes' or 'fears', and of the narrator's speculation or 'foresight', both of which are enough to create the 'horrible or banal reality' (and/or the poetic object upon which this reality depends) which, as we were told on the first page, only a few privileged readers will have been able to 'decipher' or 'guess' [*adivinar*]: in a world now ruled by Tlönian laws, we have all become 'possibilitarians' who, like Ulrich

[73] Ibid. 28 [28].

in Musil's *The Man Without Qualities*, 'do not shrink from reality but treat it, on the contrary, as a mission and an invention':[74]

Here I conclude the personal part of my narrative. The rest, when it is not in their hopes or their fears, is at least in the memories of all my readers. If our foresight is not mistaken, a hundred years from now someone will discover the hundred volumes of the *Second Encyclopedia of Tlön*. Then, English, French, and mere Spanish will disappear from this planet. The world will be Tlön.[75]

The effectiveness of this use of allusion and the dramatic intensity which it provides, is clearly crucial for a writer who has decided that 'the composition of vast books is a laborious and impoverishing extravagance', and therefore 'to pretend that these books already exist, and then to offer a résumé, a commentary'.[76] But this art of the outline, which Borges is supposed to have learnt from essay-writing, is also a typically narrative strategy, one founded on narrative 'desire'. The multiple references, in the narrator's commentary, to memory (in expressions such as 'to remember', 'to partially reproduce', 'only one memorable feature', etc.), and to prediction and speculation ('to calculate', to 'conjecture', 'it is reasonable to suppose', etc.) also function as the narrative filters which turn the discontinuous pattern of notes (the narrator's disjointed report) into a meaningful one, in response to the reader's perception of the text as the desired yet feared progression towards an inevitable end. The narrator's report implies a process of selection and subordination—i.e. of abstraction from the here and now—so that the paratextual structure described previously as a structure of supplementation or a series of metonymic approximations forever displaced from an original object, is also a system of metalinguistic disjunction: it is a mnemonic which is geared towards totalization both retrospectively and prospectively, and designed to guarantee verisimilitude. Alongside the notions of invention, speculation, and imagination, of fortuity and the unaccountability of 'unbelievable systems' which are said to abound in Tlön, the credibility of the fiction relies upon a network of intricate interrelations (references, allusions, quotations from the encyclopedia) by which apparently contingent textual elements which coexist as a result of an association of ideas are nevertheless 'conjoined' according to a certain logic. The notion of 'system' in Tlön is elaborated in relation to that of subordination, or hypostatization, the system being 'the subordination of all aspects of the universe to any one of them'.[77] To abstract is to hypostatize, to draw one aspect out and to lift it above all others: the more elliptical the subordination of whole to part, the more authoritatively

---

[74] Musil, *The Man Without Qualities*, 'If there is such a thing as a sense of reality, there must also be a sense of possibility', i. 12.

[75] Borges, *Fictions*, 32 ['Aquí doy término a la parte personal de mi narración. Lo demás está en la memoria (cuando no en la esperanza o en el temor) de todos mis lectores', *Ficciones*, 34]; and ibid. 33 ['Si nuestras previsiones no yerran, de aquí a cien años alguien descubrirá los cien tomos de la Segunda Enciclopedia de Tlön. Entonces desaparecerán del planeta el inglés, el francés y el mero español. El mundo será Tlön', 36].

[76] Ibid. 13 [12].   [77] Ibid. 24 [24].

the abstracted effect imposes the reality of the described object—whether it exists or not. Both the acknowledgement of the nature of narrative as a process of omission and distortion and the conditions of the verisimilitude of 'Tlön' are in fact created and reinforced by the initial and supposedly 'lengthy' exposition—in the presence of mirrors and friends—of Bioy Casares's 'great scheme for writing a novel in the first person, using a narrator who omitted or corrupted what happened'.[78]

The actualization of the pure ideal world of Tlön in the narrative itself—its narrative 'translation'—necessarily calls for a subjection of the infinite potentiality of its ideas to a contrived and sequential organization. It involves a conflict between chaos (the unchecked proliferation of fragments generated by imagination and speculation to the point of chaotic indistinguishability, such as the Hrönir), and a certain form of order, even when the 'story' is open-ended (when its beginning and ending are only alluded to[79]). The discovery of textual fragments is already depicted in terms of an opposition between what is fragmentary and what is complete, between 'invention' and 'plan' or 'scheme'. The narrator's initial discovery of Volume XI is described as a 'substantial methodical fragment of the complete history of an unknown planet . . . all clearly stated, coherent'.[80] Then follow the narrator's speculation as to the possible creators of that encyclopedia, capable of 'subordinating this invention to a strict systematic plan',[81] and the final remark before the outline of Tlönian principles about the 'apparent contradictions in the eleventh volume' which are 'the basis for proving the existence of the others, so lucid and clear is the scheme maintained in it'.[82] In Tlön itself, the tension between the conceptual claims of the encyclopedia and the arbitrary system of classification—the arbitrary rules of language—which they depend upon, is taken so far that it ceases, apparently, to exist as such: philosophy, metaphysics, and theology display a total submission to the a-logical semiotic links that bring the most incongruous, incompatible elements 'magically'[83] together by simple relations of similarity and difference. On the other hand, contradictions or paradoxa arise from the account of the Tlönian's metaphysical principles. I am not referring to the 'false' contradictions which Borges characteristically points out (e.g. the

---

[78] Ibid. 17 ['una vasta polémica sobre la ejecución de una novela en primera persona, cuyo narrador omitiera o desfigurara los hechos', 13].

[79] Hence what Walter Moser sees as the 'two levels' on which Borges's fictions develop: 'On the episodic level of the narrative action, the initial problem is usually solved and the narrative concluded. On the level of reflective thought, the mystery acquires the dimension of an infinite and insoluble philosophical problem', which leads Moser to state that 'It is this ambivalent balance between the open-ended and the concluded that Borges's narrative pieces share with the genre of the fragment' ('Fragment and Encyclopedia', 112); he concludes that 'there is no final synthesis in this formulation of the dialectic of fragmentation and totalization' (p. 116).

[80] Borges, *Fictions*, 21 [*Ficciones*, 19].

[81] Ibid. 22 ['individuos capaces de subordinar la invención a un riguroso plan sistemático', 20].

[82] Ibid.

[83] For Borges's notion of 'magical causality' which is essential to all his stories and essays, see his essay 'El arte narrativo y la magia', in *Discusión*, 226–32.

surprising multiplication of nouns, philosophies, and sciences in Tlön 'despite' the Tlönians' lack of belief in their justification—which is in fact perfectly consistent), but to the fact that the narrator's description of the Tlönian's allegiance to idealist principles betrays a markedly self-conscious process, the abstracting requirements of which are hardly compatible with the adherence to the only reality of instant present perceptions. Idealism here is presented as a willed doctrine, not as the inescapable human condition. Consciousness becomes it own object: Tlönians, we are told, are acutely aware that materialism is the opposed doctrine (an example of extreme abstraction), a 'scandal' which thinkers have taken upon themselves to 'formulate' and clarify', despite the fact that 'the language of Tlön is by its nature resistant to the formulation of this paradox'. Not only is there a choice in this resistance, but the charge used against the existence of materialism is one of 'verbal fallacy'—an argument which doubly implies the reflection of language upon itself.[84] This reflexiveness achieves new subtleties when we read not only that Tlönians (choose to) consider metaphysics as 'a branch of fantastic literature', but that 'metaphysicians of Tlön *are not looking for* truth or verisimilitude; they seek amazement' (emphasis added).[85] Is this the kind of judgement that was said to operate outside the field of cause and effect, relying only on associations of ideas? Above all, as the narrator/annotator continues immediately thereafter, 'they *know* that a system is nothing other than the subordination of all the aspects of the universe to some one of them' (emphasis added), a statement which, to say the least, seriously questions the refutation of objective truth.[86] This demonstration of abstract thinking is definitively reinforced by the most abstract of considerations, that of the non-acceptance of abstract generalizations formulated in phrases such as 'all aspects of the universe':

Even the phrase 'all the aspects' can be rejected, since it presupposes the impossible inclusion of the present moment, and of past moments . . .

or again

Even so, the plural, 'past moments' is inadmissible, since it supposes another impossible operation.[87]

These remarks lead potentially to endless yet 'impossible' abstractions of abstractions, at the same vertiginous speed with which the Hrönir are mentally multiplied, in spite of the fact that 'each state of mind is irreducible': 'the mere act of giving it a name, that is of classifying it, implies a falsification of it'.[88] The increas-

---

[84] Borges, *Fictions*, 25–6 [*Ficciones*, 24–6].

[85] Ibid. 24 ['Los metafísicos de Tlön no buscan la verdad ni siquiera la verosimilitud: buscan el asombro. Juzgan que la metafísica es una rama de la literatura fantástica', 23–4].

[86] Ibid. ['Saben que un sistema no es otra cosa que la subordinación de todos los aspectos del universo a uno cualquiera de ellos', 24].

[87] Ibid. 24–5 ['Hasta la frase "todos los aspectos" es rechazable, porque supone la imposible adición del instante presente y de los pretéritos'; and 'Tampoco es lícito el plural "los pretéritos", porque supone otra operación imposible', 24].

[88] Ibid. 24 [23].

ing number of clues which enable the narrator and his friends gradually to acquire a total picture of Tlön—concomitantly with the gradual intrusion of Tlön into the whole of reality—also goes together with a shift from the perception of arbitrariness to that of method: 'To begin with, Tlön was thought to be nothing more than a chaos, a free and irresponsible work of the imagination; now it was clear that it is a complete cosmos, and that the strict laws which govern it have been carefully formulated, albeit provisionally.'[89]

The paratextual or essayistic structure of 'Tlön' is representative of the majority of Borges's narratives, since it revolves around the problem of the absent centre or the illusory origin (that of a non-existing country or reality), in a way that draws particular attention, via the encyclopedia, to the 'infinitely decentred structure' of language and writing. Because the unfolding of the story is purely paratextual, 'Tlön' mimes more radically than our essayistic novels the endless supersession of aspects corresponding to the 'wrong excess of history' or 'bad infinite' warned against by Hegel. On the one hand, 'Tlön' subordinates and compromises the endless possibilities of Tlön. On the other, the essaying of Tlönian principles in narrative also corresponds to the 'trying out' of an idealism which has become dogmatic, absolute, or universal (the unreal encompasses the whole of reality); it relativizes idealist principles at the point where indetermination merges into dogmatism, the essay—and by extension essayism—being 'skeptical precisely about general laws, even general laws of skepticism'.[90] Like 'deconstructive textualism' as described by Graham Good, the laws of Tlön finally 'turn into a form of credulity, a naïve *un*realism', for they are founded on the assumption that 'we perceive *nothing but* our own constructs, which we can only endlessly deconstruct and reconstruct'.[91] At the same time, it is through the paratextual structure that the narrator, more unrestrictedly than the essayistic novelist, is able to exploit the space of a utopian realm of the mind or idea, prior to writing, that is, prior to its concretization in narrative. In the margins of narrative, the renewed recontextualizations of the essayistic text enable the narrator always to 'say otherwise', thus emphasizing the fact that reality as we perceive it is only one possible realization among others. In this sense, 'Tlön' is also paradigmatic of the 'absence of history' or of insertion into the concrete world which Hegel also contests. Paratext and text, the ideal world and its actualization, remain distinct, despite the fact that the paratext appears 'in' a text which it constitutes from beginning to end, and this demarcation is yet another reflection of the disjunctive patterns 'or/and' which prevail throughout the story. Although Tlön does not exist independently of 'Tlön' (of its narration) and even though we are all emprisoned by narratives, the abstraction holds throughout, enabling the essayistic structure to suspend the progression of a narrative meaning which it generates and to which it is never-

---

[89] Ibid. 22 ['Al principio se creyó que Tlön era un mero caos, une irresponsable licencia de la imaginación; ahora se sabe que es un cosmos y las intimas leyes que lo rigen han sido formuladas, siquiera en modo provisional', 20].

[90] Graham Good, *The Observing Self: Rediscovering the Essay* (1988), 180–1.

[91] Ibid.

theless subordinated. Between text and paratext which are, yet are not, one and the same thing, in other words, there is both redundancy and anachronism.[92]

6.3. DELIBERATE TECHNIQUES OF ANACHRONISM

It is Pierre Ménard's famous 'technique of deliberate anachronism' which makes him the realizer and challenger of the specifically literary utopia of Tlön. Pierre Ménard is a French Symbolist poet of the beginning of this century whose 'visible' work is 'easily enumerated;[93] it is divided up into the two poles of symbolist poetry and the essayistic work of an editor, annotator, reviewer, anthologist, and translator. But what makes Ménard the author (the 'genius') of a work which is 'possibly the most significant of our time', is his ambition to 'reproduce a few pages which would coincide—word for word and line for line—with those of Miguel de Cervantes'.[94] At the time of the story's narration, Ménard has already produced the ninth and thirty-eighth chapters of part I, and a fragment of the twenty-second chapter. The paratextual 'aberration' which this involves[95] seems to stretch the resources of the Montaignian essayist to—and beyond—their limits, since it is a more than literal implementation of the requisite that the essayist's imagination 'carry [him] out of [himself] into the feelings of others'; that, at its best, the essay be not only the 'imaginative re-creation', but the 'incarnation', whether of 'a man, an epoch, or a form'; that, in other words, the essayist, like Virginia Woolf's 'common reader', 'immerse' himself into the world of the author in an attempt to become him and so do justice to his or her unique individuality.[96] In fact, Borges's story requires more subtly that Ménard dismiss from the outset the all too 'easy' solution of a 'mechanical transcription' or 'copy' of the original text:'he does not want to compose another *Don Quixote* but *the Don Quixote*',[97] for it seems to him that 'to be, in some way, Cervantes, and to arrive at *Don Quixote* is 'less arduous— and consequently less interesting—than to continue being Pierre Ménard and to arrive at *Don Quixote* through the experiences of Pierre Ménard'.[98] Ménard thus rejects the Romantic notion of total identification with the author, and his text

---

[92] Interesting readings of 'Tlön, Uqbar, Orbis Tertius' include: Jaime Alazraki, 'Tlön y asterión: Metáforas epistemológicas', in *La prosa narrativa de Borges* (1983); Walter Mignolo, 'Emergencia, Espacio, "Mundos Posibles": Las Propuestas Epistemológicas de Jorge L. Borges', *Revista Iberoamericana*, 43 (1977); Frances Wyers Weber, 'Borges's Stories: Fiction and Philosophy', *Hispanic Review*, 36 (1968); James E. Irby, 'Borges and the Idea of Utopia', in L. Dunham and Ivar Ivask (eds.), *The Cardinal Points of Borges* (1971); Suzanne Jill Levine, 'Adolfo Bioy Casares y Jorge Luis Borges: La Utopía como Texto', *Revista Iberoamericana*, 43 (1977); Gérard Genette, 'L'Utopie littéraire', *Figures*, ii (1969); Stefania Mosca, *Utopía y realidad* (1983); Louis Marin, *Utopics: Spatial Play* (1984); and Pierre Jourde, *Géographies imaginaires: De quelques inventeurs du mondes au XXe siècle (Gracq, Borges, Michaux, Tolkien)* (1991).

[93] Borges, *Fictions*, 42 [*Ficciones*, 47].   [94] Ibid. 45 [52].

[95] See Compagnon, *La Seconde Main*, 366 and 370.   [96] See section 1.2 of Ch. 1.

[97] Borges, *Fictions*, 45 ['No quería componer otro Quijote—lo cual es fácil—sino el *Quijote*', *Ficciones*, 52].

[98] Ibid. 46 [53].

becomes an exceptionally long quotation, the outrageousness of which highlights the primary rule of all intertextual practice, namely that 'redundancy' or 'tautology' is a notion relative to the statement, never to the utterance which remains a unique, and unrepeatable event. The irreducible difference at the level of enunciation—the anachronism itself—is therefore maintained even (and all the more palpably) in the case of the relationship between two identical texts.[99] The result is that 'the text of Cervantes and that of Ménard are verbally identical, but the latter is almost infinitely richer':[100] 'Ménard (perhaps without wishing to) has enriched, by means of a new technique, the hesitant and rudimentary art of reading: the technique is one of deliberate anachronism and erroneous attributions.'[101]

If the 'fantastic' aspect of 'Tlön, Uqbar, Orbis Tertius' lay in the 'realization' of an idealist world, the fantastic dimension of 'Pierre Ménard, Author of Don Quixote' also lies in the realization of the Tlönian conception of literature, where all books are the permutations of a single book—the author of which is timeless and anonymous—and where therefore plagiarism does not exist.[102] In fact, the actualization of this impossible citational practice is again only alluded to, 'as though' it had been done. The most significant part of Ménard's work remains 'invisible', and this is precisely what establishes its affiliation to the idealist world of Tlön, where 'to be' is to be perceived, thought of, or imagined, where, in other words, one only needs to think or imagine something for it to be real or true. To modify perception in literature is to modify everything; since the text has no independent existence, it varies with each reading of it: 'one literature differs from another, either before or after it, not so much because of the text as for the manner in which it is read'—as Borges puts it in one of his essays.[103] Literature is a 'reversible' and 'curved' space where 'individual specificity and chronological precedence' do not apply. Hence the possibility, at any moment, of the 'most unexpected' and 'paradoxical' encounters,[104] which not only generates the banal situation where Ménard is the contemporary of Cervantes, but where 'each writer *creates* his precursors', and where 'his work modifies our conception of the past, as it will modify the future'.[105] If the time of a work is not the 'definite time of its

[99] ['La redondance, ou la tautologie, est une notion (logique) relative à l'énoncé et non à l'énonciation: quant à l'énonciation, cet événement singulier, il ne saurait y avoir de redondance. Dans la mesure où il n'y a pas d'énoncé sans énonciation . . . et où le système du texte comprend l'énoncé et l'énonciation . . . deux textes, à admettre que leurs énoncés soient identiques, ne demeureraient pas moins dans une irréductible différence qui ne tiendrait plus qu'à l'énonciation', Compagnon, *La Seconde Main*, 57].

[100] Borges, *Fictions*, 49 ['El texto de Cervantes y el de Ménard son verbalmente idénticos, pero el segundo es casi infinitamente más rico', *Ficciones*, 56].

[101] Ibid. 51 ['Ménard (acaso sin quererlo) ha enriquecido mediante una técnica nueva el arte detenido y rudimentario de la lectura: la técnica del anacronismo deliberado y de las atribuciones erroneas', 59].

[102] Ibid. 27–8 ['Es raro que los libros estén firmados. No existe el concepto del plagio . . .', 28].

[103] ['Una literatura difiere de otra menos por el texto que por la manera de ser leída', Borges, 'Nota sobre (hacia) Bernard Shaw', *Otras Inquisiciones*, 747].

[104] Genette, 'L'Utopie littéraire', in *Figures*, ii. 125 and 131.

[105] ['El hecho es que cada escritor *crea* a sus precursores. Su labor modifica nuestra concepción del pasado, como ha de modificar el futuro', Borges, 'Kafka y sus precursores', *Obras completas*, 712].

writing', but the 'indefinite time of reading', its author has no special power over it; the meaning of his work is 'ahead of it rather than behind it'.[106] The literary past of a text is its future, the relationship of 'influence' being one of pure retroaction, not anticipation. The genesis of a work in the time and history of its author's life is 'the most contingent and insignificant moment of its duration':[107] '*Don Quixote*', Ménard justifies, 'is an accidental book, *Don Quixote* is unnecessary. I can pre-meditate writing, I can write it, without incurring a tautology.'[108] So the above-mentioned apology of the (fakely modest) writer's attitude which consists in his disclaiming all paternity and all rights with regard to what he has written except those of a translator or reader, serves to proclaim the superiority of reading as 'an activity posterior to that of writing: more resigned, more civil(ized), more intellectual'.[109] It casts the 'timid' activity of the reader as the most 'violent' form of 'appropriation' and 'theft'.[110] In *Pierre Ménard*, the utmost faithfulness connoted by the intertextual practice of the 'copy' (and thus of the model, with all its mimetic implications), is coupled with the utmost unfaithfulness of an empirical or contingent reader (as opposed to a transcendental or 'implied' reader) whose active participation is such, that 'non-writing' becomes equivalent to 'rewriting'. As with *S/Z*, writing as 'rereading' 'alone saves the text from repetition' and draws it 'out of its internal chronology'.[111] And in so far as it functions as a fragment wrenched from its initial context and chronology, Ménard's long quotation contributes to foregrounding the interpolation and play on digression characteristic of essaying, and which derives from the assumption that all thought is circumstantial and everchanging—that 'one cannot see the whole of anything' (which would also apply if *Don Quixote* were to be read and rewritten as a whole). The actualization, by Ménard, of one of the novel's many virtual meanings or versions among the boundless reserve of additional glosses which exceeds it, emphasizes that, contrary to the quantifiable, visible work of writing, the invisible work of reading is indeed incommensurable. In this respect, Borges's choice of a work of such inexhaustible fecundity for world literature as *Don Quixote* for what Genette calls his '*excessive*' conception of literature, could not be more apt. For this is a work which blatantly stages its own 'difference from itself', i.e. the question of its own self-identity (including not least the question of authorship) through an internal 'dialogue' of forms and a continuing process of recontextualization by which reading and writing are merged.

[106] Genette, 'L'Utopie littéraire', 132 and 126.   [107] Ibid. 132.

[108] Borges, *Fictions*, 47 ['El Quijote es un libro contingente, el Quijote es innecesario. Puedo premeditar su escritura, puedo escribirlo, sin incurrir en una tautología', *Ficciones*, 56].

[109] ['Leer . . . es una actividad posterior a la de escribir: más resignada, más civil, más intelectuál', Borges, Prologue to the first edition of *Historia universal de la infamia* (1935), 289].

[110] In Compagnon's pattern, the citational value of the *icône*—which is identified with the classical economy of writing—bears the following characteristics: 'L'icône est une citation qui qualifie le citateur lui-même: il assume une énonciation propre malgré la reprise; le pastiche, la citation implicite, la reminiscence sont d'ordre icônique: des paroles secondes qui revendiquent leur identité, leur spécialité dans la similarité, par l'appropriation, la mainmise, la violence' (Compagnon, *La Seconde Main*, 79).

[111] Barthes, *S/Z*, IX, 'How Many Readings?', 16.

Borges himself, who is known to have begun his writing activities by imitating Cervantes,[112] displays a life-long inclination towards 'exercises of anachronism' which 'do not restitute the difficult past' but induce 'speculations and digressions'.[113] Since he rewrites others and himself, his work looks like a set of variations on, or versions of a given number of topics, a game of shifting mirrors which combines the infinitely extendable 'permutations'—in Tlönian terms—of one book. Like Barthes's work, in this sense, Borges's writings constitute a ' "repertory" of critical themes' intended for the 'virtual creator' in every reader.[114] The world of rewriting is one in which the text that is rewritten is neither completely the same nor completely other, as the title of the sequel to the volume of essays *Inquisiciones*, '*Otras Inquisiciones*', suggests. This self-translation ensures that not only every text and genre, but every writer, linguistic form, theme, character, rhetorical figure, is the appearance of another, a modification, a version, a 'pseudo', which will thus necessarily be subjected, as in Barthes, to the perspectivistic game of the 'presenting oneself as'. All modes of internal repetition are deployed via transcriptions to other contexts, recontextualizations within a genre or between one genre and another in the case of transgeneric mutations.[115] Notes or postscripts such as the ones found in 'Tlön, Uqbar, Orbis Tertius', or in 'The Approach to Al-Mu'tasim', are interpretive (or counter-interpretive) gestures which already allude to other textual or generic virtualities: in 'Tlön', the story we have been reading suddenly turns into the reprint of an article published in the *Anthology of Fantastic Literature*, while in the postscript appended to 'The Approach', interpretation is sought— only to be rejected—in the direction of a poem by a Persian mystic (*Colloquy of Birds*). According to the very logic by which Ménard reproduces fragments of *Don Quixote*, it is common, in Borges's own work, to find the identical repetition of specific lines, sequences, or pages in different texts, or a repetition of these lines or sequences with slight transpositions (reductions, amplifications, or other kinds of distortion), within or between volumes of essays and fictions,[116] thus presenting the reader with a few possible actualizations of the virtual meanings which already exceed the 'original'. The most flagrant cases of transcription are those which involve entire texts, as when books themselves are published under different titles (*Antiguas Literaturas Germánicas* (1951) becomes *Literaturas Germánicas Medievales* (1966), and *Manuel de Zoología fantástica* (1957) becomes *El Libro de Seres Imaginarios* (1967)), or when an entire essay initially published in a volume

[112] See Lelia Madrid, *Cervantes y Borges: La inversión de los signos* (1987).

[113] Prologue to Borges's volume of essays *Discusión*: 'resignados ejercicios de anacronismo: no restituyen el dificil pasado—operan y divagan con él' (Borges, *Obras Completas*, 177).

[114] Barthes, *The Grain of the Voice*, 26.

[115] 'Monsters', for Michel Lafon, the monster being 'a hypertextualized animal which has suffered transmutation' (*Borges ou La Réécriture*, 32).

[116] Or both, e.g.: 'Me sentí muerto, me sentí percibidor abstracto del mundo: indefinido temor imbuido de ciencia que es la mejor claridad de la metafísica', which appears in identical form in both *Historia de la Eternidad*, 366–7, and *Otras Inquisiciones*, 765, and, slightly transposed, in *Ficciones*, 107: 'Me sentí, por un tiempo indeterminado, percibidor abstracto del mundo' (translated as: 'For an undetermined period of time I felt myself cut off from the world, an abstract spectator', *Fictions*, 85).

of essays reappears word for word in a volume of fictions, as with 'The Approach to Al-Mu'tasim'.[117]

These duplications could be perceived as the ultimate consequence of the essayist's lack of memory and of his unwillingness to correct: Montaigne, after all, alleges that 'In these ravings of mine, what I fear is that my treacherous memory should make me inadvertently record the same thing twice', and that 'Repetition is always a bore'.[118] In fact, they are recontextualizations which constantly challenge the self-identity of any one text or genre, and of Borges's work as a whole, and which go hand in hand with the staging of the author and his 'others', as expressed by titles such as 'Borges y yo' [*Borges and I*] (in *El Hacedor*, 1960) or *El otro, el mismo* [*The Other, The Same*] (1964). As with Montaigne and Barthes, the dialectic of same and other begins with the 'dispersion' or 'diffraction' of the subject by way of a confrontation with the intertext. The essayist's position of enunciation is the living proof that 'selfhood cannot be grasped independently', that it 'can only be configured with an object',[119] to the point—as we have seen—where the essayist 'tells himself only through what surpasses, goes through, and denies him'.[120] If only because one can probably never 'begin to write without taking oneself for another',[121] the 'I' can only be grasped as another and via the other—whether this 'other' exists or is to come—analogically, metaphorically. In Borges, this is put down to the absence of new subject-matters, which requires the writer to experiment with and complexify 'point of view' or diegesis. In this sense, 'narrations' would be a more appropriate title for Borges's 'fictions', as critics have often pointed out, since what the latter mainly do is to stage a narration, which, precisely, relies on the recurring landscape of fiction to try itself out and enjoy the paradigmatic pleasure of variation. The mysterious play of voices which results from these exercises are translations of the self which recall the Montaignian and Barthesian 'drifting' of the subject among an evanescent plurality of personae—all masks of the essayist's 'impostures'—from the seemingly most authentic figure of the essayist or scholar to the explicitly fictional character, given that in his fictions Borges overwhelmingly favours the first-person narrative.[122] The confrontation of essay and narrative fiction within any one story usually makes possible the reader's adjustment to what I referred to in Chapter 1 as 'the emerging aspects of the essayist's *fictional self*'.[123] The atopian shift between contexts of enunciation, so well illustrated by 'The Approach', is again made possible by the existence of 'shifters', the markers of enunciation which are, as we know, non-referential and therefore 'always available' to any speaker as the prerequisites of 'intersubjective communication'; for—as Benveniste points out—'if in order to express his

---

[117] These are only a few of the permutations listed above all in Michel Lafon in *Borges ou La Réécriture*.

[118] Montaigne, 'On Vanity', *Essays*, III. 9, p. 1089 ['La redicte est partout ennuyeuse', 'De la vanité', *Essais*, III. ix, 939*b*].

[119] Good, *The Observing Self*, 22.   [120] Beaujour, *Poetics of the Literary Self-Portrait*, 35.

[121] Barthes, *Roland Barthes by Roland Barthes*, 'What is Influence?', 206.

[122] Cf. Borges, 'La nadería de la personalidad', in *Inquisiciones*.   [123] Klaus, 'Essay', 8.

irreducible subjectivity each speaker had at his disposal a distinct marker, there would be as many languages as there are individuals, and communication would become strictly impossible'.[124] Language solves the problem by creating a group of 'mobile' or 'empty' signs which are 'filled in' every time a speaker takes them over; and it is by identifying themselves as a unique invidual saying 'I' that each one of the speakers in turn can claim to be the 'subject' of his discourse.[125] The 'filling in' of these 'empty' or 'virtual' signs is described in Benveniste as a 'process of appropriation',[126] one which enables Pierre Ménard to appropriate *Don Quixote*, and the Borges of *Fictions* to appropriate 'The Approach' in its previous form. By extension, this is the process of appropriation which defines one's use of language and texts generally, in the terms of Bakhtin's 'dialogism':

Language, for the individual consciousness, lies on the borderline between oneself and the other. The word in language is half someone else's. It becomes 'one's own' only when the speaker populates it with his own intention, his own accent, when he appropriates the word, adapting it to his own semantic and expressive intention. Prior to this moment of appropriation, the word does not exist in a neutral and impersonal language . . . but rather it exists in other peoples's mouths, in other people's contexts, serving other people's intentions: it is from there that one must take the word, and make it one's own. Language is not a neutral medium that passes freely and easily into the private property of the speaker's intentions; it is populated—overpopulated—with the intentions of others.[127]

In the previous chapter, we saw that 'subjectivity cannot be defined outside the text: in the same way that the "I" of discourse only refers to a context of enunciation, the present tense which also characterizes "discourse" does not refer to a "reality" or "objective position in time and space" (signalled by deictics such as "here" or "now"), but to the moment at which that discourse is held.'[128] And both Montaigne and Barthes have shown that the acknowledgement and maximization of this fact corresponds to their—and our—perception of the writer's 'modernity': 'The modern scriptor is born *at the same time* as his text; he is not furnished with a being which precedes or exceeds his writing, he is not the subject of which his book is the predicate; there is no time other than that of the speech-act, and every text is written eternally *here* and *now*.'[129] What, for Benveniste, applies to discourse in the limited sense can thus be made to apply to discourse generally: because those signs (shifters) are 'devoid of material reference', because they are 'not subjected to truth-requirements', they 'cannot be misused' and 'evade all denial'.[130] However, Ménard's 'technique of deliberate anachronism', like Borges's, necessarily implies 'misuse' and 'denial' on some level which enables the displacement of one

---

[124] Benveniste, *Problémes de linguistique générale*, i. 272.   [125] Ibid.   [126] Ibid.

[127] Mikhail Bakhtin, 'Discourse in the Novel', in Michael Holquist (ed.), *The Dialogic Imagination: Four Essays by M. M. Bakhtin* (1990), 293–4.

[128] Genette, 'Frontiers of Narrative', 138–9.   [129] Barthes, *The Rustle of Language*, 52.

[130] ['Dépourvus de référence matérielle, ils ne peuvent pas être mal employés; n'assertant rien, ils ne sont pas soumis à la condition de vérité et échappent à toute dénégation', Benveniste, *Problèmes de linguistique générale*, i. 272].

text by the other to be perceived as a displacement, and which summons up the spatial and temporal circumstances in which the 'original' text was written. It is 'legitimate'—as the narrator states towards the end of the story—'to consider the "final" *Don Quixote* as a kind of palimpsest, in which should appear traces—tenuous but not undecipherable—of the "previous" handwriting of our friend'.[131] The irony behind the passing reference to these 'tenuous but not undecipherable' traces is characteristic. However slight, anachronism involves by definition the representation of an event in a historical context in which it could not have occurred or existed; but the shift, here, is of course spectacular. The time and cultural environment in which a text like *Don Quixote* can be written and represent a plausible subject-matter, as well as the connected generic and stylistic conventions of the period which determine the handling of the subject-matter in a more or less accepted way, are more than 'tenuously' at stake. Moreover, the comical and archaic enterprise which results from these temporal and spatial displacements also relies in characteristically essayistic fashion on the discrepancy between Cervantes's literary grandeur and genius and the insignificant little essayist/poet whose turn it is, in Benveniste's scheme, to fill in the 'empty' deictic signs with the 'plenitude' of a discourse which he must now 'assume'. This choice of a marginal author and of the indispensability of his paratextual activity—in relation to the literary canon—raises again the question of the 'essence' of a literature which accredits the notion that it is eternal or 'natural', that it 'goes without saying'.[132]

It is precisely the gap between the discursive markers and an 'objectivity in time and space' which these markers also record, which makes possible the play between the linguistic subjects of both Cervantes and Ménard which are interchangeable, and the authorial subjects which are not, thus safeguarding the paradox behind the story's logic that 'while everyone is Cervantes, no one else is'. And this for the very reason that meaning, which from the time of the *Essais* is no longer seen as transcending history, must be grasped in its historically, culturally limited context. In short, 'Pierre Ménard' illustrates the awareness that 'texts are *relative* to contexts', but also that 'contexts *determine* texts'.[133] This point is very well argued in Juliet Sychrova's book on idealist aesthetics, in which she asserts that the deconstructionist principle that 'where a text is rendered determinate or closed by its context, it is never in fact limited, for any context will itself be limited by a context and so on without end'[134] can—and must—be countered by the fact that 'if', for instance, 'we draw a frame round a picture, our idea of what is art can certainly be questioned. But nevertheless, given that idea, the frame does determine the picture: what is in the frame is a picture, given the conventions of

---

[131] Borges, *Fictions*, 50 ['He reflexionado que es lícito ver en el Quijote "final" una especie de palimpsesto, en él que deben trasladirse los rastros—tenues pero no indescifrables—de la "previa" escritura de nuestro amigo', *Ficciones*, 58].

[132] Barthes, *Critical Essays*, 250 [*Essais critiques*, 247].

[133] Juliet Sychrava, *From Schiller to Derrida: Idealism in Aesthetics* (1989), 164.

[134] Ibid. 177. Cf. Culler's definition of deconstruction as the 'twin principles of the contextual determination of meaning and the infinite extendability of context'.

framing'.[135] The frame, then—Sychrava continues—'need not be considered . . .
as a frame-up, an interpretive imposition that restricts an object by establishing
boundaries'—which is how Culler summarizes Derrida's view in 'The Parergon'—
'but as a useful and necessary way of making critical distinctions and thinking
systematically at all'.[136] In other words, one can read

'reflectively' or outwards, from text to context, to context-of-context—and this will always
reveal the instability of meaning. But it is also possible to read 'determinately' or inwards,
from context-of-context, to context, to text, and this is perhaps more like the way in which
we usually—as readers, not as critics—read.[137]

In this sense, 'Pierre Ménard' implements the 'double' perspective, defended by
Sychrava and which 'combines a critique of the text as context-*relative*, with an
acceptance of the text as context-*determined*', by virtue of the fact that

Literary texts are at once relative to the system that produces them, revealing in their
apparent design the textual processes that give them meaning, create them and the results
of that system, limited and determined by it

and that

It is just because the system does have limited, meaningful results or products and rules that
give those products meaning, that it is a system at all. The detection of the process in the
product does not make it any less a stable product.[138]

So paratextual law and perversion are shown mutually to include one another:
between the inside and the outside of *Don Quixote*, Ménard's apparently 'immanent' or 'reflexive' reading which emphasizes the 'relative, self-referential, unstable, processual aspect' of the text also relies on what immanent or reflexive
criticism usually ignores: 'what the text means specifically, locally, historically, in
a particular spatial and temporal context' and, therefore, 'what differentiates it
from another'.[139] The consequence is that beyond the discursive subject which is
each time unique to the particular instance of enunciation, one does not find an
'irreducible subjectivity'—in Benveniste's words—but a concept of authority which
is definable above all in terms of what Edward Said calls 'explicit and implicit rules
of pertinence' and by which a word, text, or set of texts can be recognized as belonging to a particular discourse.[140] The authority of authorship is neither absolutely
necessary nor absolutely accidental; hence Said's appropriate notion of 'contingent
authority' which perhaps best sums up the paradoxical implications of Pierre
Ménard: 'One aspect of authorship is its contingent authority, its ability to initiate

---

[135] Sychrava, *From Schiller to Derrida*, 178.   [136] Ibid. 182.
[137] Ibid. 181.   [138] Ibid. 193.   [139] Ibid. 163.
[140] 'Every sort of writing establishes explicit and implicit rules of pertinence for itself. I call these
rules *authority* both in the sense of explicit law and guiding force . . . and in the sense of that implicit
power to generate another word that will *belong* to the writing as a whole (Vico's etymology is *auctor:
autos: suis ipsius: propsius: property*)' (Said, *Beginnings: Intention and Method*, 16).

or build structures whose absolute authority is radically nil, but whose contingent authority is a quite satisfactory transitory alternative to the absolute truth.'[141] Ménard's performance is ultimately a 'fiction' for two seemingly opposed, yet inseparable reasons. First, because origins are fictions, in the sense of 'lie' and 'forgery': the text cannot be attributed any more to Ménard than it is attributed to Cervantes, the act of quoting being the reminder that writing is always displaceable from its 'proper' place, and that the signs filled with the particularity and unique-ness of each enunciation are unrestrainedly mobile, available to all. Ménard is the author of *Don Quixote* in the same way that every reader is. Yet Ménard's perform-ance is also impossible because fictions do, to some extent, have origins, or, rather, because origins are *necessary fictions*,[142] so that his appropriation of *Don Quixote* can only be enacted in the virtual dimension of a fictional and/or theoretical text.[143]

Like Ménard's *Don Quixote*, 'The Approach' is a palimpsest in which 'traces—tenuous but not undecipherable—of the previous handwriting of . . . [Borges]', appear. Here, the two absolutely identical texts confront the two anachronistically related modes of enunciation of the essayist and of the fiction-writer within Borges's work. And the 'difference' between the two modes of enunciations remains 'irre-ducible', for although world and self are only the fictional constructs of a multi-plicity of linguistically determined perceptions, this multiplicity is itself primarily dependent on the idea or shifting metaphor of time. Borges remains 'a human being anchored by an oppressive sense of reality and historical time' (and by an oppressive sense of his own consciousness), a reader who, like every reader, is 'part of a timeless eternal return and adamantly not so because of the trap of history and time-bound sensibility'.[144] This is how Borges suspends the reflexive implications not just of his essay 'A new refutation of time', of which this is the famous conclusion, but of his work as a whole:

And yet, and yet . . . Denying temporal succession, denying the self, denying the astronomi-cal universe, are apparent desperations and secret consolations. Our destiny . . . is not frightful by being unreal; it is frightful because it is irreversible and iron-clad. Time is the substance I am made of. Time is the river which sweeps me along, but I am the river; it is a tiger which destroys me, but I am the tiger; it is a fire which consumes me, but I am the fire. The world, unfortunately, is real; I, unfortunately, am Borges.[145]

---

[141] Said, *Beginnings*, 86; see also 23.   [142] Ibid. 50.

[143] On 'Pierre Ménard, author of Don Quixote', see Alicia Borinsky, 'Re-escribir y Escribir: Arenas, Ménard, Borges, Cervantes, Fray Servando', *Revista Iberoamericana*, 41 (1975), 605–16; Compagnon, *La Seconde Main*, 375 ff.

[144] Dipple, 'Borges: The Old Master', in *The Unresolvable Plot*, 53 and 63.

[145] Transl. James Irby ['*And yet, and yet . . .* Negar la sucesión temporal, negar el yo, negar el universo astronómico, son desesperaciones aparentes y consuelos secretos. Nuestro destino . . . no es espantoso por irreal; es espantoso porque es irreversible y de hierro. El tiempo es la sustancia de que estoy hecho. El tiempo es un río que me arrebata, pero yo soy el río; es un tigre que me destroza, pero yo soy el tigre; es un fuego que me consume, pero yo soy el fuego. El mundo, desgraciadamente, es real; yo, desgraciadamente, soy Borges', Borges, 'Nueva refutación del tiempo', *Obras Completas*, 771].

Radical philosophical idealism theorizes the dissolution of generic—textual, authorial—boundaries. It is a 'sufficient unreason' which, in Compagnon's words, 'erects contingence into necessity, accomplishing all virtualities; but it retains the sense of necessity, of truth which it does not threaten'; thus the 'efficiency' of the 'principle of identity' is improved rather than rejected.[146] The decision to honour or to subvert a generic contract necessarily requires something like an 'intrinsic genre' and the notion that, to some extent, every text, like the *Essais*, is 'the only one of its kind' [*unique en son genre*]. By (re-)affirming his 'reality', Borges safeguards the tension between the 'authentic' subject and the linguistic, discursive subject(s) which, as in the *Essais*, makes possible the retrospective (the 'previous' handwriting of our friend) identification or appropriation of the multiplicity of fragmentary selves by the unifying instance of the (contingent) authority described above. In other words, rules of 'pertinence' and 'belonging' make Borges's work identifiable as that of a single mind, despite and with the contribution of the paratextual proliferations by which it is continuously 'essayed' on its own margins, and even though this unity is clearly one of 'process rather than stasis'.[147]

In the end, the question which is raised in every one of Borges's writings is not whether a fragment belongs to this or that text, or to this or that literary genre, but whether or not it is 'true' (authentic) or fictitious; and in Borges's work, this distinction is encompassed by the main opposition between 'essay' ('doomed to *authenticity*—to the preclusion of quotation-marks', that is, 'condemned to error—truth'[148]) and 'fiction'. We have seen that, regardless of their external generic markers as essays or as fiction (which usually amounts to their being integrated in a volume of essays or in a volume of fictions), Borges's texts continue to pose the question of their truth or of their fictitiousness from the inside. This is the sense in which these texts are neither 'real' stories, nor 'real' essays, but a 'feigning' on both sides, 'fictions' in both cases.[149] Nevertheless, these fictions—which include the 'fiction' of theoretical speculation—also refer us to the real conventions which, in practice, make both this feigning and its perception possible. Essays of fictions and fictions of essays are produced, which rely on the complex staging of the real-in-fiction, the fictitious-in-the-real, and the fictitious-in-fiction. Indeed, our perception of the external distinction between essay and fiction is inseparable from our perception of what essay and fiction contribute to each other within any one text, and from our awareness of the way in which we are made 'constantly' to 'readjust' our expectations 'between what we demand of fiction and what we relie upon in criticism'.[150] We have had plenty of opportunities, in this and previous chapters, to examine fiction's contribution to the essay. In Chapter 1, I suggested that the word 'essay' (of a literary essay) already disorientates the reader's horizon of expectations, for if it is associated with the authority and authenticity of someone who speaks in his or her own name, it also disclaims all responsibility with regard to

---

[146] Compagnon, *La Seconde Main*, 380.   [147] Christ, *The Narrow Act*, 102.

[148] Barthes, *Roland Barthes*, 'Fatigue and Freshness', 89; and *Critical Essays*, Preface, p. xxi.

[149] Christ, *The Narrow Act*, 100.   [150] Ibid. 108.

what is after all only tried out and which is therefore closer, in a sense, to the 'as if' of fiction.[151] To present the essay straight out 'as' fiction, here, is clearly to let the literary and sceptical dimension of the philosophy which determines the genre express itself to the full. At the same time, it draws attention to the 'license' which is taken with the reader's preconceptions in practice, however wise he may be about the ambivalence of the genre theoretically. Fiction is in other words used to undermine the fictional dimension of the essay as forcefully as it is used to underline it. The essay's contribution to fiction is analogous. For Borges's fictions constantly parade their own fictitiousness; and a successful demonstration of fiction's fictitiousness depends on the foregrounding of the referential and the pragmatic contexts which the essay, precisely, is supposed to reinforce. In this sense, Borges's fictions implement the Searlean precept that they only 'pretend' to conform to the specific semantic and pragmatic rules which characterize the non-fictional statement, not occasioned and determined by a historically real context.[152] From the point of view of reading, the 'as if' of fiction is broken down into its constituent stages (the paradoxical 'is, yet is not' of fiction) in exactly the same way, according to the idea that 'competent reading of fiction has to pass from quasi-pragmatic reception to higher forms of reception which alone can do justice to the specific status of fiction'—in other words that:

The reading of fictional texts does not demand an entirely different form of reception, but rather one that asks the reader to take an additional step, which is made necessary by the very status of fiction itself. In order to apprehend fiction, the reader first has to receive it as mimesis in the type of quasi-pragmatic reading.[153]

---

[151] Cf. Tzvetan Todorov in *Critique de la critique: Un Roman d'apprentissage*, 41: 'En tant qu'énoncés, l'essai et le roman divergent: l'un se réfère au monde de individus, l'autre pas; mais ils se ressemblent dans le monde de leur énonciation: ici et là un discours non assumé, une fiction.'

[152] What this amounts to, for John Searle, is that (1) the maker of the statement does not commit himself to the truth of the expressed assertion, (2) that he does not, therefore, have to be in the position to provide evidence or reasons for the truth of the expressed statement, and (3) that the expressed proposition need not be obviously true to both the speaker and the hearer in the context of utterance, 'The Logical Status of Fictional Discourse', *New Literary History*, 6 (1975), 322. See also Barbara Herrnstein-Smith, *On the Margins of Discourse: The Relation of Literature to Language* (1978), 21, 33, and 36. The problematization of utterance and context in modern fiction (and theory) reflected by the special concern with speech-act theories, pragmatics, and discourse analysis, is what Linda Hutcheon appropriately refers to as the 'revenge of *parole*', in *A Poetics of Post-Modernism* (1988), 168, and what prompts Jonathan Culler to remark that the consideration of fiction as imitation speech act or the claim that literary works are fictional speech acts 'paradoxically urges us to treat narrators as though they were real people', *Framing the Sign* (1988), 210 and 216. The questions which I briefly touch upon here are developed at length in Jon K. Adams, *Pragmatics and Fiction* (1985); Wolfgang Iser, 'Akte des Fingierens, oder: was ist das Fiktive im fiktionalen Text?', in *Poetik und Hermeneutik* (1983); Geoffrey Leech, *Principles of Pragmatics* (1983); Stephen C. Levinson, *Pragmatics* (1983); Felix Martínez-Bonati, *Fictive Discourse and the Structures of Literature: A Phenomenological Approach* (1981); Marie-Louise Pratt, *Toward a Speech-Act Theory of Literary Discourse* (1977); and Rainer Warning, 'Staged Discourse: Remarks on the Pragmatics of Fiction', *Dispositio*, 5 (1980), 35–54.

[153] Karlheinz Stierle, 'The Reading of Fictional Texts', in Susan Suleiman and Inge Crossman (eds.), *The Reader in the Text: Essays in Audience and Interpretation* (1980), 87 and 92.

Borges's fiction insists on its conceptual or philosophical claims in order to show how aware it is of its illusory character. The liminary position of the gloss (notes, comments, bibliographical lists, postscripts, etc.) which forms the substance of most of Borges's tales, draws attention to just this contradiction. Both readers and theorists tend to rely on a distinction between the 'non-subversive' status of the gloss or footnote in non-fiction, and its 'subversive' function in fiction. In non-fiction, the gloss is intended to reduce obliquities, affirming the relation of part to whole, constantly refining its interventions towards an ever fuller interpretation of the text until the overall revelation of the latter's truth, which is also its closure. In fiction, on the contrary, the gloss, often referred to as 'marginalia', promotes digression and thus ambiguates the relationship between part and whole in a way that precludes finality. By directing itself 'inwards' rather than 'outwards', the fictional footnote or gloss subverts rather than guarantees the latter's credibility.[154] The overall fictional frame of Borges's tales emphasizes the fact that 'there is no longer anything outside the text'. And yet it is precisely by considering the paratext as paratext, and not just as the text or fiction which it constitutes from beginning to end, that justice can be done to the enactment of the critical relation within a fictional frame, that is, to the respective exploitation of the conventions of criticism and the possibilities of fiction.

So, one could say that Borges's use of essayism results in the extreme refinement of the techniques of fiction, while conversely, Borgesian fiction offsets the essay's potential in ways never explored before. In this sense, the Tlönian conditions by which one only needs to think or imagine something for it to be true, converges with and furthers the procedures of a modern genre criticism which, as I pointed out in Chapter 1, 'attempts to describe a few basic types of literature that *can* be written, not numerous kinds of work that *have* or, in the critic's view, *should* have been written'.[155] More pragmatically, what is stressed here is that the underlying presuppositions and conventions which inform our perception of distinct genres are necessarily 'in excess' of each genre respectively: the self-identity of each genre cannot be recognized otherwise than through its difference from itself. And this undeniably applies to those more 'straightforward', 'monologic', or 'aphoristic' essays which I have left out of this study, and which would no doubt gain from being read or rewritten in Ménard-like fashion. To conclude, anachronism seems to be the key to both the essay's displacement and to its survival. Adorno only focuses on the former, pessimistic aspect: the 'relevance of the essay'—he declares at the beginning of his own essay—'is that of anachronism'; 'the hour is more unfavourable to it than ever'.[156] Whether this is because 'our times correspond less

---

[154] See Shari Benstock, 'At the Margin of Discourse: Footnotes in the Fictional Text', *PMLA* 98 (1983), 204–25; Lawrence Lipking, 'The Marginal Gloss', *Critical Inquiry*, 3–4 (1977), 609–55; Susan Stewart, *Nonsense: Aspects of Intertextuality in Folklore and Literature* (1979), 74 and 108; and 'Les Notes', in Genette, *Seuils*.

[155] Paul Hernadi, *Beyond Genre: New Directions in Literary Classifications* (1972), 184.

[156] Adorno, trans. Hullot-Kentor, 170: 'Die Aktualität des Essays ist die des Anachronistischen. Die Stunde ist ihm ungünstiger als je', Adorno, 'Der Essay als Form', 47.

to the form of the essay than to essayism as a structure of thought which is expressed formally in narrative literature'—as Dieter Bachmann asserts at the end of his book on 'essay and essayism'[157]—or whether the 'contemporary displacement of the essay' can be seen to result in the 'fading' of the genre, 'as if in parasitic refuge', into not only the 'everchanging textures of fiction' but also those of journalism and criticism,[158] a genre so directly identified with bourgeois individualism can hardly be expected to survive the generalized 'dehumanization' of modern relations, one which, according to Peter Earle, 'has far exceeded the modest apprehensions of Ortega y Gasset in 1925'.[159] 'Something in the air and in recent literary theory and criticism abhors the essay', Earle notes, and sees both structuralism and post-structuralism as having had a 'hand in its decline' since about 1950.[160] And this comes down to the fact that the essay 'has not made, together with the major genres, the conceptual leap from language as a manifestation of reality to reality as a manifestation of language'.[161] Yet unlike Adorno, Earle is aware of the saving dimension of this situation. 'Ironically', he writes, 'this failure of accommodation may be the essay's hidden strength. Or, to put it another way, in its resistance to structural change it has preserved—openly or in disguise—its essential character.'[162] This sentence, the implications of which Earle does not develop, 'bears'—as Montaigne says of his *exempla*—'the seeds of a richer, bolder subject-matter', of a whole debate which I hope at least to have laid the foundations for. Whether the essay's anachronism is perceived as the genre's ability to be 'ahead' of other genres—in accordance with the prospective sense of 'rehearsal'—or as its equally significant tendency to be 'belated' in relation to other genres—when the 'rehearsal' is grasped as a repetition—one can probably rest assured with Peter Earle but also with Graham Good that 'the idea of individual personality is still flourishing outside academia *in practice*, though it has generally been ignored or attacked by academic disciplines *in theory*'; and that, since 'the essayist's inherent aesthetic and intellectual *freedom*' are at stake, there will be essays 'as long as there is an art of literary subversion'—as long, in fact, as the essay remains 'a focus of individual resistance to "systems" of various kinds, political, intellectual, and cultural'.[163] Or so one hopes.

---

[157] Dieter Bachmann, *Essay und Essayismus* (1969), 196.

[158] 'But now it has faded, as if in parasitic refuge, into the everchanging textures of fiction, journalism and criticism' (Peter G. Earle, 'On the Contemporary Displacement of the Hispanic American Essay', *Hispanic Review*, 46 (1972), 329.

[159] Ibid.

[160] 'Of course'—Earle hastens to add, 'it would be an over-simplification to blame the extenuated condition of the essay throughout the Western World on an elite of French critics whose influence, because of the very completeness of their semiological system, was predestined to wear itself out' (ibid. 330).

[161] Ibid.   [162] Ibid.

[163] Good, *The Observing Self*, 183; Peter Earle, 'On the Contemporary Displacement of the Hispanic American Essay', 330 and 333; and Good, *The Observing Self*, 185.

Bibliography

ABRAMS, M. H., *The Mirror and the Lamp: Romantic Theory and the Critical Tradition* (Oxford University Press, 1953).

ADAMS, JON K., *Pragmatics and Fiction* (John Benjamins Publishing Company, 1985).

ADAMS, RICHARD M., *Afterjoyce: Studies in Fiction after 'Ulysses'* (Oxford University Press, 1977).

ADORNO, THEODOR W., 'Der Essay als Form', in *Noten zur Literatur*, i (Suhrkamp, 1958). ET: 'The Essay as Form', trans. Bob Hullot-Kentor, *New German Critique*, 32 (1984), 151–71.

——— *Noten zur Literatur*, ii (Suhrkamp, 1961).

——— *Noten zur Literatur*, iii (Suhrkamp, 1965).

AGACINSKY, S., DERRIDA, J., KOFMAN, S., LACOUE-LABARTHE, P., NANCY, J.-L., and PAUTRAT, B. (eds.), *Mimesis des articulations* (Aubier-Flammarion, 1975).

AGHENEA, ION T., *The Prose of J. L. Borges: Existentialism and the Dynamics of Surprise* (Peter Lang, 1984).

ALAZRAKI, JAIME, *Versiones, Inversiones, Reversiones: El Espejo como modelo estructural del relato en los cuentos de Borges* (Editorial Gredos, 1977).

——— 'Tres Formas del Ensayo Contemporaneo: Borges, Paz, Cortázar', *Revista Ibero-americana*, 48 (1982), 1–20.

——— *La prosa narrativa de Jorge Luis Borges: Temas, Estilo* (Editorial Gredos, 1983).

——— (ed.), *Jorge Luis Borges* (Taurus Ediciones, 1987).

ALLARD, YVON, *Paralittératures* (Montréal, La Centrale des Bibliothèques, 1979).

ALTER, ROBERT, *Partial Magic: The Novel as a Self-Conscious Genre* (University of California Press, 1975).

ARAGON, DEBRAY-GENETTE, QUÉMAR, BELLEMIN-NOËL, BRUN, BERNARD, and MITTERRAND, HENRI (eds.), *Essais de critique génétique* (Flammarion, 1979).

ARRIVÉ, MICHEL, 'Pour une théorie des textes poly-isotopiques', *Langages*, 31 (1973), 53–63.

AUERBACH, ERICH, *Mimesis: Dargestellte Wirklichkeit in der abendländischen Literatur* (Francke, 1946).

BACHMANN, DIETER, *Essay und Essayismus* (Kohlhammer, 1969).

——— 'The *Bildungsroman* and its Significance in the History of Realism (Toward a Historical Typology of the Novel)', in Caryl Emerson and Michael Holquist (eds.), *Bakhtin: Speech Genres and Other Late Essays* (University of Texas Press, 1986).

BAKHTIN, MIKHAIL, 'Epic and Novel', 'From the Prehistory of Novelistic Discourse', and 'Discourse in the Novel', in Michael Holquist (ed.), *The Dialogic Imagination: Four Essays by M. M. Bakhtin* (University of Texas Press, 1990).

——— and MEDVEDEV, P. M., *The Formal Method in Literary Scholarship: A Critical Introduction to Sociological Poetics*, trans. A. J. Wehrle (Harvard University Press, 1985).

BAL, MIEKE, *Narratologie: Essais sur la signification narrative dans quatre romans modernes* (Klincksieck, 1977).

BALDINGER, KURT, *Semantic Theory: Towards a Modern Semantics* (Blackwell, 1980).

BARILLAUD, MARIE-CHRISTINE, 'Roland Barthes: Les Fragments, langue équivoque', *Revue Romane*, 16 (1981), 22–35.

BARNETT, RICHARD L., *Dynamics of Detour: Codes of Indirection in Montaigne, Pascal, Racine, Guilleragues* (Günter Narr, 1986).

BARRENECHEA, ANA MARÍA, *La Expresión de la irrealidad en la obra de Borges* (Paidós, 1967).

BARTHES, ROLAND, *Mythologies* (Seuil, 1957). ET: *Mythologies*, trans. Annette Lavers (Hill & Wang, 1972).

—— *Essais critiques* (Seuil, 1964). ET: *Critical Essays*, trans. Richard Howard (Northwestern University Press, 1972).

—— *Critique et vérité: Essai* (Seuil, 1966).

—— *S/Z* (Seuil, 1970). ET: *S/Z* (Blackwell, 1992).

—— *Sade, Fourier, Loyola* (Seuil, 1971).

—— *Le Degré zéro de l'écriture; Suivi de Nouveaux essais critiques*, 2nd edn. (Seuil, 1972).

—— *Le Plaisir du texte* (Seuil, 1973). ET: *The Pleasure of the Text*, trans. Richard Howell (Blackwell, 1990).

—— *Roland Barthes par Roland Barthes* (Seuil, 1975). ET: *Roland Barthes by Roland Barthes* (Macmillan, 1977).

—— *Fragments d'un discours amoureux* (Seuil, 1977). ET: *A Lover's Discourse: Fragments*, trans. Richard Howard (Hill & Wang, 1978).

—— *Le Grain de la voix: Entretiens 1962–1980* (Seuil, 1981). ET: *The Grain of the Voice: Interviews 1962–1980* (University of California Press, 1991).

—— *L'Obvie et l'obtus: Essais critiques III* (Seuil, 1982). ET: *The Responsibility of Forms: Critical Essays on Music, Art, and Representation*, trans. Richard Howard (University of California Press, 1991).

—— *Le Bruissement de la langue: Essais critiques IV* (Seuil, 1984). ET: *The Rustle of Language* (University of California Press, 1989).

—— *L'Aventure sémiologique* (Seuil, 1985). ET: *The Semiotic Challenge*, trans. Richard Howard (Blackwell, 1988).

—— and KAYSER, W., BOOTH, W. C., HAMON, PH. (eds.), *Poétique du récit* (Seuil, 1977).

BAUSCHATZ, CATHLEEN M., 'Montaigne's Conception of Reading in the Context of Renaissance Poetics and Modern Criticism', in Susan R. Suleiman and Inge Crossman (eds.), *The Reader in the Text* (Princeton University Press, 1980), 264–92.

BEAUJOUR, MICHEL, 'Autobiographie et autoportrait', *Poétique*, 32 (1977), 442–58.

—— *Miroirs d'encre: Rhétorique de l'autoportrait* (Seuil, 1980). ET: *Poetics of the Literary Self-Portrait*, trans. Yara Milos (New York University Press, 1991).

—— 'Genus Universum', *Glyph*, 7 (1980), 15–31.

—— '"Considérations sur Ciceron" (I, XL). L'Alongeail comme marque générique: La Lettre et l'essai', in *Actes du Colloque International Montaigne* (1980), 16–35.

BEHLER, ERNST, *German Romantic Literary Theory* (Cambridge University Press, 1993).

BEITCHMAN, PHILIP, 'The Fragmentary Word', *Sub-Stance*, 39 (1983), 58–74.

BELLEMIN-NOËL, JEAN, *Le Texte et l'avant-texte: Les Brouillons d'un poème de Milosz* (Larousse, 1972).

—— *Vers l'inconscient du texte* (Presses Universitaires de France, 1979).

BENJAMIN, ANDREW, *The Problems of Modernity: Adorno and Benjamin* (Routledge, 1989).

BENJAMIN, WALTER, *Der Begriff der Kunstkritik in der deutschen Romantik* (Suhrkamp, 1973).

BENNETT, TONY, *Formalism and Marxism* (Methuen, 1979).

BENNINGTON, GEOFFREY, *Sententiousness and the Novel: Laying down the Law in Eighteenth Century French Fiction* (Cambridge University Press, 1985).

BENSE, MAX, 'Über den Essay und seine Prosa', *Merkur*, 3 (1947), 414–24.

BENSMAÏA, RÉDA, *Barthes à l'essai: Introduction au texte réfléchissant* (Günter Narr, 1986). ET: *The Barthes Effect: The Essay as Reflective Text*, trans. Pat Fedkiew (Theory and History of Literature, 54; University of Minnesota Press, 1987).

BENSTOCK, SHARI, 'At the Margin of Discourse: Footnotes in the Fictional Text', *Publications of the Modern Language Association*, 98 (1983), 204–25.

BENVENISTE, ÉMILE, *Problèmes de linguistique générale*, i (Gallimard, 1966).

—— *Problèmes de linguistique générale*, ii (Gallimard, 1974).

BERGER, BRUNO, *Der Essay: Form und Geschichte* (Francke, 1964).

BERSANI, LEO, 'Proust and the Art of Incompletion', in H. Bloom (ed.), *Modern Critical Views: Marcel Proust* (Chelsea House Publishers, 1987).

BLACK, JOEL D., 'The Scientific Essay and Encyclopedic Science', *Stanford Literature Review*, 1 (1984), 134–48.

BLANCHARD, MARC ELI, *Description: Sign, Self, Desire. Critical Theory in the Wake of Semiotics* (Mouton, 1980).

BLANCHOT, MAURICE, *L'Espace littéraire* (Gallimard, 1955).

—— *Le Livre à venir* (Gallimard, 1959).

—— *L'Entretien infini* (Gallimard, 1969).

BLEZNICK, DONALD W., *El ensayo español del siglo XVI al XX* (Ediciones de Andrea, 1964).

BLOOM, HAROLD, *The Anxiety of Influence: A Theory of Poetry* (Oxford University Press, 1973).

—— DE MAN, PAUL, DERRIDA, JACQUES, HILLIS-MILLER, J., and HARTMAN, GEOFFREY (eds.), *Deconstruction and Criticism* (Routledge & Kegan Paul, 1979).

BLUMENBERG, HANS, *Die Lesbarkeit der Welt*, 2nd edn. (Suhrkamp, 1983).

BLUMENTHAL, GERDA, *Thresholds: A Study of Proust* (Summa Publications, 1984).

BOA, E., and REID, J. H., *Critical Strategies: German Fiction in the 20th Century* (Edward Arnold, 1972).

BOOTH, WAYNE C., *The Rhetoric of Fiction*, 2nd edn. (University of Chicago, 1983).

BORGES, JORGE LUIS, *Discusión* (1932), *Historia Universal de la Infamia* (1935), *Historia de la Eternidad* (1936), *Otras Inquisiciones* (1952), *El Otro, El Mismo* (1964), in *Obras Completas 1923–1972* (Emecé, 1974).

—— *Ficciones*, 9th edn. (Emecé, 1980). ET: *Fictions*, trans. Anthony Kerrigan (Calder, 1985).

BORINSKY, ALICIA, 'Re-escribir y Escribir: Arenas, Ménard, Borges, Cervantes, Fray Servando', *Revista Iberoamericana*, 41 (1975), 605–16.

BOWEN, BARBARA C., *The Age of Bluff: Paradox and Ambiguity in Rabelais and Montaigne* (University of Illinois Press, 1972).

BRADBURY, MALCOLM, and McFARLANE, J. (eds.), *Modernism (1890–1930)* (Penguin Books, 1976).

BRATOSEVICH, NICOLAS, 'El desplazamiento como metáfora en tres textos de J. L. Borges', *Revista Iberoamericana*, 43/100–1 (1977), 549–60.

BRÉE, GERMAINE, *Marcel Proust and Deliverance from Time*, trans. C. J. Richards and A. D. Truitt (Greenwood Press, 1981).

BRÉMOND, CLAUDE, *Logique du récit* (Seuil, 1973).

BROCH, HERMANN, *Hermann Broch: Kommentierte Werkausgabe*, ed. Paul Michael Lützeler, vol. 9/1, 'Schriften zur Literature 1, Kritik' (Suhrkamp, 1976); vol. 9/2, 'Schriften zur Literatur 2, Theorie' (Suhrkamp, 1976); and vol. 13/1 (Suhrkamp, 1981).

BROCH, HERMANN, *Die Schlafwandler: Eine Romantrilogie*, 3rd edn. (Suhrkamp, 1981). ET: *The Sleepwalkers* (Quartet Books, 1986).

BRODY, JULES, *Lectures de Montaigne* (French Forum, 1982).

—— 'Au-delà de 1580: L'Évolution d'une forme', *Actes du congrès de Bordeaux* (Champion-Slatkine, 1983), 195–208.

BROICH, ULRICH, PFISTER, MANFRED, and SCHULTE-MIDDELICH, BERND (eds.), *Intertextualität: Formen, Funktionen, Anglistische Fallstudien* (Niemeyer, 1985).

BROOKE-ROSE, CHRISTINE, *A Rhetoric of the Unreal: Studies of Narrative and Structure, especially the Fantastic* (Cambridge University Press, 1981).

BROOKS, PETER, *Reading for the Plot: Design and Intention in Narrative* (Oxford University Press, 1984).

BRUFORD, W. H., *The German Tradition of Self-Cultivation: 'Bildung' from Humboldt to Thomas Mann* (Cambridge University Press, 1975).

BRUSS, ELIZABETH, *Autobiographical Acts: The Changing Situation of a Literary Genre* (Johns Hopkins University Press, 1976).

BÜRGER, PETER, *Theory of the Avant-Garde*, trans. M. Shaw (University of Minnesota Press, 1984).

—— '*Passé simple*: The Essay as an Autobiographical Form in J.-P. Sartre', *Modern Language Notes*, 102/2 (1987), 1182–90.

—— *Prosa der Moderne* (Suhrkamp, 1988).

BUSH, DOUGLAS (ed.), *Oxford History of English Literature*, v. *English Literature in the Earlier Seventeenth Century (1600–1660)* (Oxford University Press, 1962).

BUTLER, CHRISTOPHER, *Interpretation, Deconstruction, and Ideology: An Introduction to Some Current Issues in Literary Theory* (Oxford University Press, 1984).

BUTOR, MICHEL, *Essais sur les Essais* (Gallimard, 1968).

BUTRYM, ALEXANDER J. (ed.), *Essays on the Essay: Redefining the Genre* (University of Georgia Press, 1989).

CAGNON, MAURICE, *Éthique et esthétique dans la littérature française du XXème* (Anma Libri, 1978).

CALI, ANDREA, *Pratiques de lecture et d'écriture (Ollier, Robbe-Grillet, Simon)* (Nizet, 1980).

CANTARUTTI GIULIA, *Aphoristikforschung im deutschen Sprachraum* (Peter Lang, 1984).

CARROLL, DAVID, *Paraesthetics: Foucault, Lyotard, Derrida* (Methuen, 1987).

CAVE, TERENCE, *The Cornucopian Text: Problems of Writing in the French Renaissance* (Oxford University Press, 1979).

—— 'The Mimesis of Reading in the Renaissance', in John D. Lyons and Stephen G. Nichols, Jr. (eds.), *Mimesis: From Mirror to Method, Augustine to Descartes* (University Press of New England, 1982).

—— *Recognitions: A Study in Poetics* (Oxford University Press, 1988).

CAWS, MARY ANN, *Reading Frames in Modern Fiction* (Princeton University Press, 1985).

CELEYRETTE-PIETRI, NICOLE, *De rimes et d'analogies: Les Dictionnaires des poètes* (Presses Universitaires de Lille, 1985).

CERTEAU, MICHEL DE, *Heterologies: Discourse on the Other*, trans. B. Mazzorni (University of Minnesota Press, 1986; trans. from the French).

CHADBOURNE, RICHARD M., 'A Puzzling Literary Genre: Comparative Views of the Essay', *Comparative Literature Studies*, 20 (1983), 133–53.

CHAMBERS, ROSS, *Meaning and Meaningfulness: Studies in the Analysis and Interpretation of Texts* (French Forum, 1979).

—— *Story and Situation: Narrative Seduction and the Power of Fiction* (Manchester University Press, 1984).

CHAMPIGNY, ROBERT, *Pour une esthétique de l'essai: Analyses critiques (Breton, Sartre, Robbe-Grillet)* (Minard, 1967).

CHAPMAN, DAVID WAYNE, 'The Essay as a Literary Form', D.Phil. thesis, Texas Christian University, 1985.

CHARLES, MICHEL, *Rhétorique de la lecture* (Seuil, 1977).

—— 'Bibliothèques: Essai', *Poétique*, 9 (1978), 1–27.

—— 'La Lecture critique', *Poétique*, 9 (1978), 129–51.

—— 'Digression, régression (Arabesques)', *Poétique*, 40 (1979), 395–407.

—— *L'Arbre et la source* (Seuil, 1985).

CHASE, CYNTHIA, *Decomposing Figures: Rhetorical Readings in the Romantic Tradition* (Johns Hopkins University Press, 1986).

CHATMAN, SEYMOUR, *Story and Discourse: Narrative Structure in Fiction and Film* (Cornell University Press, 1978).

CHRIST, RONALD, *The Narrow Act: Borges's Art of Allusion* (New York University Press, 1969).

CHRISTENSEN, INGER, *The Meaning of Metafiction: A Critical Study of Selected Novels by Sterne, Nabokov, Barth, Beckett* (Oslo Universitetsforlaget, 1981).

CLARK, KATHERINA, and HOLQUIST, MICHAEL, *Mikhail Bakhtin* (Belknap Press of Harvard University Press, 1984).

CLEMENTE, JOSÉ EDMUNDO, *El ensayo* (Ediciones Culturales Argentinas, 1961).

COCKING, J. M., *Proust: Collected Essays on the Writer and his Art* (Cambridge University Press, 1982).

COHN, DORRIT, *The Sleepwalkers: Elucidations of Hermann Broch's Trilogy* (Mouton, 1966).

COLIE, ROSALIE L., *Paradoxica Epidemica: The Renaissance Tradition of Paradox* (Princeton University Press, 1966).

—— *The Resources of Kind: Genre-Theory in the Renaissance* (University of California Press, 1973).

COMMENT, BERNARD, *Roland Barthes, Vers le neutre* (Christian Bourgois, 1991).

Communications, 11 (1968), Special issue: 'Le Vraisemblable'.

Communications, 36 (1982), Special issue: 'Roland Barthes'.

COMPAGNON, ANTOINE, *La Seconde Main, ou Le Travail de la citation* (Seuil, 1979).

—— *Nous, Michel de Montaigne* (Seuil, 1980).

CORE, GEORGE, 'Stretching the Limits of the Essay', in Alexander J. Butrym (ed.), *Essays on the Essay: Redefining the Genre* (University of Georgia Press, 1989).

CORNETTI, JEAN-PIERRE, *Robert Musil, ou L'Alternative romanesque* (Presses Universitaires de France, 1985).

CORREDOR, EVA L., 'The Essay as Nostalgia for Form', and 'The Problematic Elements of the Novel', in id., *György Lukács and the Literary Pretext* (Peter Lang, 1987).

COULANGE, ALAIN, 'L'Étrange mode de l'alphabet', *Courrier du Centre International d'Études Poétiques*, 121–2 (1977), 20–5.

COWARD, R., and ELLIS, J., *Language and Materialism: Development in Semiology and the Theory of the Subject* (Routledge and Kegan Paul, 1977).

Critique, 423–4 (1982), Special issue: 'Roland Barthes'.

CROSSAN, JOHN DOMINIC, *Raid on the Articulate: Comic Eschatology in Jesus and Borges* (Harper and Row, 1976).

CULLER, JONATHAN, 'Paradox and the Language of Morals in La Rochefoucauld', *Modern Language Review*, 68 (1973), 28–39.

—— *Structuralist Poetics: Structuralism, Linguistics, and the Study of Literature* (Routledge & Kegan Paul, 1974).

—— *The Pursuit of Signs: Semiotics, Literature, Deconstruction* (Routledge & Kegan Paul, 1981).

—— *Barthes* (Fontana, 1983).

—— *On Deconstruction: Theory and Criticism after Structuralism* (Routledge & Kegan Paul, 1983).

—— *Framing the Sign: Criticism and its Institutions* (Blackwell, 1988).

CURTIUS, ERNST R., 'Schrift- und Buchmetaphorik in der Weltliteratur', *Deutsche Vierteljahrsschrift für Literaturwissenschaft und Geistesgeschichte* (1942), 359–411.

DÄLLENBACH, LUCIEN, 'Du fragment au cosmos (la *Comédie Humaine* et l'opération de lecture I)', *Poétique*, 40 (1979), 420–31.

—— 'Le Tout en morceaux (la *Comédie Humaine* et l'opération de lecture II)', *Poétique*, 42 (1980), 156–69.

—— *Le Récit spéculaire: Essai sur la mise en abyme* (Seuil, 1977). ET: *The Mirror in the Text*, trans. Jeremy Whiteley and Emma Hughes (Polity Press, 1989).

DEGUY, MICHEL, 'Certitude et fiction', *Poétique*, 21 (1975), 3–7.

DE LATTRE, ALAIN, *La Doctrine de la réalité chez Proust*, 3 vols. (José Corti, 1978, 1981, 1985).

DELEUZE, GILLES, *Différence et répétition* (Presses Universitaires de France, 1968).

—— *Logique du sens* (Éditions de Minuit, 1969).

DEMERSON, G. (ed.), *La Notion de genre à la Renaissance* (Slatkine, 1984).

DERRIDA, JACQUES, *L'Écriture et la différence* (Seuil, 1967).

—— *De la Grammatologie* (Éditions de Minuit, 1967). ET: *Of Grammatology*, trans. G. C. Spivak (Johns Hopkins University Press, 1976).

—— *Marges: De la Philosophie* (Éditions de Minuit, 1972). ET: *Margins: Of Philosophy*, trans. Alan Bass (University of Chicago Press, 1982).

—— *La Dissémination* (Seuil, 1972). ET: *Dissemination*, trans. Barbara Johnson (University of Chicago Press, 1981).

—— *Positions* (Éditions de Minuit, 1972). ET: *Positions*, trans. Alan Bass (University of Chicago Press, 1981).

—— *L'Archéologie du frivole: Lire Condillac* (Galilée, 1973).

—— *Glas* (Galilée, 1974).

—— 'Le Parergon'/'The Parergon', in *La Vérité en peinture* (Flammarion, 1978). ET: *The Truth in Painting*, trans. Geoffrey Bennington (University of Chicago Press, 1987).

—— *La Carte postale de Socrate à Freud et au-delà* (Aubier-Flammarion, 1980).

—— *L'Oreille de l'autre: Otobiographies, transferts, traductions* (Textes et débats avec J. Derrida, ed. Claude Lévesque et Christie V. McDonald) (VLB Editeur, 1982).

—— 'La Loi du genre', in *Parages* (Galilée, 1986). ET: 'The Law of Genre', trans. Avital Ronell, *Glyph*, 7 (1980), 203–29.

DESCOMBES, VINCENT, *Proust: Philosophie du roman* (Éditions de Minuit, 1987).

DESMOND, WILLIAM, *Art and the Absolute: A Study of Hegel's Aesthetics* (State University of New York Press, 1986).

DEWS, PETER, *Logics of Disintegration: Post-Structuralist Thought and the Claims of Critical Theory* (Verso, 1988).

—— 'Adorno, Post-Structuralism, and the Critique of Identity', in Andrew Benjamin, *The Problems of Modernity: Adorno and Benjamin* (Routledge, 1989).

DIPPLE, ELIZABETH, *The Unresolvable Plot: Reading Contemporary Fiction* (Routledge, Chapman and Hall, 1988).

DOBRÉE, BONAMY, *English Essayists* (Collins, 1946).

—— (ed.), *Oxford History of English Literature*, vii. *English Literature in the Early Eighteenth Century (1700–1740)* (Oxford University Press, 1959).

DONATO, EUGENIO, '"A Mere Labyrinth of Letters": Flaubert and the Quest for Fiction, a Montage', *Modern Language Notes* 89 (1974), 885–910.

—— 'The Ruins of Memory: Archeological Fragments and Textual Artifacts', *Modern Language Notes*, 93 (1978), 575–96.

—— 'Topographies of Memory', *Sub-Stance*, 21 (1978), 37–48.

DONOGHUE, DAVID, *Ferocious Alphabets* (Faber & Faber, 1981).

DOUBROVSKY, SERGE, 'Une écriture tragique', *Poétique*, 47 (1981), 329–54.

DUBOIS, JEAN, 'Dictionnaire et discours didactique', *Langages*, 19 (1970), 35–47.

DUBROW, HEATHER, *Genre* (Methuen, 1982).

DUCROT, OSWALD, and TODOROV, TZVETAN, *Dictionnaire encyclopédique des sciences du langage* (Seuil, 1972).

DUNHAM, L., and IVASK, IVAR (eds.), *The Cardinal Points of Borges* (University of Oklahoma Press, 1971).

DURZAK, MANFRED, (ed.), *Hermann Broch: Perspektiven der Forschung* (Wilhelm Fink Verlag, 1972).

EAGLETON, TERRY, *Criticism and Ideology: A Study in Marxist Literary Theory*, 2nd edn. (Verso, 1978).

—— *Literary Theory: An Introduction* (Blackwell, 1983).

—— *The Function of Criticism: From 'The Spectator' to Post-Structuralism* (Verso, 1984).

EARLE, PETER G., 'El ensayo hispanoamericano como experiencia literaria', in Kurt L. Levy and Keith Ellis (eds.) *El ensayo y la crítica literaria . . .* (University of Toronto, 1970), 23–32.

—— 'On the Contemporary Displacement of the Hispanic American Essay', *Hispanic Review*, 46 (1978), 329–41.

—— 'El ensayo hispanoamericano: Del modernismo a la modernidad', *Revista Iberoamericana*, 48 (1982), 47–57.

—— and MEAD, ROBERT G., *Historia del ensayo hispanoamericano* (Ediciones de Andrea, 1973).

ECHAVARRÍA, ARTURO, *Lengua y Literatura de Borges* (Ariel, 1983).

ECO, UMBERTO, *L'Œuvre ouverte* (Seuil, 1965).

—— *A Theory of Semiotics* (Indiana University Press, 1976).

—— *The Role of the Reader: Exploration in the Semiotics of Texts* (Hutchinson, 1979).

—— *Semiotics and the Philosophy of Language* (Macmillan, 1984).

EHRLICH, HÉLÈNE-HÉDY, *Montaigne: La Critique et le langage* (Klincksieck, 1972).

EMERSON, CARYL, and HOLQUIST, MICHAEL (eds.), *Bakhtin: Speech Genres and Other Late Essays*, trans. Vern W. McGee (University of Texas Press, 1986).

Ensayistas (Los), 1 (1976); 5 (1978); 10–11 (1981); 14–15 (1983).

L'Esprit Créateur, 22 (1982), special issue: 'Roland Barthes'.

L'Esprit Créateur, 27 (1987), special issue: 'Paratextes'.

Études Françaises, 11 (1975), special issue: 'Le Fragment/La Somme'.

Études Littéraires, 5 (1972), special issue: 'L'Essai'.

Europe, 741–2 (1991), special issue: 'Robert Musil/Hermann Broch'.

EXNER, RICHARD, 'Zum Problem einer Definition und einer Methodik des Essays als dichterischer Kunstform', *Neophiologus*, 46 (1962) 169–82.

FARASSE, GÉRARD, 'Héliographie', *Revue des Sciences Humaines*, 151 (1973), 435–57.

FEKETE, JOHN (ed.), *The Structural Allegory: Reconstructive Encounters with the New French Thought* (University of Minnesota Press, 1984).

FELMAN, SHOSHANA (ed.), *Literature and Psychoanalysis. The Question of Reading: Otherwise* (Johns Hopkins University Press, 1982).

FELPERIN, HOWARD, *Beyond Deconstruction: The Uses and Abuses of Literary Theory* (Oxford University Press, 1985).

FISH, STANLEY, *Self-Consuming Artifacts: The Experience of Seventeenth-Century Literature* (University of California Press, 1974).

FLAHAUT, FRANÇOIS, *La Parole intermédiaire* (Seuil, 1978).

FONTANIER, PIERRE, *Les Figures du discours* (Flammarion, 1977).

FOSTER, DAVID W., 'Para une Caracterización de la *Escritura* en los Relatos de Borges', *Revista Iberoamericana*, 43/100–1 (1977), 337–55.

FOUCAULT, MICHEL, 'Le Langage à l'infini', *Tel Quel*, 15 (1963), 44–53.

—— *Les Mots et les choses: Une Archéologie des sciences humaines* (Gallimard, 1966). ET: *The Order of Things: An Archeology of the Human Sciences* (Vintage Books, 1973).

—— *L'Archéologie du savoir* (Gallimard, 1969).

—— 'Qu'est-ce qu'un auteur?', *Bulletin de la Société Française de Philosophie*, 3 (1969), 73–104.

FOWLER, ALASTAIR, *Kinds of Literature: Introduction to the Theory of Genres and Modes* (Oxford University Press, 1982).

FOWLER, ROGER, *Linguistics and the Novel* (Methuen, 1977).

—— *Linguistic Criticism* (Oxford University Press, 1986).

FRAISSE, LUC, *Le Processus de la création chez Marcel Proust: Le Fragment expérimental* (José Corti, 1988).

FRANK, MANFRED, 'The Infinite Text', *Glyph*, 7 (1980), 70–101.

FRIEDMAN, ALAN, *The Turn of the Novel* (Oxford University Press, 1966).

FRIEDRICH, HUGO, *Montaigne* (Gallimard, 1968).

FRISÉ, ADOLF, 'Roman und Essay: Gedanken u.a. zu Hermann Broch, Thomas Mann und Robert Musil', in *Plädoyer für Robert Musil* (Rowohlt, 1987).

FRYE, NORTHROP, *The Anatomy of Criticism: Four Essays* (Princeton University Press, 1957).

—— *The Secular Scripture: A Study of the Structure of Romance* (Harvard University Press, 1976).

FUENTES, CARLOS, *Cervantes o la crítica de la lectura* (Editorial Joaquin Mortiz, 1976).

GALAY, JEAN-LOUIS, 'Esquisses pour une théorie figurale du discours', *Poétique*, 20 (1974), 389–415.

—— *Philosophie et invention textuelle: Essai sur la poétique d'un texte Kantien* (Klincksieck, 1977).

—— 'Problèmes de l'œuvre fragmentale: Valéry', *Poétique*, 31 (1977), 337–67.

GARCÍA PONCE, JUAN, *La errancia sin fin: Musil, Borges, Klosowski* (Editorial Anagrama, 1981).

GARZILLI, ENRICO, *Circles without Center: Paths to the Discovery and Creation of the Self in Modern Literature* (Harvard University Press, 1972).

GASCHÉ, RODOLPHE, 'The Scene of Writing: A Deferred Outset', *Glyph*, 1 (1977), 150–71.

—— *The Tain of the Mirror: Derrida and the Philosophy of Reflection* (Harvard University Press, 1986).

GENETTE, GÉRARD, *Figures*, i (Seuil, 1966).

—— *Figures*, ii (Seuil, 1969).

—— *Figures*, iii (Seuil, 1972). ET: *Narrative Discourse: An Essay in Method*, trans. Janet E. Lewin (Cornell University Press, 1980).

—— 'Genres, "types", modes', *Poétique*, 32 (1977), 389–421.

—— *Introduction à l'architexte* (Seuil, 1979).

—— *Palimpsestes: La Littérature au second degré* (Seuil, 1982).

—— *Figures of Literary Discourse* (inc. 'Frontiers of Narrative'), trans. Alan Sheridan (Columbia University Press, 1982).

—— *Nouveau discours du récit* (Seuil, 1983).

—— *Seuils* (1987).

—— JAUSS, HANS-ROBERT, SCHOLES, ROBERT, and VIËTOR, KARL (eds.), *Théorie des genres* (Seuil, 1986).

GIRARD, RENÉ, *Mensonge romantique et vérité romanesque* (Grasset, 1961).

—— (ed.), *Proust: A Collection of Critical Essays* (Greenwood Press, 1977).

GLAUSER, ALFRED, *Montaigne paradoxal* (Nizet, 1972).

GOFFMAN, ERVING, *Frame Analysis: An Essay on the Organization of Experience* (Harper and Row, 1974).

GÓMEZ-MARTINEZ, JOSÉ-LUIS, *Teoría del ensayo* (Ediciones Universitarias de Salamanca, 1981).

GOOD, GRAHAM, *The Observing Self: Rediscovering the Essay* (Routledge, 1988).

GOODHEART, EUGENE, *The Skeptic Disposition: Deconstruction, Ideology and Other Matters* (Princeton University Press, 1984).

GOSVIG OLESEN, SÖREN, *La Philosophie dans le texte* (Éditions Trans-Europ-Repress, 1982).

GRAFF, GERALD, *Literature Against Itself: Literary Ideas in Modern Society* (University of Chicago Press, 1979).

GRANDEROUTE, ROBERT, *Le Roman pédagogique de Fénelon à Rousseau* (Slatkine, 1985).

GRAY, FLOYD, *Le Style de Montaigne* (Nizet, 1958).

—— 'Montaigne and Sebond: The Rhetoric of Paradox', *French Studies*, 28 (1974), 134–45.

—— *La Balance de Montaigne: Exagium/essai* (Nizet, 1982).

—— and TÉTEL, MARCEL (eds.), *Textes et intertextes: Études sur le XVIème siècle pour Alfred Glauser* (Nizet, 1979).

GREENBERG, MITCHELL, *Detours of Desire: Readings in the French Baroque* (Miami University, 1984).

GREIMAS, ALGIRDAS JULIEN, *Sémantique structurale*, 2nd edn. (Presses Universitaires de France, 1986). ET: *Structuralist Semantics: An Attempt at Method*, trans. D. McDowell, R. Schleifer, and A. Velic (University of Nebraska Press, 1983).

—— *Du sens I: Essais sémiotiques* (Seuil, 1970).

—— *Du sens II: Essais sémiotiques* (Seuil, 1983). ET: *On Meaning: Selected Writings in Semiotic Theory*, trans. P. Perron and F. Collins (University of Minnesota Press, 1987).

—— and COURTÈS, JOSEPH, 'The Cognitive Dimension of Narrative Discourse' (trans. from the French by M. Rengstorf), *New Literary History*, 7 (1976), 433–47.

GRIVEL, CHARLES, and VARGA, A. KIBÉDI, *Du linguistique au textuel* (Van Gorcum, 1974).

GROSS, JOHN (ed.), *The Oxford Book of Essays* (Oxford University Press, 1991).

GUILLÉN, CLAUDIO, *Literature as System: Essays toward the Theory of Literary History* (Princeton University Press, 1971).

HAAS, GERHARD, *Studien zur Form des Essays und zu seinen Vorformen im Roman* (Max Niemeyer, 1966).

—— *Essay* (Metzler, 1969).

HALL, MICHAEL L., 'The Emergence of the Essay and the Idea of Discovery', in Alexander J. Butrym (ed.), *Essays on the Essay: Redefining the Genre* (University of Georgia Press, 1989).

HAMBURGER, MICHAEL, 'Essay über den Essay', *Akzente*, 12 (1965), 290–2.

HAMON, PHILIPPE, 'Un discours contraint', *Poétique*, 16 (1973), 411–45.

—— 'Clausules', *Poétique*, 24 (1975), 495–526.

—— 'Texte littéraire et métalangage', *Poétique*, 31 (1977), 261–84.

HARARI, JOSUÉ, V., *Textual Strategies: Perspectives in Post-Structuralist Criticism* (Cornell University Press, 1979).

HARDISON, O. B., Jr., 'Binding Proteus: An Essay on the Essay', in Alexander J. Butrym (ed.), *Essays on the Essay: Redefining the Genre* (University of Georgia Press, 1989).

HARLAND, RICHARD, *Superstructuralism: The Philosophy of Structuralism and Post-Structuralism* (Methuen, 1987).

HARRISON, THOMAS, *Essayism: Conrad, Musil, Pirandello* (Johns Hopkins University Press, 1992).

HART, THOMAS R., 'The Literary Criticism of Jorge Luis Borges', *Modern Language Notes*, 78 (1963), 489–503.

HARTMAN, GEOFFREY, *Beyond Formalism: Literary Essays 1958–1970* (Yale University Press, 1970).

—— *The Fate of Reading and Other Essays* (University of Chicago Press, 1975).

—— *Criticism in the Wilderness: The Study of Literature Today* (Yale University Press, 1980).

—— *Saving the Text: Literature/Derrida/Philosophy* (Johns Hopkins University Press, 1981).

HASSAN, IHAB, *The Dismemberment of Orpheus: Toward a Post-Modern Literature* (Oxford University Press, 1971).

HAWKES, TERENCE, *Structuralism and Semiotics* (Methuen, 1977).

HAWTHORN, JEREMY (ed.), *Narrative: From Malory to Motion Pictures* (Edward Arnold, 1985).

HEATH, STEPHEN, *Vertige du déplacement: Lecture de Barthes* (Fayard, 1974).

HEGEL, G. W. F., *Phänomenologie des Geistes*, ed. Johannes Hoffmeister (Felix Meiner, 1952). ET: *Phenomenology of Spirit*, trans. A. V. Miller (Oxford University Press, 1979).

—— *Vorlesungen über die Ästhetik*, ed. Rüdiger Bubner (Reclam, 1977). ET: *Aesthetics: Lectures on Fine Art*, trans. T. M. Knox, 2 vols. (Clarendon Press, 1975).

HELLER, ERICH, *In the Age of Prose: Literary and Philosophical Essays* (Cambridge University Press, 1984).

HERNADI, PAUL, *Beyond Genre: New Directions in Literary Classifications* (Cornell University Press, 1972).

HERRNSTEIN-SMITH, BARBARA, *Poetic Closure: A Study of How Poems End* (University of Chicago Press, 1969).

—— *On the Margins of Discourse: The Relation of Literature to Language* (University of Chicago Press, 1978).

HILLIS-MILLER, J., 'The Critic as Host', in Harold Bloom *et al.* (eds.), *Deconstruction and Criticism* (Routledge & Kegan Paul, 1979).

—— *Fiction and Repetition: Seven English Novels* (Blackwell, 1982).

HIRSCH, E. D., Jr. *Validity in Interpretation* (Yale University Press, 1967).

HOECK, LEO H., *La Marque du titre: Dispositifs sémiotiques d'une pratique textuelle* (Mouton, 1981).

HOLLOWELL, JOHN, *Fact and Fiction: The New Journalism and the Nonfiction Novel* (University of North Carolina Press, 1971).

HOLMES, ALAN, *Robert Musil, 'Der Mann ohne Eigenschaften': An Examination of the Relationship between Author, Narrator and Protagonist* (Bouvier Verlag, 1978).

HOLQUIST, MICHAEL, *Dialogism: Bakhtin and his World* (Routlegde, 1990).

—— (ed.), *The Dialogic Imagination: Four Essays by M. M. Bakhtin* (University of Texas Press, 1990).

HOLUB, ROBERT C., *Reception Theory: A Critical Introduction* (Methuen, 1984).

HOOKWAY, CHRISTOPHER, *Scepticism* (Routledge, 1990).

HORST, KARL AUGUST, *Kritischer Führer durch die deutsche Literatur der Gegenwart: Roman, Lyrik, Essay* (Nymphenbürger, 1962).

HORST NEUMANN, PETER, 'Das Eigene und das Fremde: Über die Wünschbarkeit einer Theorie des Zitierens', *Akzente*, 4 (1980), 292–305.

HUBER, LOTHAR, and WHITE, JOHN J. (eds.), *Musil in Focus: Papers from a Centenary Symposium* (Institute of Germanic Studies, London, 1982).

HULLOT-KENTOR, BOB, 'Title Essay', *New German Critique*, 32 (1984), 141–50.

HUMPHRIES, JEFFERSON, 'The Otherness in Common/Places', *L'Esprit Créateur*, 24 (1984), 48–56.

HUTCHEON, LINDA, *Narcissistic Narrative: The Metafictional Paradox* (Wilfrid Laurier University Press, 1980).

—— *A Theory of Parody: The Teachings of Twentieth-Century Art Forms* (Methuen, 1985).

—— *A Poetics of Postmodernism: History, Theory, Fiction* (Routledge, 1988).

HUXLEY, ALDOUS, *Collected Essays* (Chatto and Windus, 1960).

IMBRIE, ANN E., 'Defining Nonfiction Genres', in Barbara Kiefer Lewalski (ed.), *Renaissance Genres: Essays on Theory, History, and Interpretation* (Harvard University Press, 1986).

IRBY, JAMES E., 'Borges and the Idea of Utopia', in L. Dunham and Ivar Ivask (eds.), *The Cardinal Points of Borges* (University of Oklahoma Press, 1971), 35–45.

ISER, WOLFGANG, *Der Akt des Lesens* (Wilhelm Fink, 1976). ET: *The Act of Reading: A Theory of Aesthetic Response* (Johns Hopkins University Press, 1978).

—— *Der implizite Leser: Kommunikationsformen des Romans von Bunyan bis Beckett*. ET: *The Implied Reader: Patterns of Communication in Prose Fiction from Bunyan to Beckett* (Johns Hopkins University Press, 1974).

—— 'Akte des Fingierens, oder: Was ist das Fiktive im fiktionalen Text?', in *Poetik und Hermeneutik* (Wilhelm Fink, 1983).

JACOBS, CAROL, *The Dissimulating Harmony: The Image of Interpretation in Nietzsche, Rilke, Artaud, and Benjamin* (Johns Hopkins University Press, 1978).

JACOBS, JÜRGEN, and KRAUSE, MARKUS, *Der deutsche Bildungsroman: Gattungsgeschichte vom 18. bis zum 20. Jahrhundert* (Beck, 1989).

JACK, IAN (ed.), *Oxford History of English Literature*, x. *English Literature 1815–1832* (Oxford University Press, 1963).

JAKOBSON, ROMAN, *Essais de linguistique générale* (Seuil, 1963).

JAKOBSON, ROMAN, *Huit questions de poétique* (Seuil, 1977).

JAMES, HENRY, 'The Science of Criticism', in Roger Gard (ed.), *The Critical Muse: Selected Literary Criticism* (Penguin Classics, 1987).

JAMESON, FREDRIC, *Marxism and Form: Twentieth-Century Dialectical Theories of Literature* (Princeton University Press, 1971).

—— *The Prison-House of Language: A Critical Account of Structuralism and Russian Formalism* (Princeton University Press, 1972).

JAPP, UWE, 'Das Buch im Buch: Eine Figur des literarischen Hermetismus', *Neue Rundschau*, 4 (1975), 651–70.

JAUSS, HANS ROBERT, *Literaturgeschichte als Provokation* (Suhrkamp, 1970).

JAY, MARTIN, *Adorno* (Fontana Paperbacks, 1984).

JAY, PAUL, *Being in the Text: Self-Representation from Wordsworth to R. Barthes* (Cornell University Press, 1984).

JEFFERSON, ANN, *The Nouveau Roman and the Poetics of Fiction* (Cambridge University Press, 1980).

—— '*Mise en abyme* and the Prophetic in Narrative', *Style*, 17 (1983), 196–208.

—— and ROBEY, DAVID (eds.), *Modern Literary Theory: A Comparative Introduction* (Bastford Academic and Educational, 1982).

JENNY, LAURENT, 'La Stratégie de la forme', *Poétique*, 27 (1976), 257–81.

JOHNSON, BARBARA, *The Critical Difference: Essays in the Contemporary Rhetoric of Reading* (Johns Hopkins University Press, 1980).

—— 'Outwork, or Disseminating Prefacing', introductory note to Derrida, *Dissemination* (1981).

JOHNSTON, GEORGIA, 'The Whole Achievement in Virginia Woolf's *Common Reader*', in Alexander J. Butrym (ed.), *Essays on the Essay: Redefining the Genre* (University of Georgia Press, 1989).

JOLLES, ANDRÉ, *Formes simples* (Seuil, 1972; trans. from the German).

JOSIPOVICI, GABRIEL, *The Lessons of Modernism and Other Essays* (Macmillan, 1977).

—— *The World and the Book: A Study of Modern Fiction*, 2nd edn. (Macmillan, 1979).

JOURDE, PIERRE, *Géographies imaginaires: De quelques inventeurs du mondes au XXe siècle (Gracq, Borges, Michaux, Tolkien)* (José Corti, 1991).

JOUVE, VINCENT, *La Littérature selon R. Barthes* (Éditions de Minuit, 1986).

KADIR, DJELAL, *Questing Fictions: Latin America's Family Romance* (University of Minnesota Press, 1986).

KAMBOUCHNER, DENIS, 'Le Labyrinthe de la présentation', *Critique*, 368 (1978), 41–62.

—— 'The Theory of Accidents', *Glyph*, 7 (1980).

KARRER, WOLFGANG, *Parodie, Travestie, Pastiche* (Wilhelm Fink, 1977).

KAUFMANN, WALTER, *Hegel: Text and Commentary* (Hegel's Preface to his System in a New Translation with Commentary on Facing Notes) (University of Notre Dame Press, 1977).

—— *Hegel: A Reinterpretation* (University of Notre Dame Press, 1978).

KAUFFMANN, R. LANE, 'The Skewed Path: Essaying as Unmethodical Method', in Alexander J. Butrym (ed.), *Essays on the Essay: Redefining the Genre* (University of Georgia Press, 1989).

KERMODE, FRANK, *The Sense of an Ending: Studies in the Theory of Fiction* (Oxford University Press, 1967).

—— *Continuities* (Routledge and Kegan Paul, 1968).

—— *Novel and Narrative* (Glasgow University, 1972).

—— *The Genesis of Secrecy: On the Interpretation of Narrative* (Harvard University Press, 1979).

KESSLER, MICHAEL, and LÜTZELER, PAUL MICHAEL (eds.), *Hermann Broch: Das dichterische Werk* (Stauffenburg Verlag, 1987).

KIEFER LEWALSKI, BARBARA (ed.), *Renaissance Genres: Essays on Theory, History, and Interpretation* (Harvard University Press, 1986).

KLAUS, CARL, 'Essay', in Robert Scholes and Carl Klaus (eds.), *Elements of Literature*, 4th edn. (Oxford University Press, 1991).

KLOTZ, VOLKER, 'Zitat und Montage in neuerer Literatur und Kunst', *Sprache im technischen Zeitalter*, 60 (1976), 259–77.

KNOX, ISRAEL, *The Aesthetic Theories of Kant, Hegel, and Schopenhauer* (Humanities Press, 1958).

KÖHN, LOTHAR, *Entwicklungs-und Bildungsroman: Ein Forschungsbericht* (Metzler, 1969).

KOLLER, WERNER, *Einführung in die Übersetzungswissenschaft* (Quelle und Meyer, 1979).

KOSTELANETZ, RICHARD (ed.), *Essaying Essays: Alternative Forms of Exposition* (Out of London Press, 1975).

KOTIN-MORTIMER, ARMINE, *La Clôture narrative* (José Corti, 1985).

KRAPOTH, HERMANN, *Dichtung und Philosophie: Eine Studie zum Werk Hermann Brochs* (Bouvier Verlag, 1971).

KRISTEVA, JULIA, *Semiotikè: Recherches pour une sémanalyse* (Seuil, 1969).

—— *Le Texte du roman: Approche sémiologique d'une structure discursive transformation nelle* (Mouton, 1970).

—— *La Révolution du langage poétique* (Seuil, 1974).

—— 'From Symbol to Sign', in Toril Moi (ed.), *The Kristeva Reader* (Blackwell, 1986).

—— 'Word, Dialogue, and Novel', in Toril Moi (ed.), *The Kristeva Reader* (Blackwell, 1986).

KRITZMAN, LAWRENCE, *Destruction/Découverte: Le Fonctionnement de la rhétorique dans les 'Essais' de Montaigne* (French Forum, 1980).

—— (ed.), *Fragments: Incompletion and Discontinuity* (New York Literary Forum, 1981).

KRUPNICK, MARK, *Displacement: Derrida and After* (Indiana University Press, 1983).

KRYSINSKI, WLADIMIR, *Carrefours des signes: Essais sur le roman moderne* (Mouton, 1981).

LACOUE-LABARTHE, PHILIPPE, 'La Fable', *Poétique*, 1 (1970), 51–63.

—— 'Le Détour (Nietzche et la rhétorique)', *Poétique*, 5 (1971), 53–76.

—— 'L'Imprésentable', *Poétique*, 21 (1975), 53–95.

—— and NANCY, JEAN-LUC, 'Le Dialogue des genres: Textes de Shaftesbury, Hemsterhuis, Schelling', *Poétique*, 21 (1975), 148–75.

—— —— *L'Absolu littéraire: Théorie de la littérature du Romantisme allemand* (Seuil, 1978).

—— —— 'Genre', *Glyph*, 7 (1980).

LAFON, MICHEL, *Borges ou La Réécriture* (Seuil, 1990).

LAFOND, JEAN, *Les Formes brèves de la prose et le discours continu (XVIe–XVIIe siècles)* (Librairie Philosophique, 1984).

LAGOS, RAMONA, *Jorge Luis Borges, 1923–1980: Laberintos del espíritu, interjecciones del cuerpo* (Ediciones del Mall, 1986).

LÄMMERT, EBERHARD, *Bauformen des Erzählens* (Metzler, 1955).

LAMY, M. N., 'Le Dictionnaire et le métalangage', *Cahiers de Lexicologie*, 36 (1980–1), 95–110.

LANG, BEREL, *The Anatomy of Philosophical Style: Literary Philosophy and the Philosophy of Literature* (Blackwell, 1990).

LARUELLE, FRANÇOIS, *Machines textuelles: Deconstruction et libido d'écriture* (Seuil, 1976).

—— *Les Philosophies de la différence (Introduction critique)* (Presses Universitaires de France, 1986).

LAVERS, ANNETTE, *Roland Barthes: Structuralism and After* (Methuen, 1982).

LAWSON, HILARY, *Reflexivity: The Post-Modern Predicament* (Hutchinson, 1985).

LEAVIS, Q. D., *Fiction and the Reading Public* (Penguin Books, 1965).

LECERCLE, JEAN-JACQUES, *Philosophy Through the Looking-Glass: Language, Nonsense, Desire* (Hutchinson, 1985).

LEECH, GEOFFREY, *Semantics: The Study of Meaning*, 2nd edn. (Penguin Books, 1981).

—— *Principles of Pragmatics* (Longman, 1983).

LEITCH, VINCENT, *Deconstructive Criticism: An Advanced Introduction* (Hutchinson, 1983).

LEJEUNE, MICHEL, *Le Pacte autobiographique* (Seuil, 1975).

—— *Je est un autre: L'Autobiographie, de la littérature aux médias* (Seuil, 1980).

LELLOUCHE, RAPHAËL, *Borges ou L'Hypothèse de l'auteur* (Balland, 1989).

LENTRICCHIA, FRANK, *After the New Criticism* (Methuen, 1980).

LERNER, LAURENCE, *The Frontiers of Literature* (Blackwell, 1988).

LEVAILLANT, JEAN, *Écriture et génétique textuelle: Valéry à l'œuvre* (Presses Universitaires de Lille, 1982).

LEVINE, SUZANNE JILL, 'Adolfo Bioy Casares y J. L. Borges: La Utopía como Texto', *Revista Iberoamericana*, 43 (1977), 415–32.

LEVINSON, STEPHEN C., *Pragmatics* (Cambridge University Press, 1983).

LEVY, KURT L., and ELLIS, KEITH (eds.), *El ensayo y la crítica literaria en Iberoamérica* (University of Toronto, 1970).

LEWIS, PHILIP E., *La Rochefoucauld: The Art of Abstraction* (Cornell University Press, 1977).

LIPKING, LAWRENCE, 'The Marginal Gloss', *Critical Inquiry*, 3–4 (1977), 609–55.

LLEWELLYN, JOHN, *Derrida on the Threshold of Sense* (Macmillan, 1986).

LODGE, DAVID, *The Modes of Modern Writing: Metaphor, Metonymy, and the Typology of Modern Literature* (Cornell University Press, 1977).

LONGUET-MARX, ANNE, *Proust, Musil: Partage d'écritures* (Puf, 1986).

LOTMAN, IURI, 'Le "Hors-texte" et les liaisons extratextuelles de l'œuvre poétique', *Change*, 6 (1971), 12–23.

LUFT, DAVID, *Robert Musil and the Crisis of European Culture 1880–1942* (University of California Press, 1980).

LUKÁCS, GEORG VON, *Die Seele und die Formen: Essays* (Egon Fleischel und Co., 1911). ET: *Soul and Form: Essays*, trans. Anna Bostock (MIT Press, 1974).

—— *The Theory of the Novel: A Historico-Philosophical Essay on the Forms of Great Epic Literature*, trans. Anna Bostock (Merlin Press, 1971). ET: *Die Theorie des Romans: Ein geschichtsphilosophischer Versuch über die Formen der großen Epik* (Luchterhand, 1981).

LÜTZELER, PAUL MICHAEL, *Hermann Broch. Ethik und Politik: Studien zum Frühwerk und zur Romantrilogie 'Die Schlafwandler'* (Winkler Verlag, 1973).

LYOTARD, JEAN-FRANÇOIS, *Le Différend* (Minuit, 1984).

MACADAM, ALFRED J., 'Translation as Metaphor: Three Versions of Borges', *Modern Language Notes*, 90 (1975), 747–54.

—— 'Lenguaje y Estética en *Inquisiciones*', *Revista Iberoamericana*, 43/100–1 (1977), 637–43.

McCormick, John, *Fiction as Knowledge: The Modern Post-Romantic Novel* (Rutgers University Press, 1975).

Macdonell, Diane, *Theories of Discourse: An Introduction* (Blackwell, 1986).

McFarlane, Ian D., and Maclean, Ian (eds.), *Montaigne: Essays in Memory of Richard Sayce* (Oxford University Press, 1982).

McGowan, Margaret, *Montaigne's Deceits: The Art of Persuasion in the 'Essais'* (University of London Press, 1974).

McHale, Brian, *Postmodernist Fiction* (Methuen, 1987).

Macherey, Pierre, 'Borges and the Fictive Narrative', in Jaime Alazraki (ed.), *Critical Essays on Jorge Luis Borges*, 77–82.

McKinley, Mary B., *Words in a Corner* (French Forum, 1981).

Madrid, Lelia, *Cervantes y Borges: La inversión de los signos* (Editorial Pliegos, 1987).

Mallac, Guy de, and Eberbach, M., *Barthes* (Éditions Universitaires, 1971).

Man, Paul de, *Allegories of Reading: Figural Language in Rousseau, Nietzsche, Rilke, and Proust* (Yale University Press, 1979).

—— *Blindness and Insight: Essays in the Rhetoric of Contemporary Criticism* (Methuen, 1983).

Mandelkow, Karl Robert, *Hermann Broch's Romantrilogie 'Die Schlafwandler': Gestalt und Reflexion im modernen deutschen Roman* (Carl Winter, 1962).

Marin, Louis, *Le Récit est un piège* (Minuit, 1978).

—— *Utopics: Spatial Play* (Humanities Press, 1984; trans. from the French by R. A. Vollrath).

Martínez-Bonati, Felix, *Fictive Discourse and the Structures of Literature: A Phenomenological Approach* (Cornell University Press, 1981).

Massuh, Gabriela, *Borges: Una estética del silencio* (Editorial de Belgrano, 1980).

Mayenowa, Maria Renata, 'Expressions guillemetées: Contribution à l'étude de la sémantique du texte poétique', in A. J. Greimas and R. Jakobson *et al.*, (eds.), *Sign, Language and Culture* (Mouton, 1970), 645–57.

Mehlman, Jeffrey, *A Structural Study of Autobiography: Proust, Leiris, Sartre, Lévi-Strauss* (Cornell University Press, 1974).

Meleuc, Serge, 'Structure de la maxime', *Langages*, 3 (1963), 69–99.

Melville, Stephen W., *Philosophy Beside Itself: On Deconstruction and Modernism* (Manchester University Press, 1986).

Merivale, Patricia, 'The Flaunting of Artifice in Nabokov and Borges', in Jaime Alazraki (ed.), *Critical Essays on Jorge Luis Borges*, 141–52.

Metschies, Michael, *Zitat und Zitierkunst in Montaigne's 'Essais'* (Droz, 1966).

Metzer, Sarah E., 'Pascal's *Pensées*: Economy and Interpretation of Fragments', *Stanford French Review*, 6 (1982), 207–21.

Metzing, Dieter (ed.), *Frame Conceptions and Text Understanding* (W. de Gruyter, 1980).

Meyer, Hermann, *Das Zitat in der Erzählkunst: Zur Geschichte und Poetik des europäischen Romans* (Metzler, 1961).

Michaud, Ginette, 'Fragment et dictionnaire: Autour de l'écriture abécédaire de Barthes', *Études Françaises*, 18 (1983), 57–78.

Mignolo, Walter, 'Emergencia, Espacio, "Mundos Posibles": Las Propuestas Epistemológicas de J. L. Borges', *Revista Iberoamericana*, 43 (1977), 357–79.

Miller, Norbert, 'Die Rolle des Zitierens', *Sprache im technischen Zeitalter*, 1–4 (1961–2), 164–9.

Missac, Pierre, 'Aphorisme et paragramme', *Poétique*, 67 (1986), 301–14.

MITCHELL, W. J. T., *On Narrative* (University of Chicago Press, 1981).

—— *Against Theory: Literary Studies and the New Pragmatism* (University of Chicago Press, 1985).

Modern Fiction Studies, 19 (1973), special issue: 'Jorge Luis Borges'.

MOI, TORIL (ed.), *The Kristeva Reader* (Blackwell, 1986).

MOLLOY, SYLVIA, '"Dios Acecha en los Intervalos": Simulacro y Causalidad Textual en la Ficción de Borges', *Revista Iberoamericana*, 43 (1977), 381–97.

—— *Las letras de Borges* (Editorial Sudamericana, 1979).

MON, FRANZ, *Texte über Texte* (Luchterhand, 1970).

MONTAIGNE, MICHEL DE, *Œuvres complètes*. Textes établis par Albert Thibaudet et Maurice Rat (Bibliothèque de la Pléiade, Gallimard, 1962). ET: Montaigne, *The Complete Essays* ed. M. A. Screech (Penguin, 1991).

MONTANDON, ALAIN (ed.), *Le Point final* (Actes du Colloque International de Clermont-Ferrand, 1984).

MORAWSKI, STEFAN, 'The Basic Function of Quotation', in A. J. Greimas, R. Jakobson, *et al.* (eds.), *Sign, Language and Culture* (Mouton, 1970), 690–705.

MORETTI, FRANCO, *The Way of the World: The 'Bildungsroman' in European Culture* (Verso, 1987).

MORSON, GARY SAUL, and EMERSON, CARYL, *Mikhail Bakhtin: Creation of a Prosaics* (Stanford University Press, 1990).

MOSCA, STEFANIA, *Utopía y realidad* (Monte Avila Editores, 1983).

MOSER, WALTER, 'L'Encyclopédie romantique: Le Brouillon de Novalis', in *Le Genre/Die Gattung/Genre* (Colloque International de Strasbourg, 1979), 500–9.

—— 'Fragment and Encyclopedia: From Borges to Novalis', in L. Kritzman (ed.), Fragments: Incompletion and Discontinuity (New York Literary Forum, 1981) 111–28.

MOURALIS, BERNARD, *Les Contre-littératures* (Presses Universitaires de France, 1975).

MOUREY, JEAN-PIERRE, 'Le Texte et sa fiction chez Jorge Luis Borges: Mirages et miroirs', *Poétique*, 45 (1981), 67–78.

—— *Jorge Luis Borges: Vérité et univers fictionnels* (Pierre Mardaga Editeur, 1988).

MUSIL, ROBERT, *Tagebücher, Aphorismen, Essays und Reden*, ed. Adolf Frisé (Rowohlt, Hamburg, 1955).

—— *Prosa, Dramen, Späte Briefe*, ed. Adolf Frisé (Rowohlt, 1957).

—— *Der Mann ohne Eigenschaften* (Rowohlt, 1978). ET: *The Man Without Qualities*, 3 vols., trans. Eithne Wilkins and Ernst Kaiser (Secker and Warburg, 1953, 1954, and 1960).

—— *Briefe 1901–1942*, ed. Adolf Frisé (Rowohlt, 1981).

NANCY, JEAN-LUC, 'Logodaedalus (Kant écrivain)', *Poétique*, 21 (1975), 24–52.

New Literary History, 6 (1975), special issue: 'On Narrative and Narratives'.

New Literary History, 13 (1982), special issue: 'Narrative Analysis and Interpretation'.

Nineteenth Century Fiction, 33 (1978), special issue: 'Narrative Endings'.

NISBET, H. B. (ed.), *German Aesthetic and Literary Criticism: Winckelmann, Lessing, Hamann, Herder, Schiller and Goethe* (Cambridge University Press, 1985).

NOGUEZ, DOMINIQUE, 'Qu'est-ce que la paralittérature?', *Scolies*, 2 (1972).

NORDAHL LUND, STEFFEN, *L'Aventure du signifiant: Une lecture de Barthes* (Presses Universitaires de France, 1981).

NORRIS, CHRISTOPHER, *Deconstruction: Theory and Practice* (Methuen, 1982).

—— *The Deconstructive Turn: Essays in the Rhetoric of Philosophy* (Methuen, 1983).

NORTON, GLYN P., *Montaigne and the Introspective Mind* (Mouton, 1975).

NOVALIS (Friedrich von Hardenberg), *Novalis Schriften*, ed. Paul Kluckshorn and Richard Samuel, 4 vols. (Stuttgart, 1960–75).

NUÑO MONTES, JUAN, *La filosofía de Borges* (Fondo de Cultura Económica, 1986).

O'HARA, DANIEL, BOVE, PAUL, and SPANOS, WILLIAM (eds.), *The Question of Textuality: Strategies of Reading in Contemporary American Criticism* (Indiana University Press, 1982).

OHMANN, RICHARD, 'Speech Acts and Definition of Literature', *Philosophy and Rhetoric*, 4 (1971), 1–19.

O'NEILL, JOHN, *Essaying Montaigne: A Study of the Renaissance Institution of Writing and Reading* (Routledge & Kegan Paul, 1982).

PALMER, F. R., *Semantics* (Cambridge University Press, 1976).

PARRET, HERMAN, *Semiotics and Pragmatics: An Evaluative Comparison of Conceptual Frameworks* (Johns Benjamins Publishing Company, 1983).

—— APOSTEL, LEO, GOCHET, PAUL, VAN OVERBEKE, MAURICE, *et al.* (eds.), *Le Langage en contexte: Études philosophiques et linguistiques de pragmatique* (John Benjamins, 1980).

PELLICER, ROSA, *Borges: El estilo de la eternidad* (Libros Portico, 1988).

PÉREZ, ALBERTO C., *Realidad y suprarealidad en los cuentos fantásticos de J. L. Borges* (Ediciones Universal, 1971).

PÉREZ, ALBERTO JULIÁN, *Poética de la prosa de J. L. Borges: Hacia una crítica Bakhtiniana de la literatura* (Editorial Gredos, 1986).

PERRONE-MOISÉS, LEYLA, 'L'Intertextualité critique', *Poétique*, 27 (1976), 372–84.

PHILLIPS GRIFFITHS, A. (ed.), *Philosophy and Literature* (Cambridge University Press, 1984).

PIEROLA, ALBA OMIL DE, 'Jorge Luis Borges: Del ensayo a la ficción narrativa', in Kurt L. Levy and Keith Ellis (eds.) *El ensayo y la crítica literaria* . . . (University of Toronto Press, 1970), 155–60.

PIERSSENS, MICHEL, *La Tour de Babil* (Minuit, 1976).

Poétique, 69 (1987), special issue: 'Paratextes'.

POIRIER, RICHARD, *The Performing Self: Compositions and Decompositions in the Languages of Contemporary Life* (Chatto and Windus, 1971).

POPKIN, RICHARD H., *The History of Scepticism from Erasmus to Descartes* (Van Gorcum, 1961).

PRATT, MARY-LOUISE, *Toward a Speech-Act Theory of Literary Discourse* (Indiana University Press, 1977).

PRENDERGAST, CHRISTOPHER, *The Order of Mimesis: Balzac, Stendhal, Nerval, Flaubert* (Cambridge University Press, 1986).

PRINCE, GERALD, *Narratology: The Form and Function of Narrative* (Mouton, 1982).

PROUST, MARCEL, *Contre Sainte-Beuve* (Gallimard, 1954). ET: *Against Sainte-Beuve and Other Essays*, trans. John Sturrock (Penguin, 1988).

—— *Le Carnet de 1908* (Gallimard, 1976).

—— *À la recherche du temps perdu* (Folio). ET: *Remembrance of Things Past*, trans. C. K. Scott Moncrieff, Terence Kilmartin, and Andreas Mayor (Random House, 1981).

—— *Selected Letters*, ii. *1904–1909*, ed. Philip Kolb, trans. Terence Kilmartin (Oxford University Press, 1989).

PUCCINI, DARIO, 'Borges como crítico literario y el problema de la novela', in Kurt L. Levy and Keith Ellis (eds.), *El ensayo y la crítica literaria* . . . (University of Toronto Press, 1970), 145–53.

PUGH, ANTHONY R., *The Birth of 'À La Recherche du Temps Perdu'* (French Forum Publishers, 1987).

QUEMADA, BERNARD, 'Du glossaire au dictionnaire: Deux aspects de l'élaboration des énoncés lexicographiques dans les grands répertoires du XVIIe siècle', *Cahiers de Lexicologie*, 20 (1972), 97–128.

QUINT, DAVID, *Origin and Originality in Renaissance Literature: Versions of the Source* (Yale University Press, 1983).

RABKIN, ERIC, *Narrative Suspense: 'When Slim Turned Sideways . . .'* (University of Michigan, 1973).

RAIMOND, MICHEL, *La Crise du roman: Des lendemains du naturalisme aux années 20* (José Corti, 1966).

RASCH, WOLFDIETRICH (ed.), *Friedrich Schlegel: Kritische Schriften* (Hanser Verlag, 1970).

RECCHIO, THOMAS E., 'A Dialogic Approach to the Essay', in Alexander J. Butrym (ed.), *Essays on the Essay: Redefining the Genre* (University of Georgia Press, 1989).

RÉE, JONATHAN, *Philosophical Tales: An Essay on Philosophy and Literature* (Methuen, 1987).

REEDER, CLAUDIA, 'Paradoxe du (para)texte', *L'Esprit Créateur*, 24 (1984), 36–48.

REGOSIN, RICHARD L., *The Matter of my Book: Montaigne's 'Essais' as the Book of the Self* (University of California Press, 1977).

RENDALL, STEVEN, 'In Disjointed Parts/*Par articles décousus*', in Laurence Kritzman (ed.), *Fragments: Incompletion and Discontinuity* (New York Literary Forum, 1981).

RENIERS-SERVRANCKX, ANNIE, *Robert Musil: Konstanz und Entwicklung von Themen, Motiven und Strukturen in den Dichtungen* (Bouvier Verlag, 1972).

REST, JAIME, *El laberinto del universo: Borges y el pensamiento nominalista* (Ediciones Librerías Fausto, 1976).

REY, ALAIN, 'A propos de la définition lexicographique', *Cahiers de Lexicologie*, 6 (1965), 67–80.

—— 'Les Dictionnaires: Forme et contenu', *Cahiers de Lexicologie*, 7 (1965), 65–102.

—— *L'Enjeu des signes: Lecture de Nietzsche* (Seuil, 1971).

—— *Encyclopédies et dictionnaires*, 'Que Say-je?', series no. 2000 (Presses Universitaires de France, 1982).

REY-DEBOVE, JOSETTE, 'La Définition lexicographique: Recherches sur l'équation sémique', *Cahiers de Lexicologie*, 8 (1966), 71–94.

—— 'Autonymie et métalangue', *Cahiers de Lexicologie*, 2 (1967), 15–27.

—— 'Le Dictionnaire comme discours sur la chose et discours sur le signe', *Semiotica*, 1 (1969), 185–95.

RICARDOU, JEAN, *Problèmes du nouveau roman* (Seuil, 1967).

—— *Pour une théorie du nouveau roman* (Seuil, 1971).

—— *Nouveaux problèmes du roman* (Seuil, 1978).

RICE, DONALD, and SCHOFER, PETER, '*S/Z*: Rhetoric and Open Reading', in *L'Esprit Créateur* (1982), 20–34.

RICHARD, JEAN-PIERRE, *Micro-lectures* (Seuil, 1979).

—— 'Nappe, charnière, interstice, point', *Poétique*, 47 (1981), 293–302.

RICHTER, DAVID H., *Fable's End: Completeness and Closure in Rhetorical Fiction* (University of Chicago Press, 1974).

RICHTER, JEAN PAUL, *Sämtliche Werke*, ed. Eduard Berend, 37 vols. (Berlin, 1952–3).

—— *Horn of Oberon: Jean Paul Richter's School for Aesthetics*, trans. Margaret Hale (Detroit, 1973).

RICOEUR, PAUL, *La Métaphore vive* (Seuil, 1975).

—— (ed.), *La Narrativité* (Editions du CNRS, 1980).

—— *Temps et récit*, i (Seuil, 1983).

—— *Temps et récit*, ii: *La Configuration du temps dans le récit de fiction* (Seuil, 1984).

—— *Temps et récit*, iii: *Le Temps raconté* (Seuil, 1985).

RIDER, FREDERICK, *The Dialectic of Selfhood in Montaigne* (Stanford University Press, 1973).

RIFFATERRE, MICHAEL, *La Production du texte* (Seuil, 1979).

—— 'La Syllepse intertextuelle', *Poétique*, 40 (1979), 496–501.

RIGOLOT, FRANÇOIS, 'Montaigne et la poétique de la marge', *Actes du Colloque International Montaigne* (1980), 140–74.

—— *Le Texte de la Renaissance: Des rhétoriqueurs à Montaigne* (Droz, 1982).

—— 'Prolégomènes à une étude du statut de l'appareil liminaire des textes littéraires', *L'Esprit Créateur*, 27 (1987), 7–18.

—— *Les Métamorphoses de Montaigne* (Presses Universitaires de France, 1988).

RIHA, KARL, *'Cross-Reading' und 'Cross-Talking': Zitat, Collagen als poetische und satirische Technik* (Metzler, 1971).

RIMMON-KENAN, SHLOMITH, *Narrative Fiction: Contemporary Poetics* (Methuen, 1983).

ROBERT, MARTHES, *Roman des origines et origines du roman* (Gallimard, 1972).

ROBINSON, JUDITH, 'L'Architecture ouverte de *La Jeune Parque*', *Poétique*, 37 (1979), 63–82.

RODRÍGUEZ MONEGAL, EMIR, 'El ensayo y la crítica en la América hispanica', in Kurt L. Levy and Keith Ellis (eds.), *El ensayo y la crítica literaria* . . . (University of Toronto, 1970), 221–7.

—— 'Borges y la *Nouvelle Critique*', *Revista Iberoamericana*, 38 (1972), 367–90.

ROGER, PHILIPPE, *Roland Barthes, Roman* (Grasset, 1986).

ROHNER, LUDWIG, *Der deutsche Essay: Materialien zur Geschichte und Ästhetik einer literarischen Gattung* (Luchterhand, 1966).

—— *Consequences of Pragmatism: Essays 1972–1980* (Harvester Press, 1982).

RORTY, RICHARD, *Philosophy and the Mirror of Nature*, 3rd edn. (Blackwell, 1986).

ROUSSET, JEAN, *Narcisse romancier* (José Corti, 1986).

ROUTH, H. V., 'The Origins of the Essay Compared in English and French Literature', *Modern Language Review*, 15 (1920), 28–40 and 143–51.

RYAN, MARIE-LAURE, 'Fiction as a Logical, Ontological, and Illocutionary Issue', *Style*, 18 (1984), 121–39.

SABRY, RANDA, 'Quand le texte parle de son paratexte', *Poétique*, 69 (1987), 83–100.

SACKS, SHELDON, *On Metaphor* (University of Chicago Press, 1978).

SAID, EDWARD W., *Beginnings: Intention and Method* (Johns Hopkins University Press, 1975).

—— *The World, the Text, and the Critic* (Faber and Faber, 1984).

SARDUY, SEVERO, *Barroco* (Editorial Suramericana, 1974).

SAYCE, RICHARD, *The Essays of Montaigne: A Critical Exploration* (Weidenfeld and Nicolson, 1972).

SCHAEFFER, JEAN-MARIE, 'Du texte au genre: Notes sur la problématique générique', *Poétique*, 53 (1983), 3–18.

—— 'Note sur la préface philosophique', *Poétique*, 69 (1987), 35–44.

SCHLEGEL, AUGUST WILHELM, *Course of Lectures on Dramatic Art and Literature*, trans. J. Black (London, 1846).

SCHLEGEL, FRIEDRICH, 'Kritische Fragmente', in Wolfdietrich Rasch (ed.), *Friedrich Schlegel: Kritische Schriften* (Hanser Verlag, 1970).

—— 'Athenäums-Fragmente' in W. Rasch (ed.), *Friedrich Schlegel: Kritische Schriften* (Hanser

Verlag, 1970). ET: 'Athenäum Fragments', in K. Wheeler (ed.), *German Aesthetic and Literary Criticism: The Romantic Ironists and Goethe* (Cambridge University Press, 1984).

SCHLEGEL, FRIEDRICH, 'Ideen' in W. Rasch (ed.), *Friedrich Schlegel: Kritische Schriften* (Hanser Verlag, 1970). ET: 'Ideas', in David Simpson (ed.), *The Origins of Modern Critical Thought* (Cambridge University Press, 1988).

—— 'Brief über den Roman' in W. Rasch (ed.), *Friedrich Schlegel: Kritische Schriften* (Hanser Verlag, 1970). ET: 'Letter about the Novel', in K. Wheeler (ed.), *German Aesthetic and Literary Criticism: The Romantic Ironists and Goethe* (Cambridge University Press, 1984).

—— 'Über Goethes "Meister"' in W. Rasch (ed.), *Friedrich Schlegel: Kritische Schriften* (Hanser Verlag, 1970). ET: 'On Goethe's "Meister"', in K. Wheeler (ed.), *German Aesthetic and Literary Criticism: The Romantic Ironists and Goethe* (Cambridge University Press, 1984).

SCHLEIFER, RONALD, *A. J. Greimas and the Nature of Meaning: Linguistics, Semiotics, and Discourse Theory* (Croom Helm, 1987).

SCHOLES, ROBERT, *Structuralism in Literature: An Introduction* (Yale University Press, 1974).

—— *Fabulation and Metafiction* (University of Illinois Press, 1979).

—— *Semiotics and Interpretation* (Yale University Press, 1982).

—— and KELLOGG, ROBERT, *The Nature of Narrative* (Oxford University Press, 1966).

—— and KLAUS, CARL (eds.) *Elements of the Essay* (Oxford University Press, 1969).

—— —— *Elements of Literature*, 4th edn. (Oxford University Press, 1991).

SCHON, PETER M., *Vorformen des Essays in Antike und Humanismus: Ein Beitrag zur Entstehungsgeschichte der 'Essais' von Montaigne* (Franz Steiner, 1954).

SCHRADER, MONIKA, *Mimesis und Poiesis* (De Gruyter, 1975).

SCHRAMKE, JÜRGEN, *Die Theorie des modernen Romans* (Beck, 1974).

SCHRAMM, ULF, *Fiktion und Reflektion: Überlegungen zu Musil und Beckett* (Suhrkamp, 1967).

SEARLE, JOHN R., *Speech Acts: An Essay in the Philosophy of Language* (Cambridge University Press, 1969).

—— 'The Logical Status of Fictional Discourse', *New Literary History*, 6 (1975), 319–32.

SERRA, EDELWEISS, 'La Estrategia del Lenguaje en *Historia Universal de la Infamia*', in *Revista Iberoamericana*, 43 (1977), 275–84.

SHAPIRO, GARY, and SICA, ALAN, *Hermeneutics* (University of Massachussets Press, 1984).

SHARMA, VIJAY L., *Virginia Woolf as Literary Critic: A Revaluation* (Arnold–Heinemann, 1977).

SIMPSON, DAVID (ed.), *The Origins of Modern Critical Thought: German Aesthetic and Literary Criticism from Lessing to Hegel* (Cambridge University Press, 1988).

SINGER, PETER, *Hegel* (Oxford University Press, 1983).

SONTAG, SUSAN, *Against Interpretation and Other Essays* (Dell, 1967).

—— *L'Écriture même: À propos de Roland Barthes* (Christian Bourgois, 1982).

STABB, MARTIN S., *In Quest of Identity: Patterns in the Spanish-American Essay of Ideas 1890–1960* (University of North Carolina Press, 1967).

—— *Jorge Luis Borges* (Twayne Publishers, 1970).

STAPLETON, LAURENCE, *The Elected Circle: Studies in the Art of Prose* (Princeton University Press, 1973).

STARK, JOHN, 'Borges's "Tlön, Uqbar, Orbis Tertius" and Nabokov's *Pale Fire*: Literature of Exhaustion', *Texas Studies in Literature and Language*, 14 (1972).

—— *The Literature of Exhaustion: Borges, Nabokov, and Barth* (Duke University Press, 1974).

STAROBINSKI, JEAN, *Words upon Words: The Anagrams of Ferdinand de Saussure* (Yale University Press, 1979; trans. from the French).

—— *Montaigne en mouvement* (Gallimard, 1982).

STEFFEN, HANS (ed.), *Die deutsche Romantik* (Vandenhoeck & Ruprecht, 1989).

STEINECKE, HARTMUT, *Das Schlafwandeln: Zur Deutung des Motivs in Hermann Brochs Trilogie*

STEINER, GEORGE, *Language and Silence: Essays 1958–1966* (Faber & Faber, 1967).

—— *In Bluebeard's Castle: Some Notes towards the Re-definition of Culture* (Faber & Faber, 1971).

—— *After Babel: Aspects of Language and Translation* (Oxford University Press, 1975).

—— *On Difficulty, and Other Essays* (Oxford University Press, 1978).

STEVICK, PHILIP, *The Chapter in Fiction: Theories of Narrative Division* (Syracuse University Press, 1970).

STEWART, SUSAN, *Nonsense: Aspects of Intertextuality in Folklore and Literature* (Johns Hopkins University Press, 1979).

STIERLE, KARLHEINZ, 'L'Histoire comme exemple, l'exemple comme histoire: Contribution à la pragmatique et à la poétique des textes narratifs', *Poétique*, 10 (1972), 176–99.

—— 'The Reading of Fictional Texts', in Susan Suleiman and Inge Crossman (eds.), *The Reader in the Text* (Princeton University Press, 1980), 83–105.

STRELKA, JOSEPH P., *Kafka, Musil, Broch und die Entwicklung des modernen Romans* (Forum, 1959).

STROUD, BARRY, *The Significance of Philosophical Scepticism* (Clarendon Press, 1989).

Studies in 20th Century Literature, 5 (1981), special issue: 'Roland Barthes'.

STURROCK, JOHN, *Paper Tigers: The Ideal Fictions of Jorge Luis Borges* (Oxford University Press, 1977).

Sub-Stance, 56 (1988), special issue: 'Reading In And Around' (on paratexts).

SULEIMAN, SUSAN R., 'Le Récit exemplaire: Parabole, fable, roman à thèse', *Poétique*, 32 (1977), 468–89.

—— and CROSSMAN, INGE (eds.), *The Reader in the Text: Essays on Audience and Interpretation* (Princeton University Press, 1980).

SUTHERLAND, JAMES (ed.), Oxford History of English Literature, vi. *English Literature of the Late Seventeenth Century* (Oxford University Press, 1969).

SWALES, MARTIN, *The German Bildungsroman from Wieland to Hesse* (Princeton University Press, 1978).

SWIGGERS, PIERRE, 'La Grammaire dans l'encyclopédie: Signe et sens', *Romanische Forschungen*, 93 (1981), 122–37.

SYCHRAVA, JULIET, *Schiller to Derrida: Idealism in Aesthetics* (Cambridge University Press, 1989).

SZONDI, PETER, *Poésie et poétique de l'idéalisme allemand* (Éditions de Minuit, 1975).

TAMAYO, MARCIAL, and RUIZ-DÍAZ, ADOLFO, *Borges: Enigma y Clave* (Editorial Nuestro Tiempo, 1955).

TANNER, TONY, *City of Words: American Fiction 1950–1970* (Jonathan Cape, 1971).

TEGAI HUGHES, GLYN, *Romantic German Literature* (Edward Arnold, 1979).

Tel Quel (Seuil, 1968), special issue: 'Théorie d'ensemble'.

Tel Quel, 47 (1971), special issue: 'Barthes'.

TERRASSE, JEAN, *Rhétorique de l'essai littéraire* (Les Presses de l'Université de Québec, 1977).

Texte, 1 (1982), special issue: 'L'Autoreprésentation: Le Texte et ses miroirs'.

Texte, 'L'Intertextualité: Intertexte, autotexte, intratexte', 2 (1983).

—— 'Roland Barthes', 34–5 (1984).

—— 'Traduction/Textualité/Translatability', 4 (1985).

THIERKOPF, DIETRICH, 'Nähe und Ferne: Kommentare zu Benjamin's Denkverfahren', *Text + Kritik*, 31–2 (1979), 3–18.

THOMPSON, ELBERT N. S., *The Seventeenth-Century English Essay* (University of Iowa Humanistic Studies, 1926).

TODOROV, TZVETAN, *Littérature et signification* (Larousse, 1967).

—— *Poétique de la prose, suivi de: Nouvelles recherches sur le récit* (Seuil, 1971).

—— *Théories du symbole* (Seuil, 1977).

—— *Symbolisme et interprétation* (Seuil, 1978).

—— *Les Genres du discours* (Seuil, 1978).

—— 'Bakhtine et l'altérité', *Poétique*, 40 (1979), 502–13.

—— *Critique de la critique: Un roman d'apprentissage* (Seuil, 1984).

TORGOVNICK, MARIANNA, *Closure in the Novel* (Princeton University Press, 1981).

TOURNON, ANDRÉ, *Montaigne: La Glose et l'essai* (Presses Universitaires de Lyon, 1983).

Triquarterly, 25 (1972), special issue: 'Borges'.

UNGAR, STEVEN, 'Parts and Holes: Heraclitus/Nietzche/Blanchot', *Sub-Stance*, 14 (1976), 126–41.

—— *Roland Barthes: The Professor of Desire* (University of Nebraska Press, 1983).

URELLO, ANTONIO, *Verosimilitud y estrategia textual en el ensayo hispanoamericano* (Premia editoria, 1986).

URMSON, J. O., and RÉE, JONATHAN (eds.), *The Concise Encyclopedia of Western Philosophy and Philosophers* (Unwin Hyman, 1989).

USPENSKY, BORIS, *A Poetics of Composition: The Structure of the Artistic Text and Typology of a Compositional Form* (University of California Press, 1973; trans. from the Russian).

VALIS, NOËL M., 'El prólogo de prólogos y J. L. Borges', *Los Ensayistas*, 3 (1978), 856–8.

VAN DIJK, TEUN A. (ed.), *Pragmatics of Language and Literature* (North Holland Publishing Company, 1976).

—— *Text and Context: Explorations in the Semantics and Pragmatics of Discourse* (Longman, 1977).

VERNON, J., *The Garden and the Map: Schizophrenia in Twentieth-Century Literature and Culture* (University of Illinois Press, 1973).

VIGNERON, ROBERT, 'Creative Agony', in René Girard (ed.), *Proust: A Collection of Critical Essays* (Greenwood Press, 1977).

VOLEK, EMIL, '"Aquiles y la Tortuga": Arte, Imaginación, y la Realidad según Borges', *Revista Iberoamericana*, 43 (1977), 293–310.

—— *Cuatro claves para la modernidad: Análisis semiótico de textos hispánicos (Aleixandre, Borges, Carpentier, Cabrera Infante)* (Editorial Gredos, 1984).

VUARNET, JEAN-NOËL, *Le Discours Impur* (Editions Galilée, 1973).

WALKER, HUGH, *The English Essay and Essayists* (Dent, 1915).

WARNING, RAINER, 'Staged Discourse: Remarks on the Pragmatics of Fiction', *Dispositio*, 5 (1980) 35–54.

WATT, IAN, *The Rise of the Novel: Studies in Defoe, Richardson and Fielding* (Penguin Books, 1979).

WAUGH, PATRICIA, *Metafiction: The Theory and Practice of Self-Conscious Fiction* (Methuen, 1984).

WEISGERBER, JEAN, 'The Use of Quotation in Recent Literature', *Comparative Literature*, 22 (1970), 36–45.

WEISSENBERGER, KLAUS (ed.), *Prosakunst ohne Erzählen: Die Gattungen der nicht-fiktionalen Kunstprosa* (Max Niemeyer, 1985).

WELLEK, RENÉ, and WARREN, AUSTIN, *Theory of Literature*, 3rd edn. (Pelican Books, 1982).

WHEELER, KATHLEEN (ed.), *German Aesthetic and Literary Criticism: The Romantic Ironists and Goethe* (Cambridge University Press, 1984).

—— *Romanticism, Pragmatism and Deconstruction* (Blackwell, 1993).

WHEELOCK, CARTER, *The Mythmaker: A Study of Motif and Symbol in the Short Stories of J. L. Borges* (University of Texas Press, 1969).

WHITE, ALLON, *The Uses of Obscurity: The Fiction of Early Modernism* (Routledge & Kegan Paul, 1981).

—— *Tropics of Discourse: Essays in Cultural Criticism* (Johns Hopkins University Press, 1978).

WHITE, HAYDEN, 'The Question of Narrative in Contemporary Historical Theory', *History and Theory*, 23 (1984), 1–33.

WHITE, LAURENCE L., 'Modern Traditions of the Essay', D. Phil. thesis, University of North Carolina, 1987.

WIEDMANN, AUGUST, *Romantic Art Theories* (Gresham Books, 1986).

WILDE, OSCAR, 'The Critic as Artist', in *Plays, Prose Writings and Poems* (Everyman Library, Dent, 1930).

WOLIN, RICHARD, 'The Essay as Mediation between Art and Philosophical Truth', in *Walter Benjamin: An Aesthetic of Redemption* (Columbia University Press, 1982).

WOOD, DAVID, *Philosophy at the Limit* (Unwin Hyman, 1990).

WOOLF, VIRGINIA, 'Addison', in *The Common Reader*, i.

—— 'The Modern Essay', in *The Common Reader*, i.

—— *The Common Reader*, i and ii (The Hogarth Press, 1984 and 1986).

WORTON, MICHAEL, and STILL, JUDITH (eds.), *Intertextuality: Theories and Practices* (Manchester University Press, 1990).

WÜTHENOW, RALF-RAINER, *Im Buch die Bücher oder der Held als Leser* (Europäische Verlagsanstalt, 1980).

WYERS WEBER, FRANCIS, 'Borges's Stories: Fiction and Philosophy', *Hispanic Review*, 36 (1968), 124–41.

Yale French Studies, 67 (1984), special issue: 'Concepts of Closure'.

YOUNG, ROBERT, *Untying the Text: A Post-Structuralist Reader* (Routledge & Kegan Paul, 1981).

ZIMA, PETER V., *L'Ambivalence romanesque: Proust, Kafka, Musil* (Le Sycomore, 1980).

—— *Textsoziologie: Eine kritische Einführung* (Metzler, 1980).

—— 'Bakhtin's Young Hegelian Aesthetics', in *The Bakhtin Circle Today, Critical Studies*, 1/2 (1989), ed. Myriam Diaz-Diocaretz.

ZIOLKOWSKI, THEODORE, *Dimensions of the Modern Novel* (Princeton University Press, 1969).

ZUIDERVAART, LAMBERT, *Adorno's Aesthetic Theory: The Redemption of Illusion* (MIT Press, 1991).

ZUM FELDE, ALBERTO, *Índice crítico de la literatura hispanoamericana: Los ensayistas* (Editorial Guarania, 1954).

ZUMTHOR, PAUL, *Langue, texte, énigme* (Seuil, 1975).

—— 'Le Carrefour des rhétoriqueurs: Intertextualité et rhétorique', *Poétique*, 7 (1976), 317–37.

Index (1)

Two indexes are provided here. Since the second, 'ordinary' index lists nouns, verbs and adjectives as they appear on the page, this first index should help locate the majority of these terms (listed alphabetically under each main category), affiliate them to a main concept and its opposite, and thereby trace them back to the argument(s) to which they belong. Due to the paradoxical nature of the overall 'thesis' of this book, overlappings and repetitions of terms between *and* within conceptual categories are frequent. Terms which appear virtually on every other page (such as 'essay', 'essayism', 'genre' or 'literature') have not been listed.

THE ESSAY AND OTHER GENRES/FORMS

Adage, aphorism, article, autobiography, biography, confession, criticism, dialogue, diary, dictionary, dissertation, draft, encyclopedia, epic, epilogue, *exemplum*, fable, footnote, foreword, fragment, gloss, heading, index, journal, letter, magazine, maxim, notebooks, notes, novel, *parergon*, *Pensée*, periodical, play, poem, portrait, postscript, preface, prologue, quotation, *résumé*, review, romance, self-portrait, sentence, sermon, short story, table, *topos*, tract, treatise.

RECEPTION

Apprenticeship, *Bildung*, common man, (common) reader, (common) opinion, clarity, comprehensibility, convention, cultivation, desire, detective, dialectic, dialogue, difficulty, education, empirical, enlightenment, entertainment, esoteric, everyman, experience, expository, formation, heuristic, hope, implied reader, impressionist, incomprehensibility, individualism, inquisition, obscurity, pact, place, point of view, polyphony, popularizing, position, posture, propaedeutics, reading, readability, reader, readerly, reception, rereading, Romanticism, speech, subjectivity, teaching, thread (*see* Indirection), vulgarizing.

MAIN OPPOSITIONS INVOLVED IN THE BOOK

ABSOLUTE VS RELATIVE: Certainty, constant, definitive, epic, eternal, firm, fixed, impersonal, invariable, monologic, mystics, selfless, solid, stable, stasis, timeless, unchanging, universal vs change, circumstance, context, contingency, degree, deictics, dialogic, difference, diversity, dynamic, flattening, here and now, indifferent, individual, insignificant, interchangeable, many-sidedness, markers, mobility/mobilizing, motion, movement, multilingual, multiplicity, multi-temporal, novelness/novelization, partial, particularity, perspective, pertinence, play, plurality, point of view, polyphonic, relativization, scepticism, shifters, singular, specific, standpoint, temporal, vantage-point, variety, version, viewpoint, weighing.

CENTRING VS INDIRECTION: Etymology, centralizing, homeland, key-words, mana words, naming/nomination, punctuation, recentring, recontextualisation, sufficient words, typography (*see also* Linearity, Closure, Method) vs accessory, adjacency, adjective, adjunct, allegation, allusion, alongside, ambulation, analogical, angle, approximation, aside, atopia, auxiliary, decentring, deporting, derived, detachment, detour, deviance, deviation, digression, dispensability, distancing, diversion, eccentric, expitextuality, errancy/erring, example, excursion/excursus, extraliterary, extrapolation, extratextual, homelessness, *hors-d'oeuvre*, *hors-texte*, invoking, key-words, mana words, meandering, oblique, ornament, para, paraliterary, parasitical, paratextuality, *parergon*, perigraphy, peripheral, peritextual, protection, punctuation, redundancy, remainder, residue, shift, skidding, skirting, subsidiary, sufficient words, suggestion, superfluous, supplementary, tangents, typography, unnamable, variant, variation, version, wandering, warping.

FICTION VS NON FICTION (lie vs truth): affabulation, as if, bogus, character, fables, fabulating, fake, falsifying, fantastic, fantasy, feigning, fictional, fictionalizing, figural, forgery, image, imagination, *in potentia*, lie, magical, marvellous, metaphor, myth, novel, oniric, scepticism, short story, theory, unscientific, untruth, utopia, verisimilitude, virtuality (q.v.) vs authenticity, authorial, authority, autobiography, biography, confession, diary, discourse/discursive, extraliterary, mimesis, persuasion, philosophy, pre-literary, science, theory, truth.

FORMLESSNESS VS METHOD: aconceptual, alogical, accidental, antistructural, antisystematic, arbitrary, baggy, chance, chaos, disorderly, formlessness, fortuitous, fortune, haphazard, informal, inversion, irrationality, looseness, lots and dices, nominalism, play, poetic, randomness, reversal, speech, shapelessness, spontaneity, surprise, systematics, typography (incl. bold, chapter, italics, punctuation, title, typeface, underlining), unmethodical, unreason vs argument(ative), conceptualization, control, definition, didactic, dissertation, doctrinal, dogmatic, domination, emphasis, expository, frame, heading, head-word, hierarchy, intention, irreversible, mastery, maxim, method, necessity, order, philosophy, preconception, predetermination, prescriptive, presupposed, purpose, rationality, reason, sententious, structure, subordination, system, tract, treatise, typography (*see above*).

FRAGMENT VS WHOLE: *see* Virtual vs Actual; Juxtaposition vs Linearity; Reducing/Expanding vs Closure; Formlessness vs Method; Looking Forward/Looking Back; Centring vs Indirection; Absolute vs Relative; Trivial vs Serious; Reception.

JUXTAPOSITION VS LINEARITY: Aggregate, alphabet, antirhetorical, associative, atonal, bits, blanks, breaking off/up/into, catalogue, chasm, compilation, cutting up, dictionary, disconnection, discontinuity, discrepancy, disintegration, disjunction, dislocation, dismemberment, disparity, dispersal, disruption, dissemination, dissolution, dissonance, ellipsis, enumeration, gap, heteroclitic, heterogeneous, heterology, hiatus, inadequation, incommensurability, incompatibility, interpolation, interruption, juxtaposition, list, *Nebeneinander*, non-homogeneity, numbering/numerical, parataxis, part, piece, pile, poem/poetry, synchronic, rhetoric, rift, rupture, scattered, series, simultaneity, systematics, tabular, unclassifiability vs argument, beginnings, cause/effect, classification, consecutive, consequence, continuity, deduction, definition, diachronic, endings, filtering, first/last, fleshing out, frame, gradual, hierarchy, last, linear, memory, *Nacheinander*, narrative, omission, philosophy, plot, progression, recollection, rhetoric, selection, sequence, subordination, successive, systematic, thread, tonal.

LOOKING FORWARD VS LOOKING BACK: Adumbrations, announcement, antecedents, antedating, anteriority, anticipating, apprenticeship, attempt, conception, craving, desire, draft, drill, early, embryonic, ephemeral, evanescence, exercises, experiment, foreboding, foreword, future, hope, index, longing, looking forward to, metonymy, neotenous, notes, occasional, outline, *parergon*, potentiality, preceding, precipitous, precursor, preface, prefiguring, preliminary, pre-literary, prelude, premature, preparatives, previous, prior, project, prolepse, prologomena, prologue, propaedeutics, prospective, prospectus, provisional, quest, quotation, raw, rehearsal, search, seek, *Sehnsucht*, skeleton, sketch, staging, striving, temporary, tentativeness, test(ing), transient, transition, trial, trying out, yearning vs annotations, appendice, belatedness, commentary, criticism, epilogue, filiation, footnote, index, late, memory, metonymy, nostalgia, obsolescence, outmodedness, past, post-date, post-liminary, predecessor, quotation, retroaction, retrospective, secondary, second-hand, *Sehnsucht*, sources, survival.

NATURE VS CULTURE (natural vs artificial; primary vs secondary): Adamic, afresh, amnesia, anew, anti-memory, artlessness, child(like), creation, essence, etymology, ignorance, immediacy, initiating, innocence, innovation, invention, naivety, naturalizing, new, novelty, oral, origin(ality), presence, primal, primary, proper, renewal, renovation, speech, spontaneity vs artful, artifice, arty, belief, commonplace, consensus, convention, copy, culture, demystification, denaturalization, *doxa*, ideology, imitation, intermediate, invention, language, mediation, medium, memory, middle, mimesis, mirror, mnemonic, model, mystification, myth(ology), norm, opinion, origin(ality), orthodoxy, parroting, quotation, received opinion, re-creation, renewal, renovation, rewriting, secondariness, second-hand, *status quo*, topic, transindividual, verisimilitude.

PHILOSOPHY VS ART: Cognitive, epistemology, intellectual, judgement, philosophy, rational, reason, theory *vs* Aesthetic, feeling, irrationality, poetic, soul, unconscious. *See* Virtual vs Actual; Juxtaposition vs Linearity; Formlessness vs Method; Absolute vs Relative; Fiction vs Non Fiction; Trivial vs Serious; Reception.

PRIMARY VS SECONDARY: Creation *vs* criticism; *see* Looking Forward/Looking Back; Centring/Indirection; Sameness vs Otherness; Nature/Culture.

REDUCING/EXPANDING VS CLOSURE: Addition, *alongeail*, archi-literature, anti-systematic, becoming, blowing up, boundless, brief, ceaseless, circle, closure, concise, condensed, contradiction, counterencyclopedia, crisis, cycle, deferment, deficiency, delay, denial, deporting, dialogism, *différance*, dilatory, displacement, drifting, ellipsis, encyclopedia, essence, excessive/exceeding, expansion, growth, incompletion, inconclusiveness, indefinite, indeterminacy, inexhaustible, infinity, in progress, invasion, irony, lack, length(ening), limitless, linguistics, mana words, mode/modal, Modernism, neoteny, never-ceasing, never-ending, non-exhaustive, non-identity, non-totalizing, novelization, open-endedness, overflow, overgloss, overrun, oxymoron, palimpsest, paradox, perpetual, processual, recessive, regression, retreat, romanticization, scepticism, sign, spacing, sufficient words, surplus, suspension, systematics, tension, transgression, unattainable, unchecked, uncompleted, under erasure, unfinished, unlimited, unnaming, writerly, writing vs arrest, *Aufhebung*, check, classical, closure, completion, comprehensive, conclusive, constant, definite, definitive, determinacy, encyclopedia, ending, exhaustive, finality, finished, finite, foreclosed, frame, fulfilment, integral, overarching, overall, perfection, readerly, regulation, resolution, resting-place, restrained, result, solution, stable/stabilization, standstill, stasis, sticking, system(atic), synthesis, teleological, telos, totality/totalization, transcendental, ultimate, unity, wholeness.

SAMENESS VS OTHERNESS: amnesia, annotation, appropriation, authorial, autobiography, autonomy, classical, cogito, confession, consciousness, copy, creation, diary, discourse/ discursive, duplication, enunciation, essence, forgetfulness, 'I', identity, illocutionary, independence, individualism, intention, iterability, lyricism, meditation/meditative, memory, *mise en abyme*, monotony, nature (q.v.), ownership, parroting, personal(ity), plagiarism, portrait, posture, presence, proper, property, purpose, redundancy, repetition, replay, reprint, reproduction, resurgence, rewriting, sameness, selfhood, self-contained, self-sufficient, speech-act, specific, subjectivity, tautology, uniqueness, utterance vs analogical, alienation, allegation, alteration, alterity, citation, collective, copy, correction, dehumanization, detachment, disappropriation, distortion, estrangement, exile, extraneous, extrapolation, falsifying, filtering, foreign, imposture, indirection (q.v.), *locus*, memory, *mise en abyme*, misquoting, misreading, mnemonic, mutation, non-identity, omission, otherness, palimpsest, permutation, point of view, portrait, quotation (marks), reconfiguration, reflexiveness, repetition, rewriting, secondary, second-hand, selection, strangeness, transformation, transindividual, translation, transplant, unlocatable, witness.

TRIVIAL VS SERIOUS: Entertainment, frivolous, impressionist, irresponsibility, superficial, surface, vacuous vs depth, profound, responsibility, serious.

VIRTUAL VS ACTUAL: Abstract, as if/as though, child(like), conjunctively, fiction, hypothesis, idea, ideal, idealism, *in potentia*, invisible, mental, mind, not yet written, poem, possibility, potentiality, probability, saying, speech, staging, subjunctive, theory, thought, universal, unrealized, unwritten, utopia, virtuality vs apprenticeship, acting out/actualization, application, *Bildung*, concrete, debasement, degradation, doing, empiricial, enactment, experience, experiment, fleshing out, itinerary, journey, material(izing), maturity, odyssey, particular, passage, path, practice/practical, pragmatic, prosaism, realization, senses/sensuous, sensibility, travel, unfolding, visible, wandering, wayfaring, writing.

Index (2)

abbreviation 254, 258
absolute 31, 39, 43–7, 49, 51, 53, 56, 63, 92, 97, 99, 103, 109–10, 130, 141, 144–5, 210–11, 216, 220–1, 224, 225, 228, 233, 245, 255, 269, 278
absorb(tion) 20, 24
abstract (*vs* concrete) 19–20, 33, 42, 48, 50, 55, 70, 71, 75, 79, 86, 103, 106, 119–20, 124, 193–4, 200, 203, 205, 214, 217, 224, 226, 230, 237, 249
abstraction/abstracting (*vs* merging) 44, 75, 86, 88, 105, 112, 119, 138, 159, 171, 194, 195, 196, 200, 204, 208, 213, 237, 240–1, 254, 266–8
accessory 76, 85, 126, 131, 169
accidental 7, 70, 77–8, 90, 107, 165, 229, 261, 264, 272, 277
aconceptual 117, 163
action/activity 41, 119, 205–6, 208, 210, 213–17, 224, 230, 238, 241, 264
actual(ity)/acting out/actualization 19, 21, 25, 41, 57–8, 79, 110, 128, 138, 144, 170, 182, 188, 191, 200, 211, 220, 223, 228–9, 231, 239, 243, 249, 253–6, 258, 264, 267, 269, 271–3
adages 14
Adamic 171
additions/adding/additional 29, 30, 55, 74, 78, 79, 82, 87, 91, 93, 95–6, 116, 131–3, 159–62, 166–7, 169, 174, 176, 180, 189, 196, 220, 265, 272
adjacency 144
adjectives 23, 78, 246, 264
adjunct 247
adumbrations 16, 26
aesthetic 5, 11, 18–19, 34–5, 46, 48–9, 54–5, 100–2, 113–15, 123, 127, 130–1, 153, 183
Aesthetics 48, 54, 61–2, 99, 108, 136, 143, 276; Adorno 102; Hegel 43, 55, 130
affabulation 192
afresh 36, 55
aggregate 101, 163–4, 235
alienation 48, 88, 225–6, 231
allegation 96
allusion 182, 253–4, 265–7, 271, 273
alogical 172, 267
alongside 112
alongeails 79, 95
alphabet 153, 163–4, 166, 168, 171–2, 174–5, 189
alteration 74, 84
alterity 25

ambulation/ambulatory 2, 42, 94
amnesia 161, 189
anachronism 29, 38–40, 93, 96–7, 111, 187, 191, 240, 251, 270–1, 273, 275–6, 278, 281–2
analogical 35, 130, 178, 274
anew 55, 86, 106–7, 124
angle 2, 3, 37, 64, 77–8, 81, 91, 101, 113, 125, 164, 174, 179, 192, 223, 238
annotations/annotator 20, 56, 72, 83, 262, 268, 270
announce(ment)/annunciation 134, 185, 222, 253
antecedents 7, 22
antedating 127
anteriority 134, 160
anticipating 26, 29, 36, 41, 47, 61–2, 140, 164, 208, 239, 272
antiquity 7, 39, 81
anti-memory 92
anti-rhetorical 88
antistructural 150–1, 154–6
anti-systematic 31, 44, 50, 63, 74, 115, 125, 147
antithesis/antithetical 8, 46, 141, 165
aphorism/aphoristic 6, 7, 32, 37–8, 101, 193, 281
appendice 173, 174, 176
application 215
apprenticeship 42, 72, 226; Wilhelm Meister's 230
appropriation 85–7, 93–4, 124, 151, 161, 177–8, 189, 254, 272, 275, 278–9
approximations/approximating 78, 109, 143, 167, 169, 172, 257, 264–6
arbitrary 3, 4, 7, 67–8, 70, 74, 78, 96, 109, 118–19, 122–3, 142–3, 146, 152, 159–60, 163, 165, 172, 174–5, 179, 182, 190, 198, 201, 207, 220–1, 229, 245, 257, 267, 269
archi-literature 53
argument(ative) 3, 5, 37–8, 59, 68, 74–5, 80–1, 83, 86, 90, 100, 104, 111, 116, 172, 205, 237
arrest 190
artful 24
artifice/artificial 8, 65, 67, 81–2, 84, 86–8, 90–2, 216, 241, 245
artless(ness) 18–19, 28, 91
article (journals) 162, 193, 260–1, 265, 273
arty 19
aside 131
as if/as though/*als ob* 3, 182–4, 186, 191, 238, 251, 253–5, 257, 263–4, 271, 273, 280

associations/associative 3, 6, 28, 35, 76, 87, 116, 143, 153, 172, 194, 218, 228, 263, 266, 268
atemporal 99, 230, 232
atonal 101, 117, 176
atopia 150, 169, 177, 179, 259, 274
attempt 2, 29, 214, 217, 230
Aufhebung 47, 50
authenticity 3, 88, 95, 114, 125, 180, 188, 256, 266, 274, 277–9, 177
author(ial) 1, 3, 5, 10, 12, 14, 18, 32, 34, 65, 69, 71, 74, 82–5, 90, 93–6, 126–9, 132–3, 137, 139, 142, 150, 154, 160–1, 176–8, 180, 183, 191, 195–6, 201, 205, 208, 210, 227, 233, 235–6, 239–40, 251, 255, 270–2, 274, 276–7, 279
authority/authoritative 3, 35, 65–9, 71, 79–80, 95–6, 101, 119, 122–3, 141, 161, 174, 176, 206–8, 210, 234, 236, 254, 279
autobiography 3, 6, 12, 20, 23, 32, 42, 70, 87, 93–4, 100, 147, 150, 153, 155, 164, 173, 177, 179, 210, 225
autonomy/autonomous 10, 17–18, 26–7, 40, 55, 86, 103, 110, 113–14, 240, 261
auxiliary 125

baggy 23
becoming 41, 45, 47, 109, 206, 222, 224–5, 228, 232, 234, 244, 265
beginning(s) 23, 75–6, 81, 90–2, 95, 97, 115, 121, 124, 131–2, 137, 160, 187, 198–9, 213–14, 217, 225, 231, 267, 269
belated(ness) 97, 134–5, 255, 260, 282
belief 13, 119, 235
Bildung 42–4, 55, 134, 226–8, 230
Bildungsroman 21, 23, 42–3, 46, 48, 197, 203, 206, 223–4, 226–33, 236
biography/biographical 1, 6, 61, 197, 214, 225, 252
bits 71, 73, 262
blanks 153, 168, 182, 195, 259, 264
blowing up 76
bogus 260, 262
bold (type) 152–3, 156–7
boundless 24, 72, 221, 244
breaking off 73, 116
breaking up/into 154, 156, 159, 195
brief 81
by-product 99, 108, 193, 247

catalogue/cataloguing 14, 65, 148–9
cause/causality 27, 76, 93, 117, 119, 153, 159, 220, 228–9, 243, 254, 263–4, 268
ceaseless 89
centralizing/centring 29, 52, 58, 77, 90, 92, 127, 138, 164
certainty 50
chance 81, 85, 261

change 66, 70–2, 74–6, 120–1, 151, 231, 233, 244, 272
chaos/chaotic 114, 216, 226, 259, 267, 269
chapter 195, 203–4, 210
character 11–12, 15, 17, 34, 160, 178, 183–4, 188, 191, 194, 197, 205, 207–10, 212, 214, 216, 218–19, 228, 231, 234–8, 248–9, 253, 255, 273
chasm 224
check 153, 170, 173, 175, 189–90, 220
child(like) 199, 207, 224–5, 231
circle/circularity 33, 34, 93, 116, 119, 161, 243, 255, 257
circumstance 32, 54, 75, 120, 149, 212, 228–9, 272, 276
citation(al) 66, 96, 156–8, 240, 253, 256, 271
clarity 34
classic(al) 14, 30, 65, 71, 126–8, 136, 138, 154, 156, 167–8, 176, 182, 189–91, 199, 243, 245
classification 59, 148, 151, 153–4, 167, 257, 267–8
closure/closed 24, 31, 37–8, 49, 52, 56, 66, 69, 73–4, 89, 92, 95–6, 118, 122–3, 125, 128, 135, 141, 144, 151–2, 160, 164, 166, 173, 176, 234, 237, 257, 276, 281
cogito 51
cognition/cognitive 21, 115, 130, 194, 200, 202, 205, 213, 215, 224
collective 14, 30–1, 65, 69, 71, 94, 179
colon 168–9
comment(ary) 20, 56, 59, 63, 65–7, 73, 80, 86, 88–9, 91–3, 95, 122, 124, 139–40, 142, 144, 156–60, 163–5, 180, 186, 192–3, 203, 208–9, 211, 223, 238, 252, 253, 255, 257, 266, 281
common: man 14, 19; opinion (*see also* opinion *and* received opinion) 66, 147, 156, 165; reader 14, 19, 33, 270
commonplace 14
compilation/compiling 7, 14, 65–6, 68, 93, 151, 157, 163, 174, 253
completion/complete 18, 26–7, 30, 67, 110, 117, 173, 224–5, 261, 267, 269
comprehensibility 54
comprehensive 41, 201
conception 248–9, 258
concept(ualization) 29, 31, 34, 41, 44–5, 48–51, 54–5, 76–8, 81, 89, 101–2, 104–7, 112–16, 119–26, 134–6, 140, 143, 152–3, 157, 164–6, 169, 171–3, 175, 189, 191, 195–6, 198, 218, 228, 235, 237, 246, 258, 267, 281–2
concise 77, 88, 91
conclusion/conclusive 20–1, 34–5, 72, 75–6, 89–90, 199, 237, 261
concrete/concretizing 20–1, 35, 37, 42, 44–6, 58, 67, 69, 79, 102, 106, 111–12, 121–2, 124, 139, 187, 200, 211, 219, 224, 228, 230–2, 237, 263, 269

condensed 252

confession: St Augustine 6; 42, 235, 246

conjunctively 219

consciousness 14–15, 35–6, 41, 43–4, 46–7, 49–52, 114, 118, 125–6, 139, 171, 199–201, 216, 223, 225, 233, 236, 239, 241–5, 268, 275, 278

consecutive 14

consensus/consensual 78, 142

consequence 159, 162, 175

constant 128, 189

context 11, 35, 51–2, 54, 56, 67, 69, 72–3, 83, 86, 93, 96, 121, 123, 132, 144, 149, 158, 170–1, 212–13, 233, 237, 240, 272–7, 280

contiguity 65, 151, 191, 264

contingency/contingent 22, 32–3, 70, 97, 146, 213, 221, 228–9, 265–6, 272, 277–9

continuity/continuous 15, 18–19, 27, 38, 73, 115–16, 119, 151, 164, 175, 179, 188, 198, 254

contradiction/contradicting 41, 68–9, 73–4, 78, 80, 100–1, 107, 110–11, 113, 117, 127, 153, 170, 192, 198, 217, 226, 233–4, 236, 252, 257, 265, 267, 281

contrary 220

control 28, 38, 42, 52, 59, 95, 126–7, 153, 168, 175–6, 190, 199, 203, 209, 233, 236, 241

convention 191

copy 93, 157, 168, 178, 252–3, 260, 270, 272

correct(ion) 79, 86, 180, 220, 253, 274

counter-encyclopedia 144, 150, 153–4, 156

counter-ideology 54, 99, 122–3, 146, 148, 162, 182–4

craving 221

creation/creating/creative 5, 9–11, 15–17, 19, 36, 41, 55–6, 66, 74, 86–7, 93, 97, 100, 106–8, 113, 121–4, 139–40, 178–9, 187–8, 200–1, 205, 218, 221, 226–7, 237, 248, 251, 254, 258, 271, 273

crisis 23, 38–9, 41–2, 48–9, 57, 72, 127–8, 155, 198, 209, 213, 238, 244

criticism/critic(al) 5, 10–14, 19–20, 23–5, 31, 36, 39–42, 45, 49–56, 63–5, 67, 74, 78–81, 87, 92–4, 99, 103–8, 113, 115, 118, 121–4, 130, 137, 139–42, 144–6, 148–55, 157–9, 161–6, 169, 174, 176–8, 183–4, 187–8, 190, 192–4, 198, 225, 227, 229, 155, 157–9, 161–6, 169, 174, 176–8, 183–4, 187–8, 190, 192–4, 198, 225, 227, 229, 233, 235, 238–9, 244–5, 256, 259, 273, 277, 279, 281–2

cultivation 42

culture/cultural 1, 9, 14, 39, 61, 66–7, 72, 93–4, 113, 119, 121–2, 124, 134, 144, 146–8, 156–7, 179, 193, 215, 245, 258, 276, 282

cutting up 160, 164, 176, 190

cycle 152, 163, 262

debasement/debased 196, 228

decentring 29, 58, 76–7, 80, 82, 88, 90, 92, 152, 178, 242, 259, 264–5, 269

deconstruction 47, 49, 58, 62–3, 123, 139–40, 144, 276

decontextualisation 159, 187

deduction/deductive 51, 116, 118, 120

deferment/deferral/deferring 29–30, 40, 47, 49, 97, 110, 112, 127, 136, 166–7, 187, 225, 234

deficiency 74, 76

definition 1–2, 7, 11, 15–16, 22, 28, 38, 50–1, 75, 77–8, 89, 99, 103, 111, 113, 116, 119, 121, 123, 131, 138, 149, 151–2, 160, 163, 166–71, 174, 177, 186, 189, 214, 218, 244

definite 216, 219, 271

definitive 162, 211

degeneration 238–9

degraded 196

degree 25

dehumanization 51, 282

deictic 275–7

delay 39

demystification 148

denaturalization 67, 118

denial 74, 143

deport(ing) 166, 172, 174, 180

depth 202, 253

derivation/derived 56, 93, 97, 123–4, 156, 264

desire (narrative) 40, 110, 178, 182, 185, 187–8, 190, 209, 224–5, 228, 242–3, 266

detachment 184

detective 243, 249–50, 259

determinacy/determinate 47, 56, 129, 222, 276–7, 280

detour 187

deviance/deviation/devious 122, 162, 168, 174, 243, 264

diachronic 8, 16, 22–3, 26, 28, 41, 91, 93, 109, 138, 169–70, 194, 205, 248, 262

dialectics/dialectical 3, 29, 45–8, 50–1, 94, 97, 101, 105, 112, 117, 134–5, 150, 174, 179, 191, 200, 208, 224, 230, 234, 257, 263, 274

dialogue/dialogism/dialogic 6, 7, 14, 21, 23, 32, 34, 47, 54–5, 93, 95, 100–1, 109, 111–13, 161, 169, 184, 189, 193–4, 210, 233–5, 236–7, 244, 272, 275; Plato 3, 6, 89–90, 103, 235, 245

diary 6, 20–1, 103, 193, 195, 203, 209–10, 235, 240

dictionary 2, 28, 131, 151–3, 156, 158, 160, 163, 167–73, 177, 181; Flaubert 156–7, 189

didactic 5, 24, 134, 152, 168, 182

difference/*différance*/differing 29–30, 35, 46–51, 57, 69, 71, 132, 134–6, 141, 143, 145, 152, 154, 157, 166, 174, 190–1, 204, 213, 228, 233–5, 248, 271–2, 281

difficulty 158
digression/digressive 30, 40, 54, 75–7, 80, 83, 86, 90, 159–60, 165, 175, 190, 194–5, 209, 240, 242, 265, 272–3, 281
dilatory 167, 185–6, 242
disappropriation 94, 143
disconnection 30, 73, 261
discontinuity/discontinuous 32, 50, 74, 80, 86, 93, 153, 159, 162, 212, 242, 266
discourse/discursive: Descartes 115; 239–41, 276–7, 279
discrepancy 59, 134, 169
disintegration 231, 264
disjunction/disjunctive/disjointed 35–6, 159, 164, 189, 264–6, 269
dislocation/dislocating 30, 32, 40, 96, 132, 150, 166, 179, 181, 212, 242
dismemberment 30, 39
disorder(ly) 20, 67, 91, 163, 167
disparity 47
dispensability 20
dispersal/dispersion 26, 57, 88, 177–9, 224, 274
displacement/displacing 17, 23–4, 30, 39, 57, 70–1, 74, 85, 87, 91, 94, 112, 138–9, 142, 144, 150, 161, 166, 171, 176, 184, 244, 265–6, 276, 278, 281–2
disruption 21, 153, 240
dissemination 26, 62, 132, 135, 143, 145, 187, 190
dissertation/dissertative 15, 33, 159, 183–4
dissolution/dissolving 21, 47, 136, 194, 196, 206
dissonance 42, 100, 225
distancing 183, 197
distortion 37, 237, 256, 267, 273
diversity/diverse 7, 34, 71, 233, 235
diversion 88–9, 94, 161, 166
doctrine/doctrinal 120, 204, 268
dogmatic 30, 50, 63, 76, 101, 115, 119, 202, 237, 269
doing (*vs* saying) 254
domination/dominant/dominating 51, 121, 140, 151, 187
doxa 66, 68–9, 74, 78, 80, 82, 87, 93, 99, 118, 147–8, 150–1, 156–7, 165–6, 171, 181
draft 18–20, 27, 30, 199; Novalis 6
drama(tic) 3–4, 6, 8, 18, 23–4, 33–4, 213, 239
drifting 150, 176–7, 189–90, 274
drill 18
duplication/duplicate 254, 262–3, 274
dynamic 16, 40, 45, 70, 79, 110, 112, 117, 129, 154, 233

early 175
eccentric/ex-centric 165–6
editor 20, 270

education/educating 21, 42–4, 226–7
effect 27, 76, 117, 153, 159, 172, 229, 263–4, 268
ellipsis/elliptical 75, 157, 164, 187, 190, 251–2, 255, 266
embedding 243
embryonic 30
emphasis 25, 105
empirical 14, 32–3, 37, 41, 53, 120, 128, 138, 179, 207–9, 272
enactment/enacting 43, 228, 281
encyclopedia 14, 30–1, 39, 41, 67, 93–4, 145–6, 148, 150–4, 156–8, 171, 173–5, 178–9, 181, 189, 199, 222, 255, 258–62, 264–7, 269; Diderot 6; Hegel 133
end(ing) 76, 91–2, 109–10, 125, 131, 147, 160, 196, 198–9, 203, 222, 227, 229–30, 249–50, 254, 265–7, 269
endless 30, 42, 47, 49, 75, 88, 94, 96–7, 127, 137, 170, 181, 186, 190, 222, 232, 236, 257, 263, 268–9
enduring 66
enlightenment 44, 55, 200
entertaining 198
entrance/entry 158, 160, 170
enumeration 116, 259
enunciation 57, 66, 87, 91, 94–6, 98, 123, 126, 139, 145, 149–50, 176–9, 241–2, 251, 271, 274–5, 278
ephemeral 120, 126, 176
epic 3, 183, 197, 199, 216–17, 224–5, 229, 231–3, 235, 241
epilogue 199
epistemology/epistemological 30–1, 42, 45, 70, 114, 119, 173, 193, 198–9, 210, 215, 226, 232, 239, 242, 244
epistles/epistolary 6, 23
epitext(ual) 20, 187, 193, 228, 240
error/errancy/erring 42, 44, 143, 167, 188, 226–7, 231, 243, 250
essence/essential 1–2, 9–10, 22–5, 27, 31, 33, 39–40, 46, 57, 61, 71, 87, 89, 101, 104–7, 109, 114, 120, 133, 142, 155, 167, 186–7, 200, 216, 220, 222, 224, 226–8, 237–8, 241–3, 248, 255, 257, 276, 282
esoteric 197
estrangement 225, 227
eternity/eternal 30, 40, 45, 114, 120, 146, 155, 180, 199, 211, 230, 233, 254, 275–6, 278; Borges 249
etymology 2–3, 16–17, 22, 29, 37, 82, 140, 143, 161, 170–1, 198
evanescence 22, 39, 49, 111, 274
everlasting 30, 40
everyman 44
excess(ive)/exceeding 19, 29, 40, 53, 57–8, 74–5, 80, 92, 111, 127, 130, 134–6, 138, 143,

145, 155, 157, 159, 162, 166–7, 179, 180–1,
185, 189, 203, 223, 225, 228, 230–2, 269,
272–3, 275, 281
example/*exemplum* 3, 7, 67–9, 74, 83, 85, 102,
108, 110–11, 161, 211, 237
excursion/excursus 159, 195, 240
exercises 18, 251, 273–4
exhausting/exhaustive 2, 74, 77, 89, 112, 116,
118, 148, 151, 158, 175, 218, 233, 254, 261
exile 30, 40
exit 158, 160, 170
expansion 208, 211
experience 2–3, 13–14, 31–2, 44–7, 71, 74, 76,
84, 105–7, 114–15, 119–20, 130, 198, 202,
205–8, 210, 212, 214–15, 218, 221, 225, 229,
231, 235, 237, 270
experiment(al) 2, 16, 26, 36, 194, 237, 239, 274
exposition/expository 5, 33, 133–4
extralinguistic 171
extraliterary 4–5, 16, 235, 252
extraneous 77
extrapolation 22, 28, 37
extrasystemic 30
extratextual 18, 20, 95, 152, 161, 166, 202, 210

fables 7
fabulating 188
failure 222
fake 262
falsifying 256, 268
fantastic 256, 259, 262–3, 265, 268, 271
fantasy/fantasizing 178, 184–5, 187–8, 220,
228, 255, 258
feeling 34, 200, 202–3, 210, 270
feigning 188, 256, 279
fiction(al)/fictitious 8, 11–12, 14–18, 21, 35–6,
58, 62, 64, 78, 88, 93, 127, 129, 133, 145,
147, 154, 159, 177, 183–4, 188, 191, 193–6,
198, 204, 208, 210, 213, 227, 236–8, 243,
247–9, 251–3, 255–6, 259–60, 262, 273–4,
278–81
fictionalizing 183, 188, 198
figural/figurative 51, 168
filiation 93, 161, 169, 176
filter 254, 256, 266
final(ity/izing) 18, 26–7, 34, 49, 51, 56, 108,
116, 119, 125, 162, 196, 229, 232, 250, 281
finished 40, 225
finite 164, 172, 211, 220, 228, 231
firm 68
first (*vs* last) 51, 79, 231
fixing/fixed 69–70, 167, 190, 217, 219, 244
flattening 76
fleshing out 19
footnotes 10, 20–1, 52, 56, 113, 139, 144, 164,
203, 240, 249, 254–5, 281
foreboding 40

foreclosed 111
foreign 78, 87, 91, 131
foreword 20, 94–6, 132–4
forgery 278
forgetfulness/forgetting 77, 84–7, 161, 175,
189, 263
Formalist 148
formation/formative 21, 42, 55, 227
formless(ness) 18, 34, 40, 81–2, 107, 230
fortuitous 266
fortune 80–2
fragment(ary)/fragmentation 2–3, 18, 20–1,
27–8, 30, 39–41, 49, 55, 62, 76–7, 82–3, 88,
91, 95–7, 99, 108, 110–11, 115, 117, 126,
136, 143–5, 151–3, 158–60, 162–5, 168–9,
171, 173–5, 177, 186–90, 193, 195, 198–9,
201, 208–9, 215, 218, 220, 224, 227–8, 231,
235–6, 240, 252, 254–5, 258, 261–2, 264–5,
267, 270, 272–3, 278–81; Schlegel 16
frame/framing 21, 52–3, 75, 78, 94–5, 124–7,
129–2, 135–7, 139, 141–3, 153, 158–9, 164,
168, 173–4, 210, 213, 242, 252, 262, 276–7,
281
frivolous 8, 19, 62, 96
fulfilment/fulfilled 40, 110, 186, 212, 230
fusion 48, 170, 187, 215, 220–1, 227
future 30, 56, 93, 132–3, 144, 148, 171, 178,
207, 219, 222, 240, 254, 257, 263, 271–2

game 12, 96, 165, 250–1, 257, 260, 263, 273
gap 18, 27, 117, 130, 148, 176, 214, 228
general(izing) 11, 14, 31, 55, 59, 60, 63, 66
69–70, 77–9, 83, 88, 91, 102, 112, 116,
119–20, 134, 136, 145, 153, 157, 179, 206,
208, 211, 215, 226, 237, 244, 268–9
Genus universum 39
gloss 20, 30, 56, 68, 76, 79, 88–9, 91–2, 98,
132, 139, 141, 146, 156–8, 161, 164, 173–4,
180, 242, 254, 272, 281
gradual 259, 262, 265, 269
graphic 175, 182, 264
growth 82, 233

haphazard 94, 117, 148, 216, 218
heading 126, 153, 164–6, 169, 174, 182
head-word 170, 189
here (and now) 32, 75, 119, 133, 180, 212, 266,
275
heteroclitic 151, 156, 158–9, 162, 165, 173
heterogeneity/heterogeneous 4, 27, 96, 130,
148–9, 151, 158, 162, 164, 173, 236, 239,
242, 263–4
heterology 134, 162, 187
heuristic 3
hiatus 42
hierarchy/hierarchical 11, 31, 39, 56, 58–9,
77, 79, 108, 110, 118, 121, 125, 143, 157,

hierarchy/hierarchical (*cont.*):
  159–60, 162, 172–4, 187, 194, 199, 220, 234–5, 243, 264
homeland 43
homeless(ness) 224, 239
homogeneity/homogeneous 27, 148–9, 151, 184, 249
hope 263, 265–6
hors-d'oeuvre 131
hors-texte 159, 166
hypertextual 253
hypothesis/hypothetical 11, 35, 64, 210, 213, 217, 219, 237, 257, 264

'I' 43, 47, 94, 178, 217, 227, 241, 274–5
idea 3, 5, 12, 18–21, 31, 34–6, 44, 48, 61, 65, 72, 74, 76, 79, 83, 85, 89, 94, 106, 156, 172, 181, 193–4, 196–203, 216, 219, 222, 226–8, 231–2, 234, 237–8, 249, 253, 256, 258–9, 263, 266, 268–9, 276
ideal 25, 46, 48, 201, 267
idealism 36–8, 43, 50–1, 62, 99, 101, 108, 136, 222, 228, 230, 256, 261, 263–4, , 266, 268–9, 271, 276, 279
identical 271, 273
identity 2, 9–10, 47, 51, 61, 94, 96, 101, 115, 134–5, 137, 141, 175, 178–9, 213, 216, 228, 230, 233–4, 236, 239, 251–2, 257, 264, 272, 274, 279, 281
ideology 80, 118, 122, 125, 129, 146, 148–9, 151, 157, 160, 162, 165–6, 183, 199, 201, 232, 234–6
ignorance 73, 80–1, 86, 88–9, 92
illocutionary 95
image 104–6, 114, 162, 172, 179, 184, 201, 206, 228
imagination/imaginative/imaginary 5, 8–11, 15, 17, 36, 44, 55, 81, 85, 103–4, 106, 111, 172, 179, 184–5, 188, 200–1, 218, 221, 229, 238, 246, 255, 256, 258–9, 261, 263, 266–7, 269–71, 281
imitation 3, 56, 65–6, 81, 97, 254, 273
immanent 44, 141
immediate 45, 48, 50, 82, 105–6, 116, 121, 124, 187
impersonal 3, 51, 67, 96, 179, 264, 275
implied reader 32–3, 272
imposture 155, 180, 184, 274
impotence 185–6, 188, 196, 205
impressionist 11, 19, 36–7
inability 198, 216–17
inadequation 134
incipit 91
incommensurable 54, 134, 228
incompatible 51
incompletion/incompleteness 18, 35, 40, 78, 222, 235, 263, 265

incomprehensibility 54, 143
inconclusiveness 91
incorporation/incorporating 21
indefinite 68, 144, 153, 160, 223, 239, 241, 272
independent 102–3, 108–13, 178, 196–7, 202, 209, 225, 237, 240, 258, 263, 271, 274
indeterminacy/indetermination 2, 6, 18, 23–4, 51, 63, 141–3, 150, 218, 244, 269
index 164–5, 173–5, 182, 261
indifferently 77, 87
indirect(ion) 3, 15, 17, 35, 54–5, 60–2, 64, 82, 149, 165, 169, 171, 174, 176, 178, 194, 196–7, 214, 237, 253, 261, 265
individual(ity)/individualism 4, 9–11, 13–14, 17, 30–2, 37, 41–2, 45, 50, 53–5, 57–8, 65–6, 71, 97, 102, 116–17, 119–21, 126, 155, 159, 179, 202, 205–8, 210, 212, 215–16, 226–31, 234, 263, 270, 271, 275, 282
inexhaustible 57, 64, 189, 272
infiltration 238, 244
infinity/infinite 40–1, 47, 49, 56–7, 75, 77, 110, 117, 135–7, 143–4, 152, 154, 157, 160–1, 164, 166–8, 171, 173, 187, 190, 199, 212, 216, 220–1, 225–6, 228, 232, 243, 259, 263–4, 267, 269, 271, 273
informal(ity) 19
initiating 21, 26
innocence/innocent 146–7, 156, 160, 171, 189
innovation/innovating 12–13, 16, 38–9, 247–8
in potentia 5–7, 15, 21, 23, 25, 43, 57, 110, 186, 200, 222
in progress 30, 54, 70, 123, 144, 150, 159, 167, 187, 215, 220, 258
inquisition(al): Borges 248, 249, 250
insignificant 76, 163, 228, 272, 276
integral 158
integration 21, 264
intellectual 101–2, 111
intention 95, 128, 159, 201, 234, 275
interchangeability/interchangeable 41–3, 74, 78, 129, 160, 174, 205, 245
interglossing 137, 144, 157, 255
intermediate/intermediary 62, 193, 198, 205
interpolation 74, 91, 142, 159, 162, 164, 220, 240, 243, 259, 265, 272
interrupt(ion) 50, 74, 82, 109, 151, 153, 159–60, 162, 164, 168, 173, 175, 189, 195, 198–9, 209
intertext(ual) 20, 56–7, 59, 64, 66–7, 71, 76, 79–80, 82, 86–8, 92–4, 96, 111, 122–4, 126, 142, 144, 157, 158–9, 163, 171, 178–9, 180–1, 189–90, 234, 247, 254, 257, 262, 271–2, 274
intratext(ual) 56, 59, 79, 86, 96, 111, 122, 142, 181, 247, 254
introduction/introducing 20, 89, 103, 133, 164, 213, 217, 254, 262

intrusion 240, 261–2, 265, 269
invariable 38, 68–9, 119–20, 122, 127–8
invasion 193, 203, 208, 217, 222, 238, 258–9, 265
invention/inventive 11, 36, 67, 86, 88, 91–2, 97, 138, 172, 188, 221, 248, 256, 261, 266–7
inversion 73, 85, 93, 146, 161, 169
invisible 271–2
invoking 182, 253
irony/ironic 41–2, 73, 77, 91, 106–9, 124, 166, 213, 225–6, 229, 244–5, 282
irrational 151, 160, 200, 207–8, 216
irresponsibility 196, 199, 251, 269
irreversible 114
italics 153, 204
iterability 68
itinerary 43

journal 193
journalism/journalistic 3, 197, 282
journey 42, 44, 48, 55, 213, 224–6, 231, 249, 259
judgement/judging 29, 33, 66, 69, 71–2, 74, 78, 81, 83, 108–9, 117, 130–1, 154, 176, 242, 263, 268
juxtaposition 34, 37, 73, 80, 93, 101, 117, 151–2, 158, 164, 216–17, 220, 243, 257, 259, 262

key-word 76, 168–70, 175, 182
knowledge 5, 12, 14, 30–3, 35, 39, 42–5, 48, 50–1, 54–5, 59, 65, 70–1, 73, 144, 148–51, 156, 171, 178, 201, 204–5, 207–8, 210, 212–13, 227, 233, 242, 254–6

lack 80, 82–3, 86, 130–2, 139, 143, 161, 166
language 35, 51–2, 55, 78, 93–4, 101, 122–4, 141, 143, 146–50, 152–4, 157–8, 161, 167–8, 171–2, 176–7, 181, 185–7, 190, 201, 222–3, 234–6, 242, 245, 256–9, 261, 264, 267–9, 275, 282
last (*vs* first) 168, 174, 181
late 175
length(ening) 6, 162, 208
letter 6, 7, 12, 14, 18, 20–1, 52, 101, 105, 173, 193, 235, 240; Diderot 6; Schiller 46; Schlegel 246
lie 83, 278
limitless 233
linear 2, 18, 27, 153, 227, 229
linguist(ic/s) 35, 52, 153, 171, 241, 276, 279
list 151, 153, 156–60, 162–3, 173–5, 190
location 10
locus/loci 65, 93, 150
logic(al) 30, 33, 44, 73–4, 76, 79, 90, 101, 111, 114, 116–18, 122; Hegel 133, 148, 153, 159, 165, 173–5, 196, 201, 211–12, 218, 228
longing 40, 110, 207–8, 230
looking forward to 41

loose(ness) 29
lots and dices 81
lyric(ism)/lyrical 3–4, 177, 184, 210, 239

magazine 12, 26
magical 172, 259, 267
mana words 168–9
many-sidedness 218
markers 276, 279
marvellous 256, 259
mastery/mastering 18, 44, 49, 53, 60, 73, 94, 132–3, 148, 151–4, 158, 164, 166, 174, 195, 223, 233, 247
material(ism) 48, 99, 201, 268
materializing 58, 258
maturity 194, 199, 224–5, 227, 231
maxim 6, 67, 69, 211; La Rochefoucauld 6
maze 243
meandering 81
mediation/mediating/mediator 29–30, 40, 45–6, 68, 71, 88, 100, 106–7, 119, 121, 123–4, 126, 128, 147, 178–9, 187, 193, 232, 258
medieval 30, 122
meditation/meditative 3, 6, 14, 32, 37
medium 17, 29, 35, 53, 211–12, 234, 242, 256, 275
memorable 261
memorization/memorizing 86–8, 91, 97, 171
memory 161, 179, 189, 201, 254, 256, 263, 265–6, 274
memoryless 179
mental 34, 36, 256, 263
merging 209
metaphor 35, 52, 62, 96, 105–6, 129, 142–3, 151, 155, 167, 169, 172, 178, 183, 190, 192, 228, 255, 265, 274, 278
method/methodical 28–9, 49–50, 59, 118, 120, 126–7, 139, 143, 152, 175, 216, 267, 269; Descartes 115
metonymy/metonymic 82, 96, 151, 166–7, 170, 178, 189, 192, 266
middle 48, 130, 198
Middle Ages 13, 206–7, 215
mimesis/mimetic 9–12, 53, 56, 66–7, 87, 93, 118, 122–3, 125, 153, 155, 159, 256, 272, 280
mind 36, 41, 63, 73, 130, 226, 238, 244–5, 256–8, 268–9, 279
mirror 64, 93–4, 96, 150, 152, 250, 255, 257–8, 260, 262, 267, 273
mise en abyme 94, 96, 130–1, 164, 242
misquoted 262
misreading 262
mnemonic 65, 67, 161, 189, 266
mobility/mobile 120, 177, 275, 278
mobilization/mobilizing 70, 149, 154, 158, 181, 189, 232, 235, 237, 264–5

mode/modal 22, 24, 28–30, 37–8, 49, 57, 79, 130, 198, 212, 237, 244, 246–7
model 9, 13–14, 26, 31–3, 37, 39, 50, 65, 69–70, 84, 159, 161, 178, 186, 272
modern(ity) 10, 13–14, 24, 26, 31, 33, 37–9, 41–3, 49–52, 54, 57, 150, 154, 173, 176, 180, 186, 189, 198, 200, 206, 209, 212, 215, 222–3, 238–9, 241–2, 245–7, 250, 252, 258, 275, 281–2,
Modernism 37, 51, 60, 127–8, 136, 138, 189, 230
monologic/monologism 54, 100–1, 189, 194, 233, 235–7, 281
monotony 255
motion 264
mots-bastants 76–7
movement 264
multilingual 161
multi-temporal(ity) 233
multiplicity/multiple 7, 21, 34, 71, 96–7, 150, 171, 177, 199, 233, 262, 264, 278–9
mutation 39
mystics/mystical 6, 103, 111, 200, 221, 225, 273
mystification 146
myth(ical) 120, 124, 146–8, 171, 241
mythology/mythologist 52, 146; Barthes 146–7

Nacheinander 220, 227
naivety 81, 114, 122, 124, 197, 217, 269
names/naming 77–8, 83, 96, 136, 154, 165–7, 170, 177, 182, 188–90, 264, 268
narrative/narration/narrating 3–4, 6, 8, 16, 18, 21, 23–4, 33–5, 53, 58, 93, 135, 147–8, 154, 157–60, 162, 167–8, 179, 183–4, 188–96, 197–8, 201–2, 204, 206, 208–9, 211–13, 216–18, 220, 223, 231–2, 237–43, 248–51, 254, 258–9, 266–7, 269, 274, 282
narratology 125, 148, 167
narrator 3, 11, 12, 19, 186–7, 196, 201, 205, 208–9, 212–13, 238, 241, 254, 256, 261
naturalizing 85–6, 97, 123, 125, 146
nature/natural 9–10, 14–15, 18, 28, 32, 40, 43, 46, 67–8, 70, 80–2, 84–5, 90–1, 97–8, 106, 120–1, 123–4, 130, 146, 152, 155–6, 160–1, 166, 171, 201, 221, 241–2, 252, 276
Nebeneinander 220, 227
necessity/necessary 108, 110, 118, 122, 130, 134, 165, 201, 216, 221, 226, 228–9, 233, 264
neoteny/neotenous 30, 35, 136
neutral(ist) 14, 32–3, 35, 122, 150, 152–3, 171, 209, 212, 234, 275
never-ceasing 219, 257
never-ending 143, 199, 225
new 10–11, 13–14, 30, 33, 55, 85, 87, 102–3, 113, 137, 139, 150, 153–4, 186, 189, 169–70, 174, 221, 248, 271, 274

nomination/nominal 153, 163–4, 168, 175, 189–90
nominalist 37, 78, 96
non-conceptual 45
non-contradiction 168–9, 212, 221
non-exhaustive 20
non-fiction 6–7, 11, 18, 20–1, 62, 129, 145, 191, 198, 208, 280–1
non-homogeneity 142
non-identity 48, 115–16, 118, 181
non-subjective 179
non-totalizing 179
non-verbal 264
non-writer/non-writing 254, 272
norm 95
nostalgia 40, 187, 207, 224, 230
notebooks 193
notes 18, 20, 29, 52, 83, 95, 101, 144, 162, 198–9, 220, 251, 254, 259, 261, 266, 273, 281; Derrida 52
not yet written 18, 20–1, 28, 35, 82, 220, 228, 258
noun 17, 22–3, 79, 160, 264–5, 268
Nouveau Roman 60
novel 8–9, 12–17, 19, 21–3, 26, 31–2, 35, 41–3, 58, 60, 99, 145, 153–4, 181, 184–8, 191–206, 208–9, 212–13, 216, 220–8, 230–1, 236, 238, 243–5, 249, 252–3, 267, 272; Schlegel 245–6
novelist 13, 18–19, 21, 139, 188–9, 197, 205, 213, 225, 269
novelness/novelistic 23–4, 58, 146, 155, 184–6, 188, 191–2, 210, 236, 244–6, 252
novelization 24, 244, 252
novelty 13, 32
number(ing) 153, 156, 159–64, 166, 168–9, 172, 182, 189, 195
numerical 158–9, 164, 174

objectivity/objective 9, 32–3, 42, 49, 119, 148, 201–2, 206, 210, 216, 225, 228, 234, 240–1, 257–8, 263–4, 268, 275–6
oblique 76–7, 81–2, 94, 163, 175, 178, 243, 261, 265, 281
obscurity 190
obsolescence/obsolete 22–3, 38–9
occasional 108
odyssey 43
omission 267
oneness 221
oniric 171
open-ended(ness)/open(ness) 4, 24, 30–1, 37, 40, 75, 77, 80, 93, 112, 118, 125, 136, 144, 151–2, 154, 175, 234, 236, 239, 244, 257, 267
opinion 68–9, 137
opposition/opposites 45–8, 62, 65, 113, 130,

134, 140–1, 145, 154, 162–3, 165–6, 169,
191, 209, 212, 235, 240–1, 249, 259, 263,
265, 267
oral 51, 253
order 3, 39, 65, 67, 71–6, 81, 105, 107, 110,
113–16, 118–20, 124–5, 143, 151, 154–6,
159–60, 163–4, 166, 172–4, 189, 215–7, 219,
228, 241, 255–7, 262, 267
origin(al) 10, 13, 28, 49, 64, 69, 73, 85–6, 89,
93, 97, 121–4, 129, 141–2, 147, 157–8,
160–1, 170–1, 176, 178, 199, 229, 254, 259,
262, 266, 269–70, 273, 276, 278
originality 11, 13–14, 56, 61, 65, 82, 85, 87–8,
93, 97–8, 123, 135, 142, 144, 179, 235,
254–5, 262
ornament 8, 29, 76, 78, 84, 92, 106
orthodoxy 66, 118, 121, 149
other(ness) 25, 47–8, 86–8, 94–5, 165, 169,
178–9, 181, 188, 221, 223, 226, 231, 234,
244, 255, 273–4
outline 19, 74, 111, 185, 251, 253–4, 266
outmoded 22–3, 38, 57, 243
overarching 31, 50, 114, 119, 129
overflow 132, 135, 155, 241
overall 59, 159
overgloss 89
overrun 30, 74, 78, 94, 126–8, 137–8, 144, 170
ownership 161
oxymoron(ic) 8, 31, 74, 78, 102, 115, 155, 165,
169, 210, 212, 217, 235, 247–8, 254–5, 265

pact 191
painting 52, 106, 131
palimpsest 170–1, 276, 278
para 27, 110, 140–1, 191
paradox(ism) 7, 9, 25, 27–30, 40–1, 55, 57, 63,
65, 73–4, 76–80, 82, 87, 90, 93, 95–7, 102,
109–12, 117, 126–7, 130–1, 135–9, 141,
145, 151, 153–5, 157, 166, 170, 173, 181,
191, 199, 201, 212, 222–3, 226, 230, 247–8,
267–8, 271, 276–7, 280
paraliterary 26–7, 59, 191
paralysis/paralyzing 181, 198, 217–18
parasite/parasitical 135, 140–1, 282
parataxis/paratactic 2–3, 18, 21, 28, 35, 54, 73,
80, 111, 115, 117, 121, 165, 187, 228, 253,
259, 264
paratext(uality) 20, 24, 27–8, 40, 49, 52–4, 56,
58, 63–4, 90, 95–6, 99, 125–30, 132,
135–41, 143–4, 153, 158, 162, 171, 175–6,
182, 184, 189, 240, 253–4, 257, 259, 264,
266, 269–70, 276–7, 279, 281
parergon 52, 96, 107–8, 110, 125, 127, 130–2,
135–6, 139–41, 277; Schopenhauer 6, 108–9
parroting 55, 68, 84
part 27, 31, 40, 43, 49, 56, 69, 71–4, 96–7, 111,
116, 119–21, 125–6, 130–1, 143, 152,

159–60, 162, 165, 201, 203, 221, 227, 241,
261, 264–6, 281
partial 115, 117, 164
particular(ity)/particularization 10, 13–14, 16,
21, 30, 32, 39, 42, 44–6, 55–7, 59–60, 65,
67, 69–71, 75, 77, 79, 82–3, 89, 100, 102,
105–6, 108, 119–20, 125, 129, 138, 145, 200,
205, 207–8, 211–12, 226, 229, 231, 277–8
passage 44, 46
past 13, 31, 35, 56, 65, 79–80, 86, 132, 148,
162, 178, 180, 216, 235, 263, 268, 271, 273
path 211
pathology 238
Pensées 6
perfection/perfect 26, 40, 222
perigraphy/perigraphical 52, 126–7, 159, 168
periodical 11, 17, 26, 197, 238
periphery/peripheral 76, 139, 162, 168–70, 175
peritext(ual) 20–1, 240
permanence/permanent 22, 30–1, 40, 72, 233
permutation/permuting 58, 257, 263–4, 271, 273
perpetual 162, 222
person(ality) 3, 6, 16, 31, 42, 194, 227, 234,
261, 266
perspective/perspectival 16–17, 34, 50, 140,
142–3, 211–12, 215, 231, 234–5, 273
persuasion 5
pertinence 277, 279
perversion/perverse/pervert 37, 127–8, 137–8,
139, 237
philosophy/philosophical 5, 13–15, 17, 21,
31–6, 38–42, 44–6, 48–9, 51–8, 62, 68,
99–100, 102, 105, 108–9, 114–15, 119,
121–32, 125, 129–1, 133, 136, 139–40, 142,
144, 147, 151, 193, 196–8, 200–5, 208–10,
212, 214, 217, 224, 228–30, 235–8, 243,
256–7, 259, 261, 263–4, 267–8, 279–81
pictorial 125
piece 27, 40, 69, 71–2, 80, 110
pile 73, 75, 77, 80
place 11, 13–14, 32, 42, 45, 149–50, 175, 179,
184, 212–13, 278
plagiarism 235, 253, 257, 271
plan(ned) 2, 72–3, 114, 267
play (drama) 1, 3–4, 21, 23–5, 125–6, 131,
142–3, 146, 149, 154, 158–9, 183, 188, 257,
274, 276
play(ful)/playing 18, 27, 121, 127, 143, 237,
272
playwright 19
plot 15, 17, 19, 43, 147, 195–6, 209, 215–16,
223, 227–8, 231, 233, 235, 238, 243, 248–9,
253, 257
plural(ity) 29, 57, 70, 79, 92, 94, 132, 150,
160–1, 176, 189–90, 234, 274
poem/poetry/poet(ic) 1, 3–5, 8–9, 11, 16,
18–19, 21, 23–4, 26, 28, 34–6, 39–40, 42,

48–9, 54, 56, 62, 72, 76, 81, 87, 93, 102–3, 105–7, 108–10, 130–1, 136, 139, 144, 147–8, 153, 171, 173, 184, 187, 195, 197, 199–202, 204–5, 209–10, 213, 219–22, 228–9, 235–6, 245, 247, 263–5, 270, 273

poetics 148, 242

poeticizing 201

point of view 12, 32–4, 71, 115, 165, 176–7, 179, 191, 235, 255, 274

polyphony/polyphonic 21, 23, 34, 206, 223, 233, 235–6, 244

popularizing 14, 19, 33

portrait/portrayal/portraying 9, 12, 26, 31, 46, 70, 106–7

position 32, 55–6, 210, 212, 235

possibility/possible 25, 34, 41, 57, 61, 64, 79, 112, 129, 171, 200–1, 214, 218–20, 222–3, 227–31, 233, 239, 243–4, 249, 253–6, 263, 265, 269, 271, 273, 281

post-dating 17, 26, 127

post-liminary 20, 89–90, 92

postpone(ment) 38, 42, 74, 187, 205, 222, 243

post-Romantic 21, 38, 199

postscript 137, 254, 261, 265, 273, 281

post-structuralism 35, 49, 51, 53, 56, 60, 62–3, 129, 137, 139, 142, 145, 282

posture 94, 150, 177–8, 184, 253

potential(ity) 4, 6, 8–9, 12, 15–19, 21, 25, 30, 36, 55, 64, 75, 82, 84, 92, 97, 101, 110, 112, 123–4, 127–8, 132, 136, 138, 144–5, 152, 163, 165, 168, 170–1, 173, 186–7, 189, 191, 202, 215, 219, 223, 228–9, 231–2, 238, 243, 248–9, 255, 264, 267, 281

practice/practical 5, 21, 26–7, 33, 37, 42, 46, 48, 52–3, 58, 60, 63, 104–5, 119, 128–9, 133, 135, 145, 191, 226–9, 279–80, 282

practitioner 38

pragmatic 2, 34, 72, 95, 103, 234, 237, 252, 280

praxis 120

preceding 28, 180

precipitous 135

preconceptions 59, 75, 125, 254, 280

precursor 16–17, 39, 108–9, 235, 245, 271

precursor-forms 7

predecessors 65, 93, 108

predetermination 75, 82, 86, 113, 120, 122–3, 233, 254

preface/prefatory 20–1, 27, 52, 103, 126, 129, 132–5, 164, 185, 196, 240, 253

prefiguring 248

preliminary 20, 27, 89–90, 92, 95–6, 112, 126, 133, 164, 184, 214

pre-literary 18–19, 28, 110

prelude 133

prematuration/premature 30, 34–5

preparatives/preparation/preparing 17, 26, 55, 73, 90–1, 95, 182, 187–8, 191

prescribing/prescriptive 75, 86, 134

presence/present 45, 79, 86–7, 91, 96, 99, 110, 132–3, 148, 162, 180, 187, 195, 219, 240–1, 257, 263, 268, 275

presupposition/presupposed 73, 79, 114

previous 93, 254, 276

primal 121

primary 11, 56, 85, 93, 97, 122–4, 140–1, 143–4, 155, 158–9, 161–2, 187

prior 171, 264

probabilities 236

process(ual) 10, 15, 29–30, 33, 38, 40–2, 45, 47, 50–1, 55–6, 70, 79, 82, 84–5, 87, 91–2, 101, 109, 118–19, 123–4, 127, 133–4, 137, 143, 152, 154, 158, 167–9, 176–7, 180, 209, 219, 224–5, 228, 232–4, 237, 242–4, 257, 262–7, 272, 275, 277, 279

profundity/profound 107, 201, 253

progress 2, 18, 59, 86, 88–9, 101, 120, 151, 163, 194, 215, 217, 248–9, 251, 262, 264

progression/progressive 17–18, 20, 24, 27, 40, 42, 48, 58, 73–4, 77, 94, 109, 112, 116, 165, 167, 172–3, 185, 192, 194, 199–200, 205, 208, 213, 231, 233, 244, 248, 258, 261–2, 264, 266, 269

project 77, 80, 185–8, 255

prolepse 185

prologomena 133

prologue 133, 251

propaedeutics 55, 135

proper 66, 77, 85, 94, 98, 123–4, 131, 168, 278

proper noun 96, 142, 184, 278

property 34, 141–2, 144, 234, 275

prosaism 196

prospective 40, 136, 162, 187, 266, 282

prospectus 185–6

protection 197

provisional 75, 108, 242, 261, 269

punctuation 153

purpose 129

quest 199, 210, 225, 231, 243, 249–50, 252, 259

quotation/quoting 139, 143, 156–8, 171, 188, 234, 256, 261–2, 265–6, 271–2, 278

quotation marks 184, 236

random(ness) 2, 58, 77, 142, 157, 160, 175

rationality/rational(izing) 46, 118, 120, 154, 175, 197, 201, 208–9, 263

raw 30, 88

reading 10, 14–15, 36, 56, 72–3, 83, 86, 90, 97, 127, 132, 141–2, 144, 148, 153, 159–61, 164, 166–7, 189–91, 199, 234, 256, 271–2, 277, 280–1

readability 189–91

reader 2, 4–5, 16, 27, 31–4, 54–5, 58, 62, 75–6, 79, 82, 83–4, 89, 95–7, 101, 112, 124–6,

154, 156, 163, 168, 172–3, 175–6, 178–9, 182, 203, 207, 210, 213, 227, 235–6, 251, 255, 262, 265–6, 272–4, 277–80

readerly 154, 166–7, 174, 189, 191

realism/realistic 13, 31, 33, 36–7, 128, 138, 157, 176, 189, 212

realization/realizing 43–4, 47, 220, 227–8, 231, 239, 269–71

reason 31, 33, 35, 71, 85, 90, 165, 172–3, 175, 200–3, 210, 223, 244

received opinion 68–9, 148, 156, 181

recentring 29, 88

reception 57, 128, 280

recessive 181, 183, 187, 245

recollection 148, 200

reconceptualization 244

reconciliation/reconciling 42, 48, 108, 130, 200, 202, 227

reconfiguration 30, 39

recontextualisation 140, 142–3, 145, 220, 240, 269, 272–4

re-creations/re-creating 9, 36, 114, 132, 227, 237–8, 252, 270

reduction 211, 273

redundancy/redundant 17, 21, 49, 60, 108, 246, 270–1

reflection/reflexive/reflective 6, 14, 19–21, 23, 31–2, 35, 38–9, 41, 44, 47–52, 54–5, 57, 59, 60–1, 64, 72, 76, 80, 87–8, 91, 93, 100–2, 105, 114, 117–19, 121, 123–4, 126, 128, 130–2, 135, 141, 145, 149, 164, 181–2, 188, 196, 198–200, 202–5, 211, 213–14, 217, 224–6, 236, 238–9, 250, 252, 258, 262, 268–9, 277–8

refusal 198

refutation 265, 268

regression/regressing/regressive 61, 73, 75, 112, 152, 167–9, 190, 217, 231, 243

regulation 22, 127, 153, 173

rehearsal/rehearsing 16–17, 20, 27, 56, 80, 82, 96–7, 144, 150, 182, 187, 193, 199, 217, 222, 241, 253–4, 282

reintegration 30, 40

relativization/relative 21, 32, 34–5, 56, 66, 70–2, 80, 97, 105, 108–9, 119–20, 124, 131, 146, 165, 194, 200, 209–12, 217, 225–6, 229, 231–2, 234–5, 242, 244, 246, 264, 269, 276–7

remainder 131, 133, 148, 169, 175, 183, 200

remembrance/remember 189, 263

Renaissance 13–14, 30, 38–40, 49, 60, 67, 97, 119, 122, 147, 150–1, 206–7, 234, 254

renew(al) 60, 149, 248

renovation 247–8

repetition/repeating 65–8, 75, 78, 85, 93, 96–8, 136, 138–9, 144–5, 150, 157, 165, 168, 180–2, 254–5, 272–4, 282

replay 39

reprint 259–60, 273

reproducing 270

rereading 9, 180, 235, 272

residue 17, 27, 50–1, 74, 115, 125, 148, 158, 211, 247

responsibility 3, 96, 146, 155, 197–8, 251, 279

resolution 226

resting-place 180

restrained 190

result 49–50

résumé 266

resurgence 38

retreat 167, 190

retroaction 272

retrospective 17, 20, 40, 162, 196, 248, 266

reversal/reversible 73, 93, 140, 143, 160, 162, 178, 271

review(er) 253, 255–6, 270

revision 28, 30, 33, 91, 213, 264

rewriter/rewriting 91, 93, 125, 133, 144, 162, 180, 220, 235, 240, 242, 252, 254, 264, 272–3, 281

rhetoric 6, 8, 18, 40, 65–9, 73, 75, 86–7, 90, 92, 93–4, 147–8, 151, 157, 160–3, 165–6, 178, 190, 235, 237, 243, 255, 273

rift 215, 232

Romance 246

Romanticism/romantic 24, 27, 38–41, 43, 46–9, 54–8, 62, 103, 108–10, 144–5, 151, 185–7, 195, 199–200, 202, 205–7, 220–3, 225–6, 230, 233–4, 245–6, 259, 270

Romanticization 24

rupture 225, 243, 259

same(ness) 47, 181, 231, 255, 273–4

saying 254

scattered 164, 167, 173–4

scepticism/sceptical 31, 35–7, 47, 50–1, 53, 58, 63, 71, 78, 87, 115, 126–7, 143, 150, 185, 229, 231, 235, 239, 256, 264, 269, 280

scholastic 31, 37, 50–1, 68, 115, 122, 212

science 5, 14, 31–3, 35, 39, 44, 46, 50–1, 53–5, 57, 62, 68, 100, 103–5, 107–9, 113–15, 119–21, 133, 147–51, 153–4, 156, 173, 183, 194, 197, 200–3, 205, 209, 212, 215, 263, 268

scope 18, 252

scriptor 180, 186–7, 191

search 44–5, 199, 222, 250

secondariness/second(ary) 20, 56, 80, 85, 93, 97–8, 123–4, 131, 140, 143–4, 158, 162, 169, 187, 196–7, 263

second-hand 253, 262, 265

seeking 40, 214

Sehnsucht 230

selection 266

self(hood) 3, 15–16, 21, 24, 30, 37, 42, 44, 48–9, 56, 63, 68, 70–2, 75, 82, 86–8, 91–5, 100, 116, 120, 126, 128–9, 132, 142, 149–50, 152, 177–9, 187, 210, 221, 224, 226–8, 230, 233, 234–5, 239, 245, 273–4, 278–9, 281
self-contained 99, 125
selfless 221
self-portrait 6, 70, 93–4, 150, 155, 177, 179, 184, 221, 253
self-sufficiency 253
semiology 146–9, 153
senses/sensuous 13–14, 32, 34, 36, 45–6, 48, 55, 105, 107, 115, 172, 200–1, 212
sensibility 44, 219
sententiae/sentences 7, 14, 29
sententious 6
sequence/sequentiality 21, 110, 128, 147, 153, 158–60, 172, 174–5, 188, 195, 216–17, 220, 227, 240, 258, 263, 267
series 101, 163, 263
serious 2, 19, 62, 148
sermon 6, 7; Donne 6
shapelessness 7, 30, 42, 71
shift 13, 17, 40, 51, 57–8, 72, 82, 88, 91–2, 96, 99, 104–5, 112, 120, 142, 170, 176–7, 182–3, 189, 234, 242, 250, 257, 260, 269, 273–4, 276, 278
shifters 95, 177, 179, 275
short 11, 18, 21, 67, 81, 162, 166, 198, 252
short story 6, 16–17, 58, 103, 147–8, 154, 156, 158, 184, 189, 242, 247, 251–3, 255, 258
showing (*vs* telling) 194, 199, 242
sign 35, 53, 78, 114, 128, 148–9, 152, 155, 171–3, 177, 217, 275–6, 278
signified 122, 134, 152, 154, 161, 168–70, 182, 191, 217, 228
signifier 35, 53, 78, 122, 134, 152, 154, 160, 168–9, 172–3, 182, 185, 190, 228, 257
simultaneity 28, 57, 74, 79, 100, 110, 127, 134, 138, 152, 191, 209, 235, 243, 254–5, 264
single 97, 142
singular 29, 57, 78–9, 94, 241, 256, 259
site 179
size 18, 58, 75, 199, 223, 252
skeleton/skeletal 19, 249
sketch 17, 29, 72
skid 157, 162, 190
skirt 163
solid/solidifying 68–9, 219 n., 257, 265
solution 109
soul 215
sources 7, 14, 30, 65–8, 83–4, 86, 93, 140–1, 178, 199, 234, 254, 256
space/spatial 5, 32, 56, 129, 132, 165, 260, 263, 275–7
spacing 134, 228
specific 56, 59, 63, 277

speculum 93, 150, 152, 258
speech/spoken 3, 18, 28, 33, 51, 78, 81–2, 87, 93, 95, 129, 147, 179, 235, 245, 253
speech-act 180, 275
speechless 45
split 39, 207
spontaneity 28
stable/stabilization 37–8, 56
staging 254
standpoint 32, 54–5, 80, 107, 122–3, 165, 212, 227
standstill 117, 220
standing out 204
stasis/static 16, 32, 40–1, 110, 112, 117, 231, 279
status quo 66, 99, 118, 171
sticking 181–2
story 3–4, 11, 23–5, 34, 43, 152, 155–6, 159–60, 162, 164, 188, 191, 197, 211, 213–14, 217, 222, 226–8, 231–3, 237–8, 241, 250–1, 262, 264–5, 273
strange(ness) 88, 94
striving 41, 109–10, 225
structuralism 53, 60, 139, 145, 148, 153, 165, 243, 282
structure 35
subject/subjectivity 14, 21, 30, 32–3, 35, 39, 42–3, 50–2, 55, 62–3, 71, 82, 87, 93–4, 96, 99–100, 114, 119–20, 126–7, 150, 156, 160–1, 164, 176–80, 183, 187, 190, 192, 198, 201–2, 205, 210, 212–14, 216, 218, 225–6, 228, 230–1, 234, 238, 240–2, 244, 259, 274–7, 279
subjunctive 219
sub-literary 16, 18, 223
subordination 10, 59, 79, 95, 116, 126–7, 140, 144, 158, 164, 220, 266–70
subsidiary 141, 215
succession/successive 73, 91, 112, 278
sufficient words 76
suggestion 254, 263
summary 253, 261
superficial 9, 19, 36, 74, 105, 182, 253
superfluous 23, 109, 133, 197, 243, 254
supersession/superseding 47, 147, 232, 269
supplement(ary) 17–18, 23, 25, 27, 29, 78–9, 89, 92, 96, 108, 130–2, 140, 143–4, 151, 157–8, 166–7, 169, 172, 174, 182–3, 187, 247, 262, 266
supra-literary 25, 223
surface 8, 26, 74, 80, 182, 253
surpassing 94, 274
surplus 69, 72, 76, 80, 132, 154, 159, 166, 169, 184
surprise 87
survival/surviving 26, 28, 57, 281
suspense 72, 160, 243
suspension/suspending 30–1, 40, 72, 78–80,

87, 111–12, 115, 119–11, 123, 142, 150, 152, 167, 171, 176, 206, 212, 242–3, 249–50, 254, 264, 269, 278

system/systematic/systematizing 2, 30–3, 39–41, 44, 46, 48–9, 50–1, 57–8, 61, 63, 65, 75, 100–1, 108, 110–11, 115–16, 118, 120, 125–7, 138, 141, 143–8, 151–4, 156–9, 161–4, 172–6, 178, 183, 185–7, 189–90, 198, 206–8, 211, 215, 217–18, 220, 224, 235, 242–5, 253–4, 257, 265–8, 277, 282

synchronic(ally) 1, 8, 16, 41, 79, 138–9, 164, 170, 191, 205

synopsis 152, 173, 175

synthesis/synthesizing 31, 40, 48, 112, 116, 135, 144, 164, 166, 174, 183, 187, 191, 200, 209–10, 215, 230, 233, 255

systematics 154, 173

tables 164–5, 173–5, 194–5

tabular 153, 158, 162

tabula rasa 86, 122

tales 208, 210, 241, 259

tangents 162–3

tautology 134, 271–2

taxonomy/taxonomic 39, 53, 64, 138, 161, 164–5, 169, 175, 189, 259

teaching 35, 237

teleology/teleological 40, 118, 233

telling 20, 194, 199, 242

telos 161, 231, 233

temporary 30–1, 75, 112–13, 116–17, 121, 123, 186, 190, 205, 211, 220, 263–4

tension 117, 124, 145

tentative(ness) 2, 230, 251, 256

test(ing) 19, 33, 42, 72, 144, 224, 226, 233

theme 8, 65, 111, 117, 120, 178

theorist 38, 53, 60, 100, 206

theory/theorizing/theoretical 11, 19–21, 27, 38–40, 42–3, 48–50, 52–4, 59–62, 99, 102–3, 105, 112–13, 115, 135–6, 138, 145, 149–50, 152, 154, 163, 173, 178, 192–6, 198, 200–1, 203–4, 209, 213, 217, 223–4, 225–8, 230, 236, 238–9, 257, 278–80, 282

thief/thievish/theft 85, 142, 144, 161, 272

thought/thinking 2, 8, 11, 17, 33–5, 41, 45–6, 48–51, 54–5, 63, 81–2, 96, 101, 115, 116, 118, 120–1, 124, 131, 134, 162, 181, 194, 197–8, 206, 213–15, 228, 237–8, 244–5, 250, 256, 263–5, 268, 271, 281

thread 216

time/temporal 5, 14, 16, 29, 32, 35, 37, 45, 47, 51, 56, 59, 70, 73, 75, 79, 96, 108, 110, 112, 119–20, 129, 132, 134, 146, 148, 159, 165–6, 191, 212, 220–1, 227–8, 231–2, 234, 237, 252, 263, 271–2, 275–8

timelessness 40, 70, 97, 118–19, 151, 257, 271, 278

title 10, 20, 77, 100–1, 126, 137, 162–3, 170, 195, 210, 273, 298

tonal 176, 191

topic(al) 2–3, 19, 42, 67, 76, 93–4, 96, 157, 164–6, 168–70, 174–5, 177, 179–80, 182, 193, 273

topological/*topos/topoi* 30, 40, 65, 93–4, 135–6, 150, 153, 156–7, 166

total(ity) 39–40, 47, 100, 110, 115–17, 121, 123, 136, 144–5, 152, 160, 203, 208, 212, 221–4, 231, 261–2, 269

totalization 18, 30, 35, 39, 41–2, 49, 55, 73, 100, 119, 132, 141, 151–2, 158, 162, 173, 181, 198, 208–9, 242, 258–9, 264, 266

tract 101, 237

trajectory 58

transcendental/transcending 32–3, 41, 44, 47–8, 53, 57, 225, 227, 272, 276

transform(ation) 20, 37, 84, 93, 219, 257

transgression/transgressive 142–3, 150, 154–5, 157, 159, 166, 174, 181, 240

transient 49, 111

transindividual 14

transition/transitory 12, 14, 20, 31, 37–9, 48, 63, 65, 105–6, 112, 116–17, 120, 122, 125, 144, 150, 155, 166, 182, 194, 207, 212, 225, 234, 255, 278

translation/translating 45, 111–12, 125, 172, 178, 180, 183–4, 191, 193, 199, 204, 211, 217, 229, 231, 253–4, 257–8, 262, 264, 267, 270, 273–4

translator 251, 255, 272

transplanting 85

transposition 273

travel 7, 10, 43, 75, 207; Goethe 230

treatise 5, 7, 15, 33, 193

trial 29, 42, 55, 146, 231, 250

trivial 2, 19, 148

truth/true 5, 9–14, 21, 25, 32, 36, 44–6, 48–9, 52, 54–5, 66–71, 74–5, 80, 85, 89, 92–3, 95, 97, 103, 106–7, 113–14, 117–23, 133–4, 147, 156, 171, 180, 182–3, 188, 196, 200–2, 205, 210–12, 221, 227, 229, 235–6, 238, 242, 251, 268, 271, 275, 278–9, 281

trying out 3, 15, 17–18, 31, 35, 79, 101, 112–13, 148–9, 186, 191, 228, 234, 237, 238, 253, 256–7, 269, 280

tutor text 159–60; word 168

typeface 142, 153, 164, 182

typography/typographical 20–30, 142, 153, 163–4, 170

ultimate 44, 106, 109, 116, 161, 164, 236

unattainable 199

unchanging 40, 128, 233

unchecked 267

unclassifiability 146
uncompleted 236, 239
unconscious 200–1, 221, 223
under erasure 143, 182, 243
underlining 182
uneducated 227
unfinished 40, 199, 244
unfolding 262, 264, 269
unifying/unified 2, 13, 22, 29, 32, 40, 129, 132, 151, 198, 206, 231, 279
unique(ness) 1, 10, 13, 32, 61, 82, 87, 96, 204, 227, 270–1, 275, 277–8
union/united/unity 29, 39–40, 47, 54, 58–9, 70, 74, 78, 91, 95–6, 102–3, 105, 108, 111, 113–14, 117, 119, 130, 132, 135, 137, 142, 147, 187, 200, 203, 209, 214, 221, 225–7, 233, 235–6, 263, 279
universality/universal 13, 21, 30–2, 39–42, 44–6, 48, 55, 63, 65–6, 69, 75, 82, 87, 93, 105–6, 108–9, 118–20, 146, 152, 200, 203, 205, 208, 212, 216, 220–2, 224, 226–9, 247; Borges 251, 254, 257, 262, 266, 268–9
unlocatable 155, 157, 176
unlimited 35
unmediated 45, 93
unmethodical 28, 59, 115, 118
unnamable 155
unnaming 265
unnecessary 272
unrealized/unrealizable 64, 231
unreason 279
unscientific 149
unsolid 257
unstable 56
unsystematic 157
untruth 47, 123
unwritten 18, 20, 97, 219, 220–2, 228
usurpation/usurping 128, 169, 238, 244, 261, 265
utopia/utopian/utopianism 39–40, 64, 87, 93, 114, 123–4, 185–7, 218, 220, 224, 231, 243, 246, 253–6, 259, 269–70

utterance 66, 87, 95, 139, 176–7, 180, 242, 244, 271

vacuity/vacuous 8, 255
vantage-point 139, 152, 161, 209
variant 199, 220
variation/varying 7, 69, 73–4, 79, 255, 271, 273–4
variety 34, 233, 244
verb(al) 17, 29, 51, 79, 104, 110, 125, 160, 172, 254
verisimilitude/*vraisemblance* 67, 71, 95, 118, 147, 158–9, 172, 191, 266–8
version 143, 217, 232, 250–1, 262, 273
viewpoint 37, 80, 132, 230
virtual(ity) 21, 39, 79, 97, 144, 178, 187, 190, 229, 258, 272–3, 275, 278–9
visible 270, 272
vulgarizing 14, 19

wandering 30, 39, 42, 81, 101, 143, 167, 175, 185, 189, 207, 211, 216, 239, 243
warping 132, 162, 174
wayfaring 43
weigh(ing) 2–3, 34, 68–9, 73, 83, 107, 112–15, 169
whole(ness) 18, 21, 27, 30–2, 39–40, 45–6, 48, 56, 62, 72, 74, 80, 86, 95, 99, 108–11, 116–17, 120, 125–6, 131, 147, 151–2, 158–9, 162, 174, 198–200, 205, 221, 227, 229, 231, 262, 264, 266, 269, 272, 281
witness 184
writer 187–8, 191, 198, 205, 218
writerly 154, 173, 185, 189
writing 132, 136, 139, 142, 144–5, 154, 157, 165, 177–9, 183–4, 186–7, 205, 217, 222, 242–3, 248, 251–3, 258–9, 269, 272–5

yearning 207, 221

zero degree 163, 171, 189